A picture is really a strange thing. Sometimes it is taken. Sometimes it is made. It's a brief pause in time that moves us from the present into presence by witnessing a moment that happened and no longer exists.

At least that's what I thought for a long time, but I misunderstood. In hindsight, I've never experienced photography as an act of presence. I wanted to. I tried to. But I never did. Photographs are ghosts.

At its best, photography is an act of flow in the creative process. I guess you could argue that I'm contradicting myself, but I'd ~~most~~ probably just argue back. Humans are full of contradictions. So are photographs — because they must be. They're made by imperfect creatures with all sorts of biases and baggage and ideas and nostalgia. They're full of selected angles and interpretations that always mean our back is turned because we can only see what is in front of us. They leave out the ugly — or include it — depending on what the photographer wants to say. Objectivity is a lie. And still, pictures are all beautiful in some way or another because they're expressions of us in a big messy world.

For Andrew Phelps and Sadie Quarrier
"Proceed and be bold."

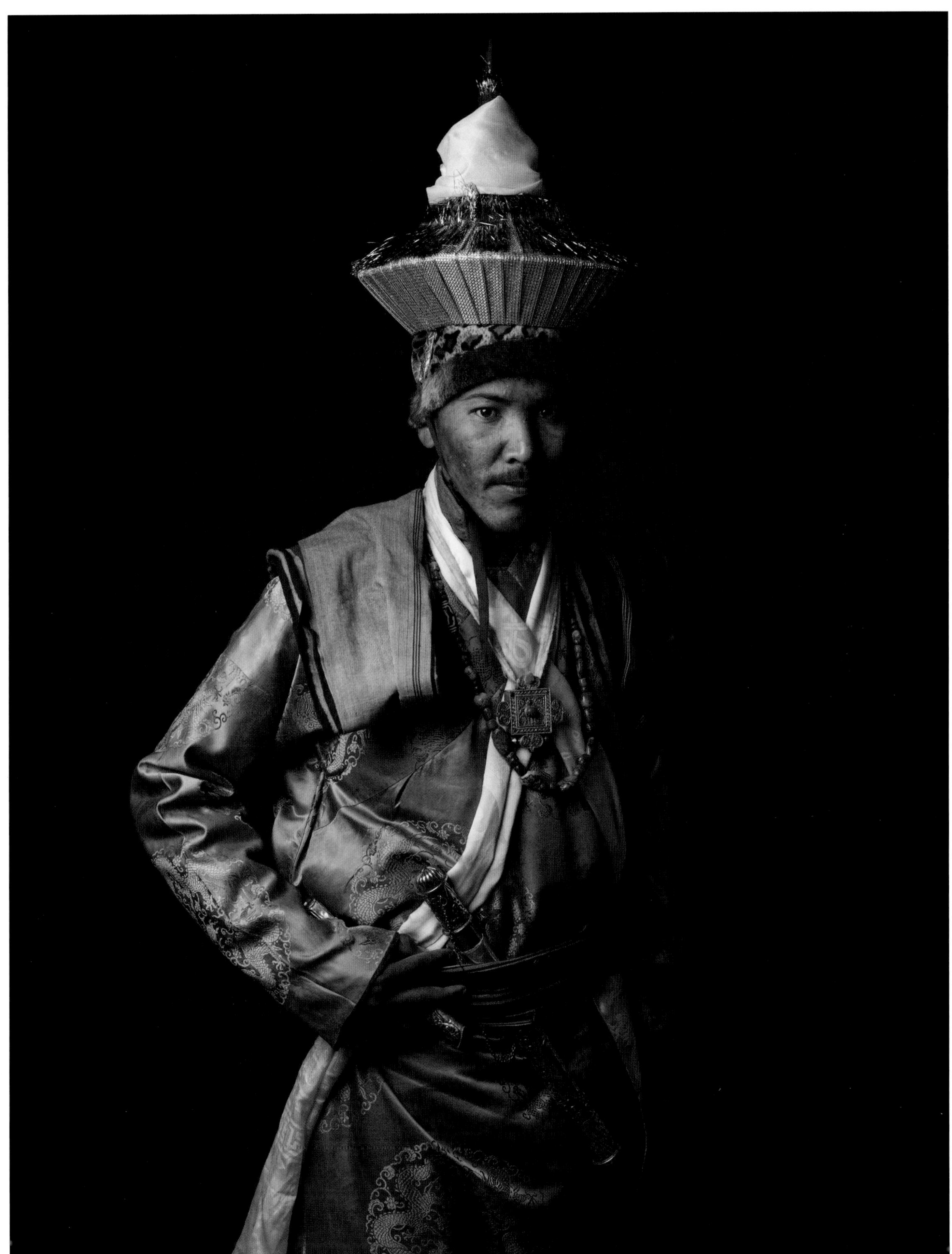

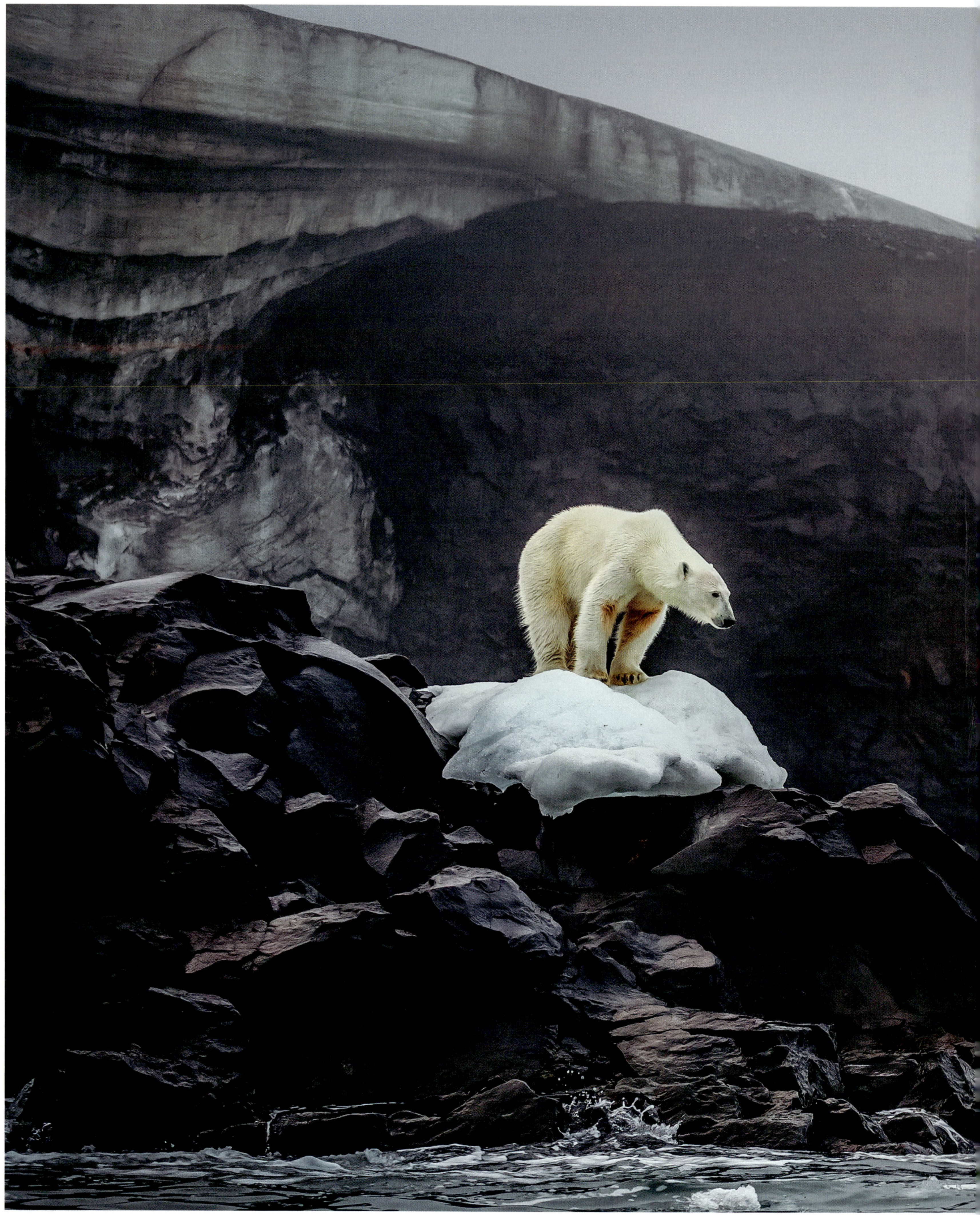

BI|POLAR

PHOTOGRAPHS FROM AN UNQUIET MIND

CORY RICHARDS

TEN SPEED PRESS
California | New York

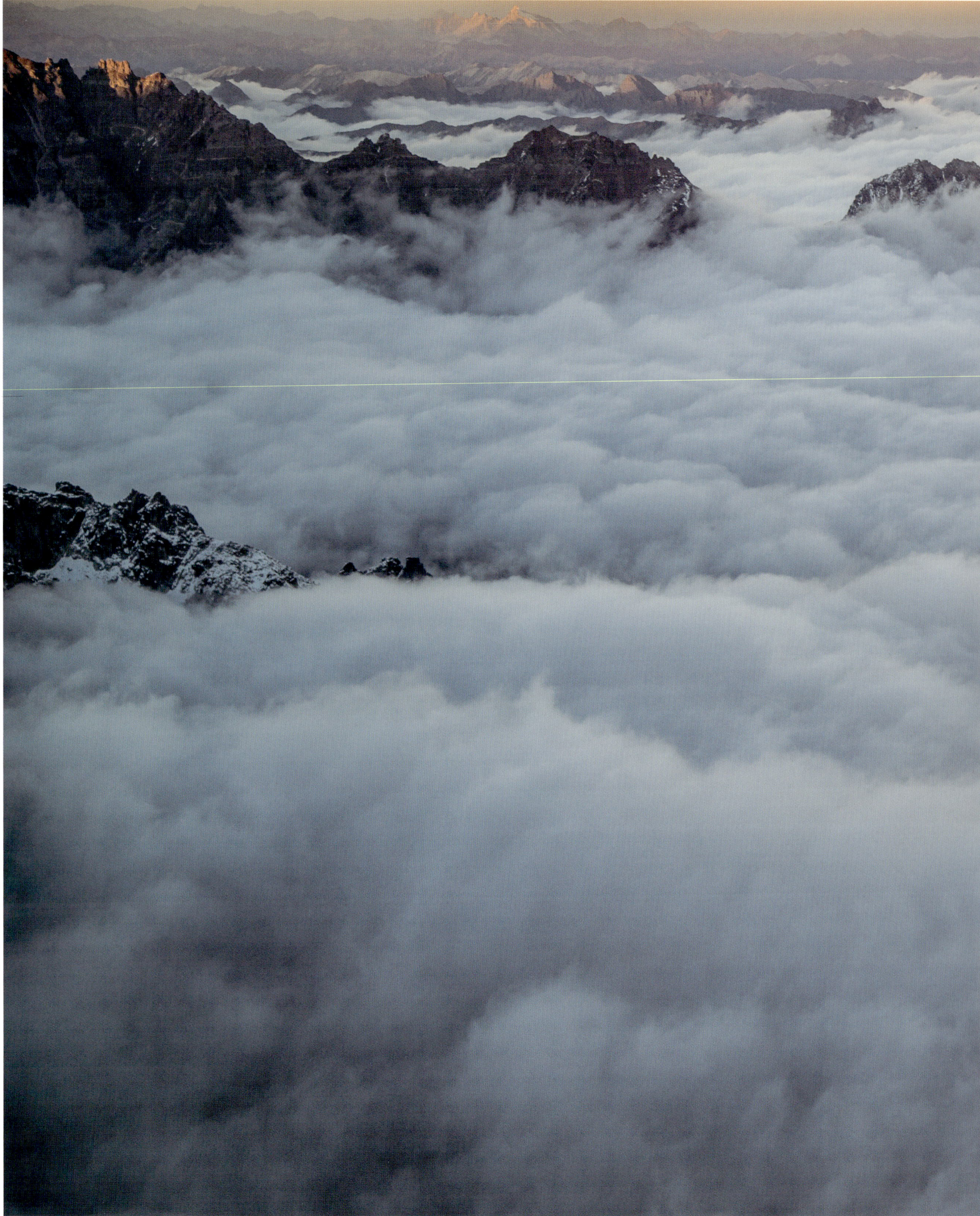

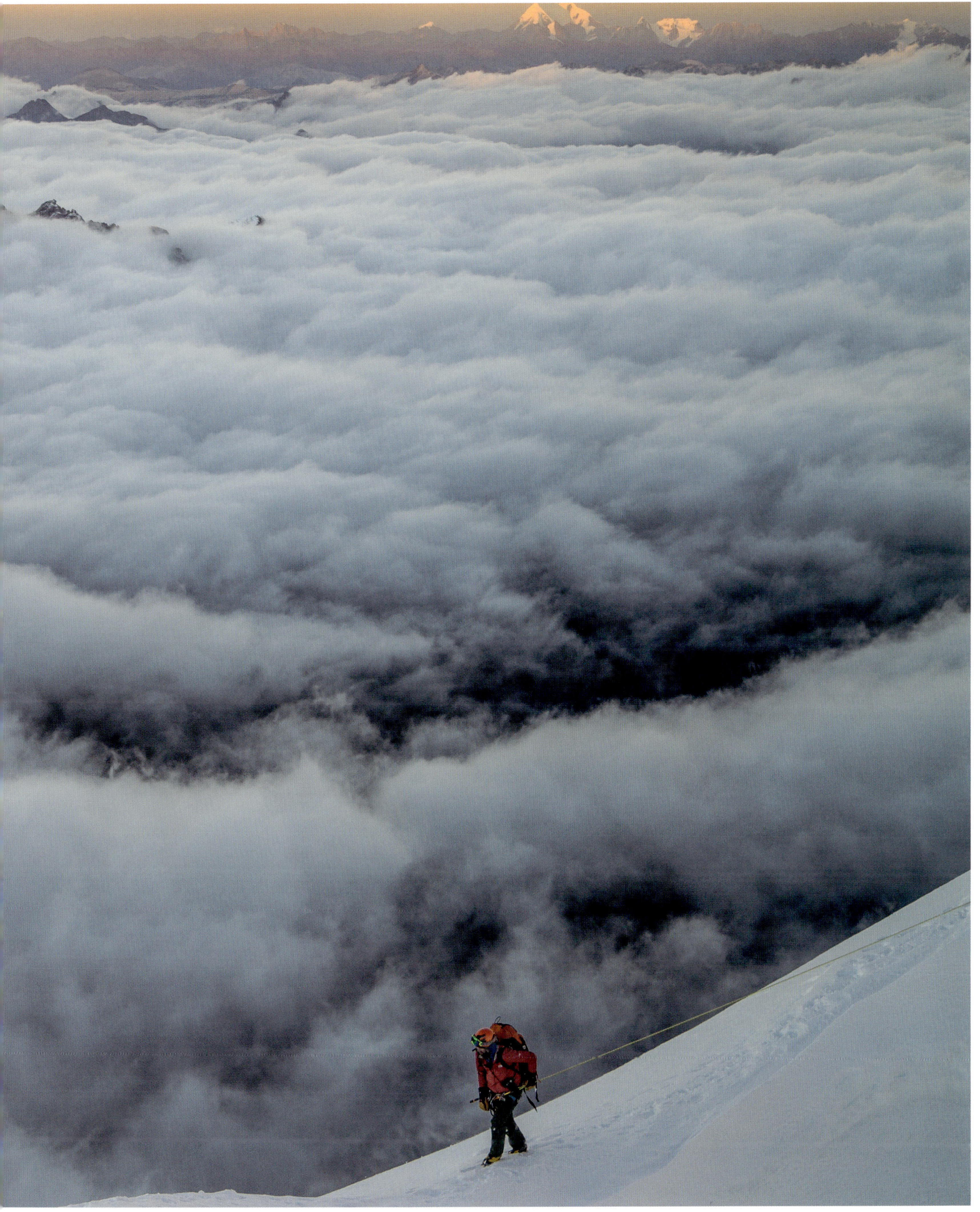

CONTENTS

EMOTION \i-ˈmō-shən\ *n*: the compass of the human heart

N

8 ◦ FOREWORD

10 ◦ POLARITY: AN INTRODUCTION

24 HOPE | FEAR

26 ◦ COLD FUSION • FRANZ JOSEF LAND, RUSSIA
40 ◦ THE EDGE OF YESTERDAY • MUSTANG, NEPAL
64 ◦ ADRIFT • THE CORAL TRIANGLE
80 ◦ THE SUM OF EARTH • THE HIMALAYA

102 CURIOSITY | INDIFFERENCE

104 ◦ AMERICAN DREAM • EVERYWHERE, UNITED STATES
114 ◦ WHEN HISTORY SMILES • MUSTANG, NEPAL

134 PRIDE | SHAME

180 ◦ THE ABSENCE OF WORDS • A COLLECTION OF FACES
204 ◦ TRUE WEST • YELLOWSTONE AND THE AMERICAN WEST

178 AWE | CONTEMPT

136 ◦ A RIVER IN AFRICA • ANGOLA, NAMIBIA, BOTSWANA, AND THE OKAVANGO DELTA
156 ◦ SUPERHUMAN SUPER HUMAN • LAKE TAHOE, CALIFORNIA, AND RED LODGE, MONTANA

218 ISOLATION | CAMARADERIE

220 ◦ BULLET HOLES IN A MAP • MYANMAR
242 ◦ ON SCREAMS & SILENCE • ON TOUR WITH THE LUMINEERS
254 ◦ ICE MARTYRS • THE SIACHEN GLACIER CONFLICT, PAKISTAN
268 ◦ A LESSON ON BELONGING • QUEEN MAUD LAND, ANTARCTICA

282 LOVE

318 ◦ ACKNOWLEDGMENTS

318 ◦ ABOUT THE AUTHOR

S

FOREWORD

By Chris Johns
former editor in chief, *National Geographic*

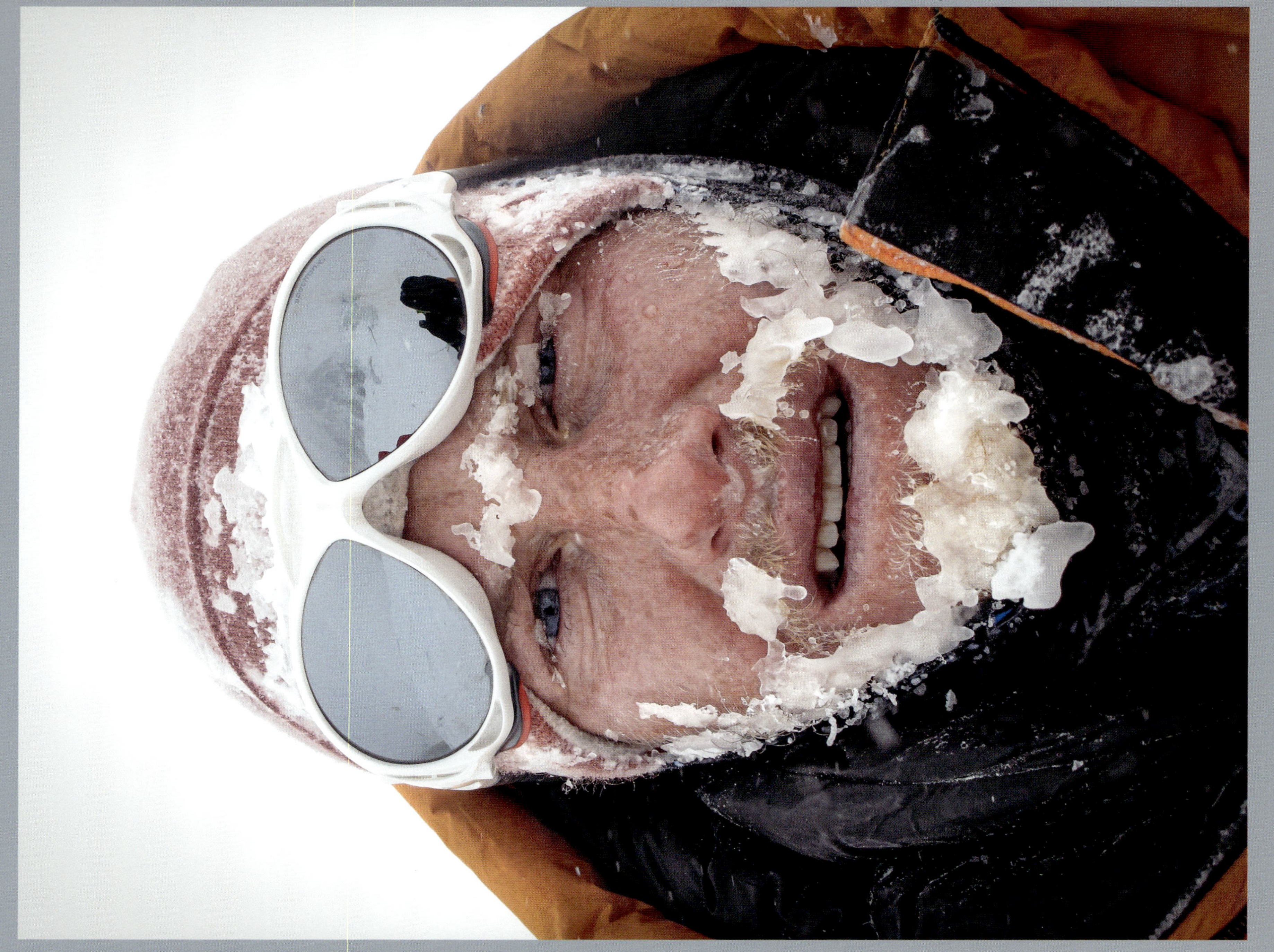

The wind is relentless, and the temperature is plummeting as Cory Richards descends from the summit of Gasherbrum II in Pakistan. He has just become one of the first Americans to climb an 8,000-meter (26,246-foot) peak in winter.

I am not aware of the film *Cold* until the *National Geographic* magazine adventure team walks into my office and says, "You have to see this."

We gather around my computer. The film trailer's score swells with drama and the screen shows, "He carried a small camera and filmed constantly." Cory emerges from beneath avalanche debris with his face covered with snow and ice, mostly ice. His ungloved right hand is rubbing his right eye as his mouth opens in a grimace. I cannot tell if he is in tears or terrified; perhaps both. No matter. He is fortunate to be alive and knows it. Cory has been pummeled on his descent of Gasherbrum II in sub-zero temperatures.

I want more—and watch all of Cory and Anson Fogel's film. It opens inside a wind-blown tent at 21,959 feet (6,693 meters) on February 2, 2011. True to the film's name, it is cold: -51°F (-46°C).

"What the fuck am I doing here?" Cory asks himself as he is photographing his climbing partners Simone Moro and Denis Urubko. "We have to get down." Simone is in a sleeping bag coughing—a deep, nasty, bloody hack—as a storm rattles the tent.

And then, "I love the mountains. I grew up in them, climbing with Dad. He taught me everything," Cory continues. "But I'm scared; so many things here trying to kill me." Cory reflects on his father, Court. "I think of the lessons I learned from my dad. How he always tells me, 'Go gently'."

I press pause to ponder that quote. I realize that if I were to ever give a photographer only two words of advice, it just might be those.

My "go gently" suggestion would be given with more than fifty years of experience as a photojournalist. There have been occasions when I had to flee an erupting volcano, dodge people shooting at me, and use my camera to bash a man with his powerful hands around my neck, but those "go quickly" experiences are rare exceptions. By doing as Court Richards advocates and embracing a "go gently" mindset, my photographs—and Cory's—are more powerful and our lives richer.

In this first experience of Cory's work, I see that he has taken an intriguing path I have long wanted to travel. So many times, as a photographer, I have been shooting still photographs when something extraordinary happened in front of my camera that made me wish I could capture video and audio, too. In *Cold*, Cory used emerging camera technology to do exactly what I had longed to do and tells deeper, more immersive personal stories.

Cory and I meet. He is energetic, sincere, and honest—all qualities I recognized in the film. He loves the mountains and the challenges they bring, as do I. In addition, using *Cold* as an example, I am in a position as editor in chief of the magazine to support a blend of still photographs, video, and audio to tell meaningful stories on digital platforms.

Cory quickly became a valuable contributor. Many photographs in this book were made during *National Geographic* assignments. And he did his assignments splendidly, but for Cory that was not enough.

As you'll see in this book, Cory is constantly searching and going beyond what the assignment demands. He is talented, curious, brave, and not afraid to take chances and make mistakes. He asks questions that often have no answer. We feel his fear. We feel his wonder. We feel his awe. We feel his frustration when life is not as it should be. And we feel Cory's voice growing stronger and becoming more poignant on these pages.

"The mountains have always been a vehicle to voice myself," says Cory. He is driven to "go gently" as his father suggests. The photographs in this book could only be made by doing so. Cory knows that thoughtlessly careening through life is costly, just as he knows that a commitment to going gently enriches his photographs and his life.

Look at the photograph of a polar bear precariously perched on a small slab of snow in Franz Josef Land (page 2). Look at the photograph of a shy young Peruvian girl with intense brown eyes and dusty wind-blown hair (page 153). Look at the photograph of a woman on crutches who is missing a left leg, mangled by a land mine in Angola (page 185). Look at the photograph of a mountaineer climbing into sunlight near the summit of Gasherbrum II (page 83).

Look at all the photographs in this book, hear Cory's voice, and go gently.

—Chris Johns, former editor in chief, *National Geographic*

Self-portrait taken after an avalanche on the descent of the first winter ascent of Gasherbrum II, Pakistan. This photograph, the events that preceded it, and the complexities of the aftermath led to Cory's deep interest in psychology, the mechanisms of the mind and heart, and the celebration of our greatest hurdles through art.

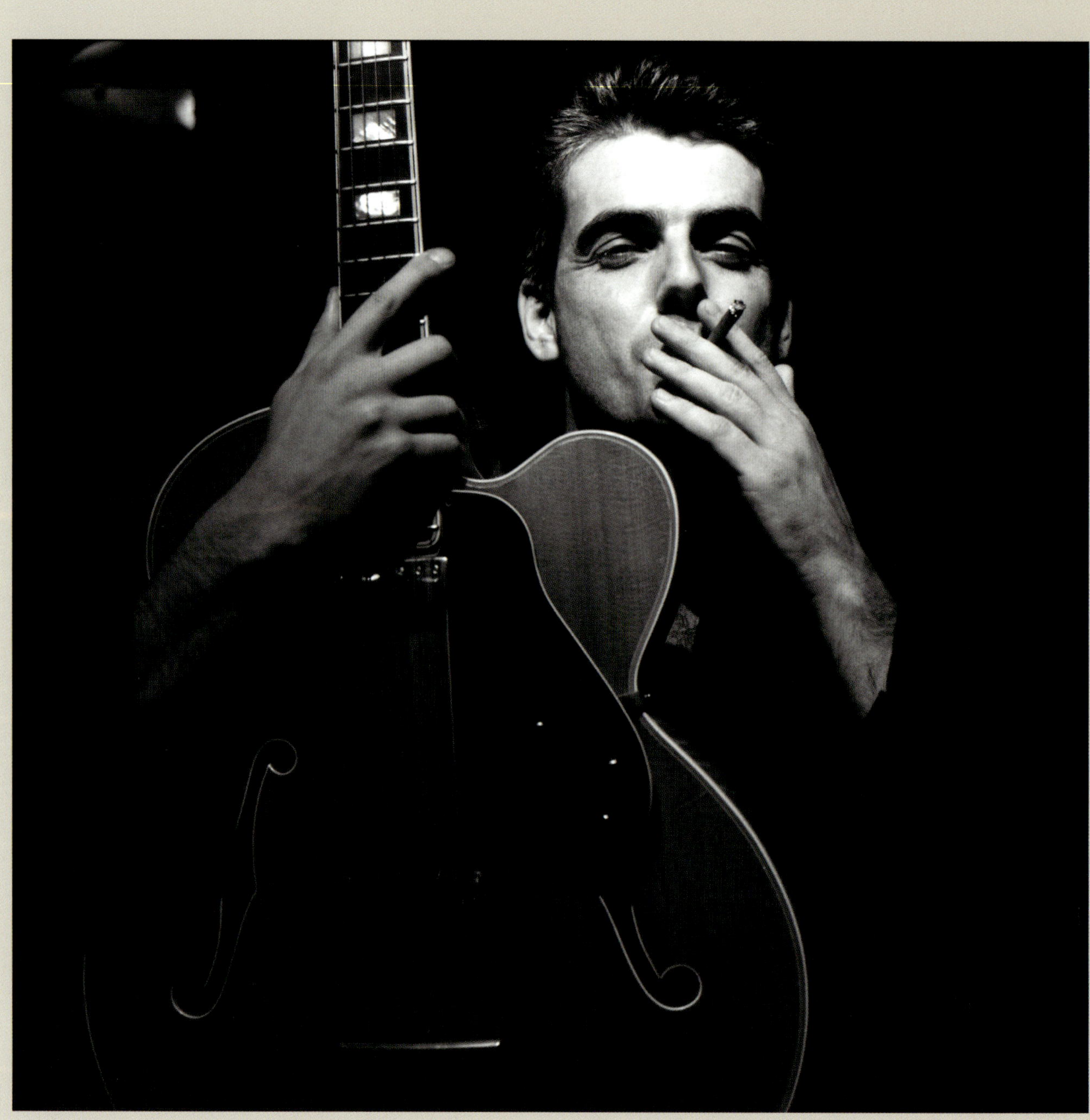

I think my lungs and eyes are confused. Art has always been like air to me. I drew obsessively as a child and pored over my family's collection of mountain books. I would fold my legs under my shirt and sit in the narrow hallway to our laundry room, thumbing through stacks of _National Geographic_ momentarily suspended between the world I knew and the one I saw in the pages. I lived through my eyes and what I saw stirred my already overwhelming sensitivity. Art resonated, because to me, it is the most complete language of emotion. In my mind, art _is_ emotion manifest.

For a number of different reasons, my life unraveled somewhat spectacularly when I was around twelve years old. I share this story in depth in my memoir, _The Color of Everything,_ but in short, my mercurial nature became overwhelming, my emotions intensified, and my ceaseless acts of defiance amplified the inner turmoil. I was at war with myself and everyone else. Eventually, I was hospitalized in the psychiatric unit of Primary Children's Hospital in Salt Lake City, Utah. After a week, I was moved to a long-term behavioral rehab center where I stayed for eight months. After running away from treatment on three occasions, I ended up briefly homeless.

This was a pivotal period in my development as an artist even though I made no art at all. The experience started to shape how I see people and the world and how it's all woven together. If art is emotion, these years would become a bottomless reservoir of inspiration. It was also during this period that I was diagnosed with bipolar 2. I was fourteen.

It can be easy to confuse a diagnosis with identity and, at the time, I understood the "bipolar" label as a sentence that would keep me perpetually trapped in turmoil. I thought my unpredictability would always consume me, that my mind was fragile, and madness was hidden just out of sight. But I misunderstood. The bipolar mind does not feel more _deeply_ . . . it rather feels more _intensely._ Emotions are ubiquitous and fire is always hot. I experience emotion right at the tip of the blue flame, the hottest part. When you live life there and you aren't careful, it can be easy to get burned. But like so many of life's hurdles, my tempestuous mind would ultimately become my greatest gift.

Early on and until very recently, I confused my sensitivity for empathy. It's important to understand the difference. Sensitivity is an internal emotional _reaction_ to external forces. Empathy is a mindful outward _response_ to the emotional experiences of others. Ironically, bipolar individuals often have trouble with empathy because we're too overcome by our sensitivity. (I still want to crawl out of my brain some days.) Thankfully, over time, I've found ways to leverage the emotional tides. Rather than a flood that I drown in, that same madness has become an ocean of reference for what I see. The gift of bipolar has been the ability to identify what emotions _look_ like, both in myself and others. I've learned that if I can see emotion, I can feel it. And when I feel it, I'm invited to respond to the emotional experience of others and the world they live in. In that way, photography has taught me empathy. In many ways, the following images and stories are an expression of that journey.

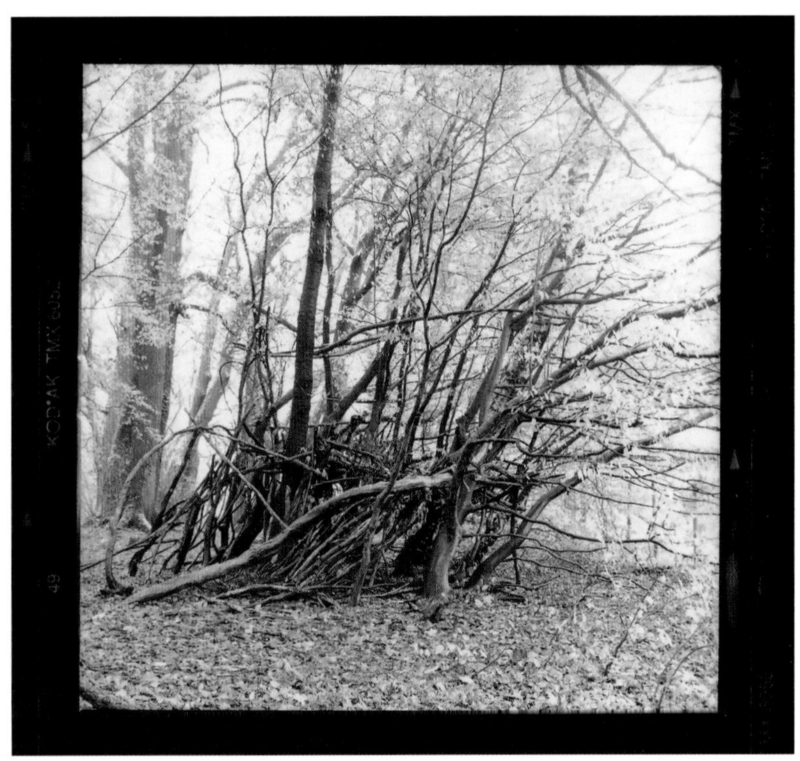

Mönchsberg, Salzburg, Austria (2001).

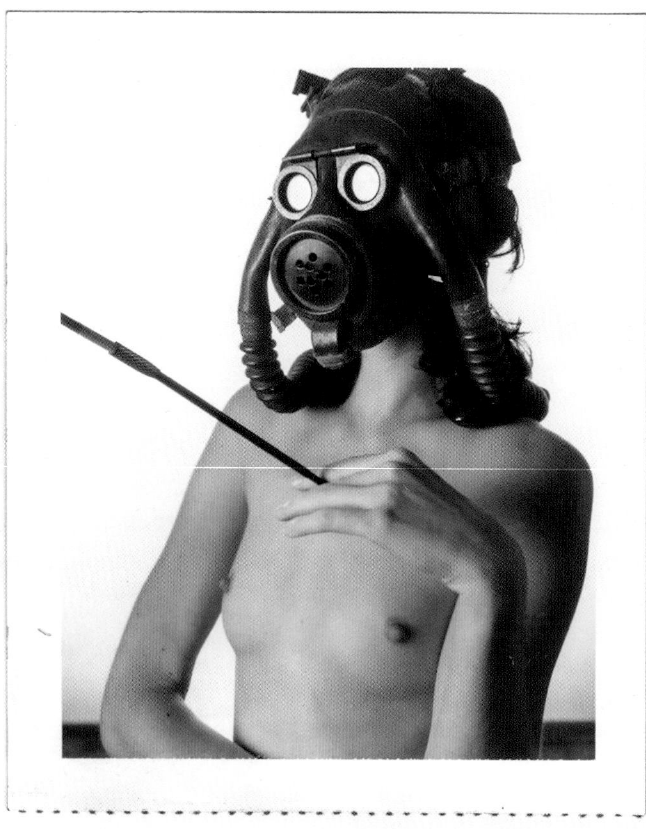

Early explorations in
concept and paradox
Seattle, Washington (2003).

I was sitting in my car one day watching tall trees bent by the Santa Ana winds sway toward the Pacific Ocean, overwhelmed by the task of organizing my photographs in a way that made sense for this book—something linear, even though my career has been anything but. I stared blankly at the palms and played back through a collage of images that seemed to blur, dazed by how full our planet is of wild landscapes and nature that looks impossible: Baobab trees and giraffes and fish with lightbulbs over their heads. Glaciers that look like frozen rivers and a perpetually curved horizon that always appears flat. A rhinoceros. An elephant. A pangolin. Humans. I've been incredibly fortunate to stand witness to so much of our world. Still, I had no idea how to arrange it all. And then I did.

By some unreasonable stroke of luck, I've photographed from Antarctica to the Arctic. My career has literally been bi-polar, an outward reflection of my *inner* extremes. And through its lessons in empathy, photography has connected me, and hopefully others, to the excruciatingly beautiful world we live in. Following that theme, I started looking at my pictures through the lens of emotional polarities.

There are many theories about the number of emotions humans experience and this is by no means a complete list. But as I dug through my work, there seemed to be some basal, recurring leitmotifs throughout the assignments—emotions that I felt as I learned the stories of others and made the pictures. The following are the major themes that emerged through the process:

Hope | Fear
Curiosity | Indifference
Pride | Shame
Awe | Contempt
Isolation | Camaraderie
Love

Every image in this book represents its emotional pole and both expressions are always present. We hope only in the presence of fear. We feel pride measured against shame. Isolation is only felt in the absence of closeness and camaraderie.

Only the final chapter, "Love," is a singular construct and stands outside of duality. This kind of love doesn't have a polarity; it is too big to be confined. In fact, I'm not sure it's an emotion at all. I also accept that love so vastly often sits beyond our reach. That's okay.

There are no introductions to the chapters aside from a brief definition of the emotions. If an image doesn't resonate, decide where you'd put it. If you don't feel anything when you see it, rip it out and throw it away! If it makes you feel deeply, tear it out and pin it on the wall. Don't know what

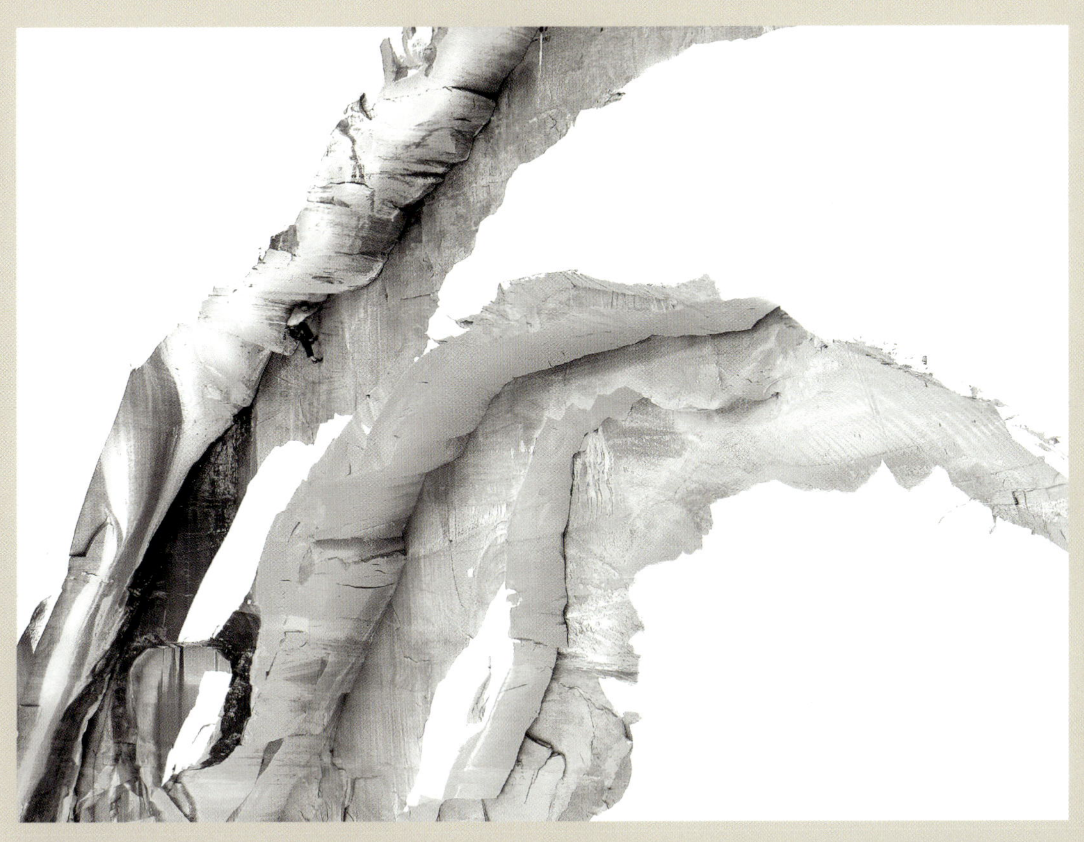

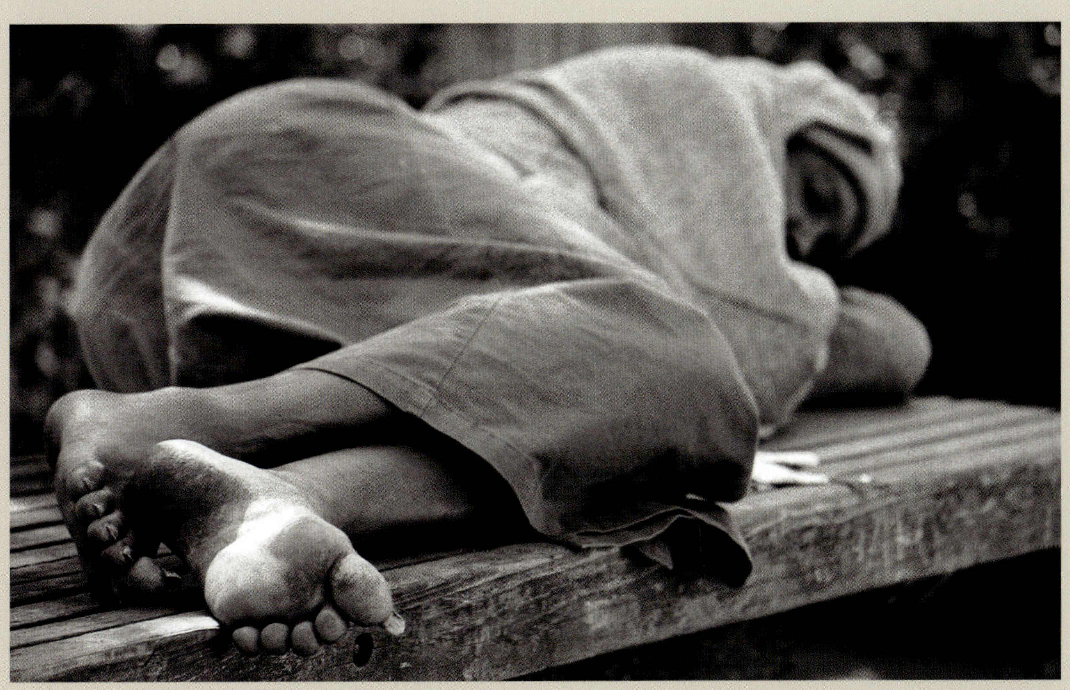

ABOVE: Early climbing work, Alex Honnold, Moab, Utah (2008).

BELOW: Early work from Seattle, Washington. At the time, I was working as a fashion photo assistant to fund climbing trips.

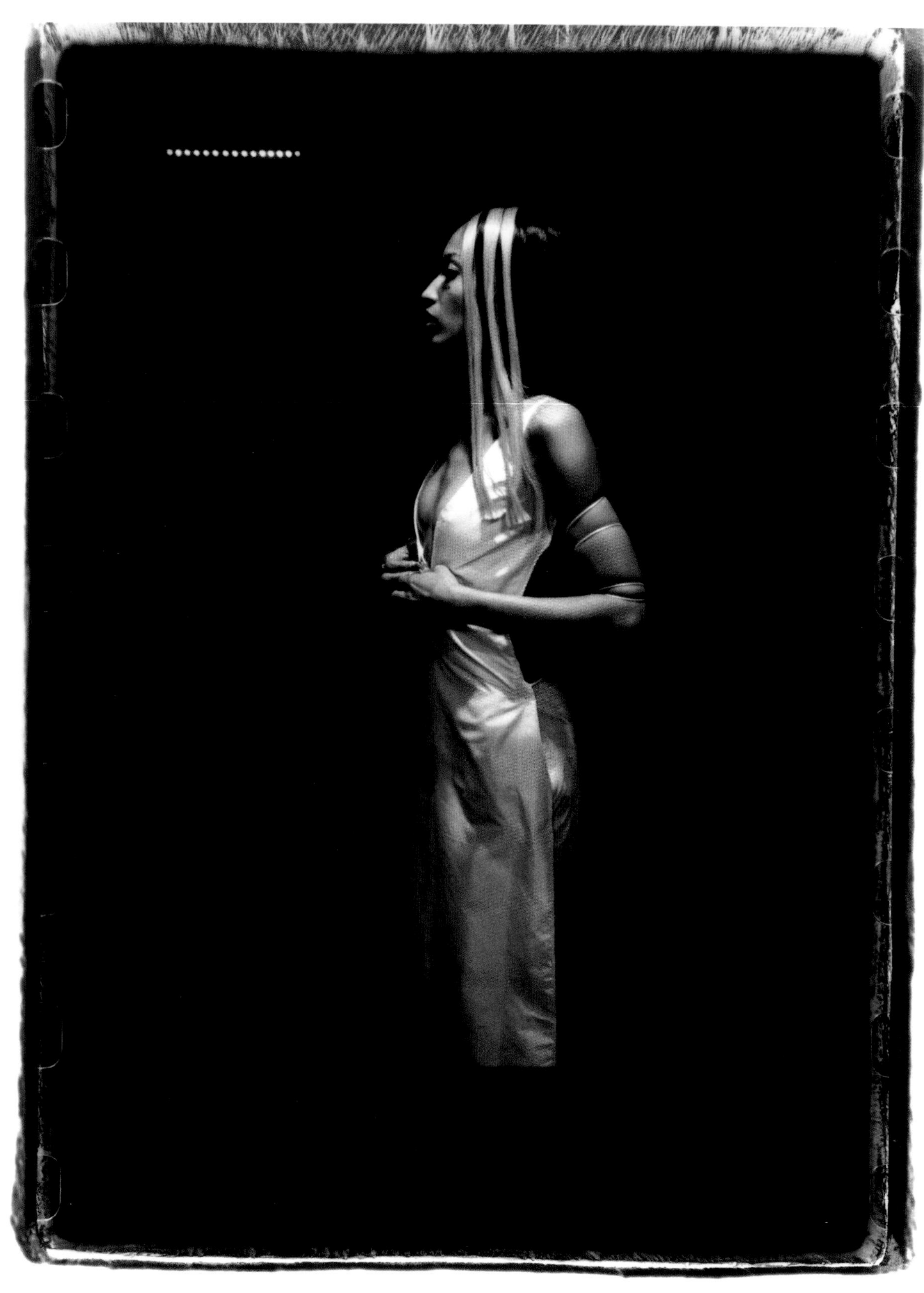

Underground fetish fashion show, Seattle, Washington (2003).

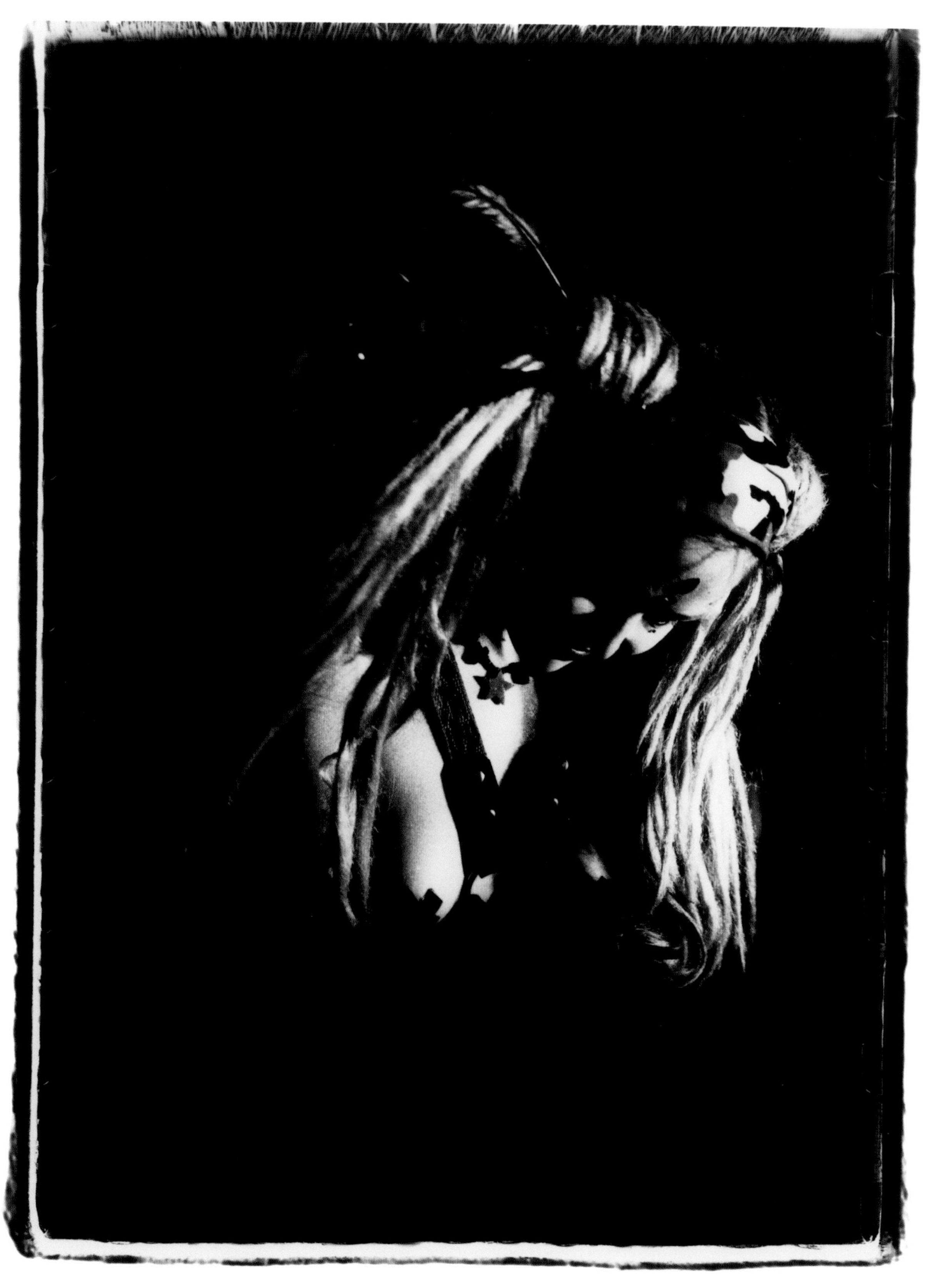

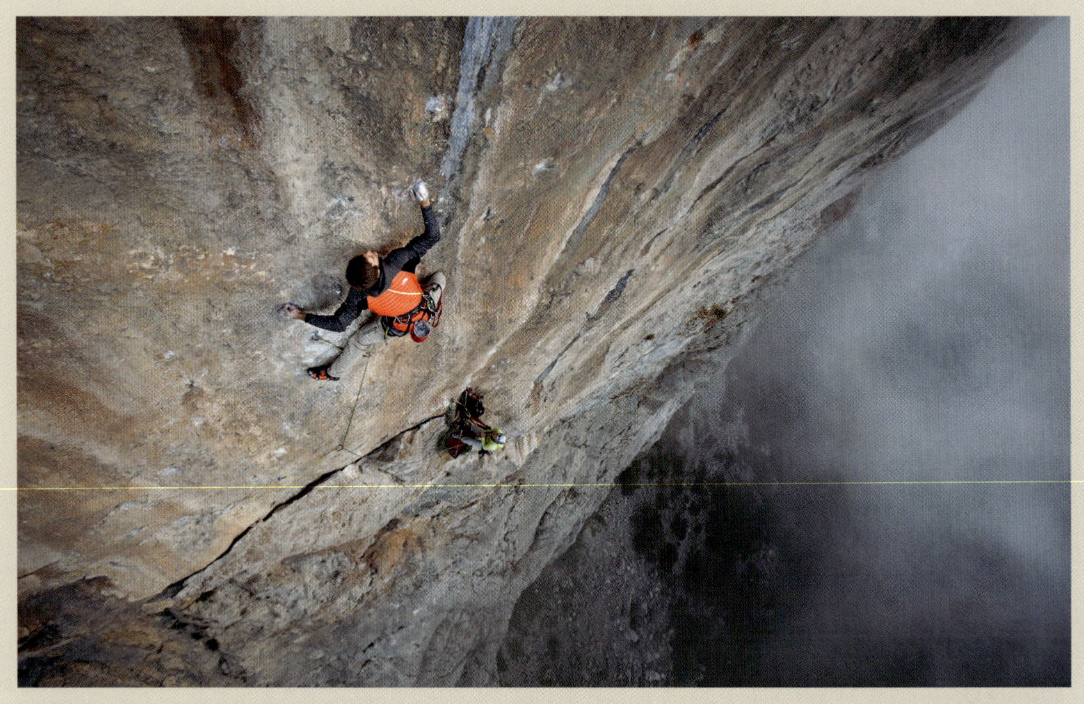

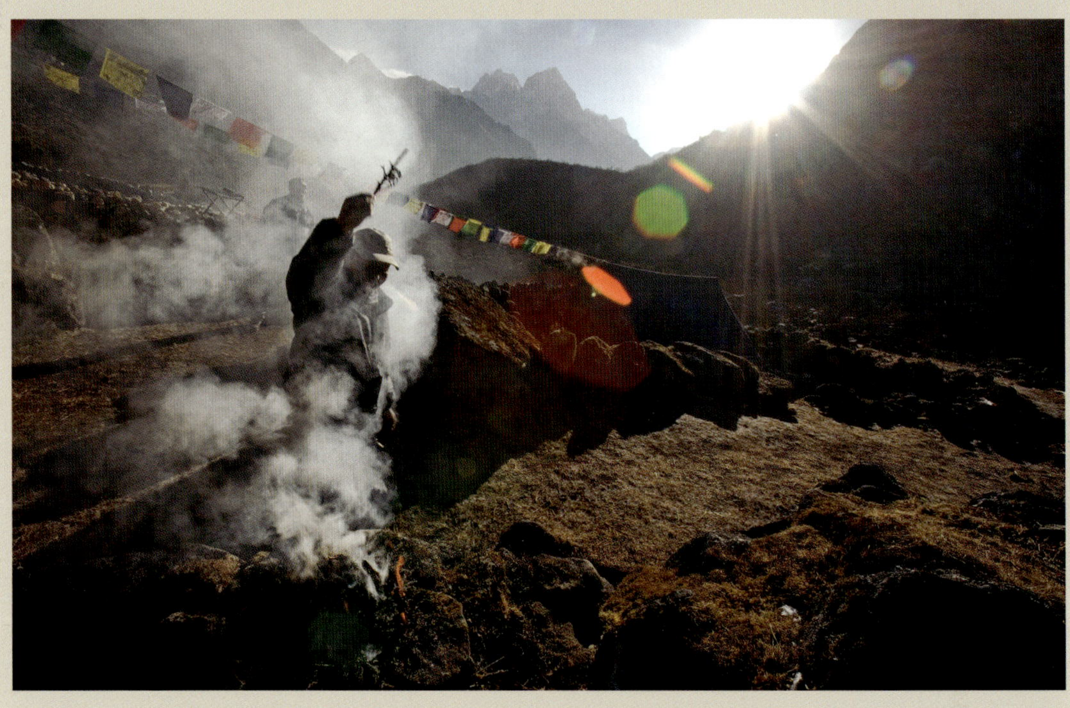

ABOVE: American climber Matt Segal in Crimea, Ukraine (2012).

BELOW: Dawa Sherpa fanning juniper smoke as a blessing for the climb ahead. Khumbu, Nepal (2008).

to feel? Sit with it. Have a glass of wine and pass the image around with your kids or at a dinner party. How do you find a needle in a haystack? You'll know when you find it.

There's an inherent messiness to this method of organizing a book. Every image can be felt a thousand different ways and just because I've slotted them into binaries doesn't mean their meanings are black and white. Emotions aren't. You'll probably experience many of these images entirely differently than I do. In that way, it's a "choose your own adventure" kind of book. It's my invitation to dialogue about what we feel and why. And when you don't know what to feel, choose love.

Story is the bedrock of humanity and art is its essential form of expression. We breathe story, and so, we breathe art. The utility of art itself is to tell stories that inform and move us to action through emotion. Photography has always been a way to anchor myself and others in moments, creating a chance to pause and ignite our hearts and minds. My greatest hope is that this book spurs conversation within yourself and with others about the ways the world moves you even when it hurts to look.

My other hope is that my work broadens the discussion around mental health, our brains, our hearts, and how we can reshape our challenges into our most creative endowments.

Salzburg, Austria, 2001

The first image I ever sell isn't a climbing picture. It has nothing to do with adventure or nature at all. It's a portrait of a musician named Knud sitting in a dark jazz club in Salzburg, Austria, washed over by a bright stage light. He's cocking his head back, pulling a long, sex-filled drag of his cigarette, and staring into the lens, squinting through the smoke. But he's not looking at me.

Somewhere over my shoulder is the woman I'd watched smile at him from the audience. She stared with upturned eyes from a gently dipped brow, holding a tiny red straw between her lips. It was a secret glance with a blast radius of lust.

I can feel her watching him now as I bend over the viewfinder and compose. She's staring at him and he's staring at me with an expression that's just for her. I can't tell if I'm in the way or exactly where I need to be. It's a two-way conversation that demands a third, and I'm learning a cardinal lesson of this medium. Photographers are both the *conduit for* and *architects of* a moment.

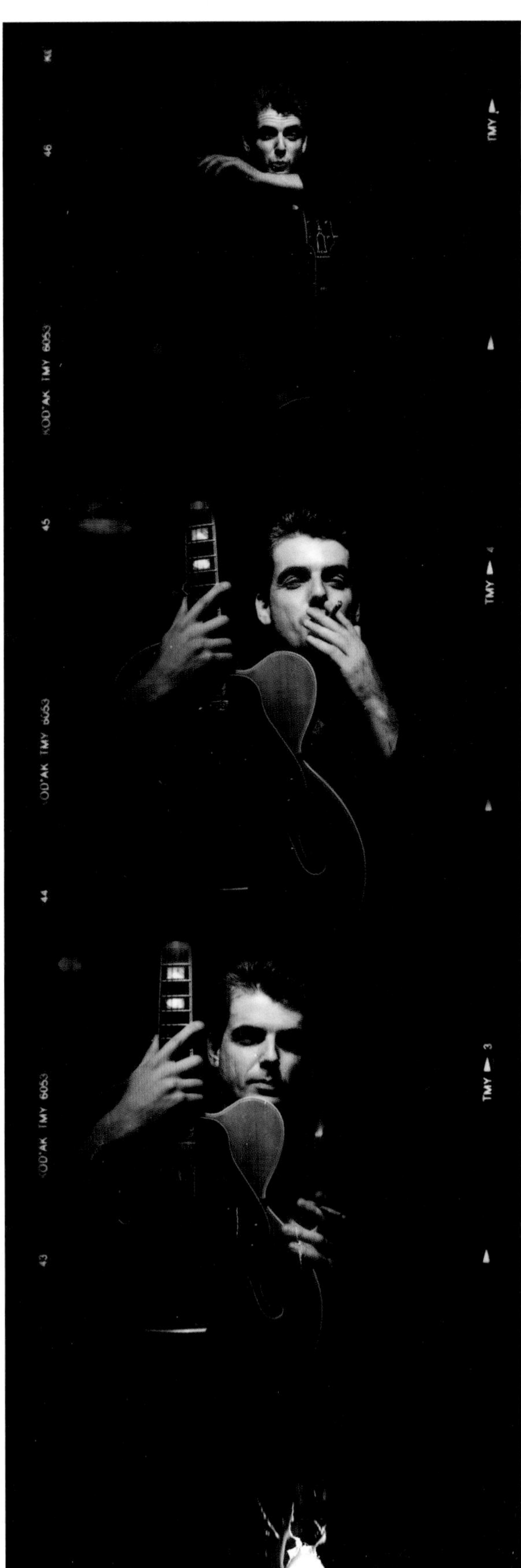

Negative proof prints of Austrian jazz musician Knud, Salzburg, Austria (2001).

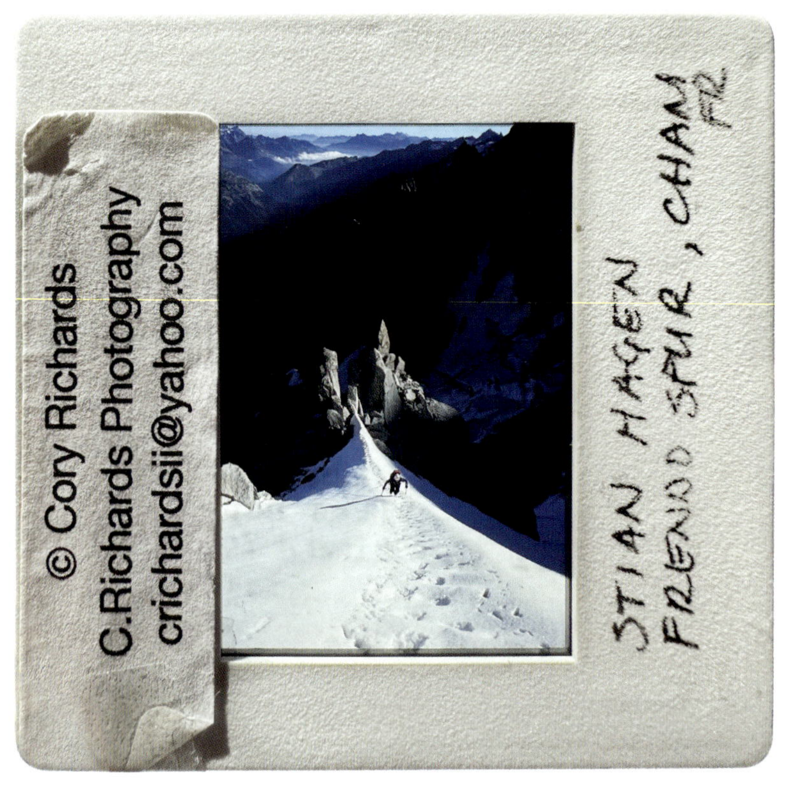

My first published image:
Norwegian climber and skier
Stian Hagen, north face of
Aiguille du Midi,
Chamonix, France (2001).

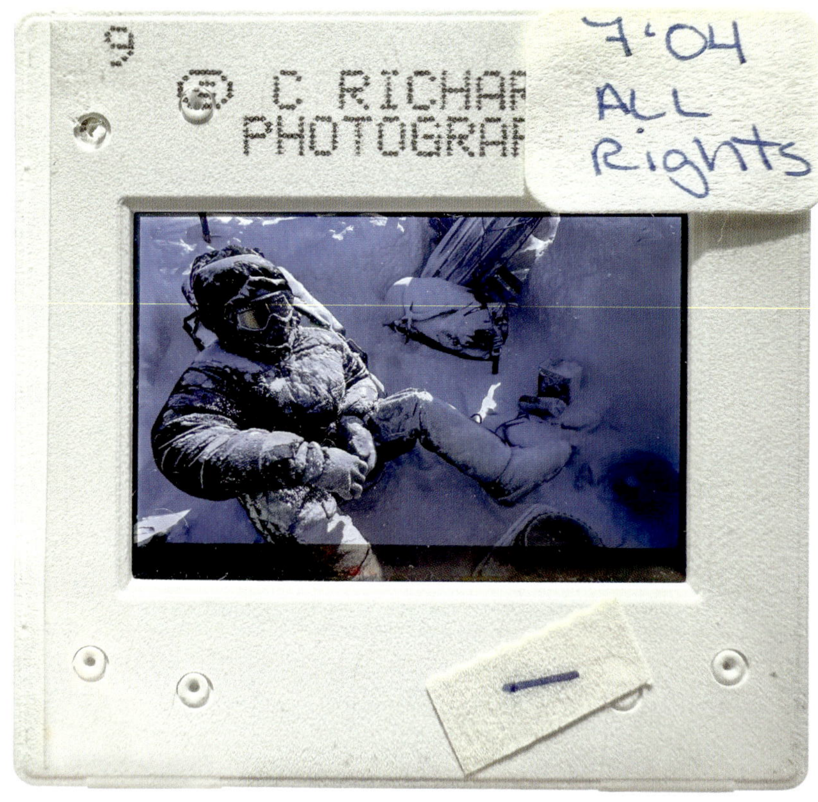

Canadian climber Dave Garrow,
Mount Logan, Yukon Territories,
Canada (2004).

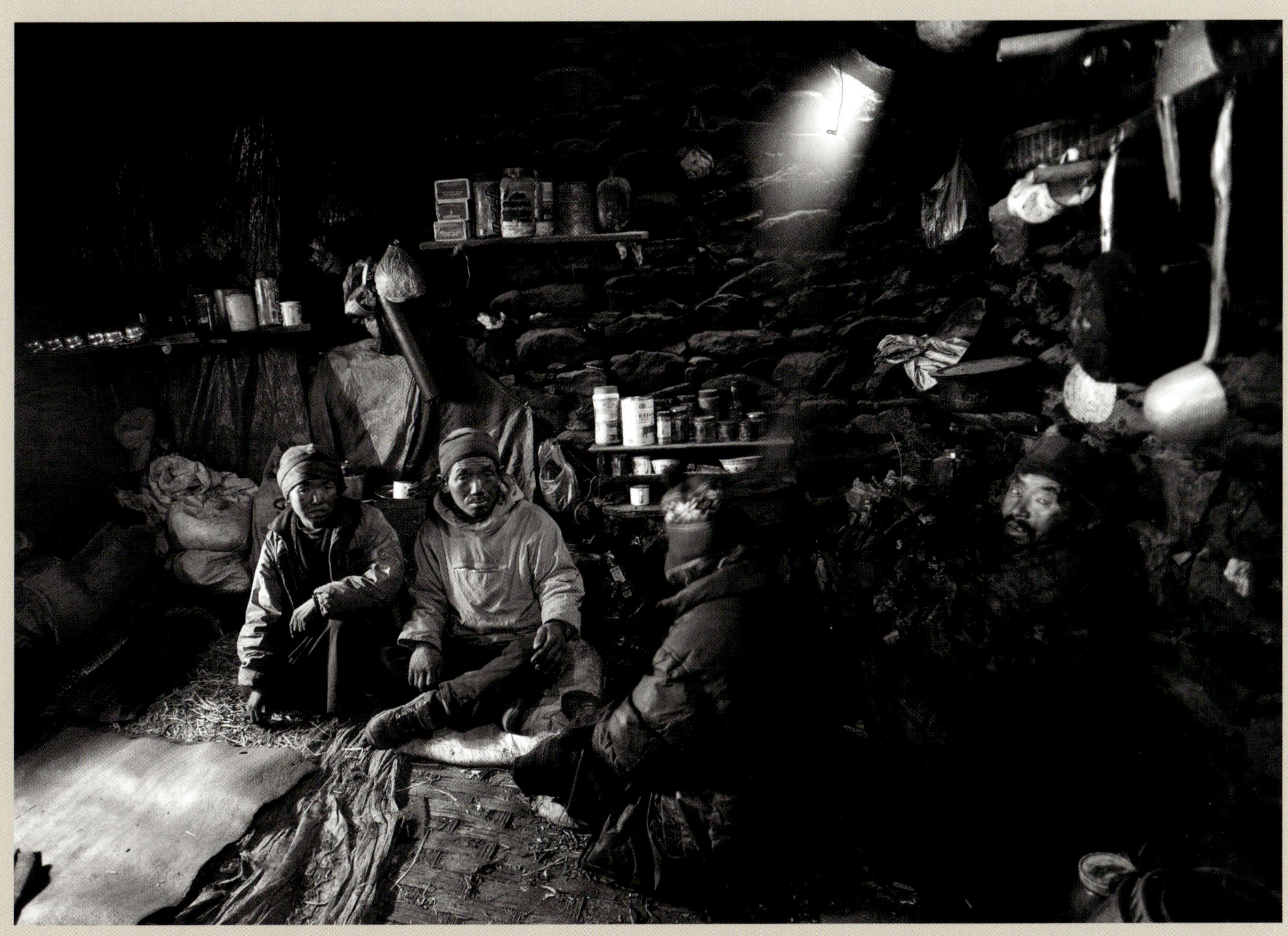

Nepali family near Thame, Khumbu, Nepal (2009).

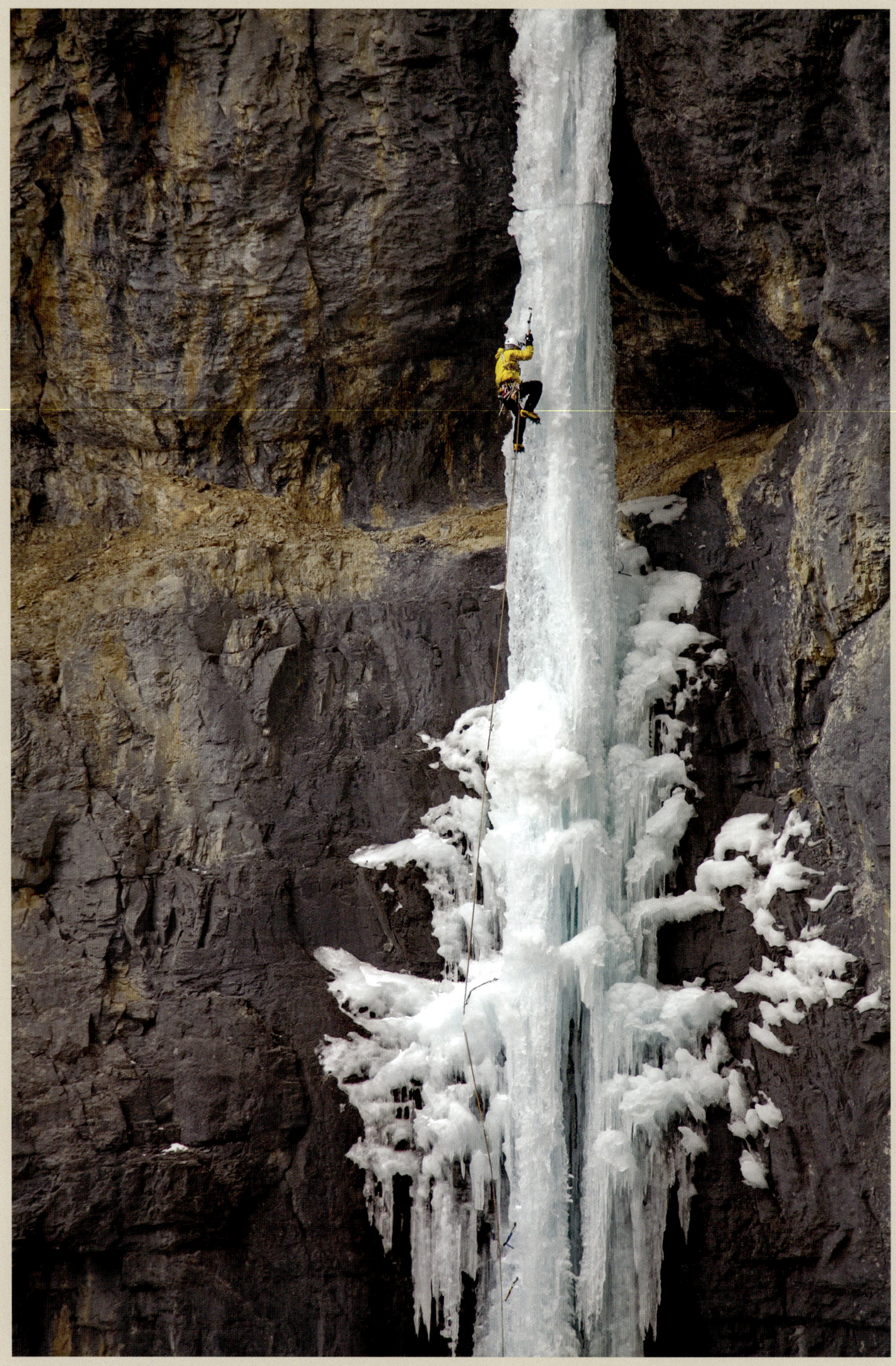

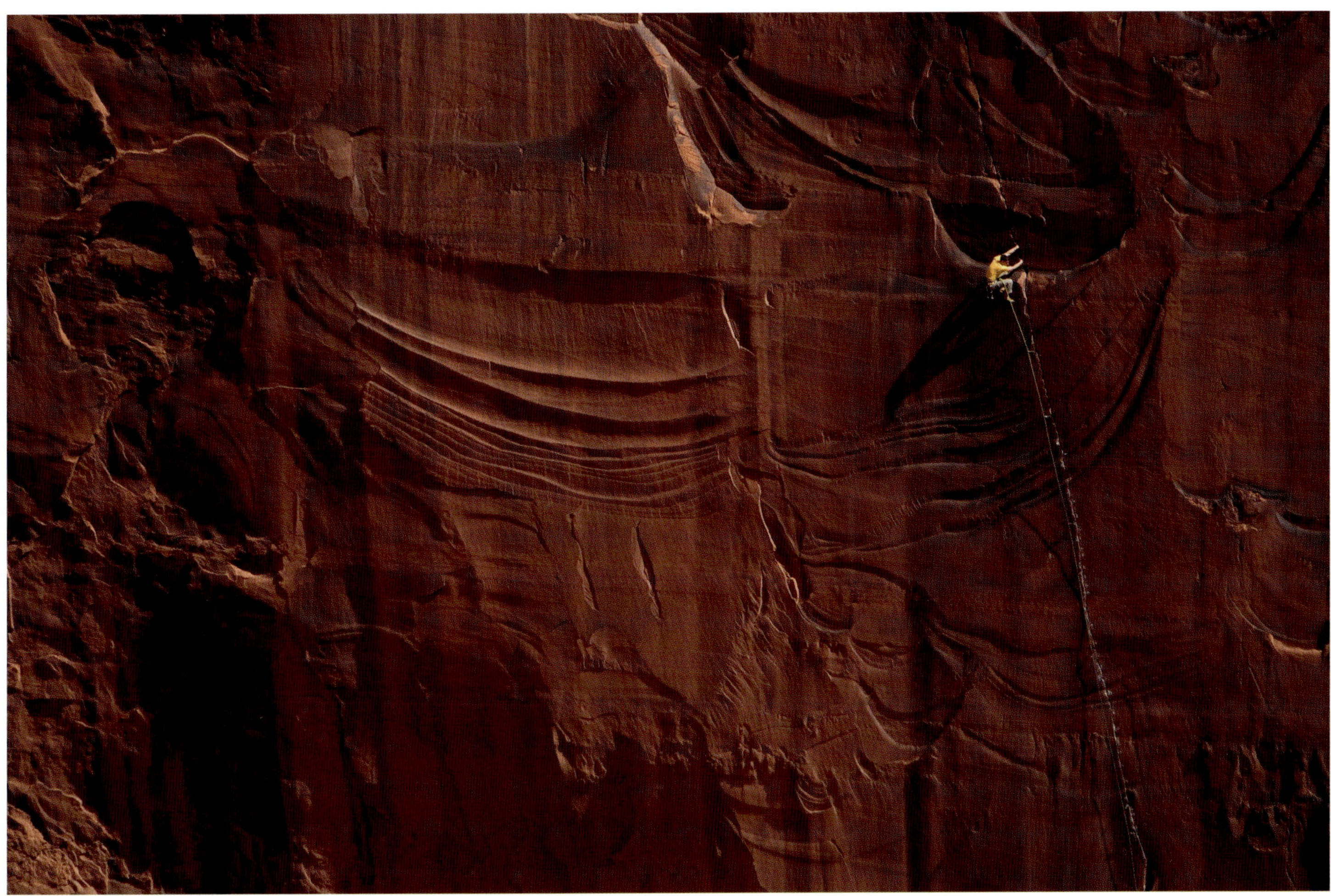

In this moment with Knud, I'm twenty and every day seems to reveal something new about this art. My eyes are open and hungry in a new way, and nothing seems too strange to photograph. Soon, I'll find my voice and initial success in climbing and exploration, using photography as a tool to expose raw emotion by stripping away the veneer that regular life demands we uphold. By reducing ourselves to survival, we somehow become more basic and emotionally complex at the same time. But adventure will never be my primary love. Eventually, when I tell people I work for *National Geographic,* they inevitably ask me what my favorite animal is. *Humans,* I always answer. We are the most complex, dynamic, and dangerous animal on Earth. I'll also come to believe that we are infinitely capable, kind, and mostly good. Photographs are simply the proof.

I look at Knud one last time and smile. I will return to this night many times in my memory when I try to understand why some photographs work and others fall flat. What has become clear is that the camera lets people speak without talking and gives the silent pieces of our hearts and the planet a voice. Without art, a person can only express in a moment. In a picture, they can scream through time. It doesn't matter if they're in front of the camera or behind it, and it doesn't matter what they are doing or where or when. They could be climbing a mountain, smoking in a club, or sleeping on a bench. Even if there is no one in the picture itself, there is always at least one person present. On this night in Austria, I learn that photography is a collaborative art and there is really no such thing as objectivity. It's always a conversation, and by witnessing a moment, we influence it and become part of it. I've often felt like an outsider. Photography is my way in.

The woman in the audience grabs my arm as I walk back into the shadows. She points at my camera and back to Knud, hands me a napkin with a scribbled number, then says three words: "I pay you." A week later, I deliver an 11-by-14-inch print in exchange for the equivalent of $60. It will take eleven more years before I shoot my first assignment for *National Geographic,* but it is a start.

ABOVE: Alex Honnold, Day Canyon, near Moab, Utah (2008).

OPPOSITE: American climber Bill Serantoni, Ghost River Wilderness Alberta, Canada (2005).

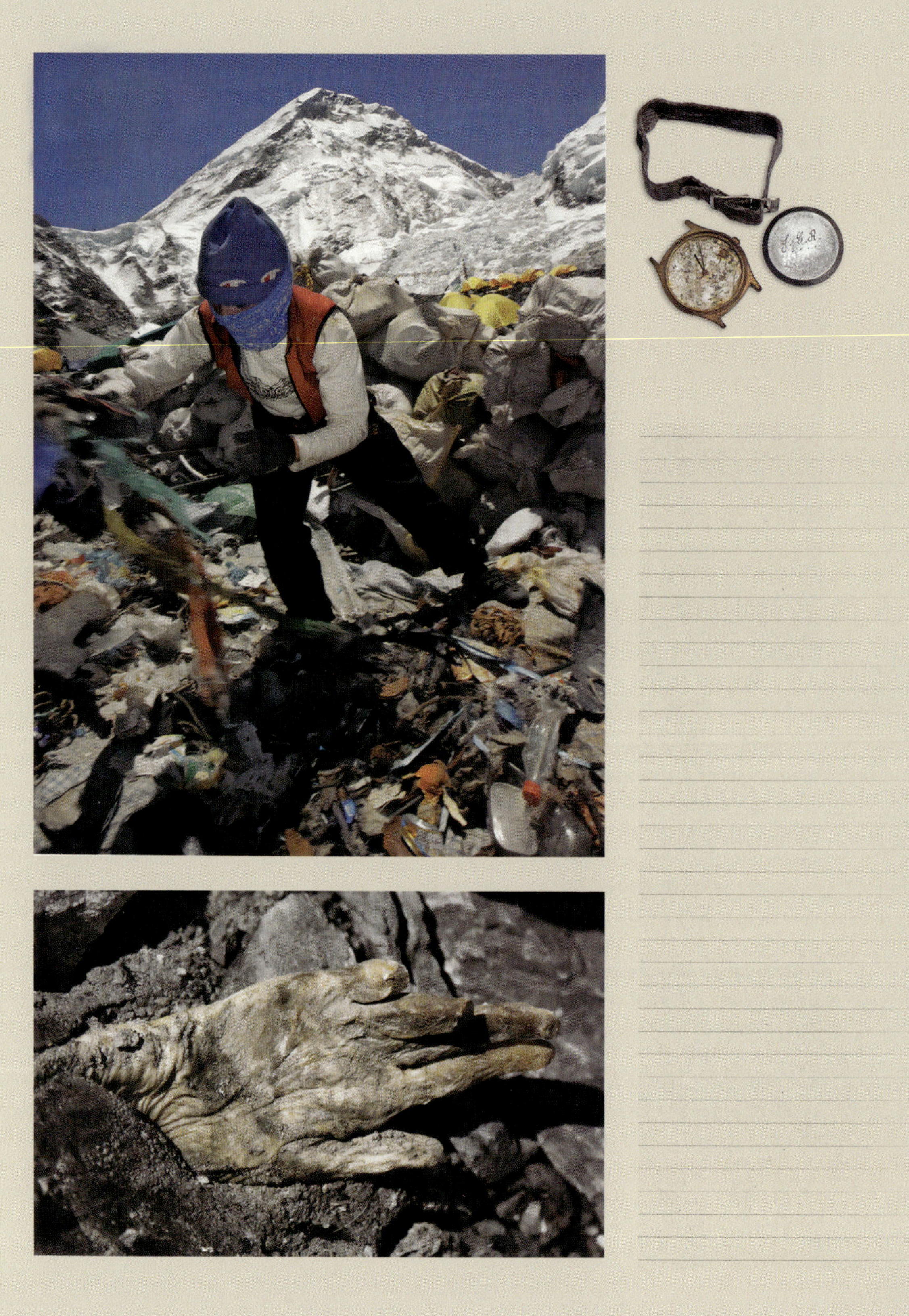

My first and second *National Geographic* publications

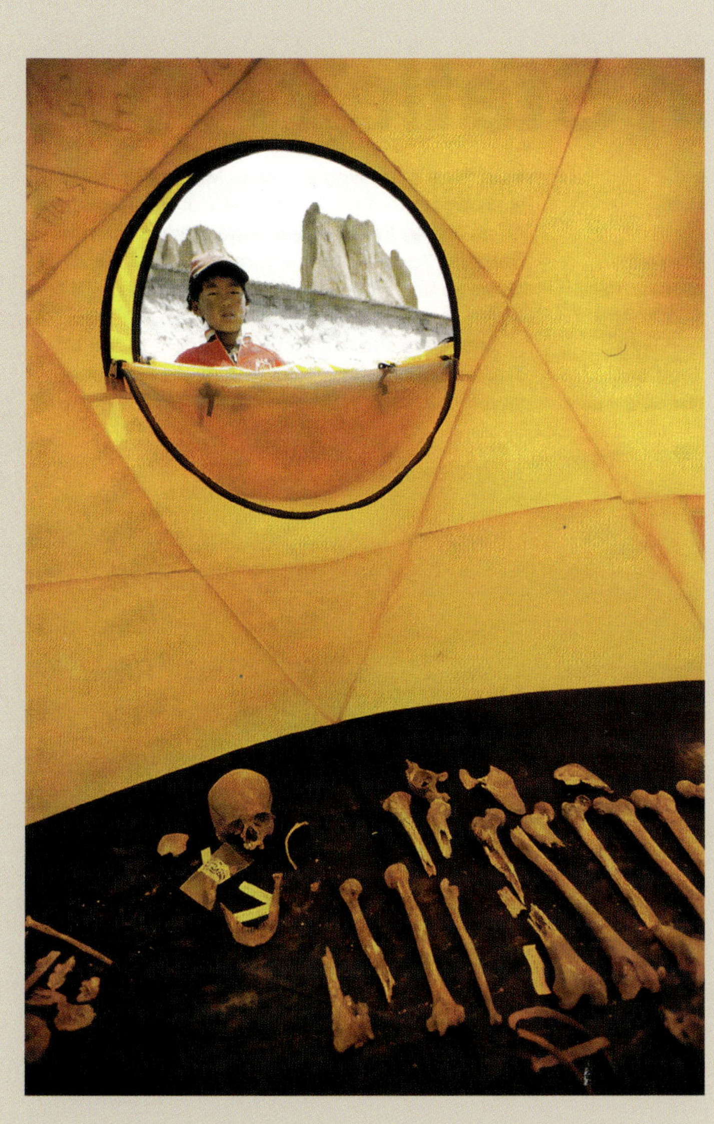

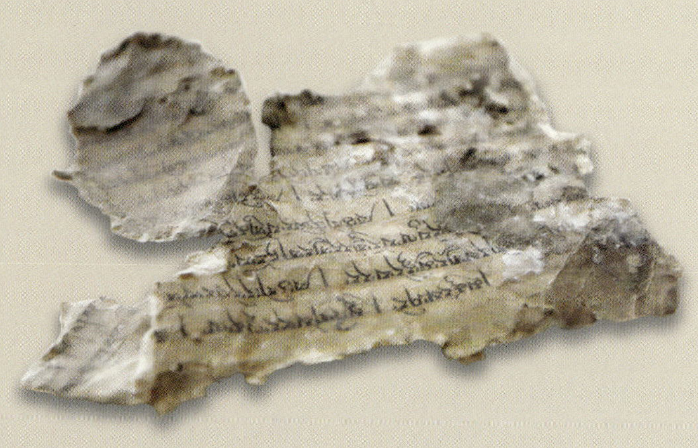

from Mount Everest and Mustang, Nepal (respectively).

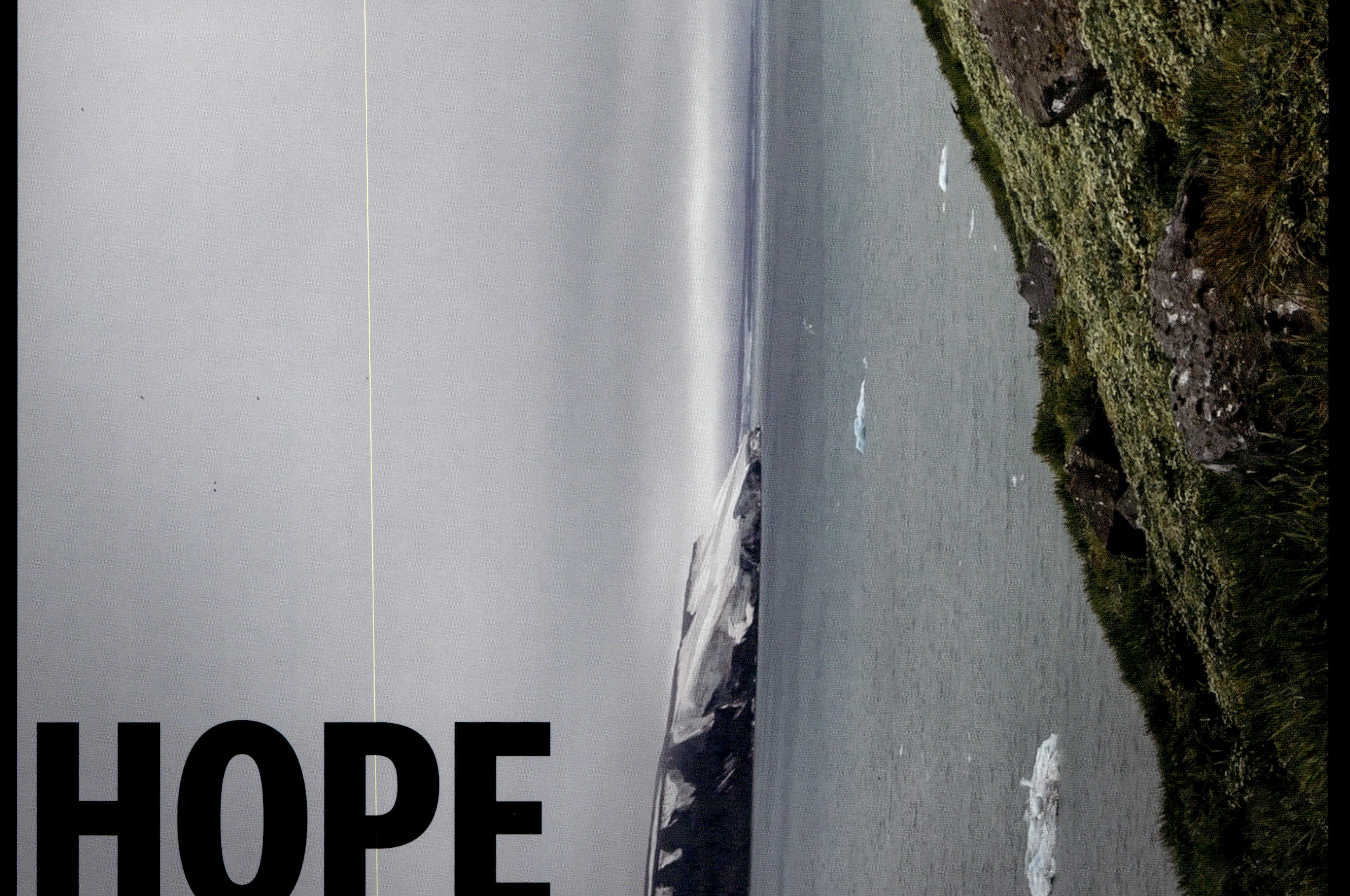

HOPE

\ˈhōp\ v: desire accompanied by expectation of or belief in fulfillment; also, expectation of fulfillment or success

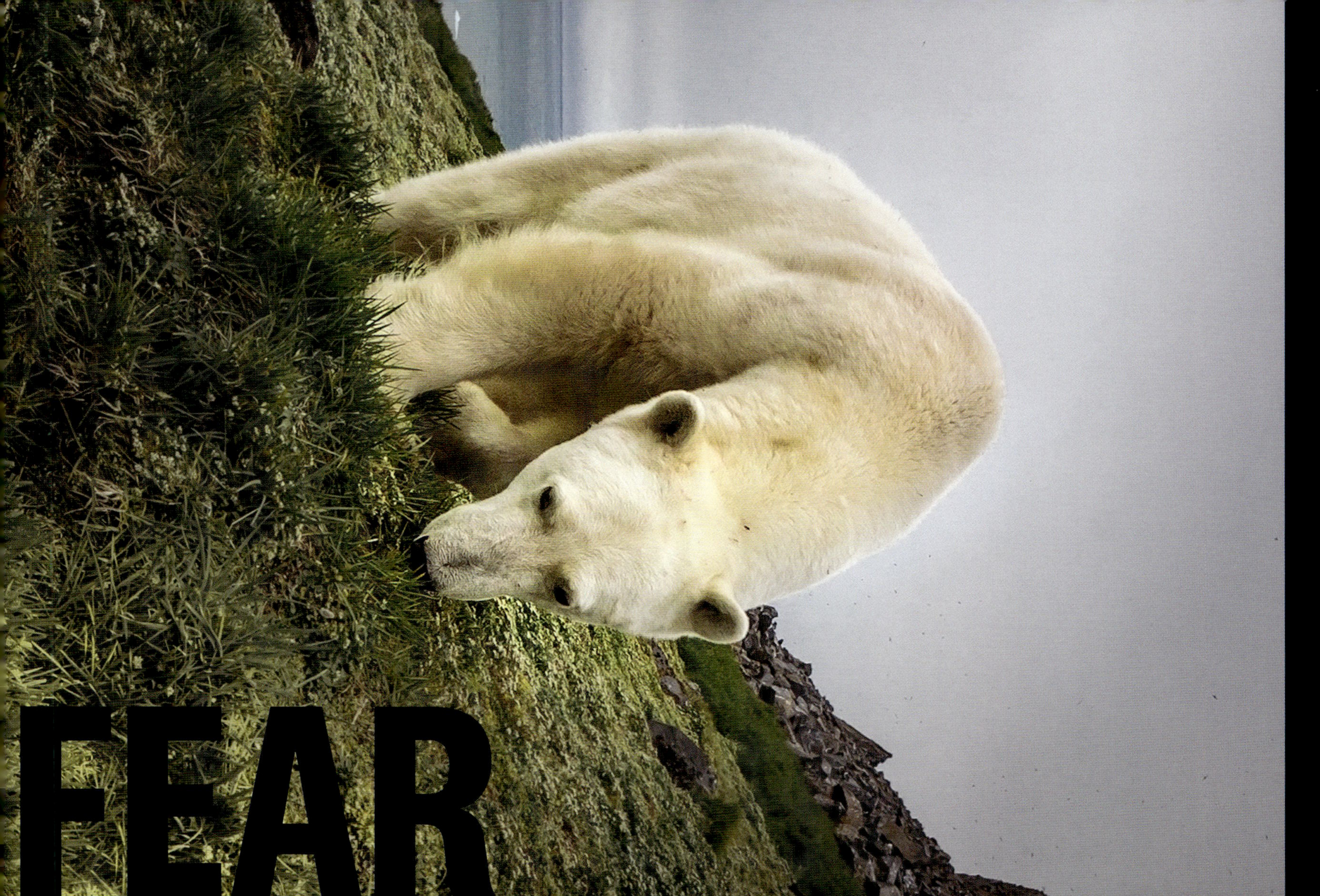

FEAR
\'fir\ *n*: a distressing emotion aroused by impending danger, evil, pain, and so on, whether the threat is real or imagined

COLD FUSION

Franz Josef Land, Russia

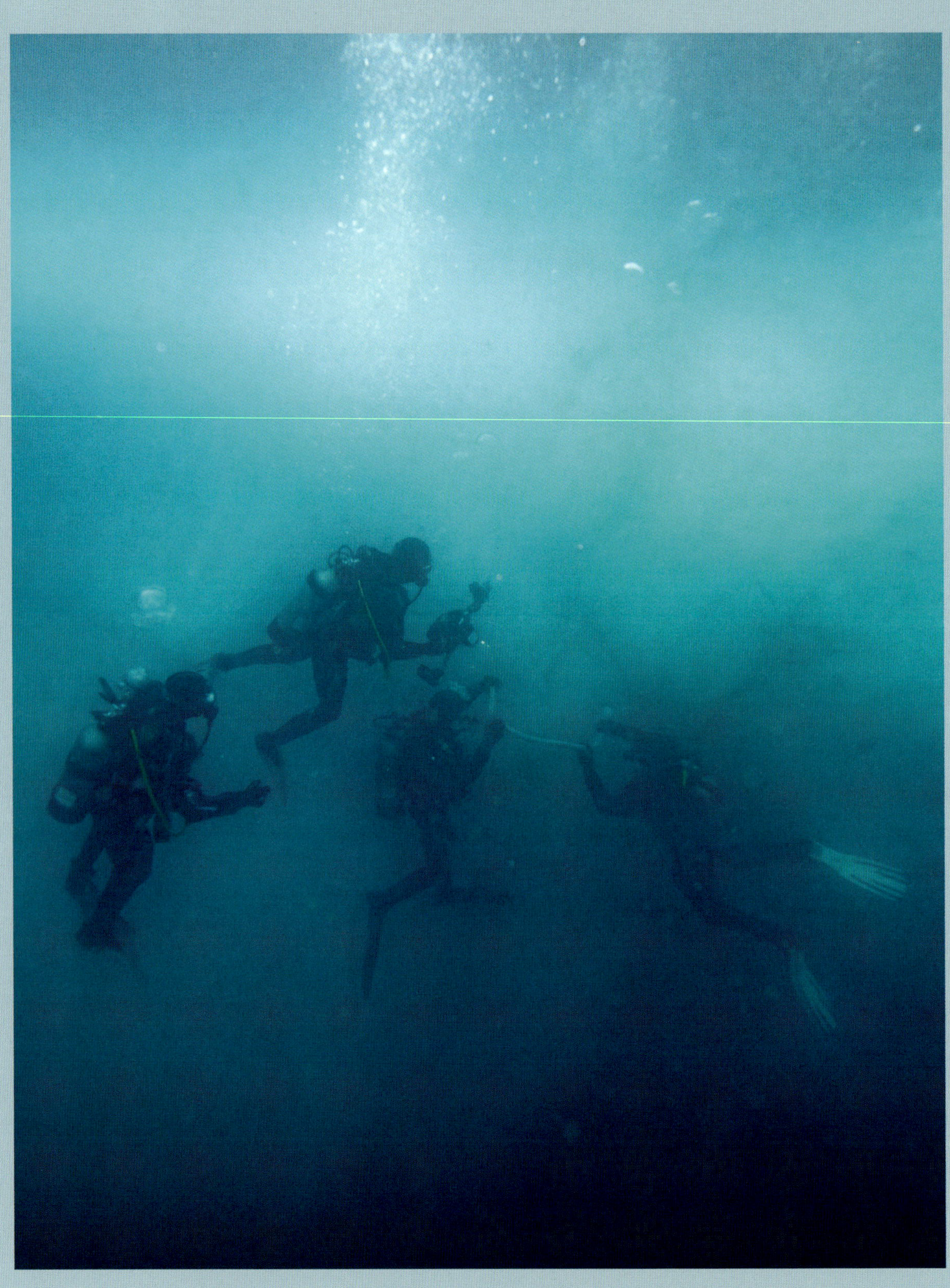

Franz Josef Land is an archipelago of 191 islands isolated deep in Russia's Barents Sea. Our interdisciplinary team of Russian and American scientists, led by Enric Sala of Pristine Seas, has been navigating the islands for more than a month. With only a handful of sparsely inhabited atolls, Franz Josef Land is one of the most intact ecosystems on Earth. Its isolation is its greatest defense, but there are still some forces that this land simply can't escape. The fact that the region remains so unspoiled is what makes it perfect for studying the shifting climate. Our goal is to help establish a new baseline of scientific data that future changes can be measured against. My job is to distill the science into pictures that might make people care.

A polar bear forages on a grassy slope.

Thousands of birds nest and screech on the angular columns of a basalt cliff.

A huddle of walruses peer at me for an underwater family portrait.

We've collected algae samples from icebergs and wandered around in whiteouts while keeping a keen eye for bears that have run out of ice. We've visited old outposts and surveyed the impacts of human habitation. We've taken samples of seawater, soil, and bones and all the days have blended because there is no night this far north. After a month, I'm tired, and even diving has become a chore.

An hour ago, I grabbed an oxygen tank from the "filled" rack, meaning it should've been full of air. When my dive watch didn't connect, I dismissed it. When my dive partner turned on his gas to get in the water, his hose blew. We should've called it right then and there. Instead, I plopped in alone for a short dive—"Don't worry, it'll be fine." Within fifteen minutes, I had absentmindedly descended too far, too fast. And now here I am in nearly black 32°F water, furiously kicking toward the little sparkle of midnight sun.

It's easy to get away with a single misstep. Maybe it didn't even feel like a mistake at all. Then we make a second mistake unknowingly correcting for or ignoring the first. Sometimes we make three more mistakes while rectifying the first two we've either forgotten or dismissed. "It'll be fine." It's only when we're under threat that we start to see the compounding effect of our actions fusing together into inescapable consequence. This is true for everything from diving to the human impact on climate and the environment.

When was the last time I slept?

Why didn't I check the tank?

Why did I get in the water alone?

How did I get so deep?

Will I pass out before or after my lungs fill with water?

When was the first commercial internal combustion engine invented?

I'm blacking out now and the world is inky and blurred. My eyes search for the surface as I feel my lips open to inhale the sea.

Instead, they are met by air, and I frantically fill my lungs long and deep. I float on my back and stare into the unending daylight, keenly aware of the string of seemingly unrelated mistakes that brought me to this moment. The earth is creaking under the strain of the human family, gasping for air as we pump massive amounts of greenhouse gasses into the atmosphere and suck up all the oxygen that remains. I bob quietly and finally remember: The first commercial internal combustion engine was invented by George Brayton in 1872, the pivotal moment that set off a perilous chain reaction that has forever changed the planet.

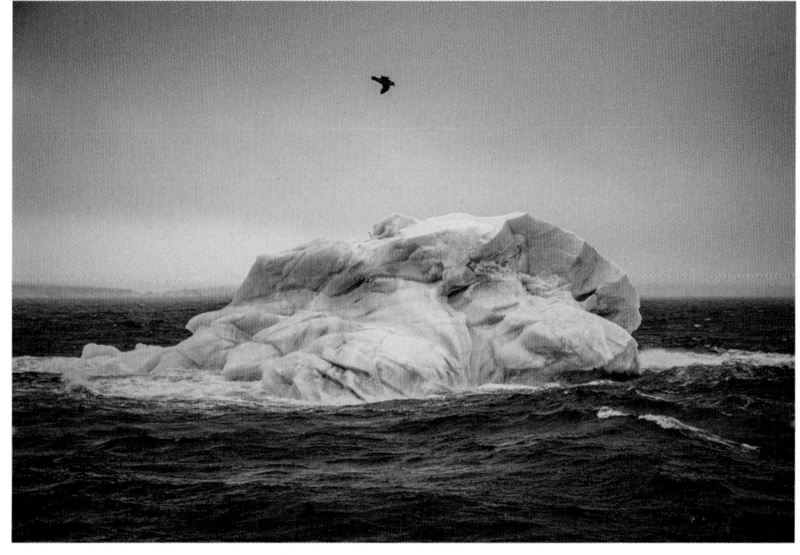

PREVIOUS: Franz Josef Land, Russia (2013). OPPOSITE: A diving team collects algae samples from an iceberg in the Barents Sea.

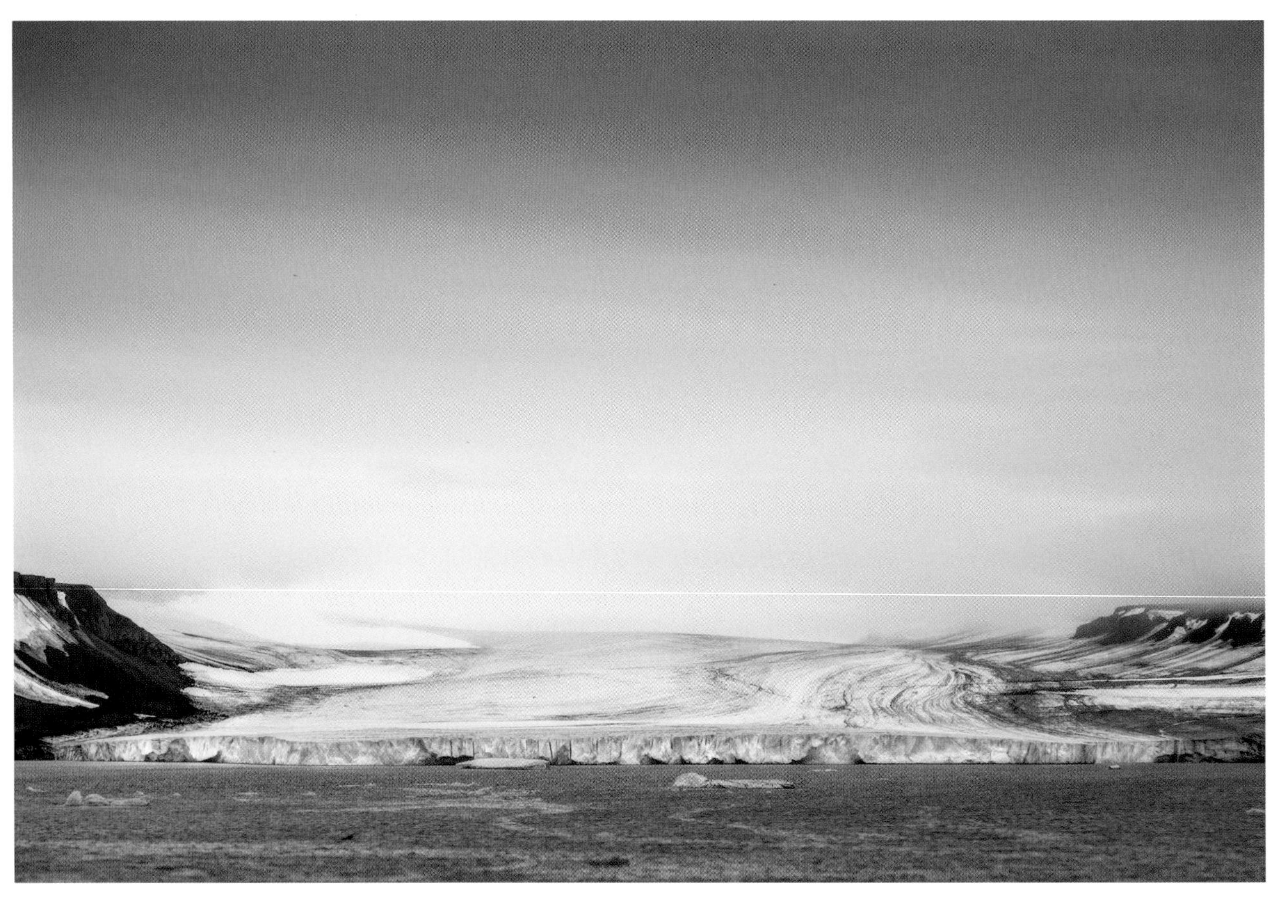

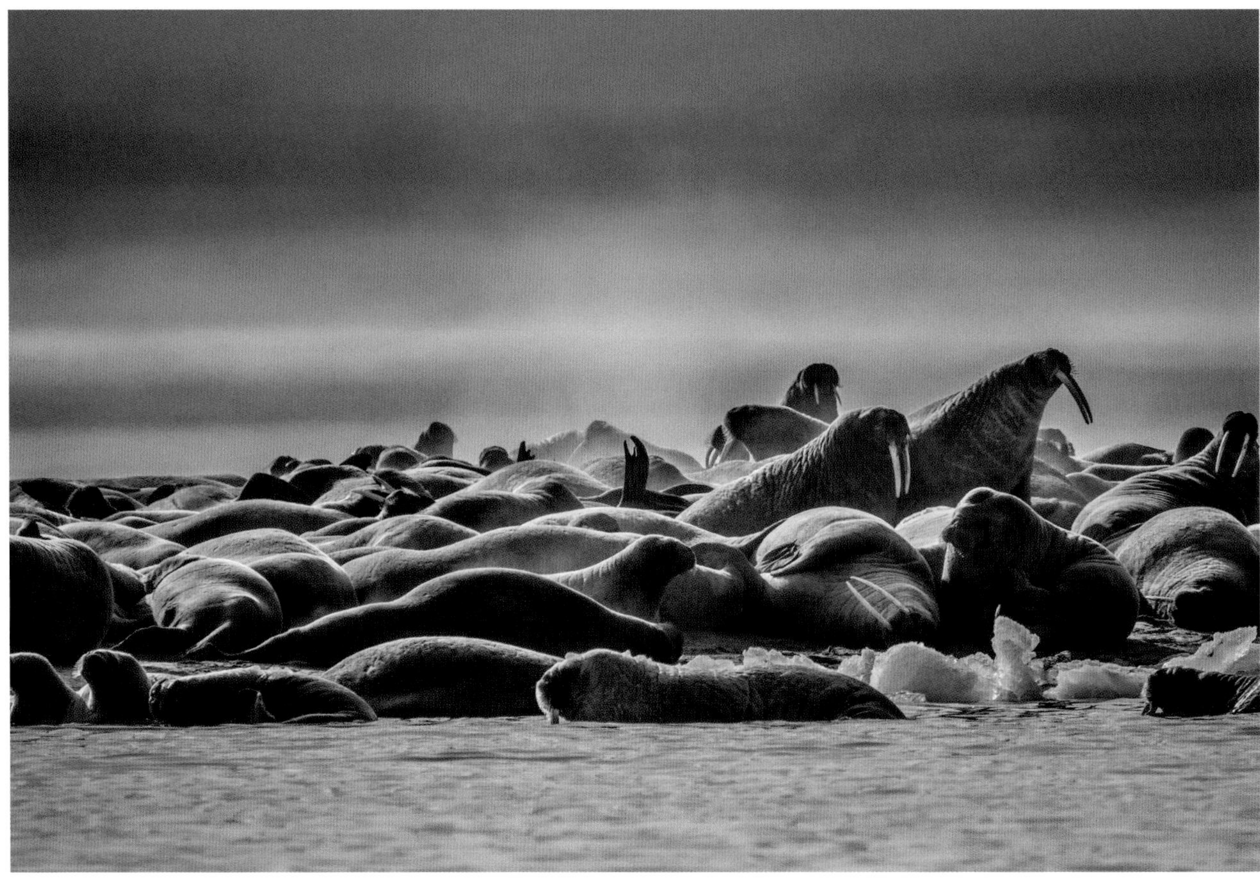

ABOVE: Glacier, Hooker Island. **BELOW:** Walrus rookery, Cape Flora.

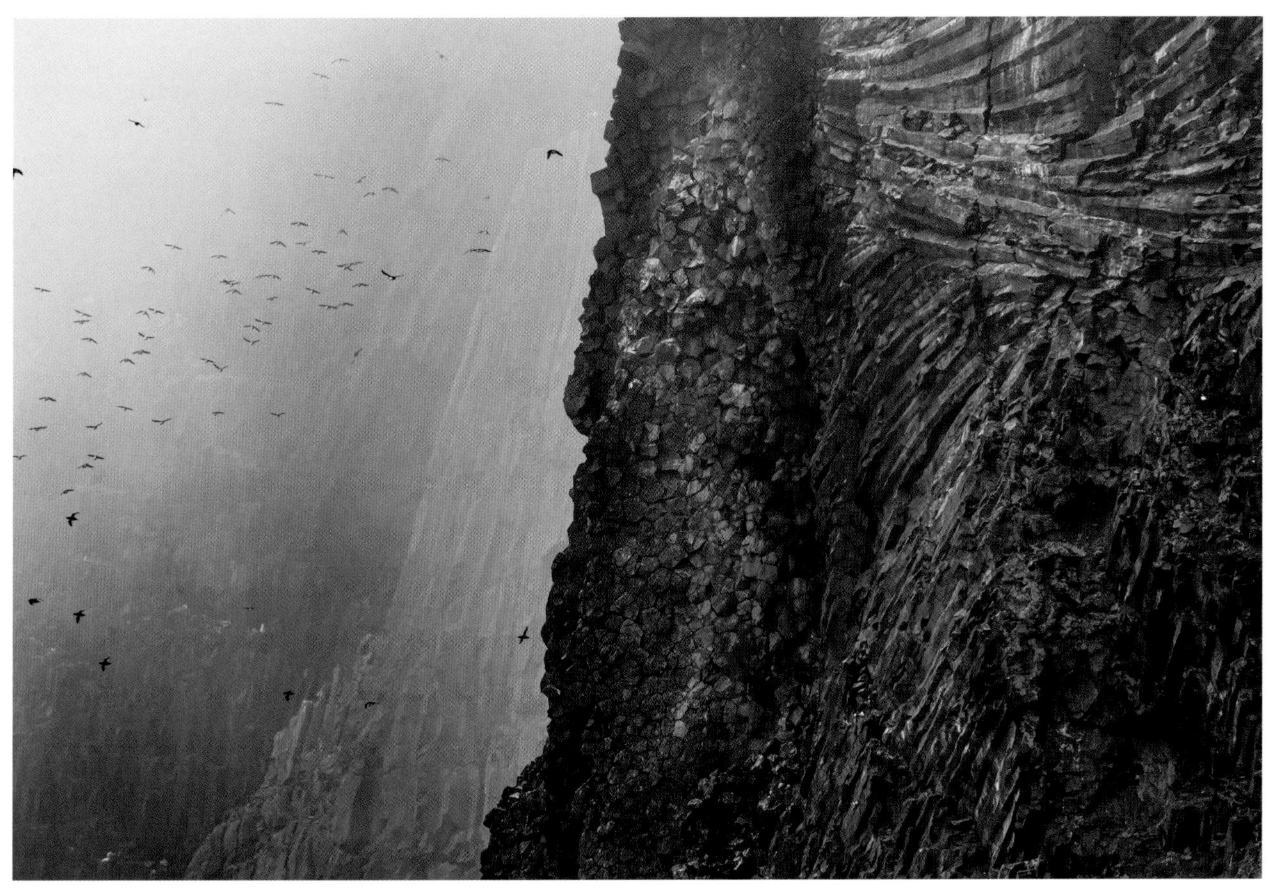

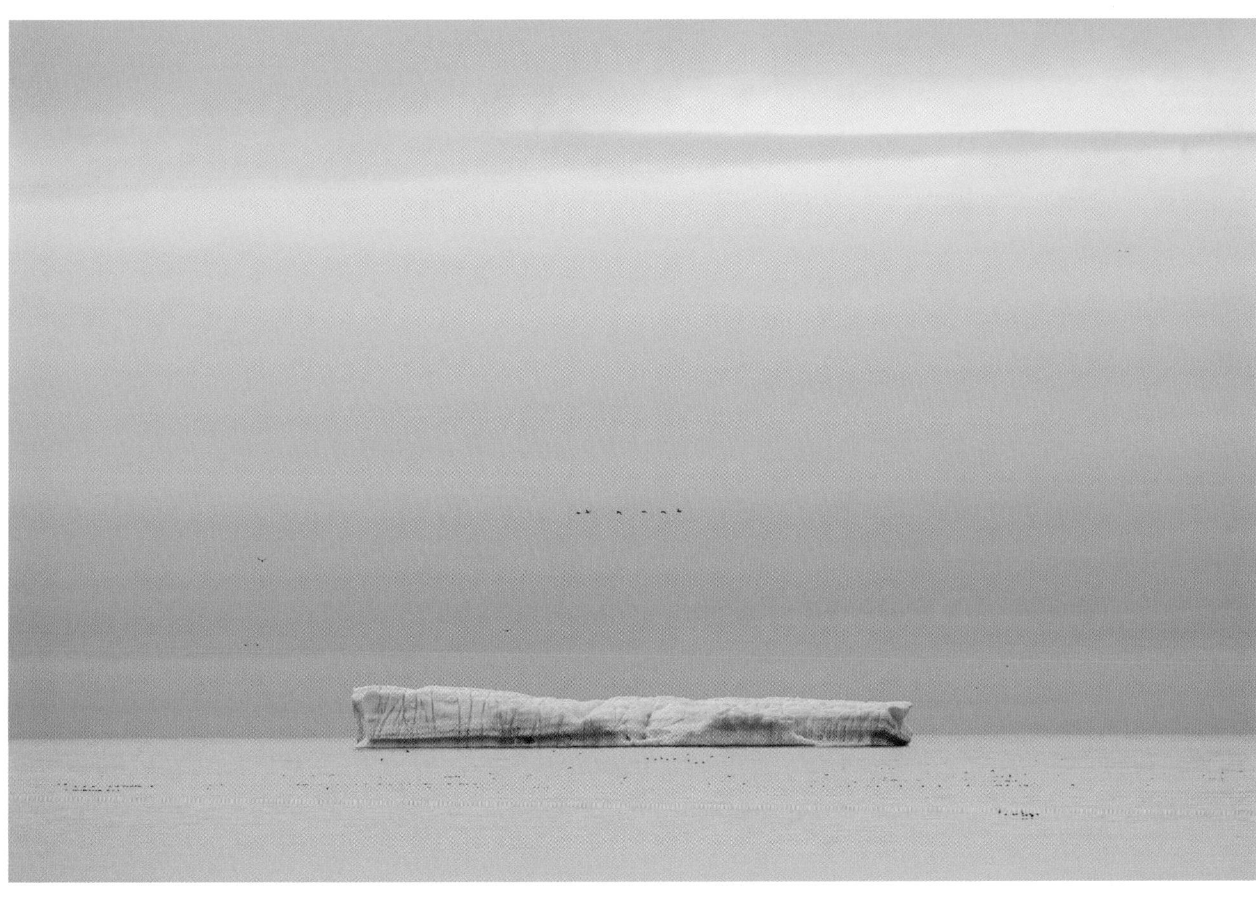

ABOVE: Basalt sea cliffs, Hooker Island. **BELOW:** Murres fly above an iceberg in the Barents Sea. **FOLLOWING:** Nesting birds at Rubini Rock, Hooker Island.

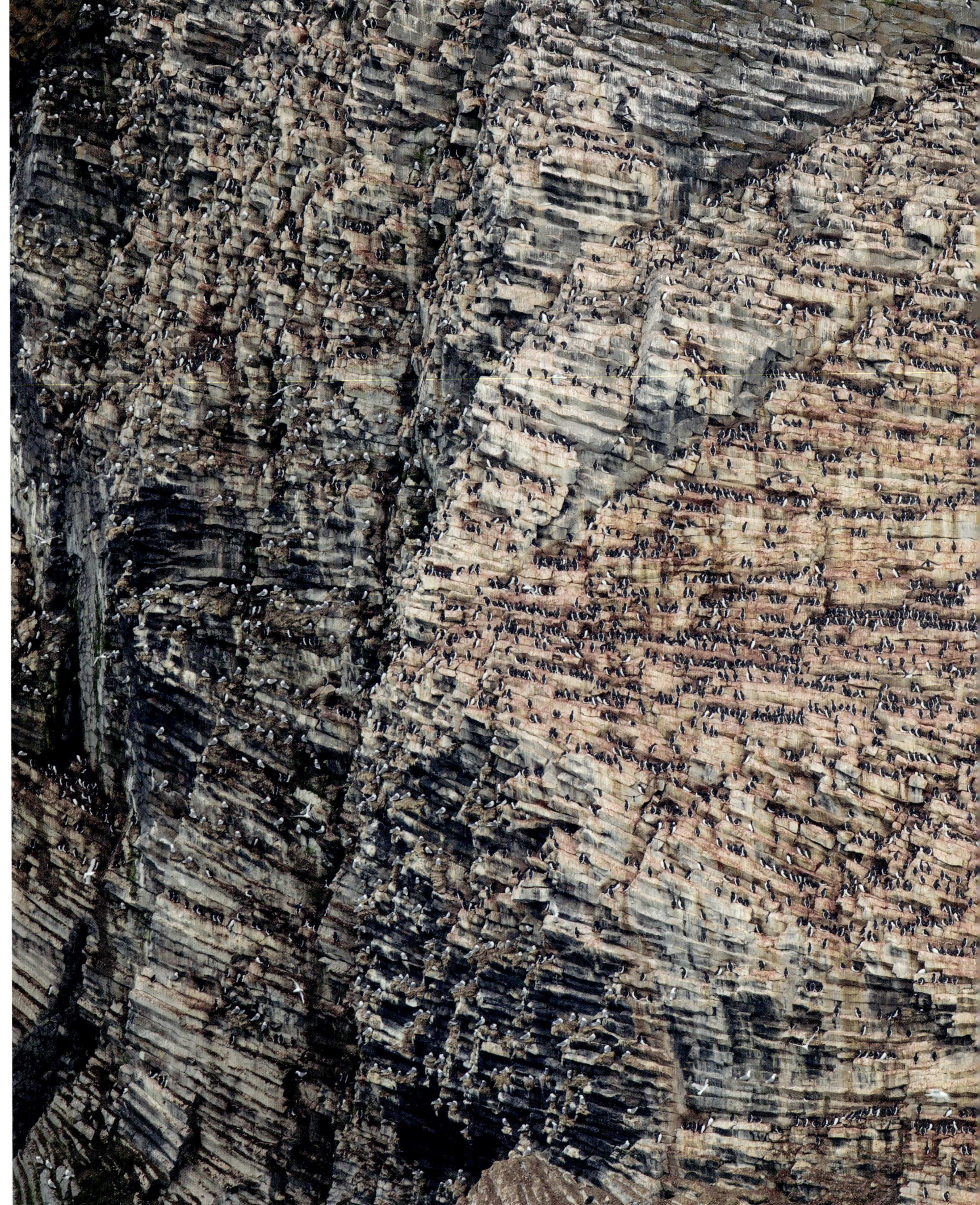

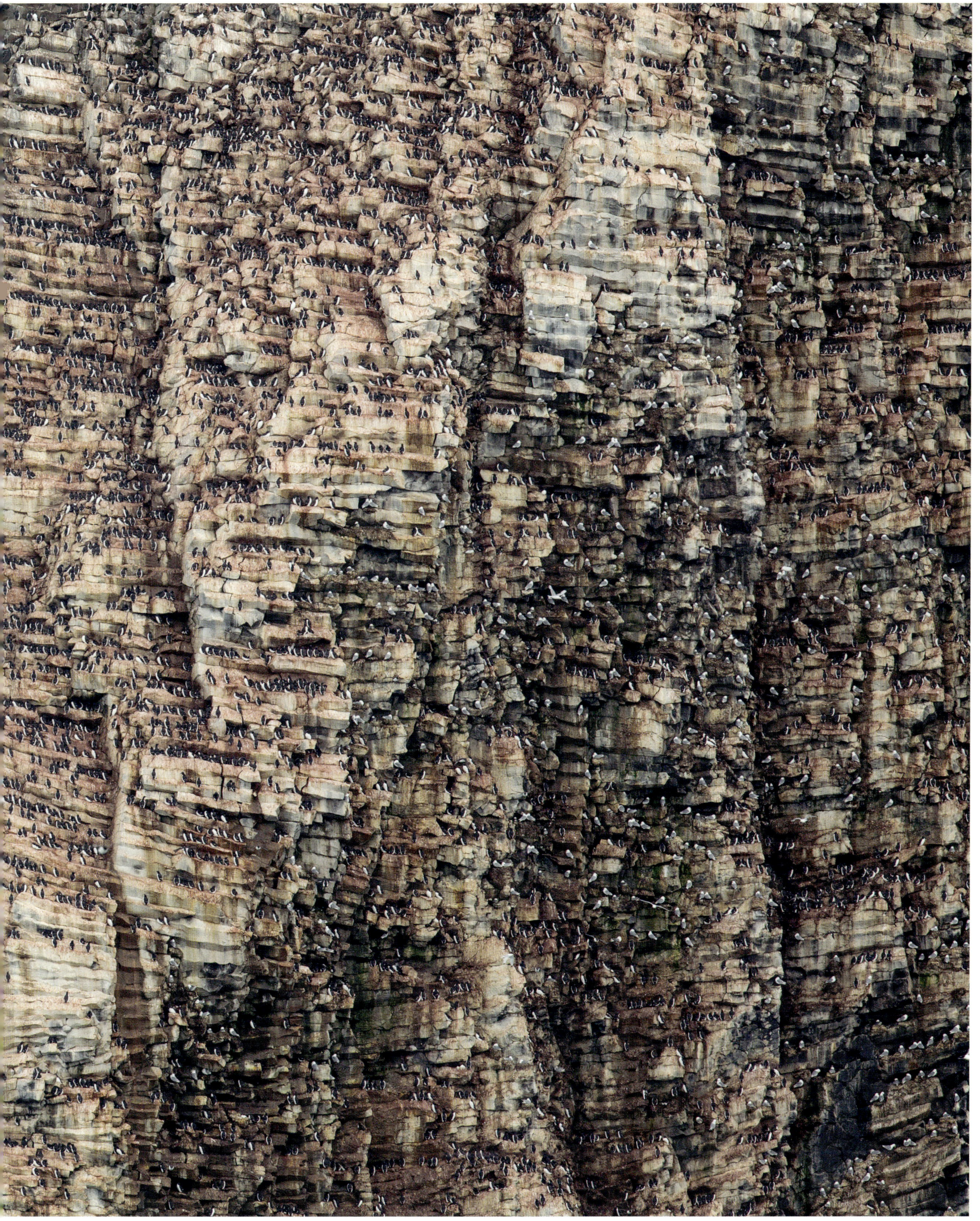

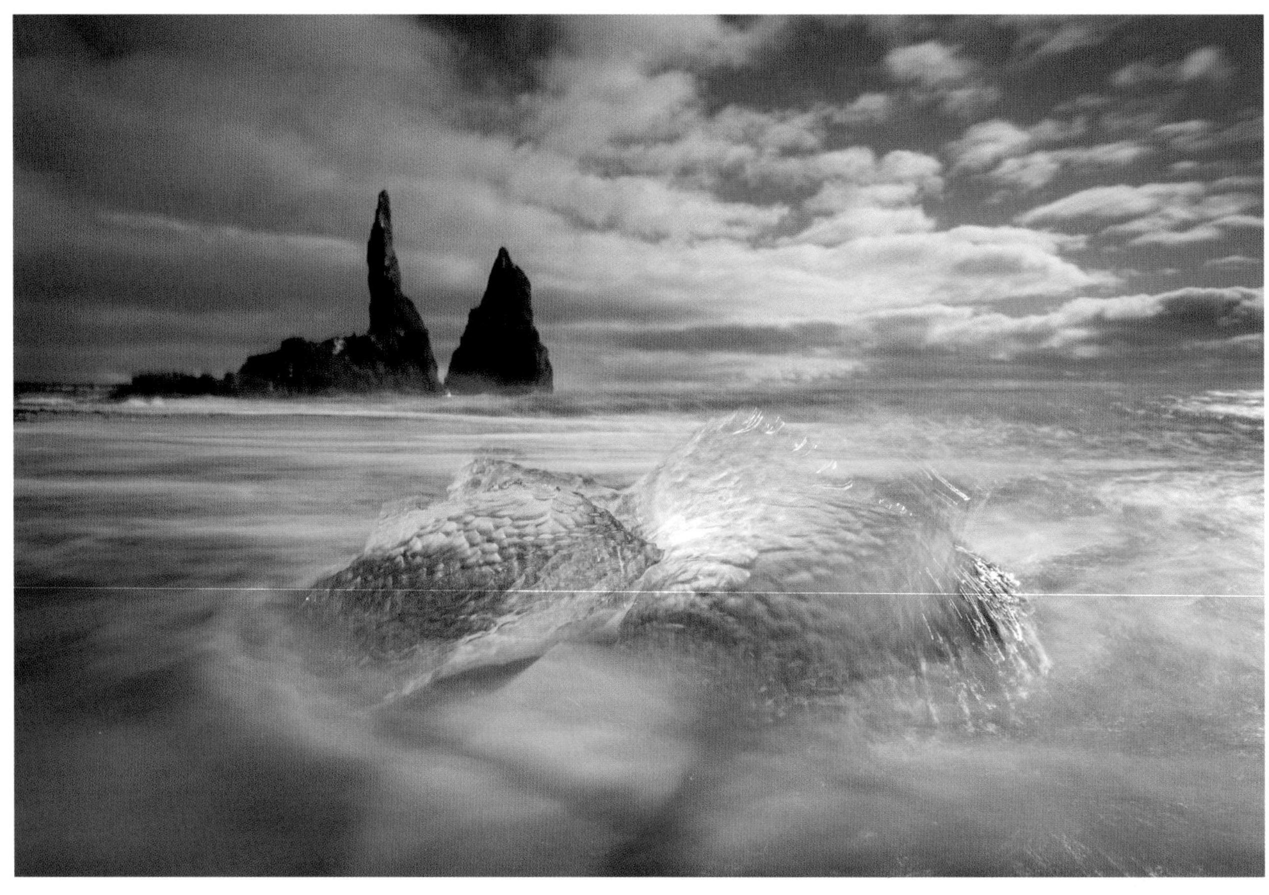

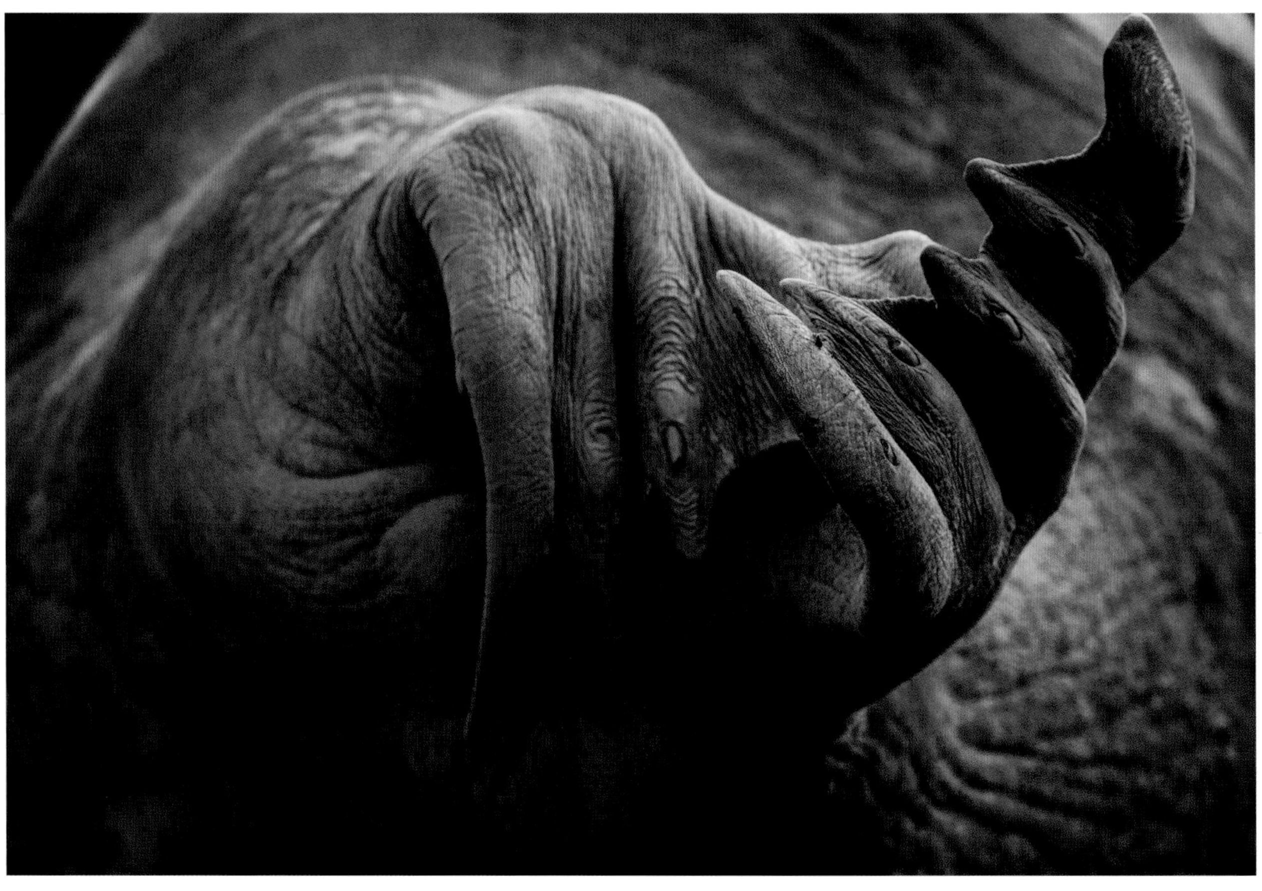

ABOVE: Ancient ice in the surf of Cape Tegetthoff. **BELOW:** Walrus hind limbs.

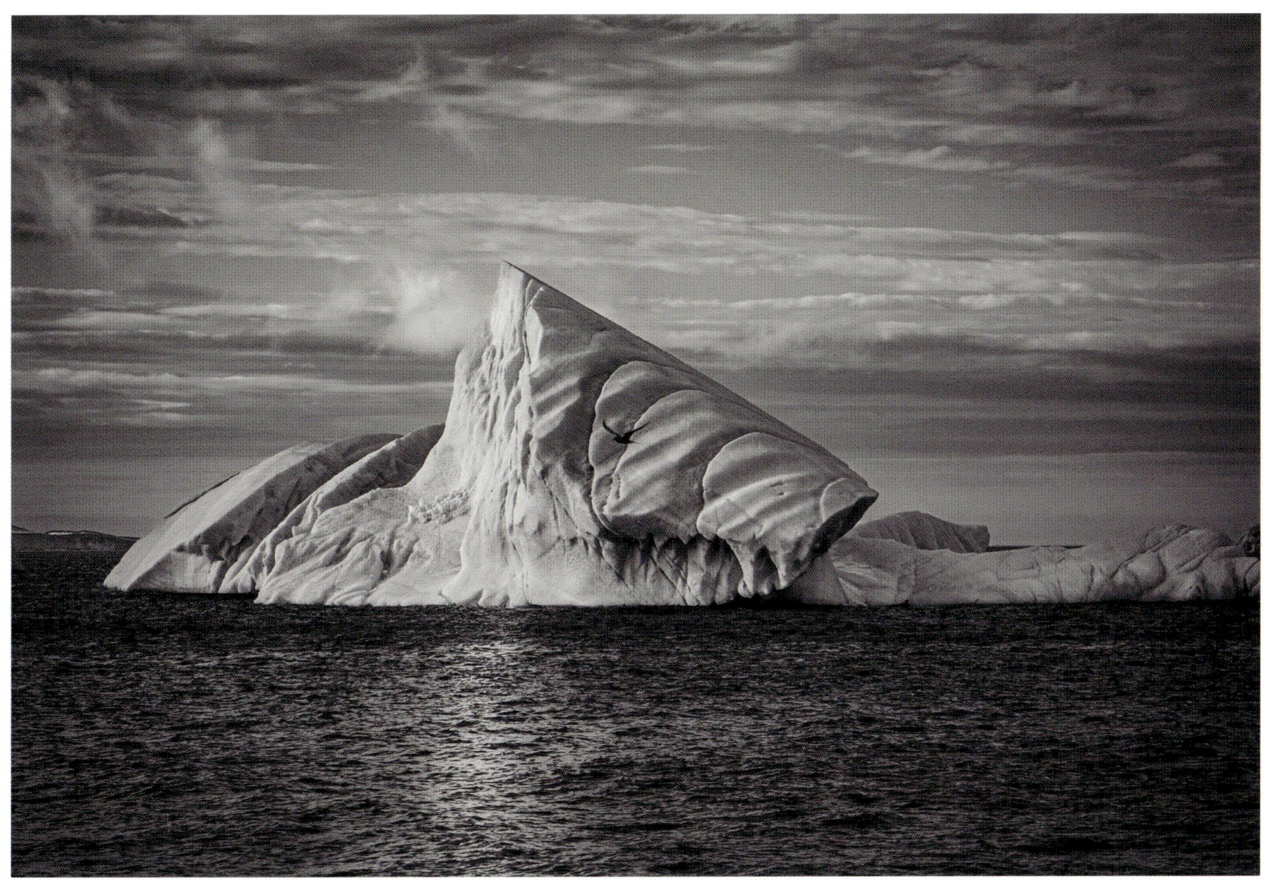

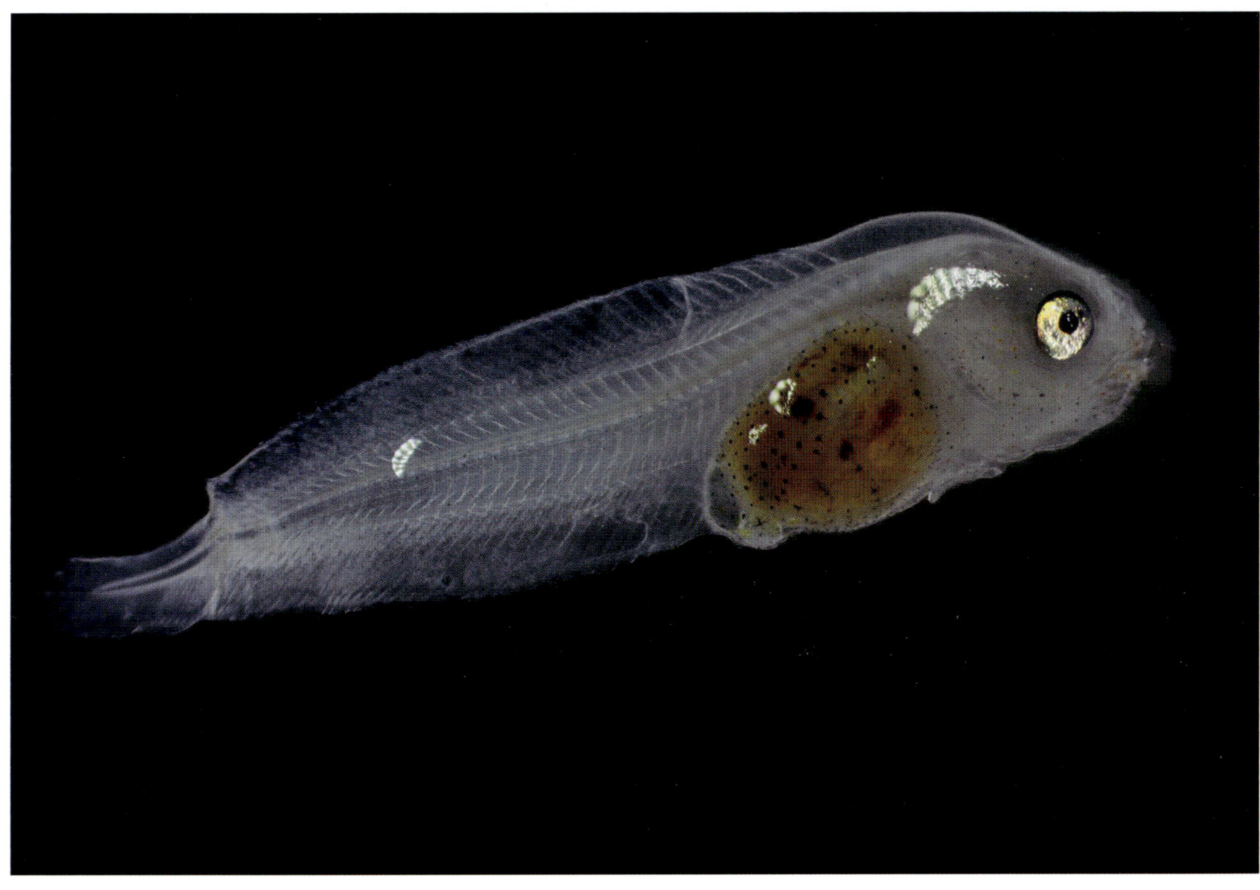

Barents Sea. **ABOVE:** Iceberg. **BELOW:** Snailfish.

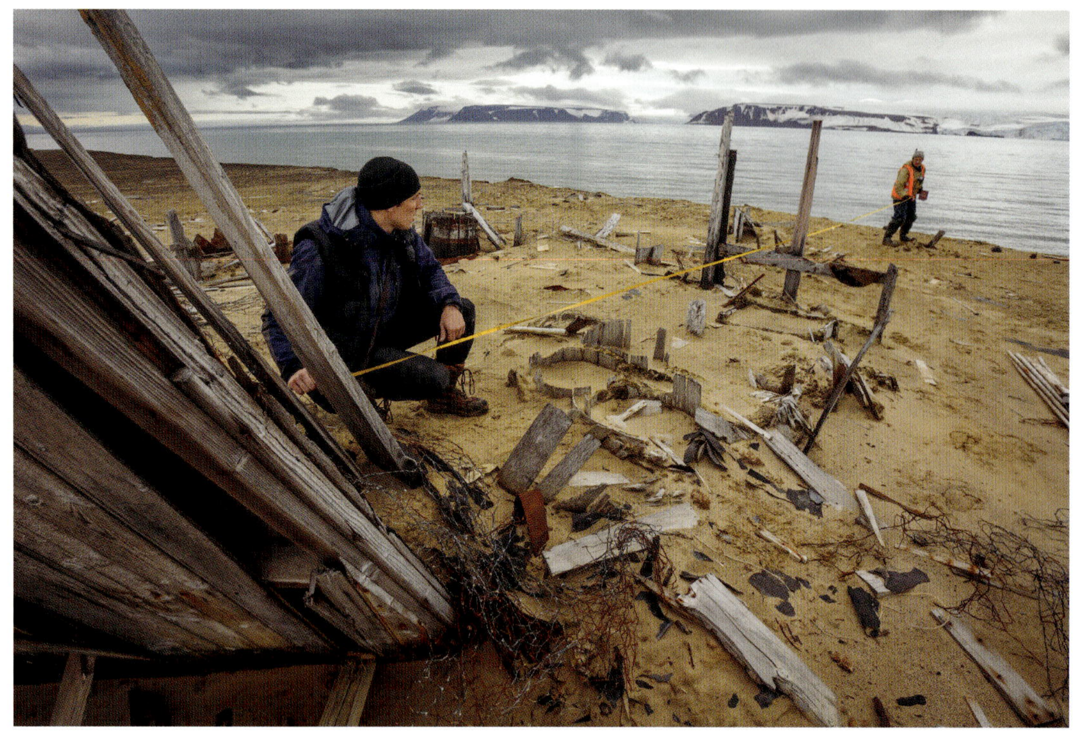

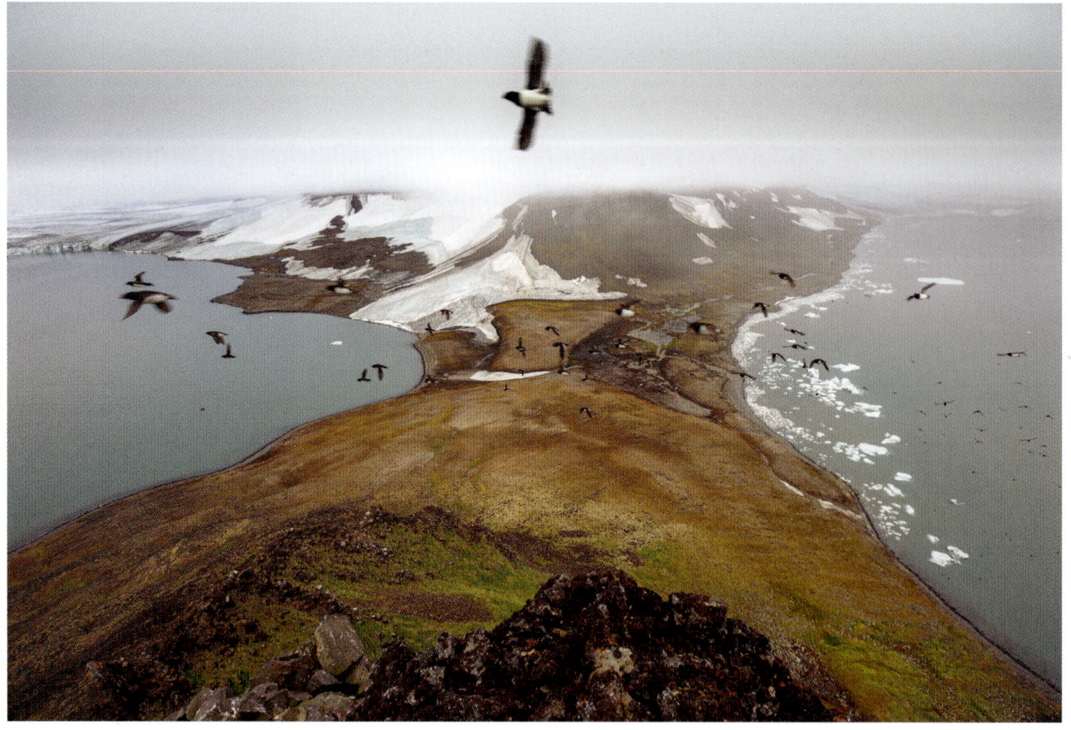

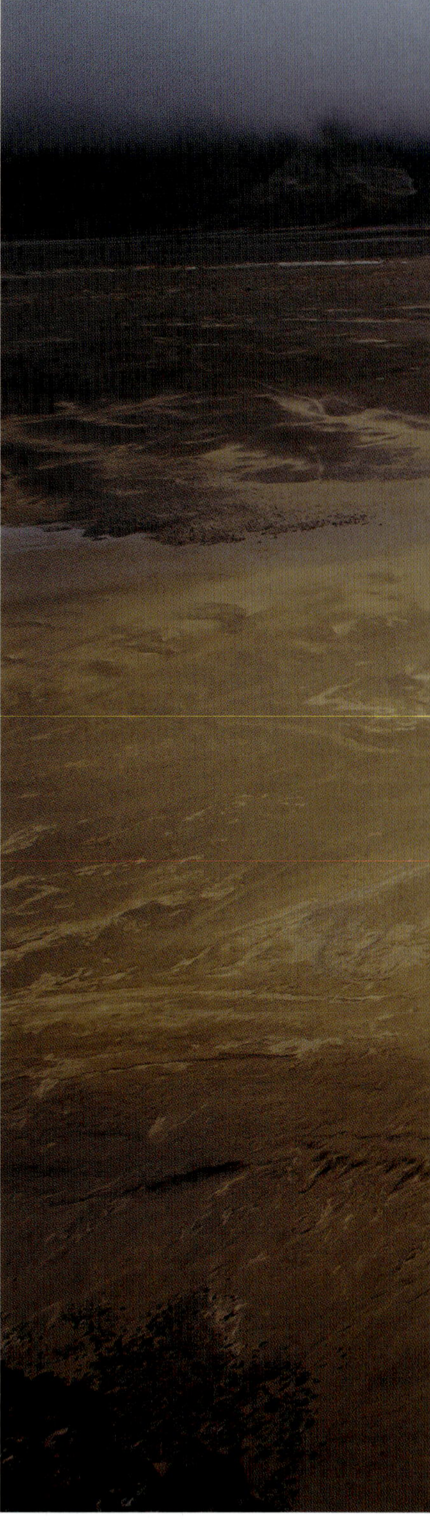

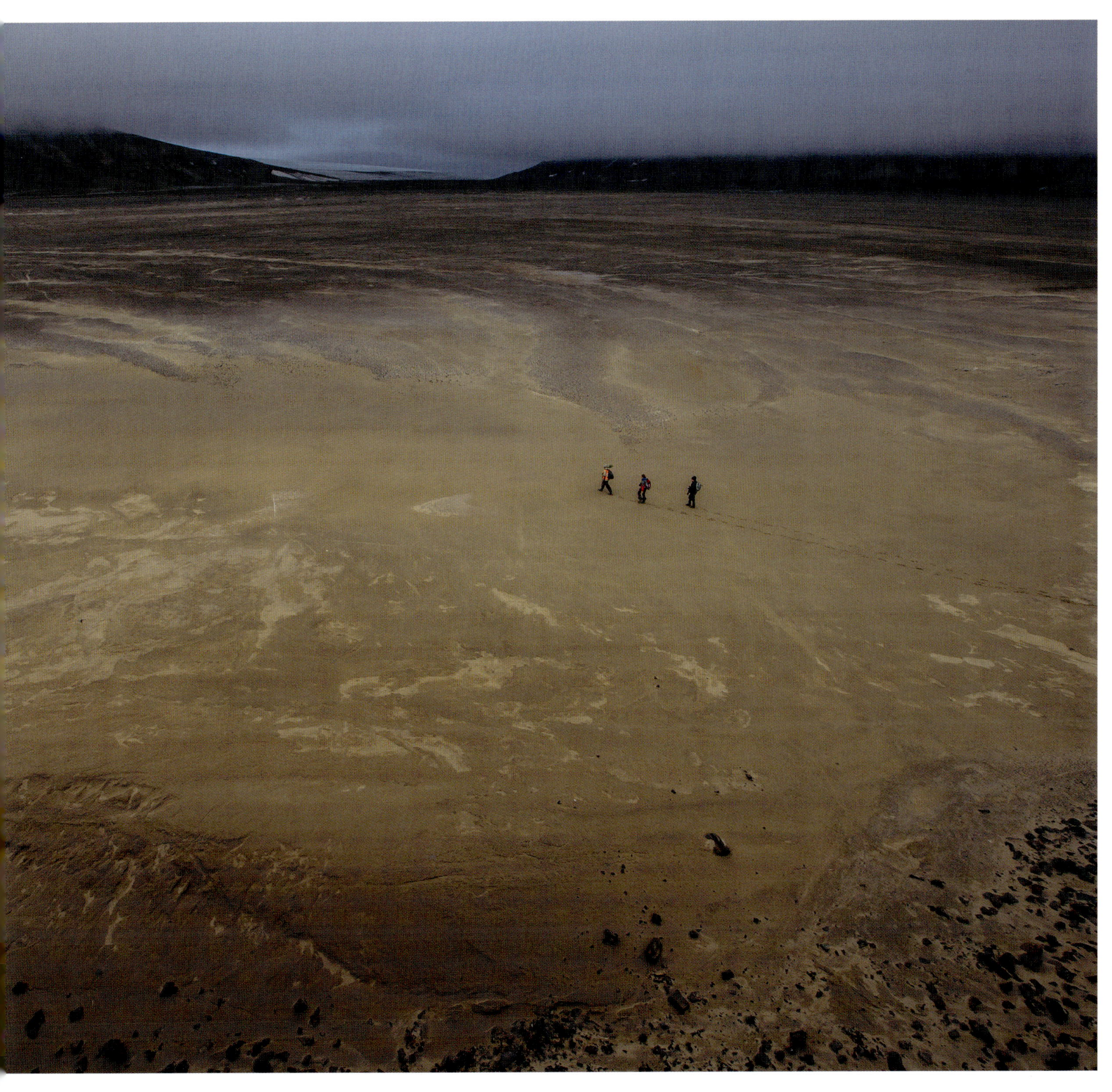

Field biologists traverse a flood plain while collecting samples of soil, algae, and whatever plant life they can find while keeping a keen eye for polar bears. **OPPOSITE, ABOVE:** Scientists measure coastal erosion from known landmarks. **OPPOSITE, BELOW:** Little Auks in flight over Hooker Island.

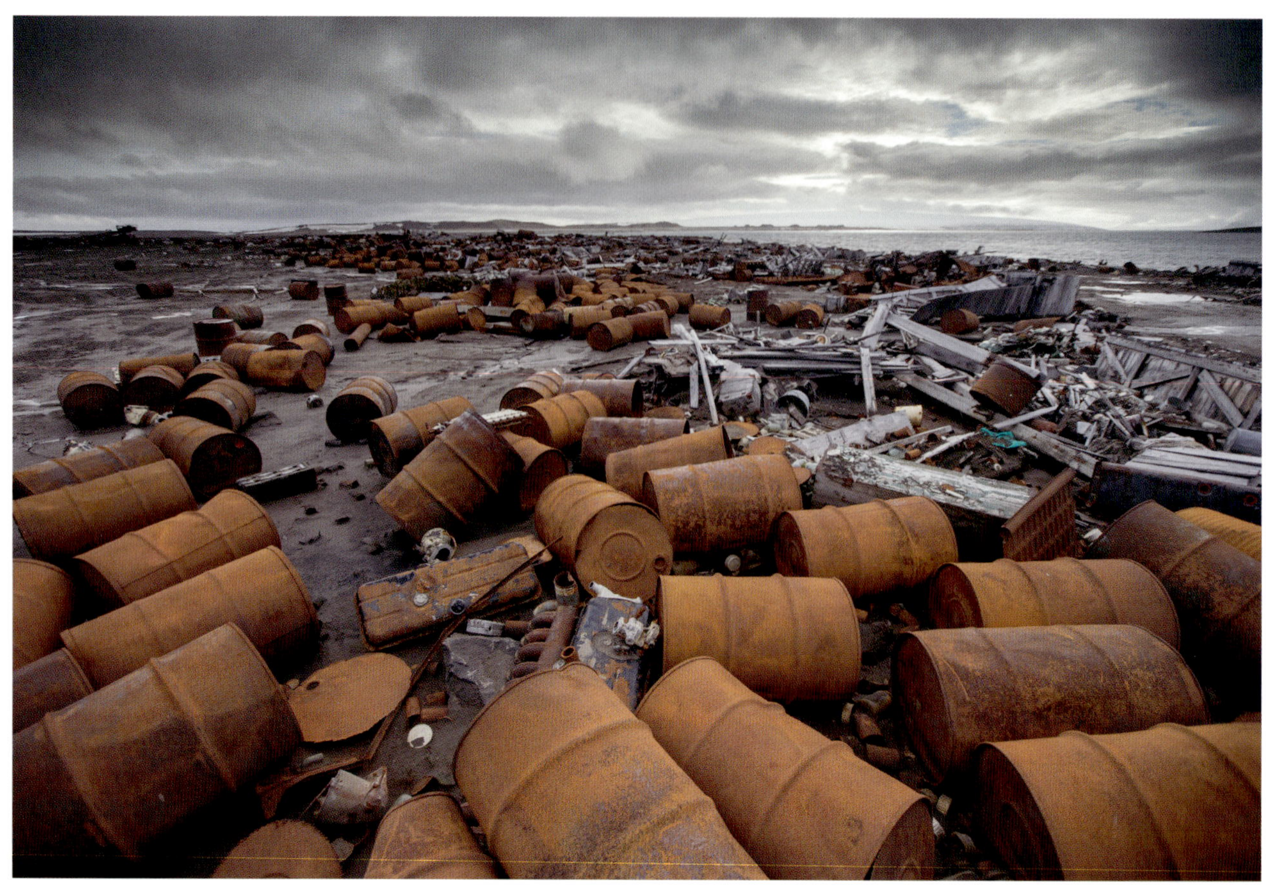

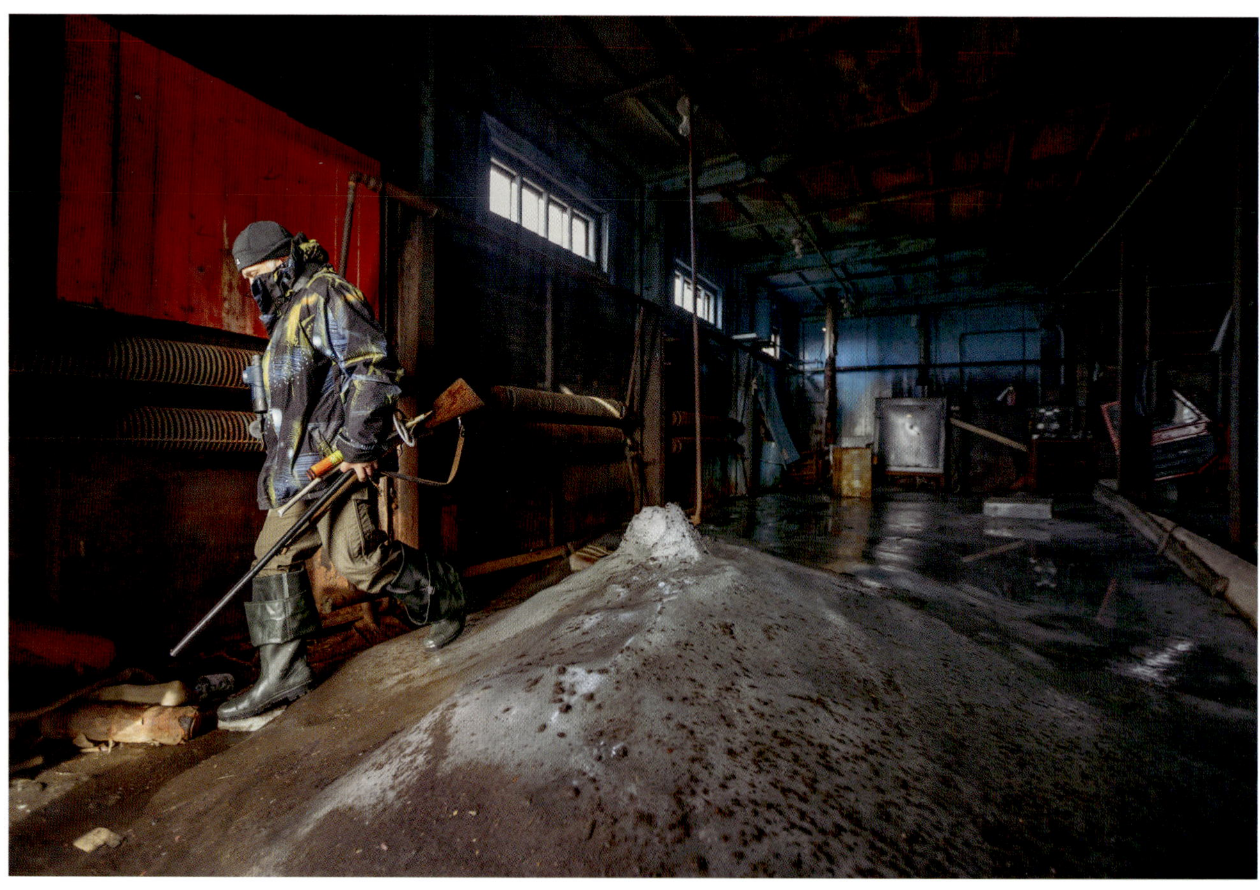

Krenkel Station, Heiss Island. **ABOVE:** Empty oil drums. **BELOW:** Checking the abandoned structures for polar bears.

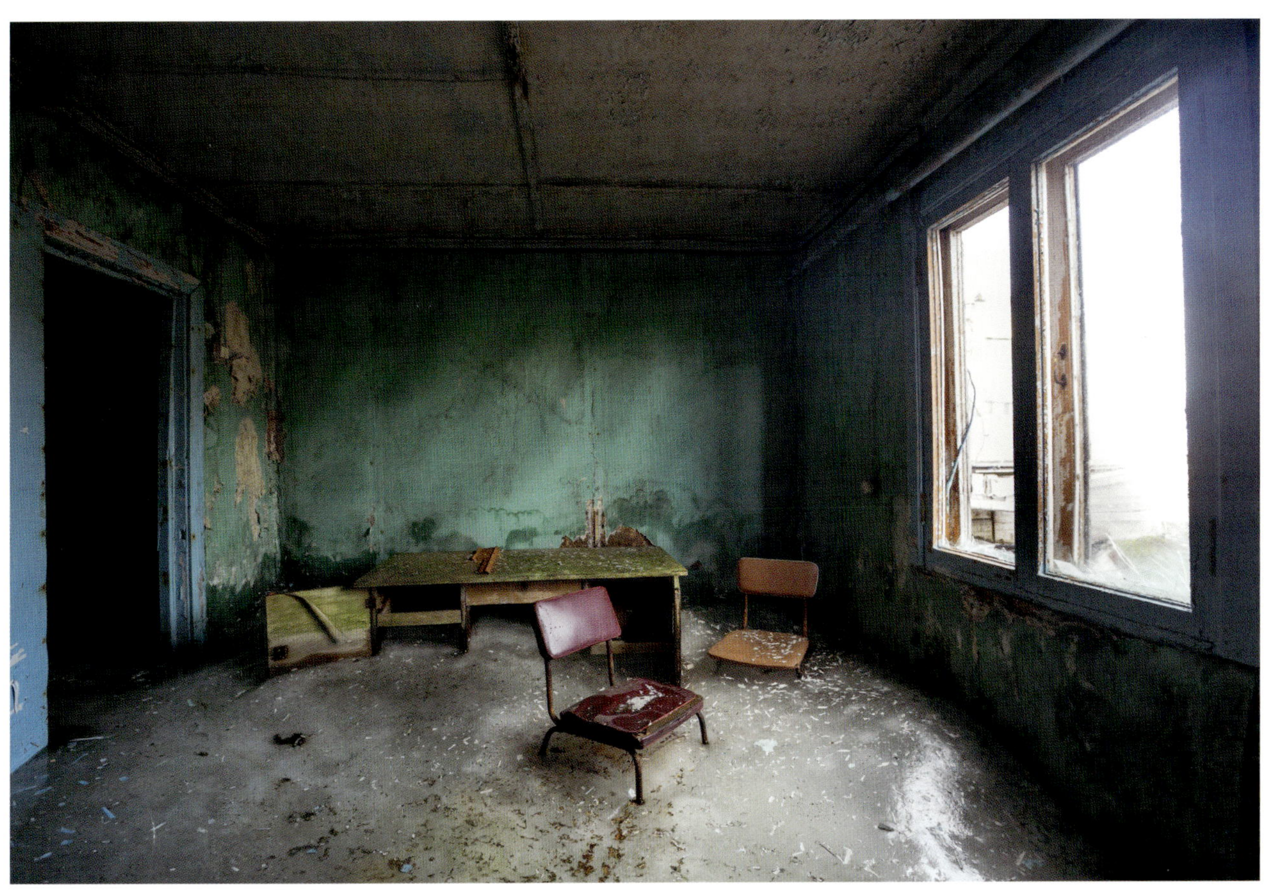

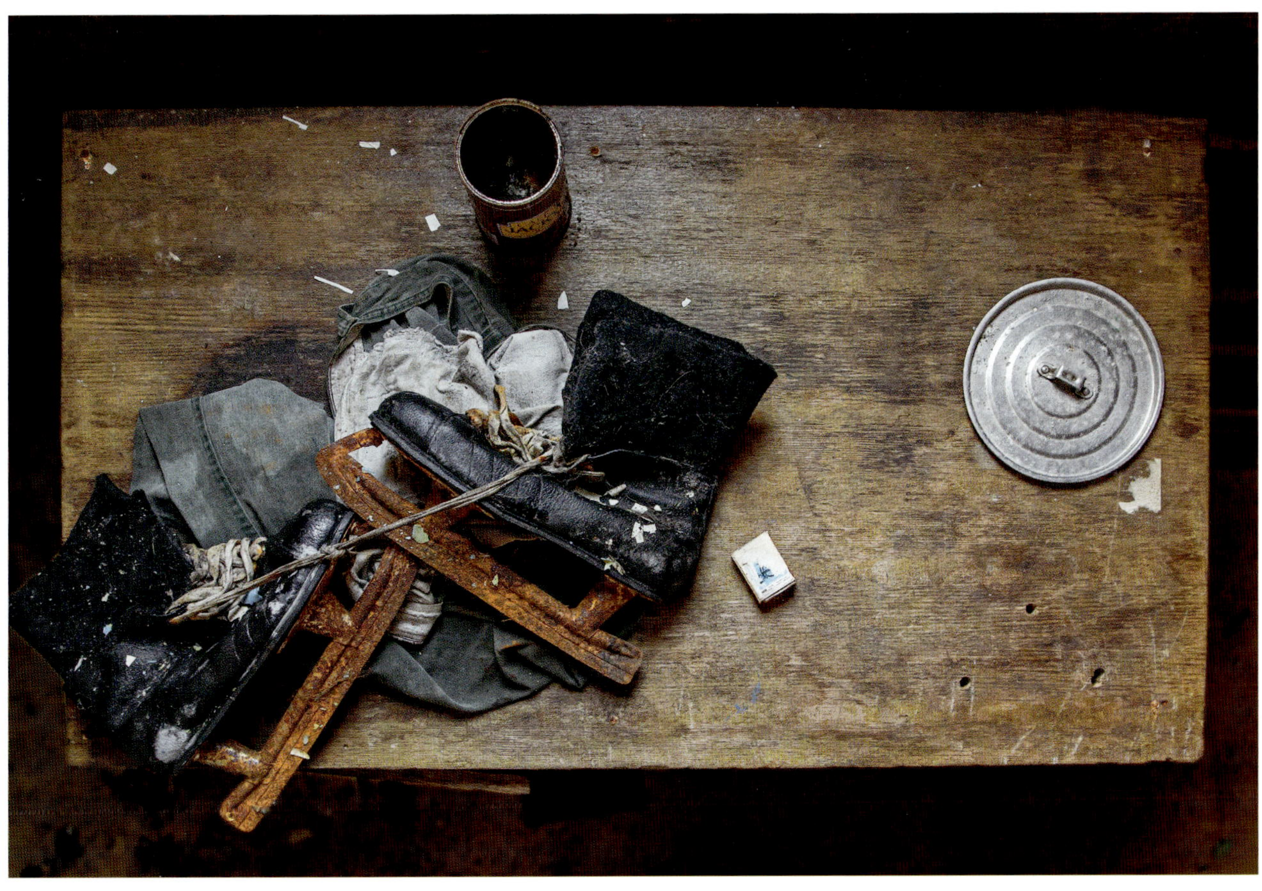

ABOVE: Frozen offices and living quarters. **BELOW:** Ice skates abandoned in haste. **FOLLOWING:** Walrus family portrait, Barents Sea.

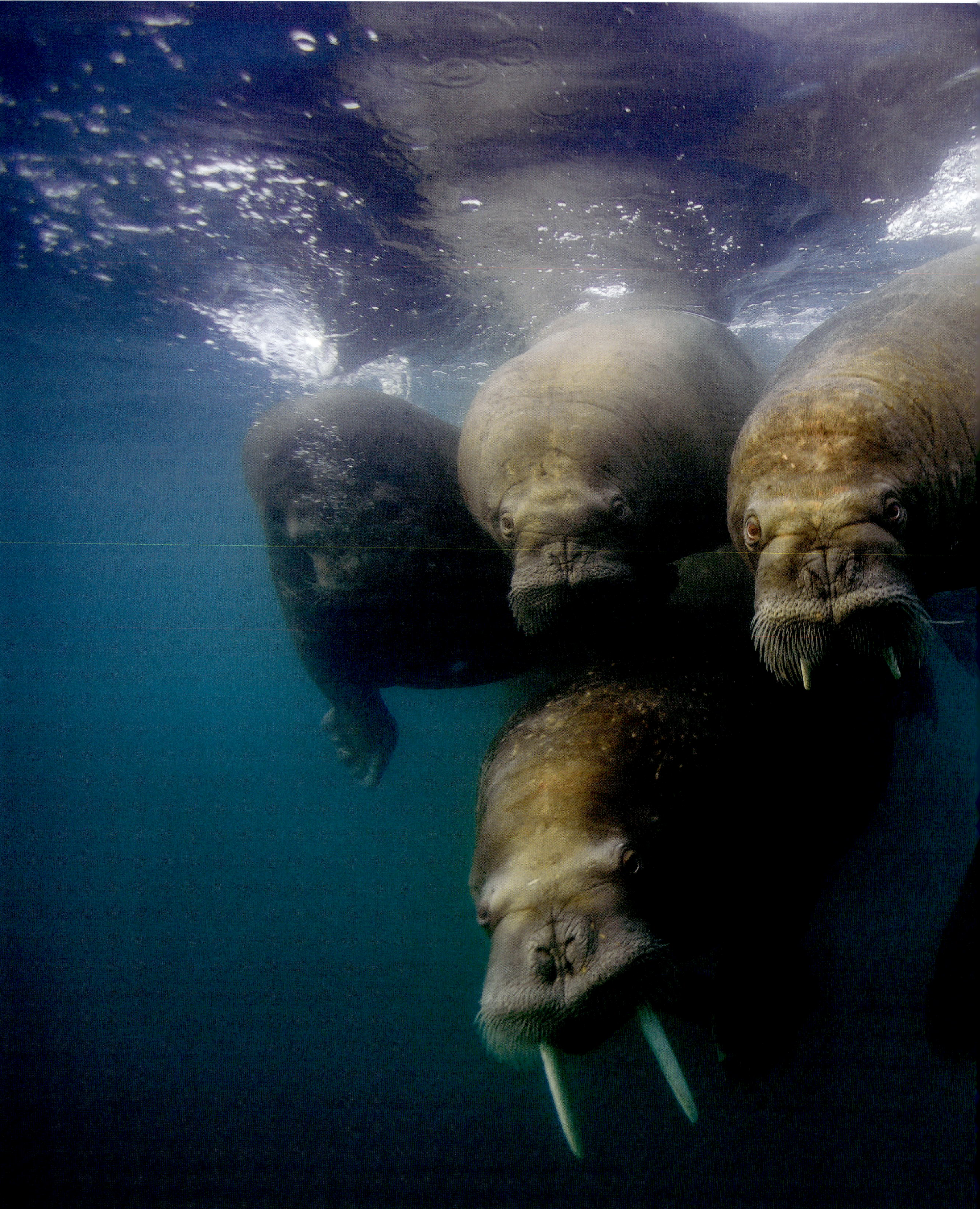

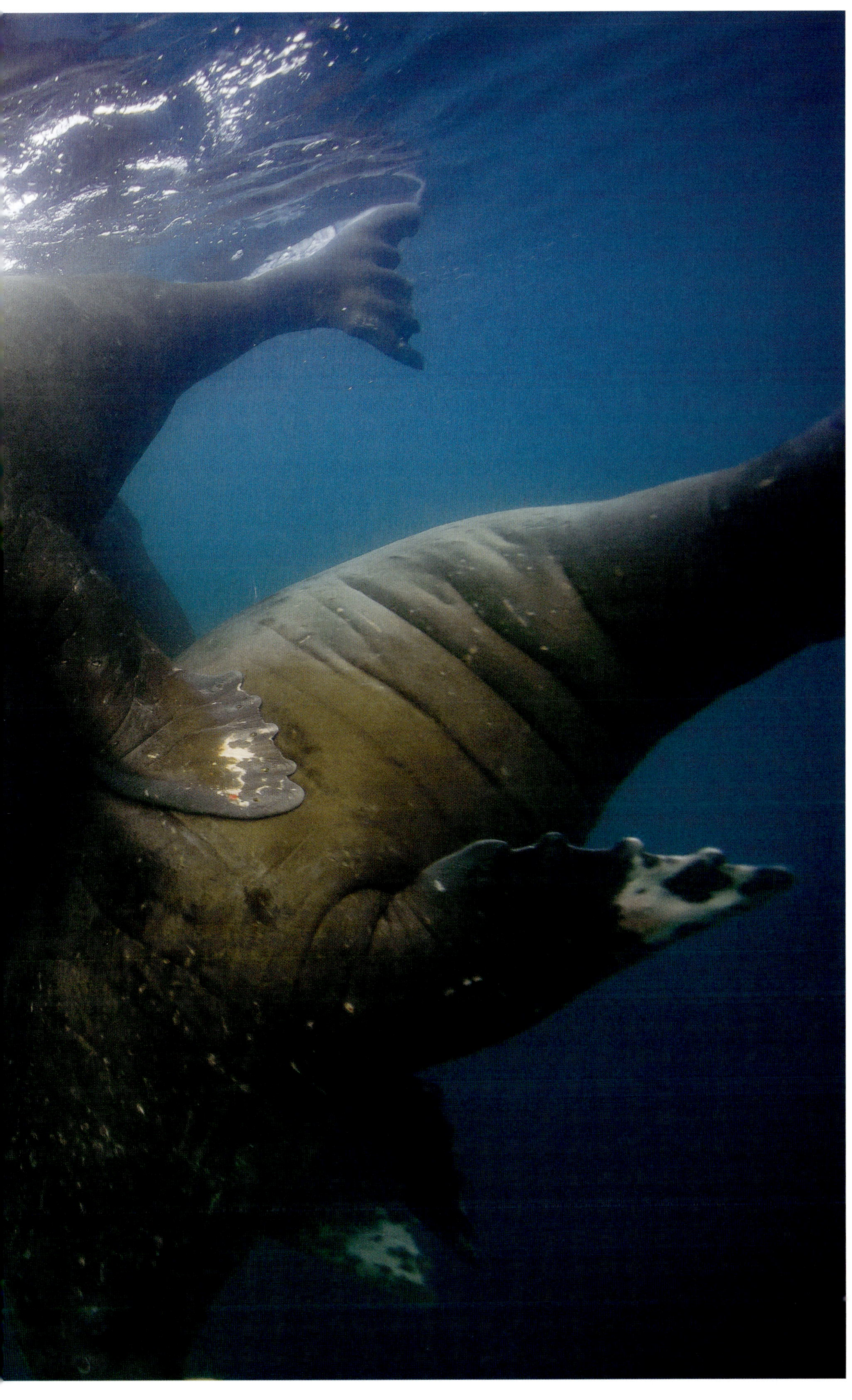

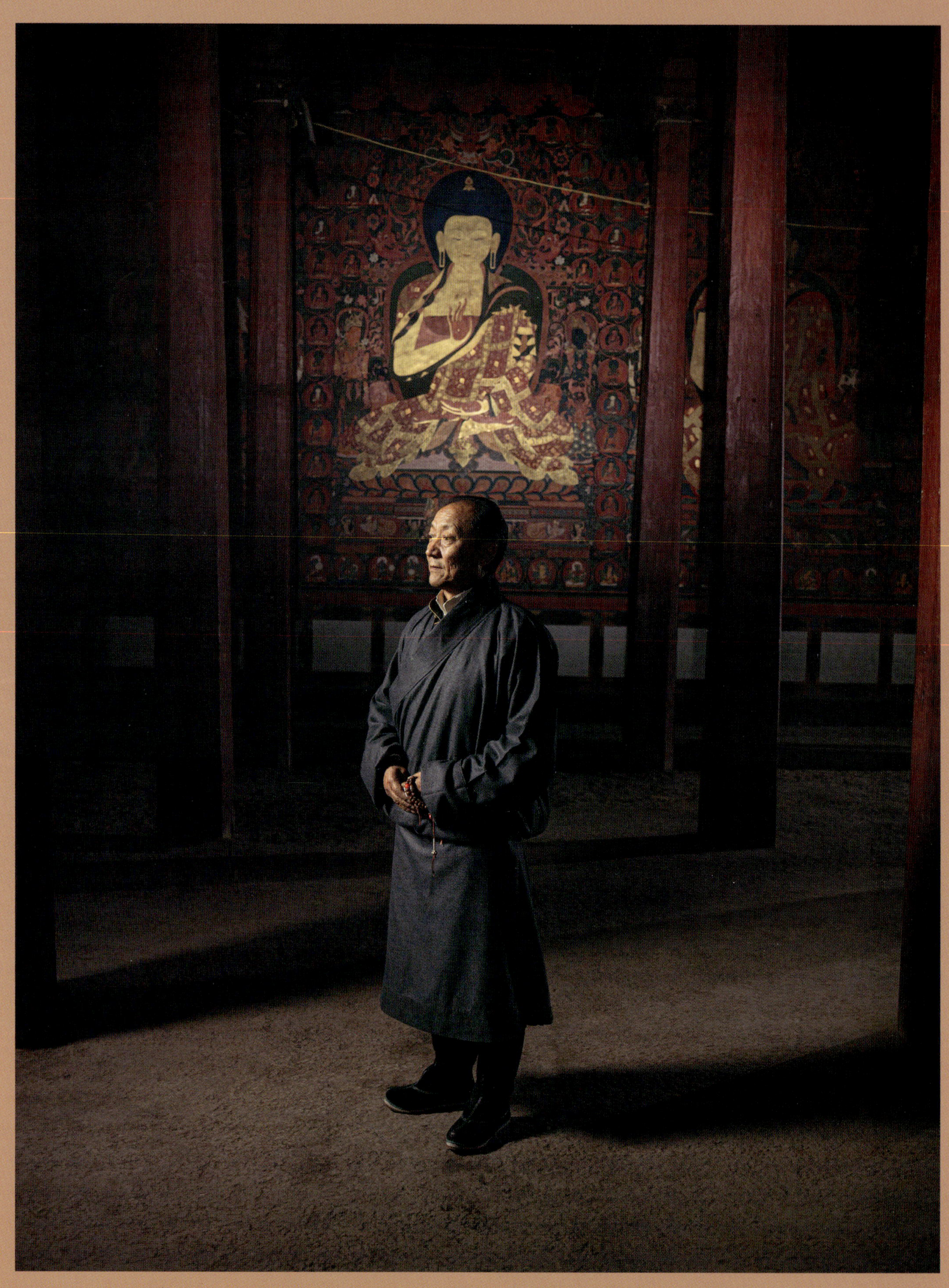

THE EDGE OF YESTERDAY

Mustang,
Nepal

The drivers exchange short beeps of their horns, signaling that they're all clear, and we speed off into the dust left in their wake. Onward.

In the decade since I first came to the Kingdom of Mustang, Nepal, a road has been carved into the canyon walls, winding its way down from the dry expanse of the Tibetan Plateau and following the ancient offshoot of the Silk Road. The kingdom is shifting and seems dustier now under the dirt kicked up by jeeps and motorcycles carrying tourists from the lowlands and trade from China.

A herd of goats brings the jeep to a halt again, and I watch a shadowed man wave a stick and whistle as the animals funnel into a narrow thoroughfare. As much as things have changed, many things remain the same. As much as the road has thrust Mustang into the future, there is a persistent timelessness here.

It's not just the texture of the culture that's changing with the road. The politics have shifted as well. In 2008, the monarchy that had held power for six centuries was dissolved and King Jigme Dorje Palbar Bista became a figurehead instead of a monarch. His power in Kathmandu was unceremoniously stripped away, leaving him as a political relic. When he died in 2016, he was succeeded by his nephew Jigme Singhe Palbar Bista. The younger Jigme was never officially a king, but to the people of Mustang, he still reigns, and they look to him for guidance, ignoring the bureaucracy from the capital hundreds of kilometers away.

As much as this assignment is about documenting the impacts of the road, it's also about Jigme. He stands in front of me dressed in a traditional chuba, thumbing the 108 prayer beads of his father's mala. Despite Jigme's relative inability to impact the decisions regarding the road, he represents a sort of cultural glue, holding the kingdom together as the traffic threatens to tear it apart. He knows that the road brings wealth, medicine, education, and trade, the same way the ancient trails of the Silk Road did. He also knows that pieces of Mustang are being lost. Children leave. The monastic system that's provided the spiritual and educational backbone of the region is threatened. And the treasure trove of ancient art that anchors the kingdom to its history is slowly being sold or stolen or simply replaced by the future that has already arrived.

As someone who has spent nearly a year of my life (collectively) in Mustang, I'm constantly fighting my biases, struggling to remain an "objective" documentarian while witnessing changes that potentially harm a culture and community I deeply care for. I try to imagine the weight that Jigme feels as I watch him quietly pray for the future. He passes the prayer beads endlessly between thumb and forefinger, balancing what was, what is, and what is to come. I take a picture and the lights pop, illuminating a golden fresco of Buddha behind him and reminding us all that nothing is forever.

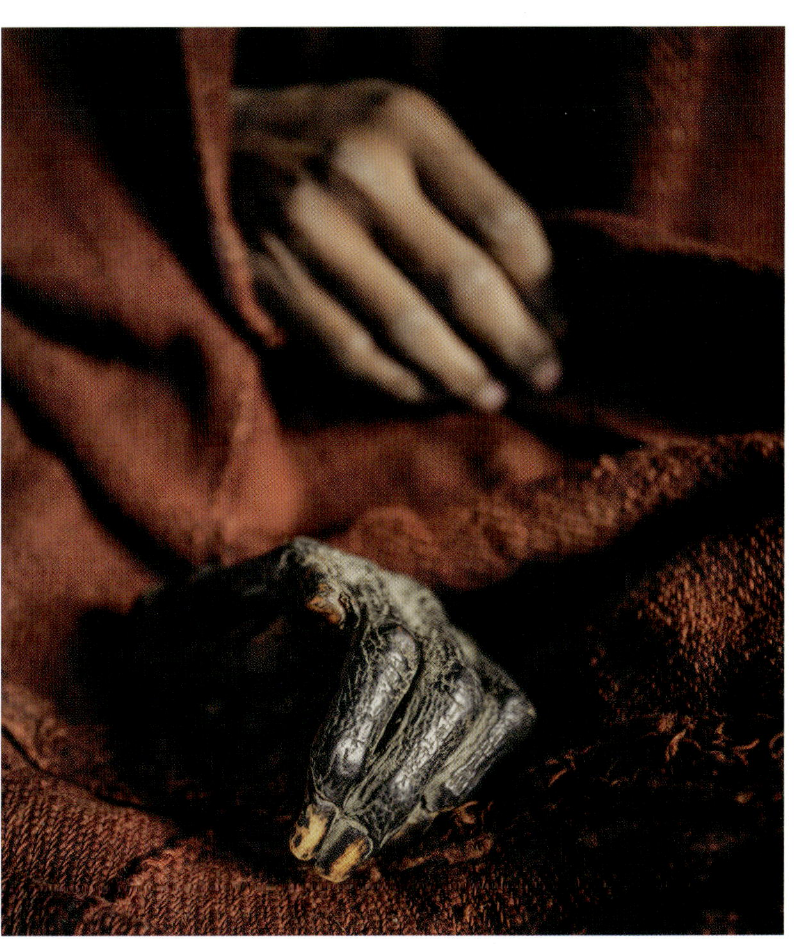

A mummified human hand rests in the robes of a monk's lap. The provenance of the hand is dubious and surrounded by rumors and myths. One posits that it is the hand of the last person who stole from the king. **OPPOSITE:** King Jigme Singhe Palbar Bista stands for a portrait in Thupchen Gompa (2019).

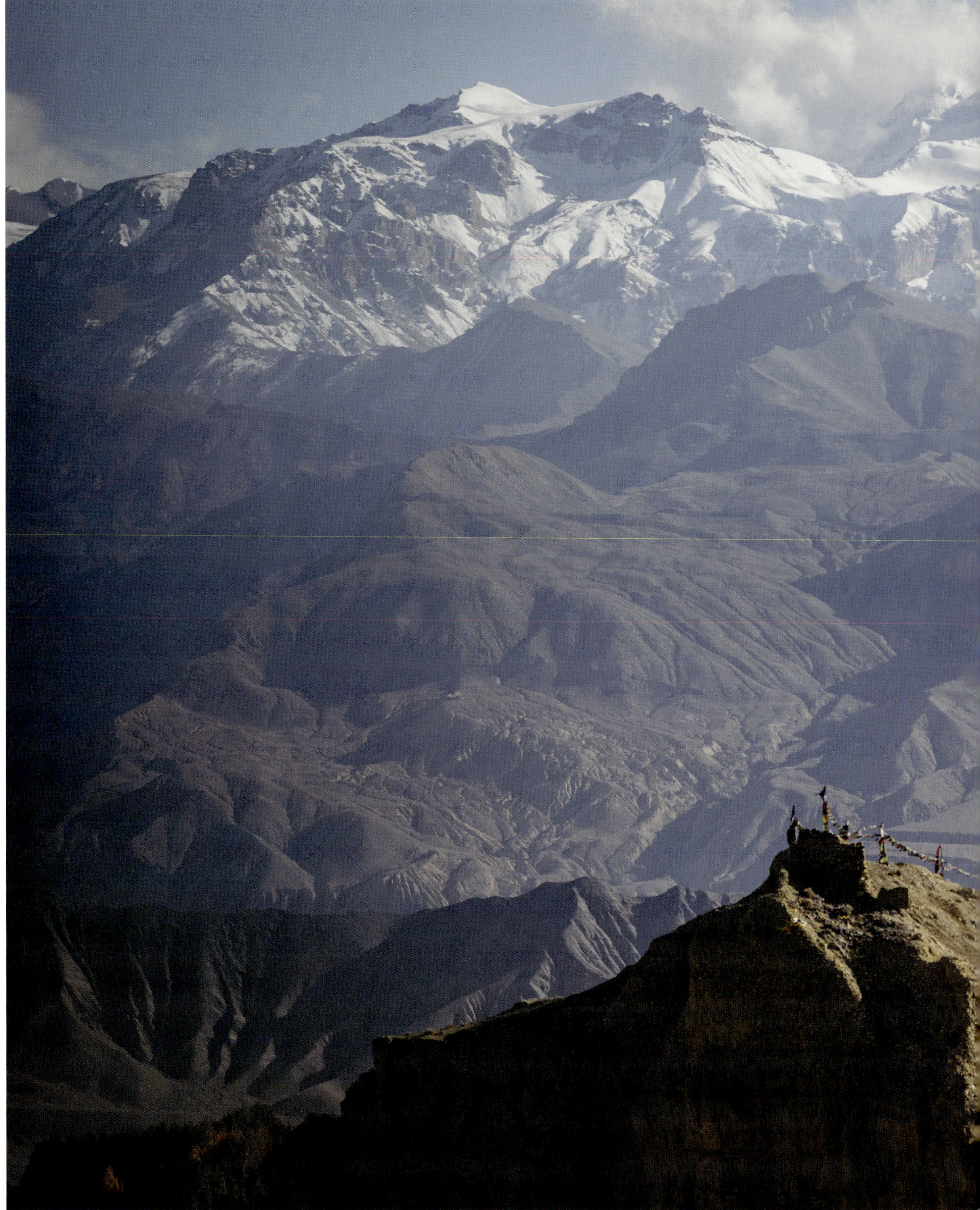

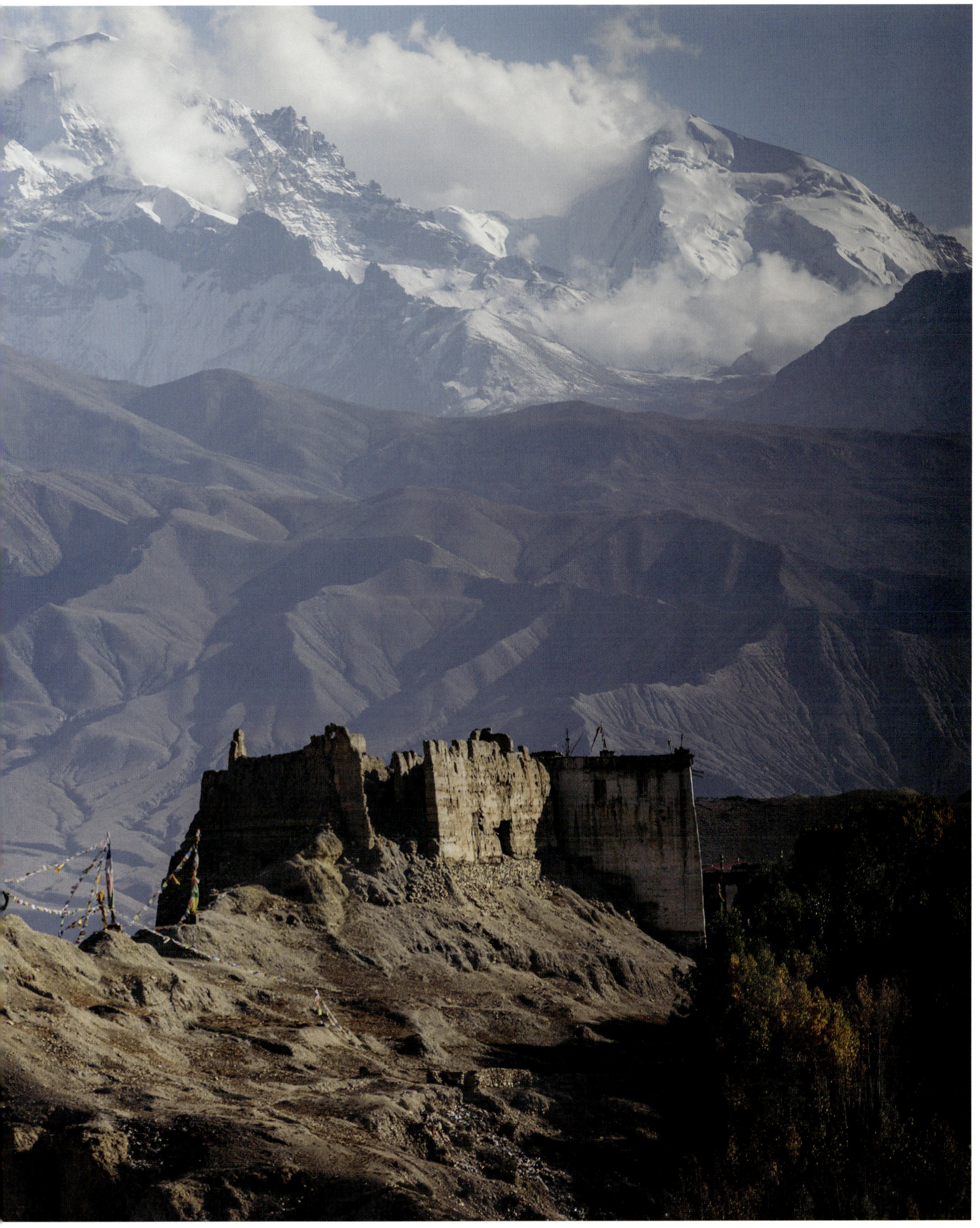

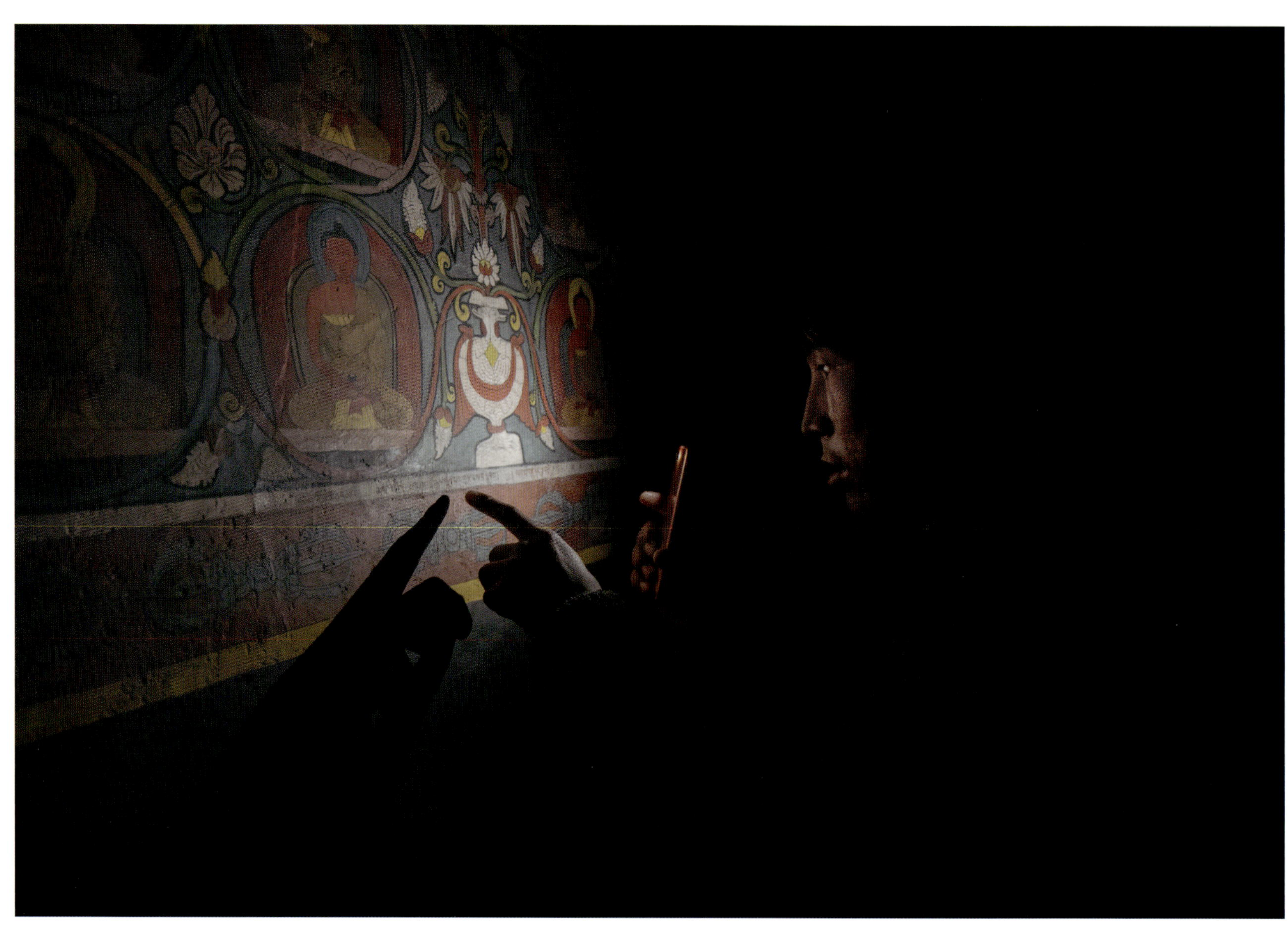

PREVIOUS: The remains of a royal palace in Tsarang, Upper Mustang. **ABOVE:** Centuries-old Buddhist frescoes read by flashlight inside Jampa Monastery in Lo Manthang, the ancient walled city and capitol of Upper Mustang.

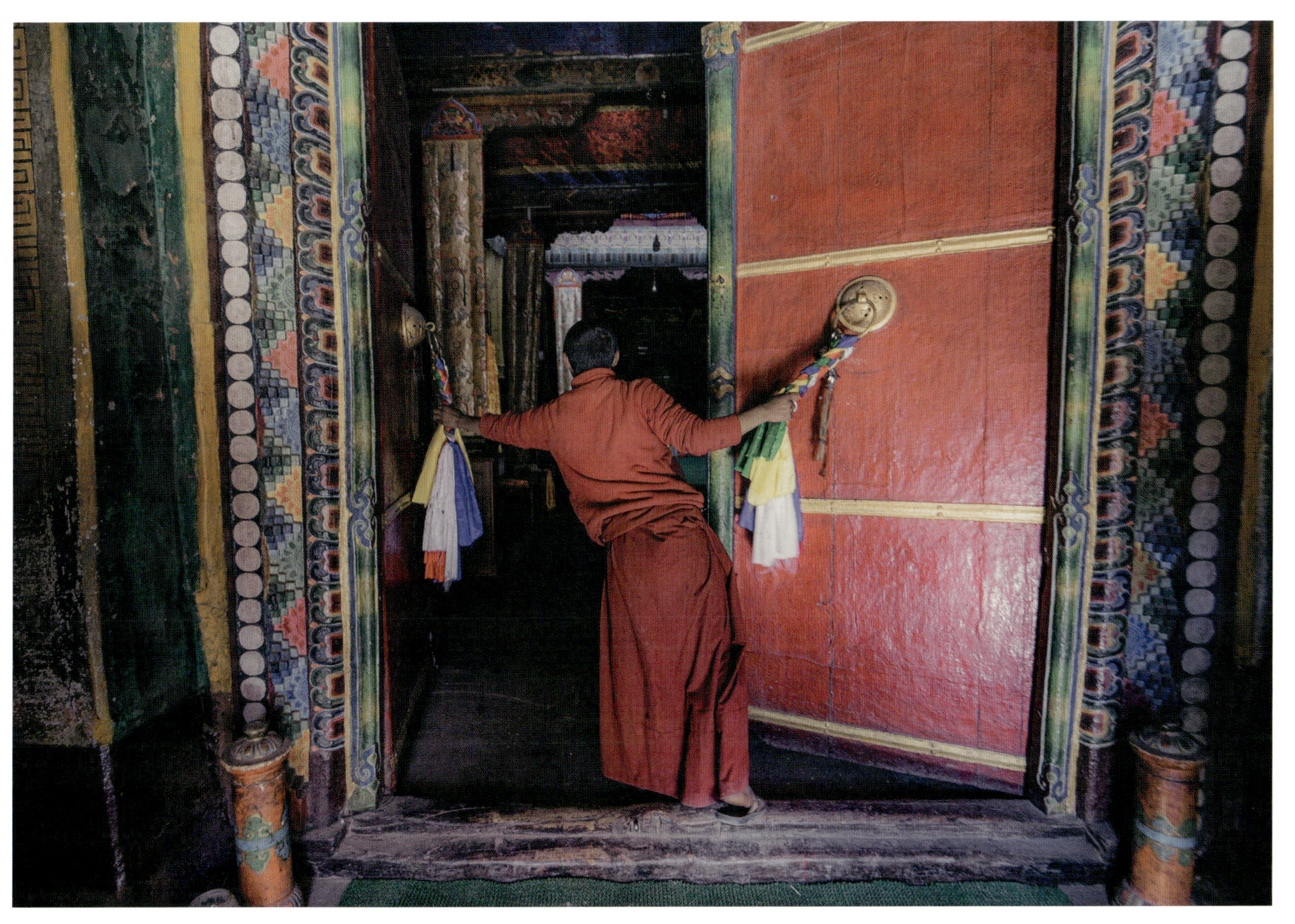

A novice monk opens the doors to Tsarang Gompa (a Tibetan temple) in Tsarang.

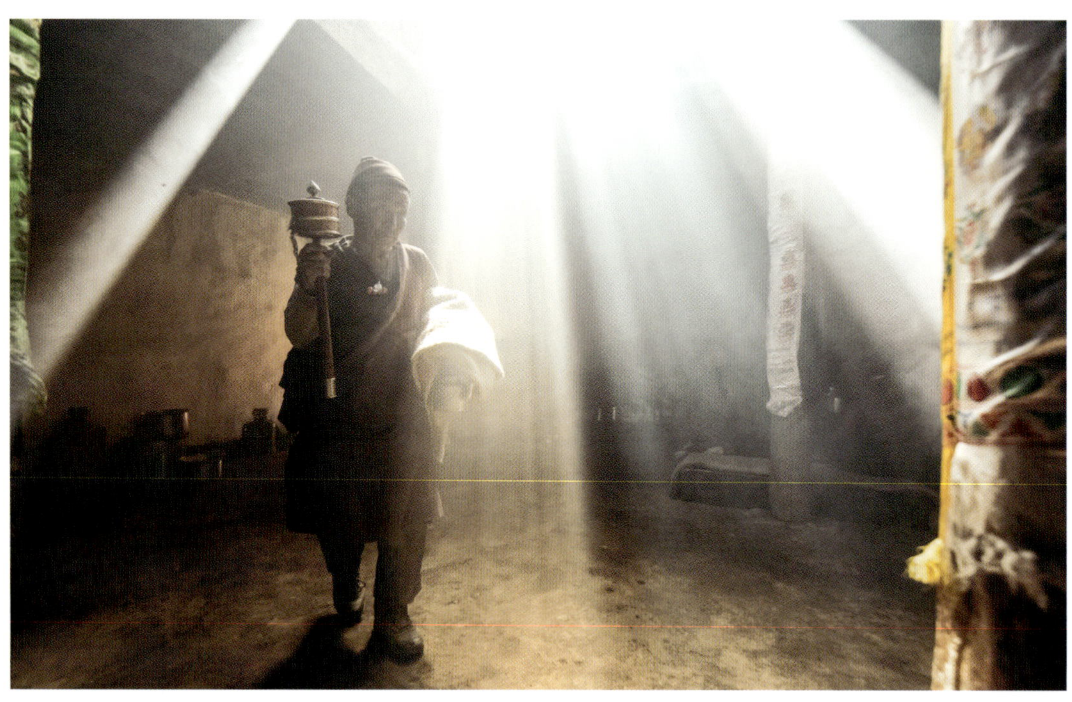

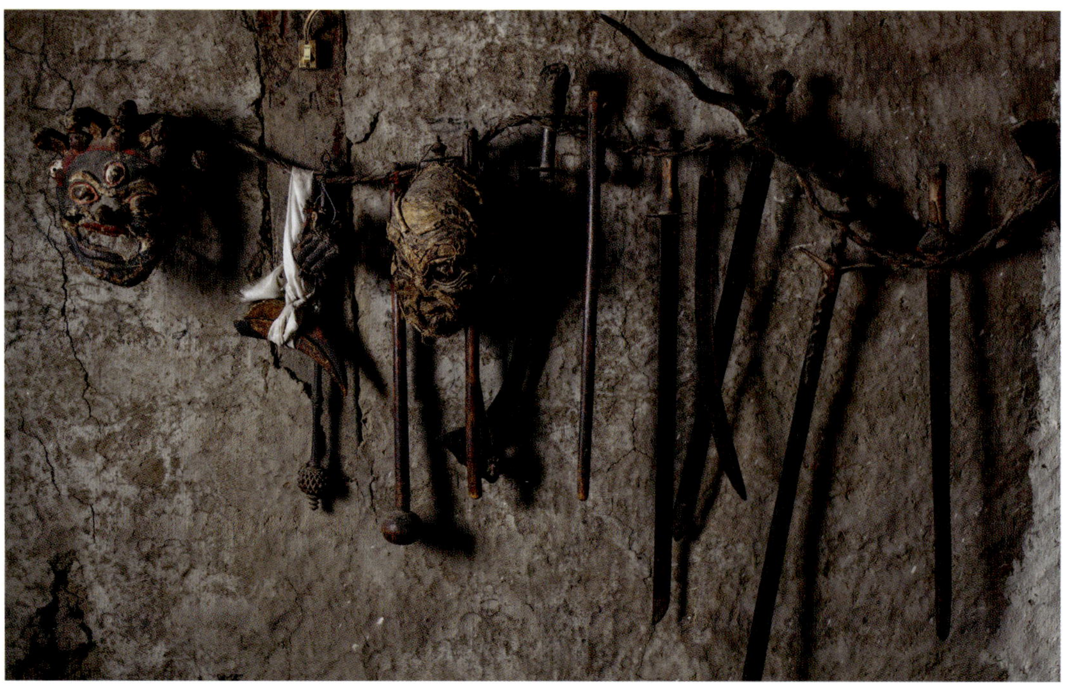

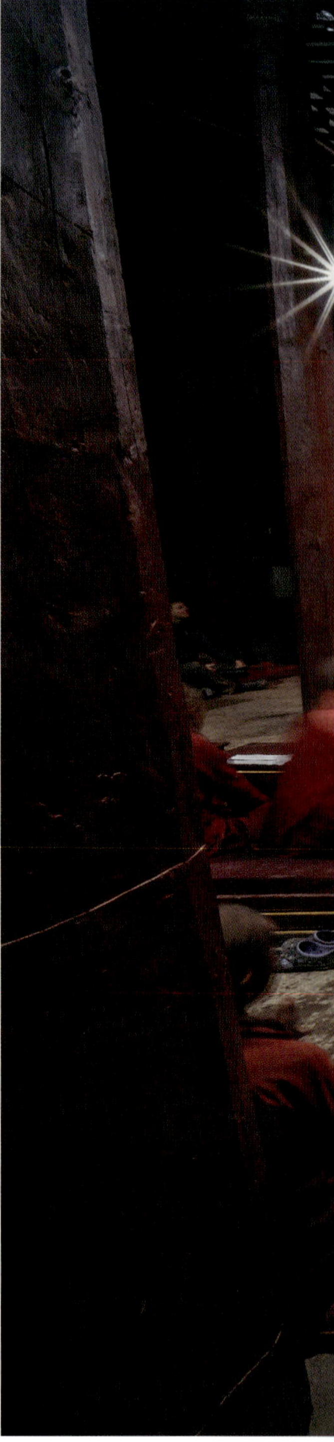

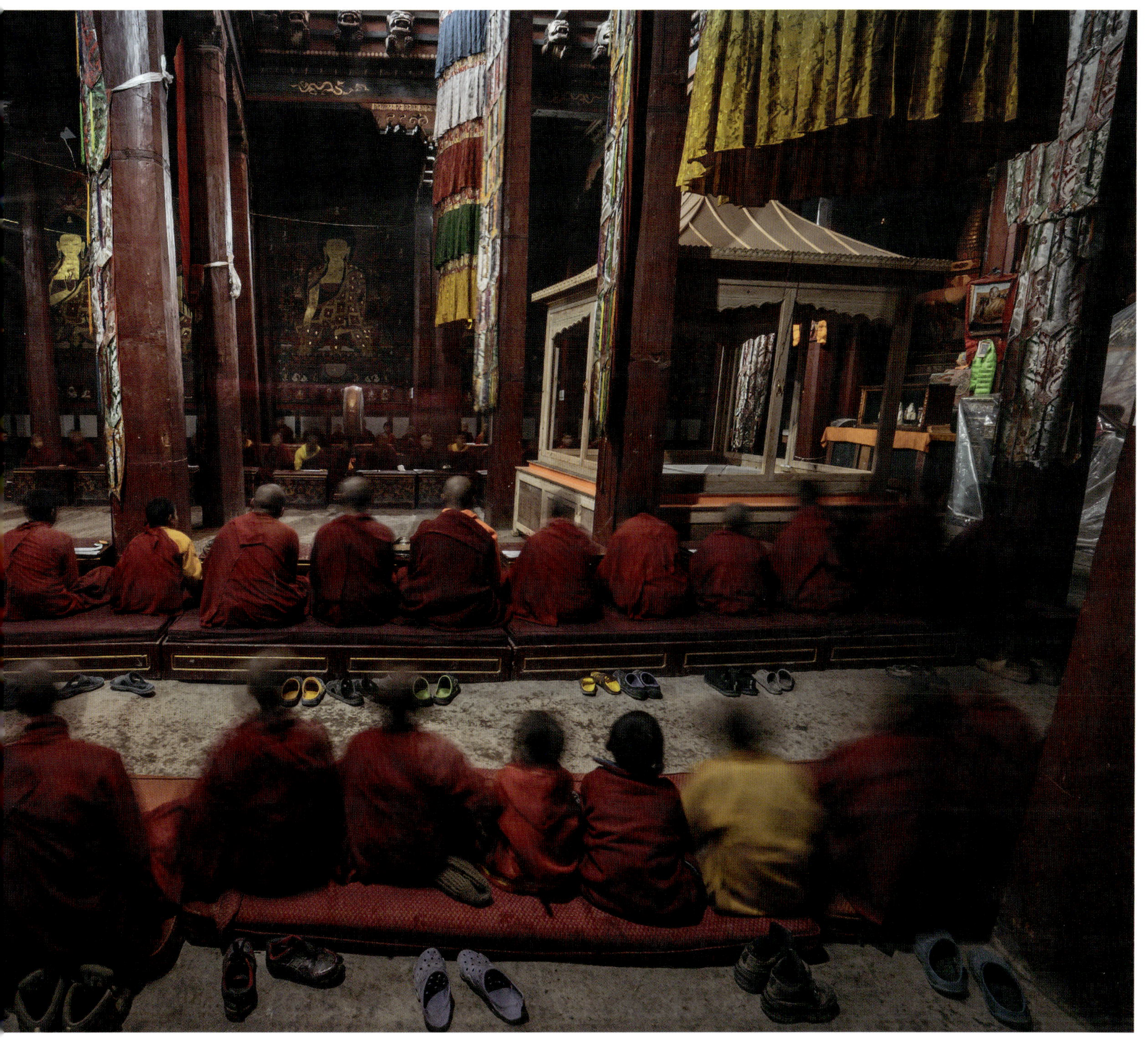

Monks sway in prayer during a puja (holy ritual), Thupchen Gompa, Lo Manthang. **OPPOSITE, ABOVE:** A Loba man spins his mani lag 'khor, a handheld prayer wheel, while reciting mantras. **OPPOSITE, BELOW:** Weapons, masks of protector deities, and other articles of war hang as protection in an abandoned palace.

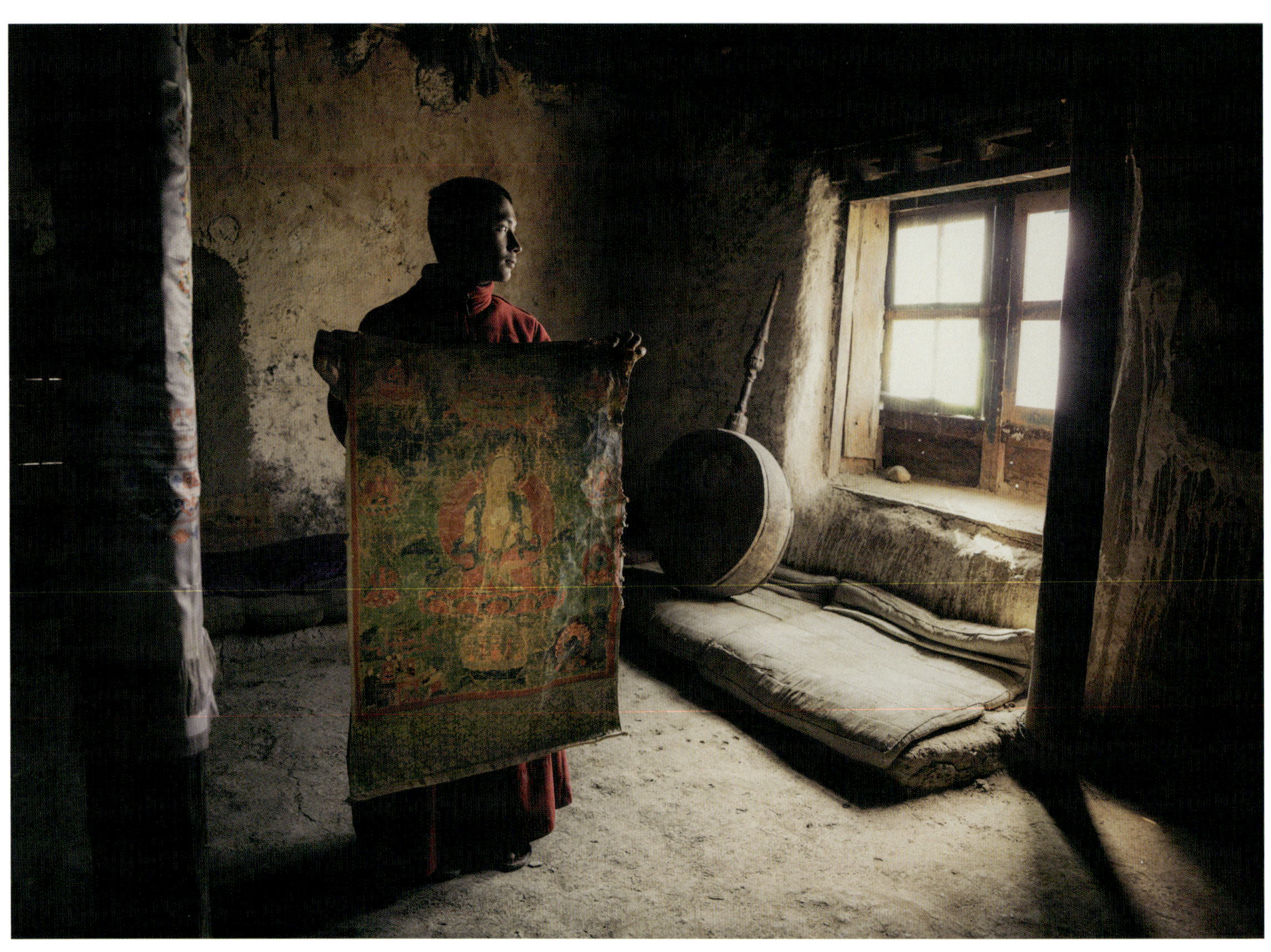

Novice monk Ngwang Phinjo holds an ancient Thanka, a traditional Buddhist painting, inside an undisclosed palace in Upper Mustang.

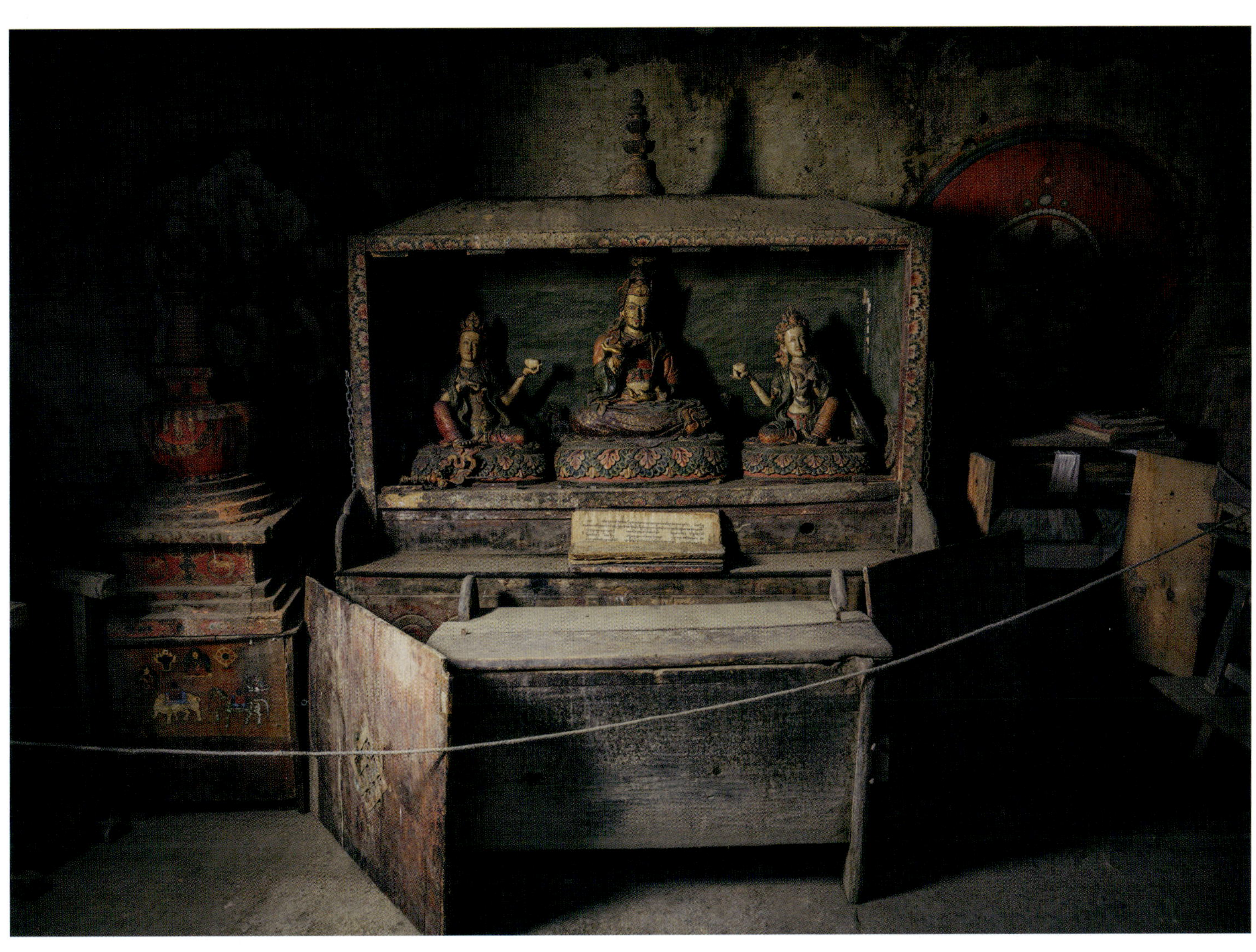

Buddhist relics from the seventeenth century rest in an undisclosed location, kept hidden for safe keeping.
FOLLOWING: Ama, a Mustangi woman, lights butter lamps in an offering of prayer, Kagbeni.

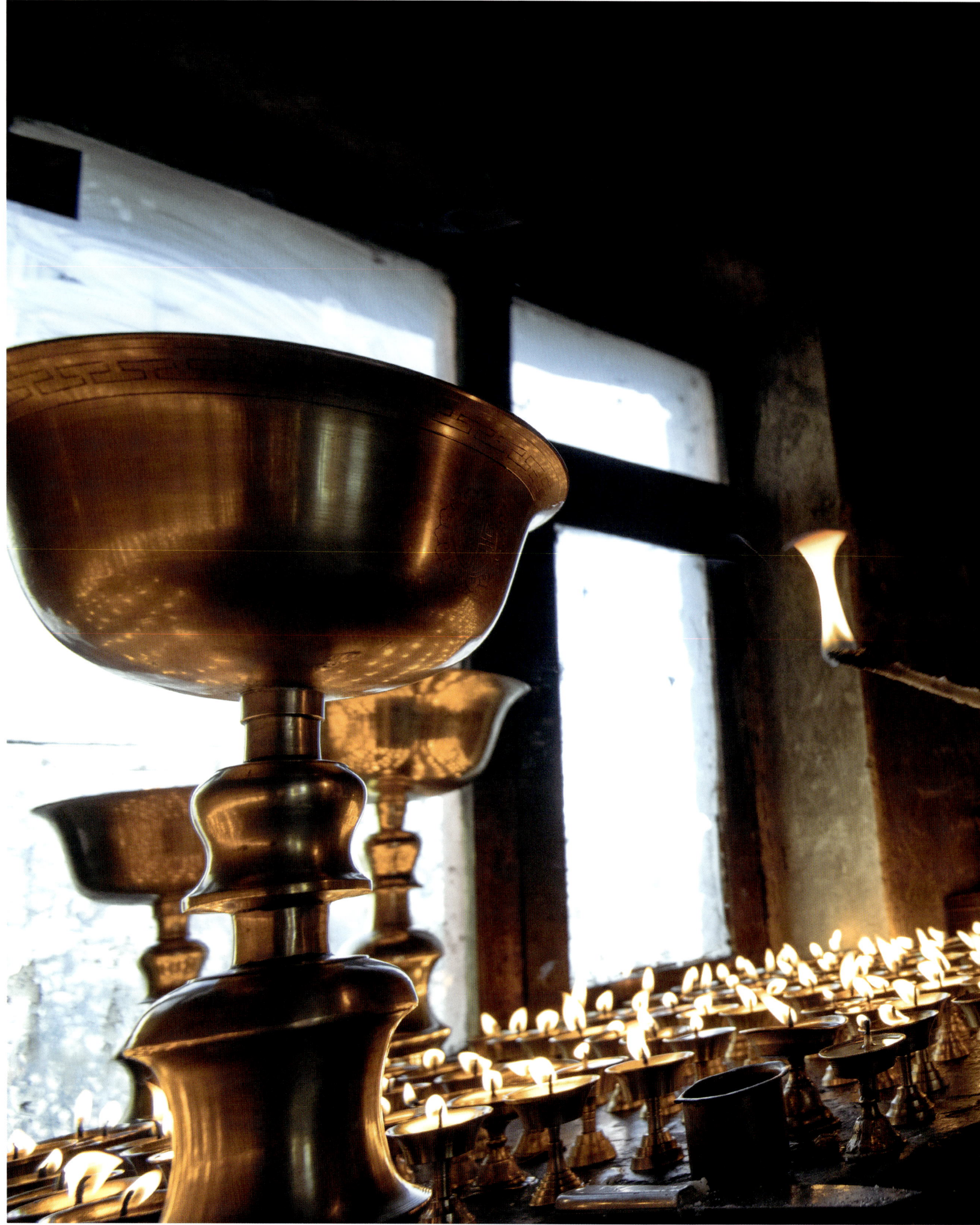

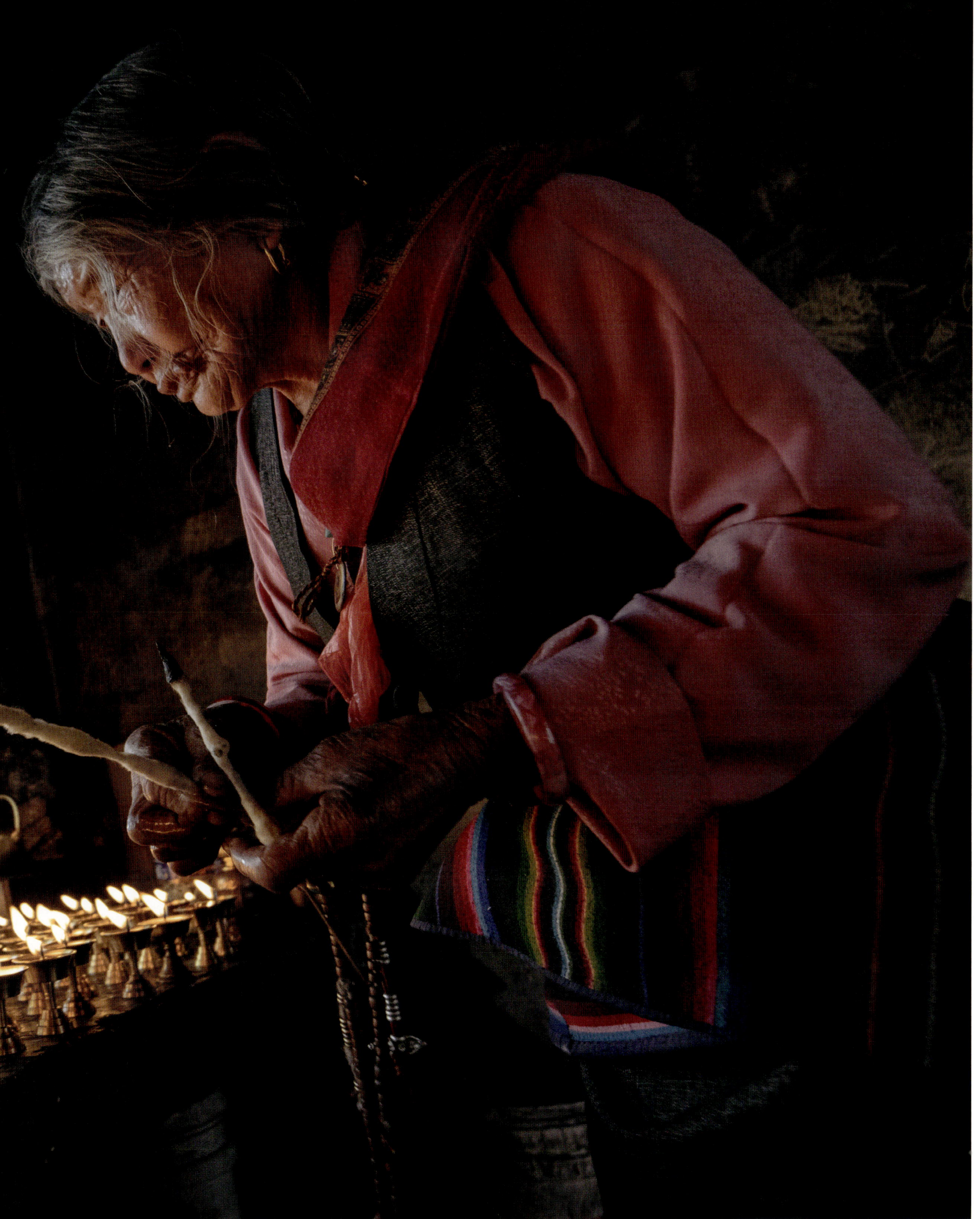

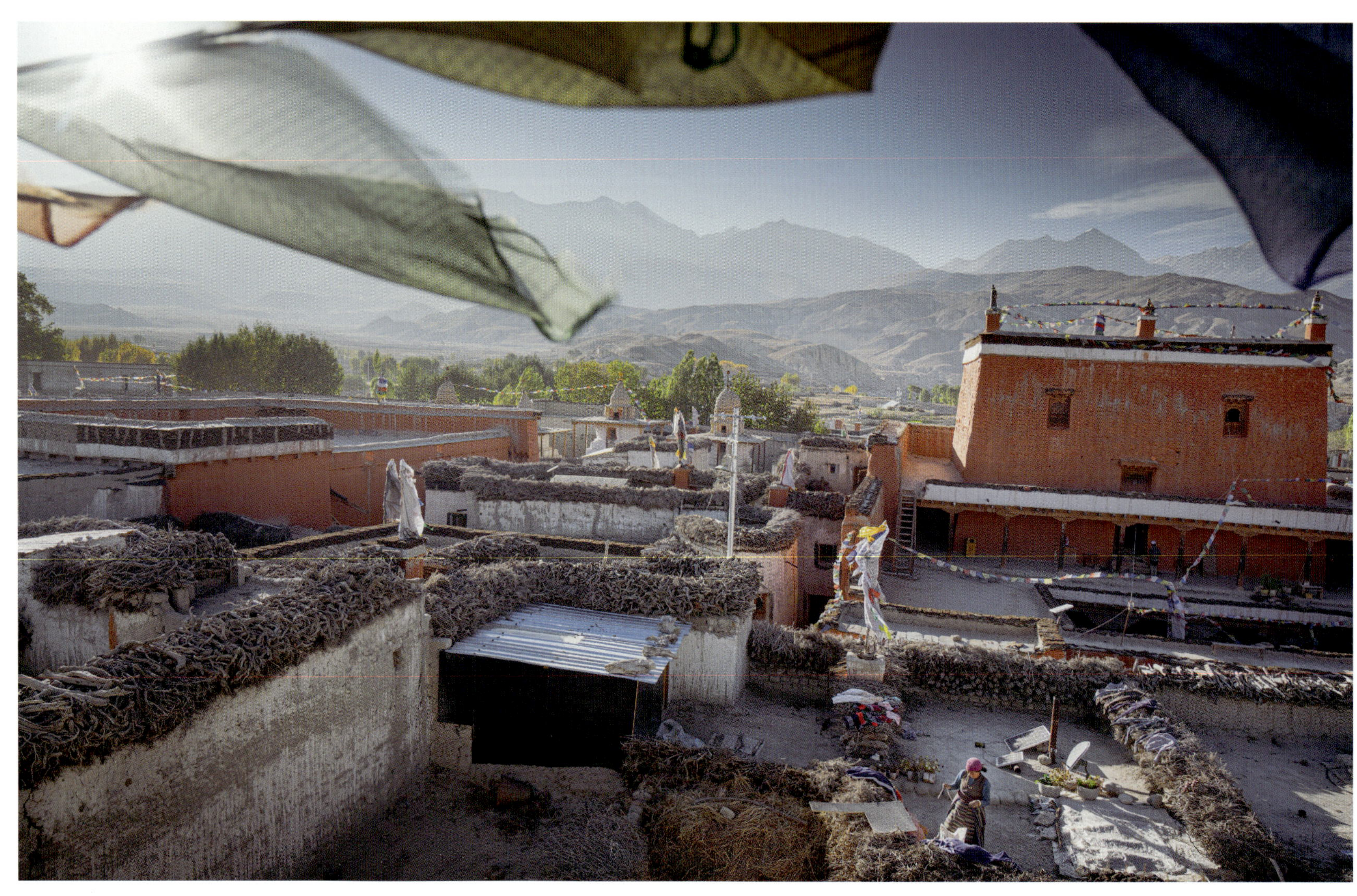

The rooftops of Lo Manthang seen from the roof of the royal palace.

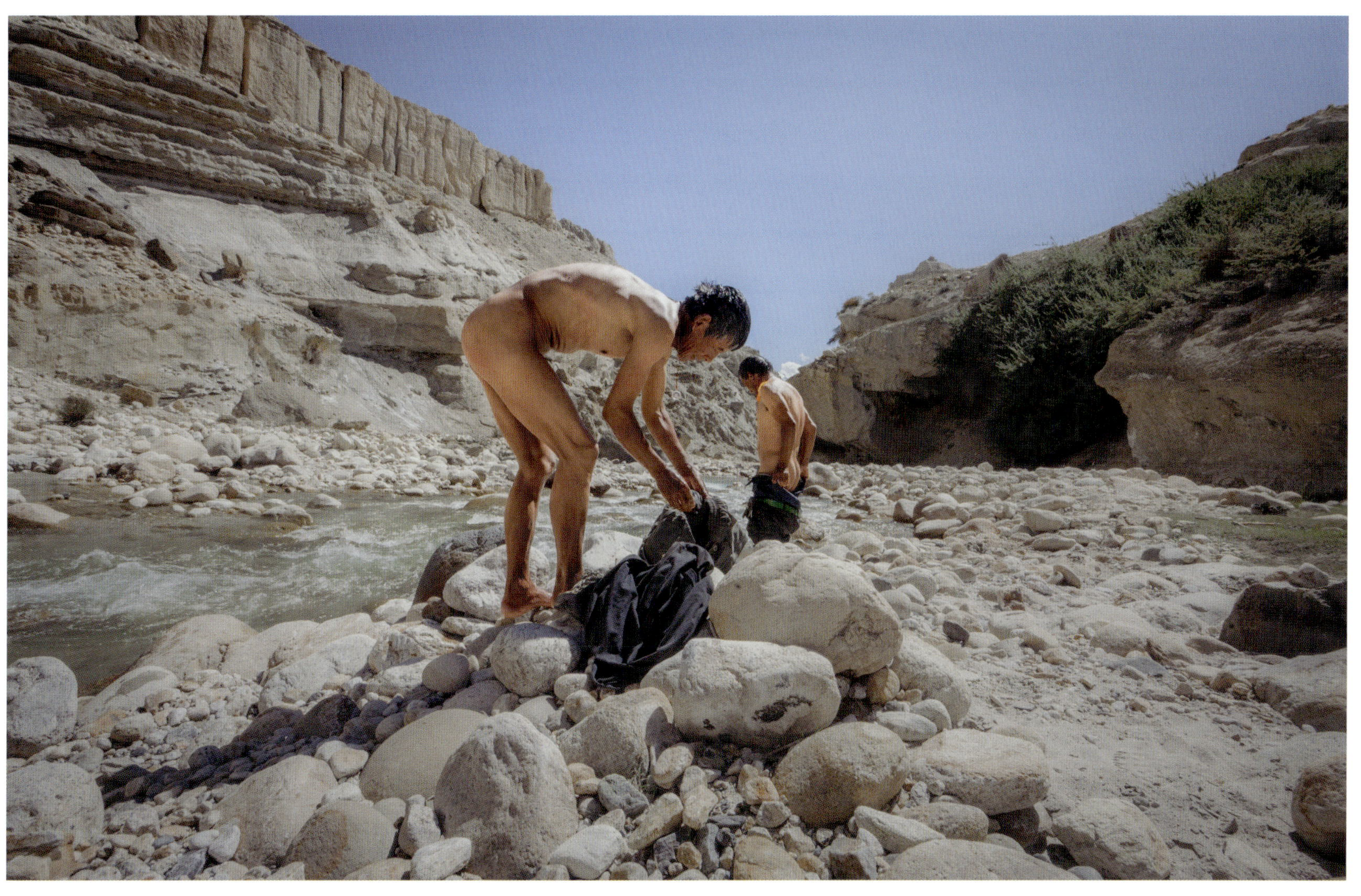

Loba men bathe and dress after performing a sky burial.

Sky burial is a charnel practice in central Asia in which the deceased's body is allowed to be scavenged as carrion, usually by vultures and other birds. The corpse is commonly prepared by ritual de-fleshing and dismembering. Seen as brutal by some, to those who practice sky burial, it is commonly understood as a human's last act of compassion as they feed their body immediately back into the natural world.

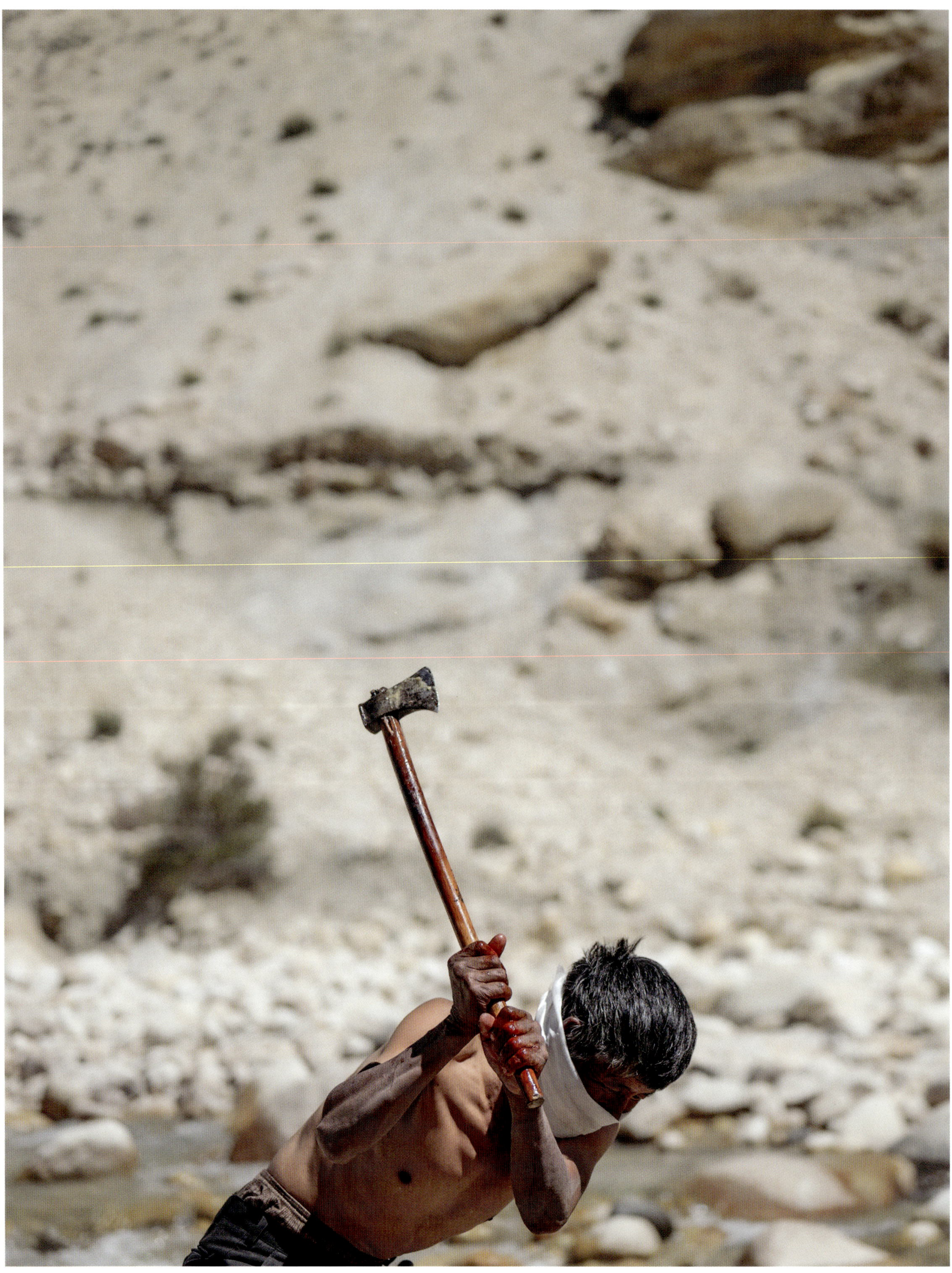

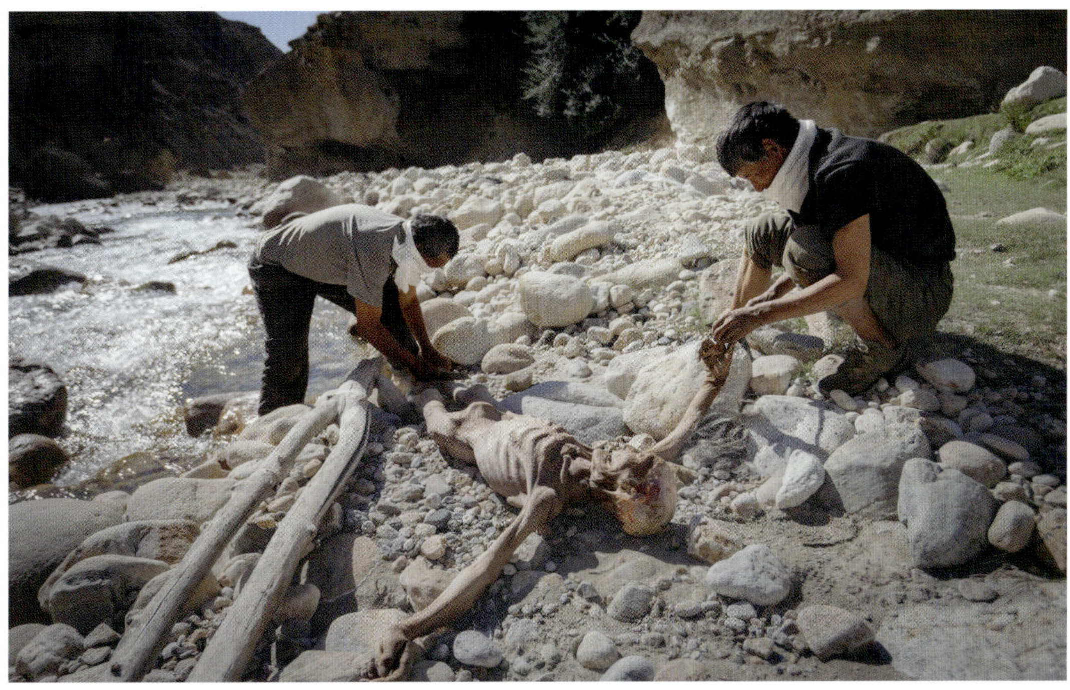

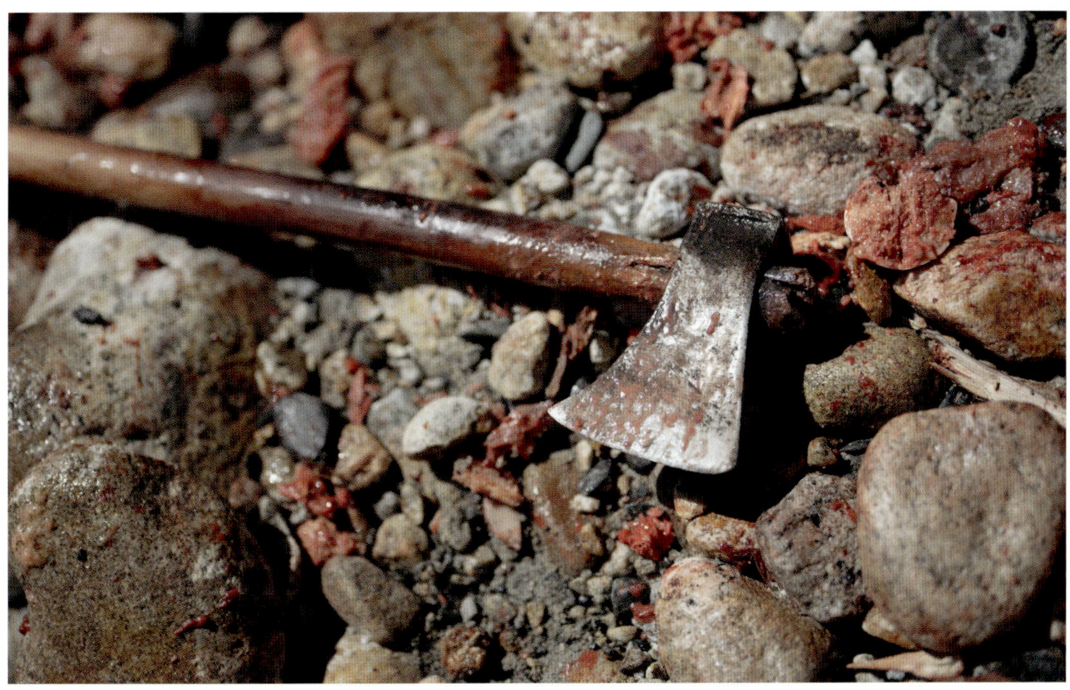

ABOVE: The body is prepared before being de-fleshed and dismembered. **BELOW:** After the ritual, the ax is set aside before being cleansed in juniper smoke. **OPPOSITE:** A Loba man uses an ax to dismember the body.

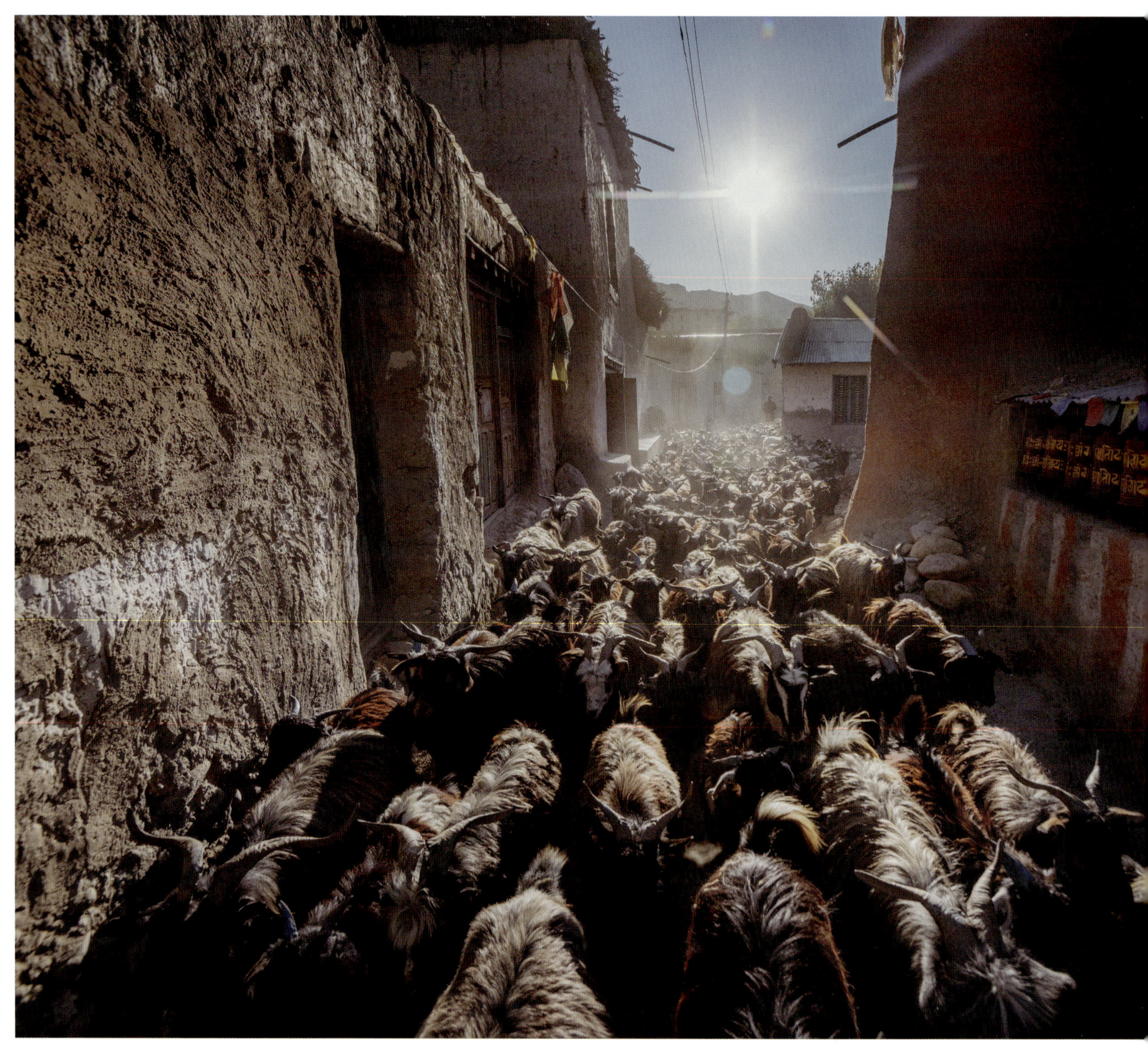

A goat herd funnels through the narrow streets of Tsarang. **OPPOSITE, ABOVE:** Tibetan and Loba traders wait at a Chinese military post for clearance to cross the border into Tibet. **OPPOSITE, BELOW:** A Loba child stands by the motorcycle her family uses to bring trade and goods across the nearby Chinese border.

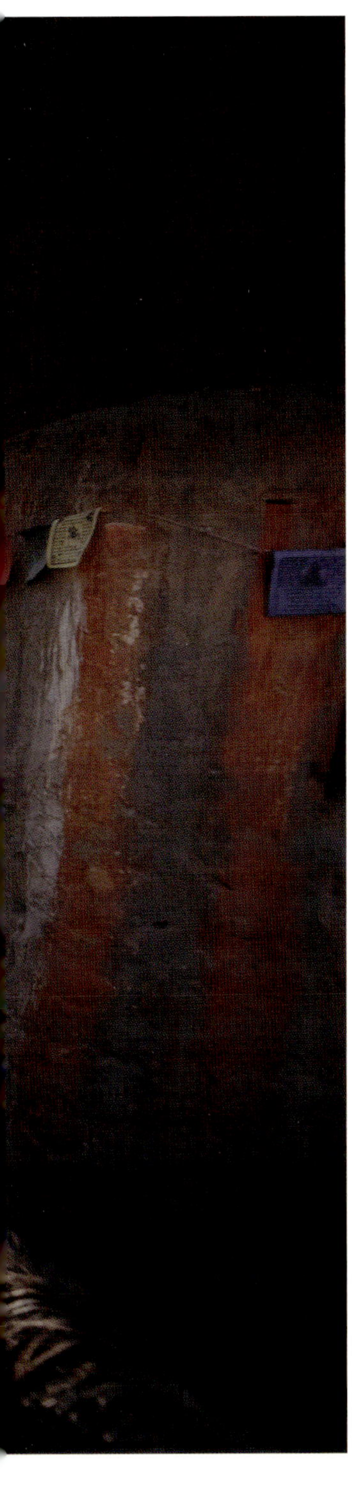

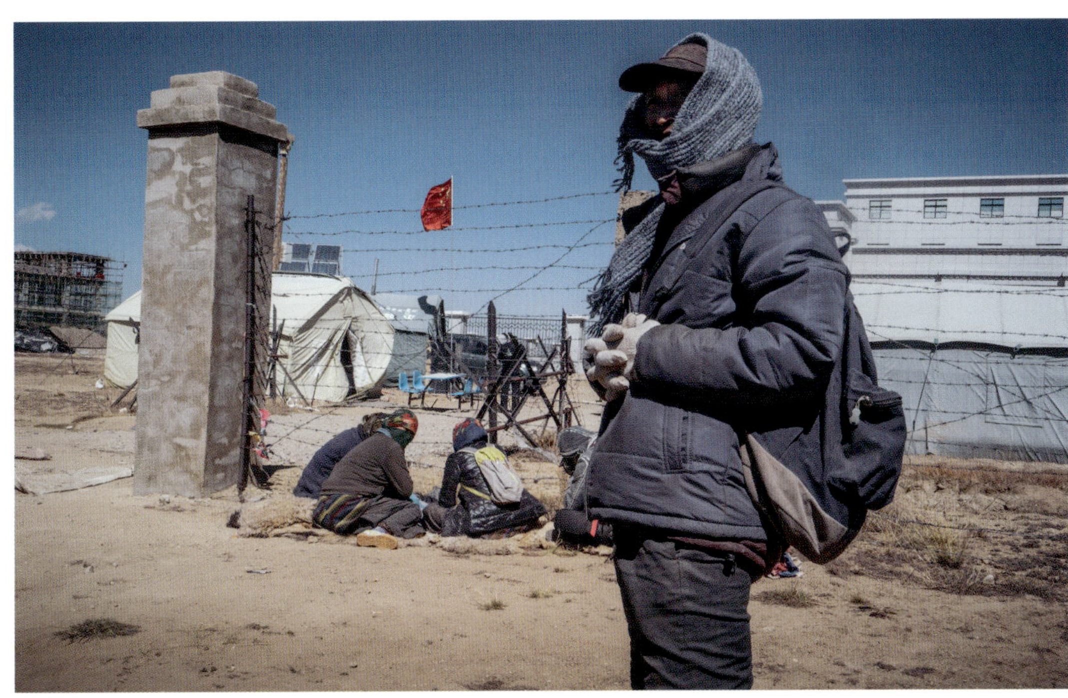

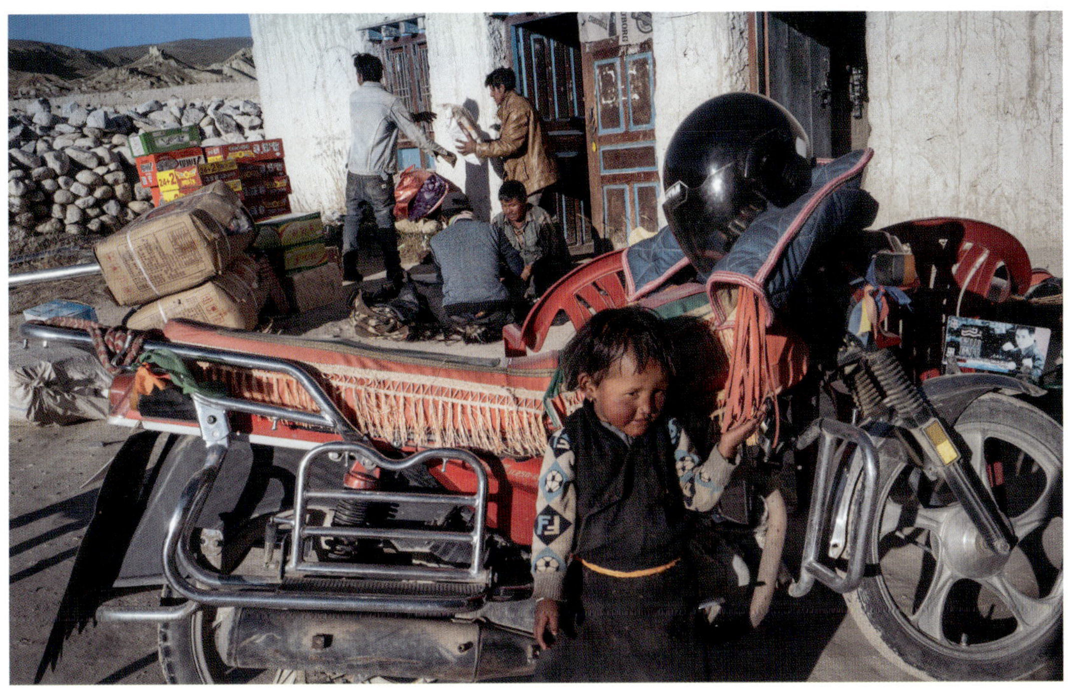

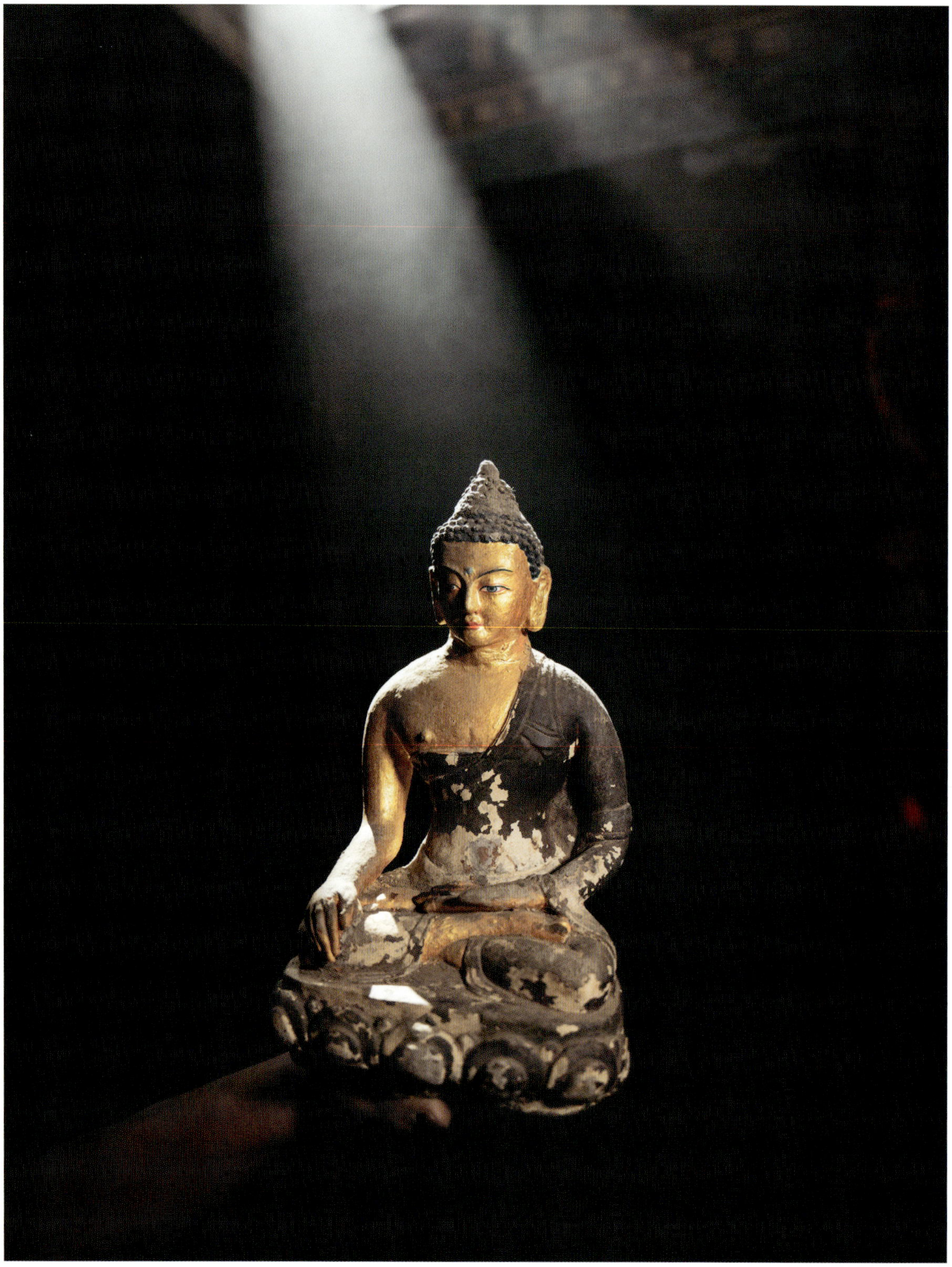

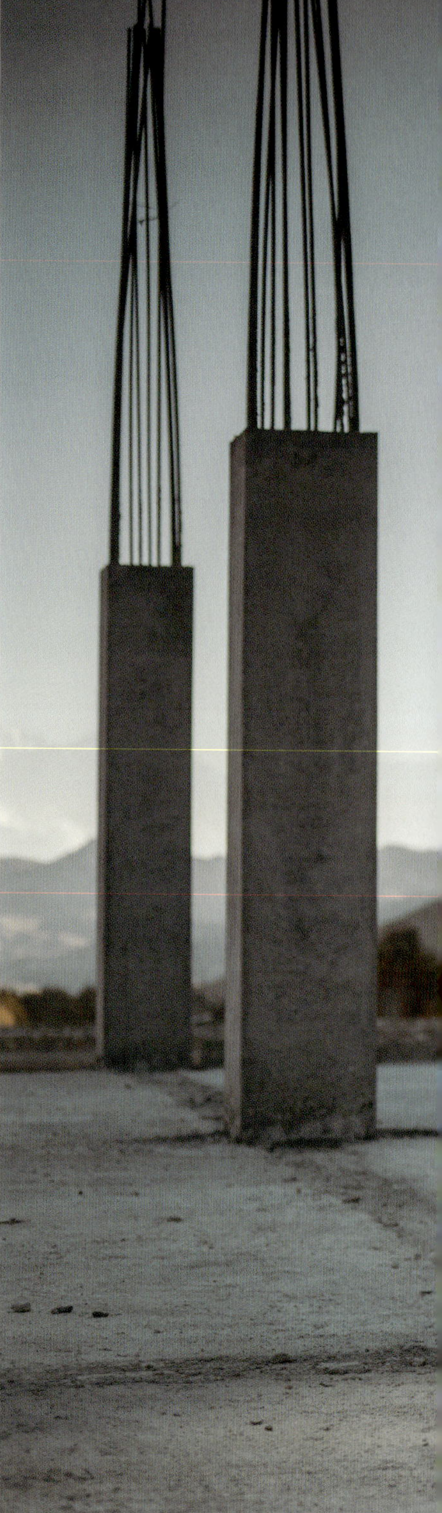

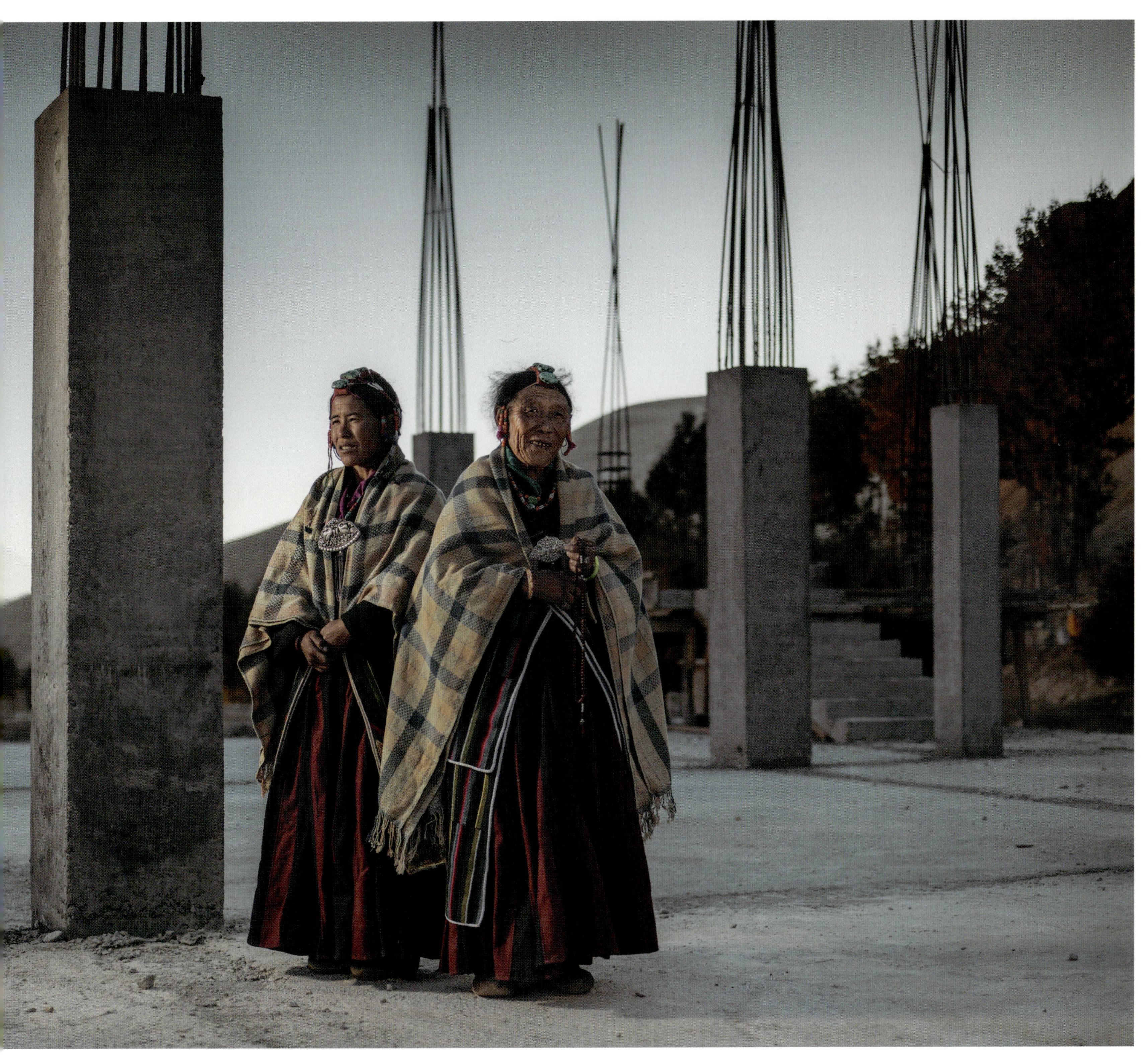

Loba women stand on the freshly poured concrete foundation of new construction in Upper Mustang. **OPPOSITE:** Fourteenth-century Buddhist effigy.

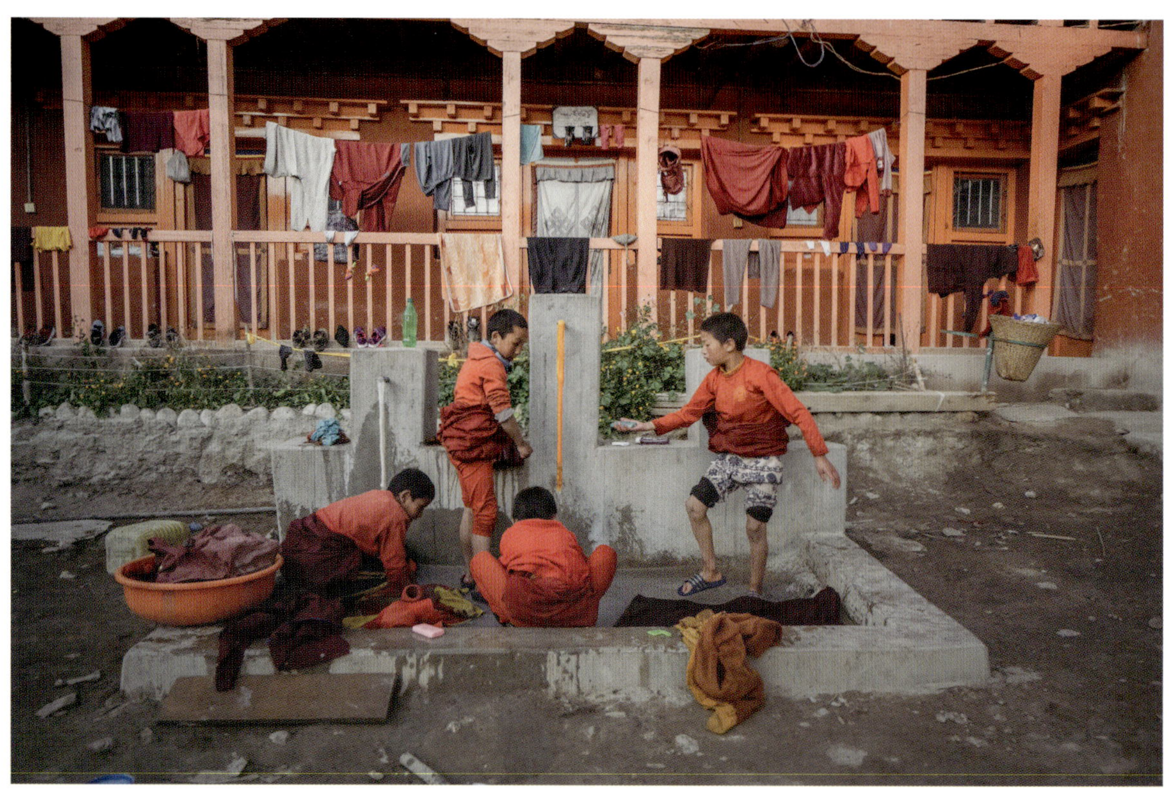

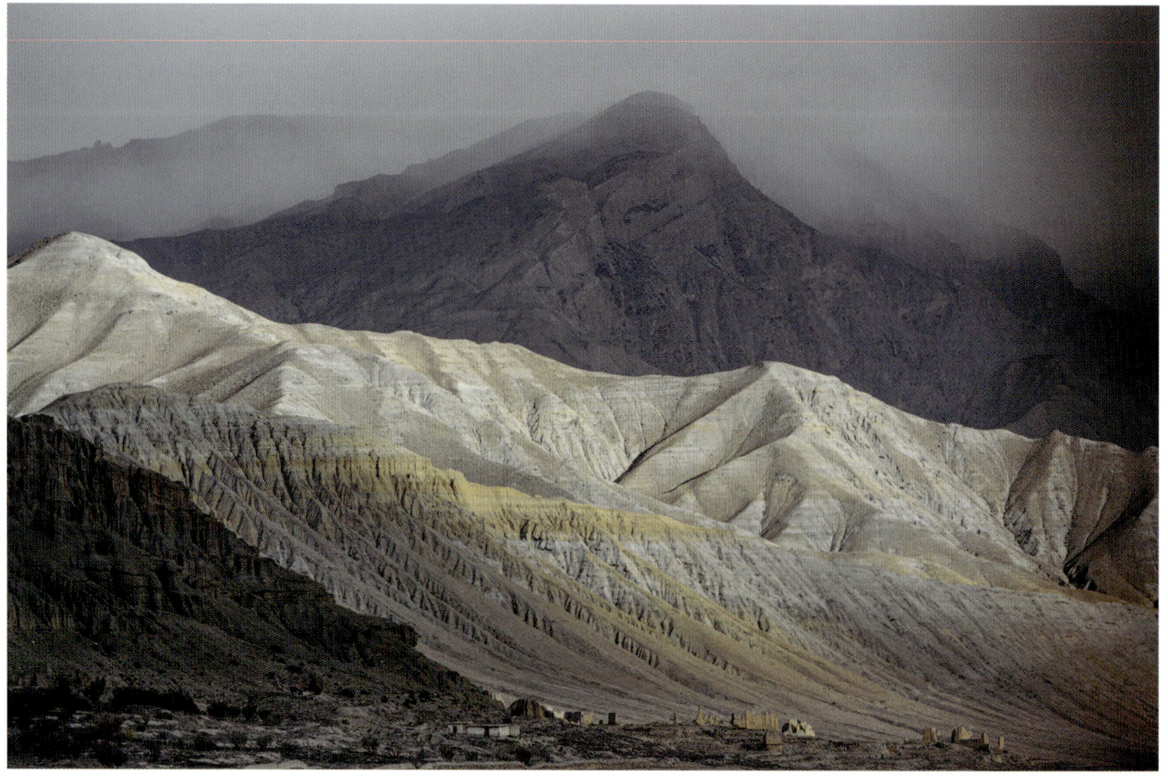

ABOVE: Novice monks do laundry at Choedhe Gompa, Lo Manthang. **BELOW:** Heavy storm clouds spill off the Tibetan Plateau.

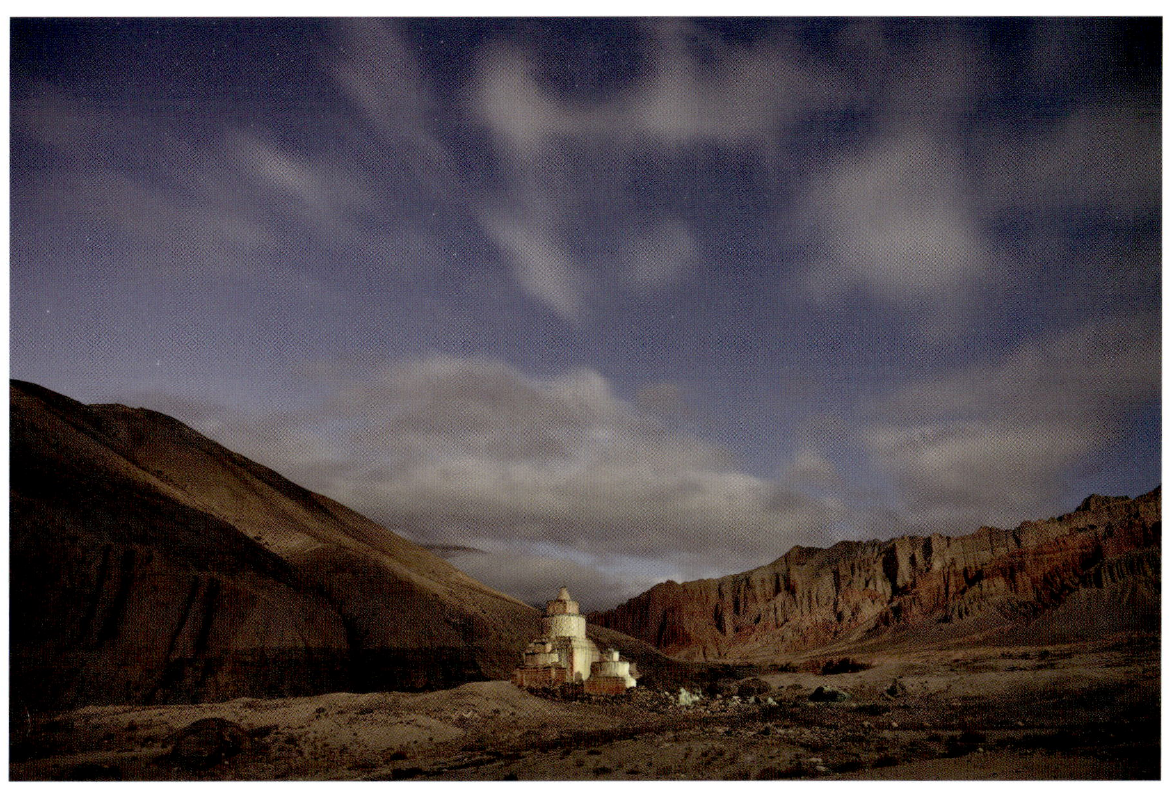

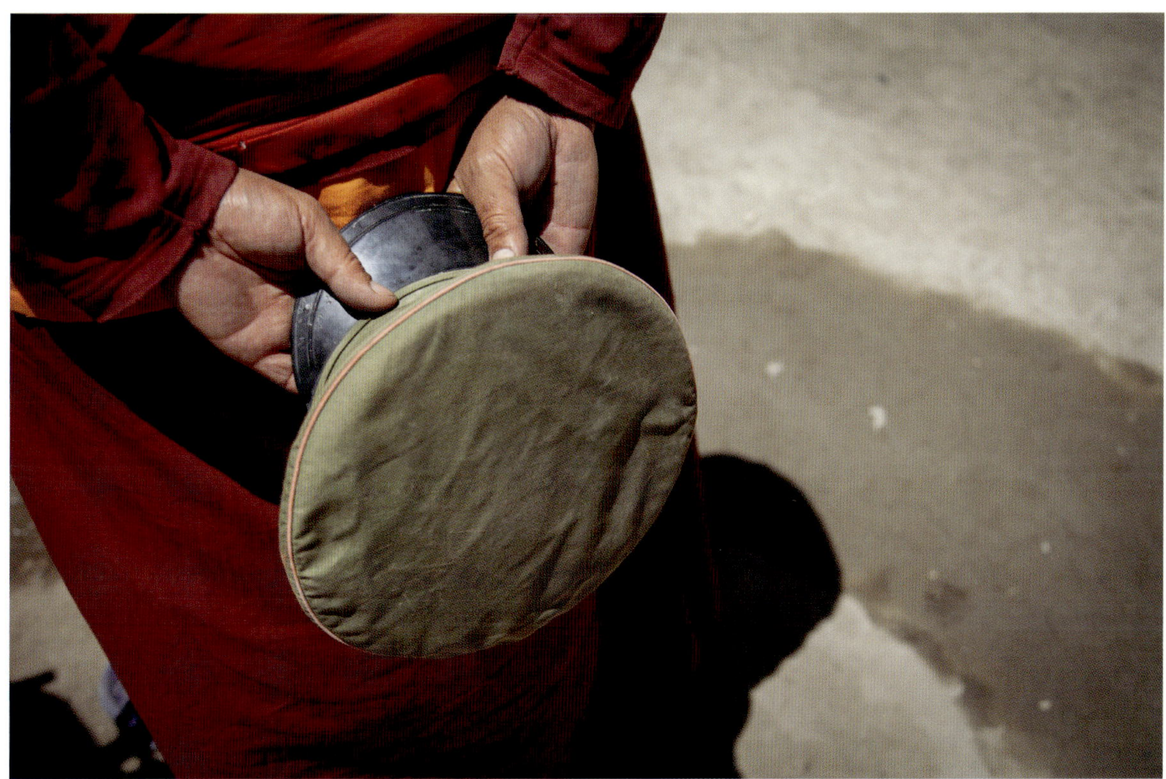

ABOVE: Khokro Chorten under the stars near Ghami, Upper Mustang. **BELOW:** An ironic fashion accessory: a monk holds a Chinese officer's cap behind his back.
FOLLOWING: Traders greet on the horizon, looking south into Nepal from the Tibetan border.

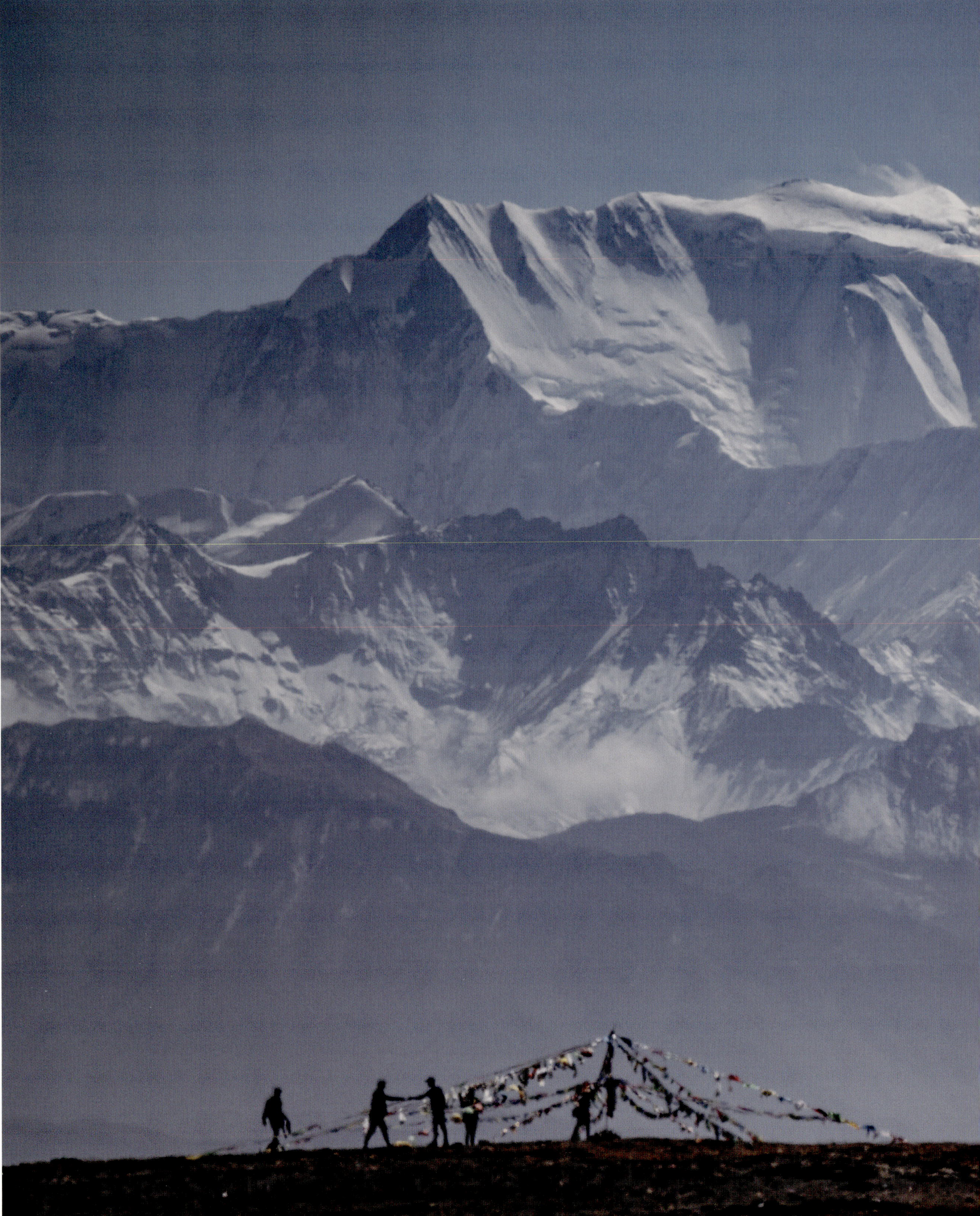

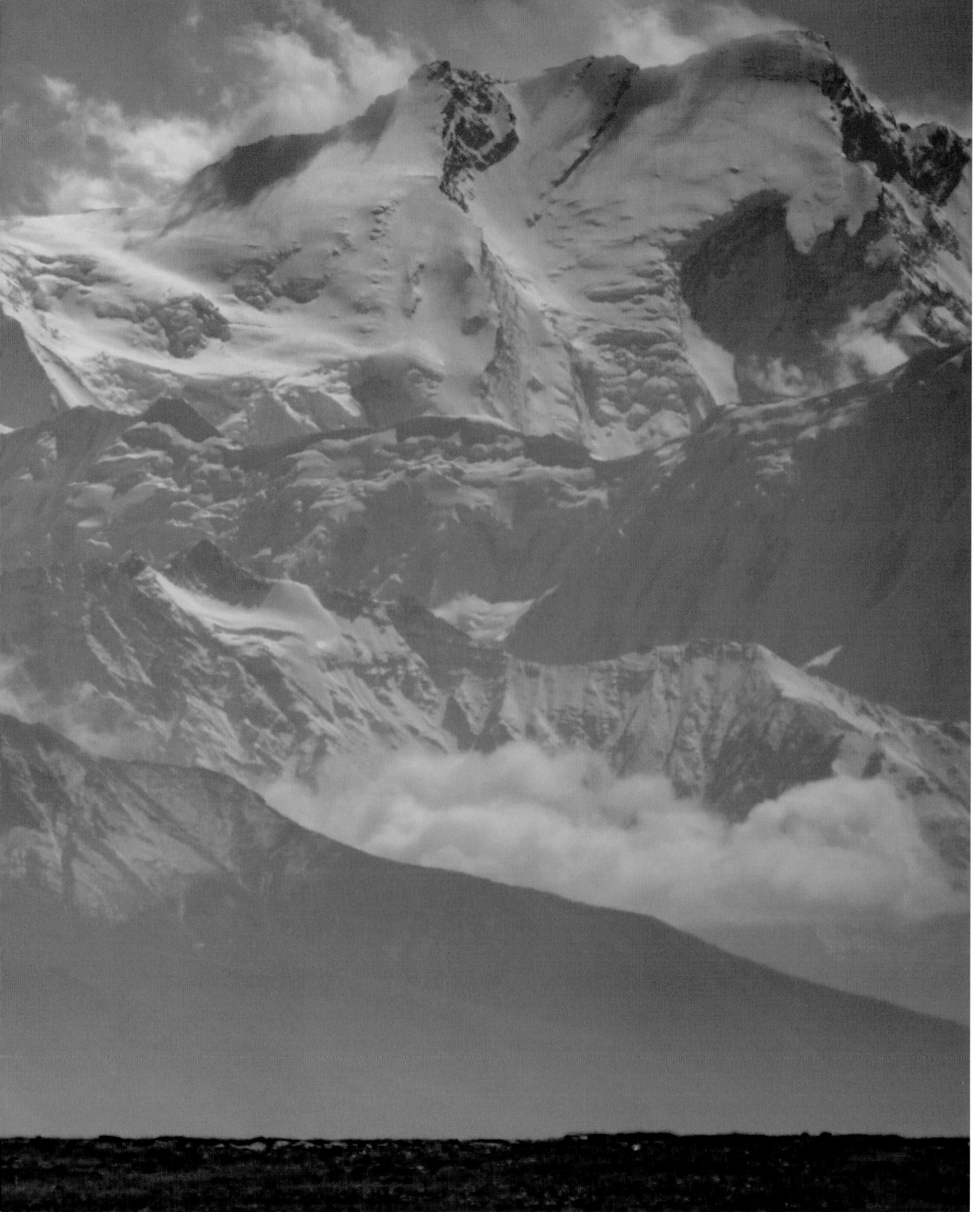

ADRIFT
The Coral Triangle

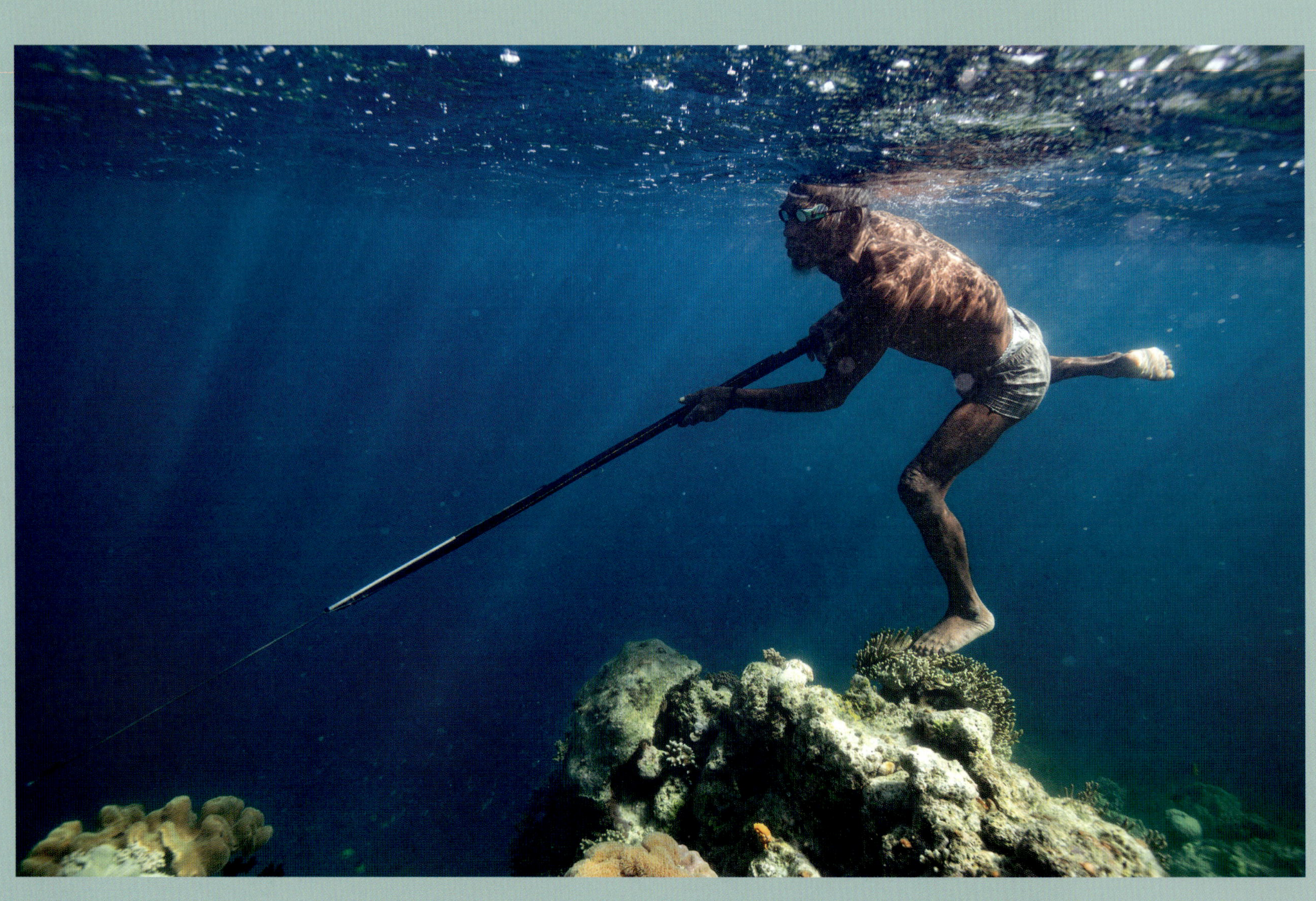

His muscles are sinewy and flex as he navigates in fluid movements from coral to coral with a long speargun gently held at the ready. He's not swimming as much as hopping and bouncing like an astronaut. An almost naked, very tan astronaut. He's as much fish as human, as much water as flesh. I've never seen anything like it. I surface and take another breath.

He's waiting now, perched and still, staring into a hollow fifteen feet below. And then, without coming up for air, he dives.

For at least a thousand years and until relatively recently, the Bajau "sea nomads" lived as traders, adrift on the abundant waters off the Philippines, Indonesia, and Malaysia. Over time, they intermarried with land-based tribes, largely holding on to their culture while assimilating into the island populations. As nations grew up around them, governments demanded permanent residency and often mandated an official declaration to Islam. Slowly, they moved off their boats, erecting stilt villages that allowed them to remain connected to the sea while claiming an address.

Mbo Tadi is probably the most photographed Bajau in the world. It doesn't hurt that he's strikingly handsome, affable, and has about 1 percent body fat. Is he twenty-five, eight-two, or four hundred years old? Some piece of him is ancient. Maybe it's his lungs, but I really can't tell. When I ask about his oldest memory, he tells me of Japanese ships with big guns lumbering through the channels as little men stared down. Did they wave? Sometimes.

He's deep now, waiting outside the hole. I surface and take another breath.

When the Bajau were forced from their nomadic subsistence lifestyle, the local reefs where they settled slowly became overfished. With no adult fish left, people started harvesting the adolescents before they reached breeding maturity. And with fewer fish to eat and trade, compounded by increasing competition from commercial fishing, some turned to other means of survival. With simple homemade explosives made for bomb fishing, whole reefs and habitats were destroyed, often claiming a hand or arm in the process.

If there's a "solution" to this situation, it's hard to see it. The Bajau have been hung in this purgatory for years. Like all cultural evolution, it comes with conflicting and paradoxical blessings and curses. Witnessing it makes me ache for something that seems irretrievably lost. But that is the nature of history. I wonder if the energy of mourning is best spent in pursuit of a future that holds on to the best pieces of the past. Regardless, the Bajau seem to be uneasily adrift again.

I duck back under the surface just as Mbo Tadi's spear shoots into the darkness. I hear it clank and see a small, dark poof of colorless blood. He collects the kill and kicks calmly toward the surface, exhaling a mercury-like trail of exhausted carbon dioxide through his nose. How long has it been? How long can this last? I hold my breath.

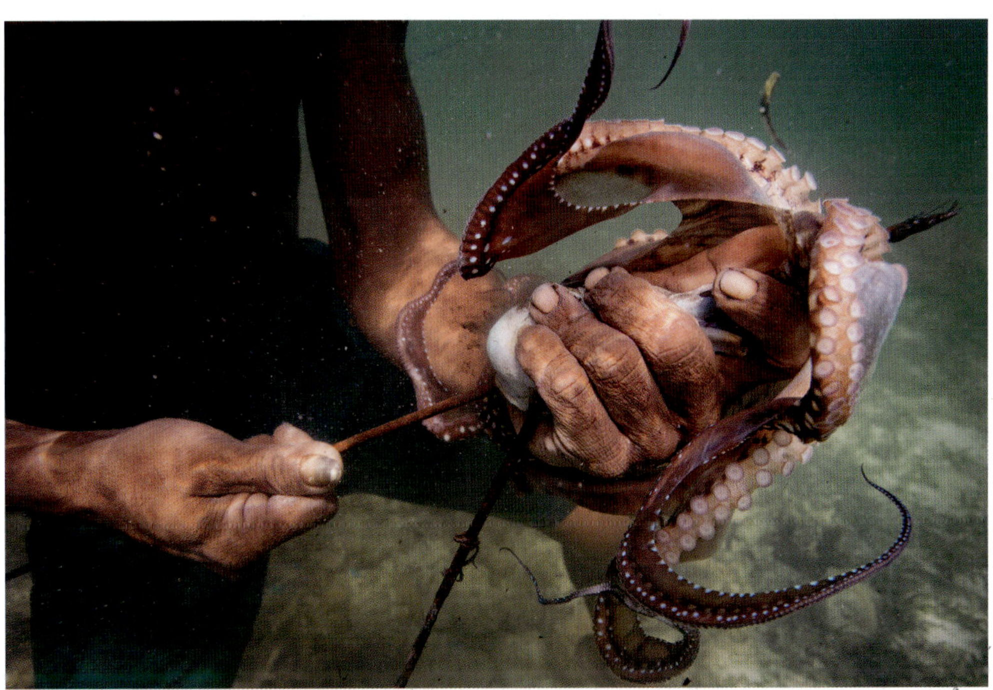

OPPOSITE: Mbo Tadi spearfishes near his home in the Wakatobi Regency, Indonesia. **RIGHT:** A spear fisherman collects a freshly harvested octopus.

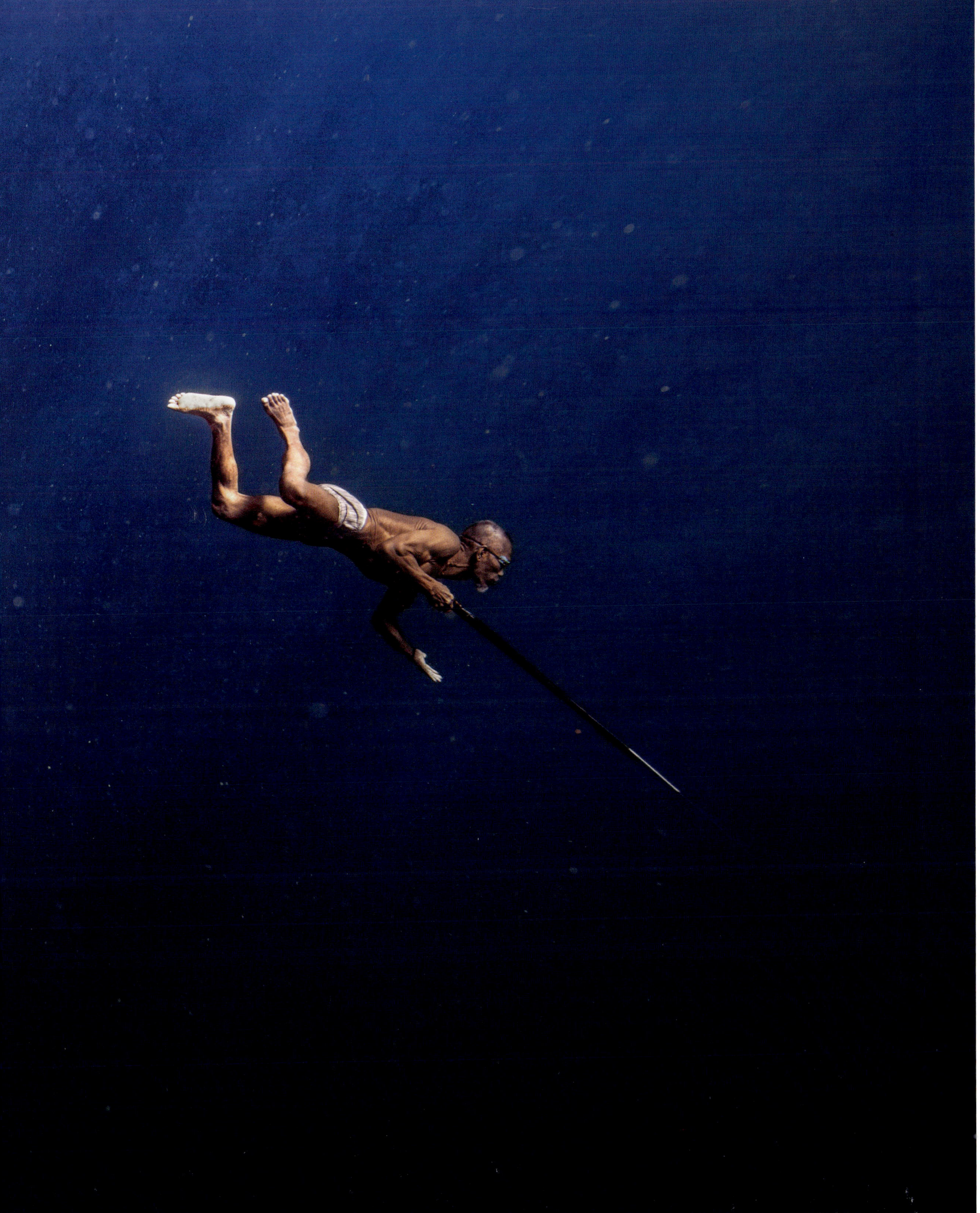

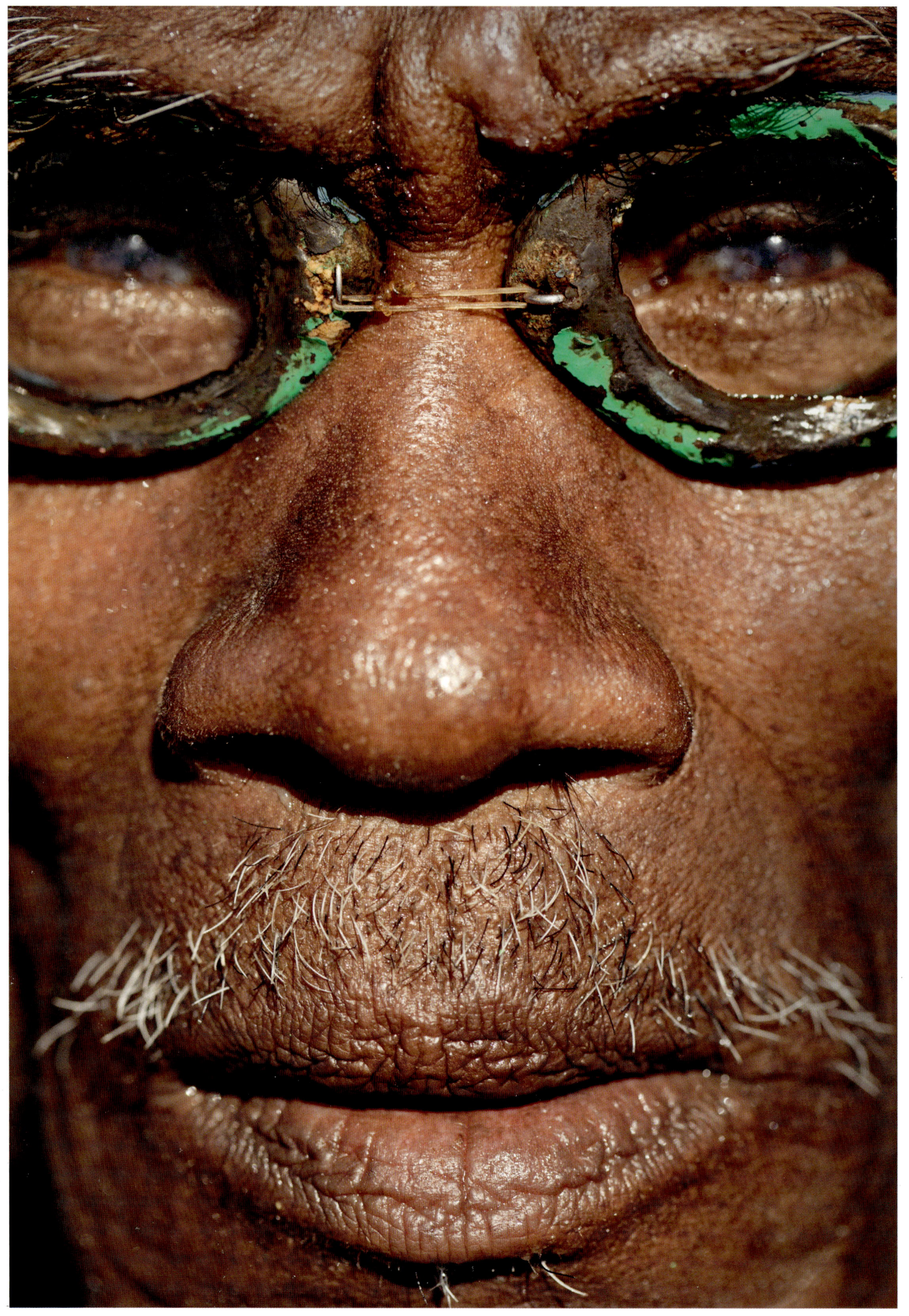

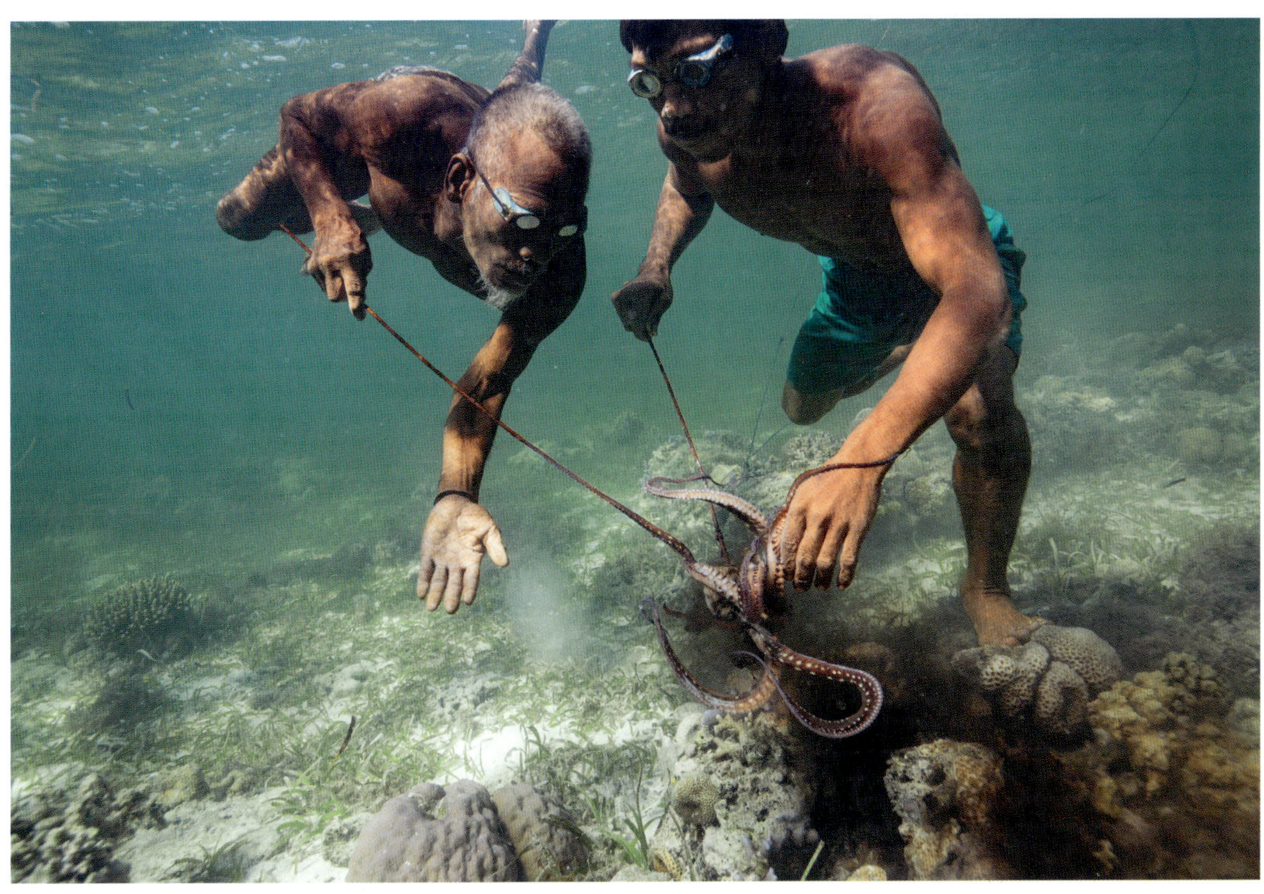

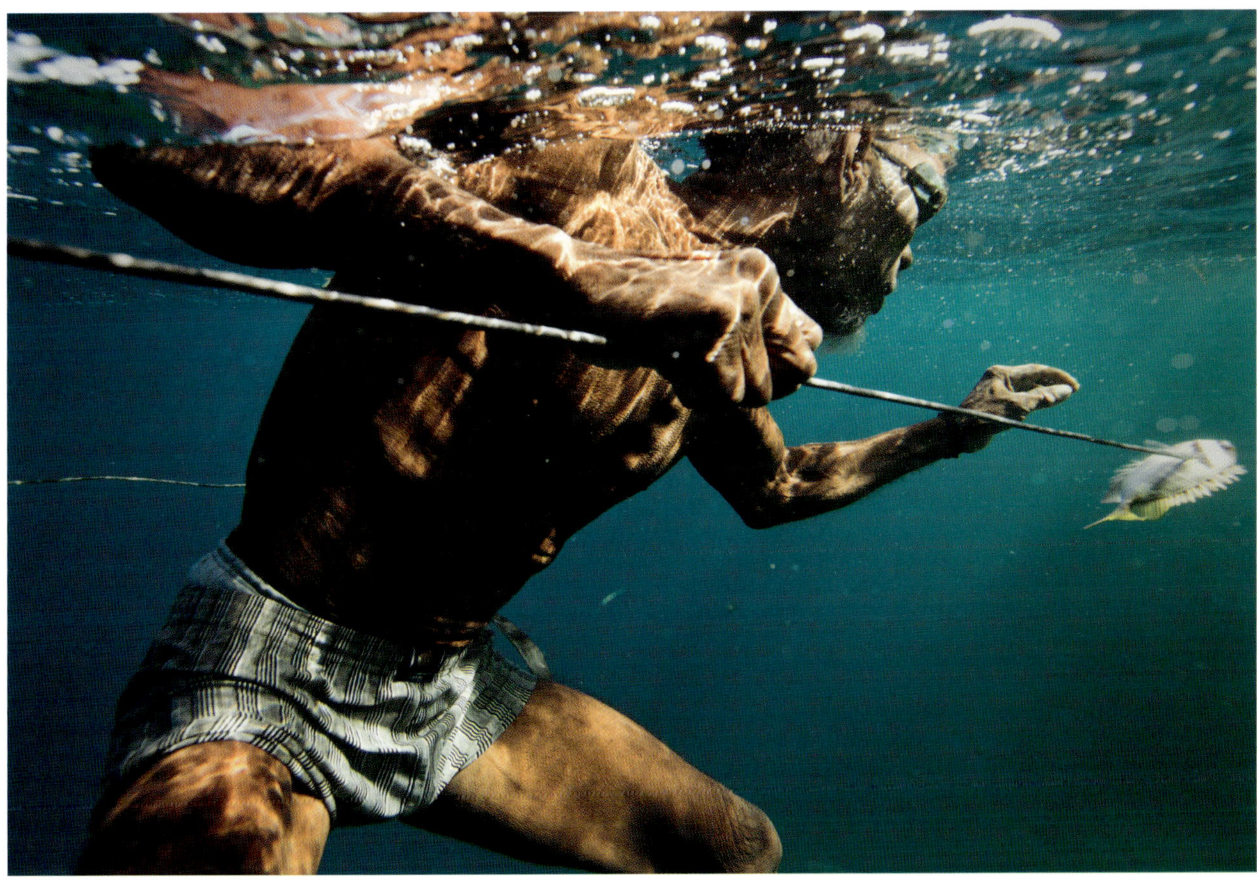

PREVIOUS: Mbo Tadi holds his breath and scans the water below for fish. ABOVE: Mbo Tadi and his son Baele harvest an octopus.
BELOW: Spearfishing near Sampela. OPPOSITE: Mbo Tadi wears the traditional Bajau Laut Carummeng (goggles) made of wood and glass.

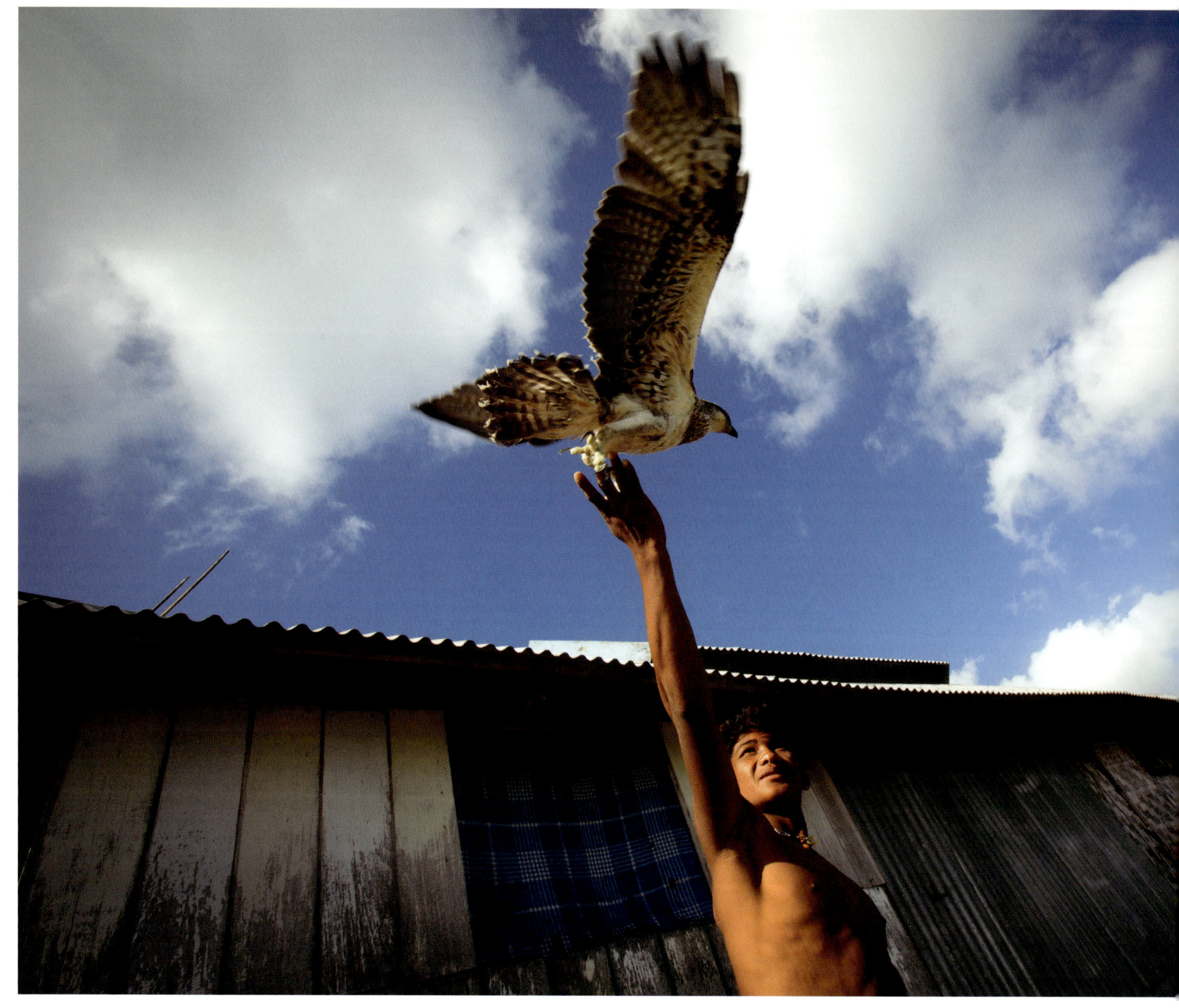

An Indonesian boy plays with a pet sea eagle in the Bajau village of LaHoa. **OPPOSITE, ABOVE:** Baele front rutters a lepa (canoe) against the cross swell while traversing a channel from LaHoa to the island of Hoga. **OPPOSITE, BELOW:** Mbo Deha, a Bajo elder who has been in prison three times for invasive fishing, bears the scars of bomb fishing. Having lost his right arm and damaged his internal organs in one accident, and lost some of his fingertips in another, he is candid about the socioeconomic pressures placed on him by the industrial fishing industry, which leads him and others to engage in more profitable means, such as bomb fishing, which yields a greater immediate harvest but kills the reefs.

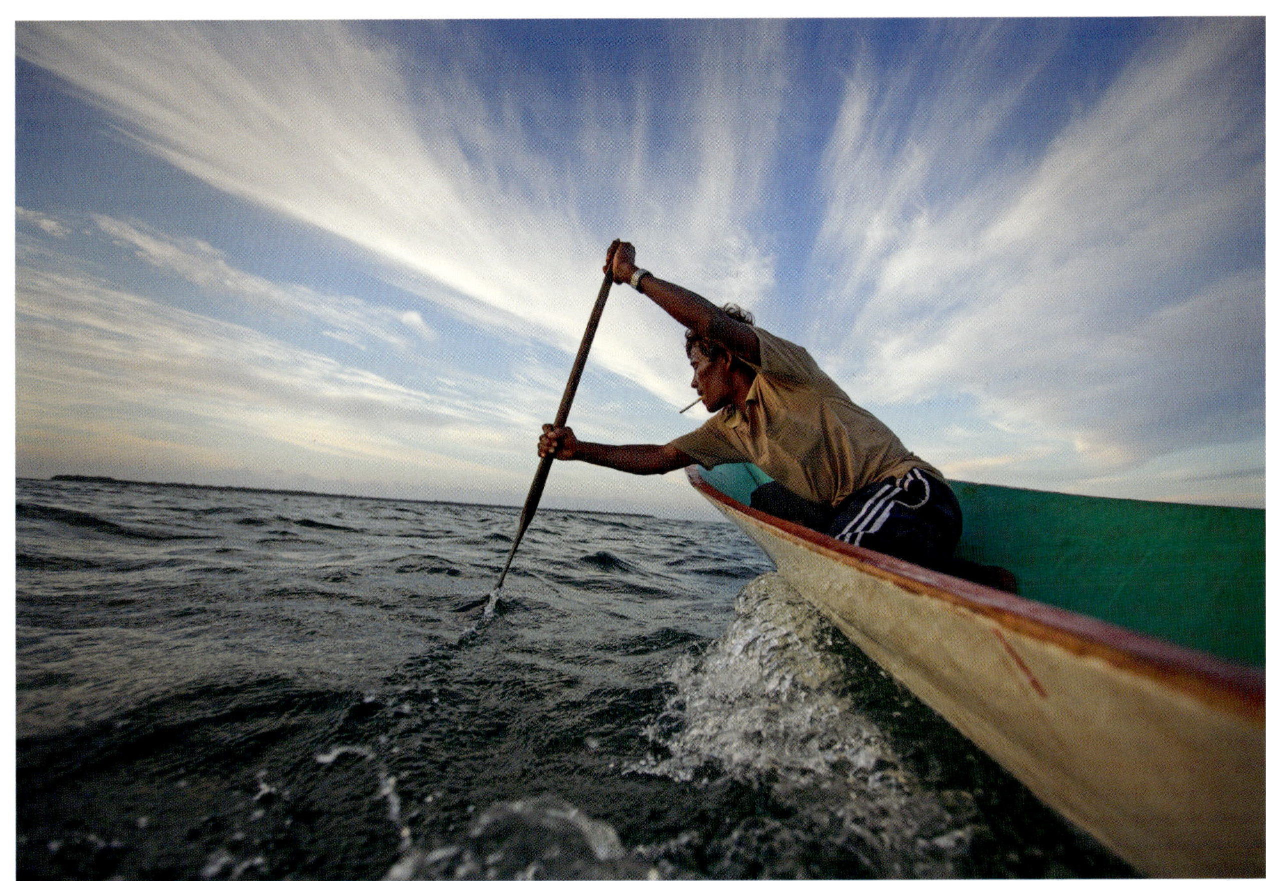

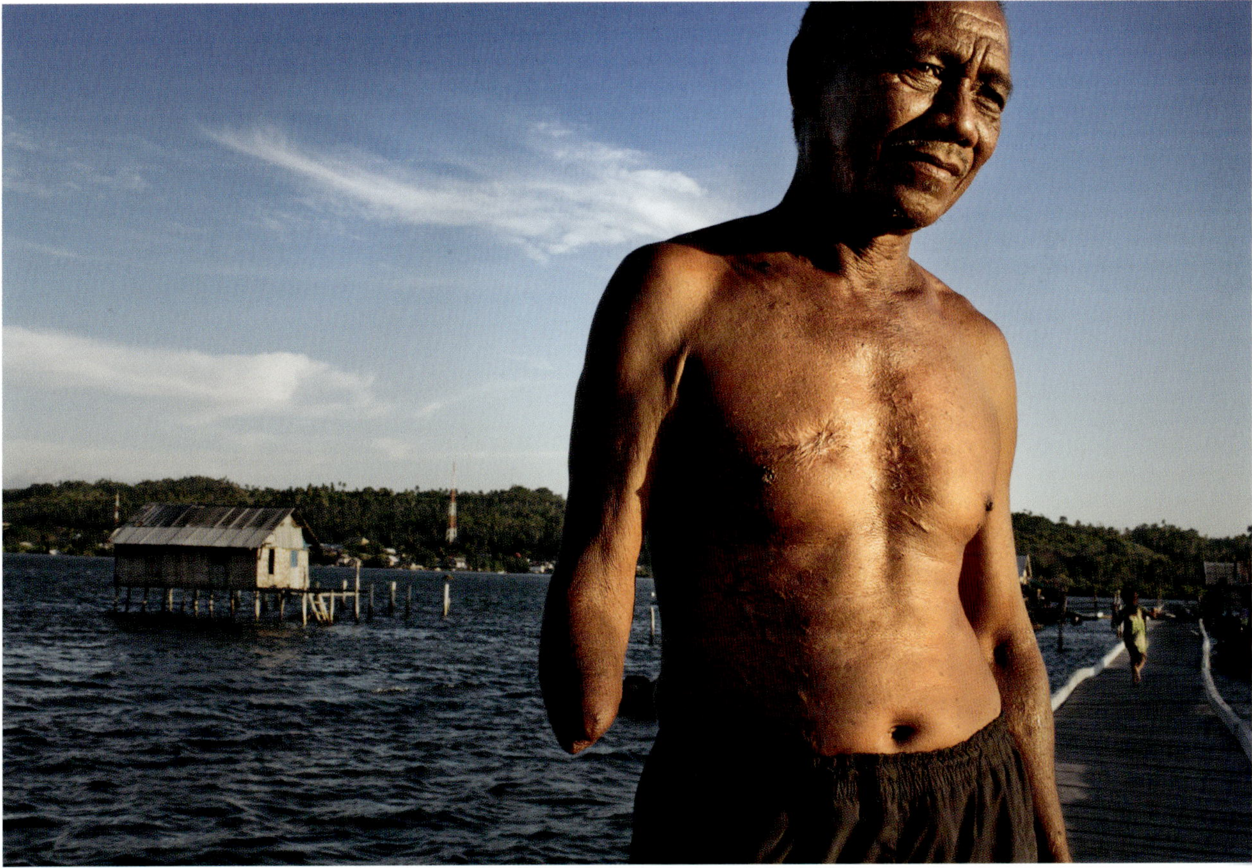

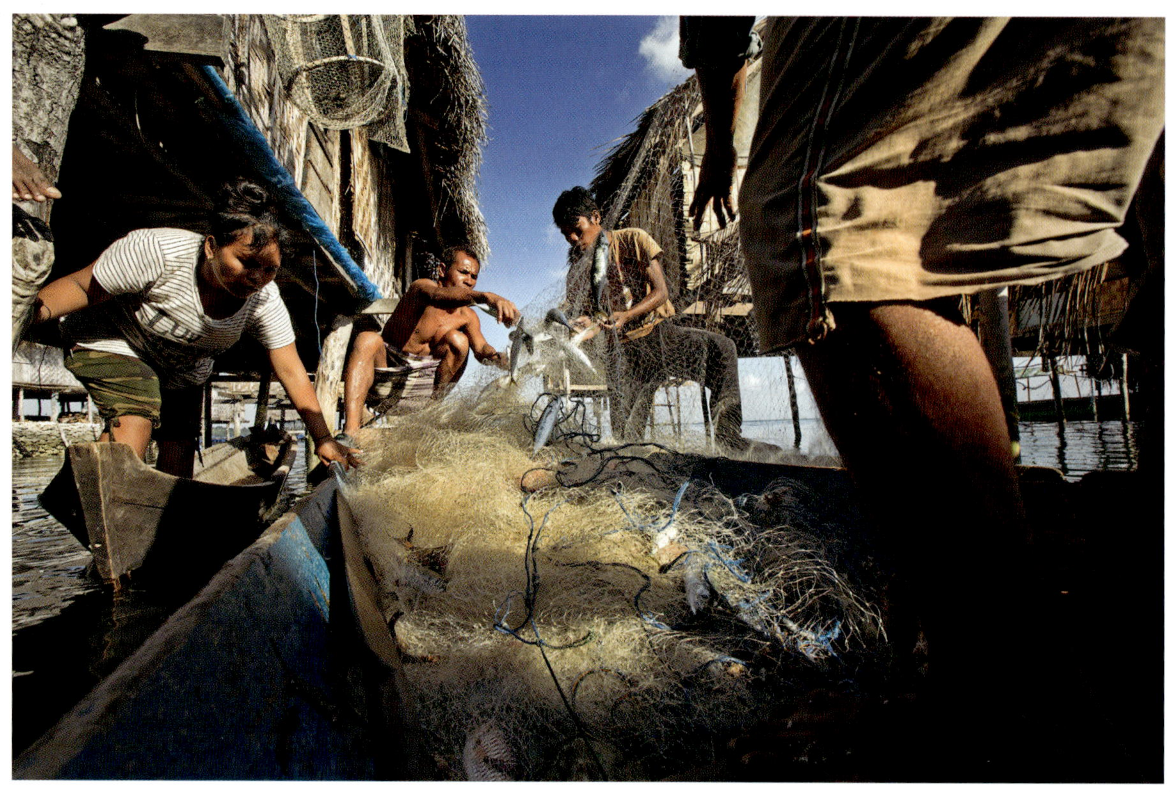

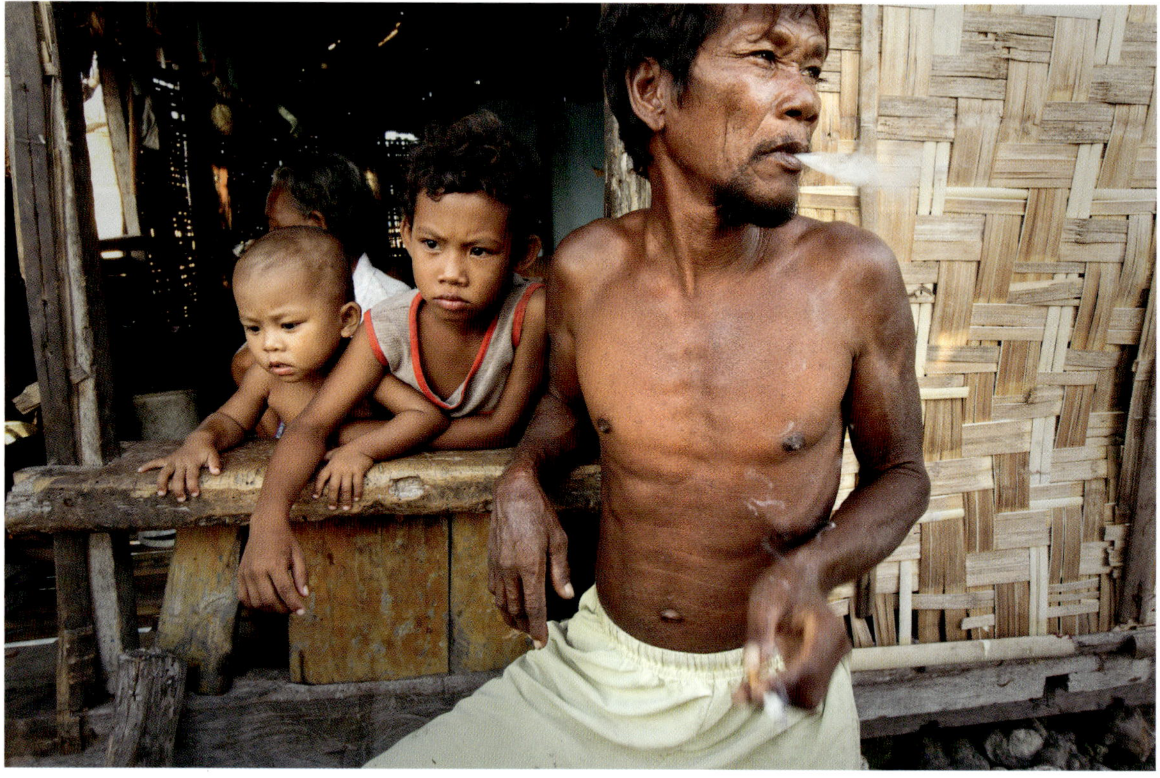

ABOVE: Mammi, La Huru, and Buntari remove their catch of gagadih (jax) to be sold at the market. **BELOW:** La Harumu, a guest in Mbo Tadi's house, scans the reef while keeping the children company. **OPPOSITE:** Mbo Lena, a Bajau elder, repairs nets for fishing.

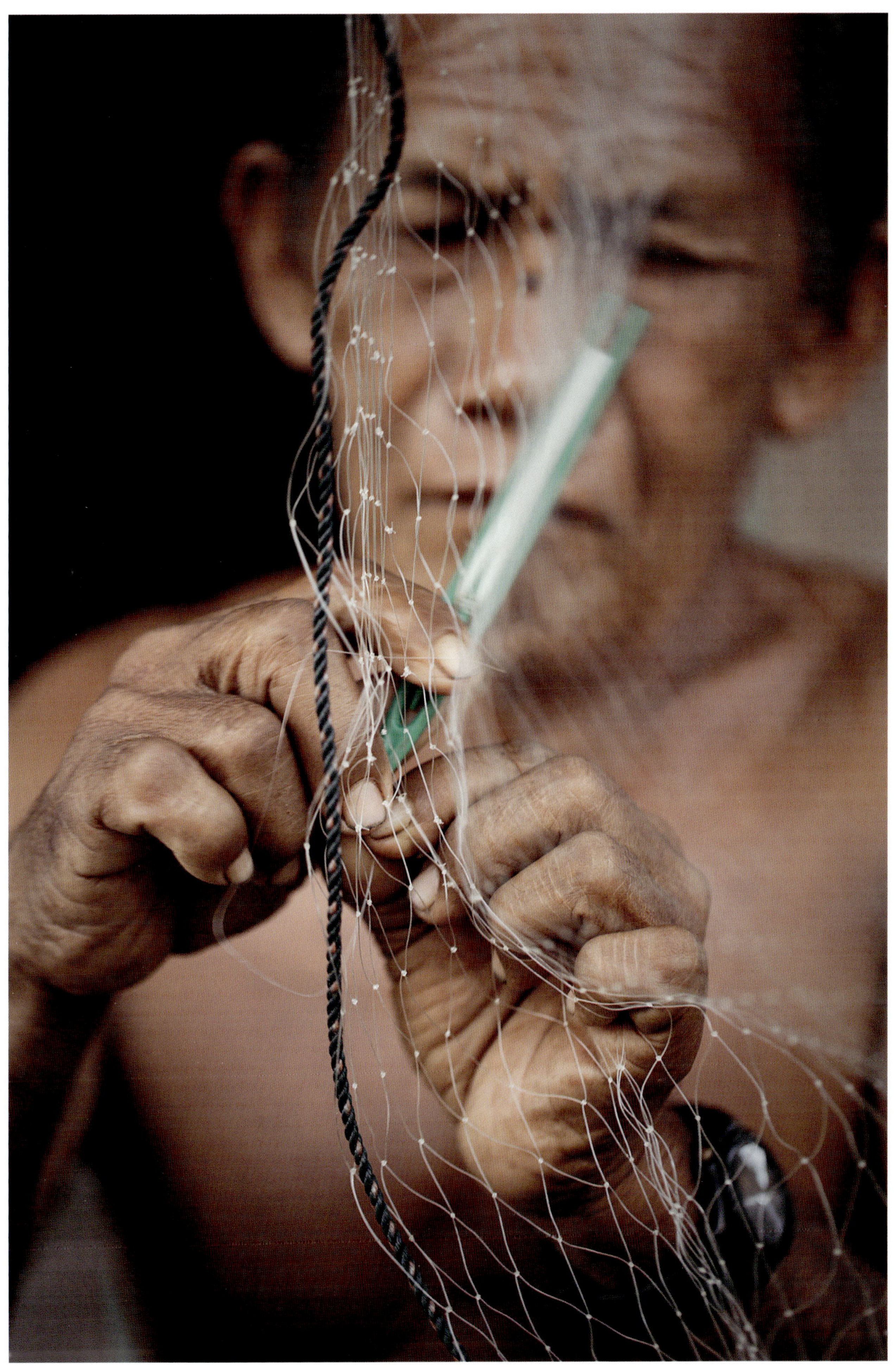

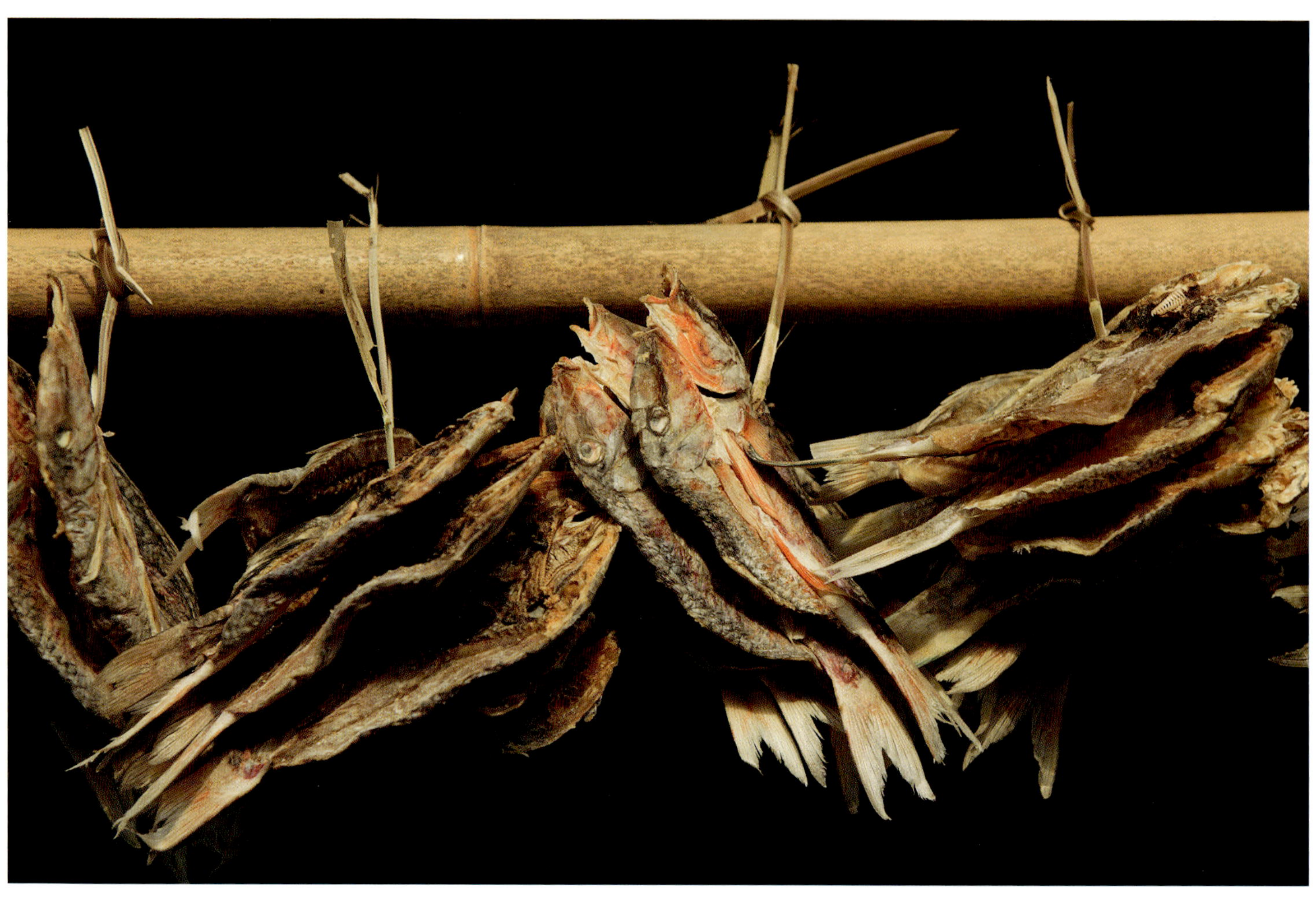

Fish dries in the late day sun, Sampela.

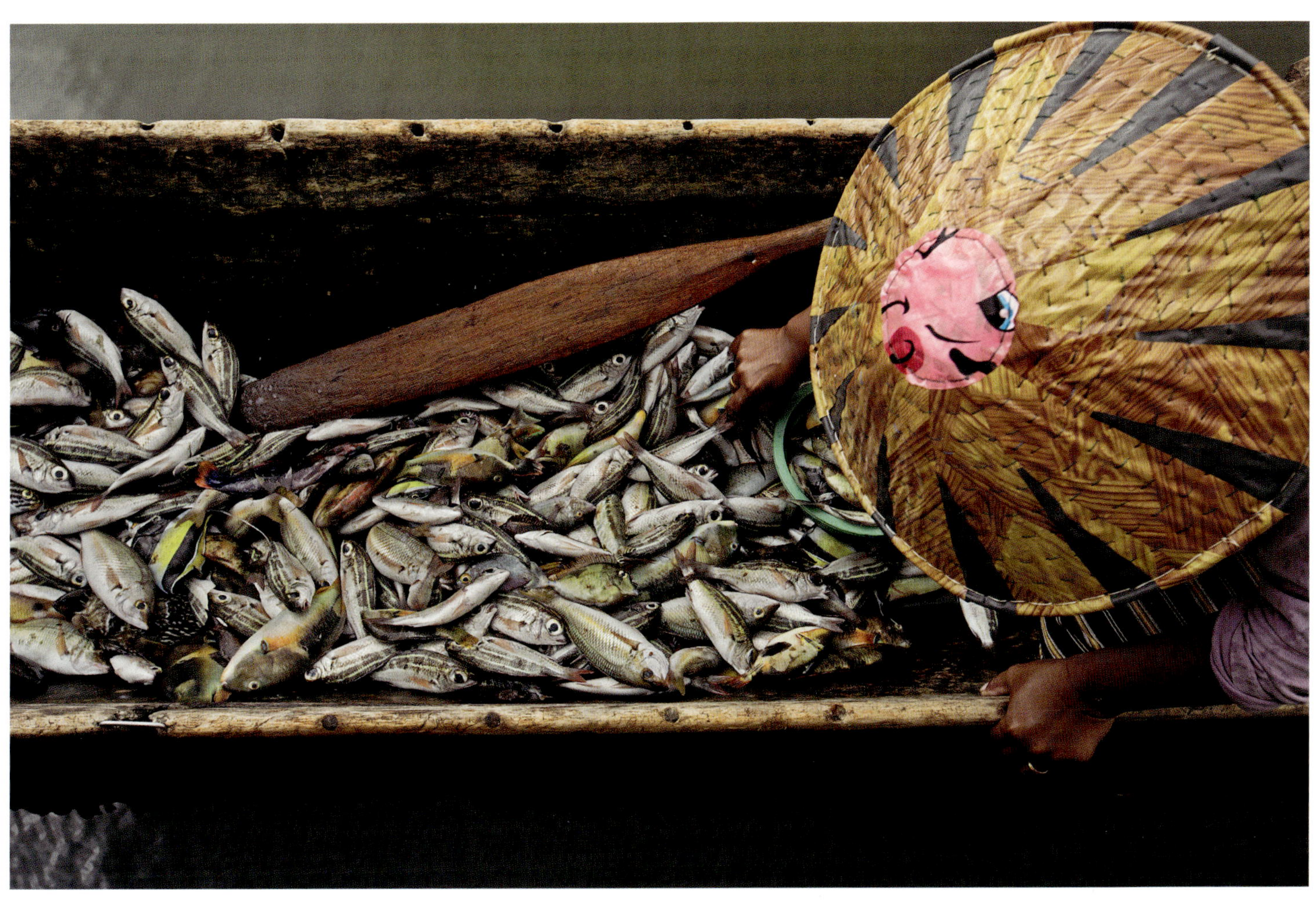

A daily harvest, likely the result of bomb fishing.

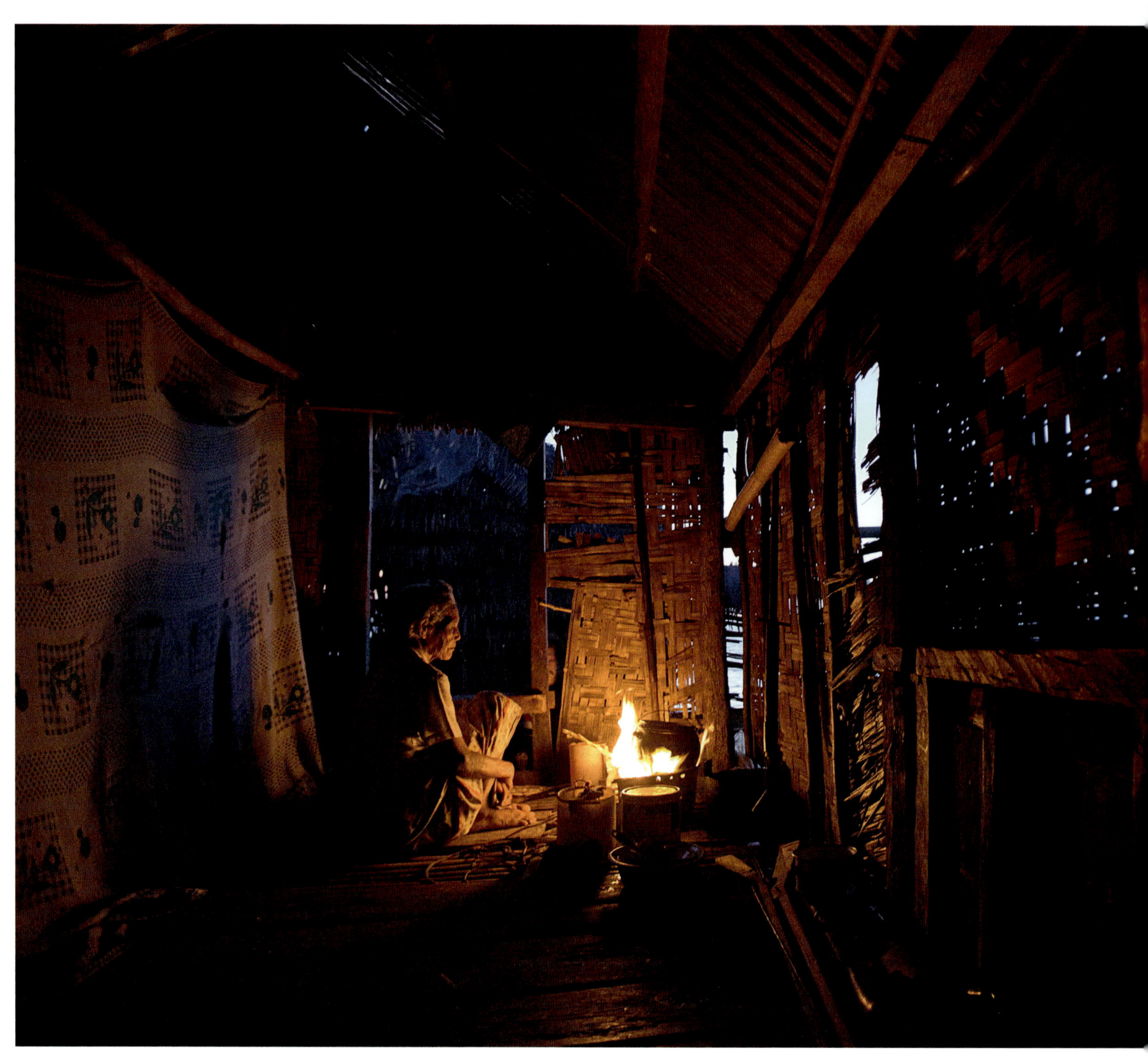

Mbo Tadi's wife, Mbo Kalong, cooking. **OPPOSITE, ABOVE:** Mbo Tadi lights his lantern early in the morning as he prepares for the day's fishing. **OPPOSITE, BELOW:** Villager La Yai out after dark, mbena mbena, or night line fishing. **FOLLOWING:** The Milky Way stretches above the lanterns of Sampela.

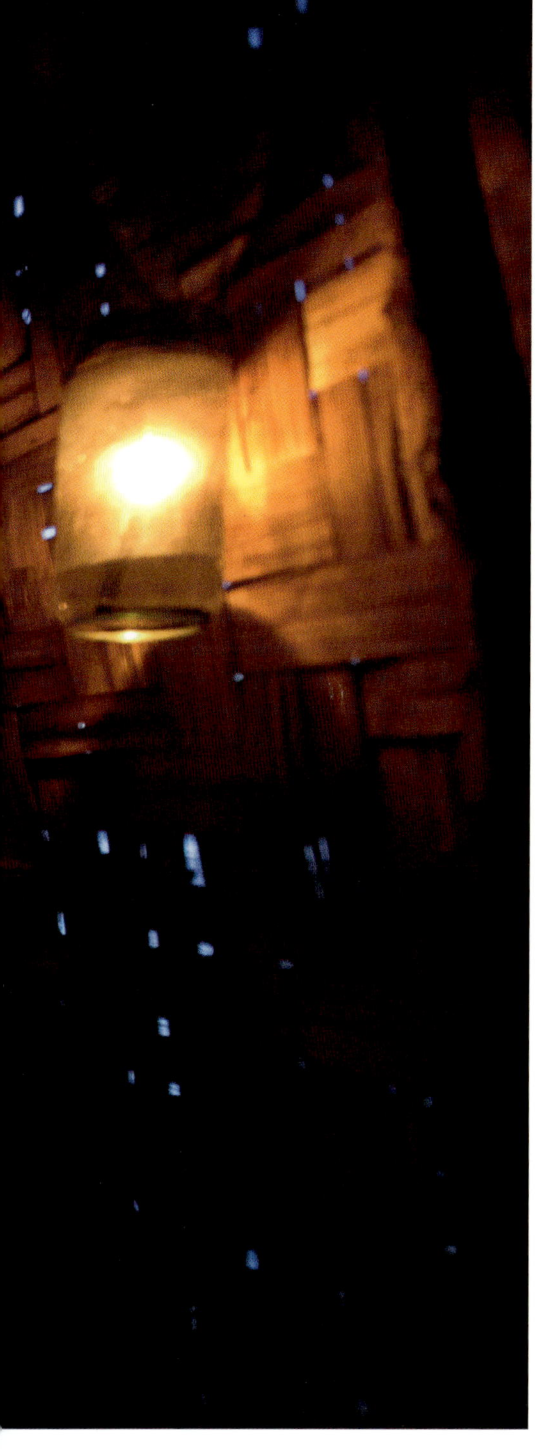

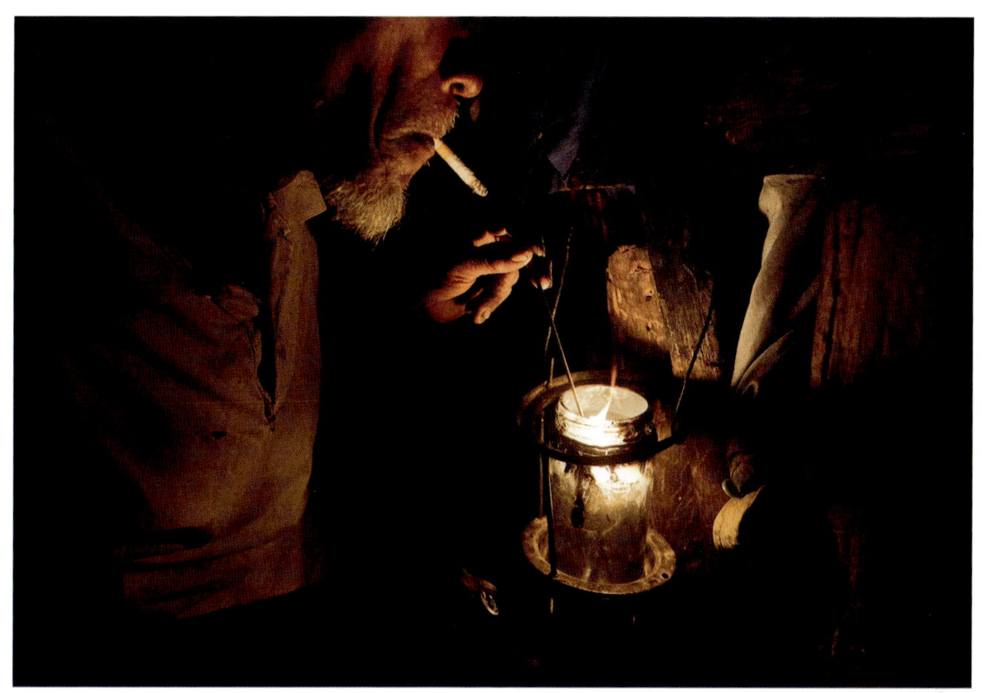

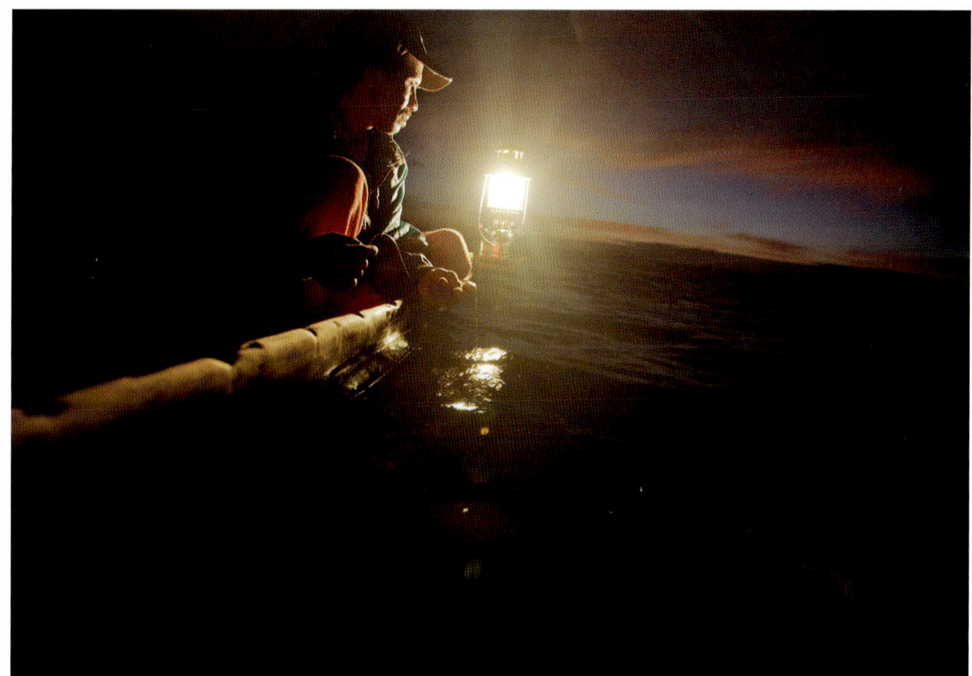

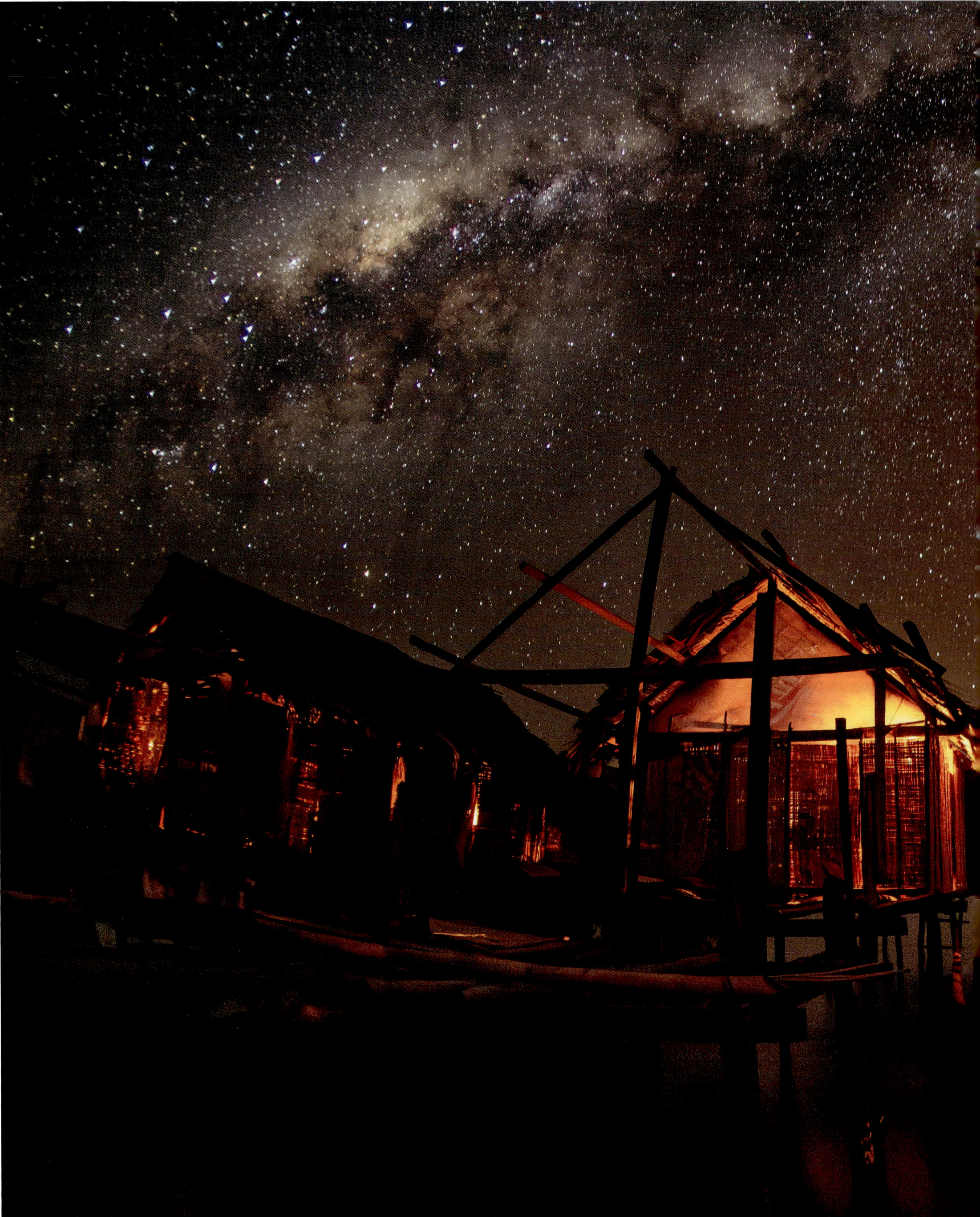

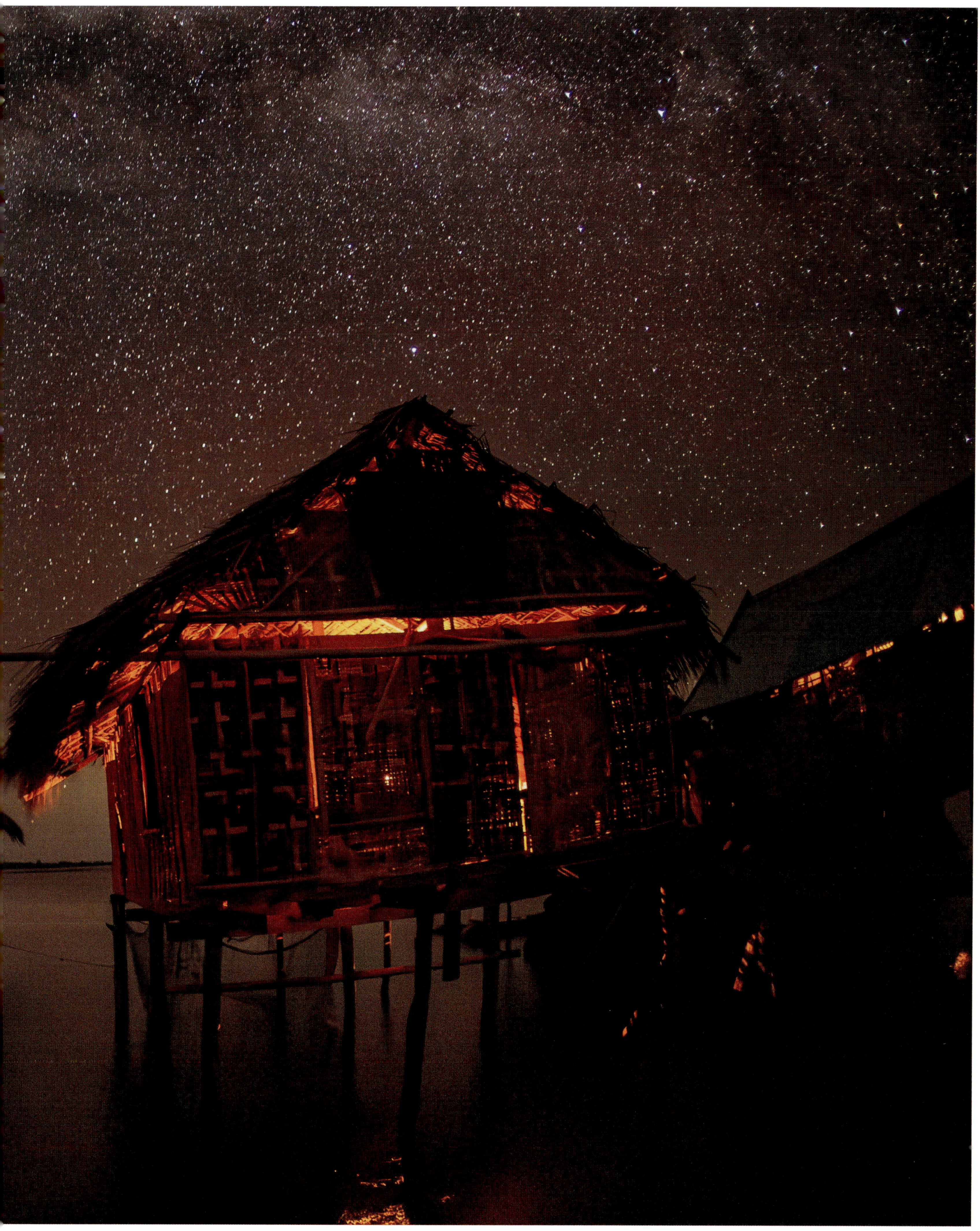

THE SUM OF EARTH

The Himalaya

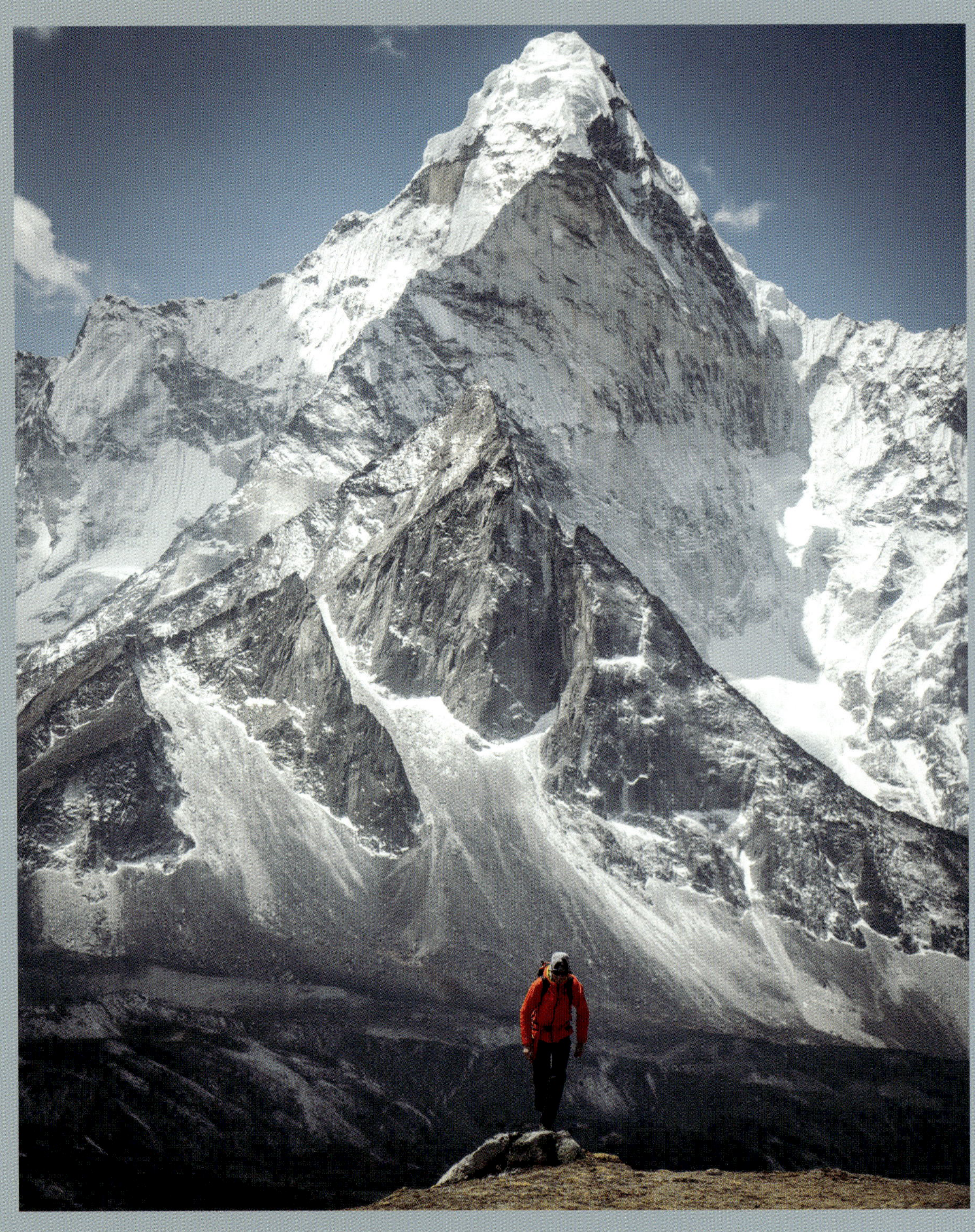

In Bön, the ancient indigenous religious tradition of the Tibetan plateau, Miyolangsangma was a malevolent demoness, haunting the world and causing mischief. It wasn't until the great Buddhist mystic Padmasambhava tamed her wickedness in the eighth century that she became an avowed guardian of Buddhism and the Dharma.

Now, holding a bowl of food in one hand and a jewel-spitting mongoose in the other, she rides a tiger through the high Himalaya as the Goddess of Inexhaustible Giving. Chomolungma, the Tibetan name for Mount Everest, is her home and she lives on the summit—my end goal . . . and only about 150 feet away. It's May 24, 2016, and I am alone with no oxygen taking the last steps to the highest point on the planet. I must admit I'm a bit disappointed that I don't see a house.

I first came to the Himalaya in the winter of 2008/2009 with German climber Ines Papert. After that first trip, I came back the following summer. And, again, in the fall. Then the winter, the next spring, and the summer after that. I'm staring at the summit in front of me now, trying to recall all the peaks, partners, wins, and near misses in these mountains over the past decade, forcing my brain to focus on something other than how cold my left pinky is. But I lose count and the list is a disjointed mess of names and mountain faces: Kwangde Shar. Tawoche. Conrad Anker. Ama Dablam. Renan Ozturk. Gasherbrum II. Lhotse. Simone Moro. Denis Urubko. Pete Athans. Steve House. Melissa Arnot. Makalu. Hkakabo Razi. Chhewang Nima. Panuru. Karma Tsering. Hilaree Nelson. Adrian Ballinger. Little gifts stacked like bricks in a big pyramid.

I close my eyes and wake up fifty feet closer to the summit. Did I blink? My nose is cold and my mouth tastes like tin. My pinky is warm, though. When was the last time I ate? A noise over my shoulder startles me and I spin slowly to see if I'm still alone. Maybe it's a tiger or a mongoose. No one is there. It's just the nylon of my down suit rubbing against itself. I look back toward the summit in search of Miyolangsangma, and, still, there is no house.

Everest holds a special place in the human psyche not because it's the most difficult or most deadly mountain to climb, but because it epitomizes the limit of what's knowable. Mythologically, mountains represent the source of creation and a trepidatious pathway to union with the divine. For those who choose to climb, mountains make the mysterious momentarily familiar, even intimate. Because Everest is the highest, it symbolizes a point of unity that pulls the surface of the planet together, as if the sum of the earth is being collected into a singularity at its apex. It's the end of the knowable world and the beginning of everything else. But these thoughts are much too big for me right now and my pinky is cold again.

I've been awake for more than thirty hours. The sky is chalky blue and the sun shines timidly. Unlike crowded days when the summit looks like a package of spilled Skittles, I'm the only one here now and I must finally accept that there is no house. That's not to say the goddess doesn't live here. I think again about the many gifts I've been given in the form of partners and climbs and pictures and everything else that has brought me to this place. *Thank you.*

I also imagine that being the goddess of inexhaustible giving can be a bit exhausting and I feel greedy when I realize that I have one more very important thing to ask of her. Just one more gift: *Please, get me down.*

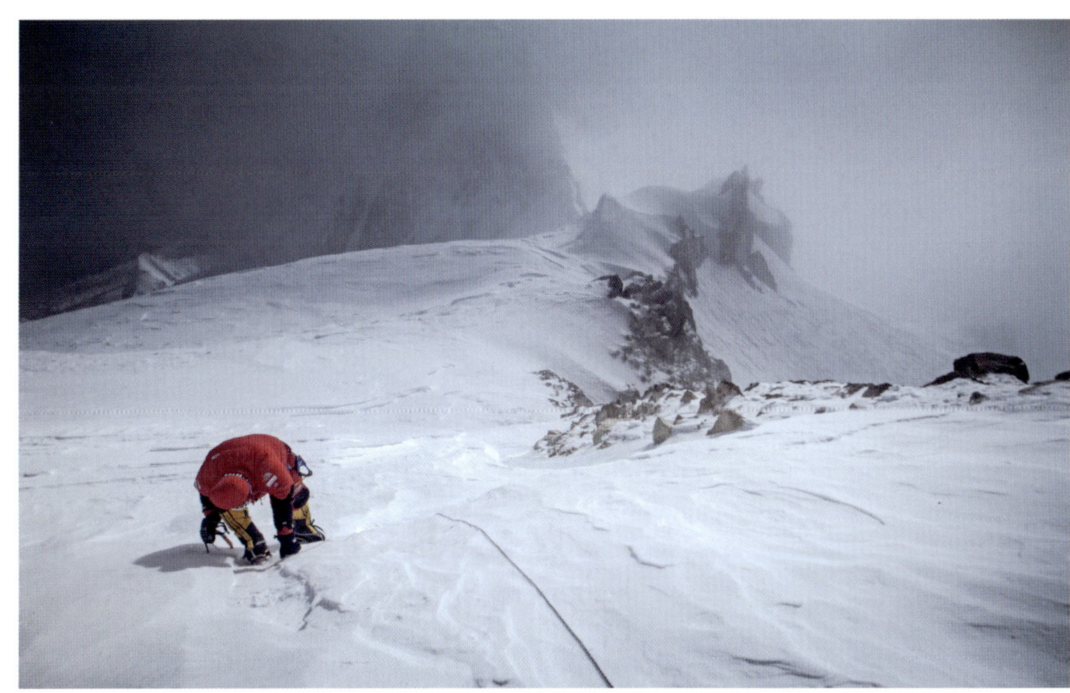

Italian climber Simone Moro attempts the first winter ascent of Gasherbrum II, the world's thirteenth-highest peak at 26,362 feet; Karakoram Himalaya, Pakistan (February 2, 2011). **OPPOSITE:** American climber Adrian Ballinger, below Ama Dablam, acclimatizes to climb Mount Everest without oxygen (2016). **FOLLOWING:** Russian-Polish climber and citizen of Kazakhstan Denis Urubko (front) and Simone Moro (behind) climb into the sunrise on Gasherbrum II.

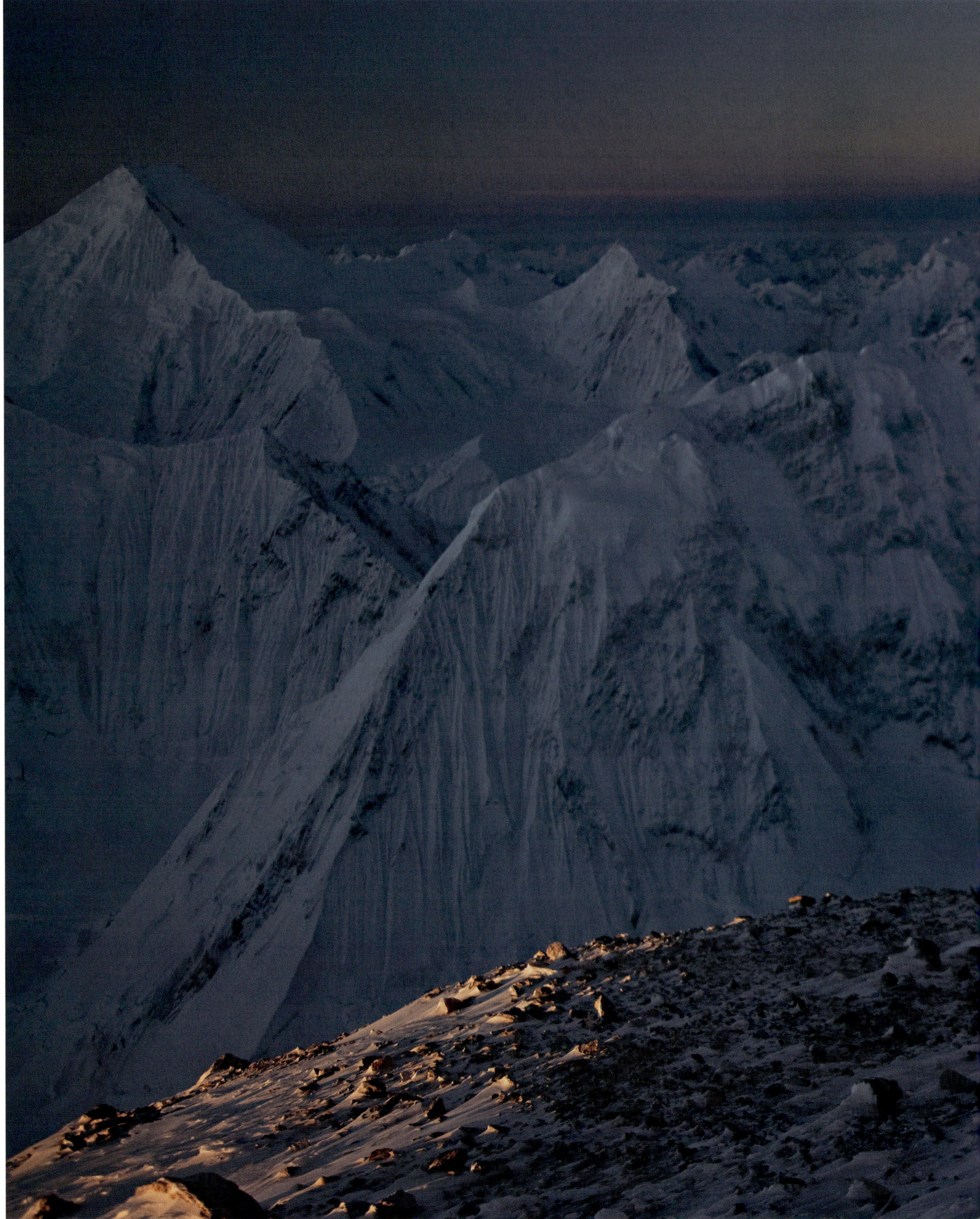

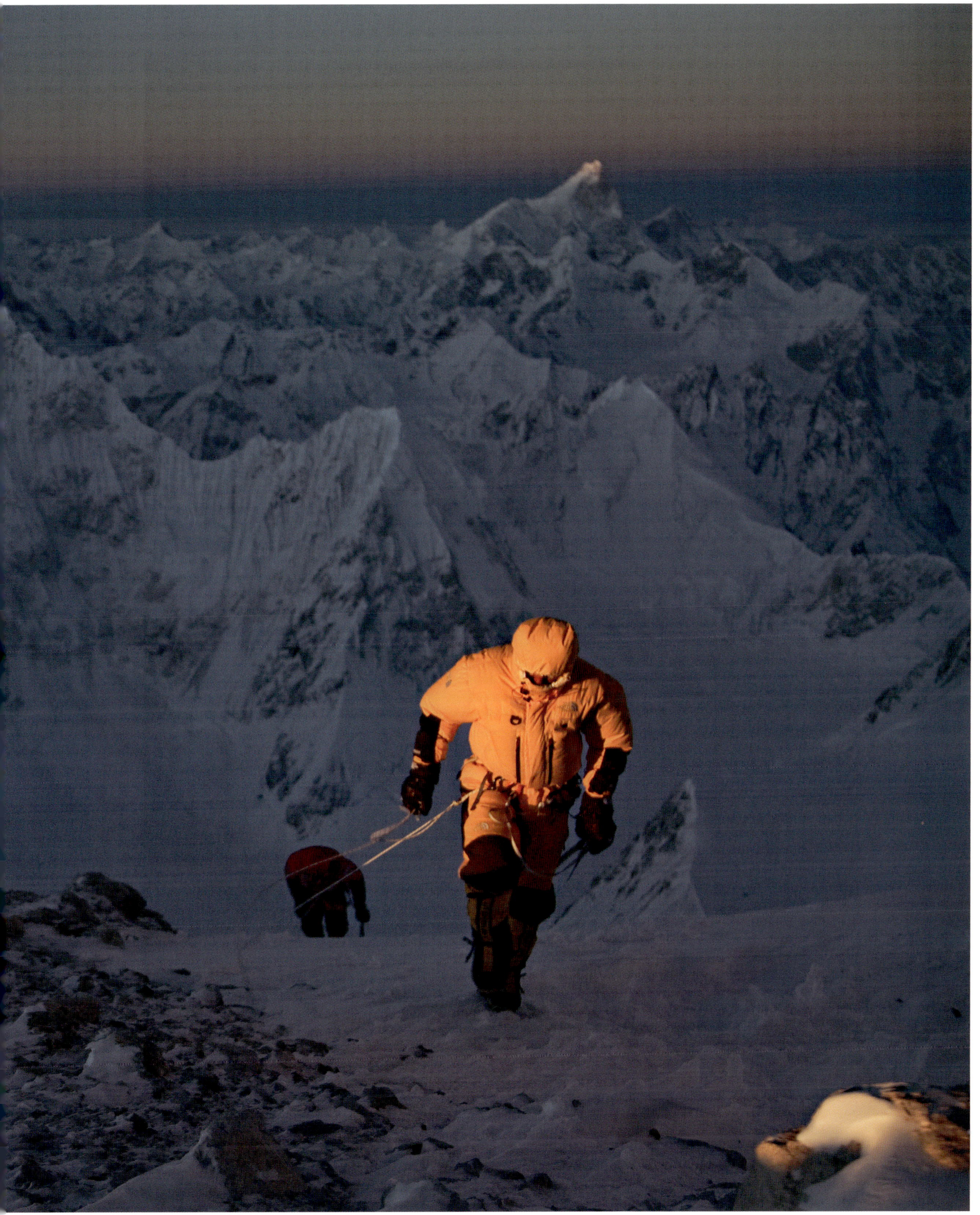

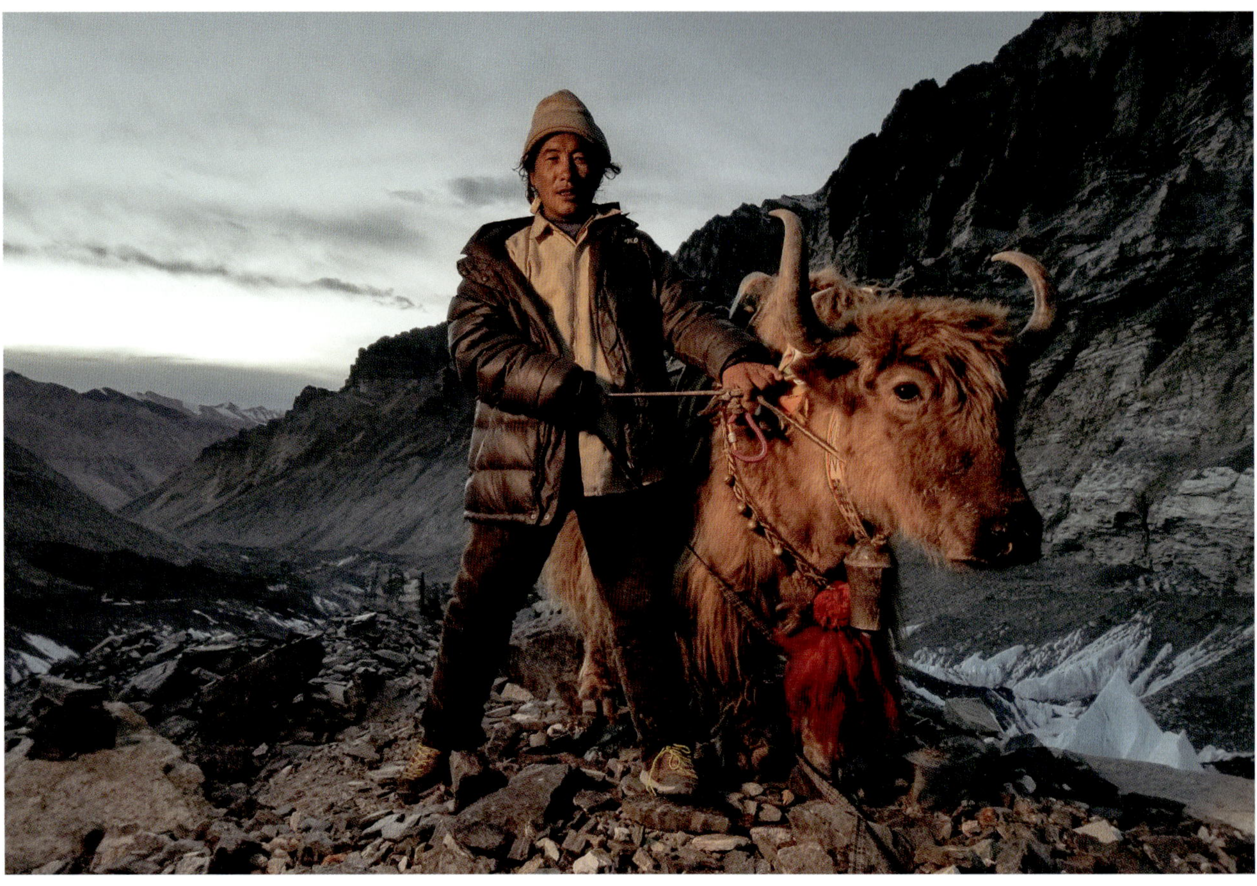

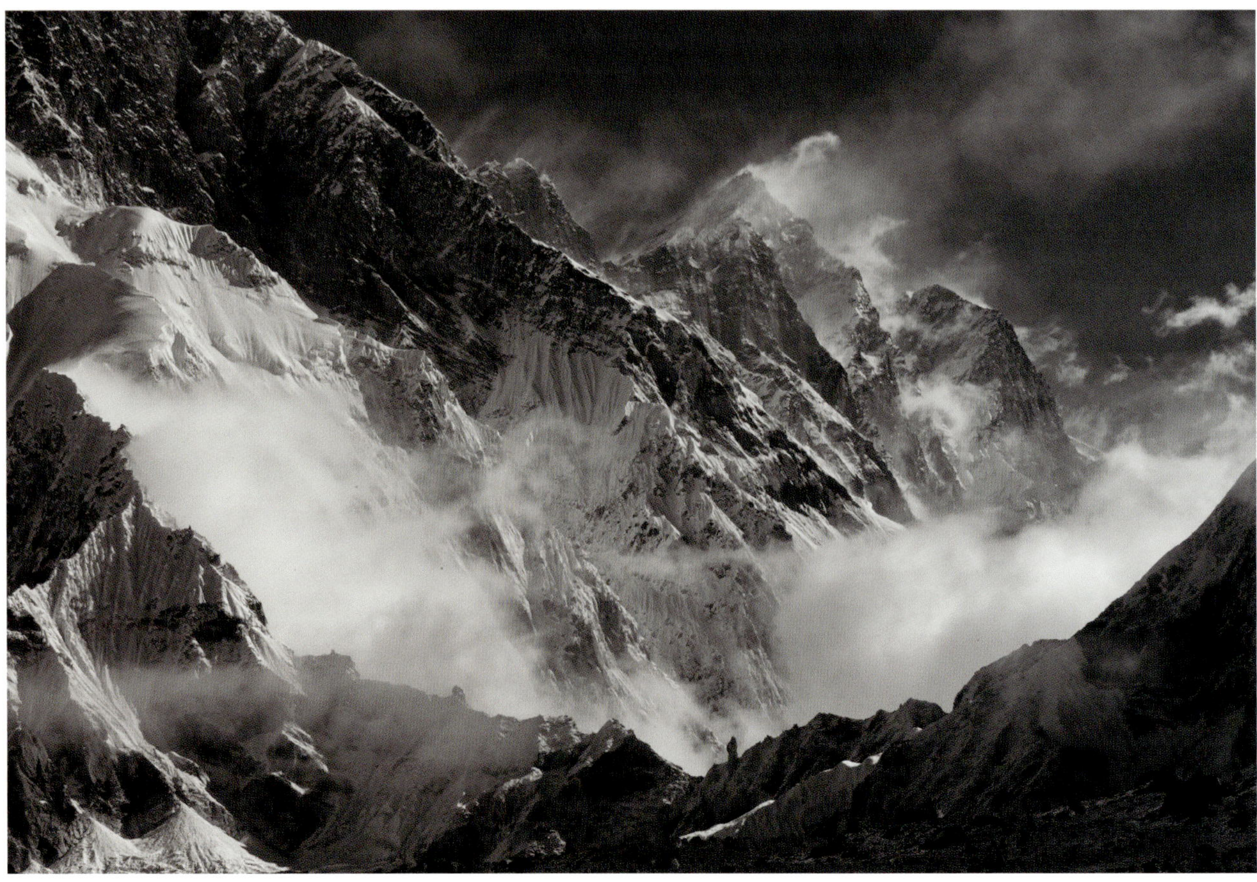

ABOVE: Tibetan yak driver; east fork of the Rongbuk Glacier, Tibet. **BELOW:** High winds on the south face of Nuptse (left) and Lhotse (right; 2009).

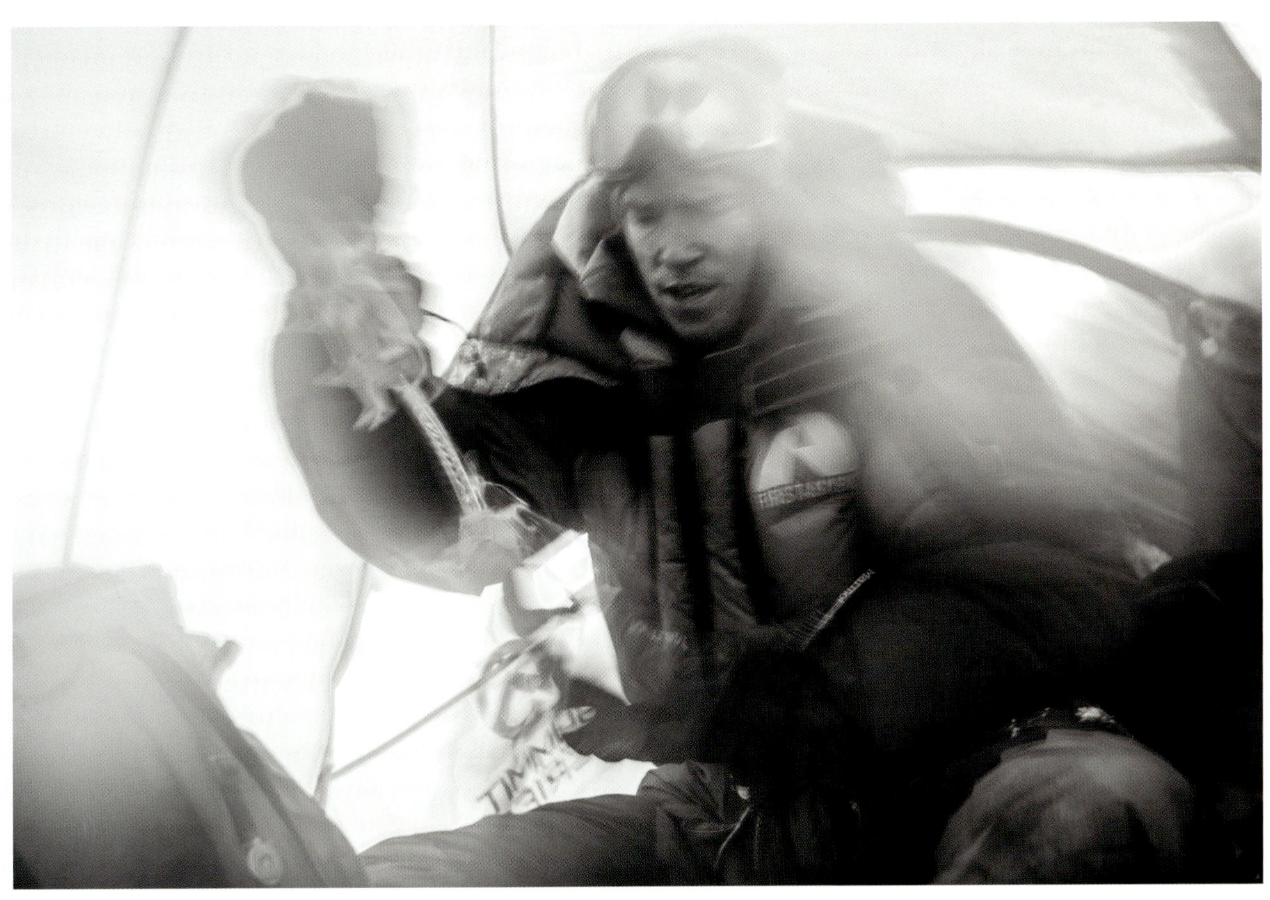

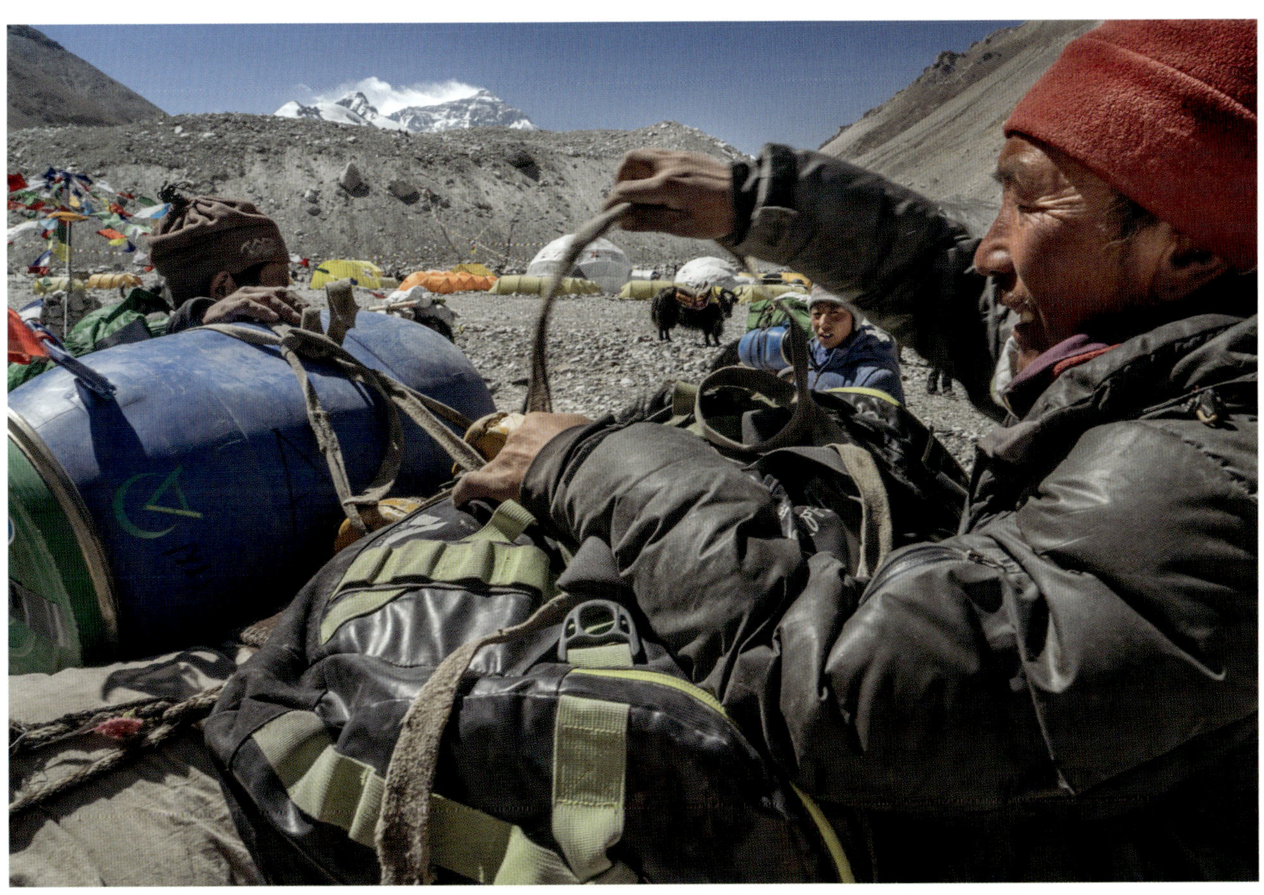

ABOVE: Adrian Ballinger packs in haste, retreating after a dangerous night of climbing without oxygen at 25,000 feet on Mount Everest's north side (2016).
BELOW: Yak herders ready loads of supplies to carry from base camp to advanced base camp on the north side of Mount Everest (2016).

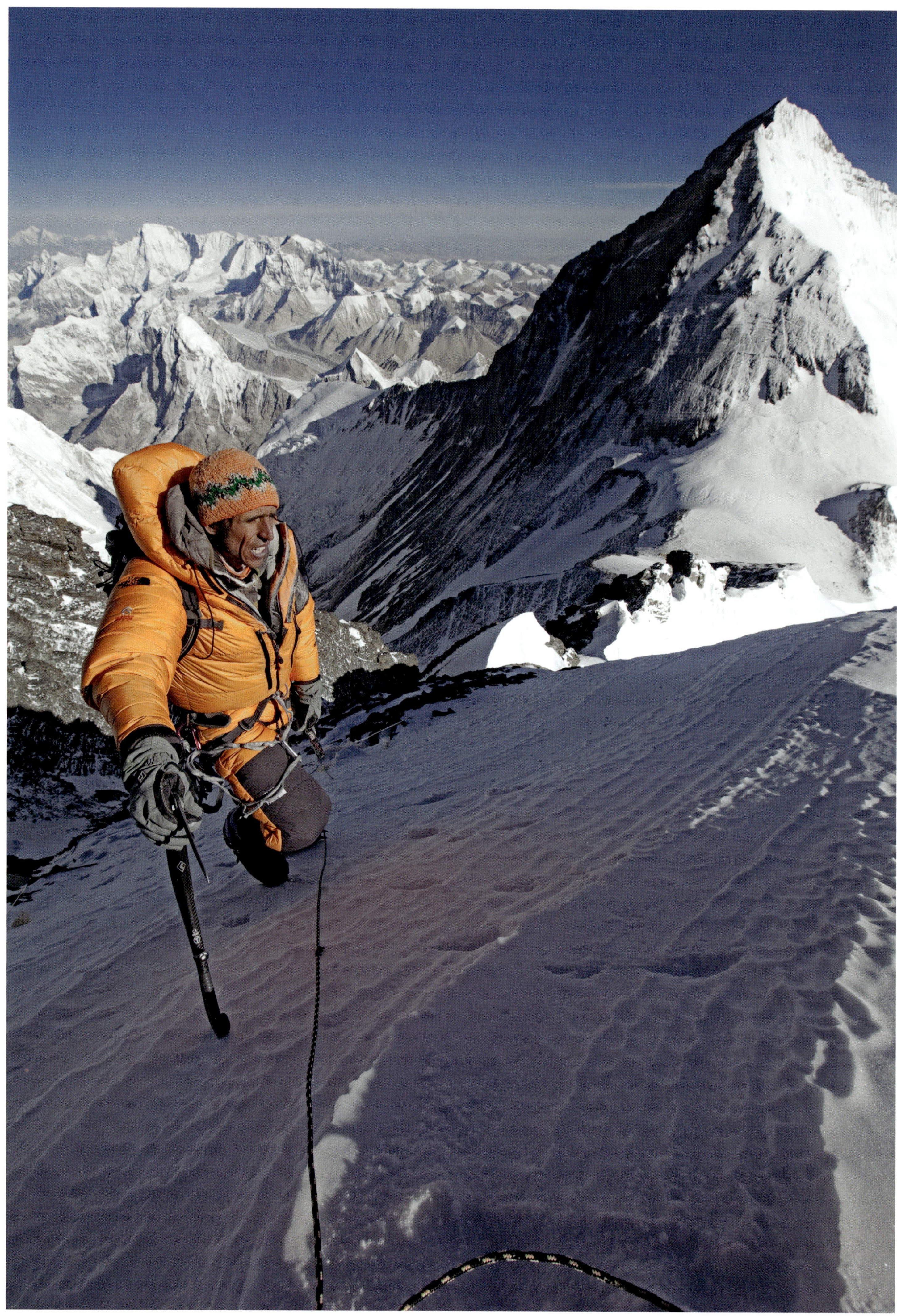

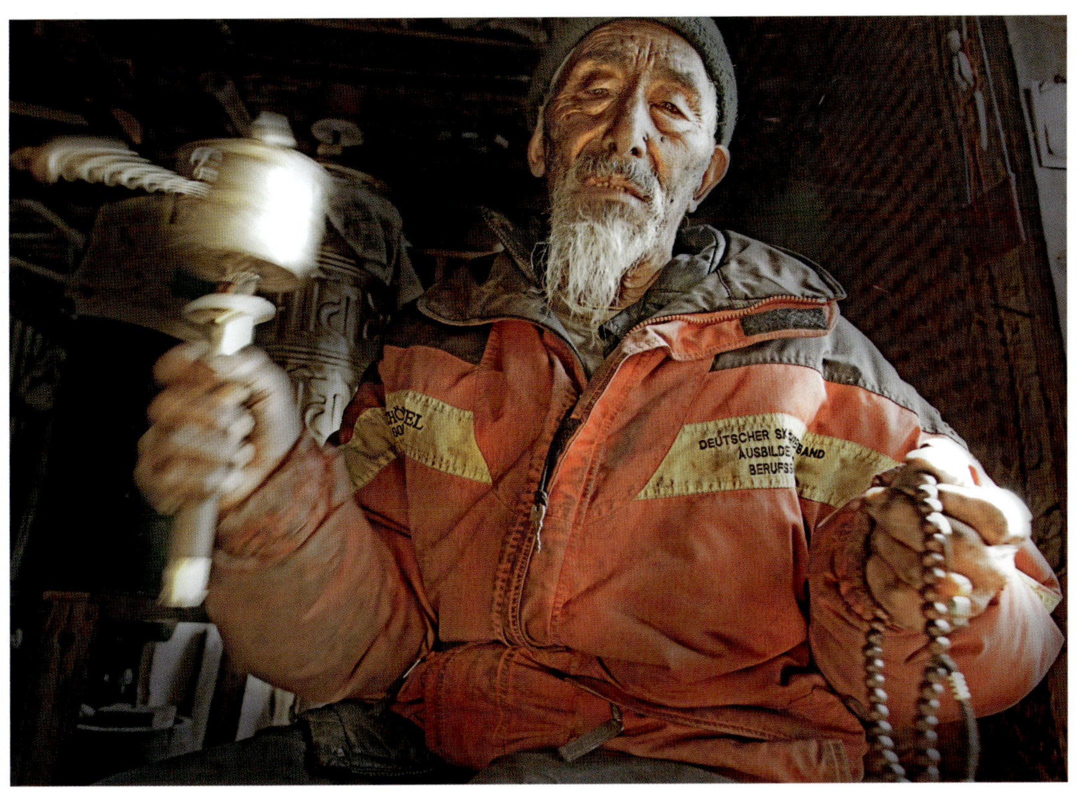

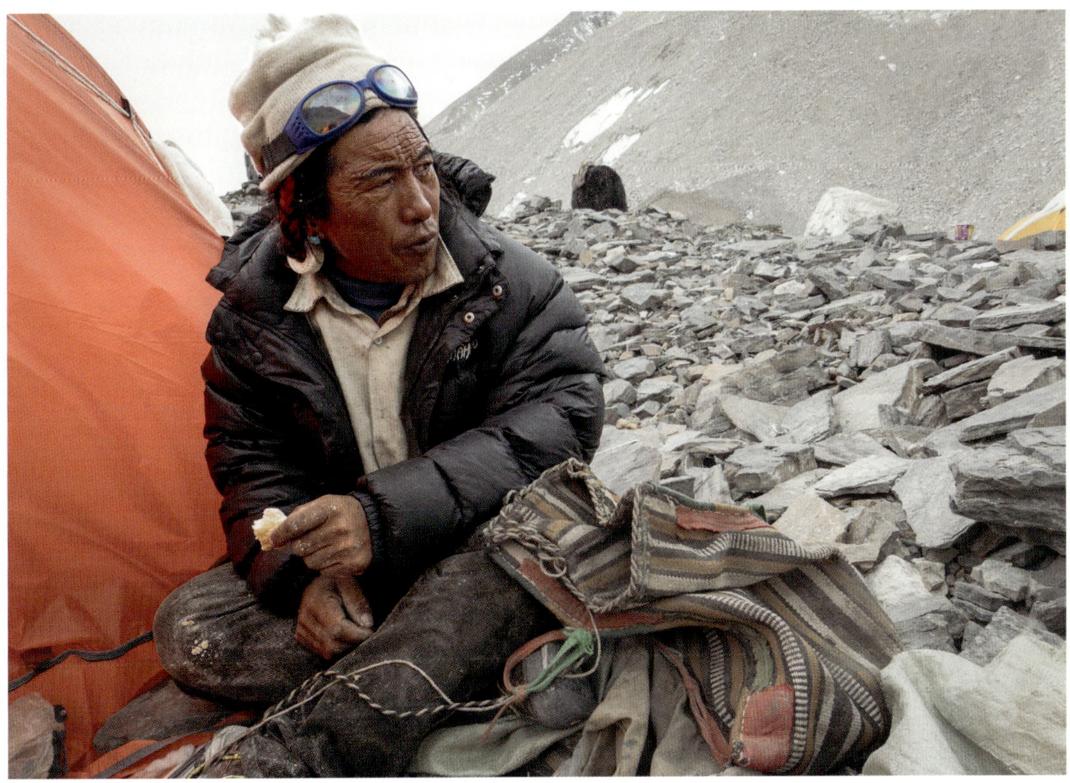

ABOVE: The late Karma Tsering Sherpa in his home in Phortse, Khumbu Valley, Nepal (2009). BELOW: A Tibetan yak driver pauses en route to advanced base camp on Mount Everest's north side (2017). OPPOSITE: Argentinian mountain guide Matoco Erroz climbs the last few feet to Lhotse's summit, the fourth-highest in the world at 27,940 feet. Mount Everest rises on the right with Cho Oyu, the world's sixth-highest mountain, in the distance (2011).

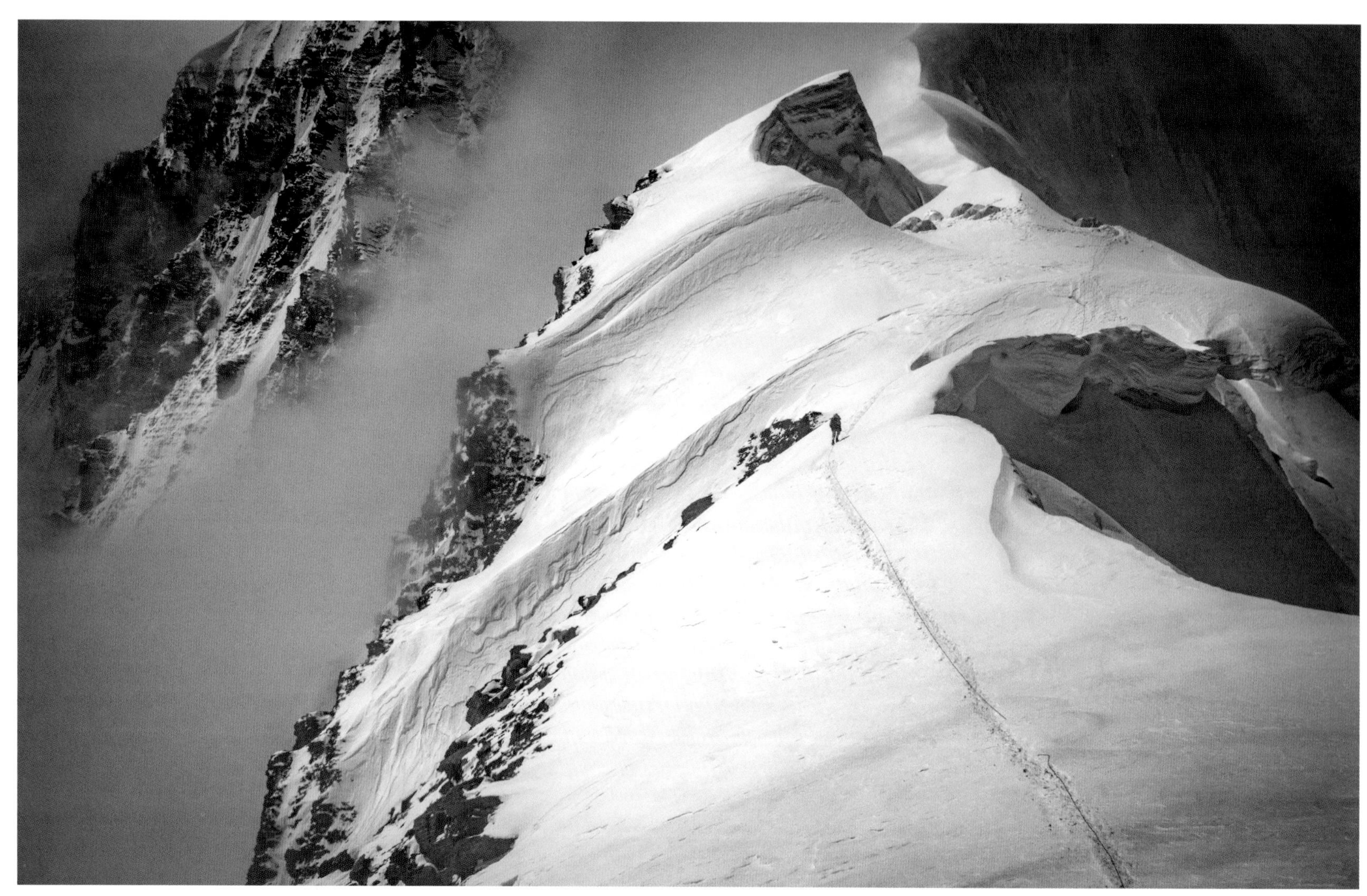

A climber descends to the North Col on Mount Everest's north side (2016).

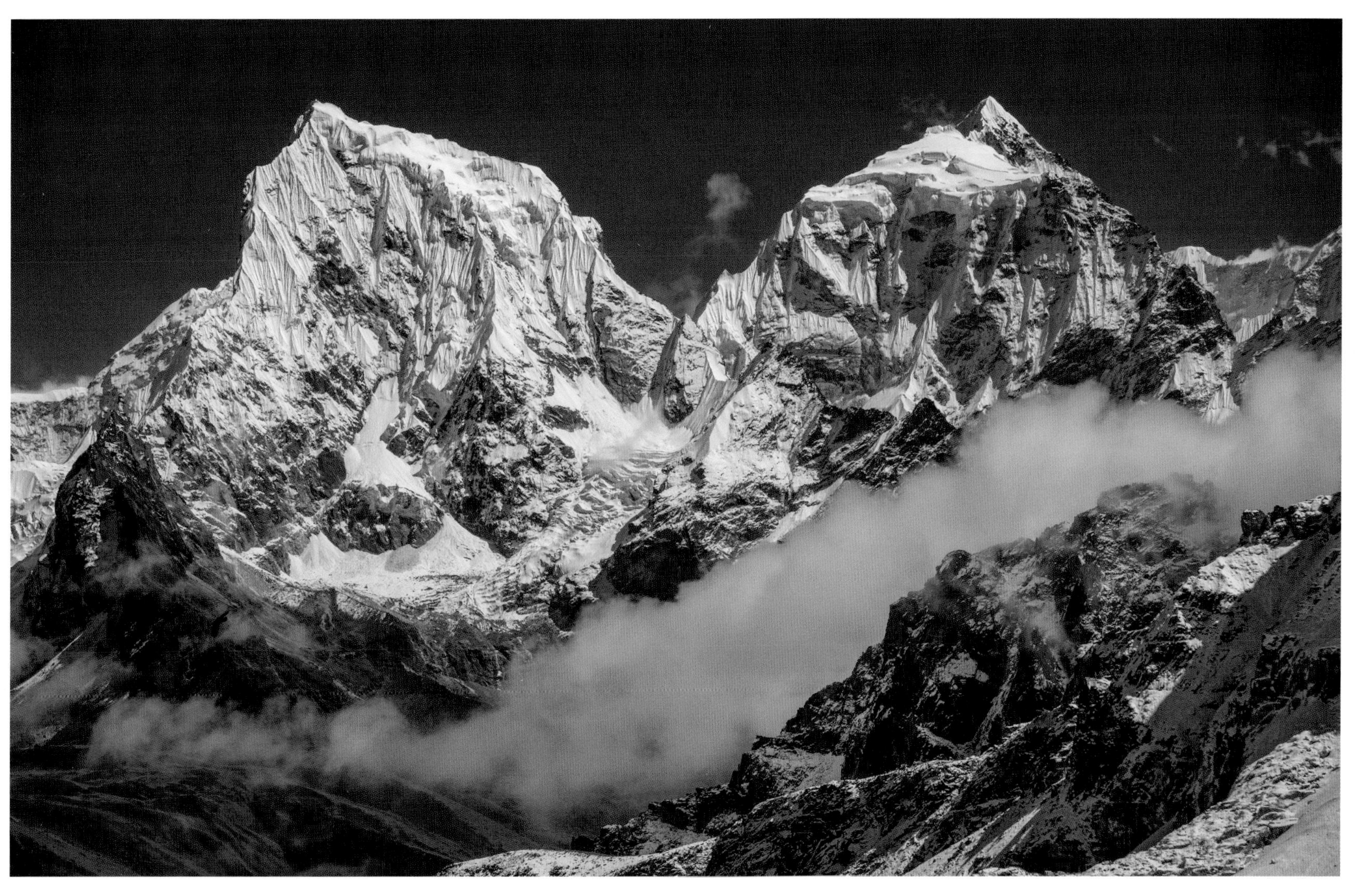

Cholatse (left) and Tawoche (right) as seen from the Renjo La Pass, Khumbu, Nepal. **FOLLOWING:** American climber Conrad Anker takes notes in his journal while spending a night out on the lower slopes of Pumori with Everest (left), Lhotse (center), Nuptse (right), and the Khumbu icefall behind.

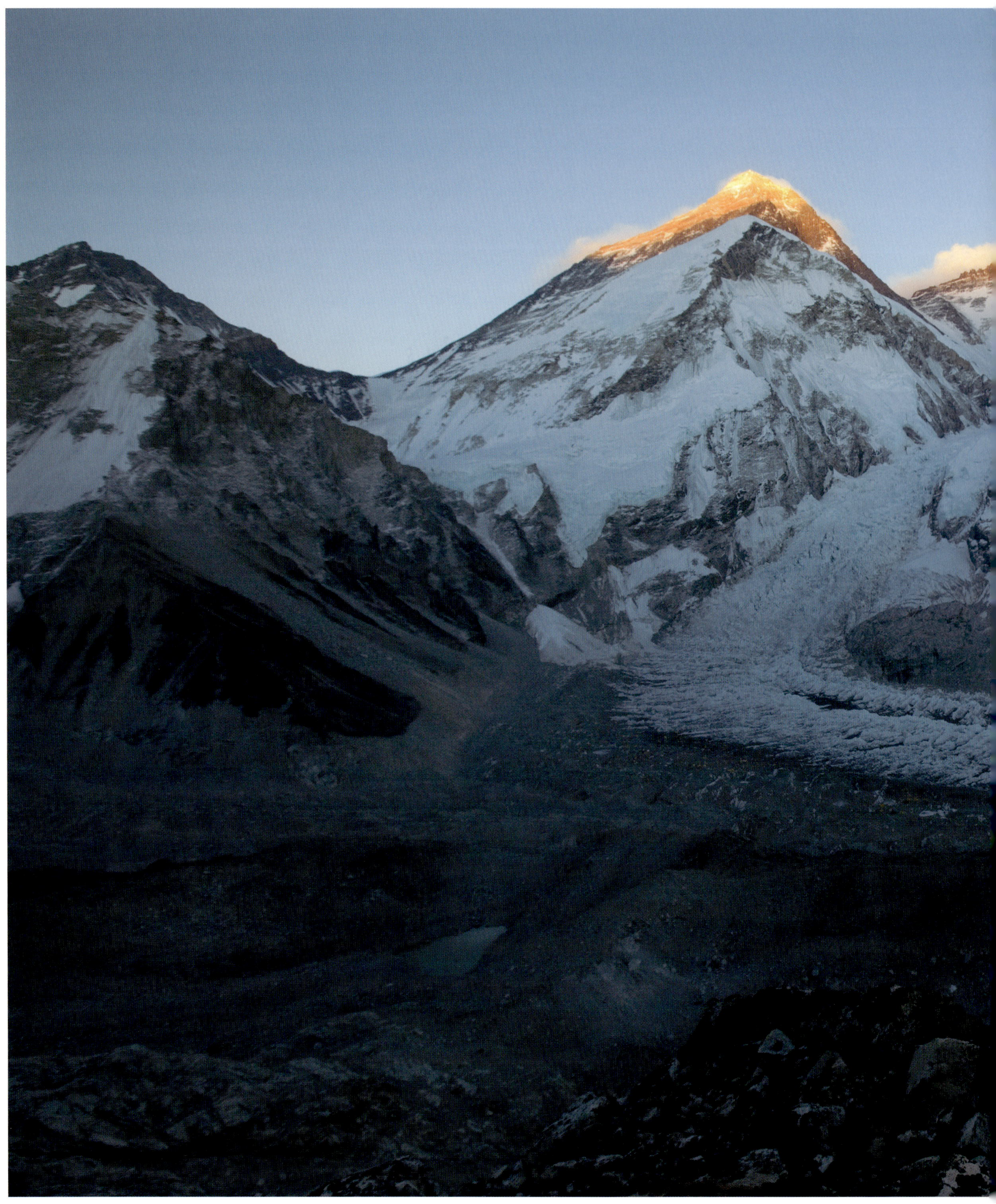

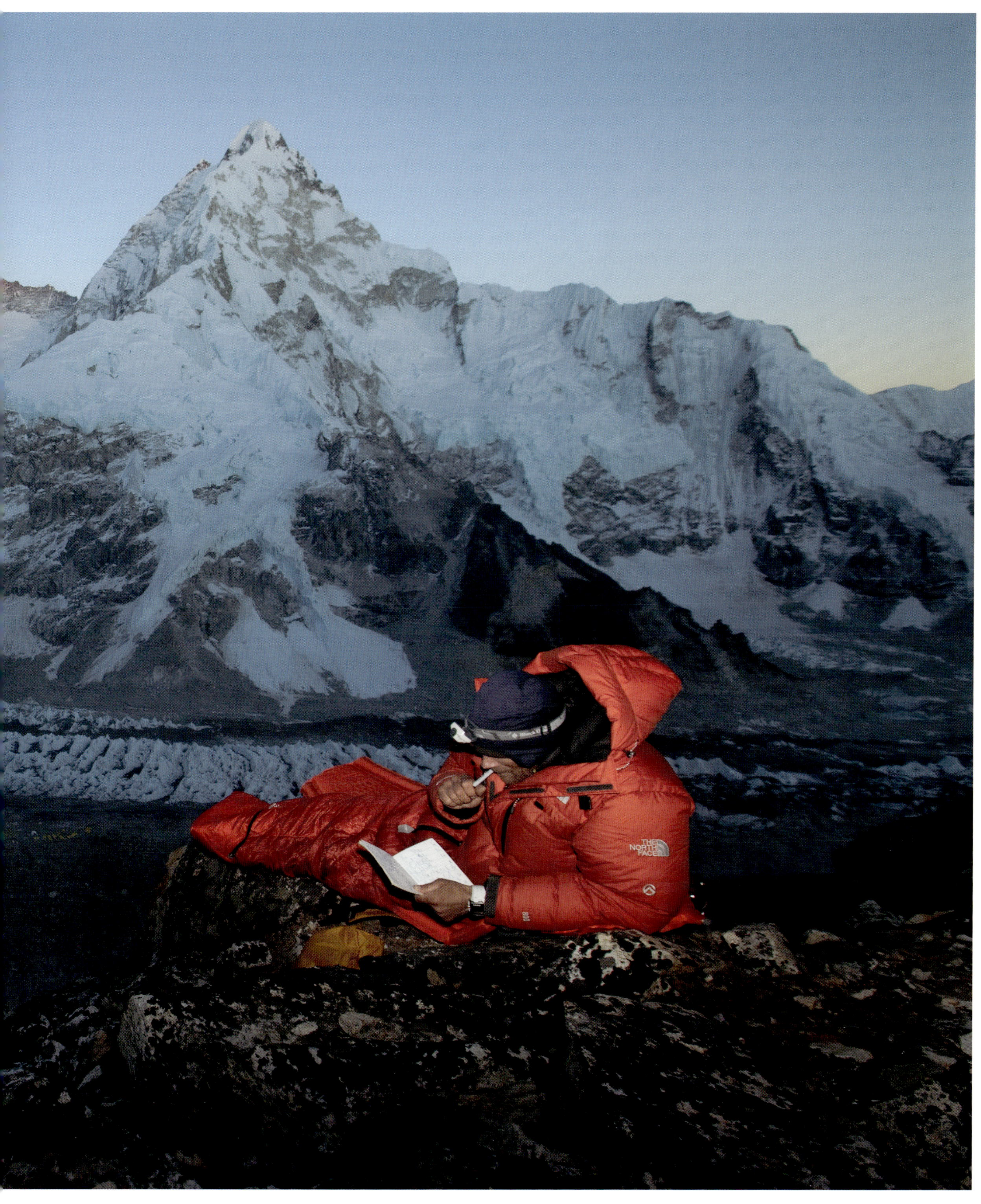

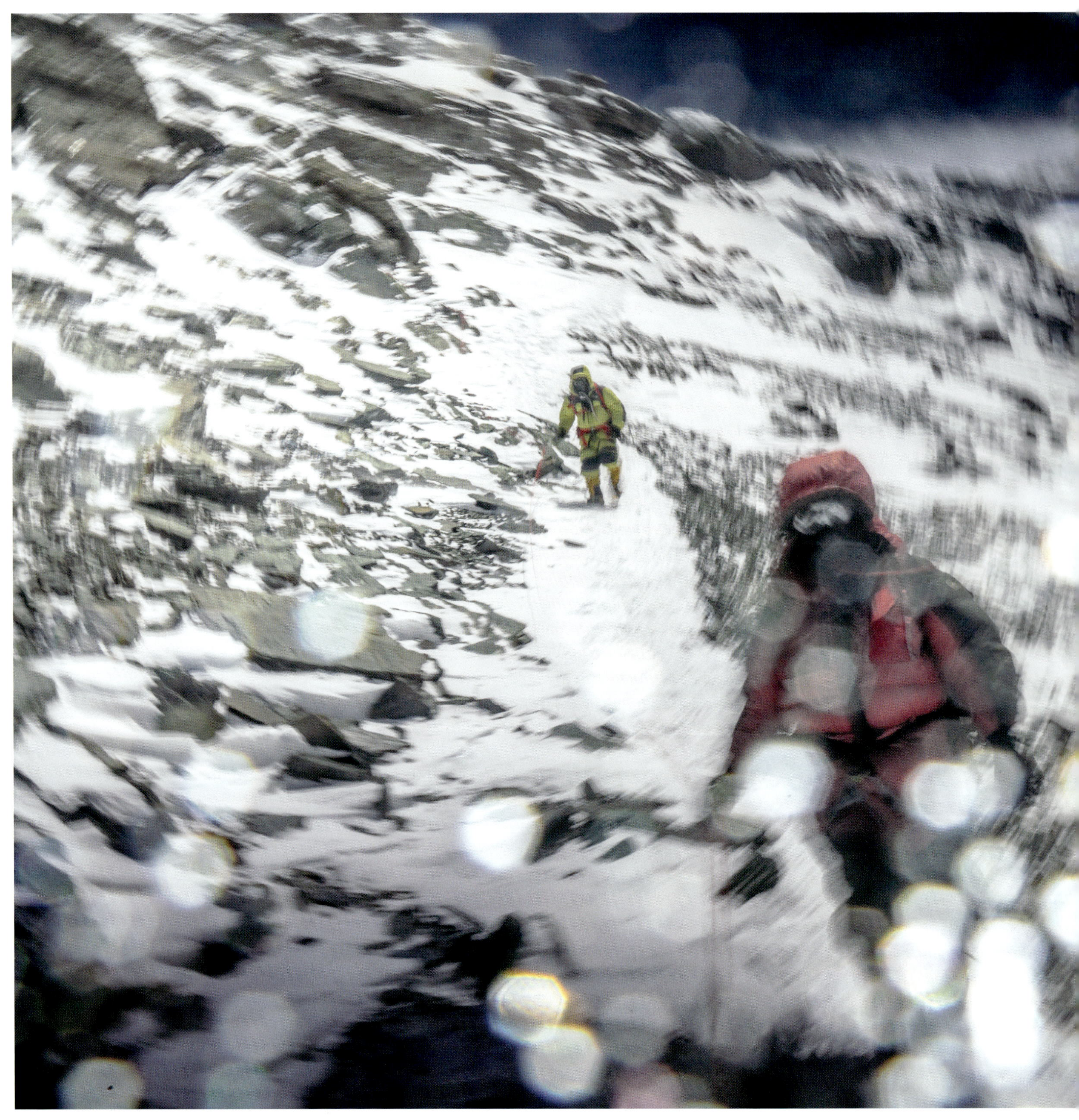

One of the most important things I was ever taught was to try to make photographs that tell what it *feels* like instead of what it *looks* like. This photograph is the closest I have ever gotten to translating the feeling of climbing at 26,247 feet; the north side of Mount Everest (2016). **OPPOSITE, ABOVE:** American climbers Freddie Wilkinson and Ben Gilmore climb on Nuptse's west ridge (2009). **OPPOSITE, CENTER:** Climbers descend through a storm on Mount Everest (2017). **OPPOSITE, BELOW:** American climber and mountain guide Kevin Mahoney (foreground) and Freddie Wilkinson (background) on Nuptse (2009). **FOLLOWING:** German climber Ines Papert acclimatizes in the Khumbu Valley (2008).

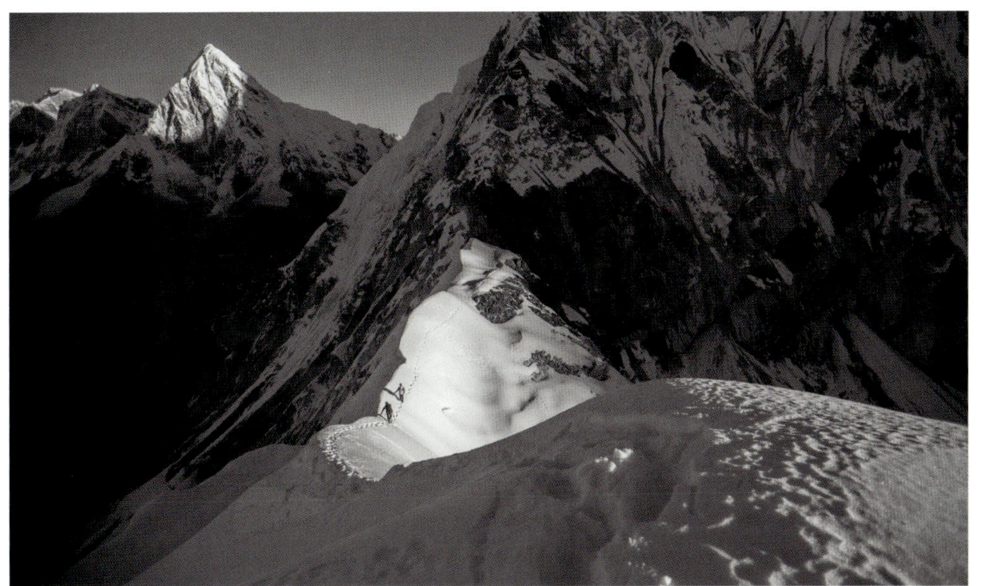

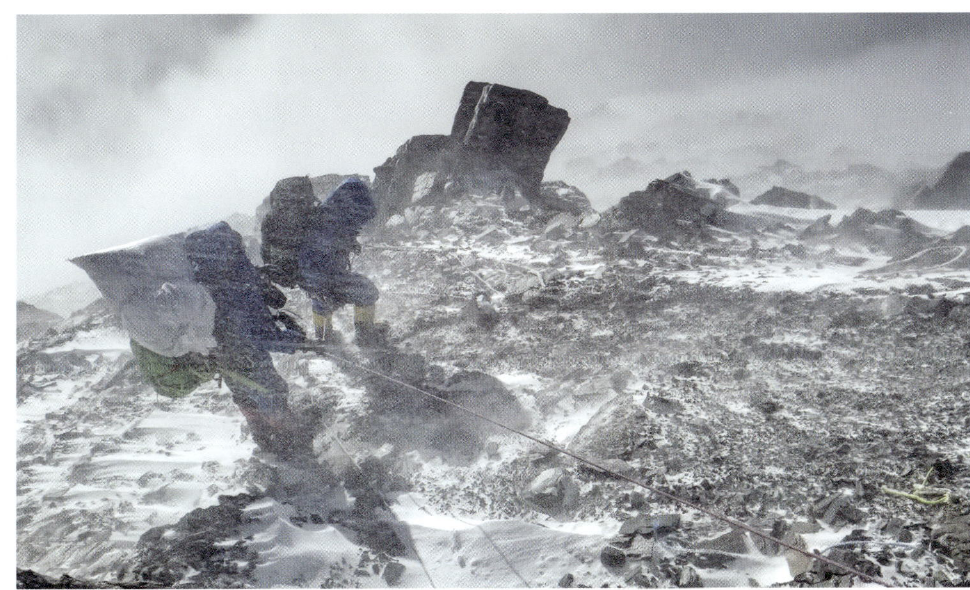

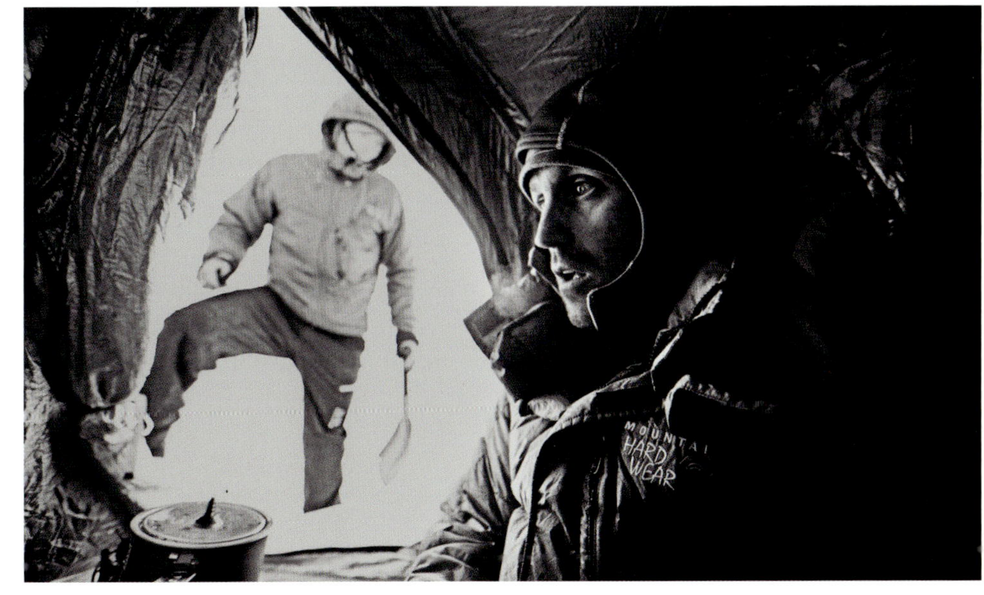

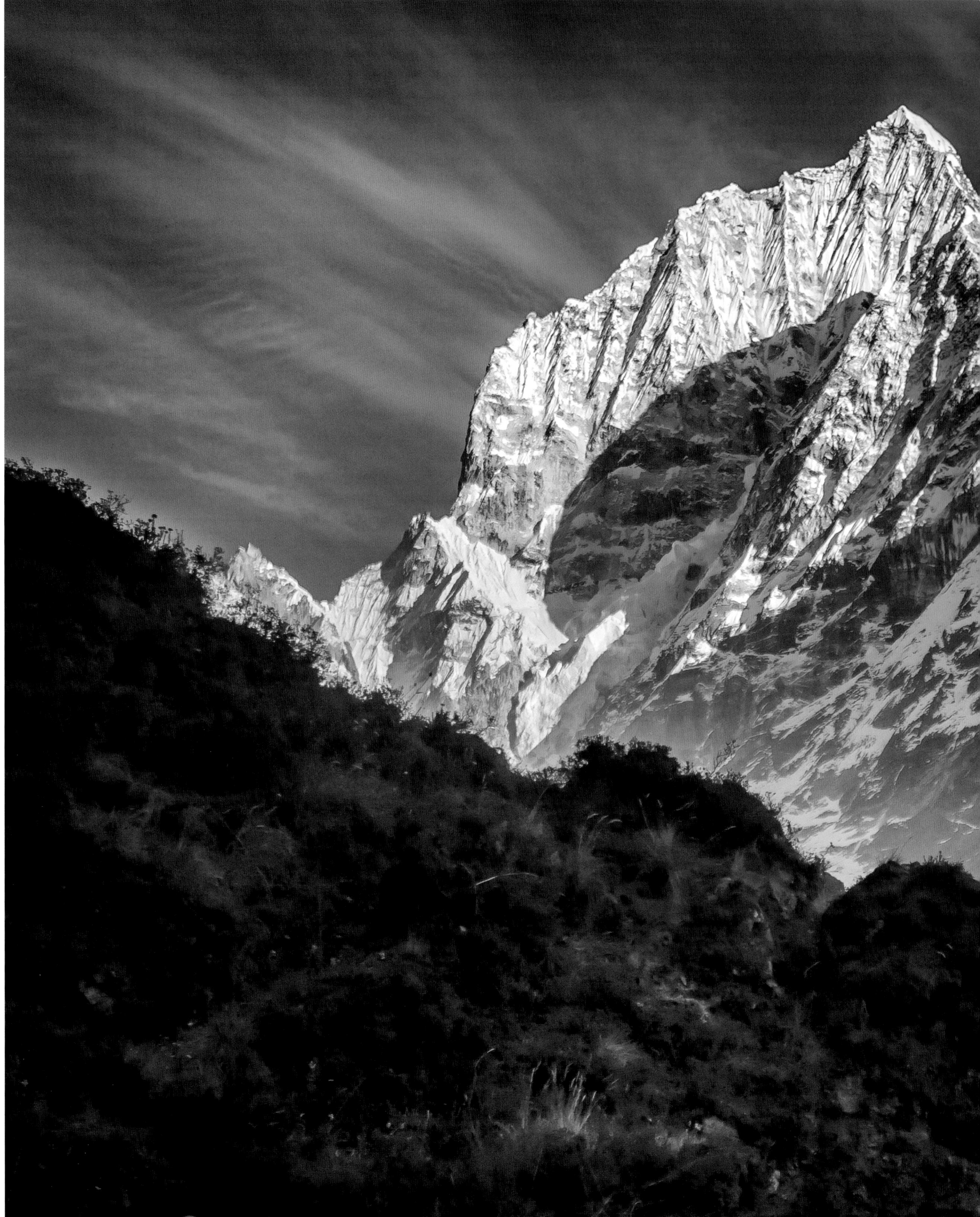

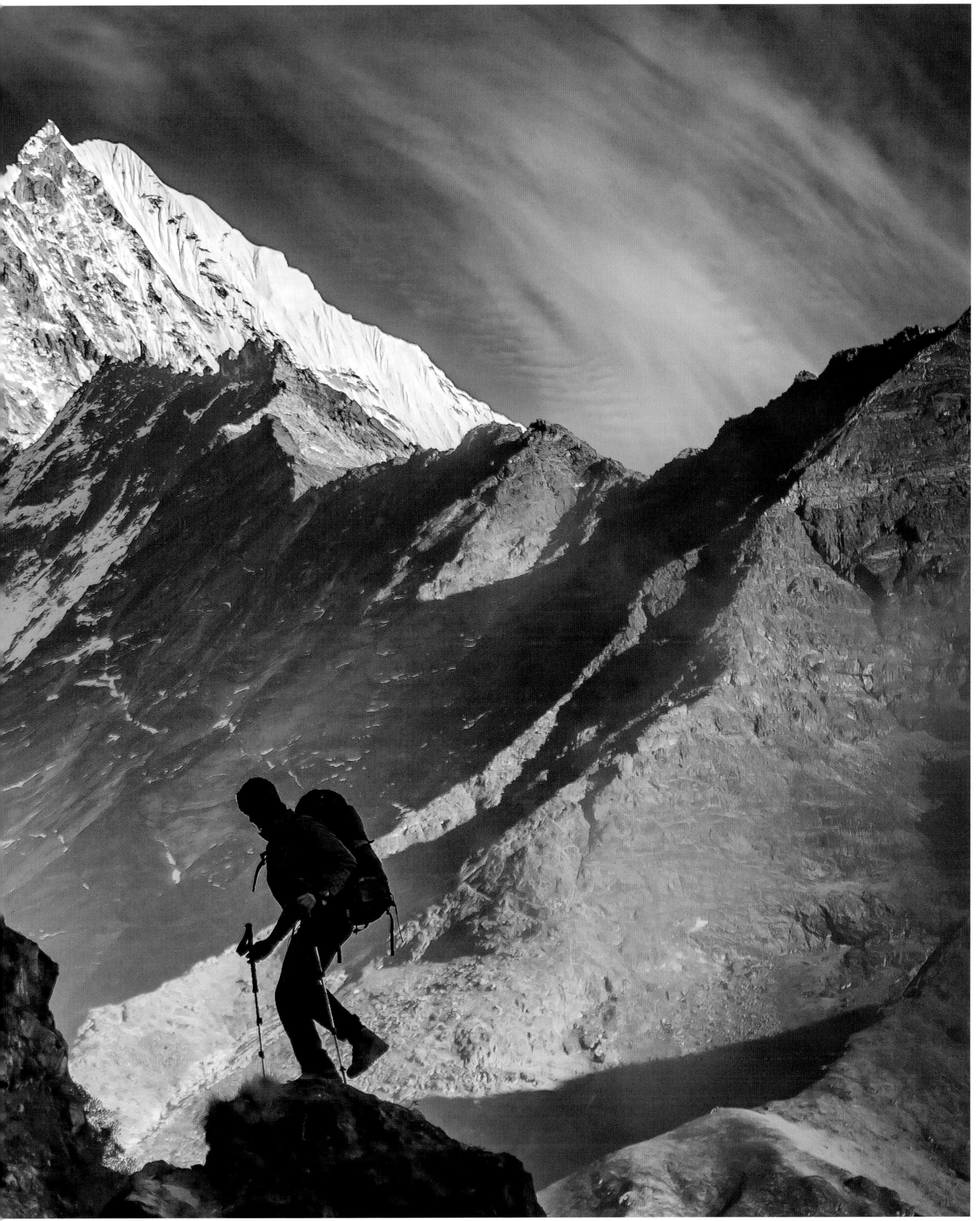

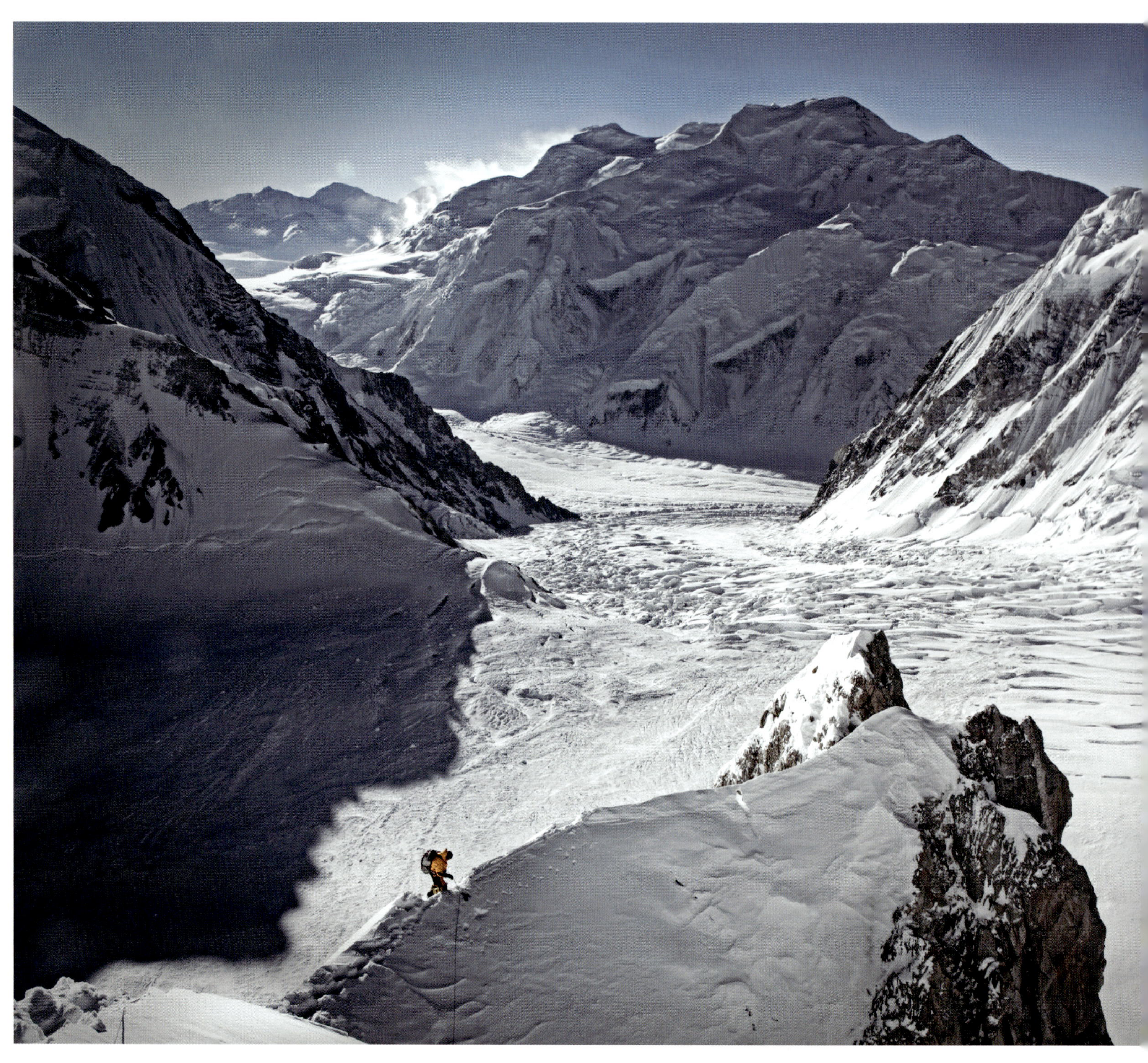

Denis Urubko acclimatizes in the Karakoram Himalaya, Pakistan (2010). **OPPOSITE, ABOVE:** Two climbers atop the third step on Mount Everest's northeast ridge just after sunrise (2016). **OPPOSITE, BELOW:** The body of Russian climber Sergei Duganov lies frozen at 7,800 meters on Lhotse, the fourth highest mountain in the world. Sergei died roughly two weeks before the photo was taken. Khumbu, Nepal (May 2010).

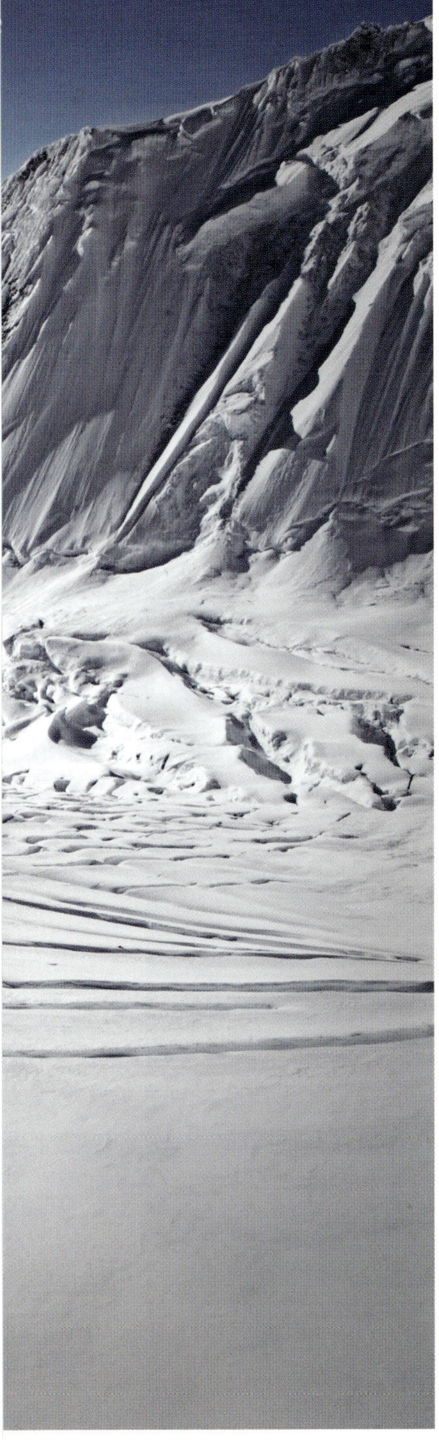

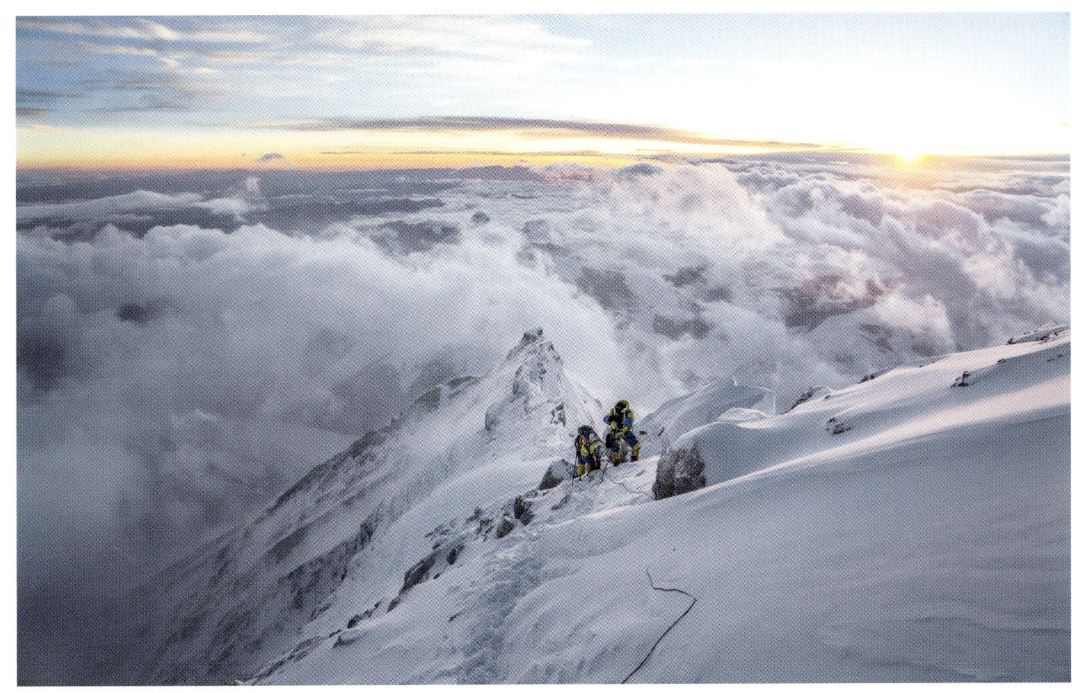

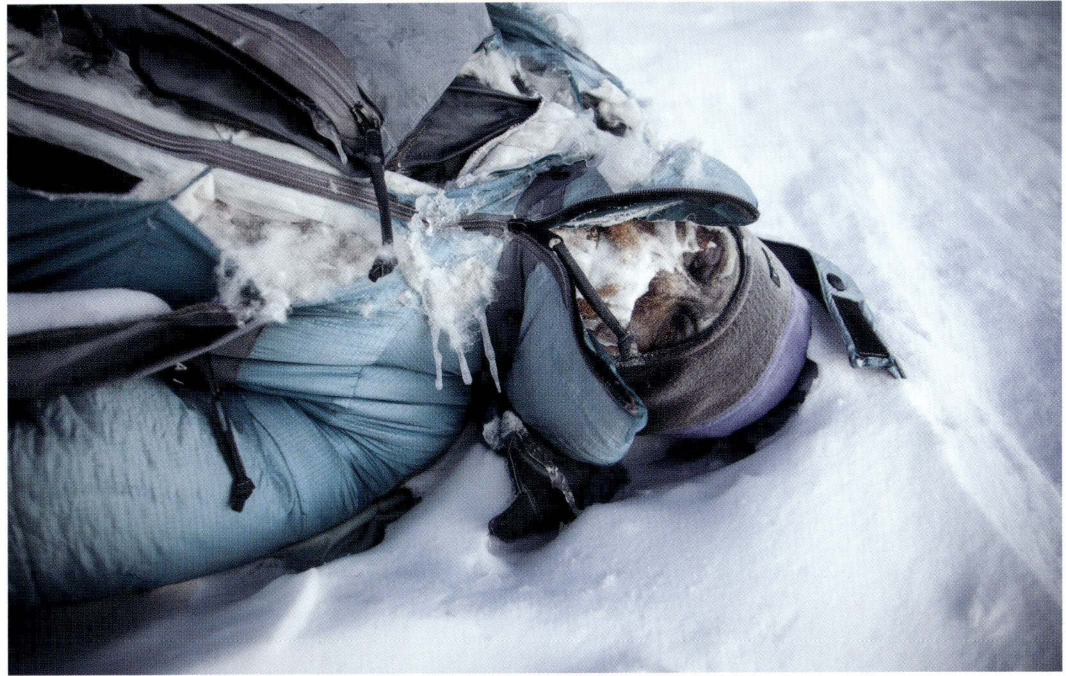

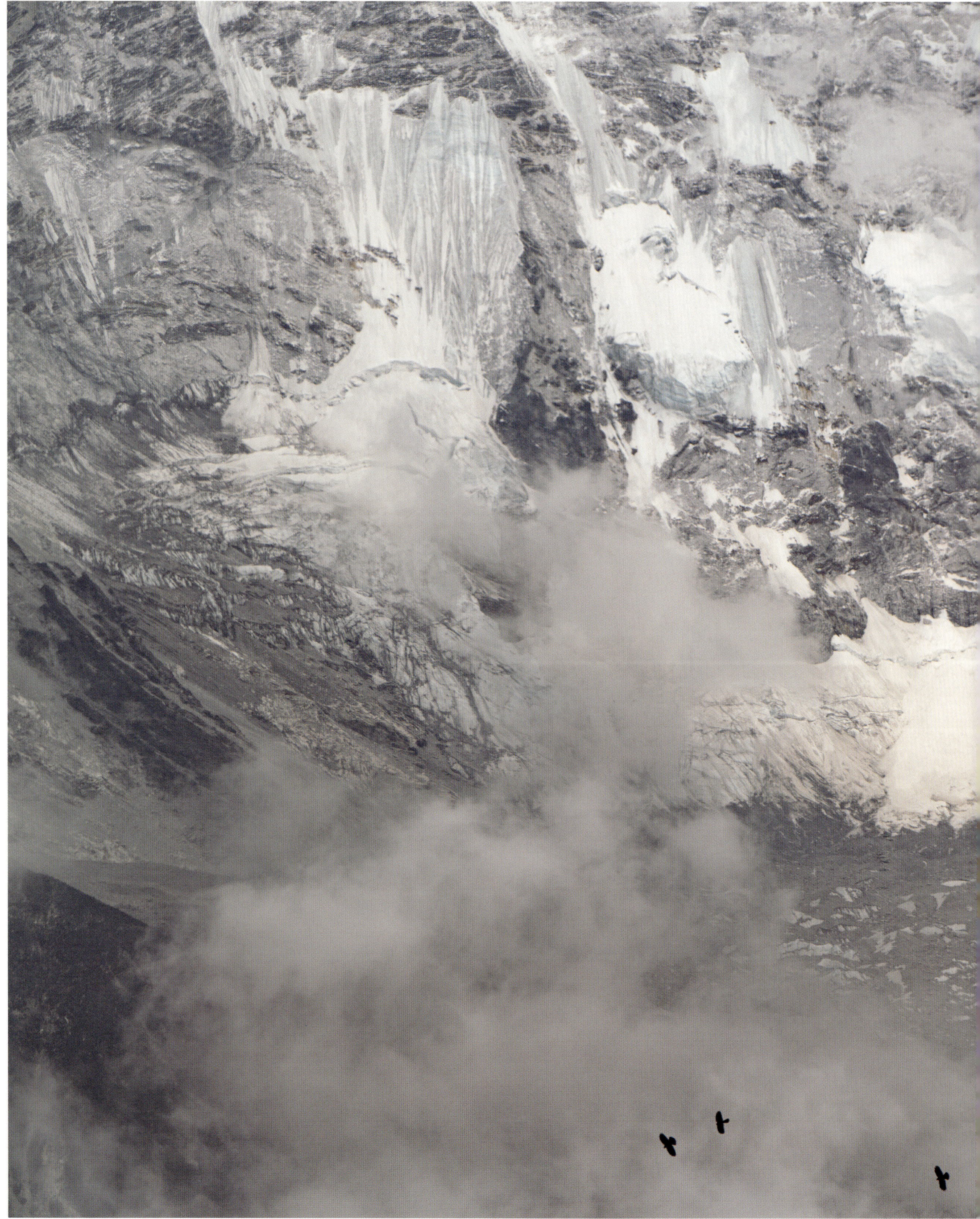

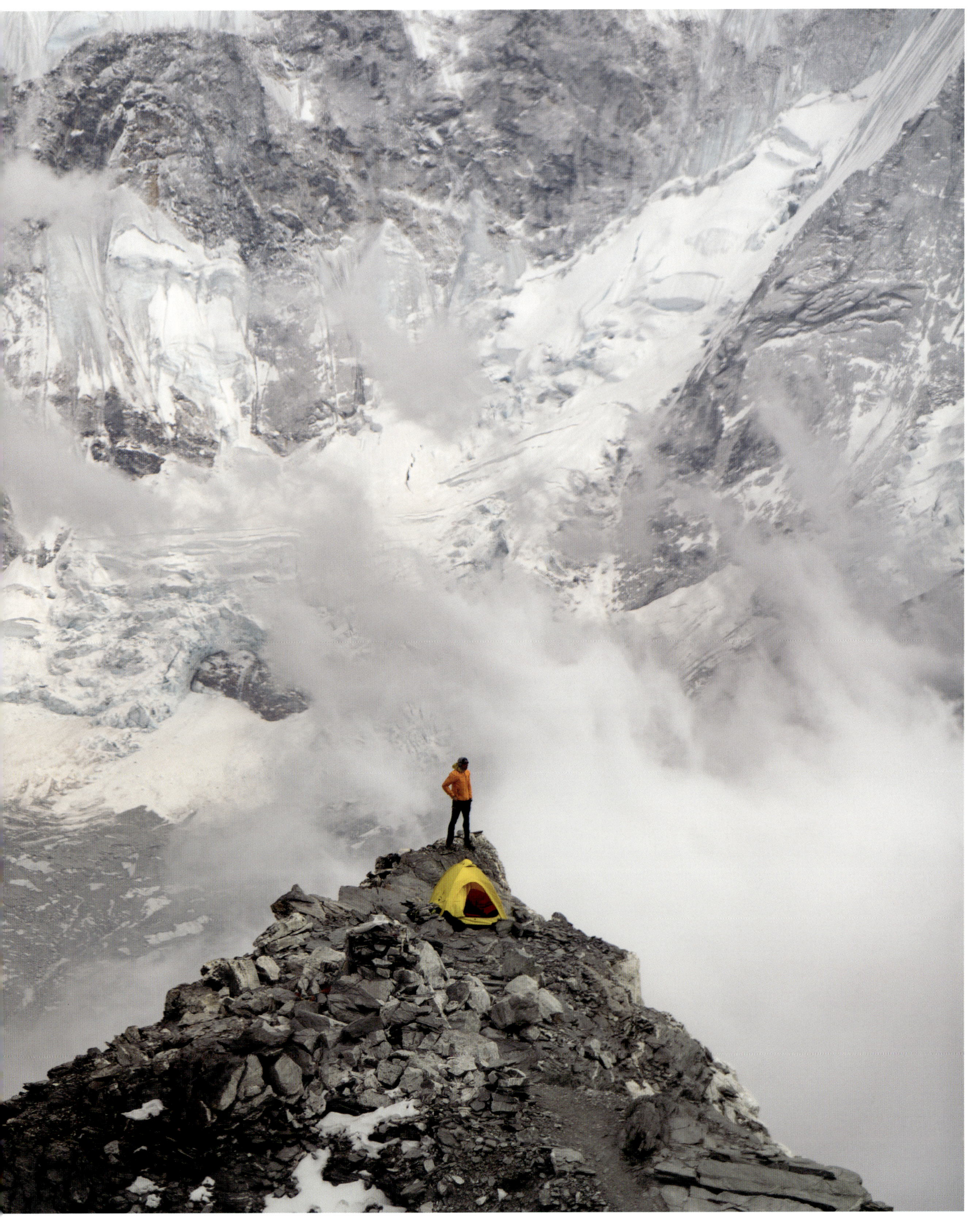

CURIOSITY

\ kyür-ē-ˈä-s(ə-)tē\ *n*: a strong desire to know or learn something

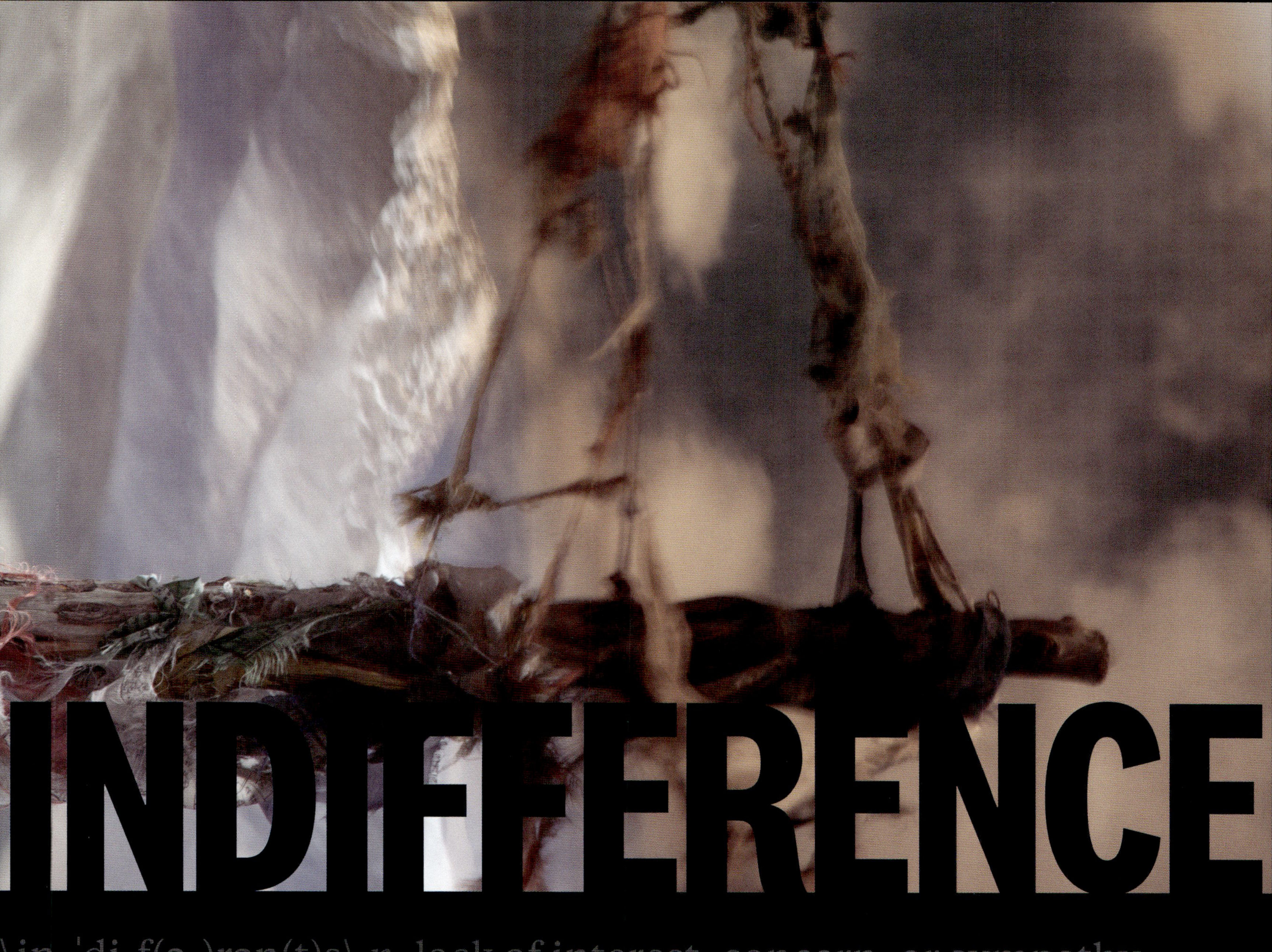
INDIFFERENCE
\in-ˈdi-f(ə-)rən(t)s\ n: lack of interest, concern, or sympathy

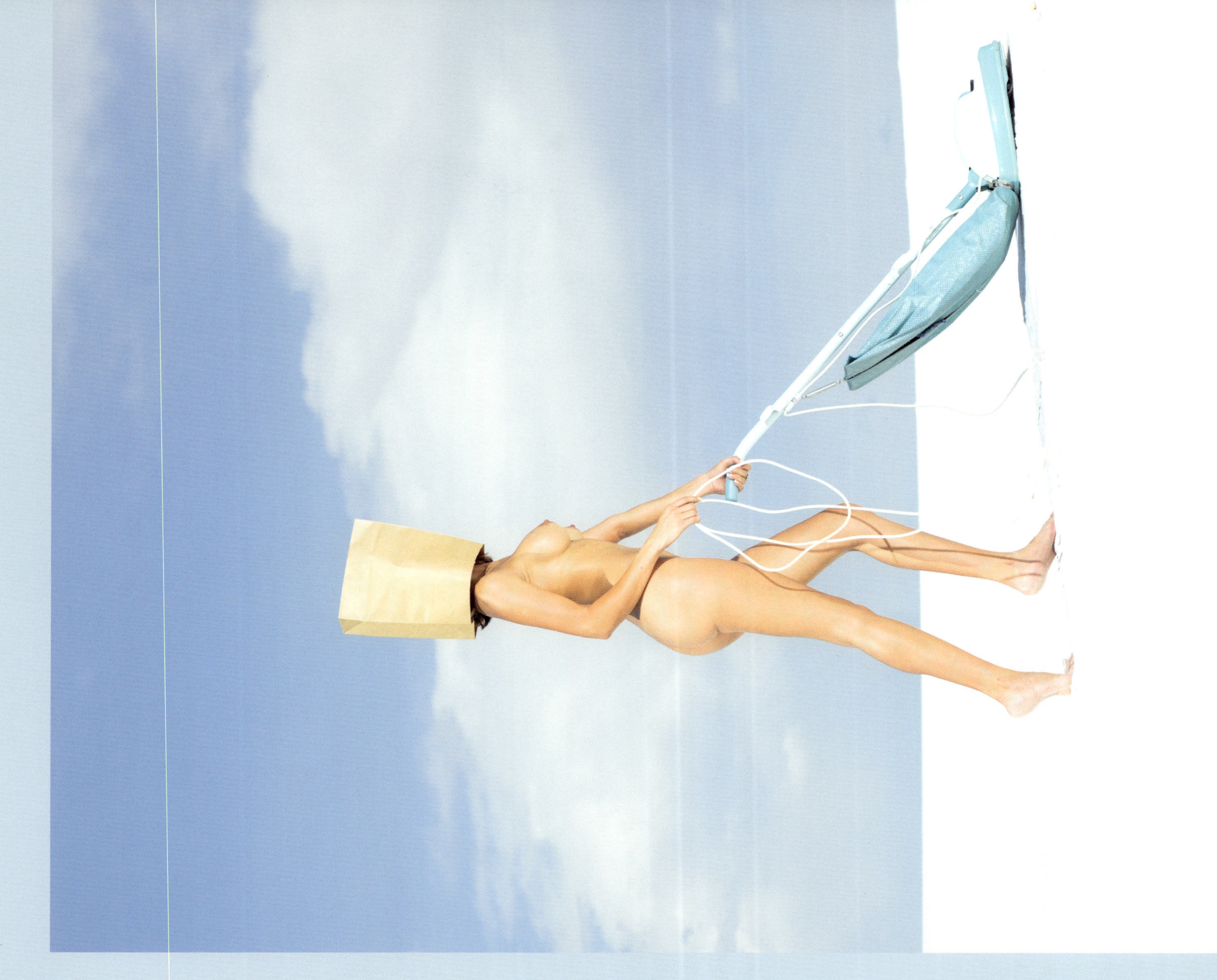

AMERICAN DREAM Everywhere,
United States

Mom: I don't get it.

Me: What's not to get? She's vacuuming the desert. With a bag over her head. And the vacuum cleaner isn't plugged in.

Mom: It just seems—bizarre.

Me: But does it make you want to know more?

Mom: Sweetheart, please don't take this the wrong way, but not really.

Me: Huh. Okay, should we go get lun—

Mom: Like, why is she naked? What's with the bag? It reminds me of those terrible pictures from the war. It's creepy. Also, why is *she* vacuuming instead of a naked man?

Me: So you *do* want to know more.

Mom: [Laughs] You shit. Okay, *yes*, Cory, I *do* want to know more.

Me: Think about all the things you learned about being a woman and what dad learned about being a man when you both were growing up. This work is about gender roles and all the things society and culture asks us to do and we do without really thinking.

Mom: But why?

Me: 'Cuz if we don't question it, how will we ever change the shit we don't like?

Mom: Okay, *duh*. No. Why the bag and why is she naked?

Me: Because we do a lot of shit blindly and we're all sort of "naked" to what culture and society is telling us to do.

Mom: *"Are."*

Me: What?

Mom: You said *"is"* when referencing plural nouns. The proper verb is "are" . . . *what culture and society* are *telling us* . . .

Me: Mom, I'm forty-one.

Mom: Exactly. You're too old to have bad grammar. [Pauses] Aren't you playing into the stereotypes then? Isn't this just more stereotypical, misogynistic bullshit? *She's* vacuuming. Why couldn't that be a man? And look at her body. Aren't you just reinforcing it all?

Me: That's the poi—

Mom: Why isn't it plugged in?

Me: I couldn't find a plug.

Mom: [Laughs again] Seriously.

Me: Futility. Same reason she's vacuuming the desert. But honestly, I think if I have to explain it this much, I probably missed the mark.

Mom: It just kinda makes me mad.

Me: 'Kay. Let's go get some foo—

Mom: Show me the next one.

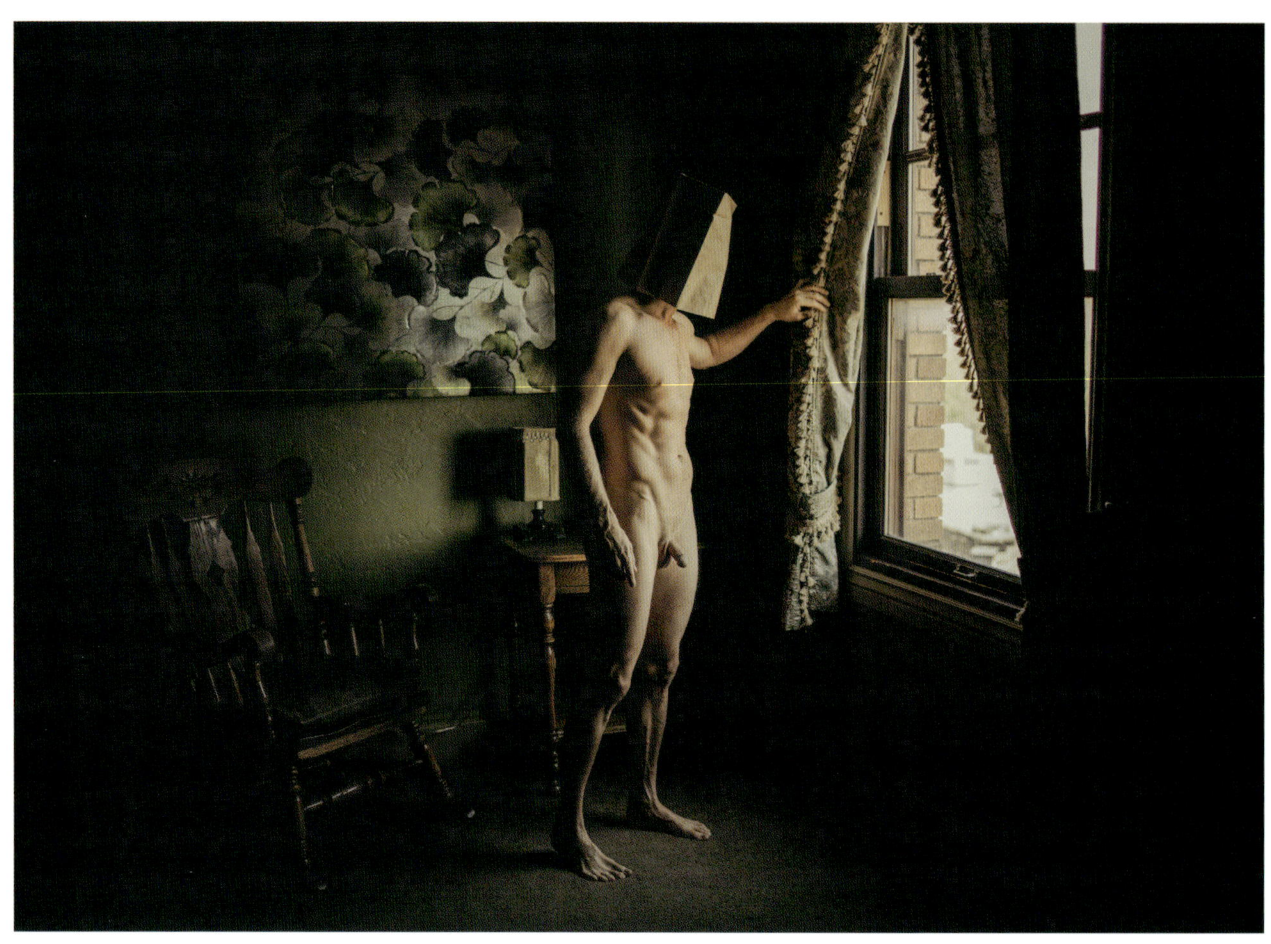

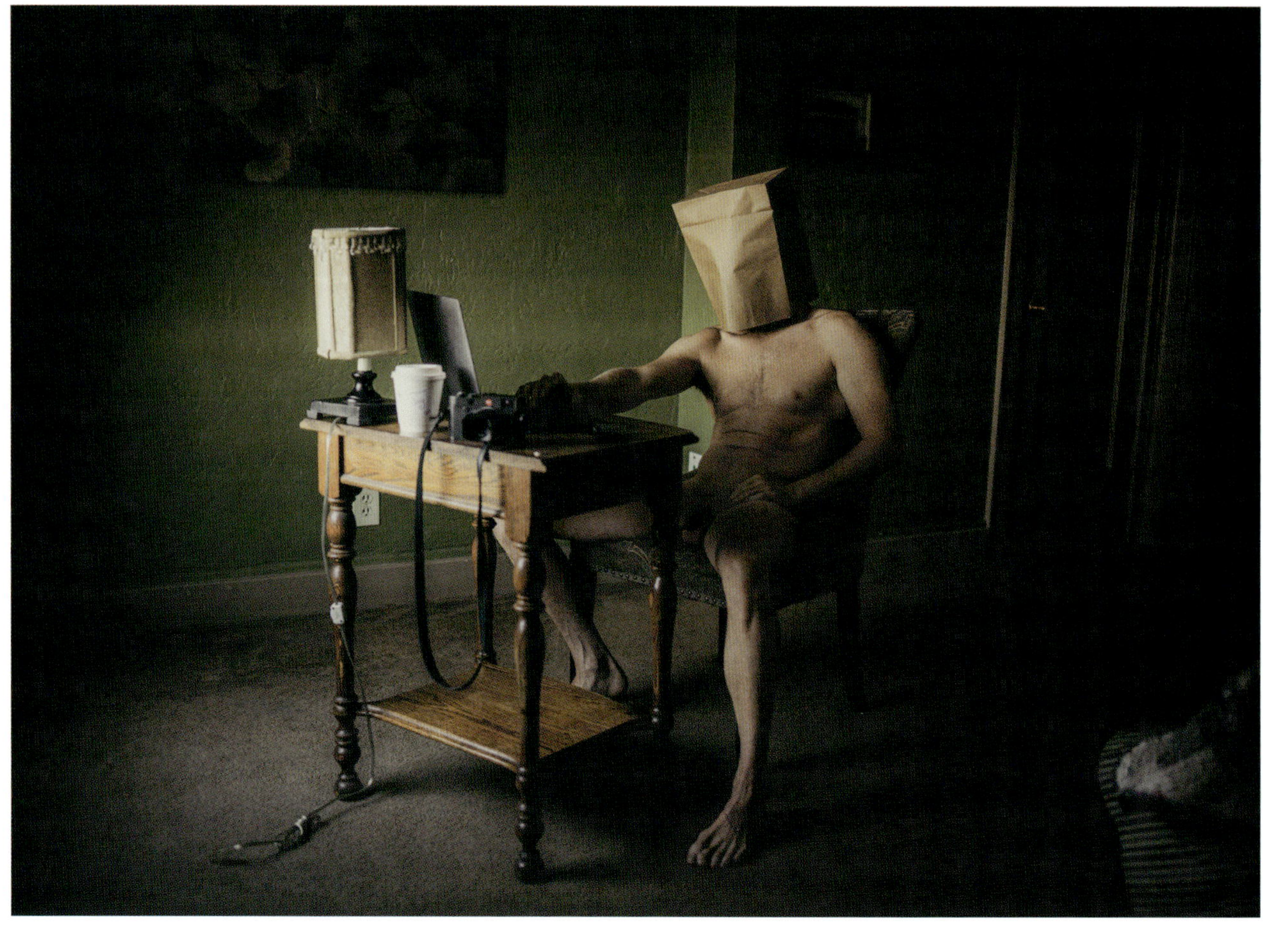

ABOVE: "Isolation" **BELOW:** "A Steady Job"

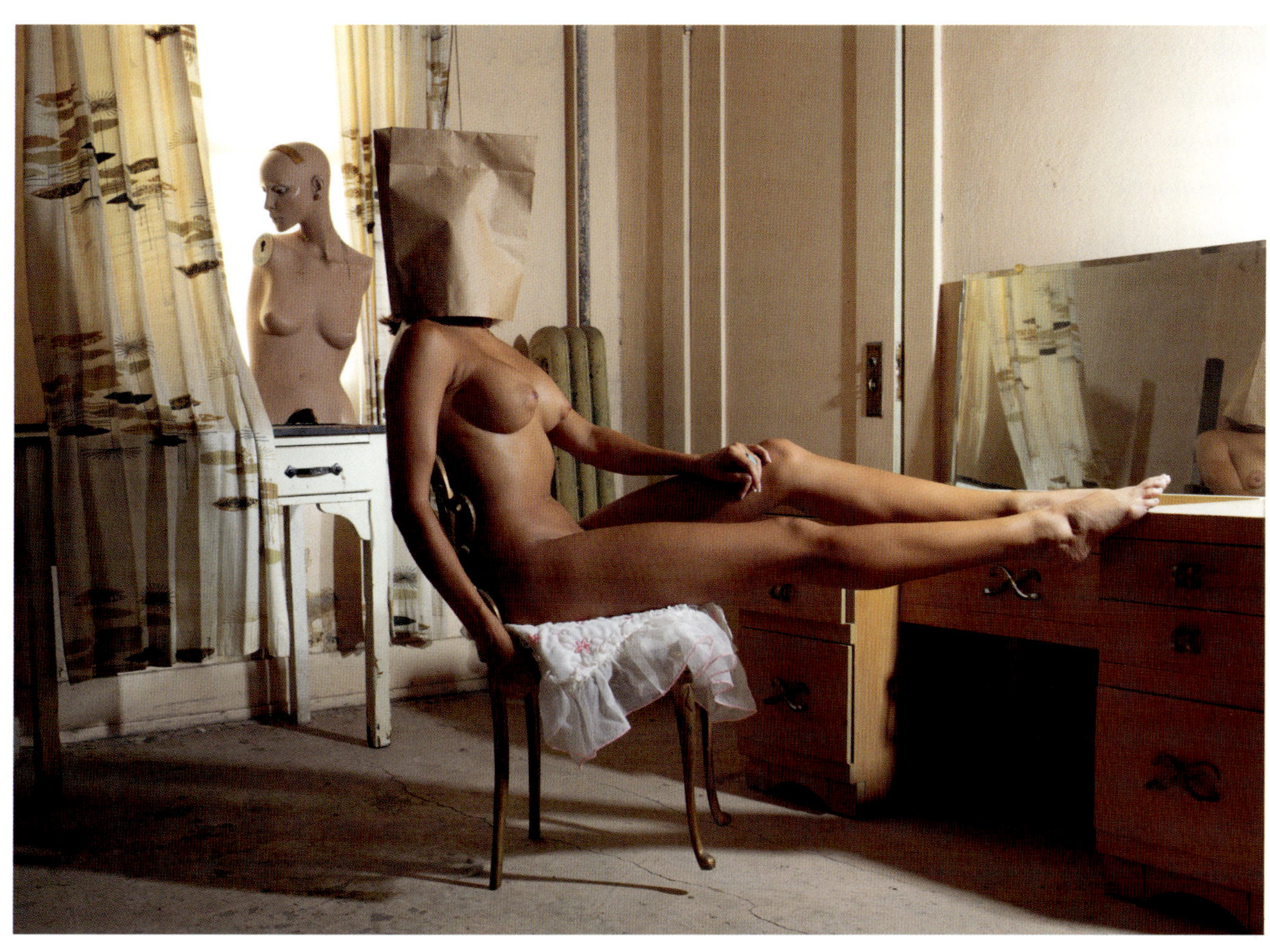

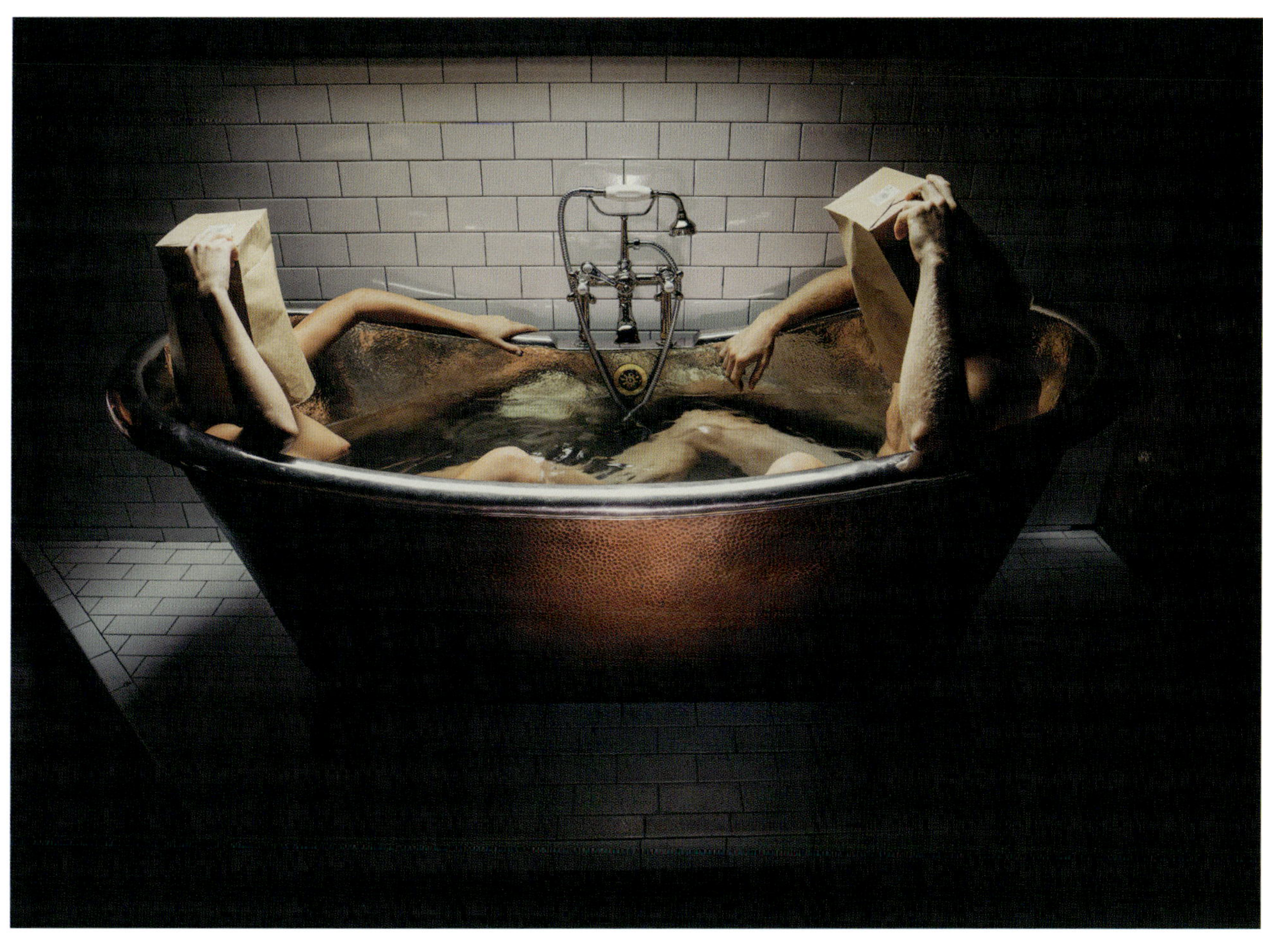

ABOVE: "Beauty Standards" BELOW: "Hopeless Romance" FOLLOWING: "Courtship"

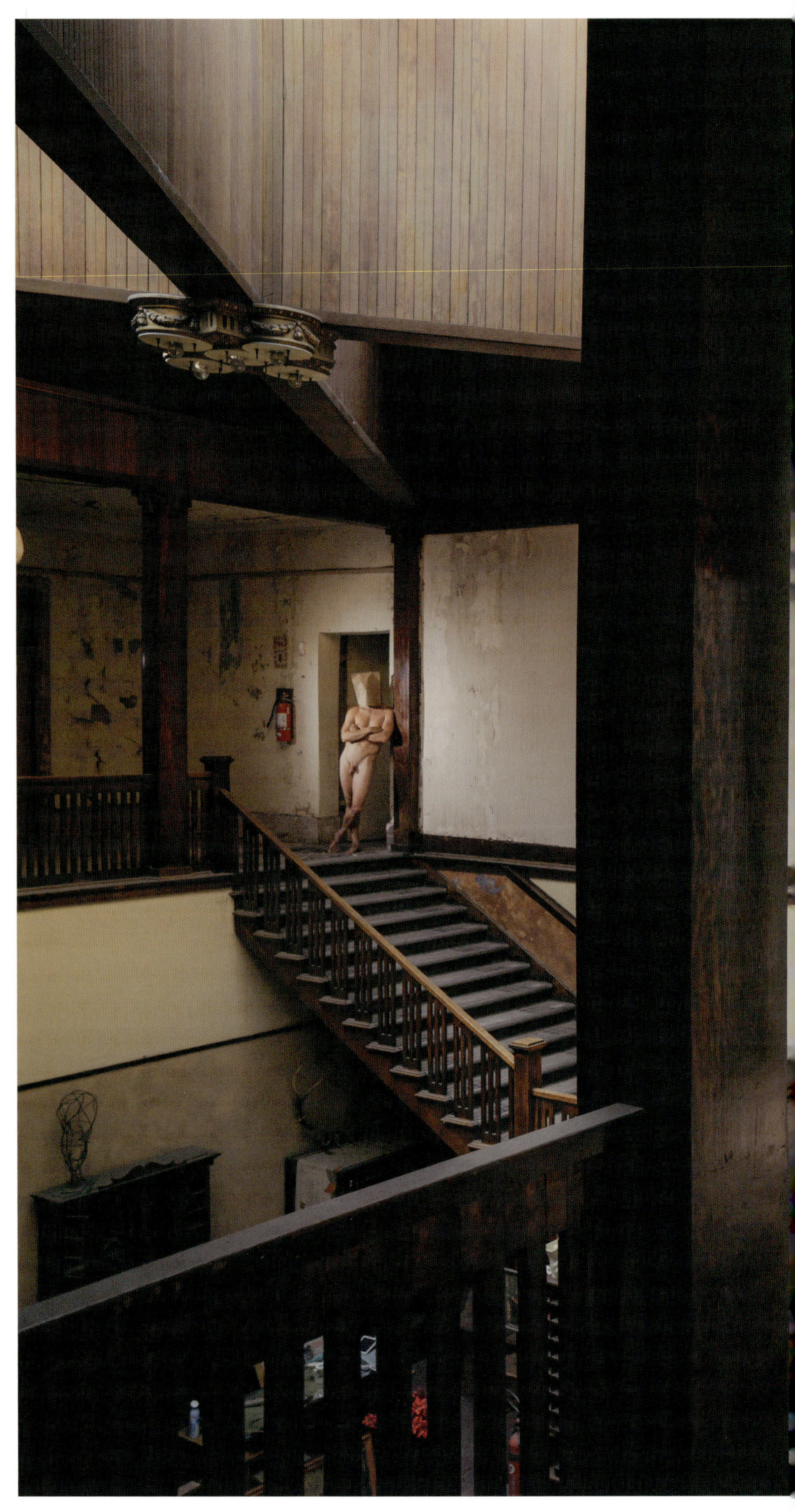

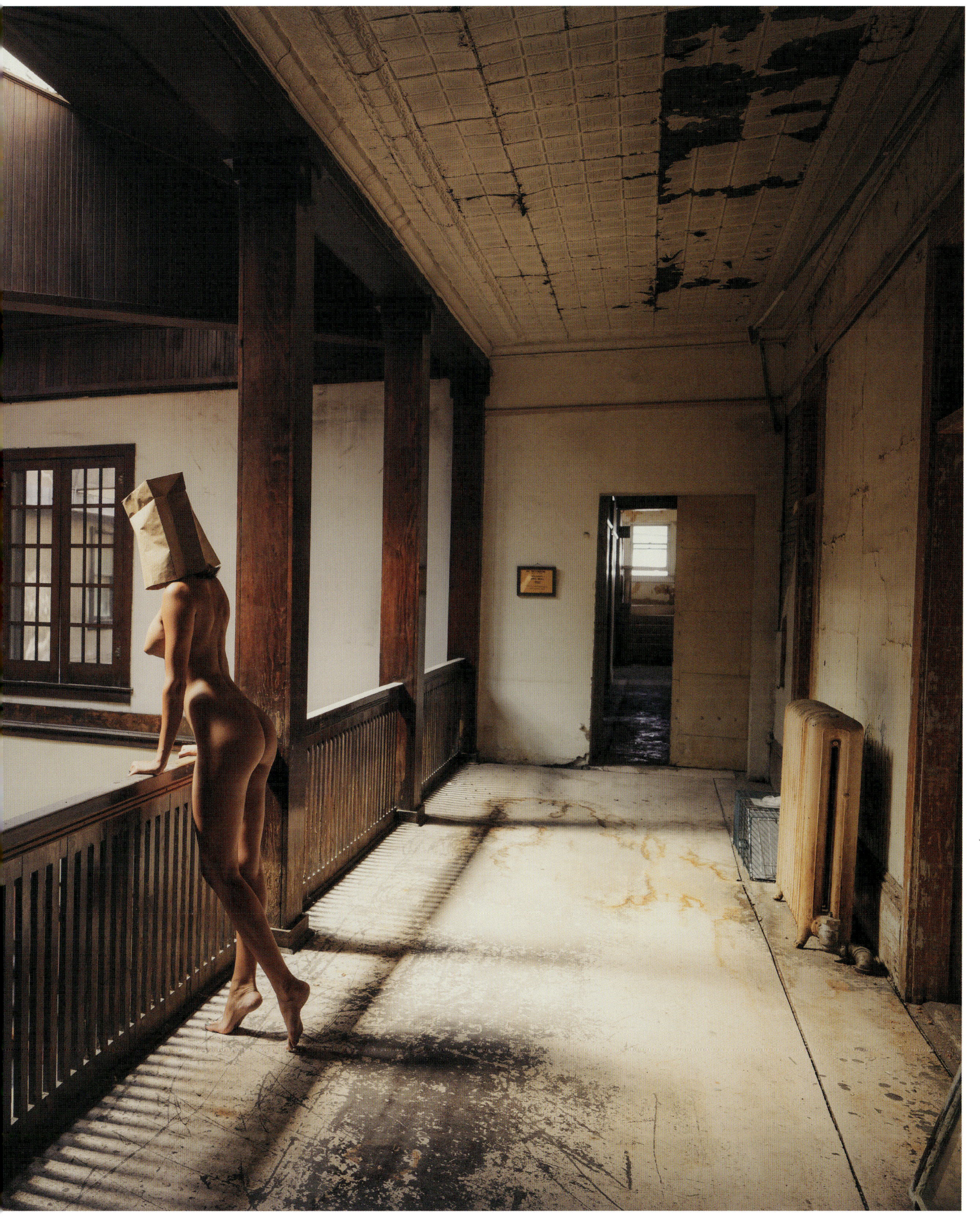

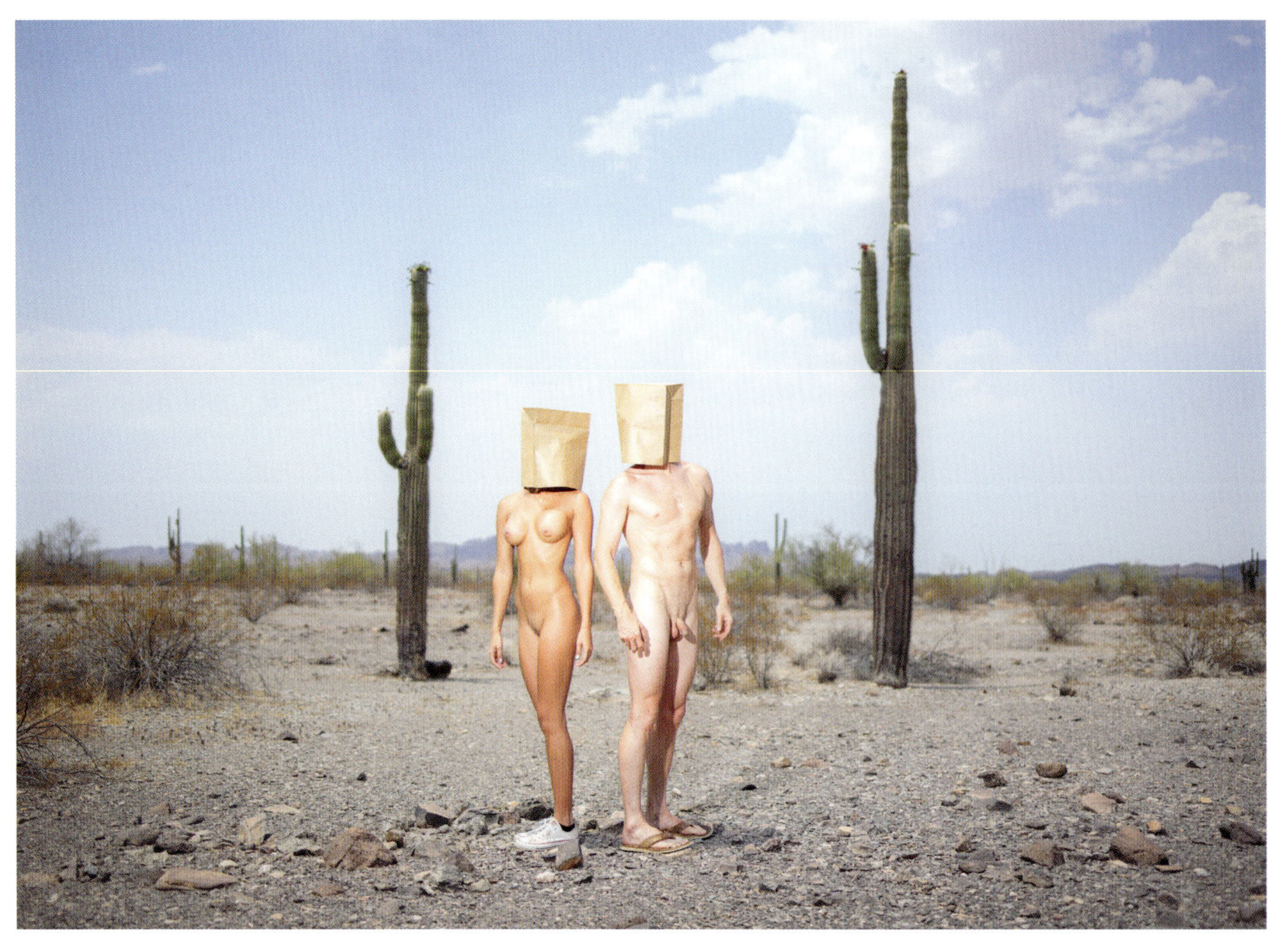

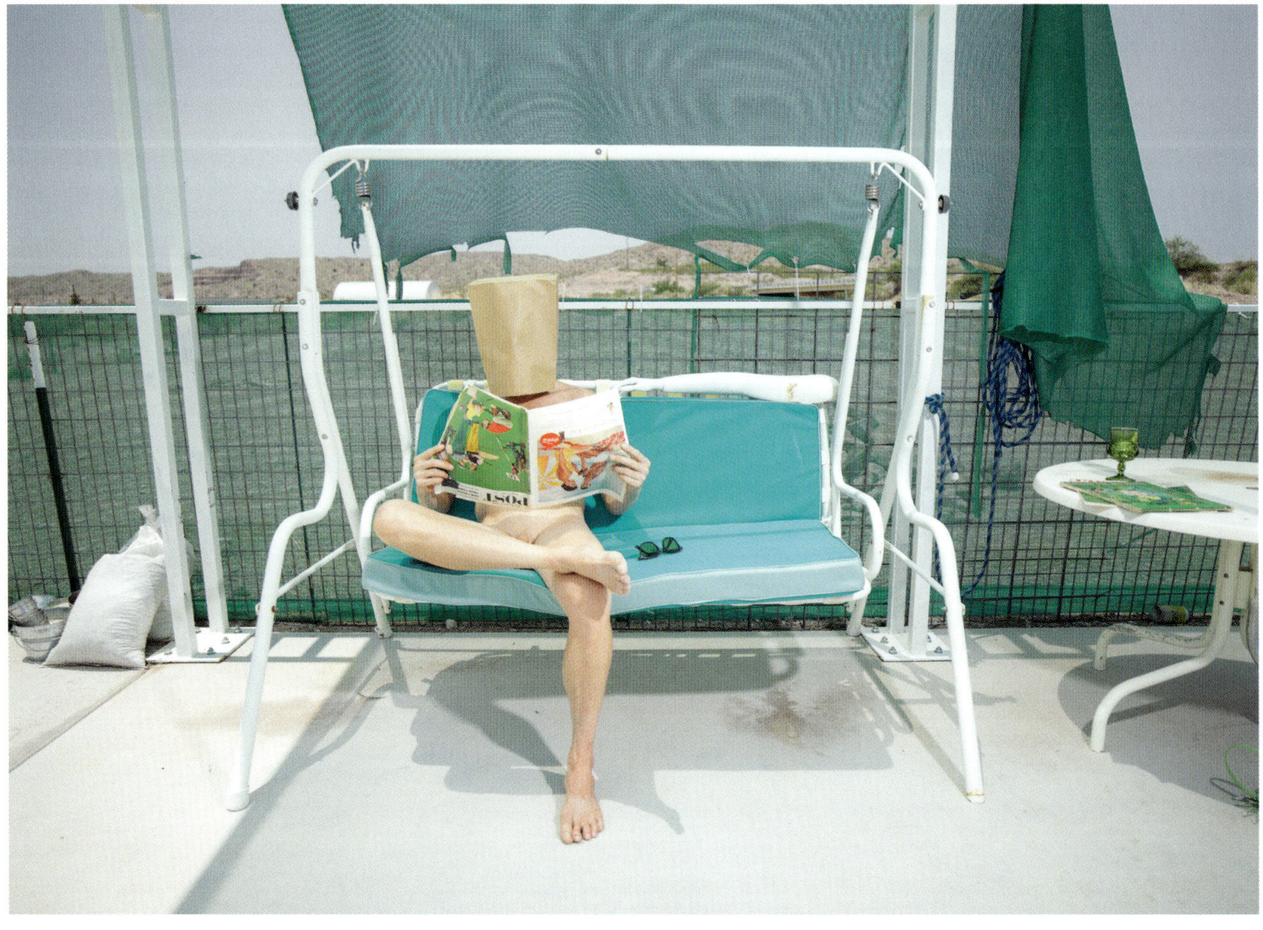

ABOVE: "The One" **BELOW:** "Two Weeks' Paid Vacation"

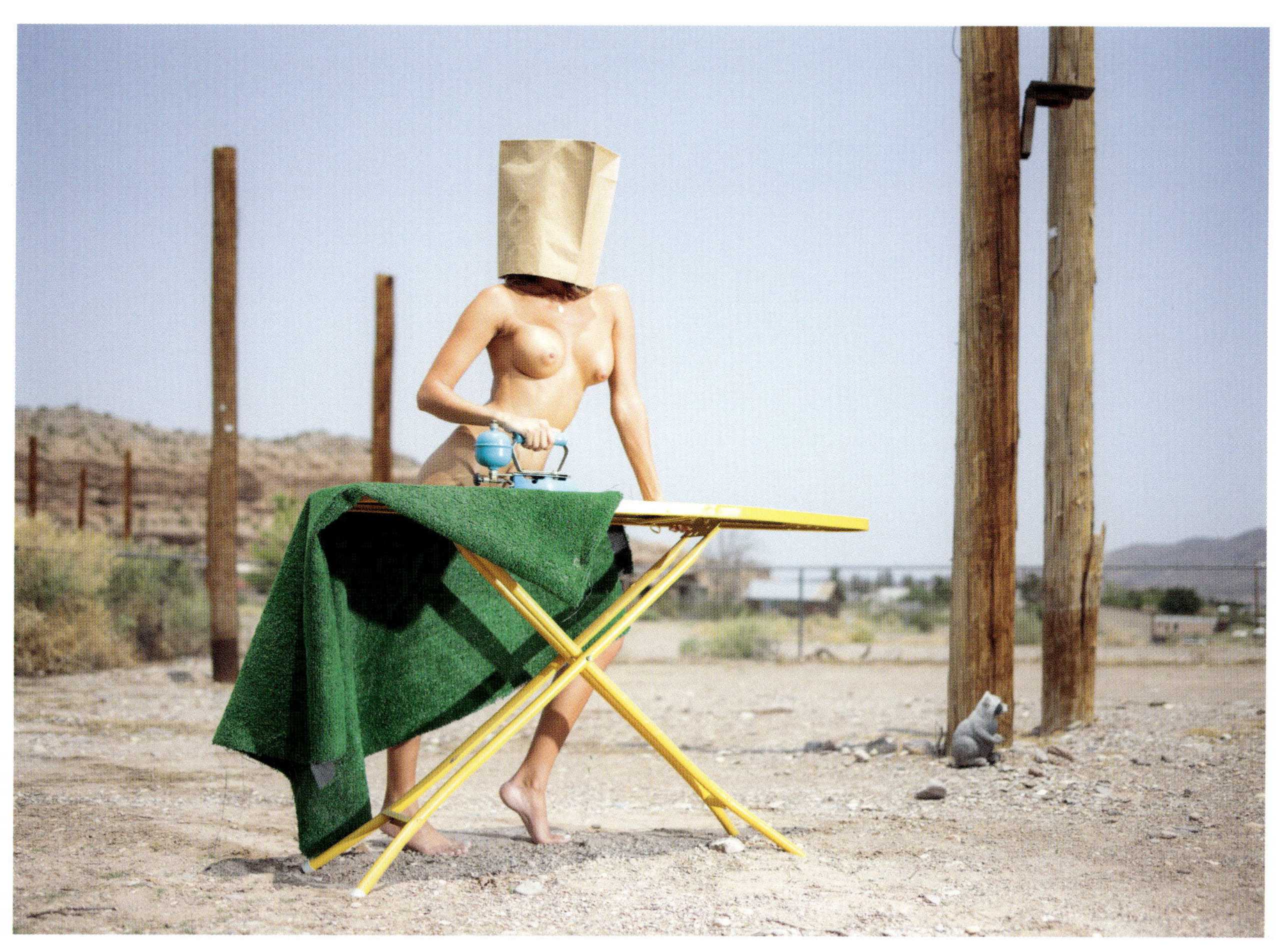

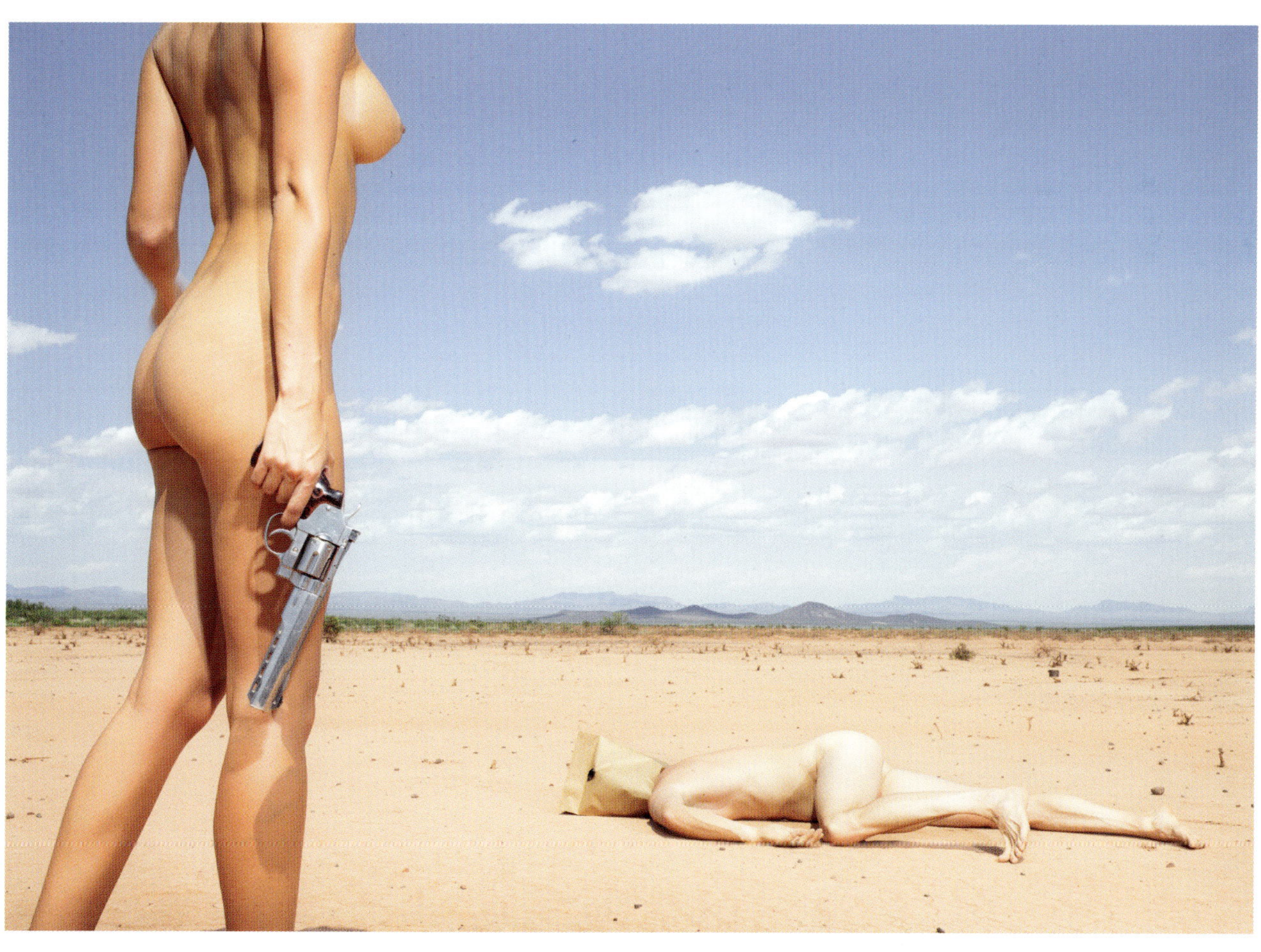

ABOVE: "A Yard" BELOW: "Female Rage" FOLLOWING: "Divorce"

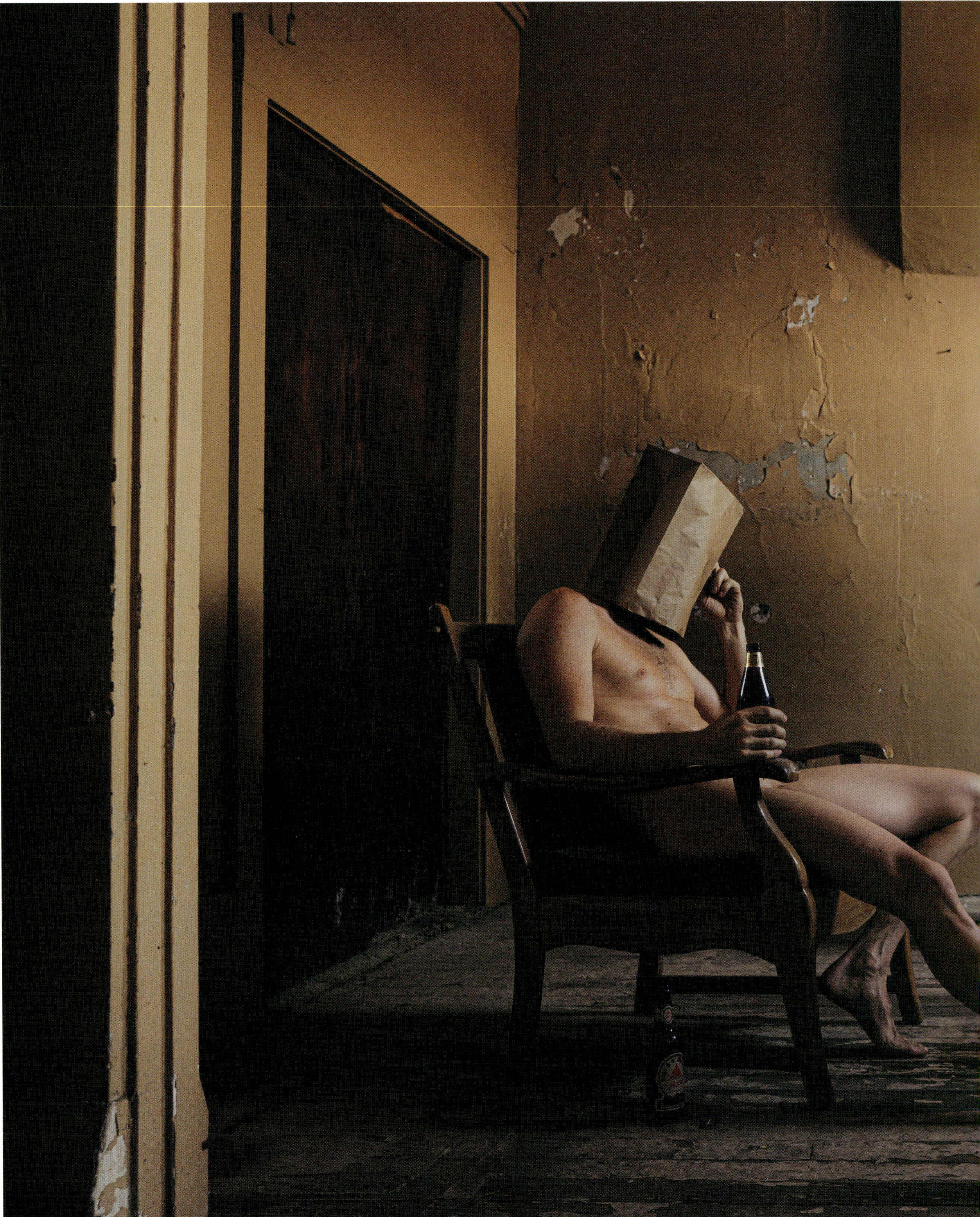

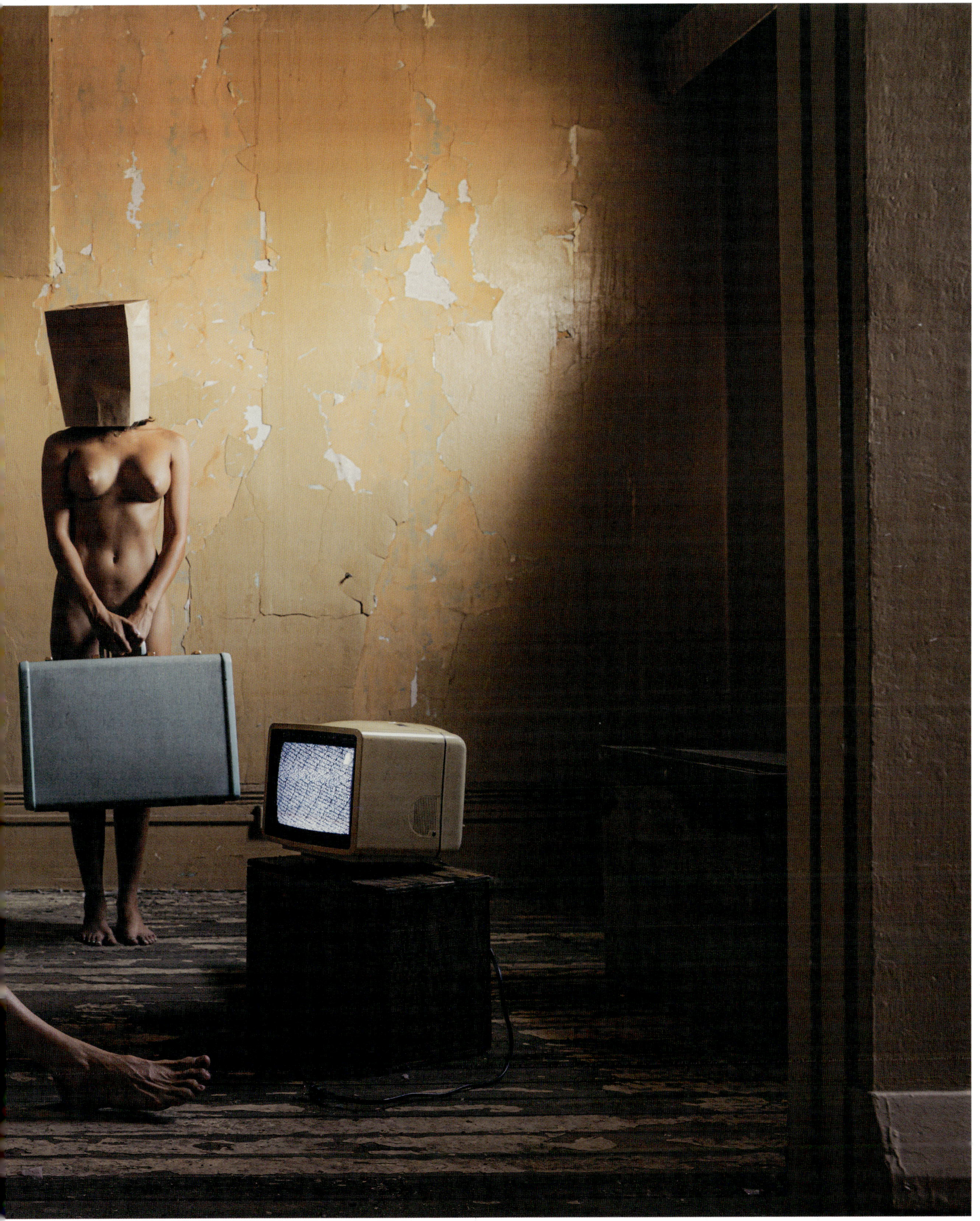

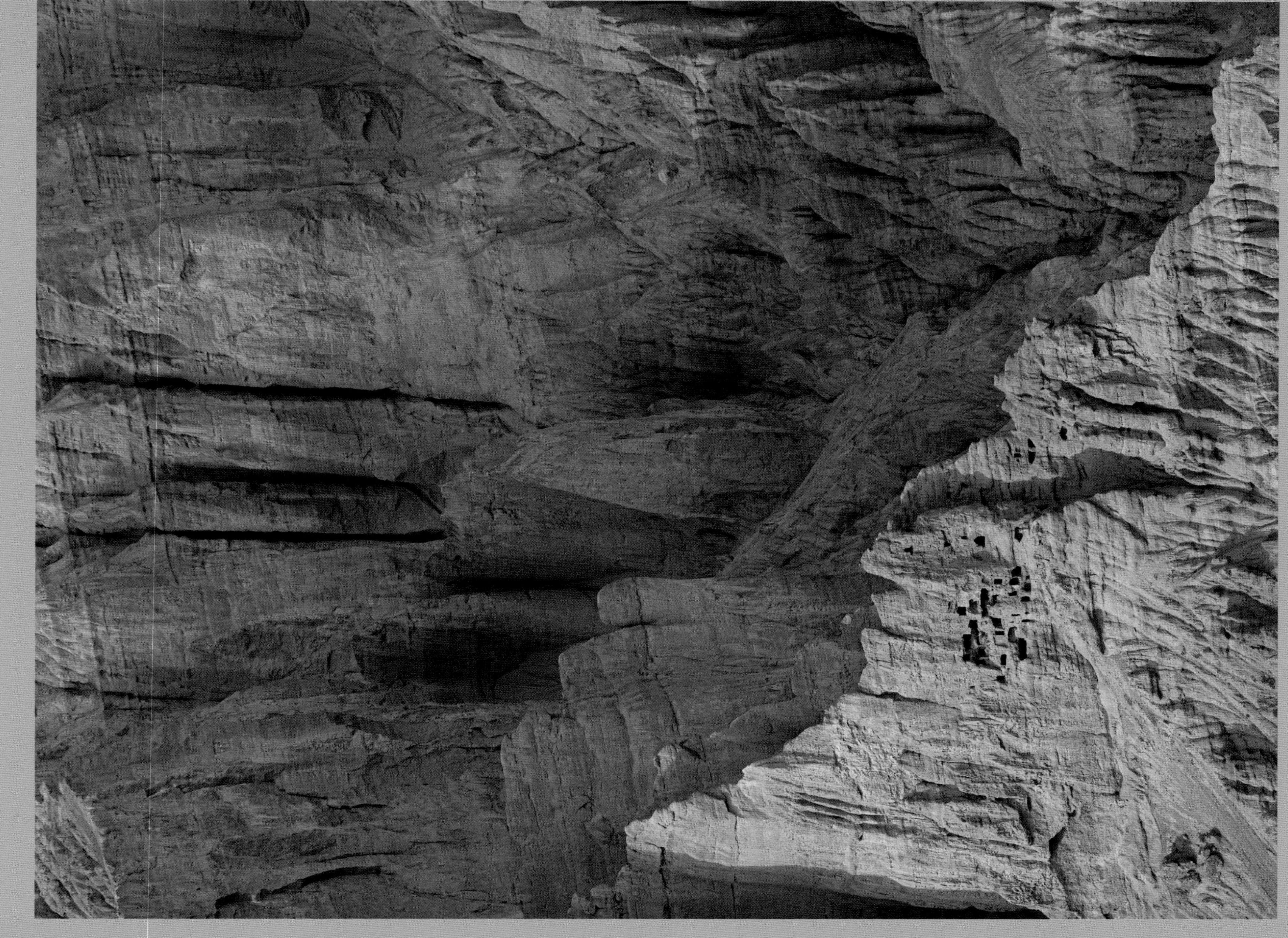

WHEN HISTORY SMILES
Mustang, Nepal

For the better part of six centuries, Mustang, Nepal, was a mystery to the western world. Nestled deep in the rugged terrain at the foot of two of the highest mountains on Earth, the region's average elevation is 13,200 feet. The kingdom was built up around the Kali Gandaki Gorge, a Grand Canyon–esque valley of tortured geography supposedly stained red by the blood of a vanquished demon. Dotting the towering cliffs are clusters of impossible hollows—thousands and thousands of inaccessible, man-hewn caves. Ancient apartment complexes easily defended. Monastic hermitages difficult to disrupt. Libraries available only to those who can levitate—or so the story goes.

For centuries, Mustang served as the most direct trade route from the Tibetan Plateau to the Indian subcontinent. Despite its importance as an offshoot of the Silk Road, the sovereignty was mostly locked away and its secrets kept safe. But in 1992, after six hundred years of solitude, the gates of the forbidden kingdom opened to the outside world and the secrets spilled out. Villages hung in the fifteenth century started serving tea to Westerners full of questions.

The team of climbers and scientists I'm a part of constitute a "rescue archeology" operation trying to unwind Mustang's past by studying the secrets of the caves before they erode and fall away into unknowable history. But for the Mustangis, spirits are everywhere and disturbing the past is cautious work. These people have lived beneath the caves for their whole lives and have either made peace with the mystery or are, at best, cautiously curious. It's only with their permission that we're allowed to explore. And even then, not everyone agrees, because our mission is for something far more intimate.

Over the past year and a half, we've spent three months in Mustang and only managed to climb or rappel into a handful of cave complexes. We've found thousands of pages of ancient manuscripts predating the second spreading of Buddhism. We've found pottery and a few beads and scraps of fabric. We've even found a human pelvis fused to a spine that was likely used in a forgotten Bon ritual. All the artifacts are interesting, but what we are really looking for are burial crypts and, specifically, human teeth.

Tooth enamel, the outer layer of a tooth, is the hardest substance in the human body. Because we need teeth to survive, enamel absorbs minerals to harden and protect our chompers. One of those minerals is strontium, an alkaline earth metal found in water, air, food, and soil.

Strontium has a robust geochemical structure that survives long after someone is buried in a cave. By measuring its signature, we can discover where a person was born. Think of it like a geotag that gets embedded in your teeth during childhood by way of what you eat and drink, starting with breast milk. If the teeth tell us someone was born in eastern Tibet, but their remains are found in northern Nepal, we can guess the rough trajectory of that person's life. If the person buried next to them was born in the jungles of the subcontinent, the picture begins to expand. When studied within the context of whoever and whatever else is found in a crypt, including fragments of material, beads, metal, and ritual adornment, information about trade is layered on top and a broader picture of our movements through time emerges.

Now hanging over the ledge, my rope cuts into the edge and showers me in grit and small pebbles. I bow my head and lower myself toward the caves. It's scary, filthy work and all I can taste is dry soil. The dark entrance to the cave is close. I'm aiming a pasty mouthful of dirt between my legs when I see it: a smooth, yellow-brown surface even with the dark hole. I lower myself another six feet and use a brush to gently sweep away the dry soil. It's a rock. Wait, no—rocks don't have eye sockets.

I exchange my large brush for a toothbrush with soft bristles and dust past the nose cavity. In time, this small, unassuming collection of caves will turn out to be the final resting place of 133 individuals. For now, I've forgotten that I'm hanging a hundred feet off the ground from two pieces of old rebar. I'm locked in a momentary confrontation with history and, suddenly, I don't remember how I got here. There are no sounds and no time. If there is dirt in my teeth, I no longer notice. I just hope any ghosts might forgive my curiosity. I don't mean to be insensitive; I'd just like to hear the stories these bones can tell. And there it is: a tooth.

OPPOSITE: A cluster of ancient habitation caves near Drakmar (2011).

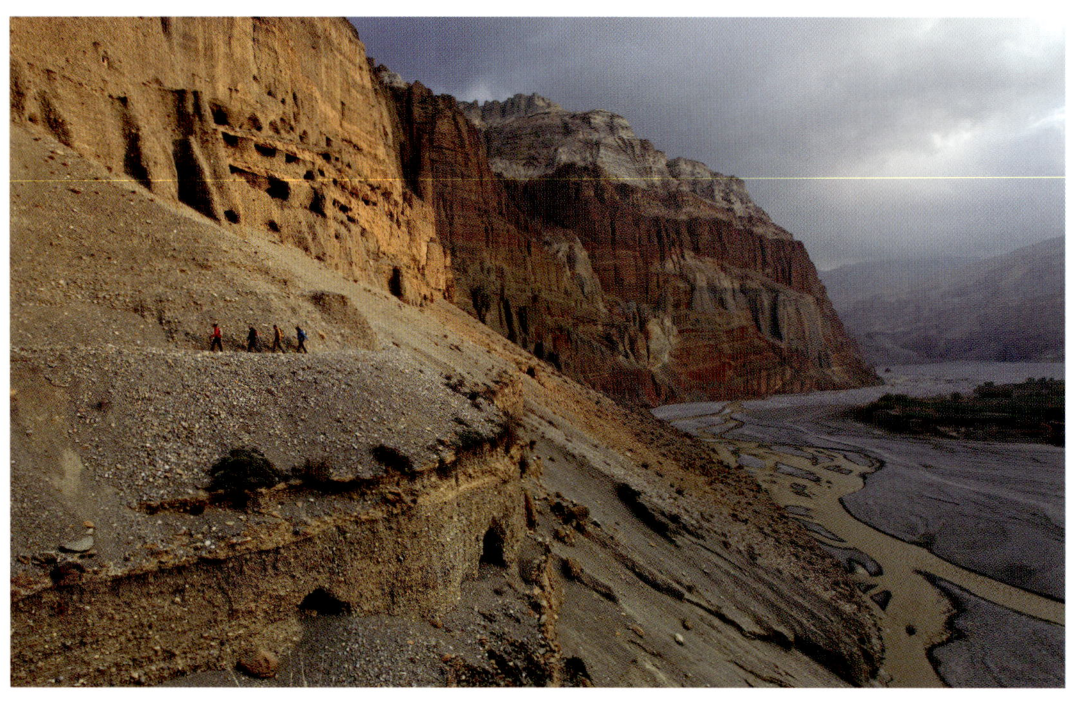

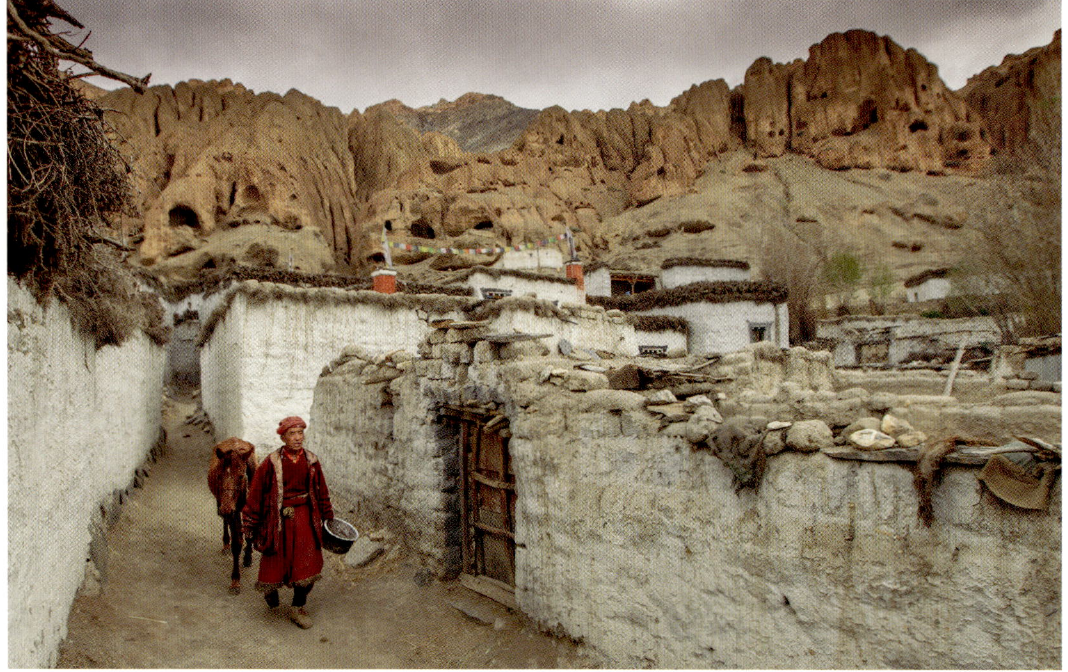

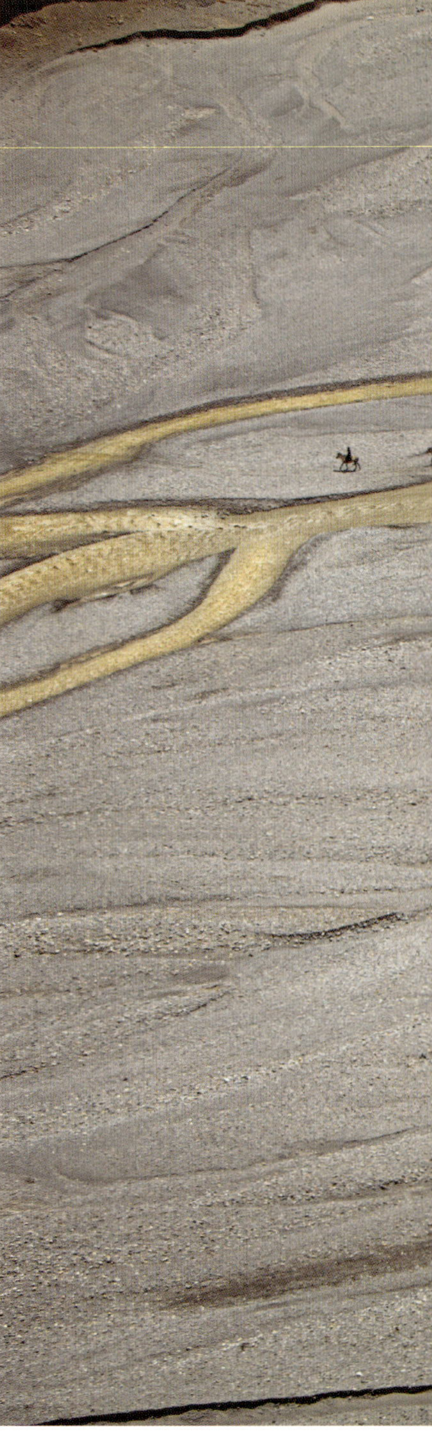

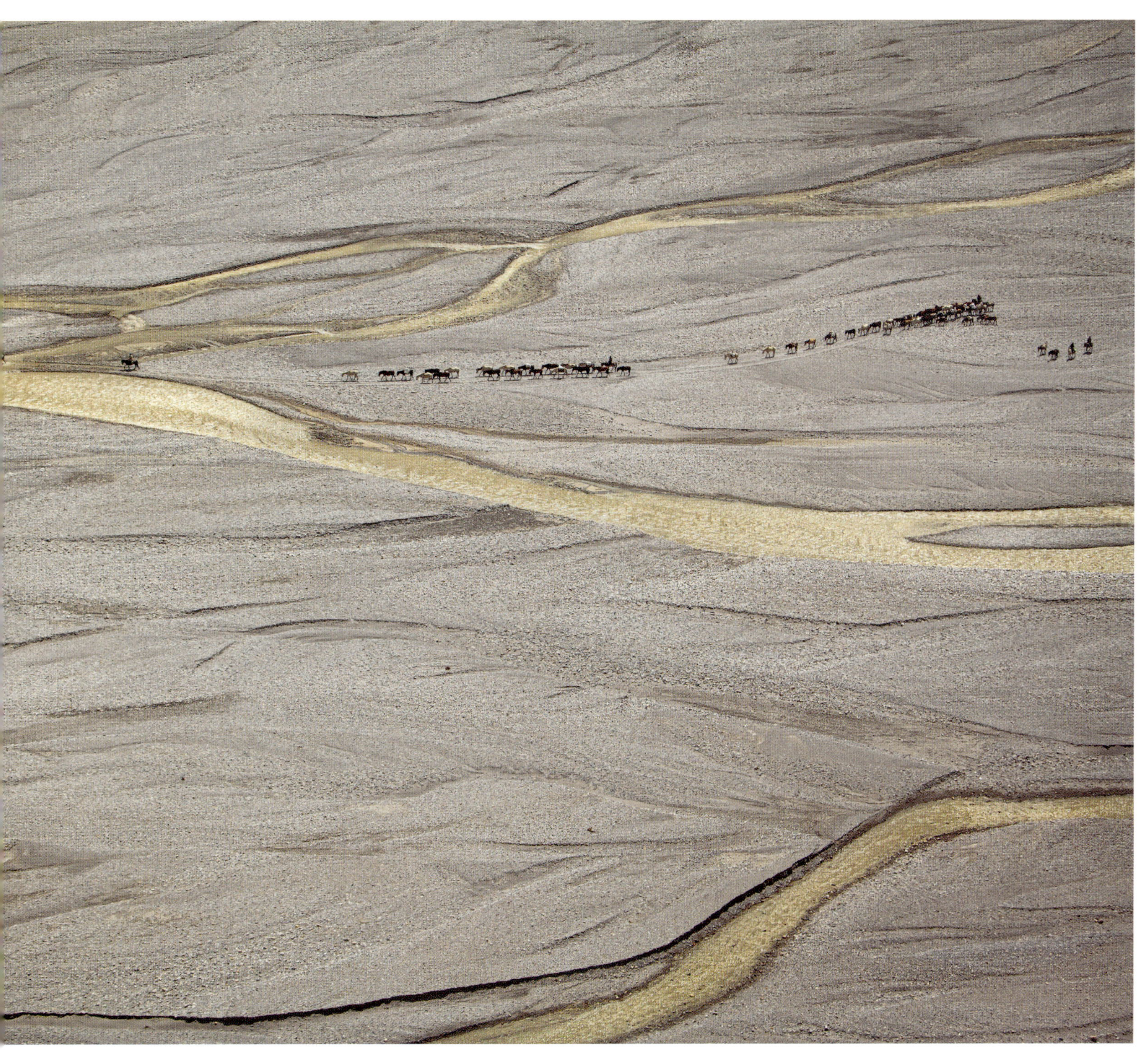

A horse train travels the floor of the Kali Gandaki Gorge, an offshoot of the Silk Road and the most direct passage from the Tibetan Plateau to the Indian subcontinent. **OPPOSITE, ABOVE:** A team of climbers and archeologists traverse beneath a cave complex near Chuksang. **OPPOSITE, BELOW:** A Lama, or Buddhist holy man, walks his horse to the well in Samdzong.

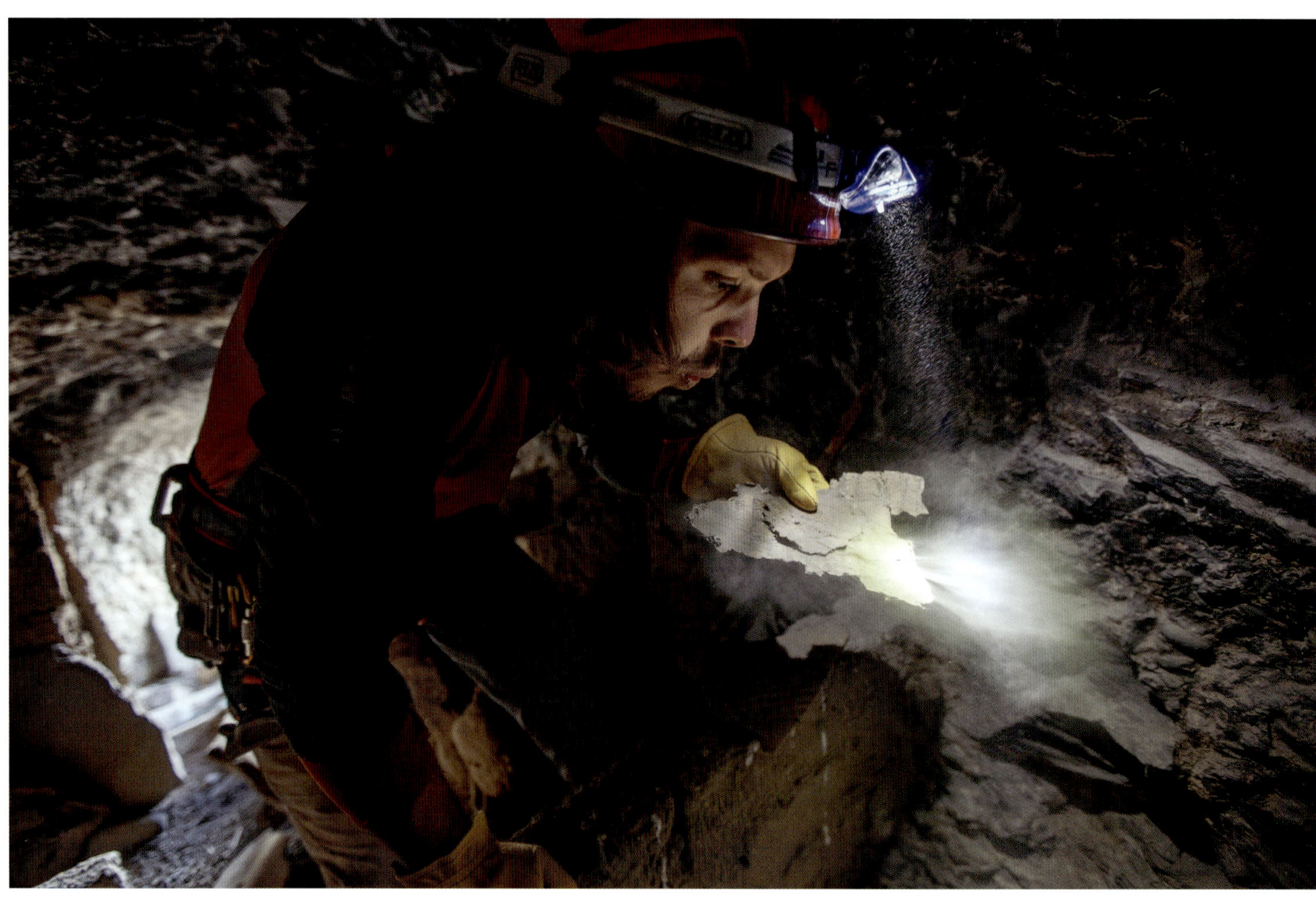

American climber Matt Segal blows dust from an ancient piece of pecha, a traditional Tibetan loose-leaf book, discovered in a cave near Somar. **OPPOSITE:** Expedition leader Pete Athans (left) and Matt Segal (right) sort climbing gear used to climb the vertical mud cliffs to access the caves. **FOLLOWING:** The landscape of Upper Mustang stretching toward Damodar.

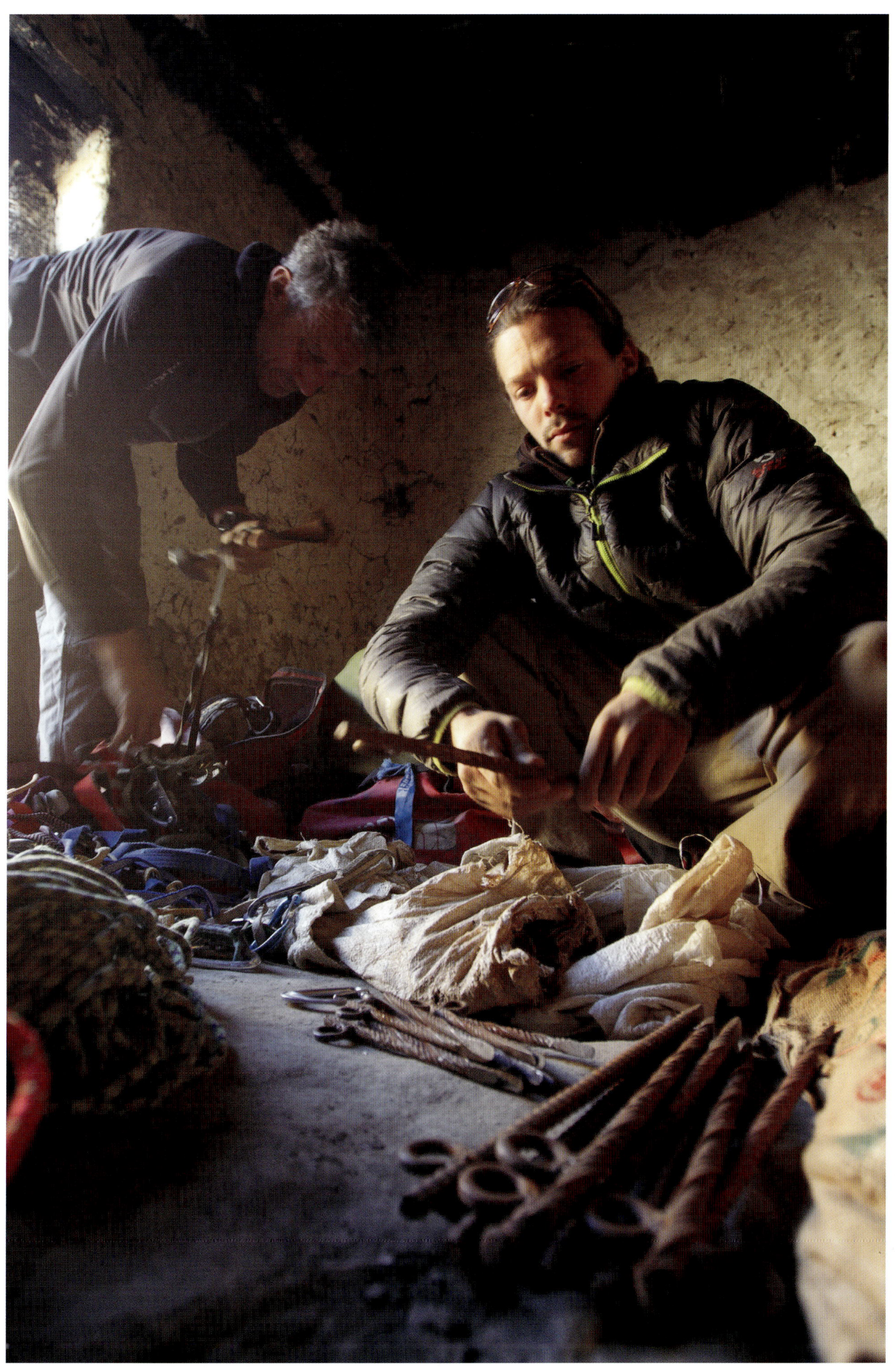

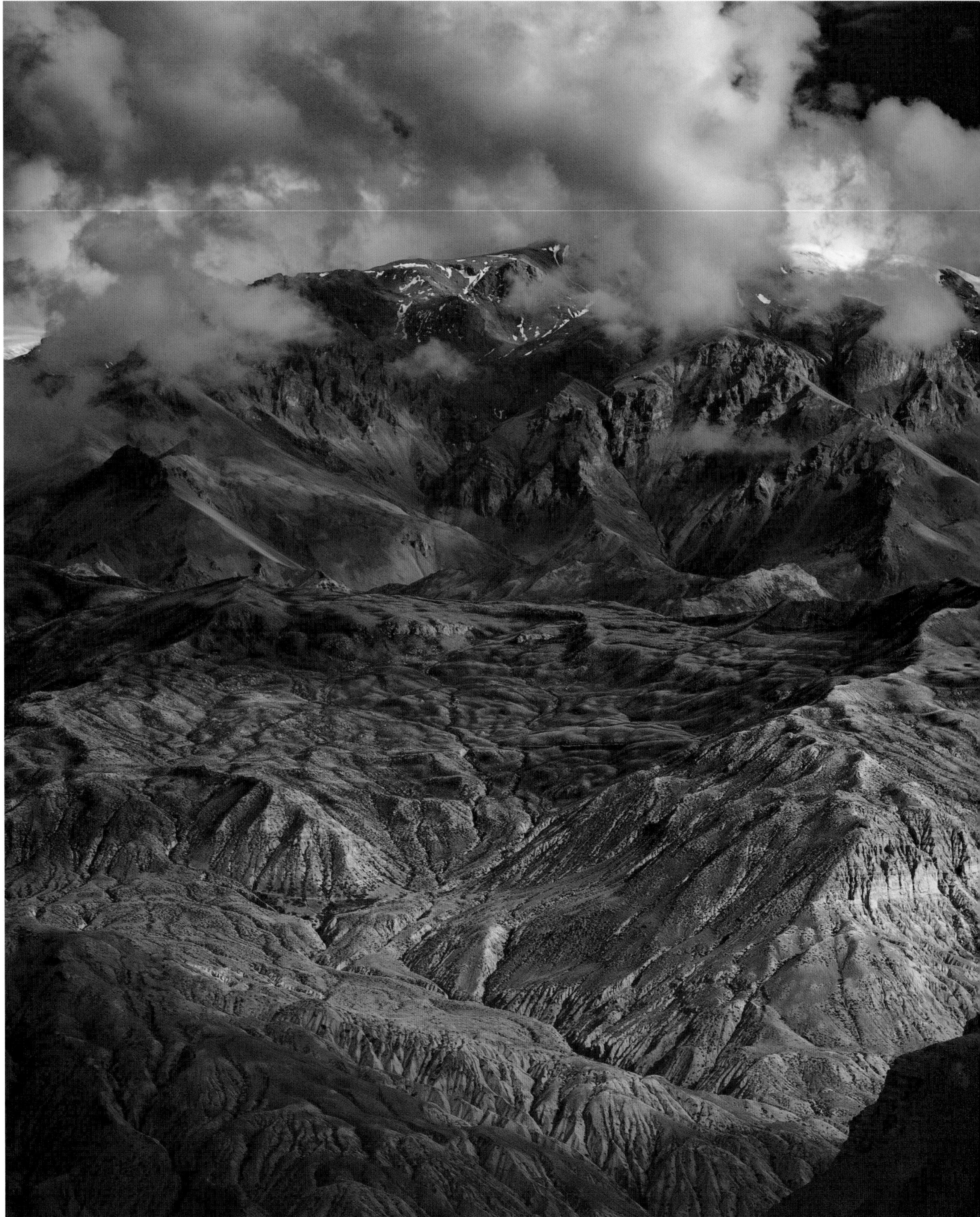

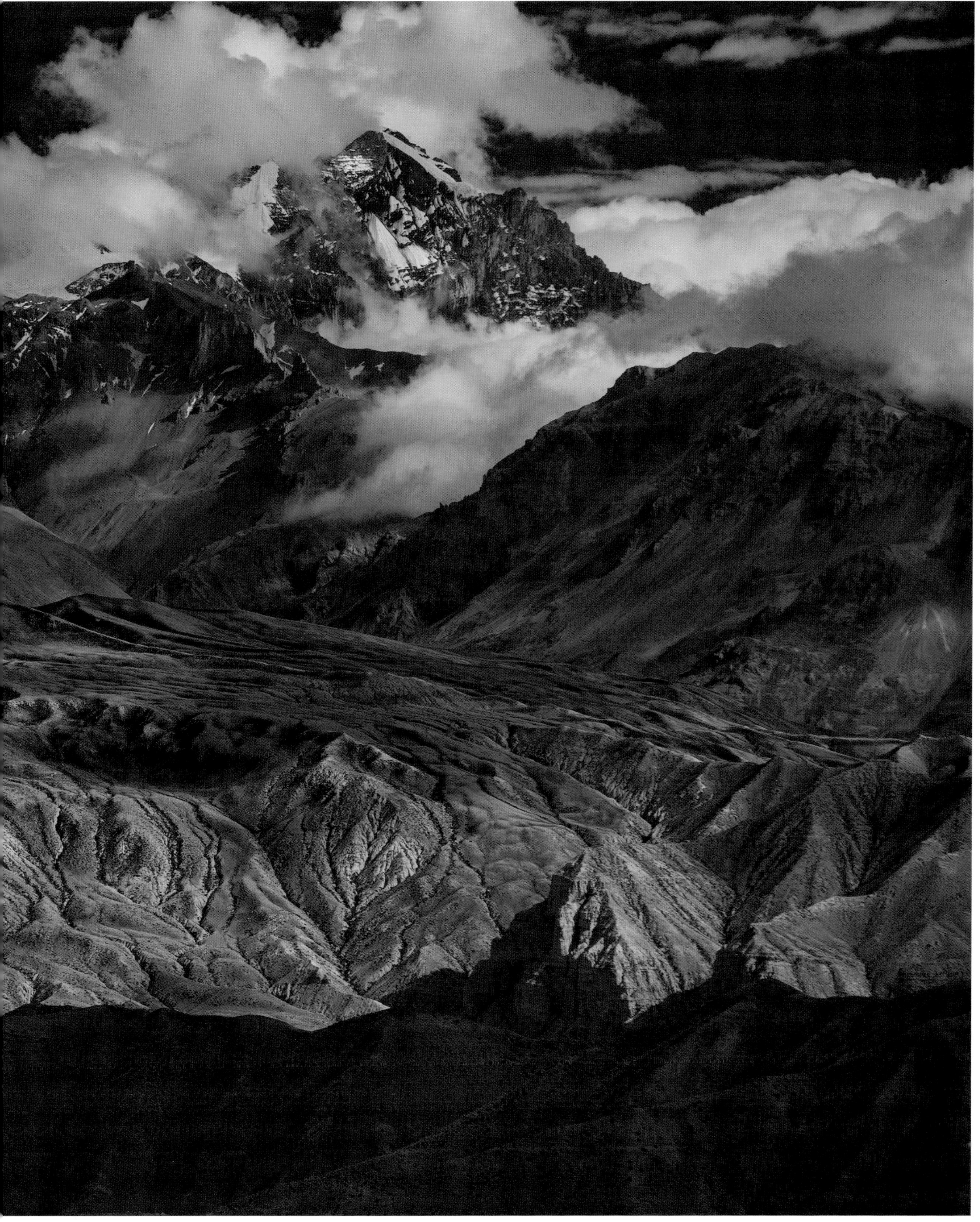

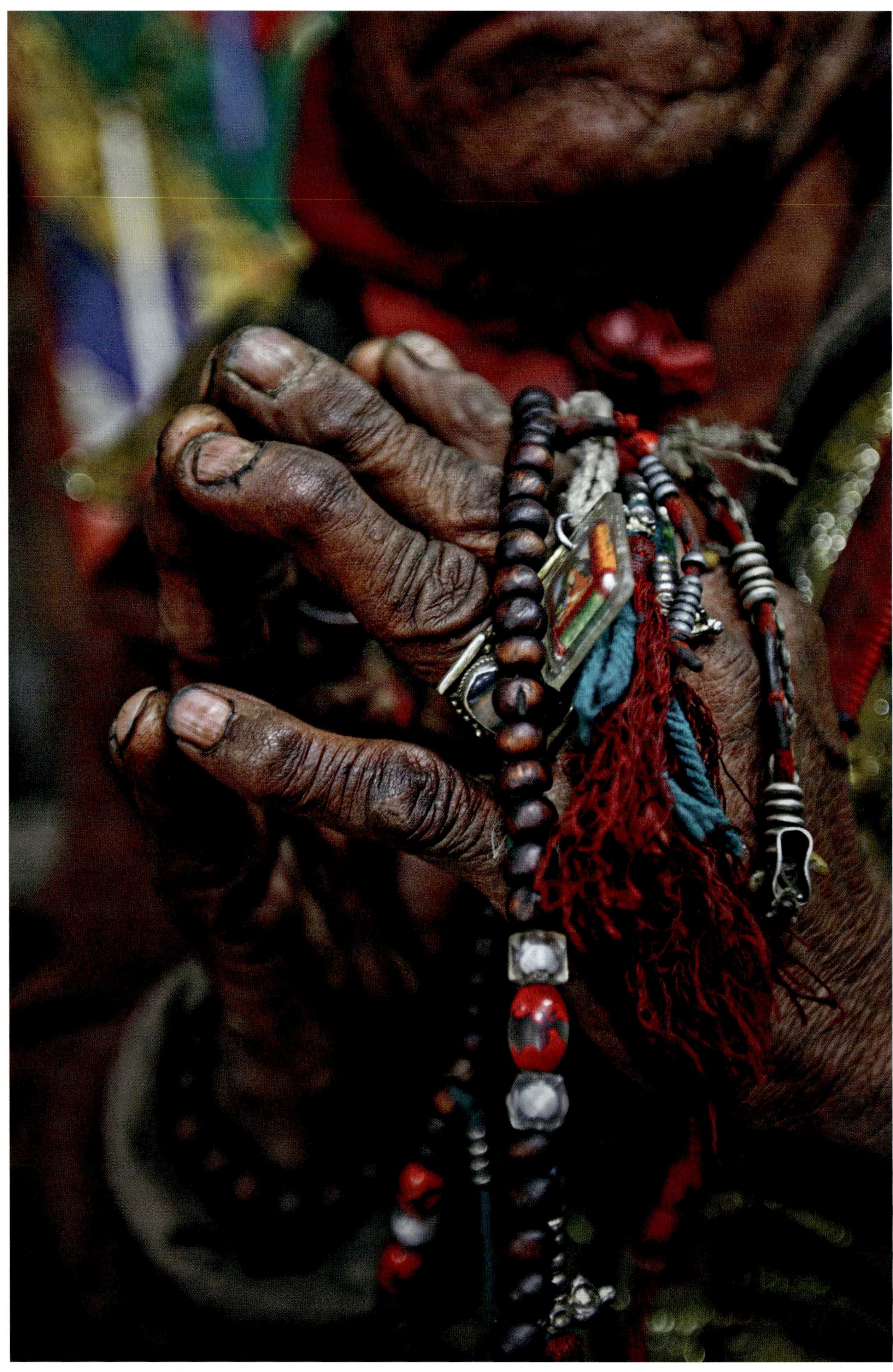

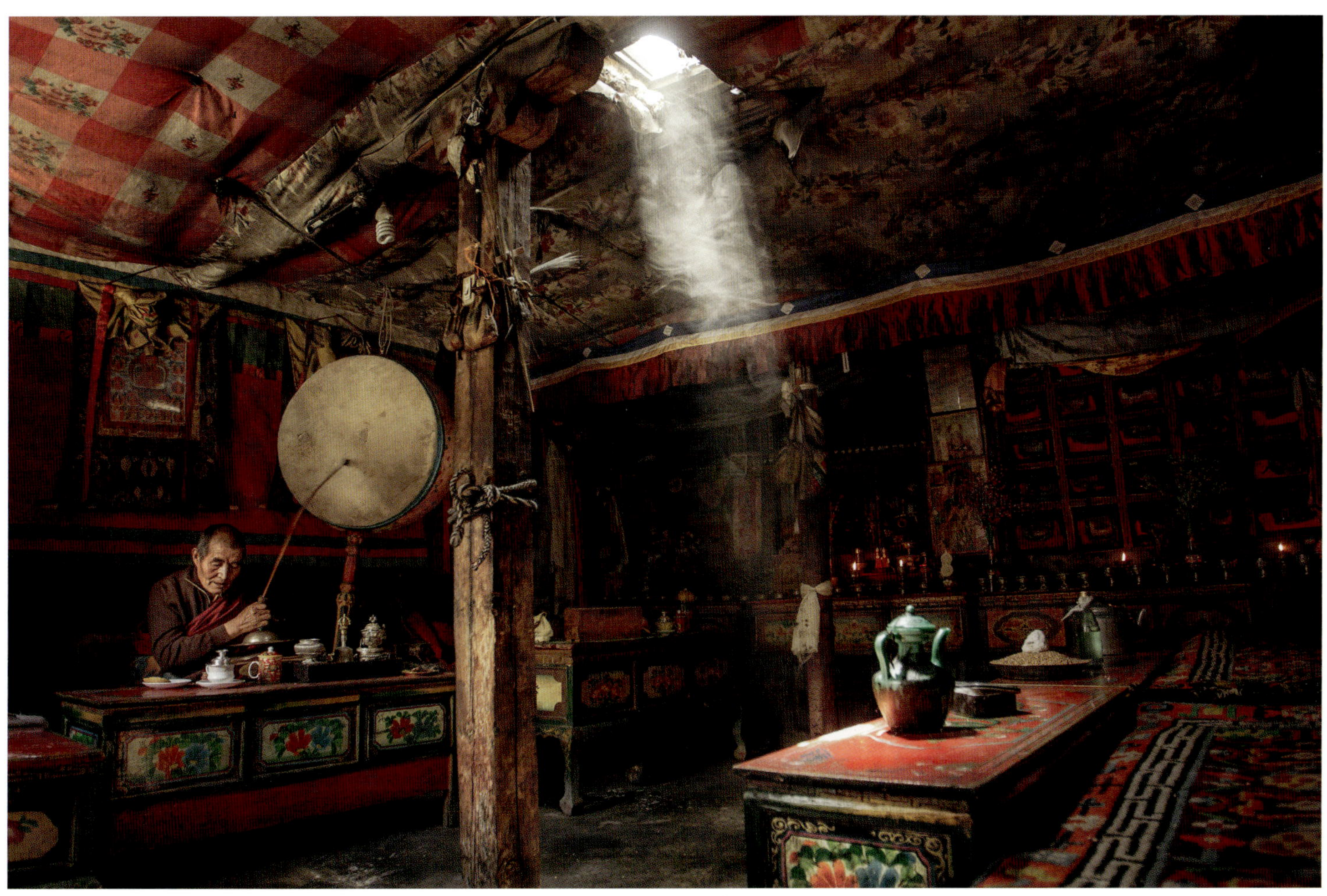

A Tibetan Buddhist Lama performs a puja (holy ritual) in a private gompa in Lo Manthang. Seen side by side, the textures of Bon and Tibetan Buddhism are easily appreciated. **OPPOSITE:** A Bon monk prays in Lubra. Bon is the indigenous religion of Tibet, though it has been argued that it only self-identified as a cohesive religion after the spread of Buddhism. Tibetan Buddhism shares its roots with ancient traditions through syncretism, the amalgamation and assimilation of different beliefs, religions, and schools of thought.

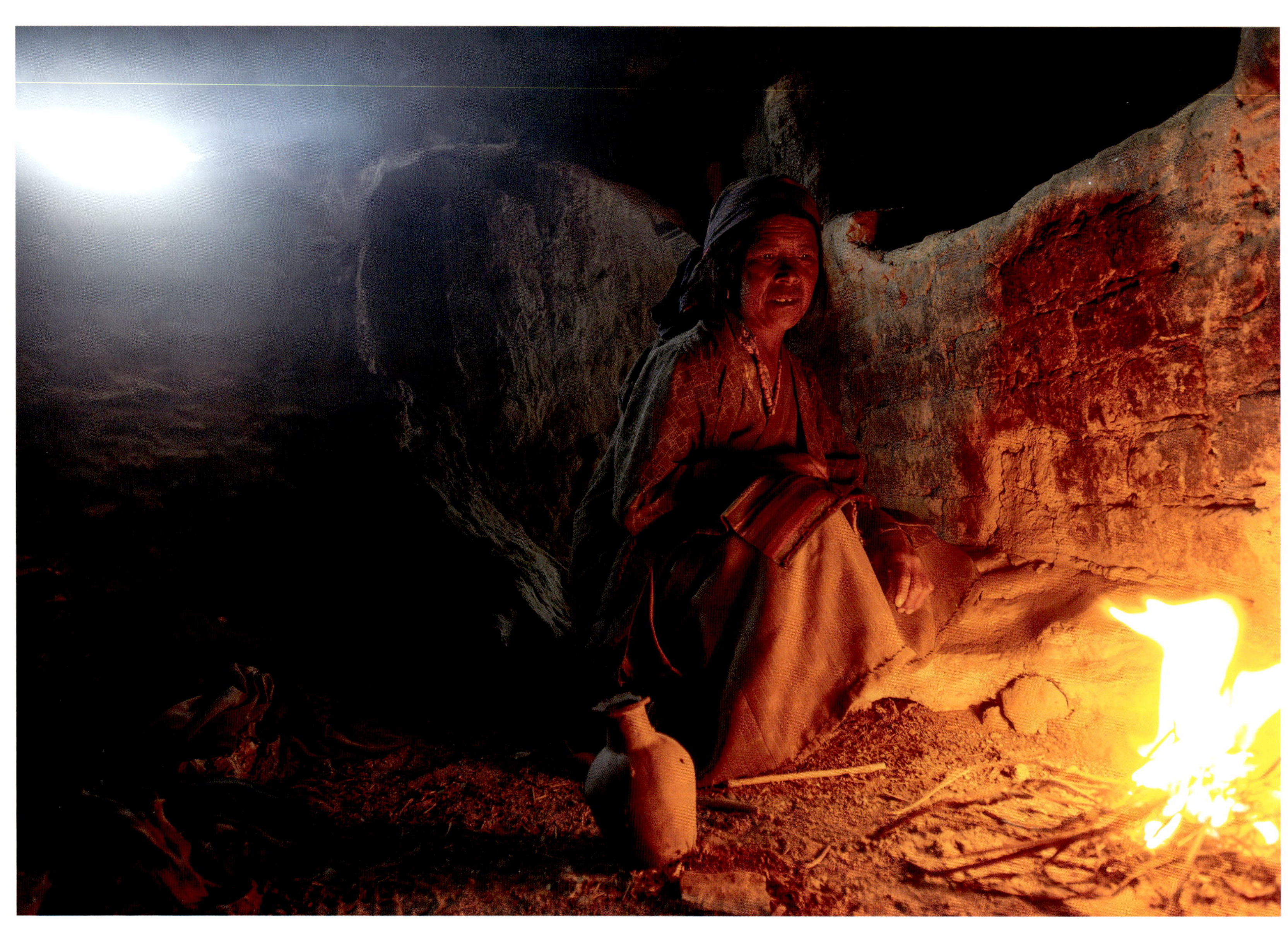

A Loba woman lights a fire in her childhood home cave; Choser, Upper Mustang.

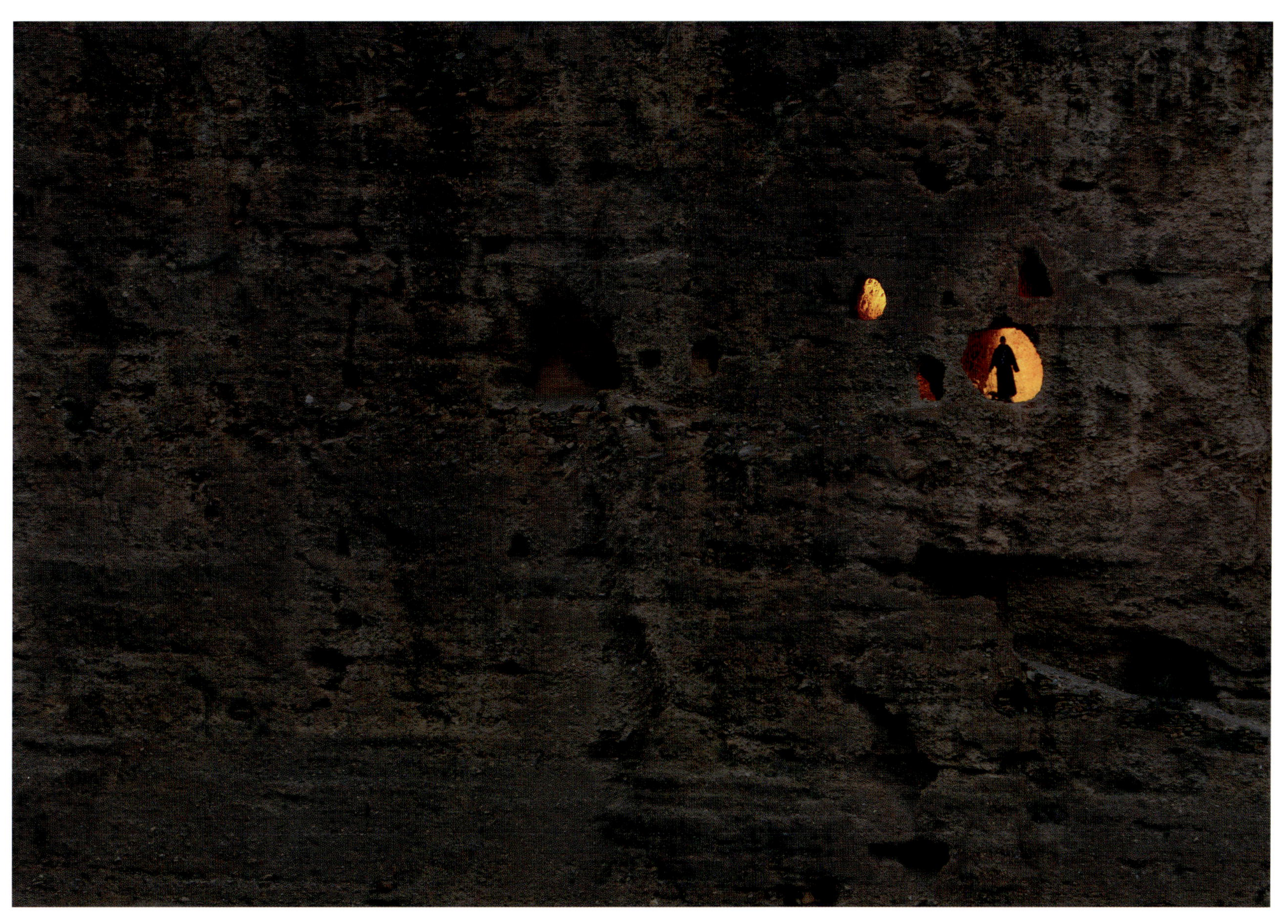

Ancient habitation caves illuminated. **FOLLOWING, LEFT:** Matt Segal climbs into a cave complex near Chuksang. **FOLLOWING, RIGHT:** The first skull discovered near Samdzong. The burial crypt in the cliffs was the final resting place of more than one hundred individuals.

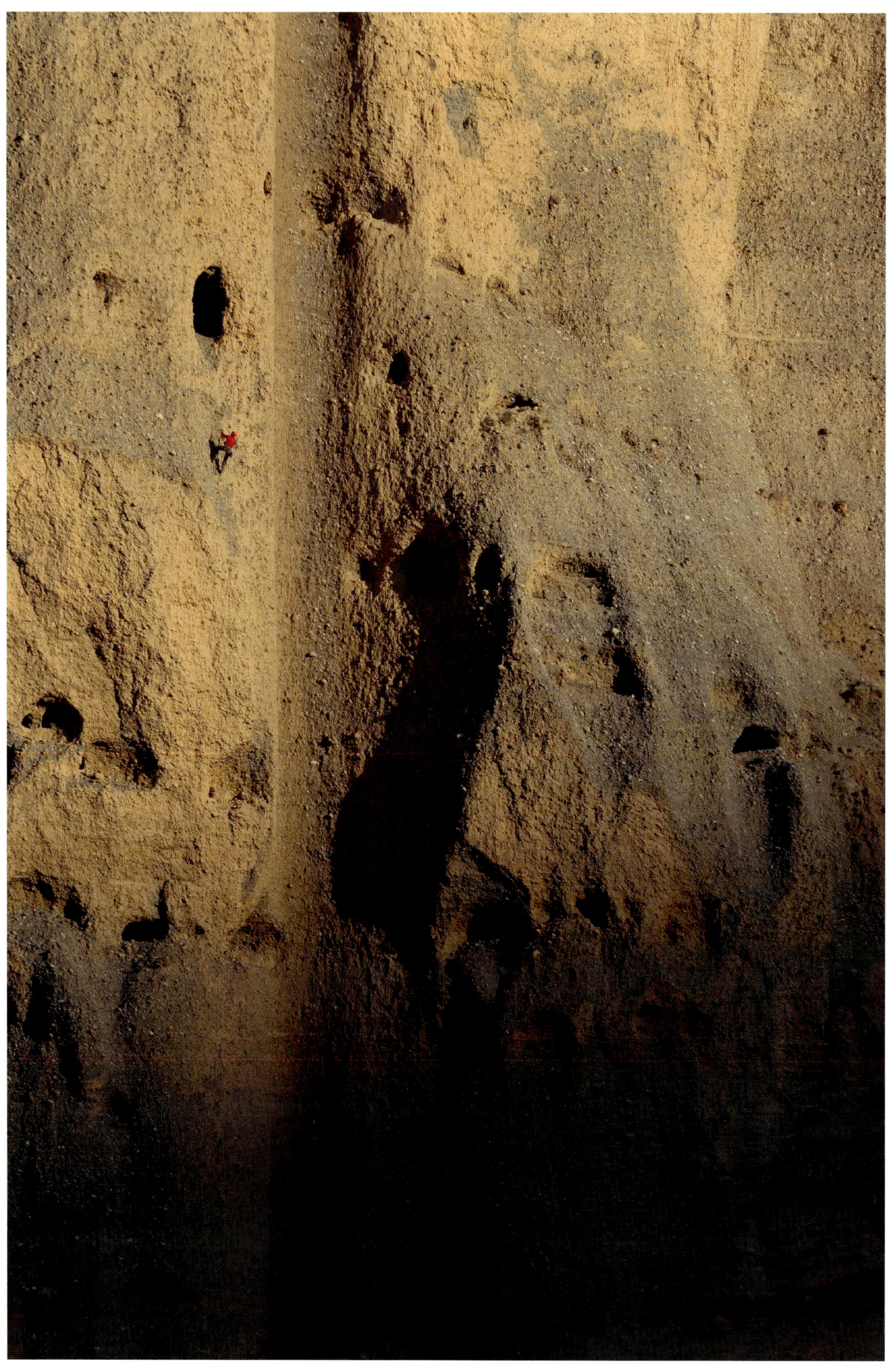

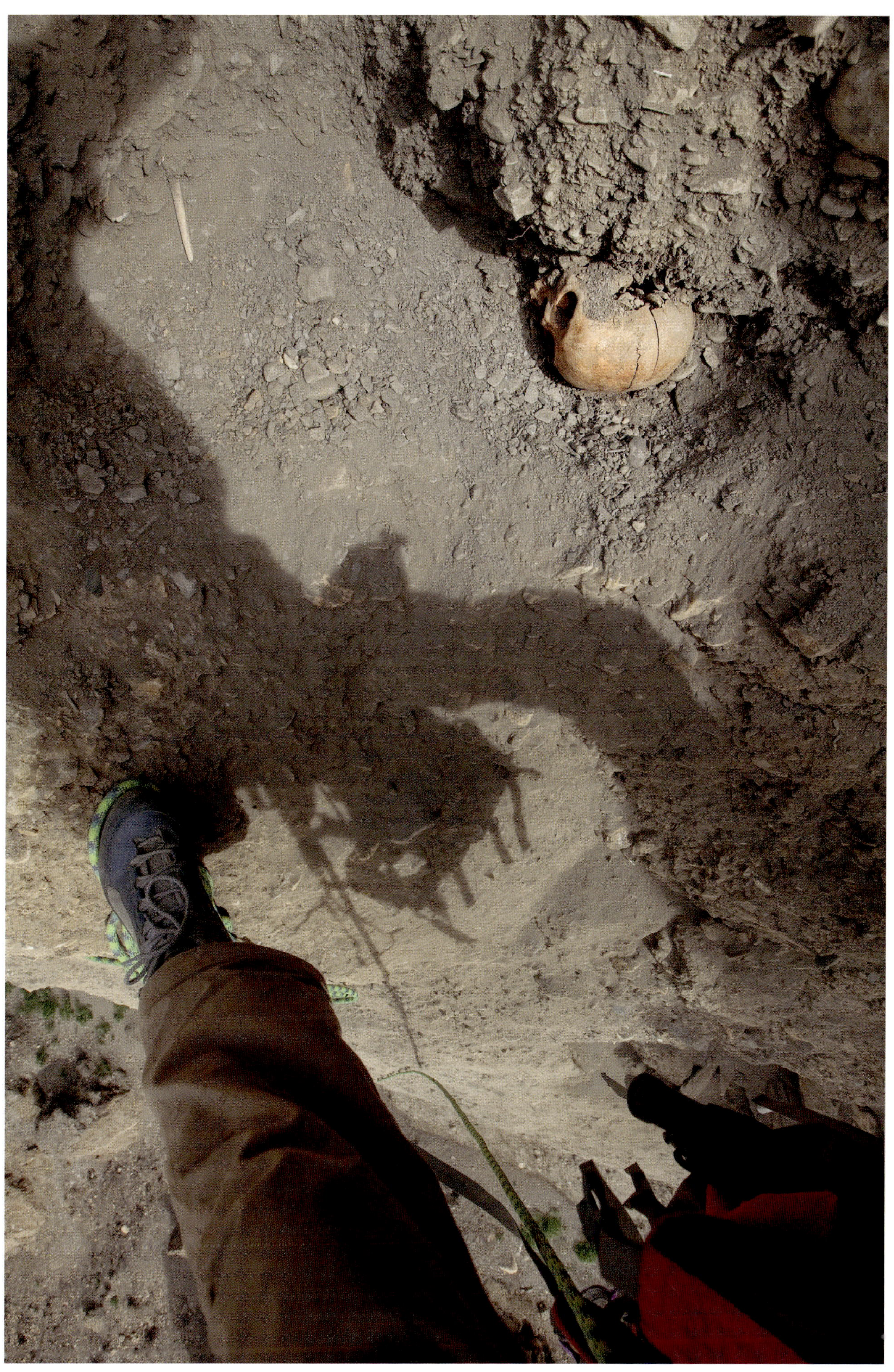

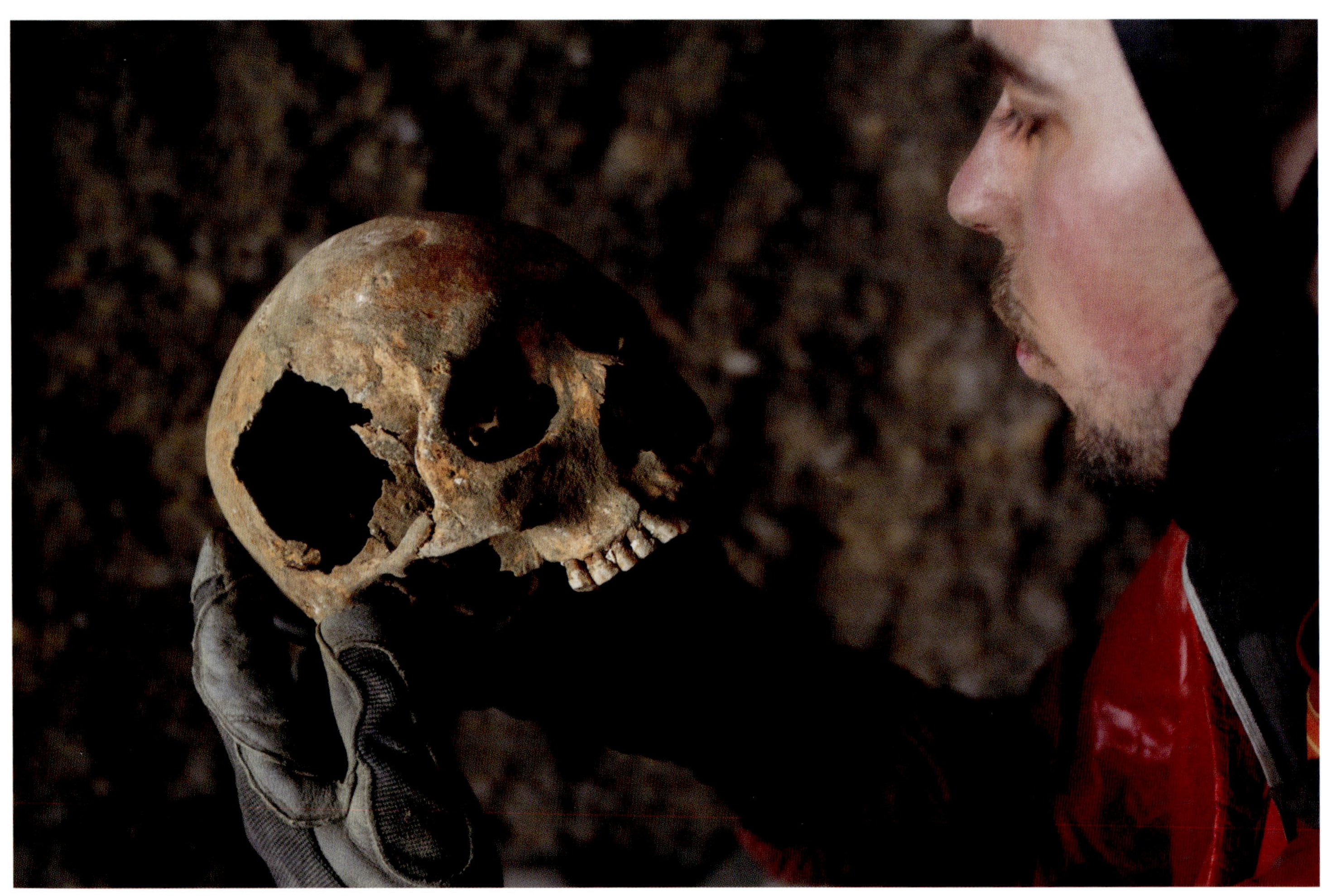

American climber and team member Ted Hesser gently pulls a skull from the burial crypt above Samdzong. The remains date from circa 500 to 800 AD.
OPPOSITE: A mummified foot from a burial crypt discovered in Mebrak. This original discovery in 1995 offered the first glimpse into the mysteries of Mustang's caves and held remains dating from circa 400 BC to 50 AD. Photographed at the Department of Archeology in Kathmandu.

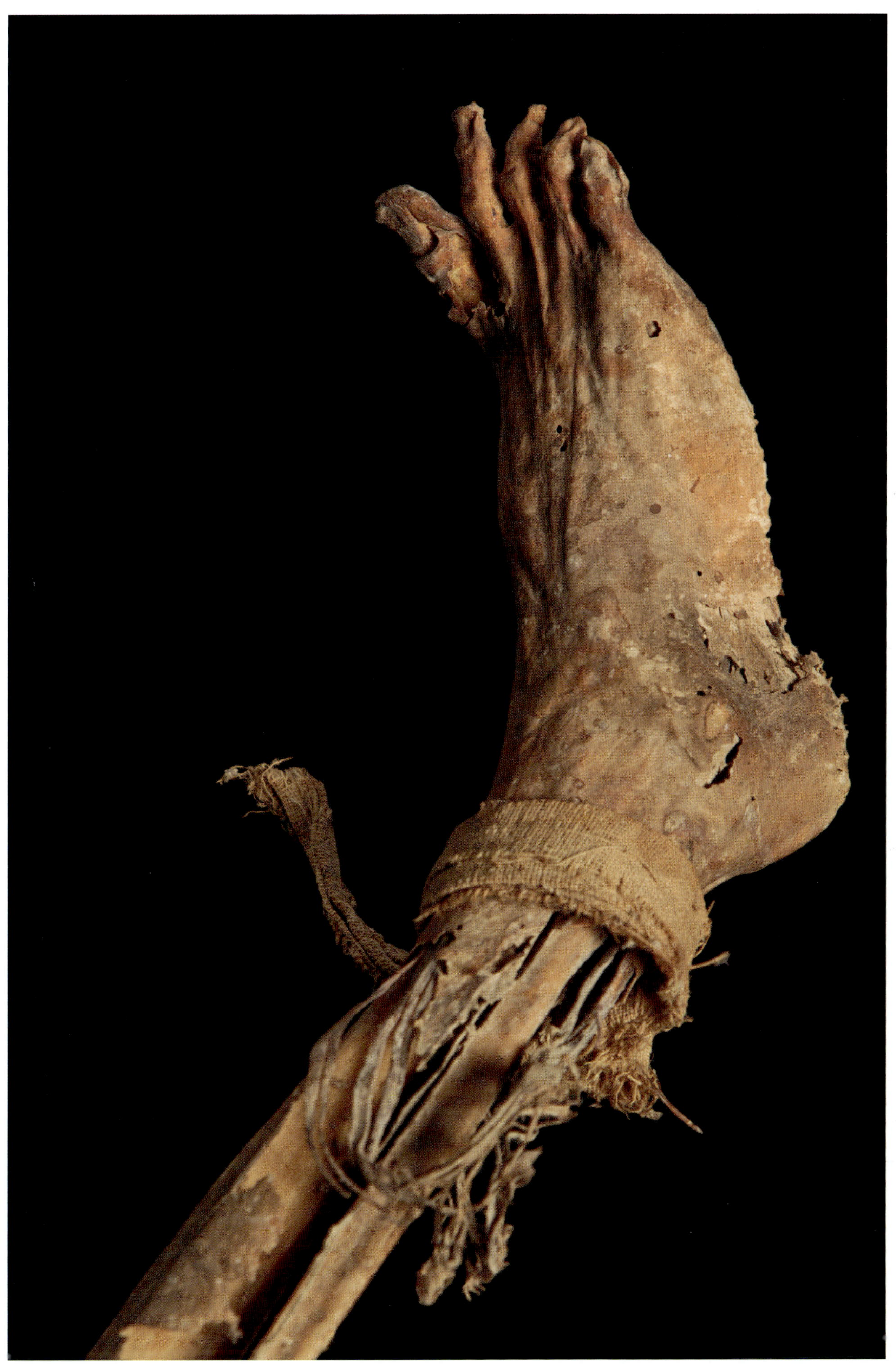

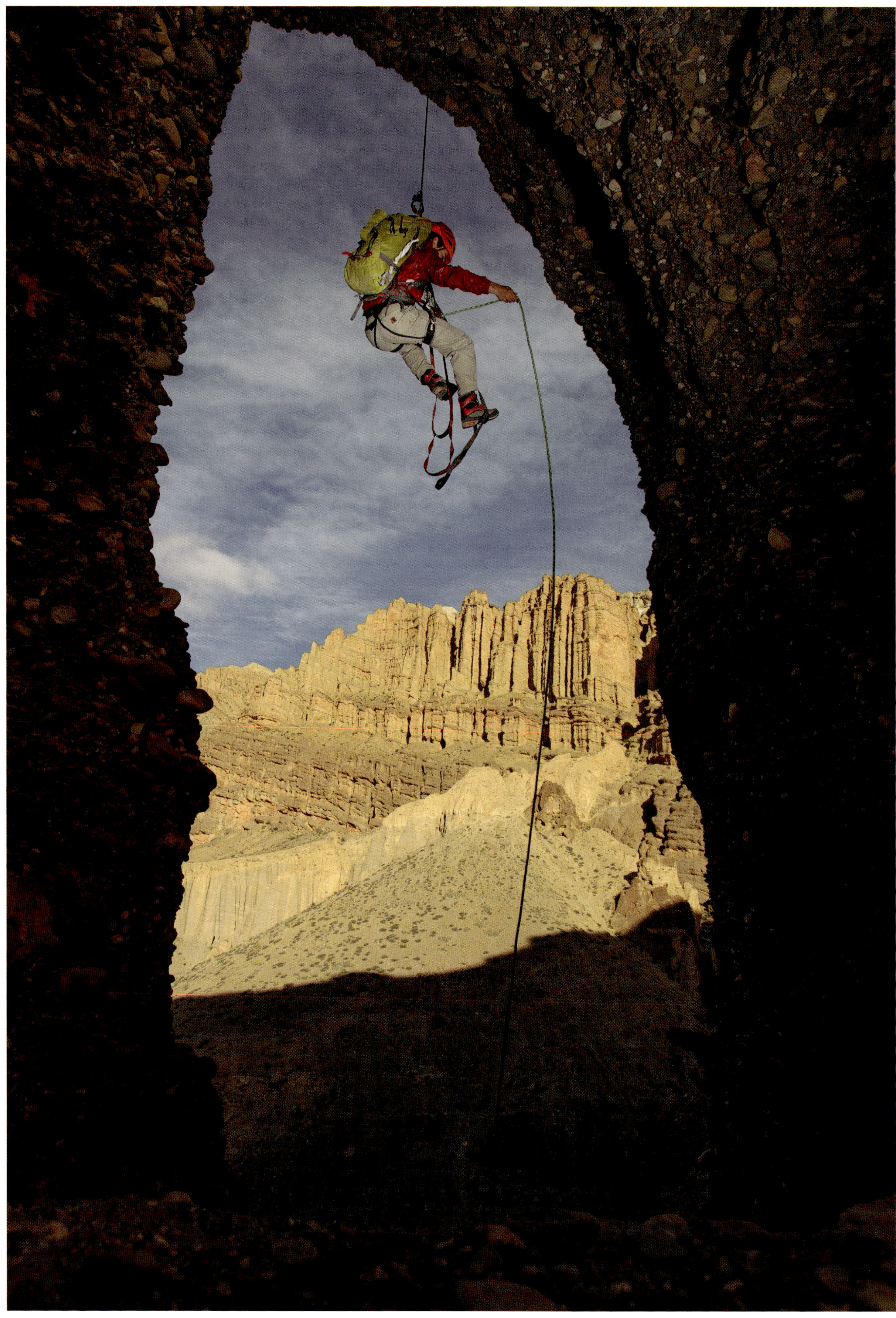

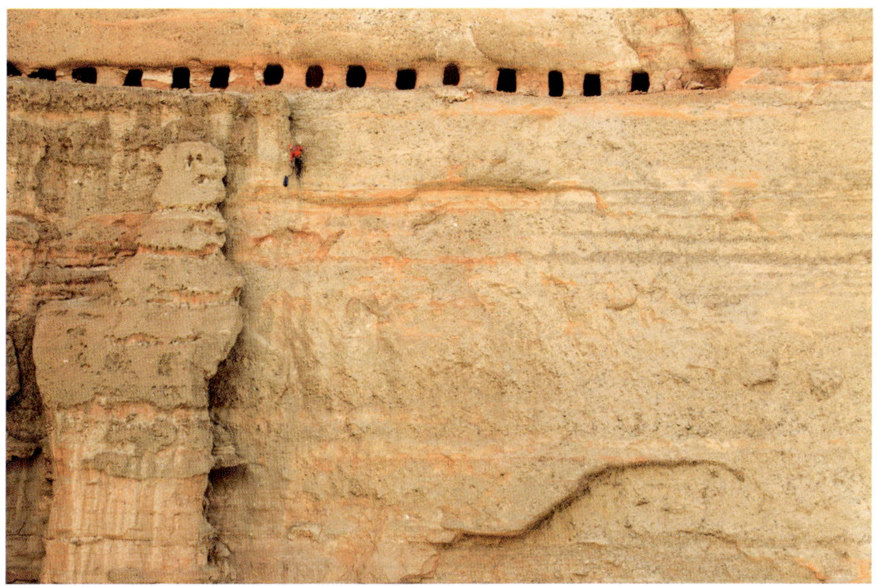

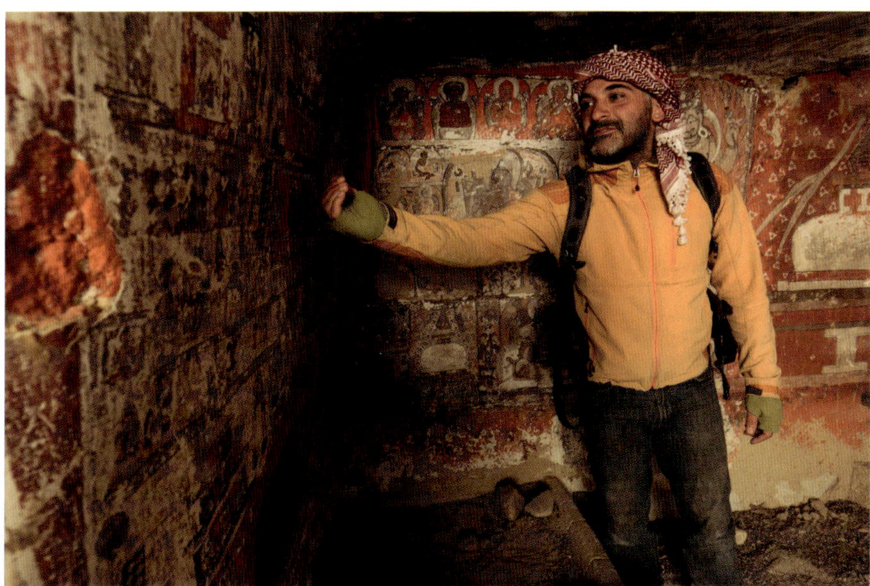

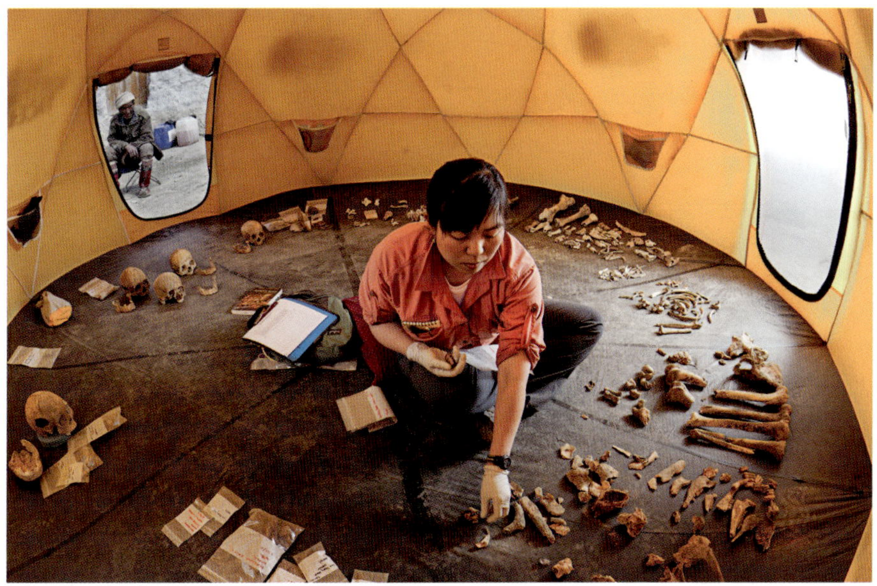

ABOVE: Matt Segal climbs into an ancient library complex near Tsele. **CENTER:** Art historian and restorer Luigi Fieni explains the frescos found in a cave meditation hermitage. **BELOW:** Bioarcheologist Dr. Jacqueline Eng catalogs findings from a burial crypt in Samdzong. **OPPOSITE:** Ted Hesser ascends a fixed rope outside the opening of a cave complex near Chuksang. **FOLLOWING:** Star trails over Tsarang.

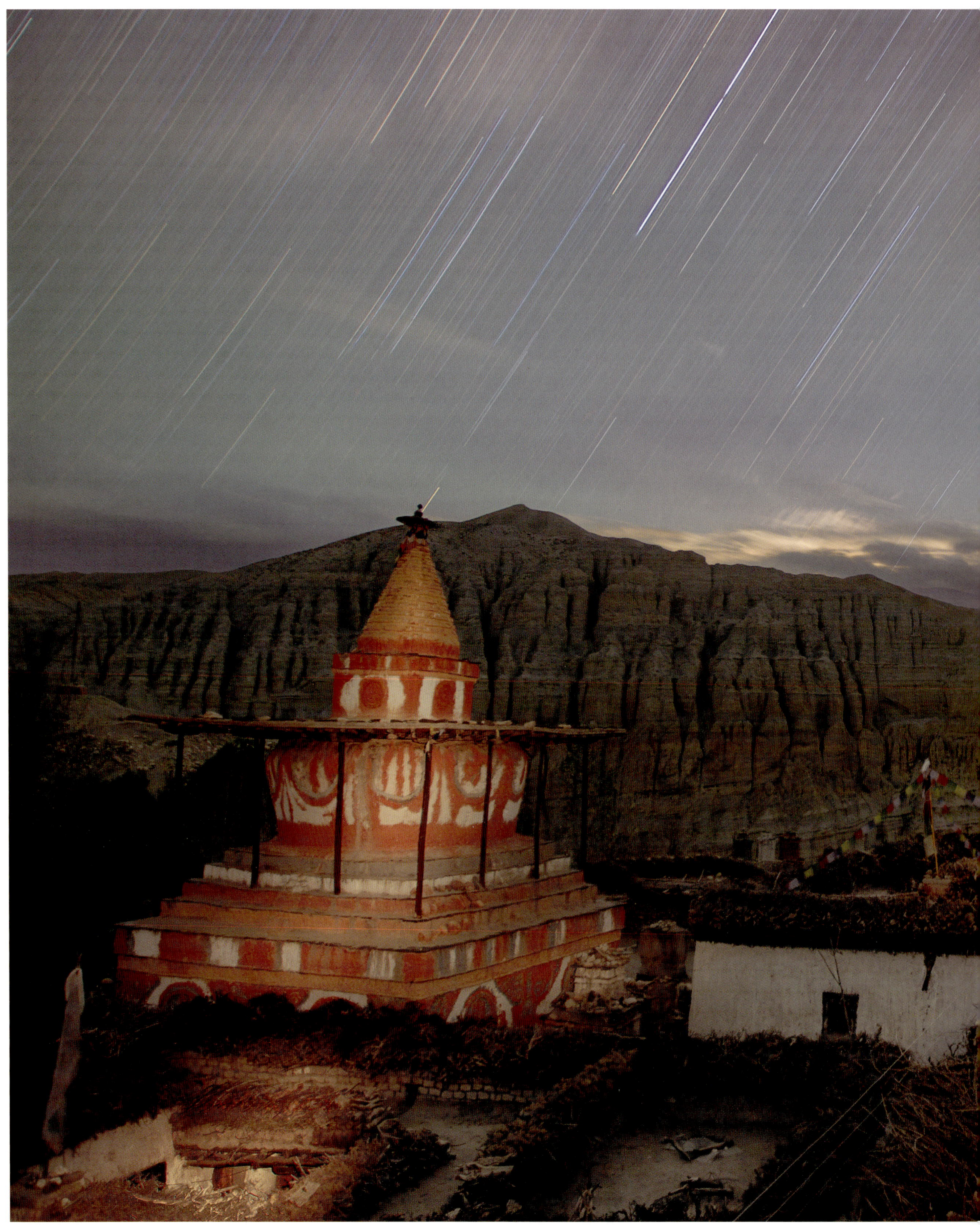

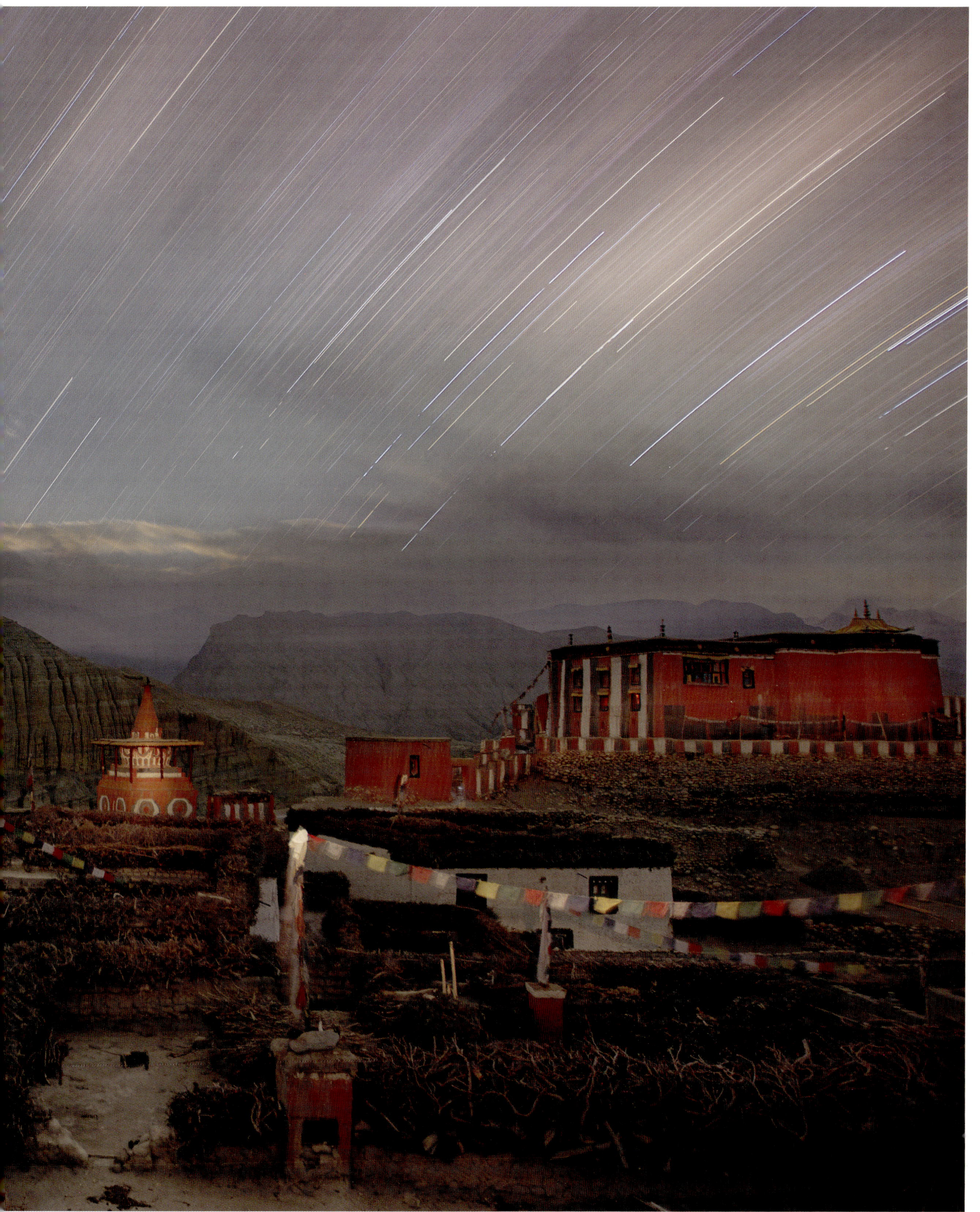

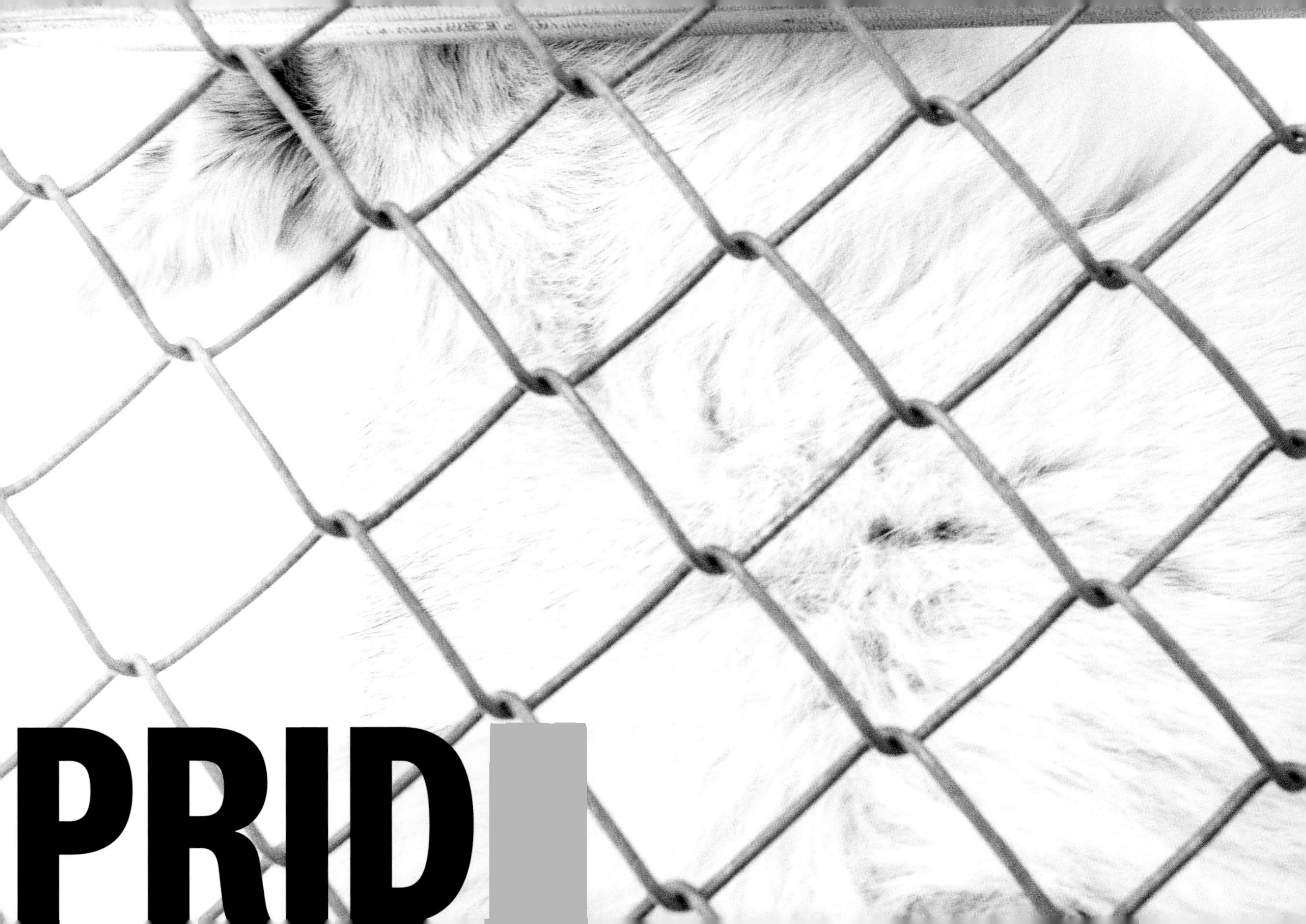
PRID

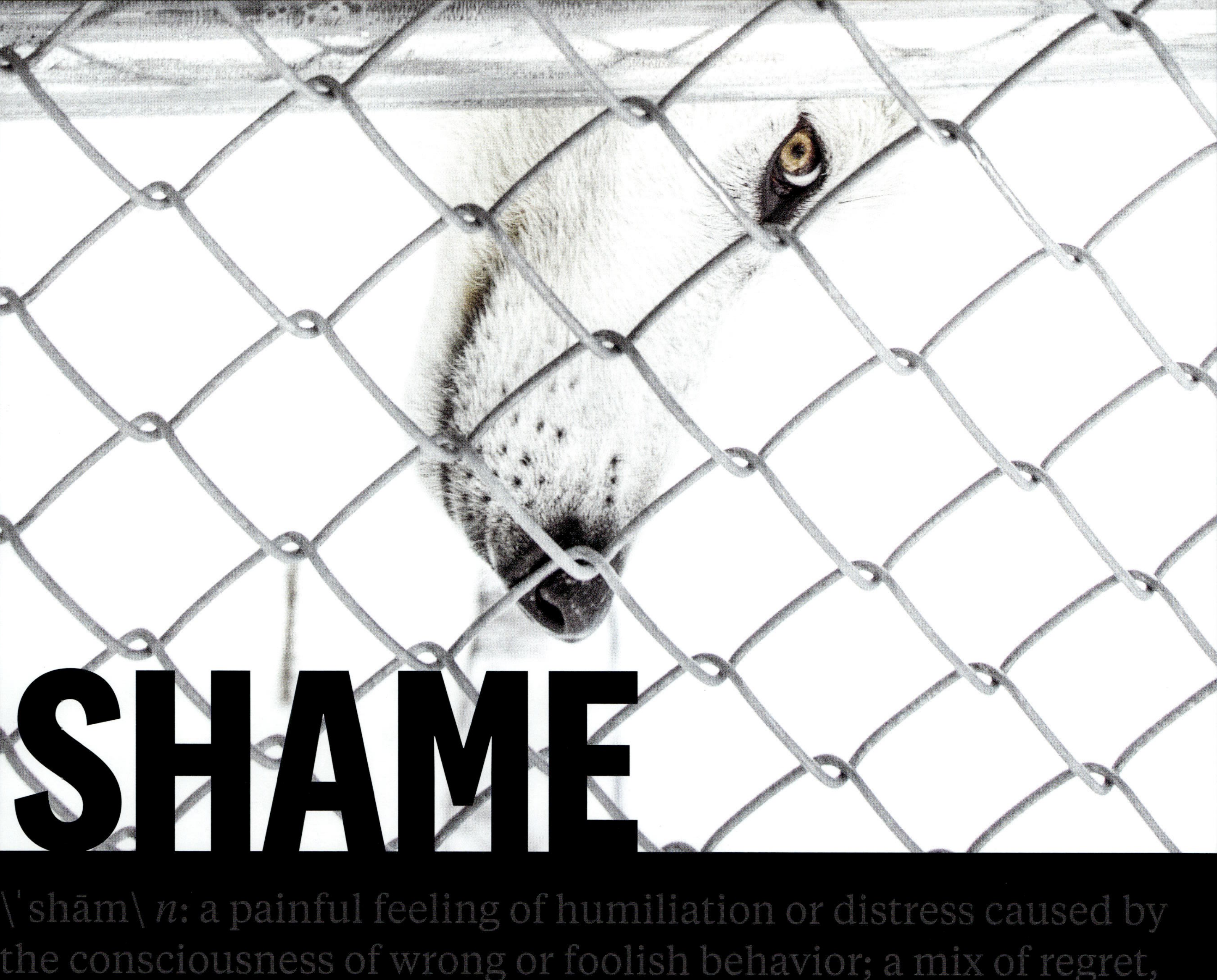

SHAME
\ˈshām\ n: a painful feeling of humiliation or distress caused by the consciousness of wrong or foolish behavior; a mix of regret, self-hate, and dishonor

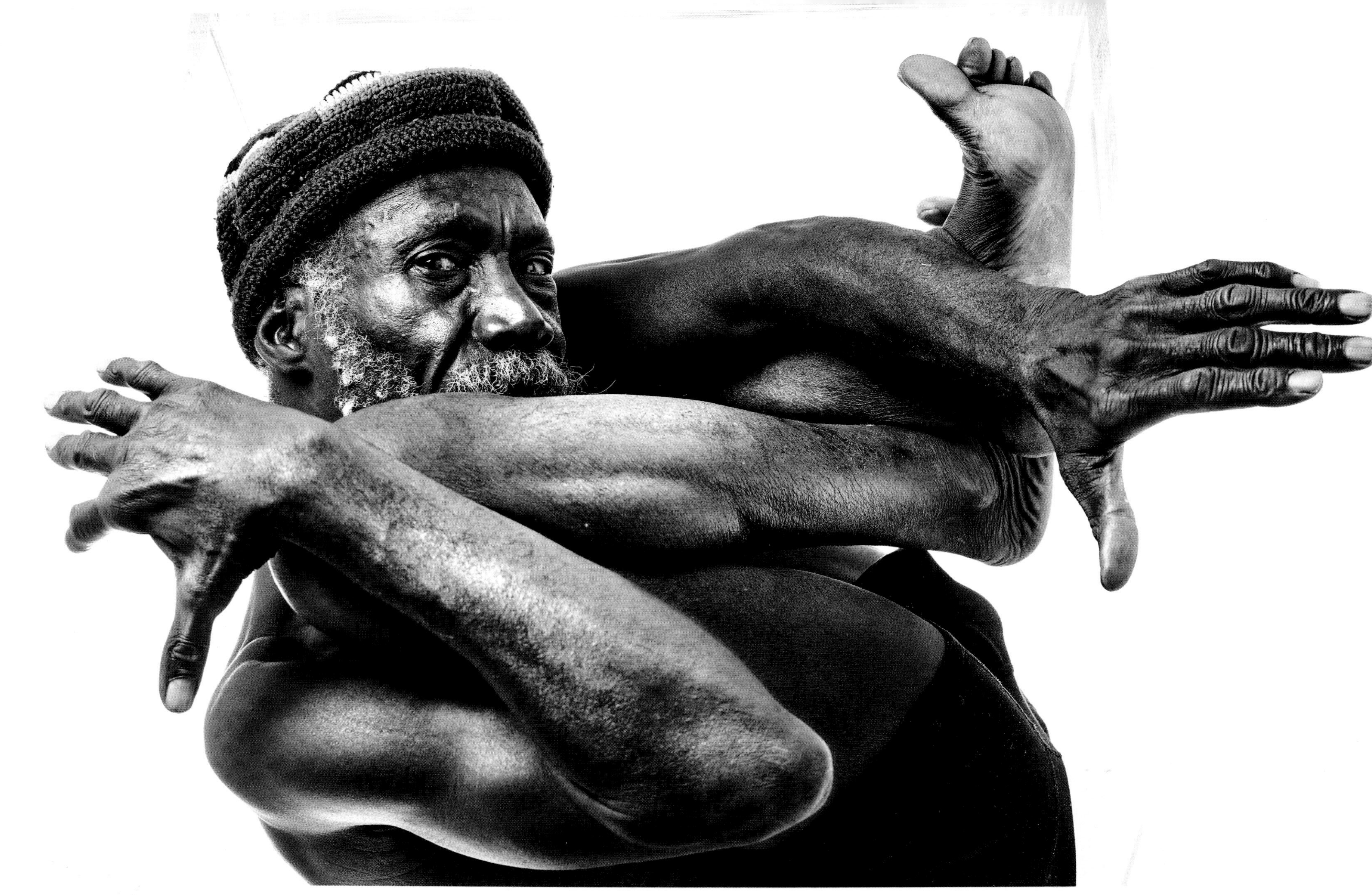

THE ABSENCE OF WORDS

A Collection of Faces

His words are muffled against the ground as he tells me about his children and how busking on Pearl Street in Boulder, Colorado, provides barely enough income to support them. After ten minutes, he goes silent, stands, and walks to his clear box.

As much as adventure photography is my bread and butter, portraiture has always been my first love. From the moment I took the portrait of Knud in the jazz club in Salzburg, I've understood that a face is capable of telling the deepest stories.

As highly social animals, we rely heavily on reading people's faces. Eye contact is crucial for communication and facial expressions help us decipher everything from pride to shame, fear and hope, and everything else. The breadth of human emotion can be revealed on a face. In the absence of words and names, portraiture is perhaps the most immediate and intimate gateway into the lives of others.

I've learned that the power of a portrait can also reside in the way I choose to frame the subject. The subtlest differences in where the eyes are looking, whether they are open or closed, the tilt of the head, the shadows the cheekbones cast—it's all a dance toward the most honest moment. Sometimes it's a stoic facade designed to guard the heart and mind from judgment. Sometimes the person in front of the camera hates the moment I choose. And that's okay . . . I hate almost every portrait that's ever been taken of me.

Ibashi-I is folded in half, pushing himself backward into the box. His skin is dark against the bright white background, and I hear it squeak against the plexiglass. He is a Black man surrounded by whiteness, folded into a clear box.

Portraits can be a canvas for commentary. If a subject is holding a gun, that tells you something. If another appears to be screaming, we want to know why and what about. Sometimes commentary is blatant, and sometimes it can be as subtle as a soft blur of motion, hinting at a sort of energy that a sharp frame can't communicate. In the case of Ibashi-I, I'm trying to say something about race in America. But the image isn't right when he's entirely encased.

I wait.

He waits.

I wait longer as he gets impatient, anticipating me to make a photo that never comes.

After five minutes, he mumbles something, extends his arms through the opening, and begins to crawl out, as if breaking the limitations of the box. Finally, I take a picture.

PREVIOUS: A wolf stares through its chain-link enclosure in a rescue sanctuary near Yellowstone National Park.

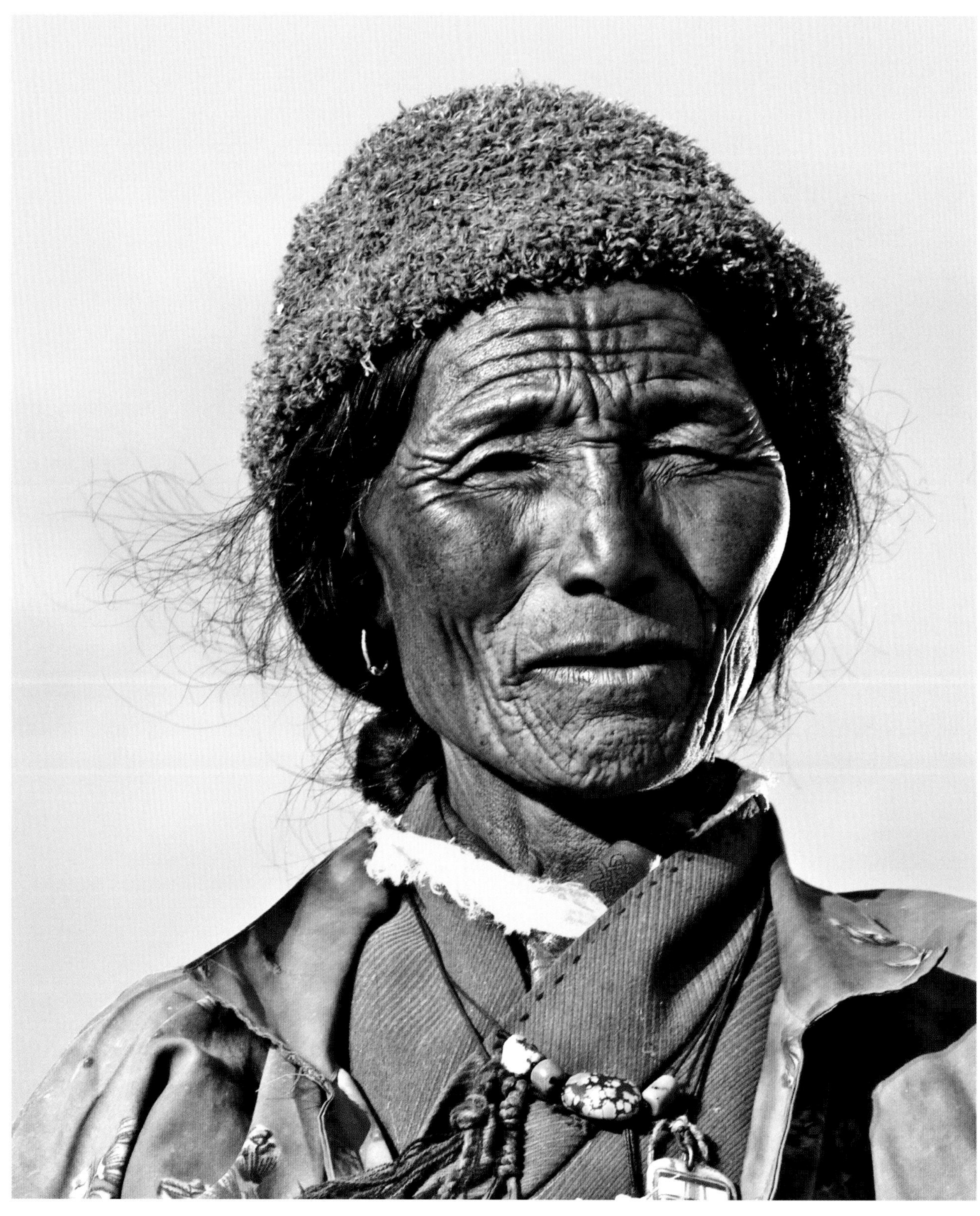

Mother and farmer, Upper Mustang, Nepal. **OPPOSITE:** Artist, poet, and hair stylist, USA.

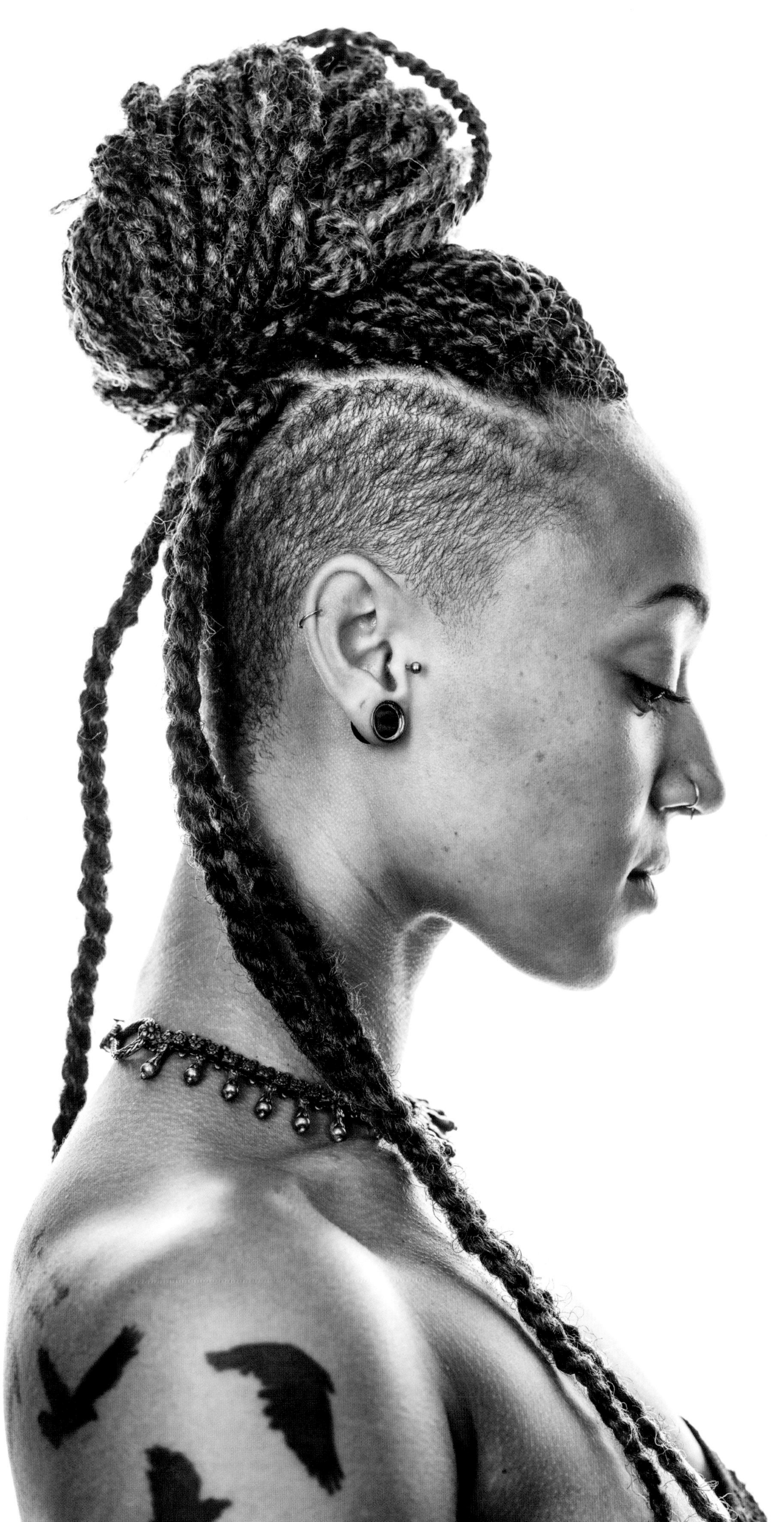

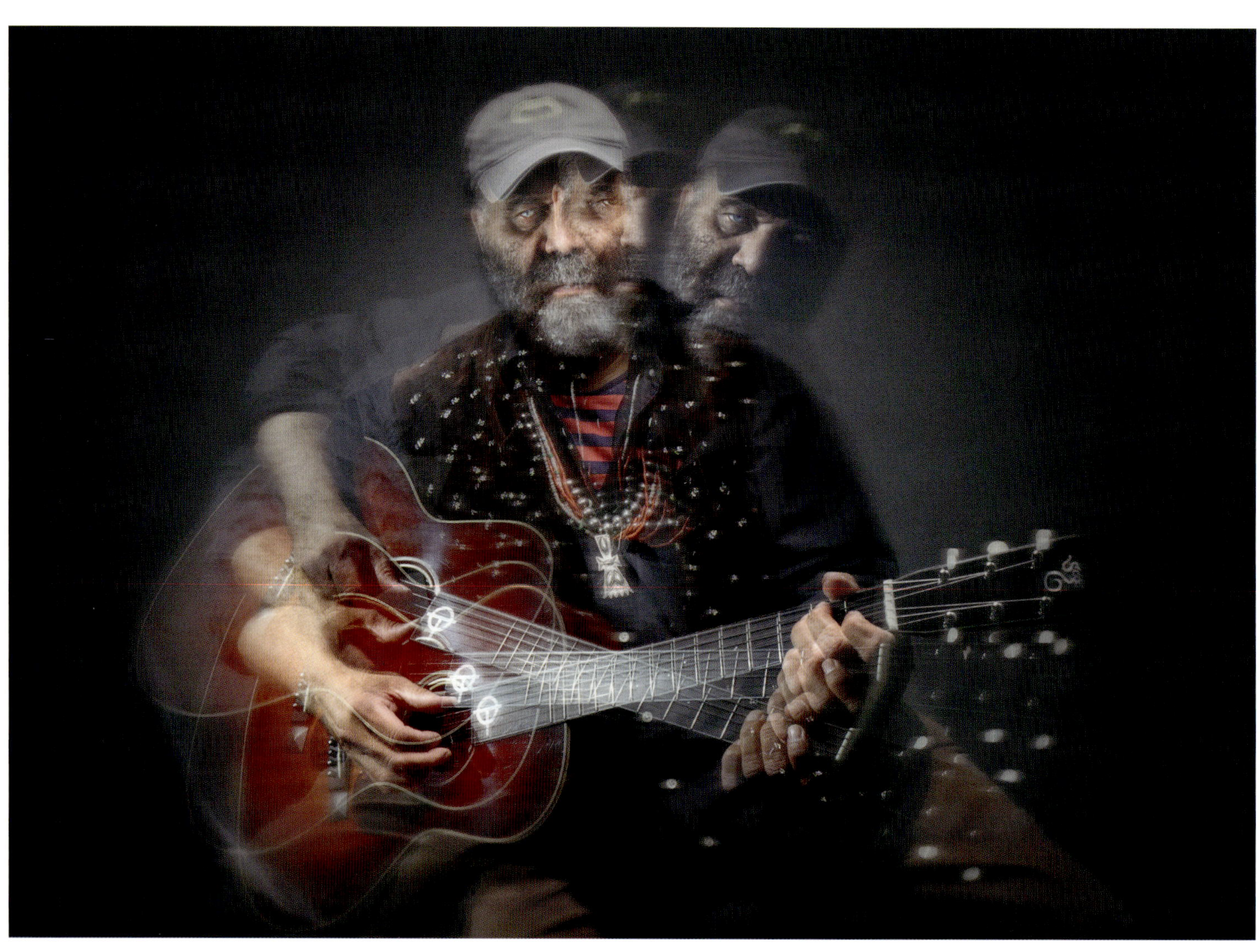

Musician and husband, USA.

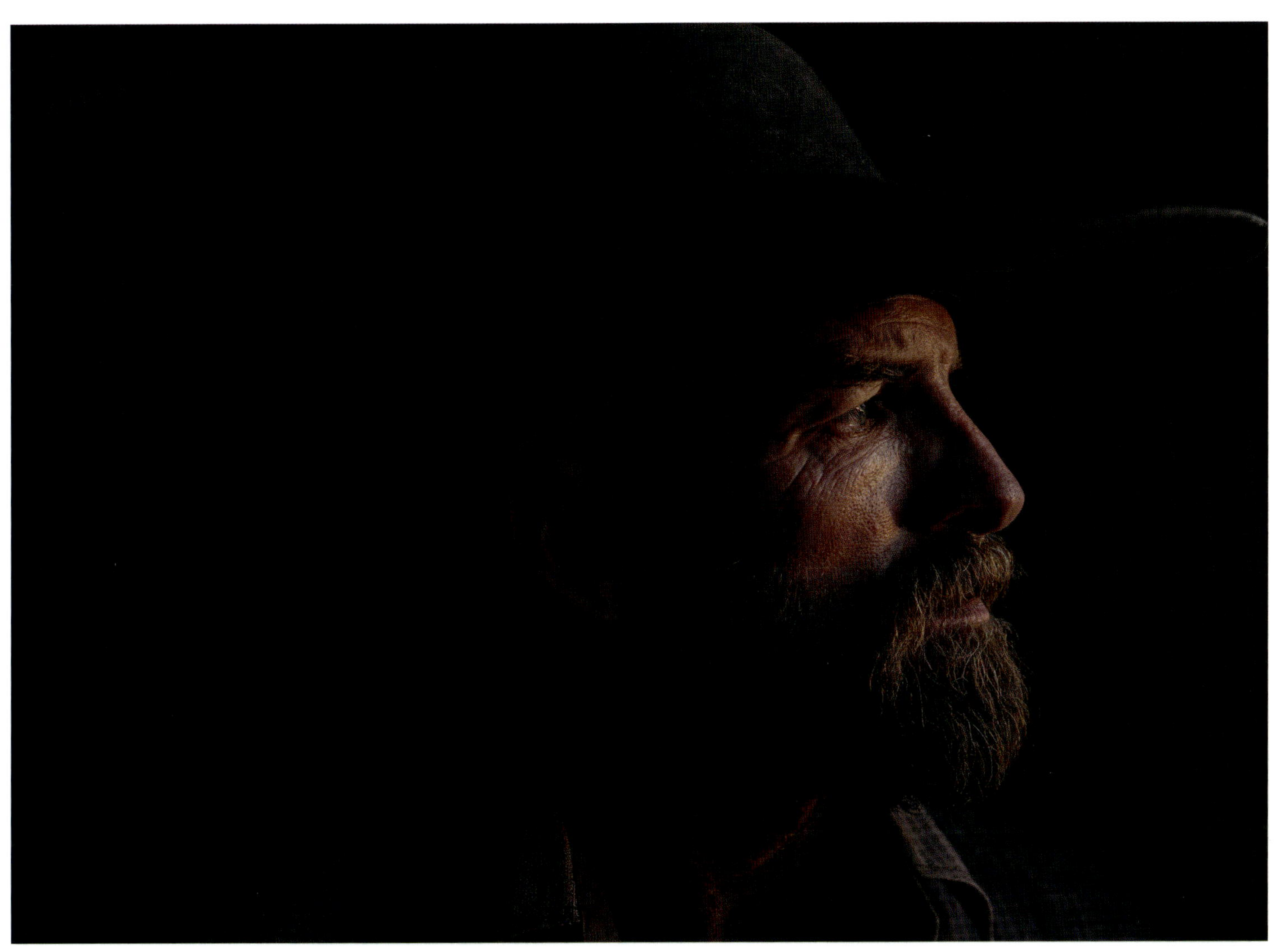

Horse trainer and rancher, USA.

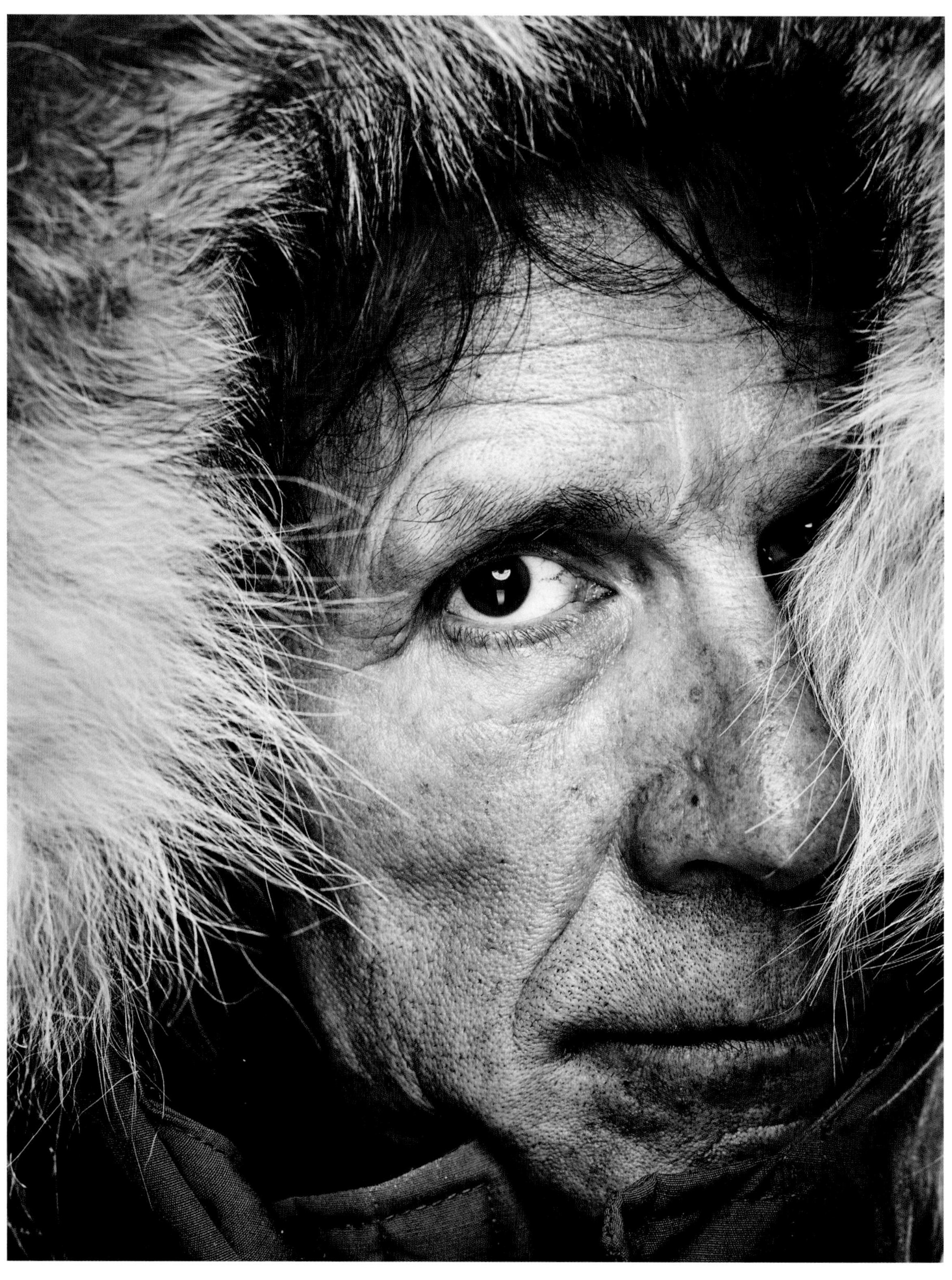

Photographer, filmmaker, and scientist, USA. **OPPOSITE:** Tea patron, Dubai, United Arab Emirates.

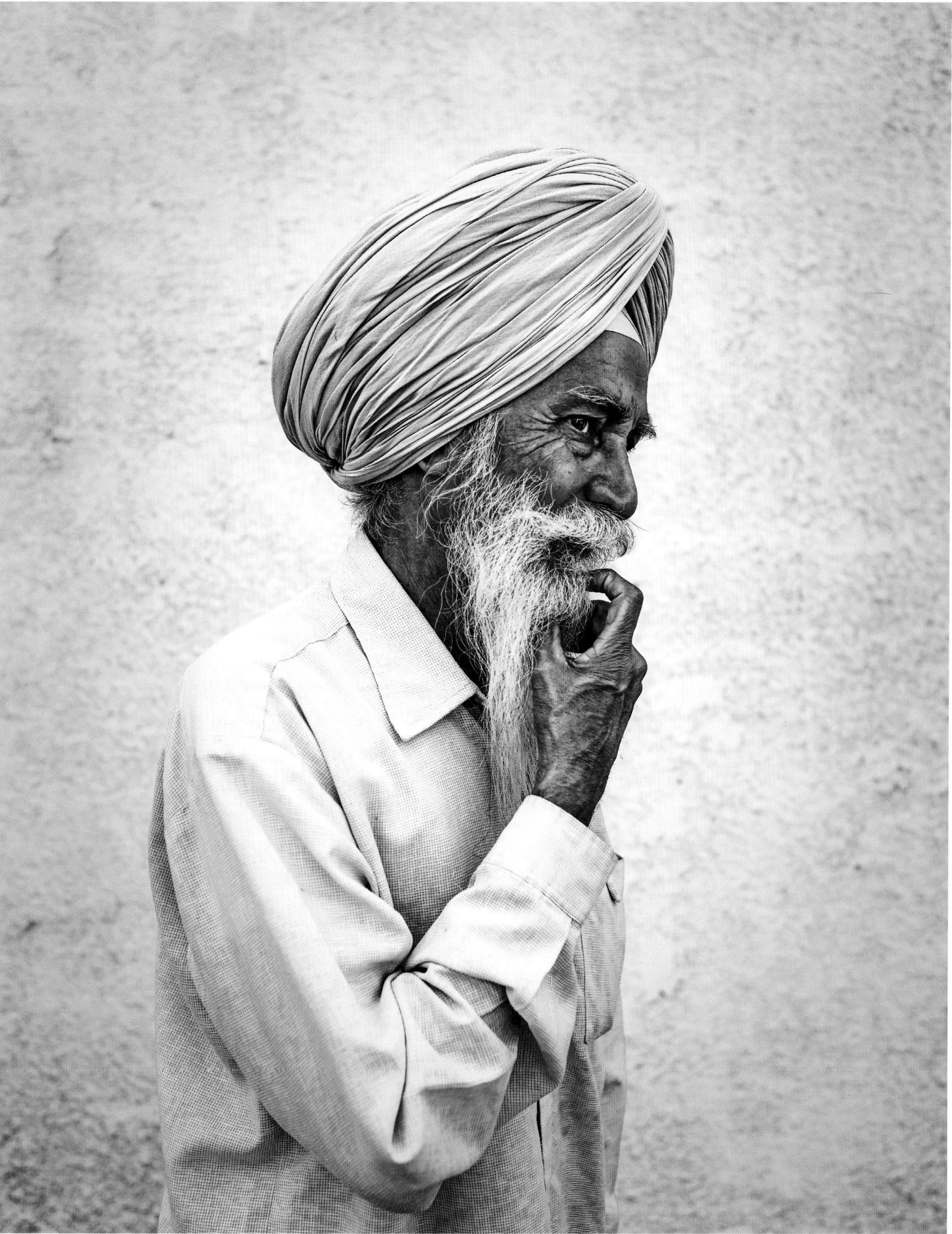

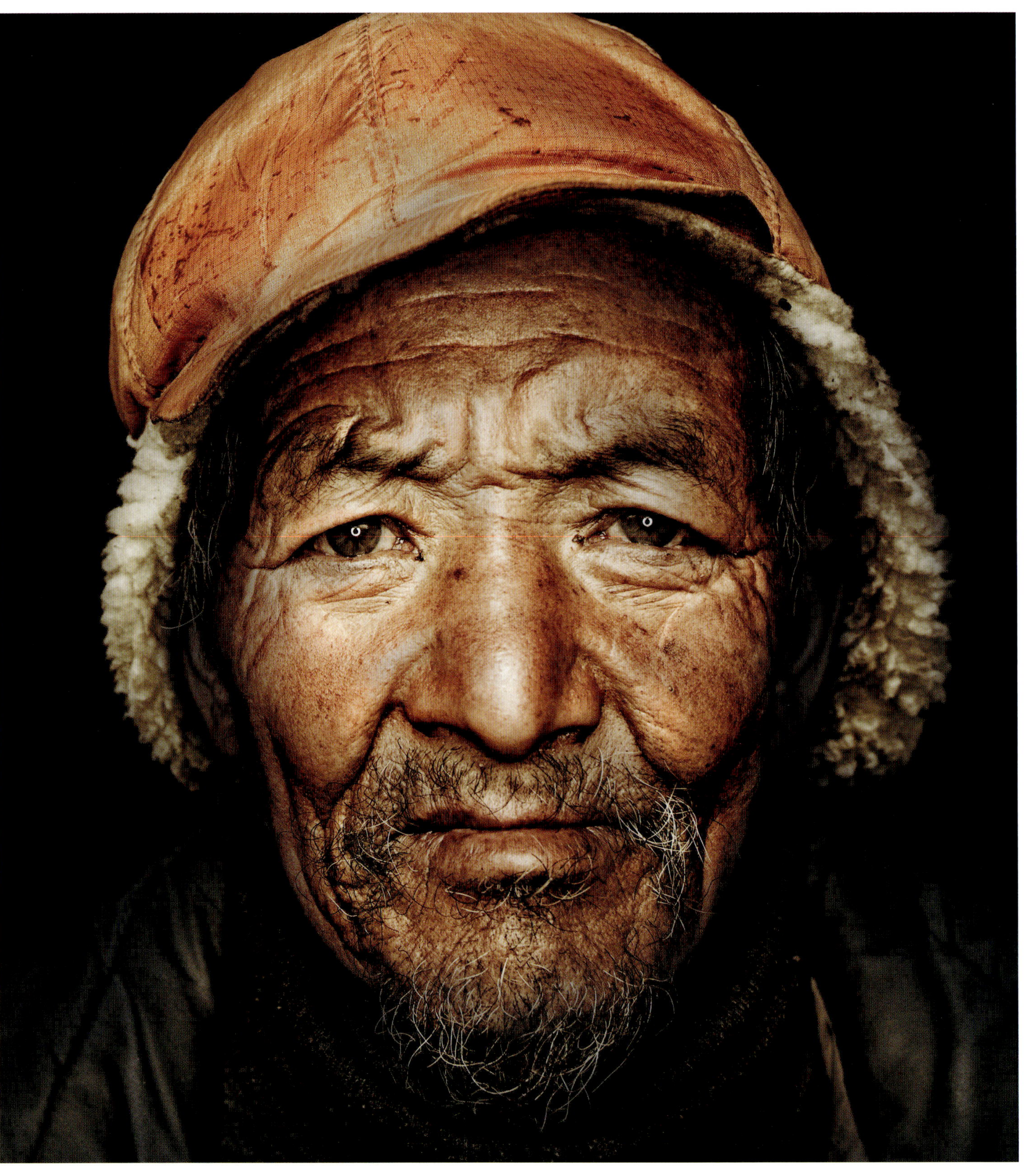

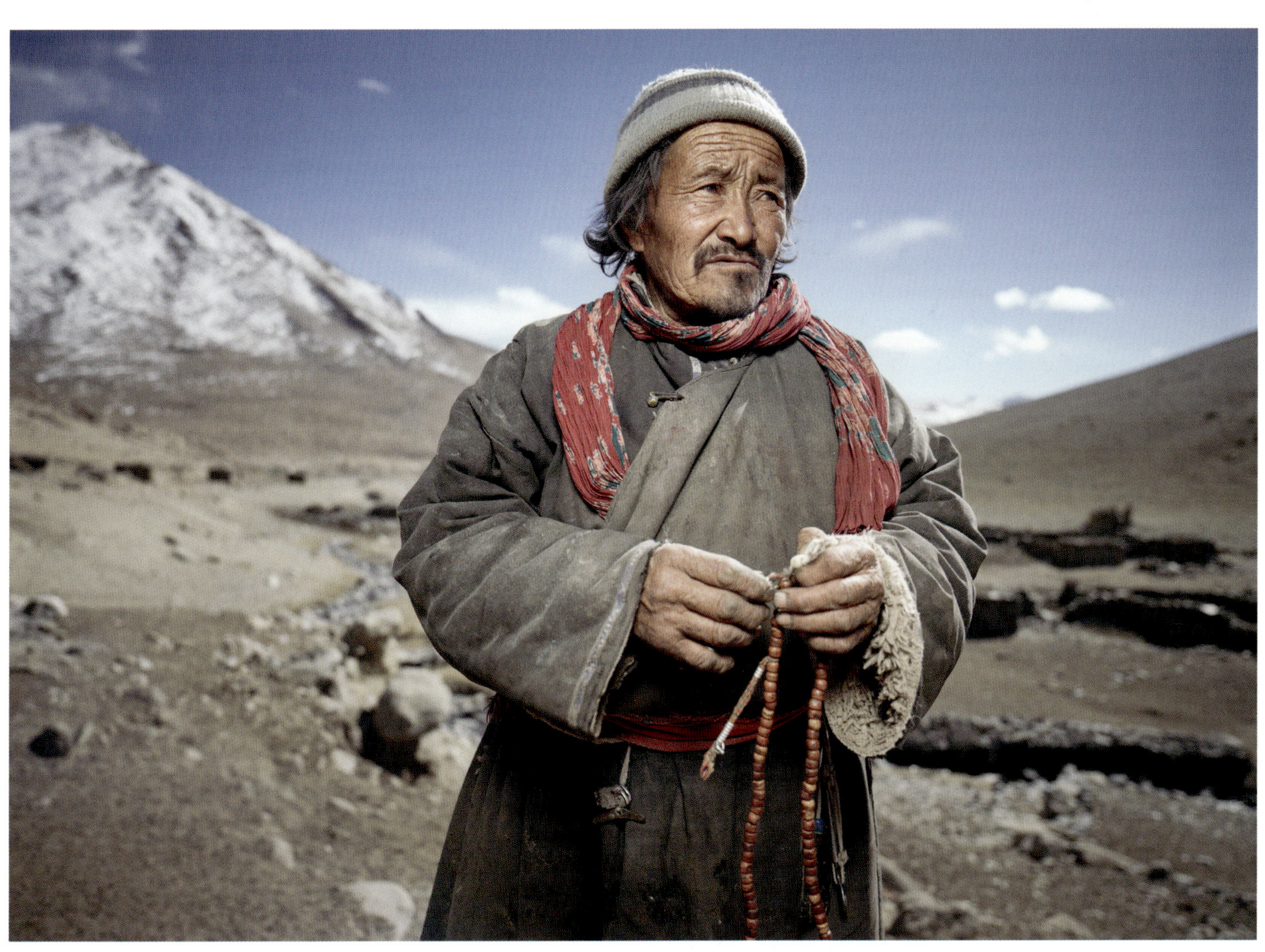

Nomadic goat herder, Ladakh, India. **OPPOSITE:** Hermitage keeper, Khumbu Valley, Nepal.

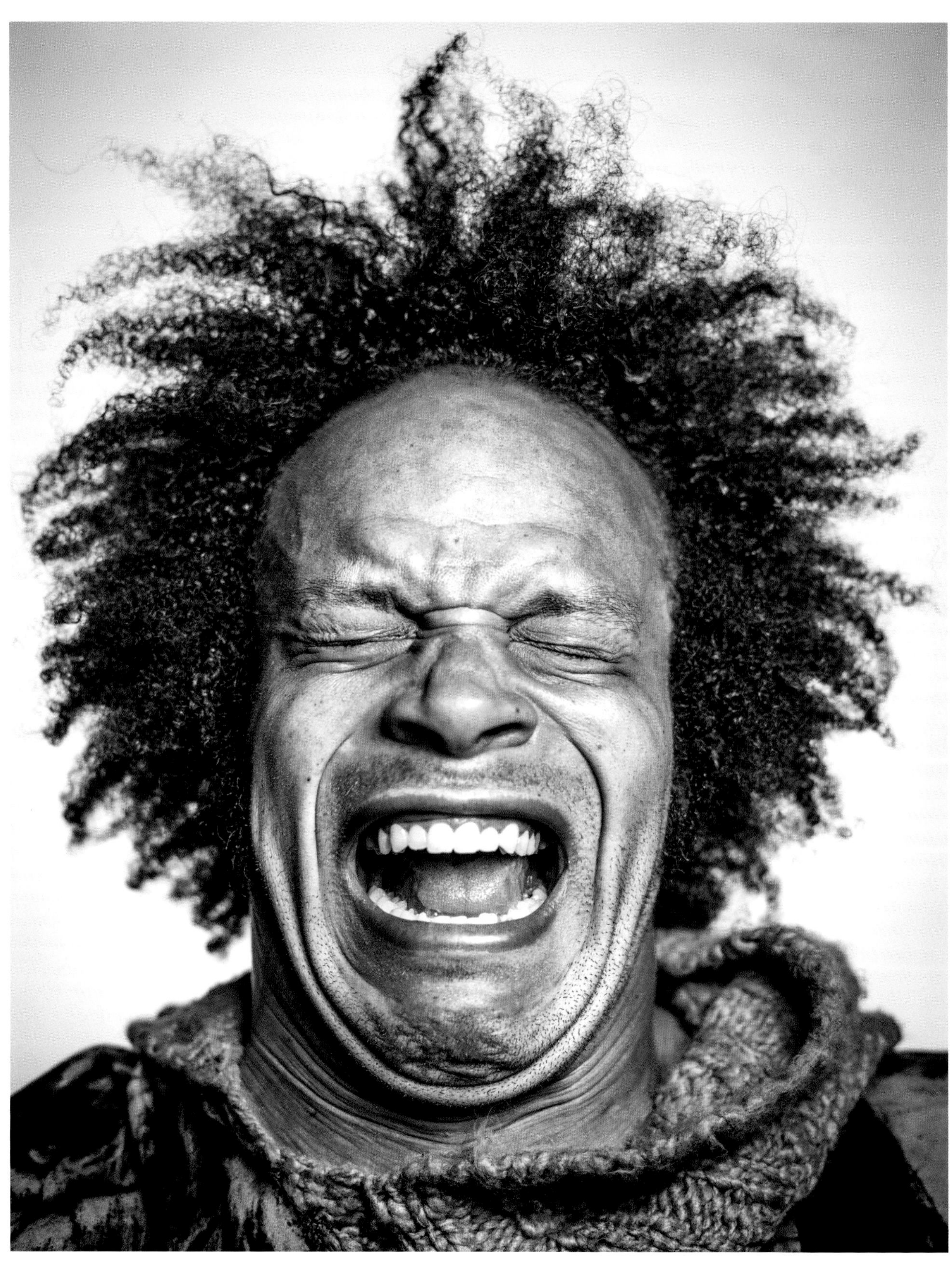

Artist and maker, USA. **OPPOSITE:** Business owner, USA. **FOLLOWING:** Day laborers, Galle, Sri Lanka.

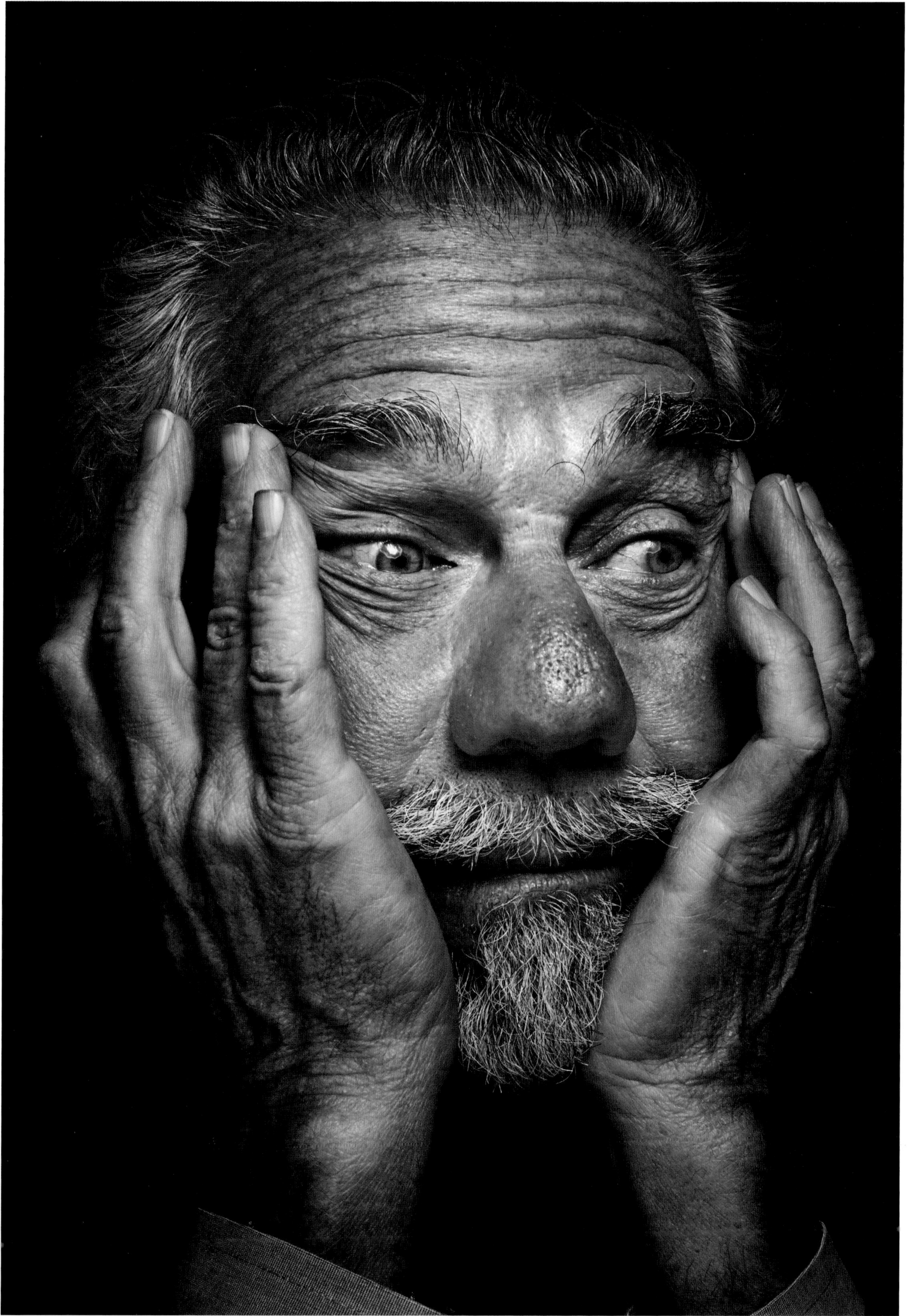

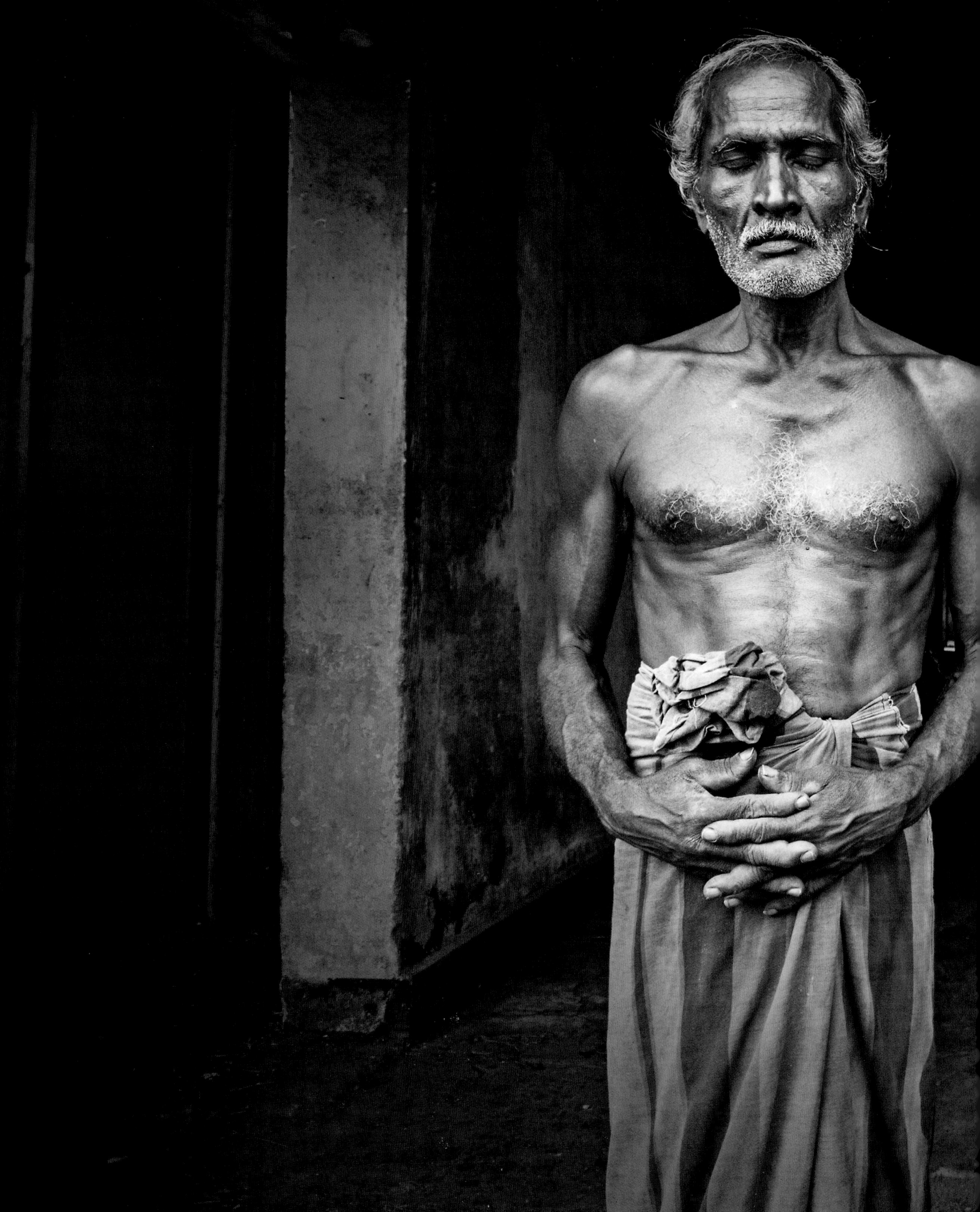

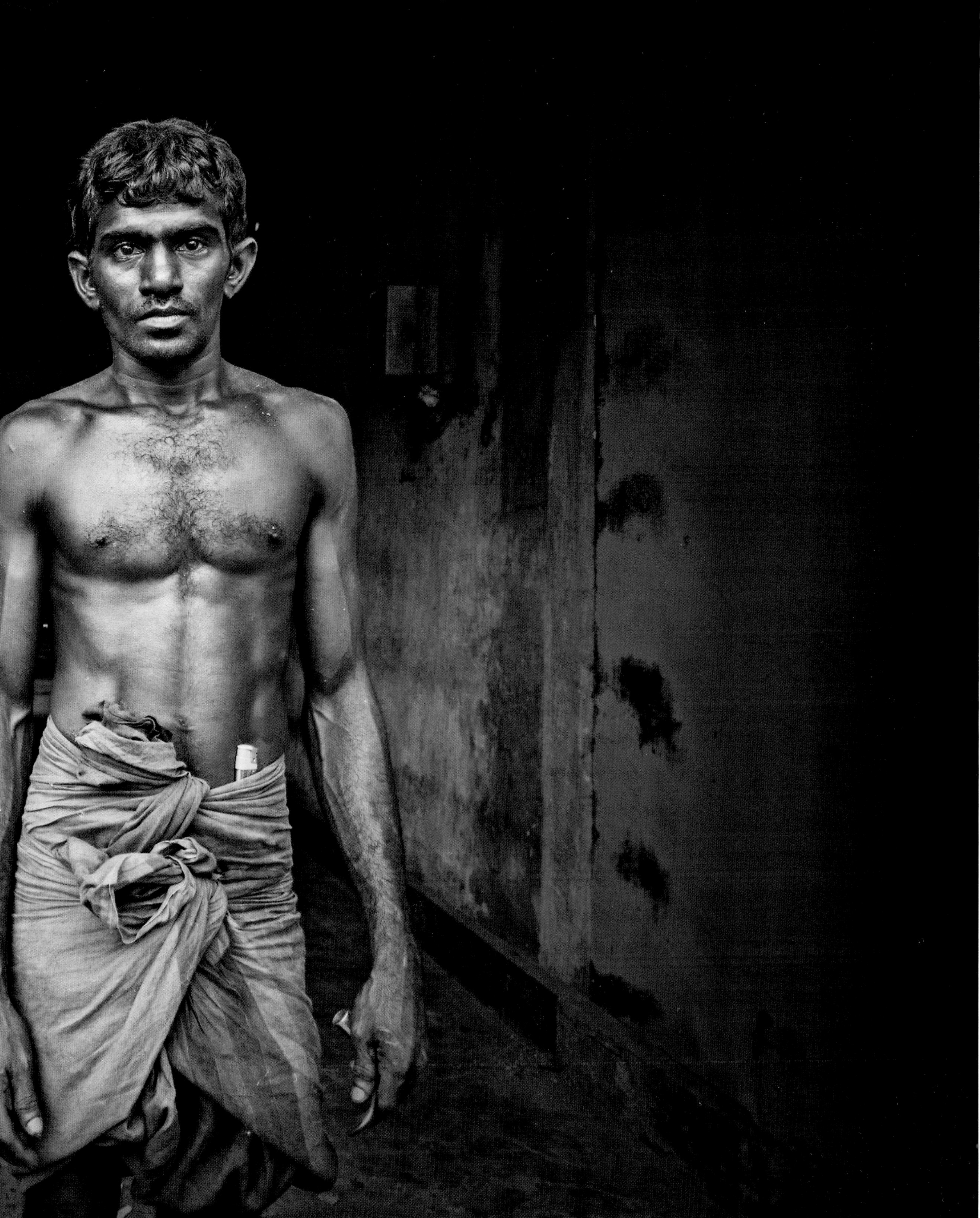

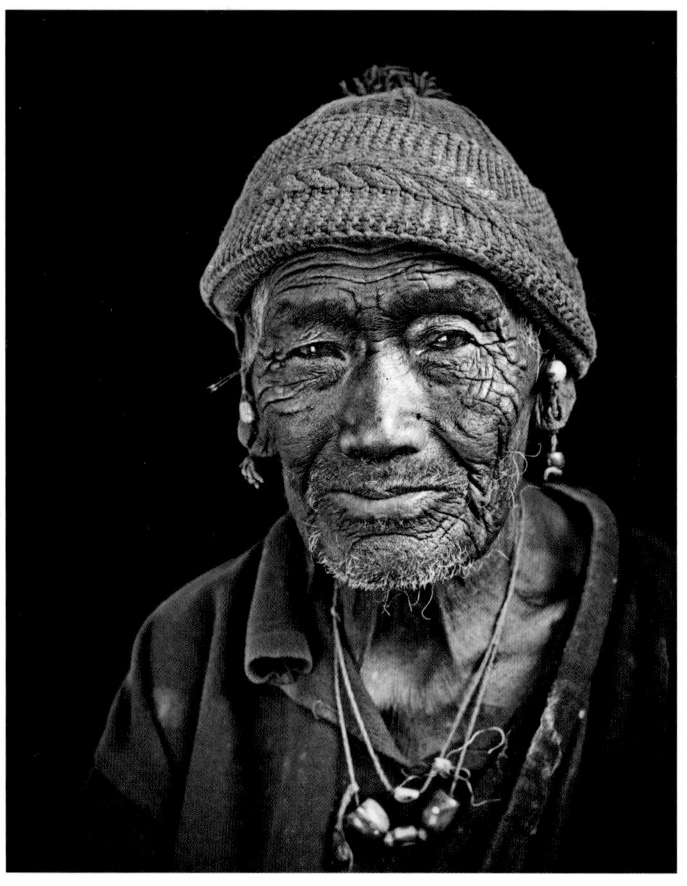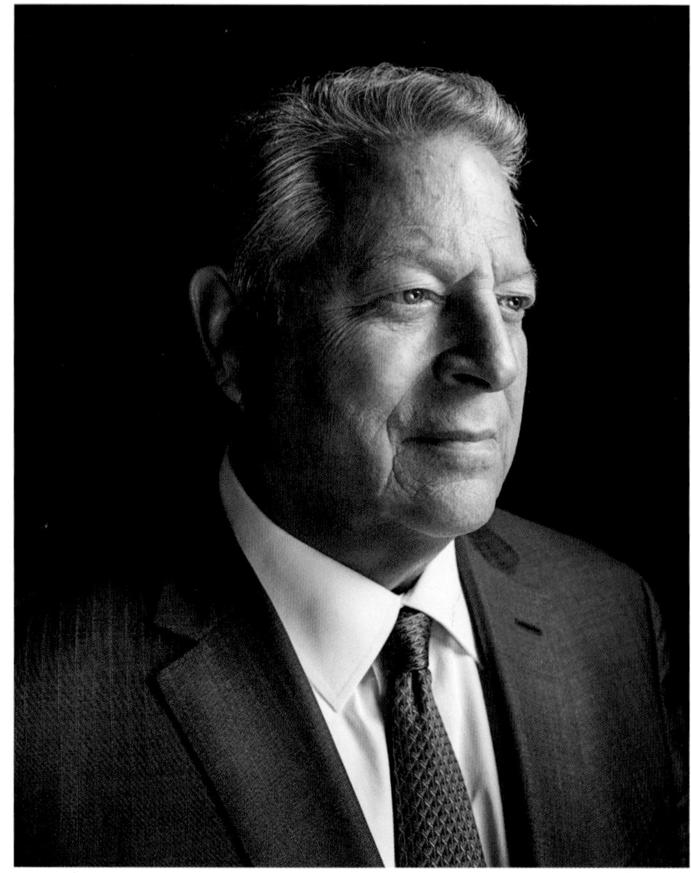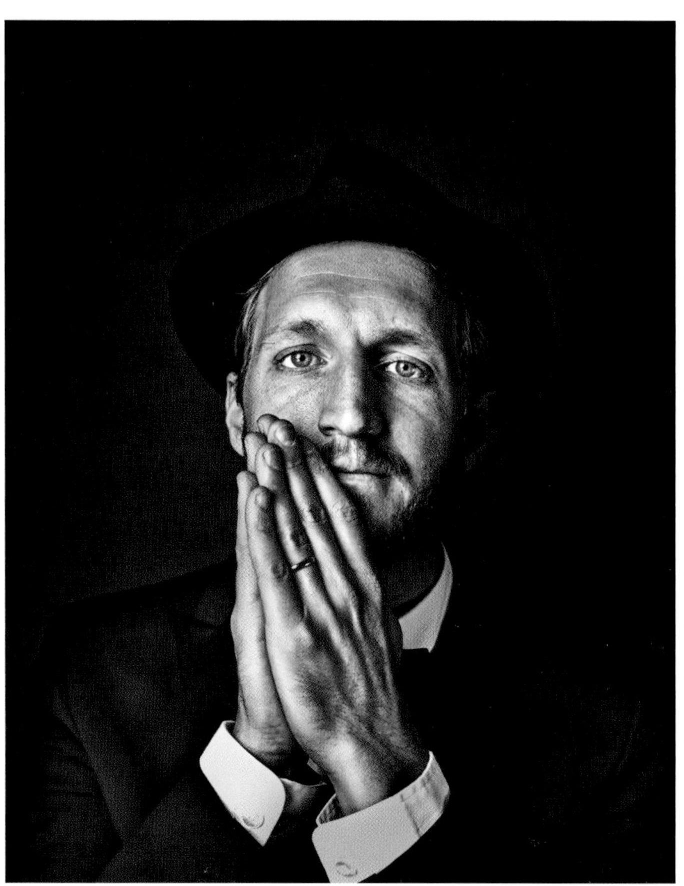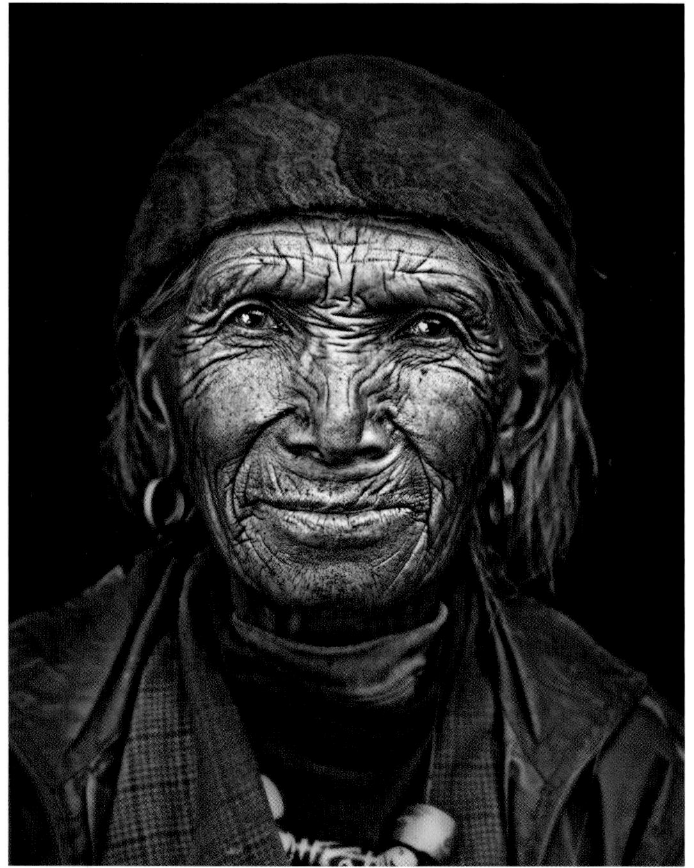

CLOCKWISE FROM TOP LEFT: Goat herder, Upper Mustang, Nepal; Climate activist and former vice president, USA; Farmer, mother, and grandmother, Phortse, Nepal; Musician, father, and husband, Italy.
OPPOSITE: Farmer and herder, Choser, Nepal.

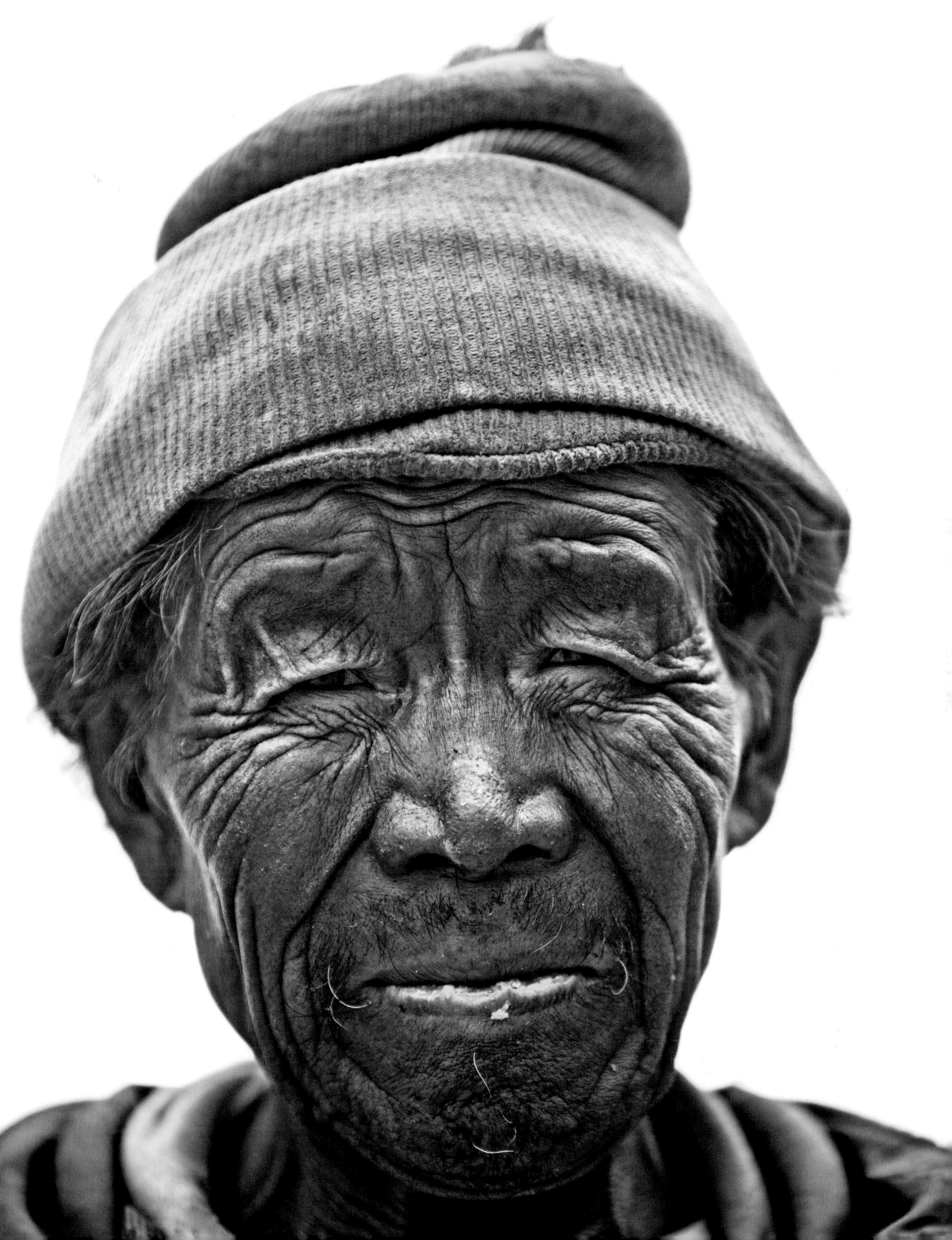

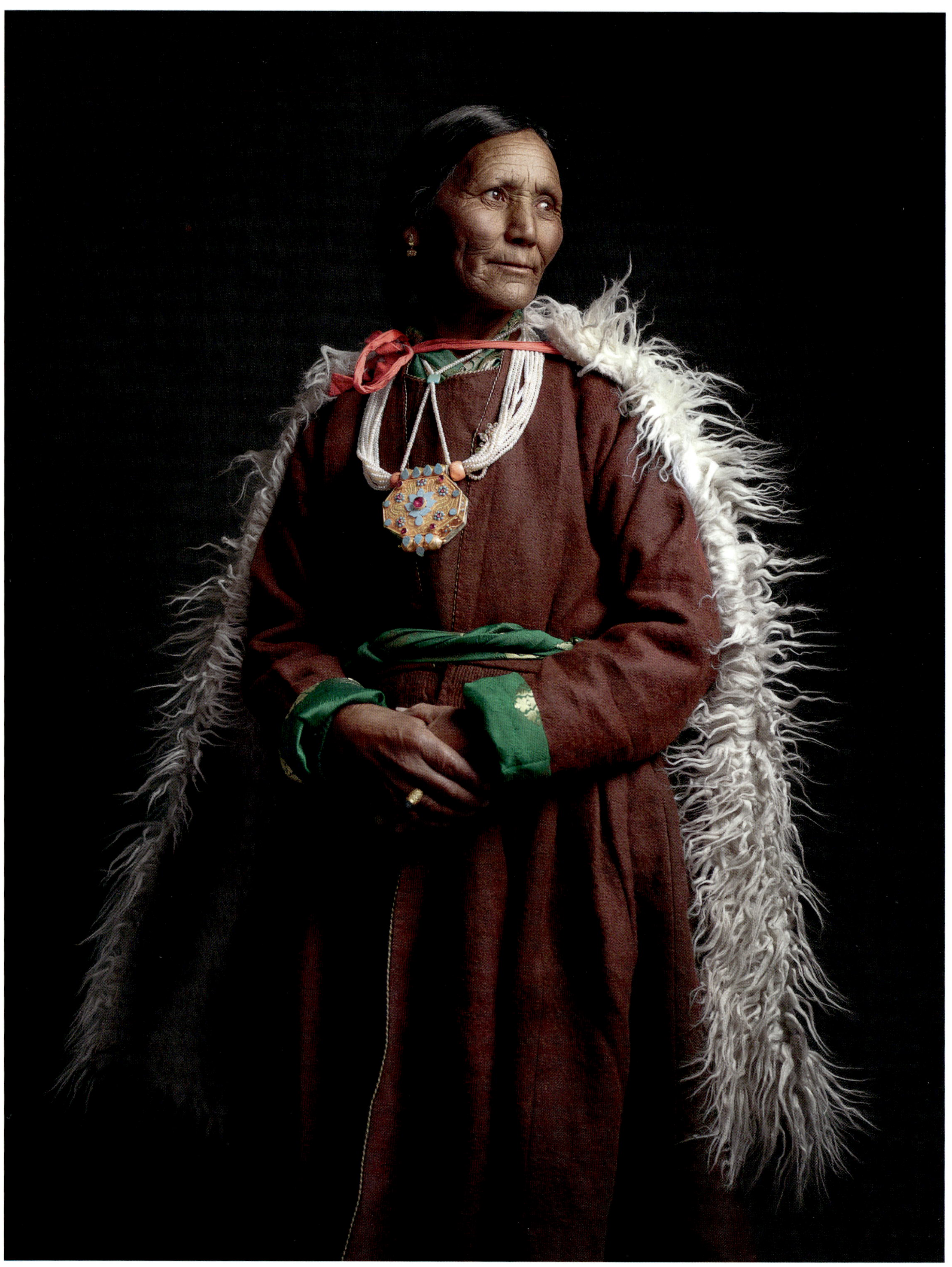

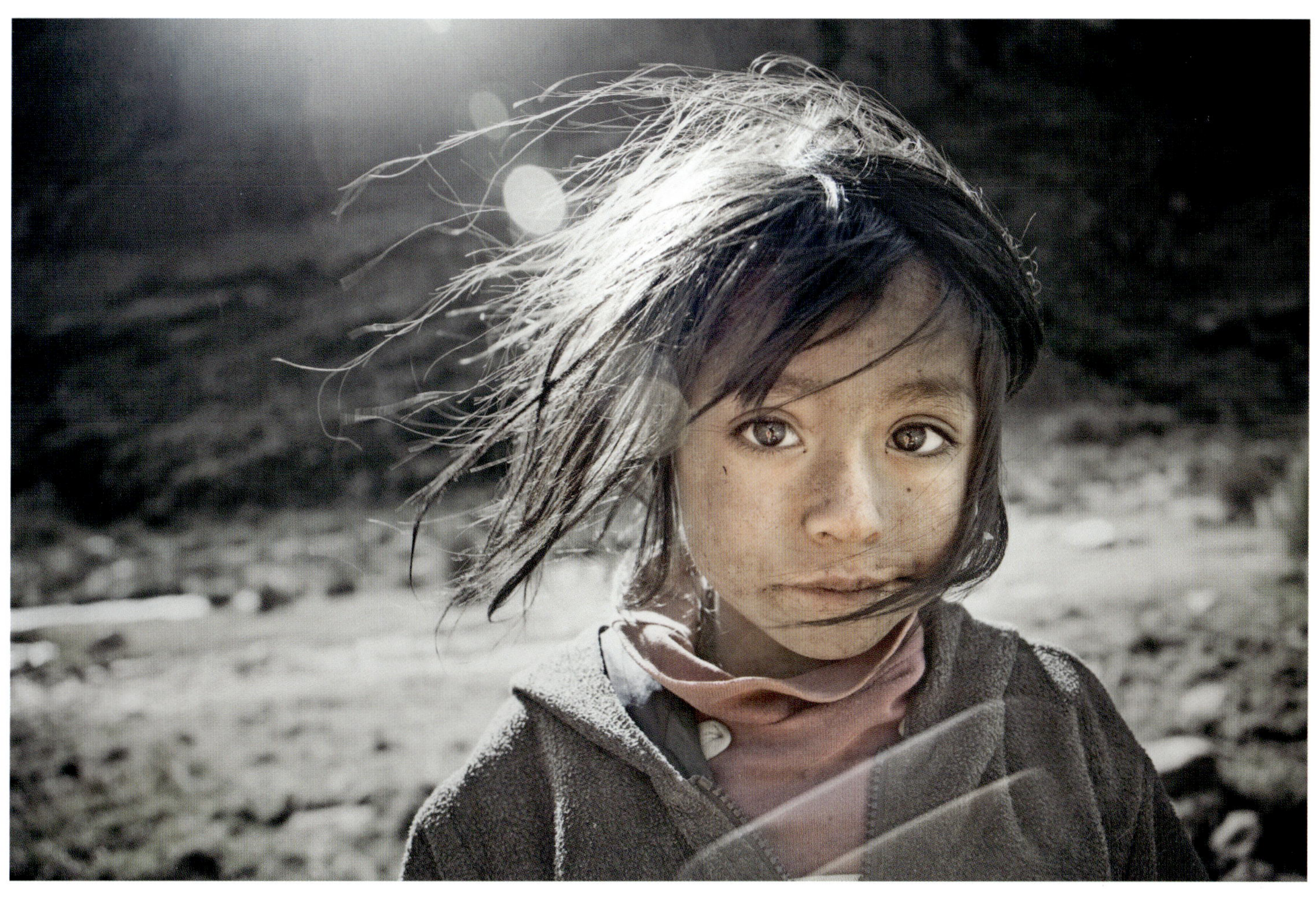

Daughter and sister, Santa Cruz Valley, Peru. **OPPOSITE:** Wedding guest, Leh, India.

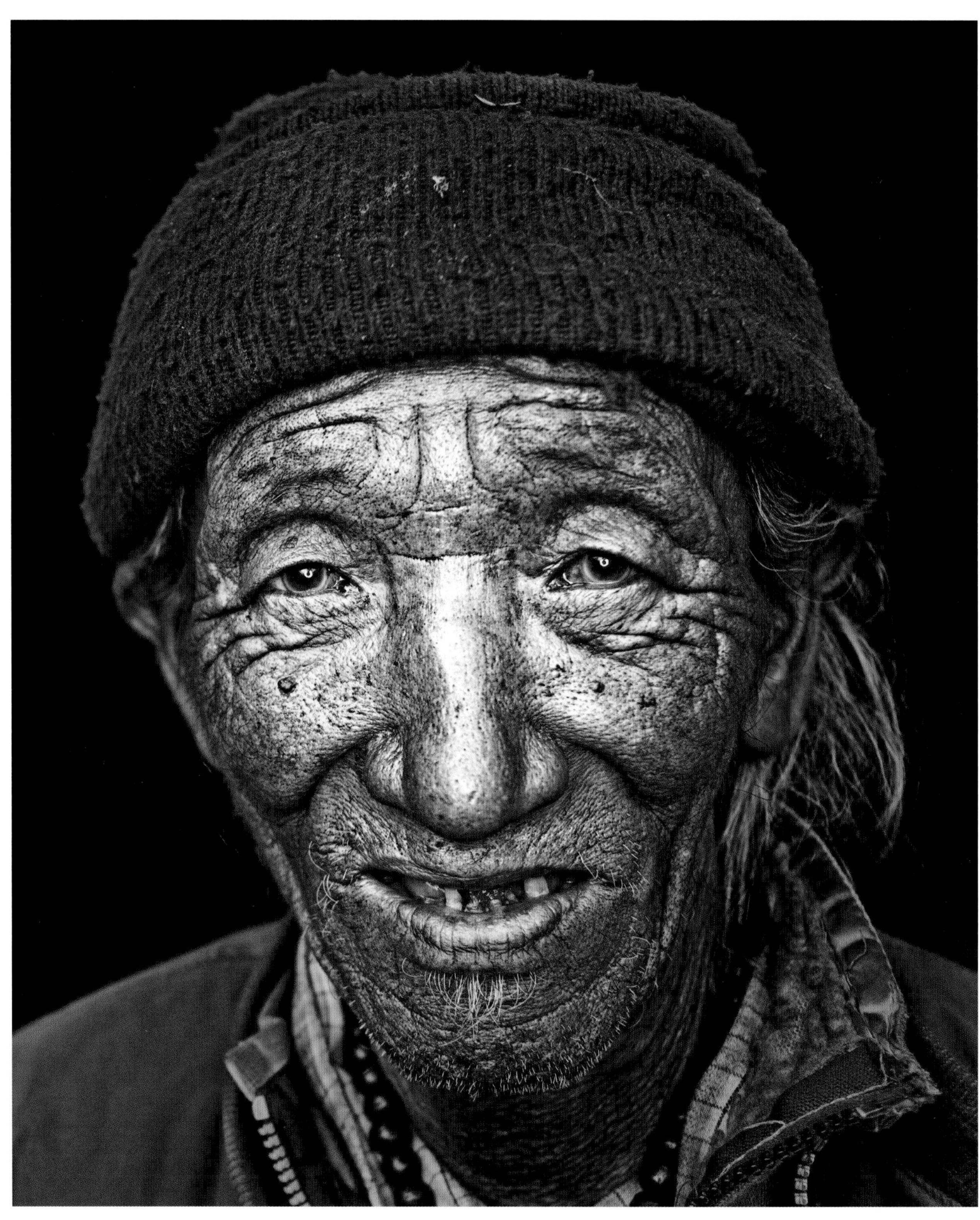

Farmer, Khumbu Valley, Nepal. **OPPOSITE:** Sculptor, USA.

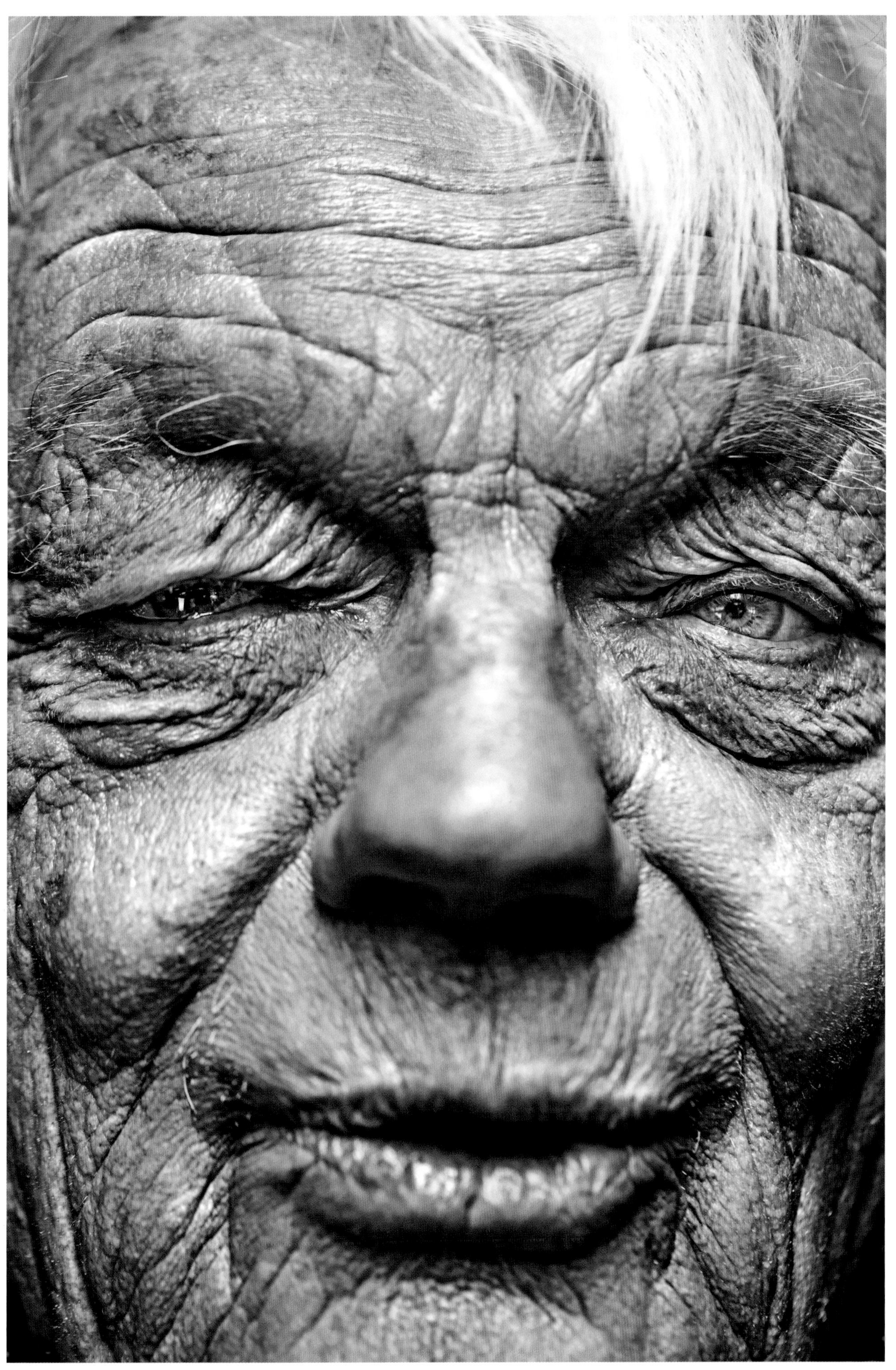

TRUE WEST

Yellowstone and the American West

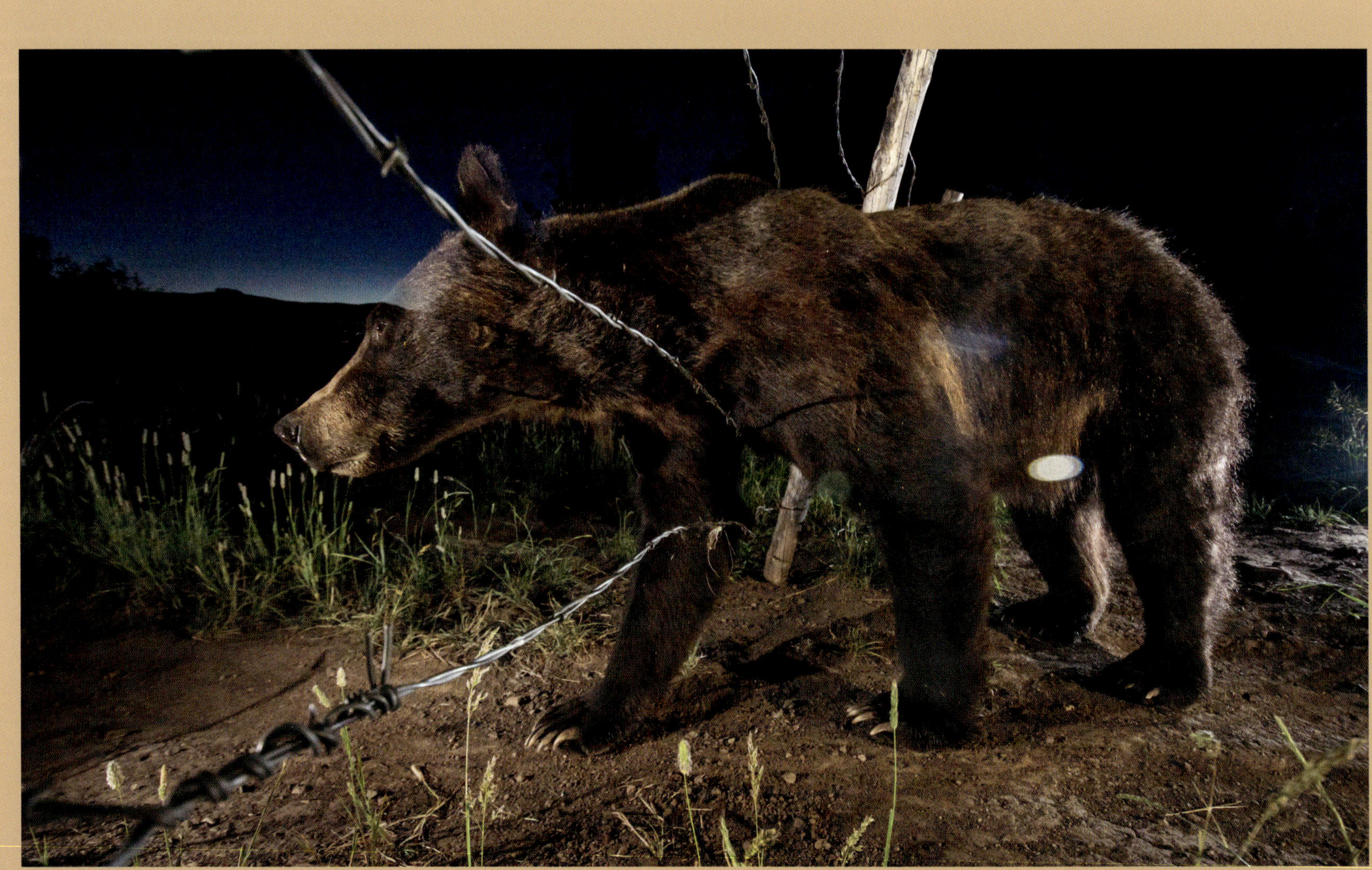

I'm on my hands and knees, alone in the wilderness, crawling like a wolf. I wonder what people might think if they could see me now, skulking my way toward a barbed wire fence and dripping with sweat.

A sharp pebble digs into the soft flesh just below my kneecap and I flinch as my body crosses an infrared tripwire. Two remote flashes fire and I hear the camera mounted to my left take a picture. I wonder what my friends who actually graduated from high school are doing exactly now.

Growing up in the Rocky Mountains, I was always at least subconsciously aware of the myths of the American West. The stories of rugged individualism balanced against the trope of the "noble savage" clashed in my mind. There is undeniable romance and mystery embedded in the landscape and stories it holds, as well as a palpable and unbreakable pride. I was also aware that something here had been lost to European expansion and the old was still at war with the new.

The history that gifted so many with the abundance of the west (and the myth that abundance was infinite) also decimated the Native American world in a slow genocide that claimed tens of millions of indigenous lives. It tore apart pristine ecosystems and drove massive populations of animals to near extinction under the rationale of an inalienable Anglo-American right to something that was never "ours" to begin with. That history lingers.

Today, the conflict persists, mostly in ideological and policy debates around land management, native rights, conservation, and just how much the government is welcome here at all. These are arguments about what was, what is, and what can be. They are also discussions about what was taken, what was lost, and what can be given back and how.

Currently, I'm on assignment to photograph the confluence and conflict of people and predators in the Greater Yellowstone ecosystem. In time, the work will expand beyond the park and its environs. But for now, I'm trying to set up a camera trap, a system capable of making pictures when I'm not present, to capture wildlife as it moves through an increasingly divided landscape crisscrossed and dissected by barbed wire and property lines. For any apex predator, either side of a fence might be the difference between safe harbor and getting shot and killed. To them, it's just an arbitrary obstacle. I reverse my crawl and approach the barbed wire fence again until I hear the camera click, making sure to avoid any stones that might puncture my knees.

I've been living in a solitary cabin in Tom Miner Basin, nestled deep in the Native historical territories of the Apsáalooke/Crow Nation, Shoshone-Bannock Tribes, Blackfeet Nation, Confederated Salish and Kootenai Tribes, and the Nez Perce Tribe. I spend my days chasing wolves, looking for clues of their frustratingly elusive presence. The barbed wire fence that's the focus of my camera trap is of particular interest because of a small tuft of hair left behind on one of the barbs. I never seem to be able to see wolves with my own eyes, instead forced to find the little breadcrumbs they leave behind. I pack up my things and head home, knowing that it might take months before the camera captures something, if it captures anything at all.

When I come back two weeks later to replace the batteries, I scroll through thousands of frames of nothing, the camera triggered by a blowing blade of grass, a magpie, or something so small I can't see it at all. There are no wolves.

Another week passes. Then another. Still nothing. I forget about the trap for a while and move on. I photograph a native bison harvest; captive wolves and bears; predators who got into livestock and were shot and killed; activists and ranchers; and game farms that rent live animals for movies. I interview and follow farmers and game wardens and park rangers. Everyone seems to know that whatever they believe is the truth—right, justified, and supported by a different set of facts—dug in like bears in winter and unwilling to budge. In some ways, it's as if the history of the west is repeating itself. The only truth I can see here is that everyone has their own.

After a month, I'm thinking it might be time to move the camera trap. Maybe the tuft of fur was just wishful thinking. I open the camera housing and scroll, expecting nothing. My eyes are blurry and disengaged when nine frames flash across the screen . . . but it's not a wolf. Instead, a subadult grizzly approaches the camera and steps delicately through the fence, unaware of what its simple action will represent to the various stakeholders in this region. It's a quiet, symbolic, and honest moment that I know will be interpreted from ideological and political polarities. Villain and victim, predator and prey . . . all of our anthropomorphic ideas momentarily upended and questioned by an instant of nature's indifference.

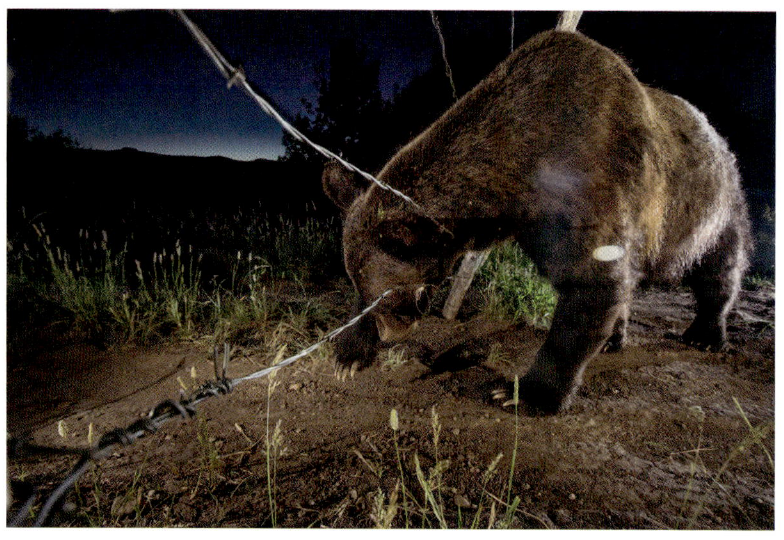
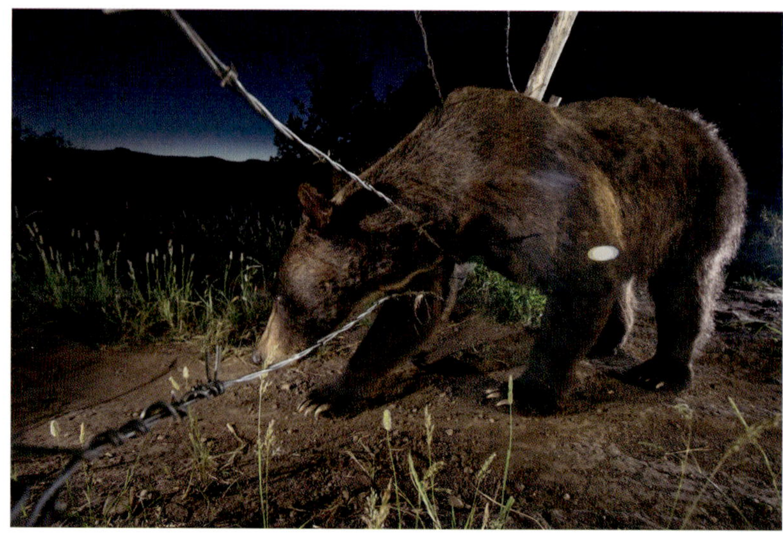
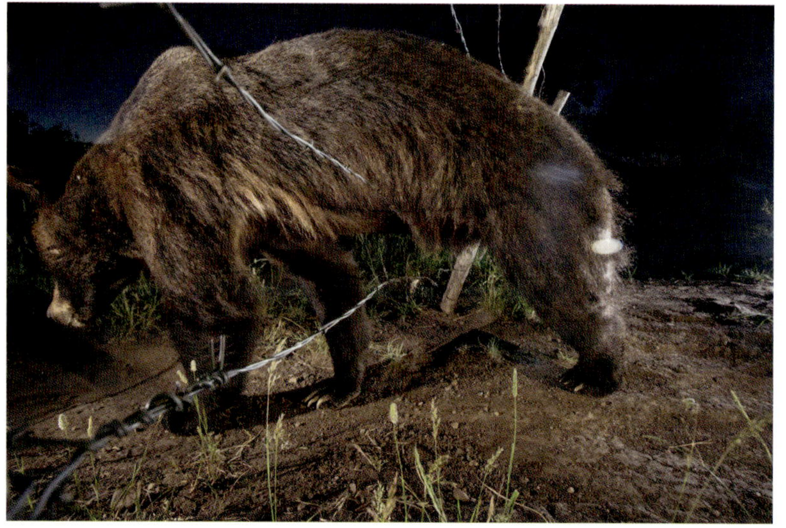
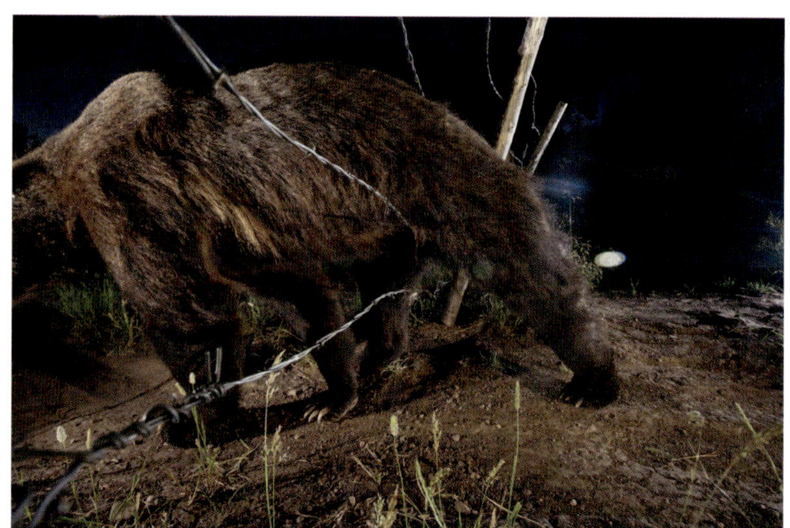

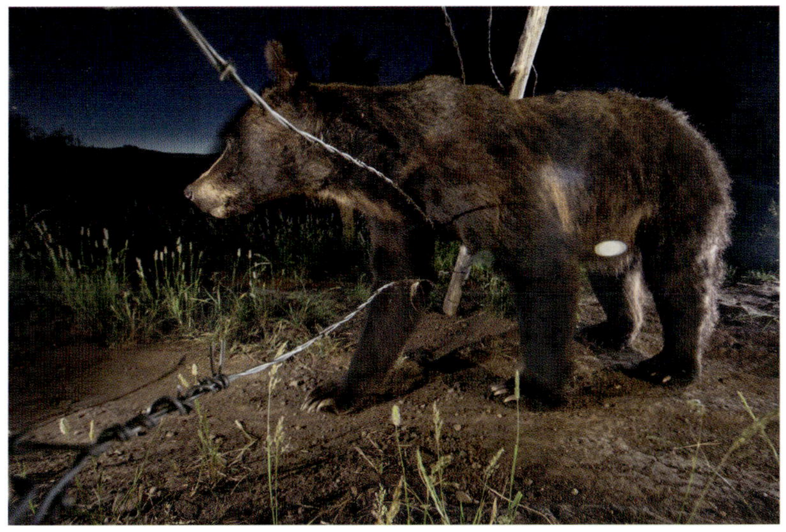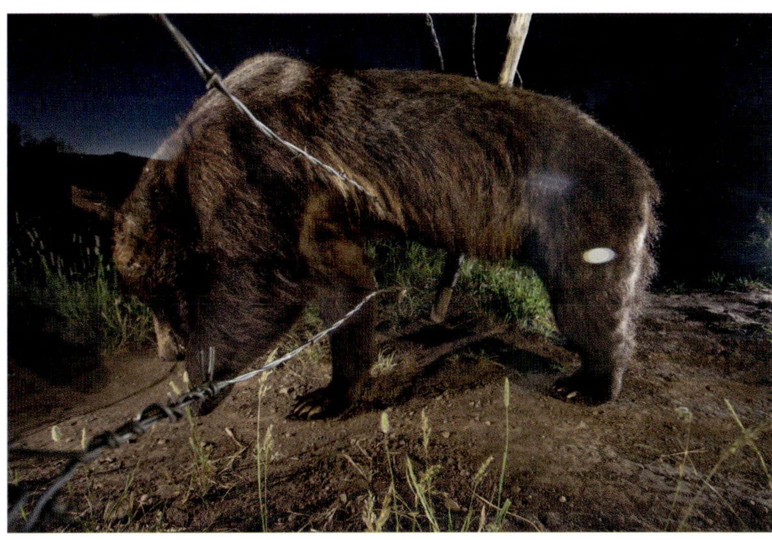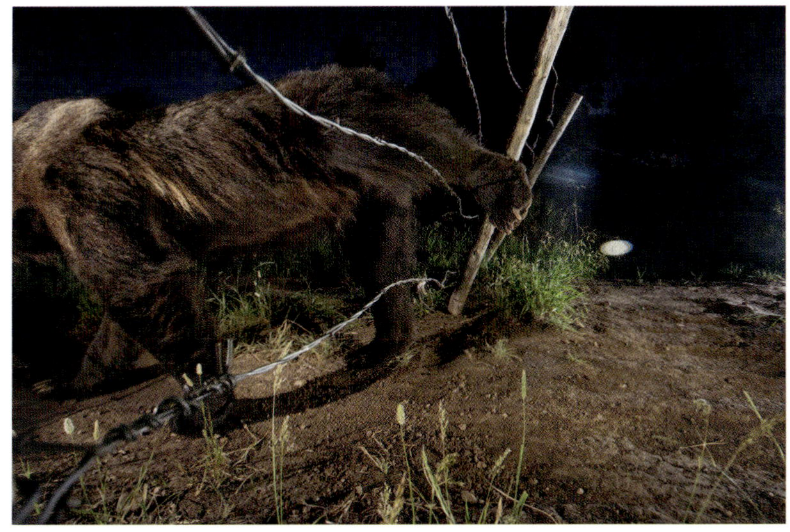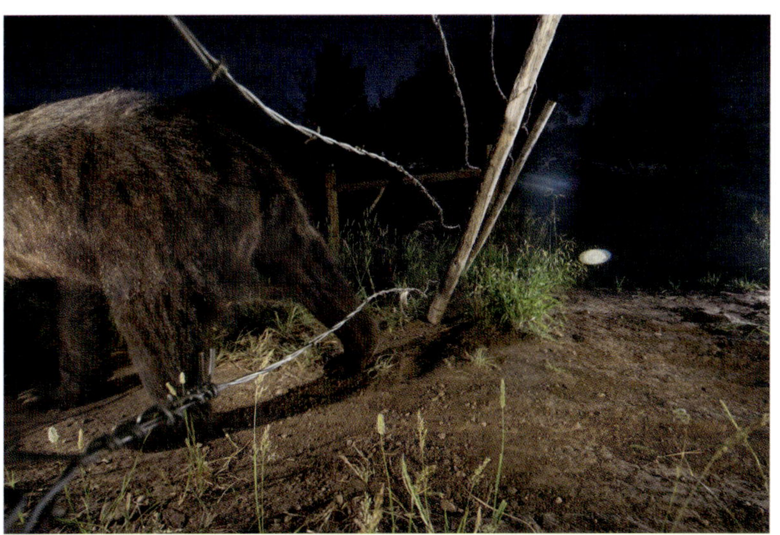

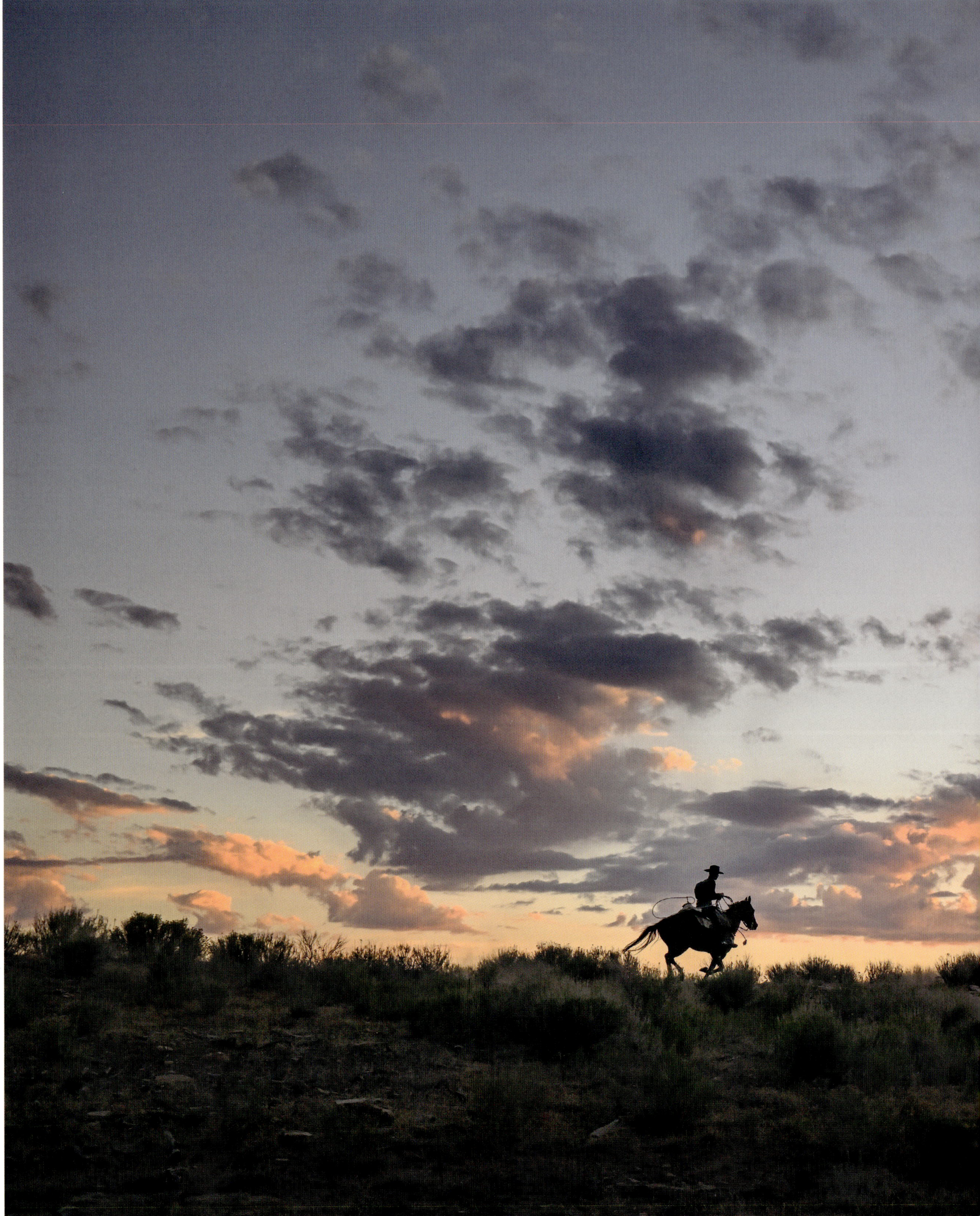

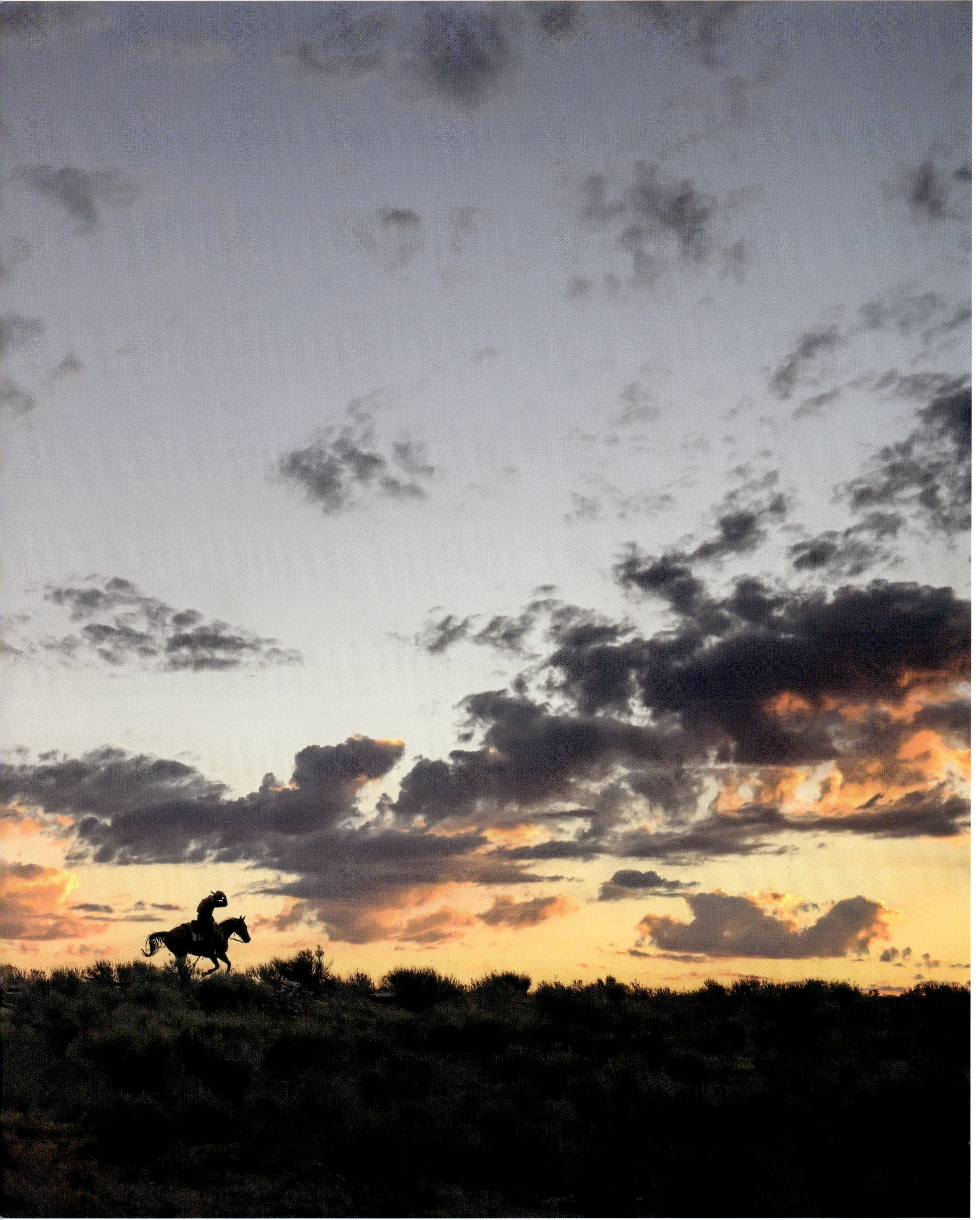

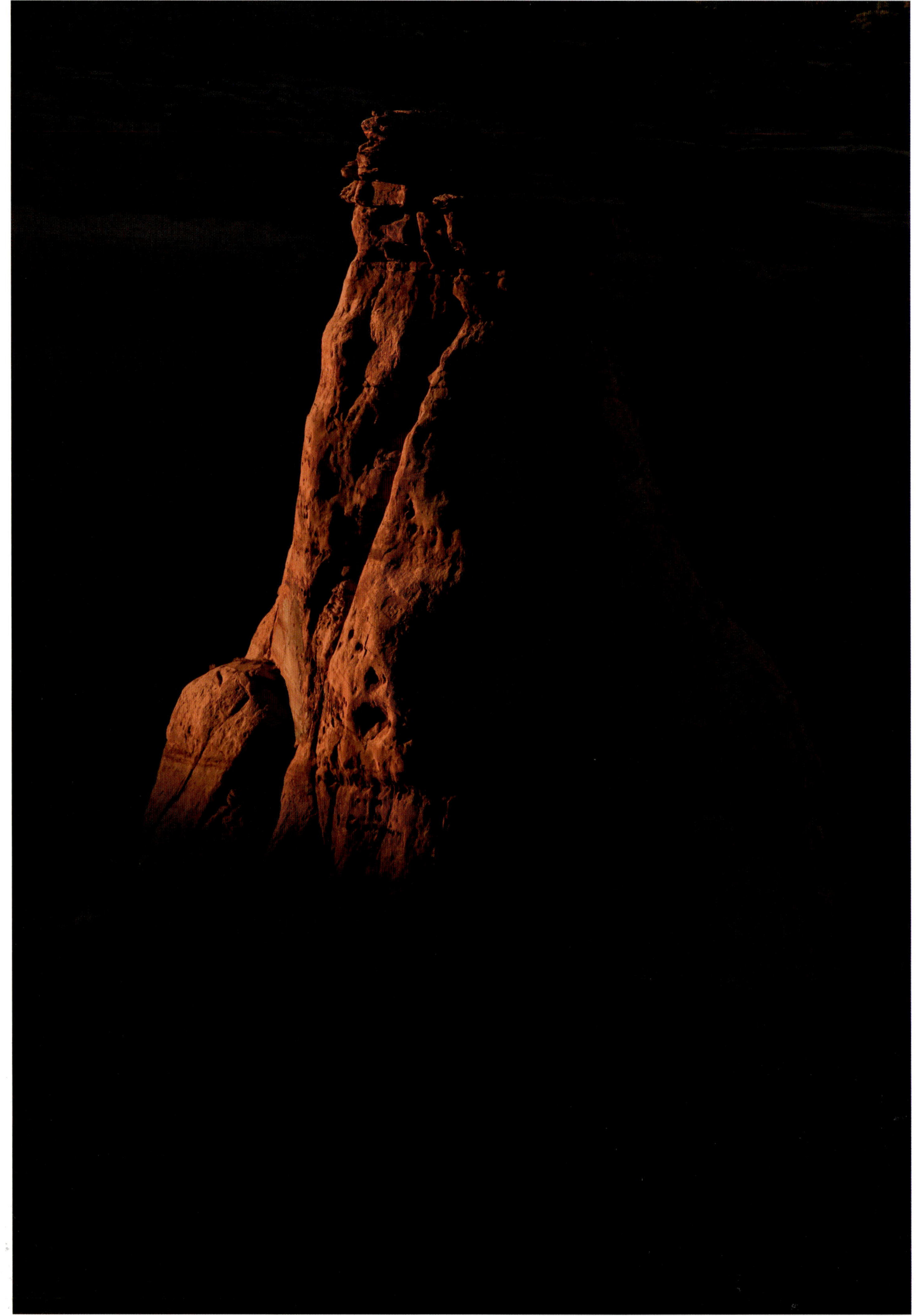

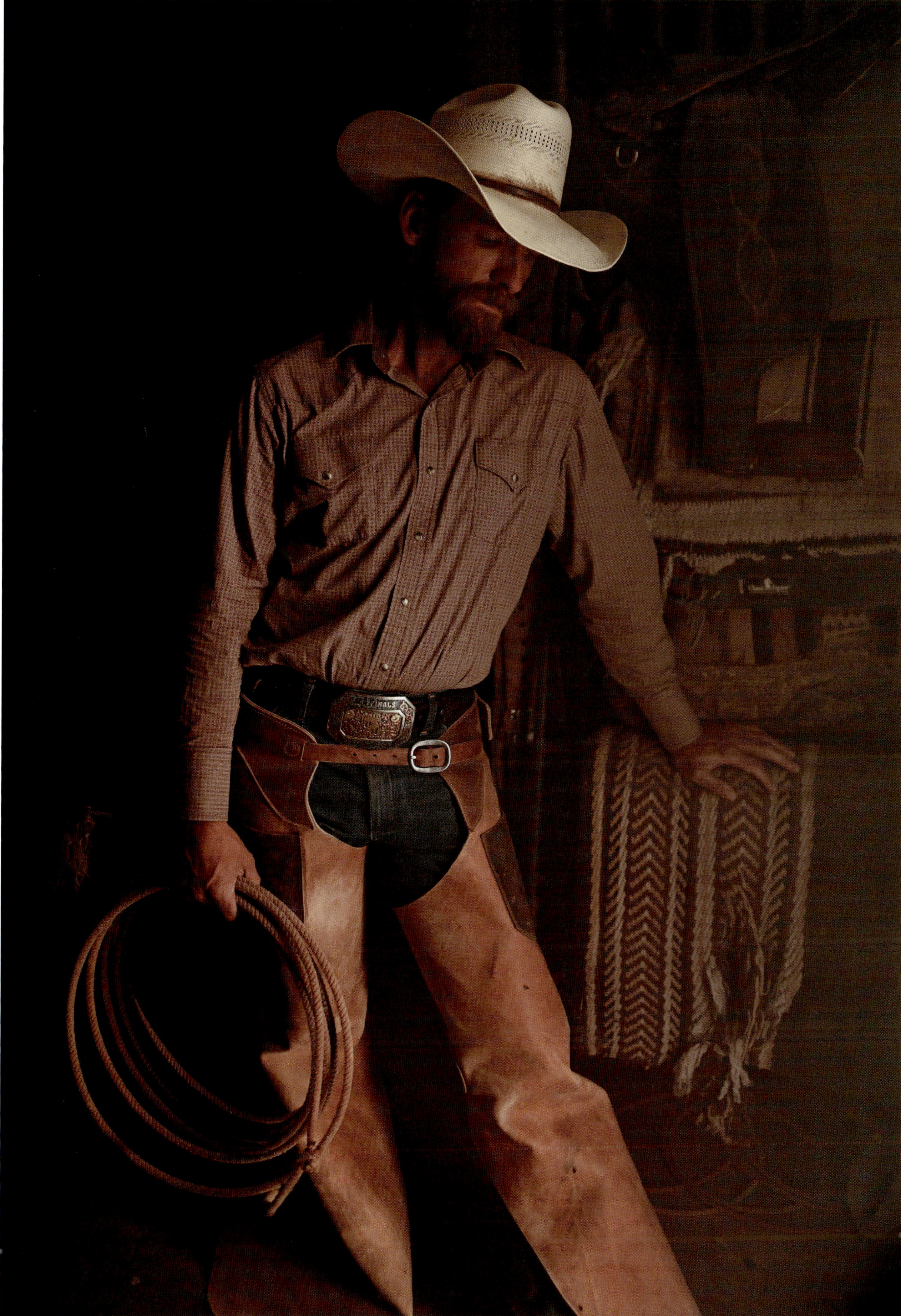

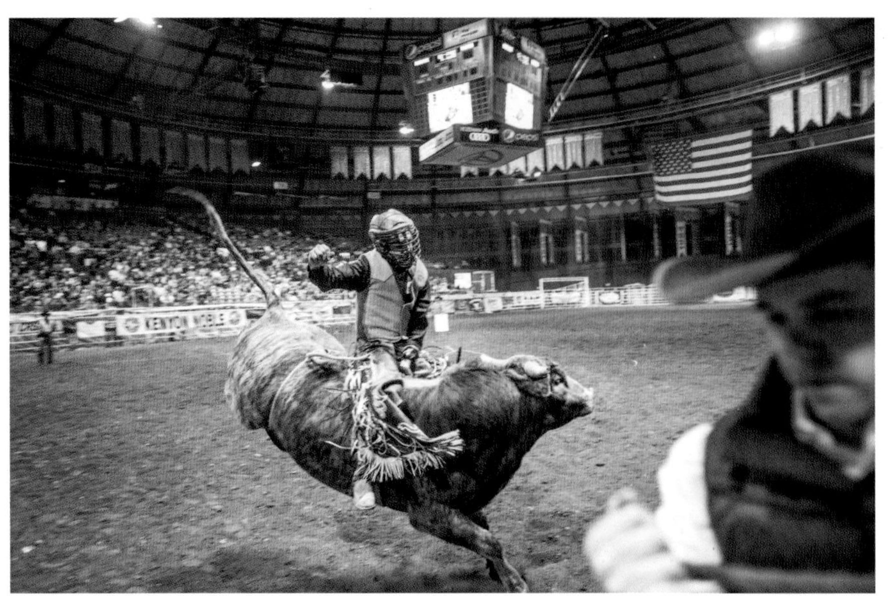

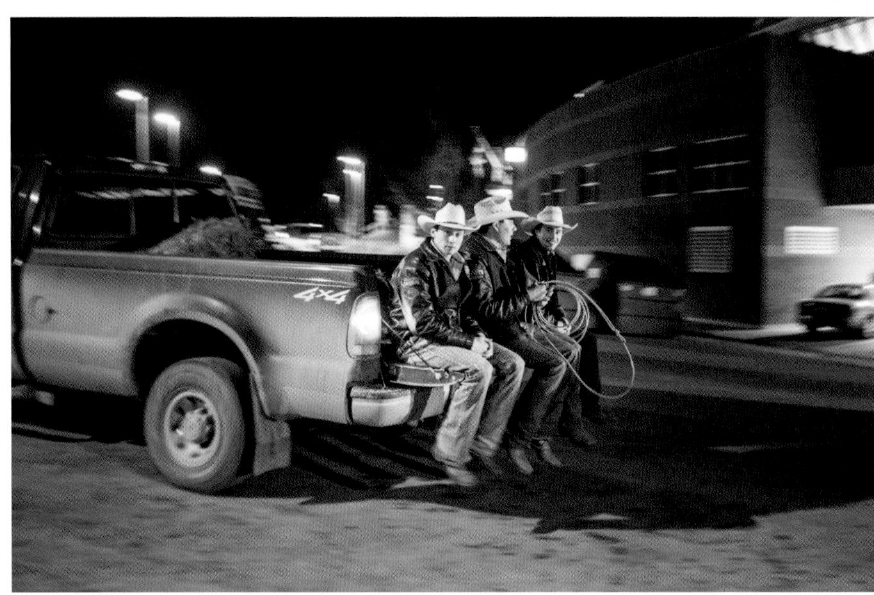

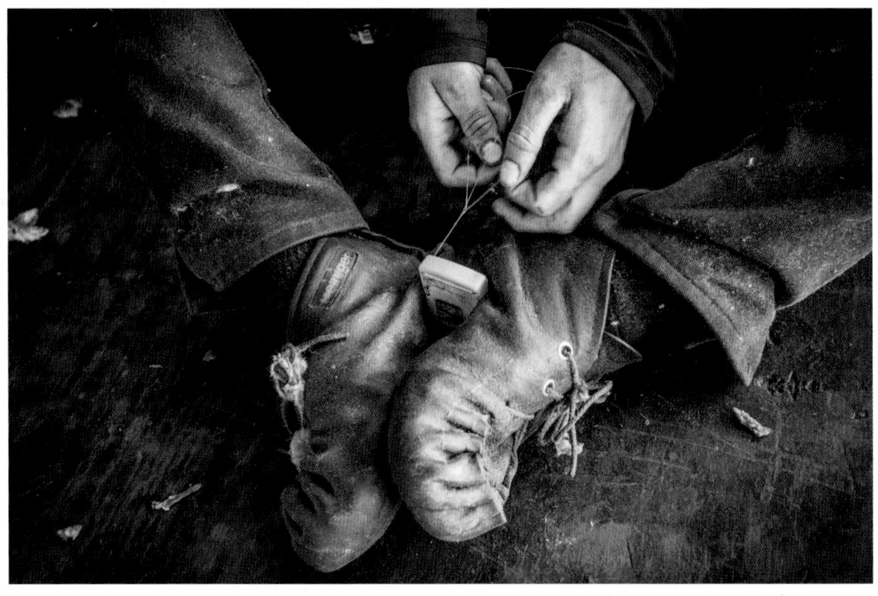

ABOVE AND CENTER: Scenes from a collegiate rodeo at Montana State University in Bozeman. **BELOW:** Mending sheep-shearing moccasins with dental floss. **PREVIOUS, LEFT:** Colorado National Monument. **PREVIOUS, RIGHT:** Jake Stephens.

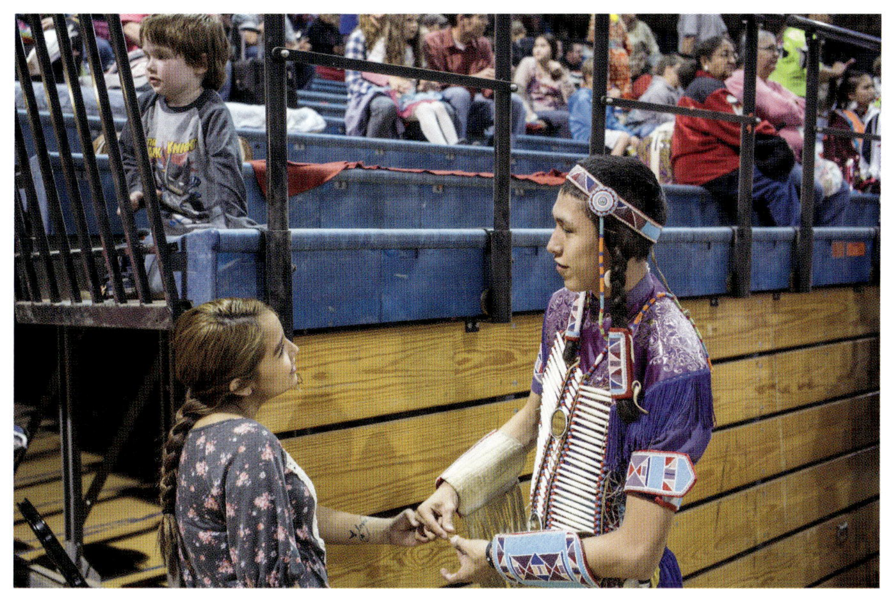

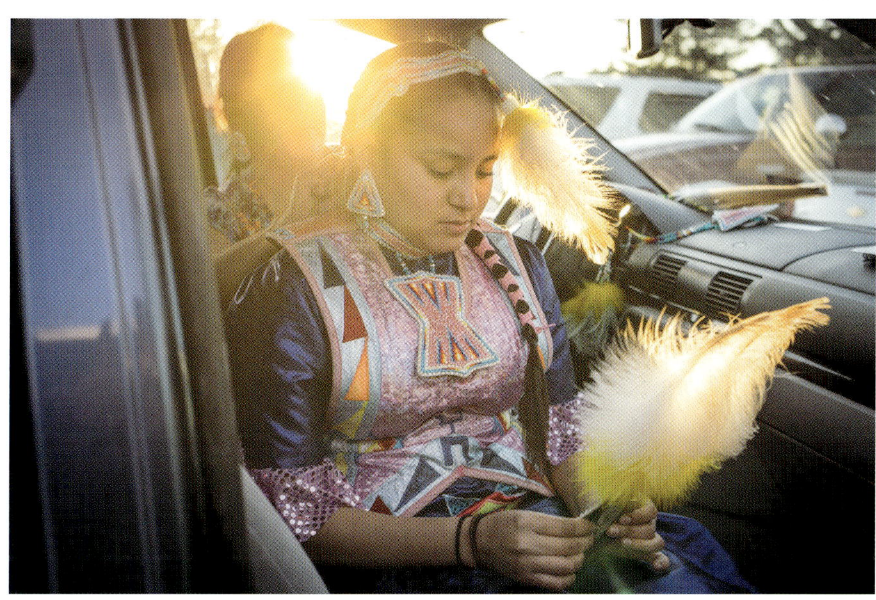

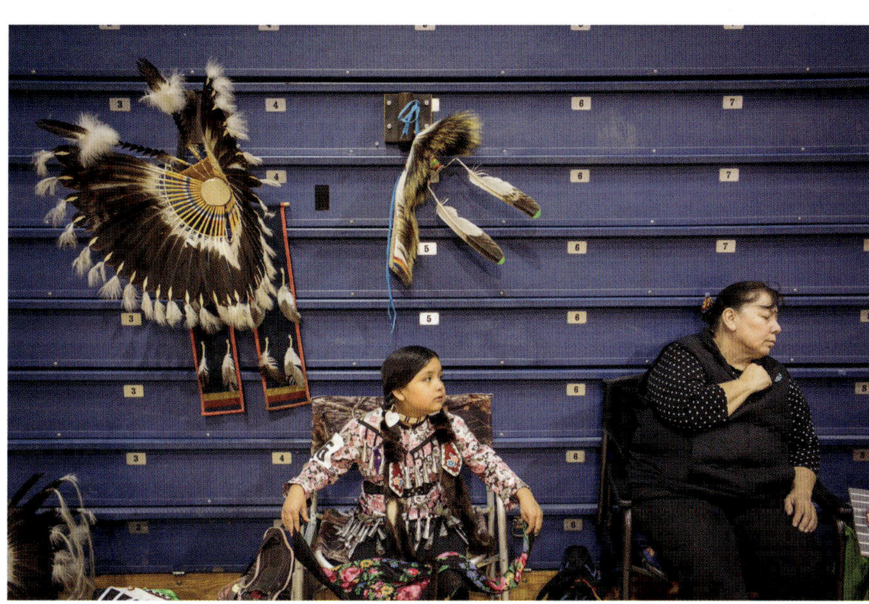

Scenes from the American Indian Council Powwow held at Montana State University.

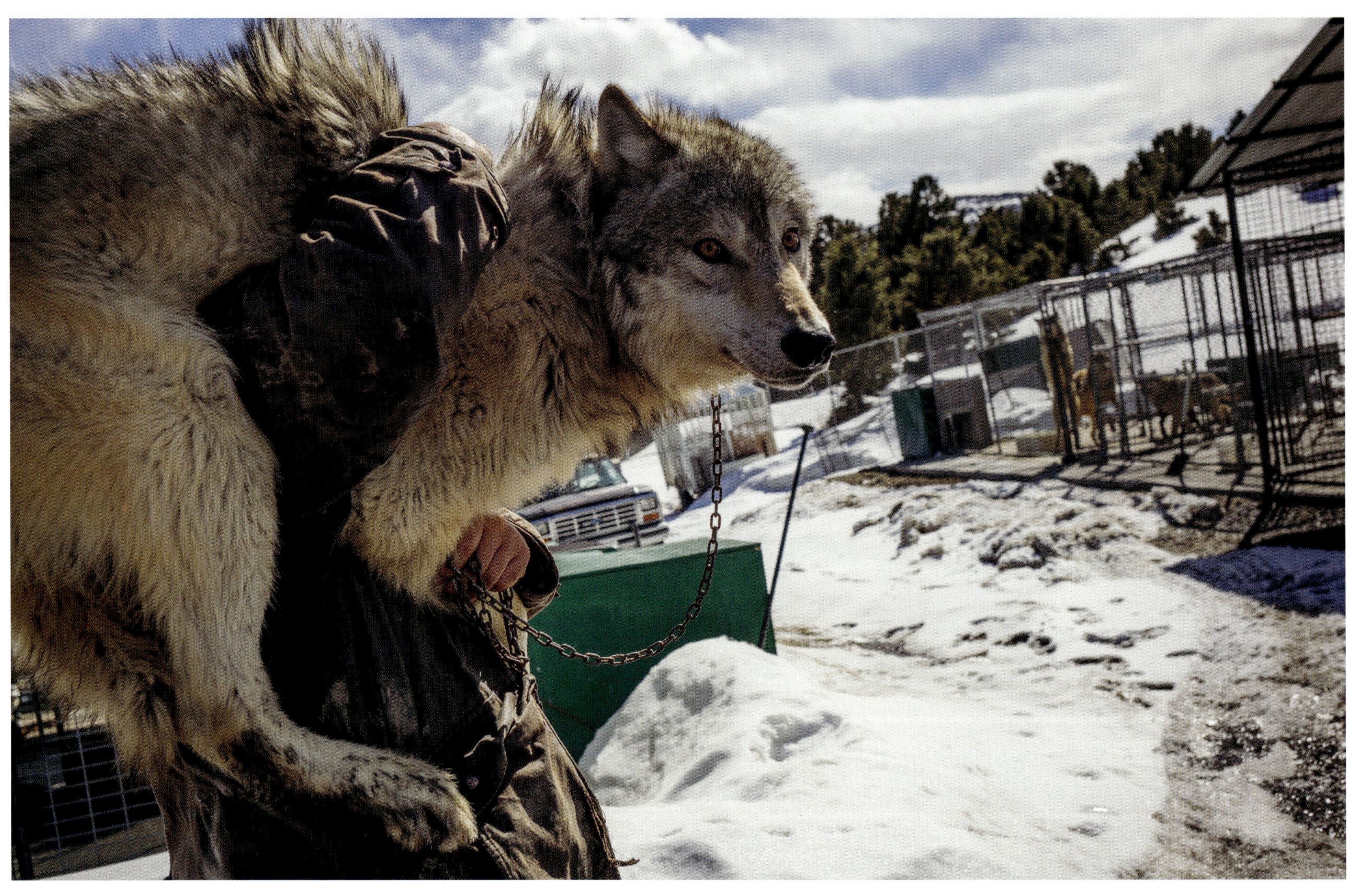

A captive wolf is carried back to its enclosure on a game farm. Many of these animals are deeply inbred, poorly cared for, and most often "rented" for use in Hollywood films, photoshoots, and even documentaries.

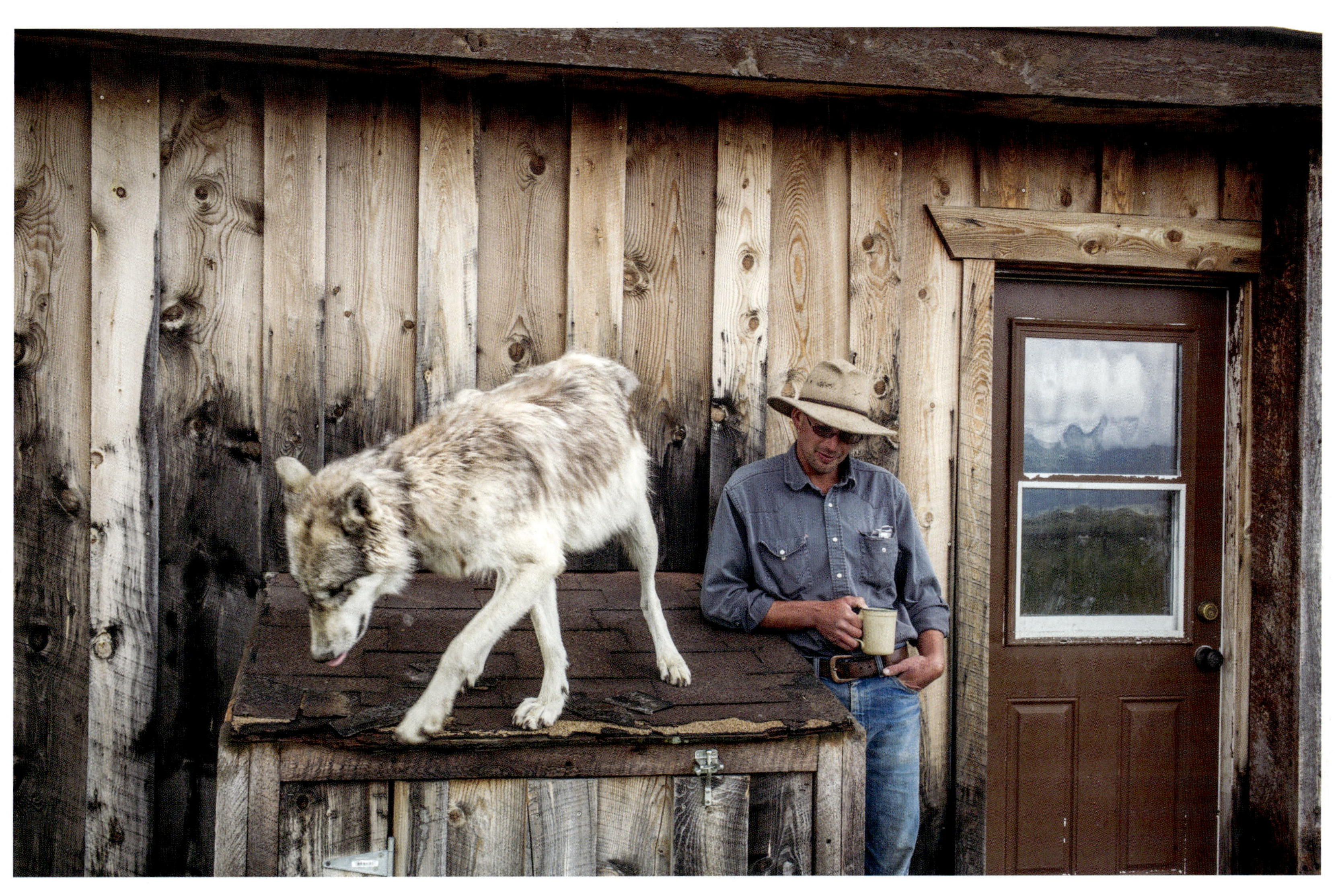

A rescued wolf plays with its caretaker in Paradise Valley, Montana. **FOLLOWING:** A grizzly bear feeds on the carcass of a culled horse (mostly likely chosen for slaughter due to illness or old age) near Yellowstone National Park.

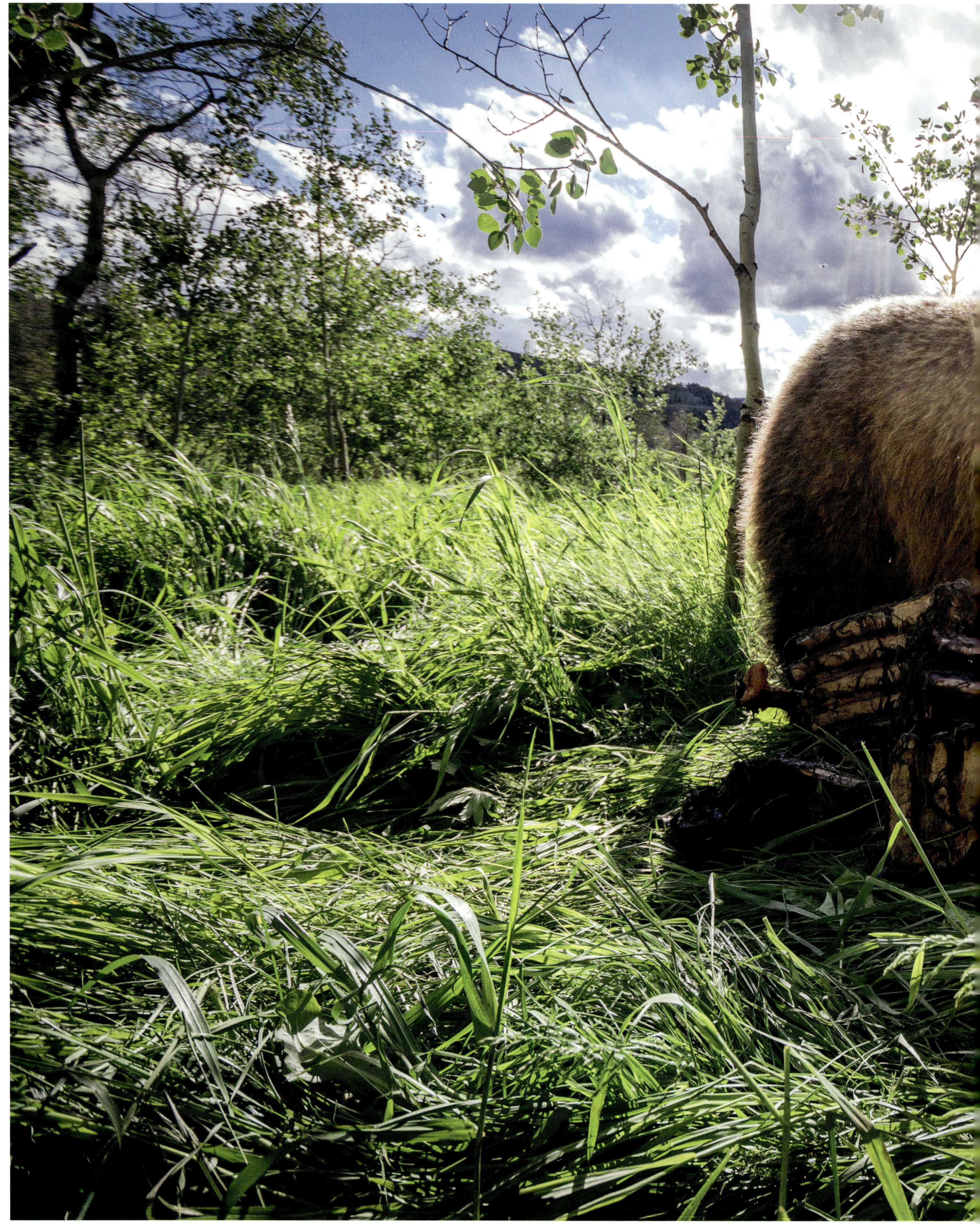

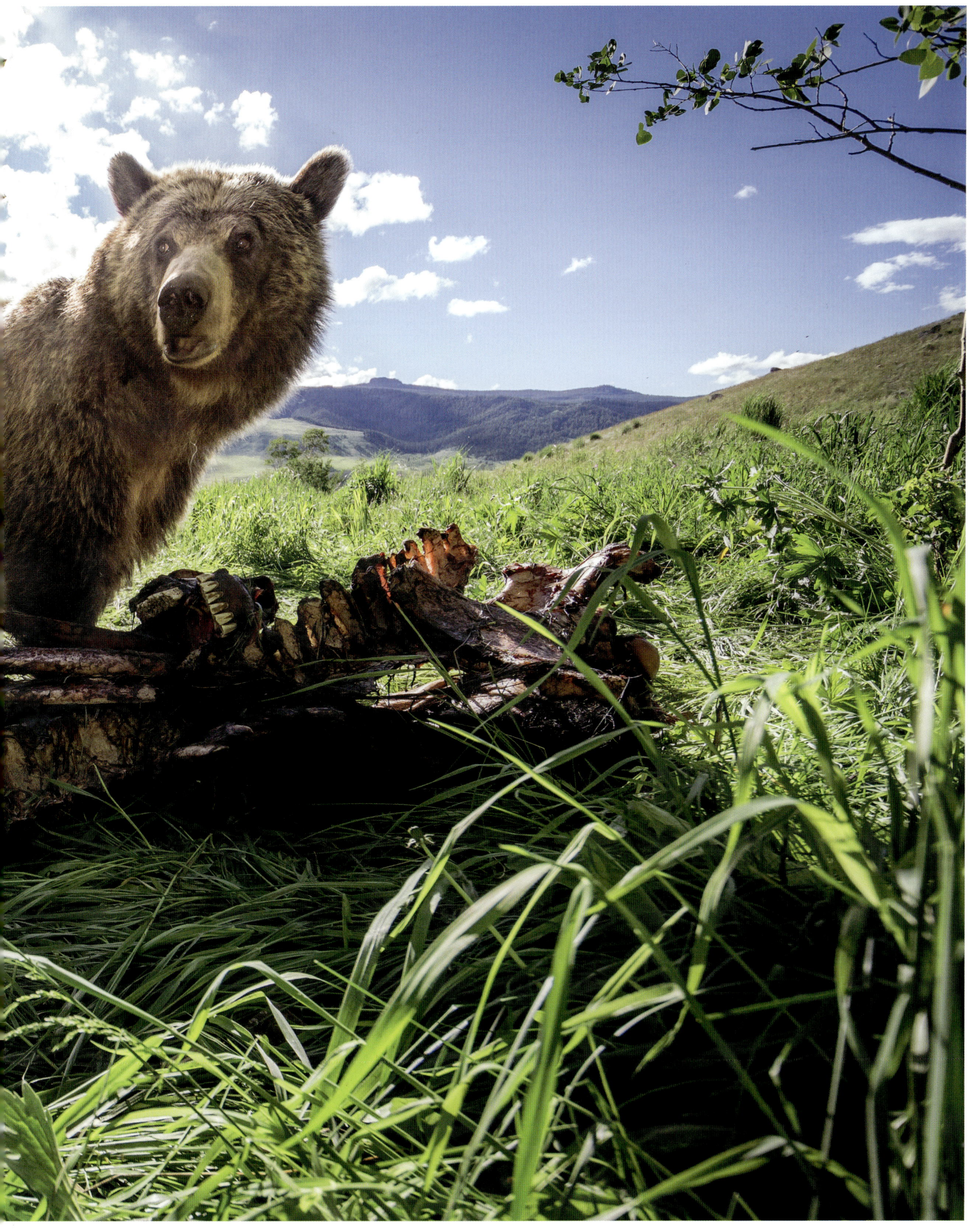

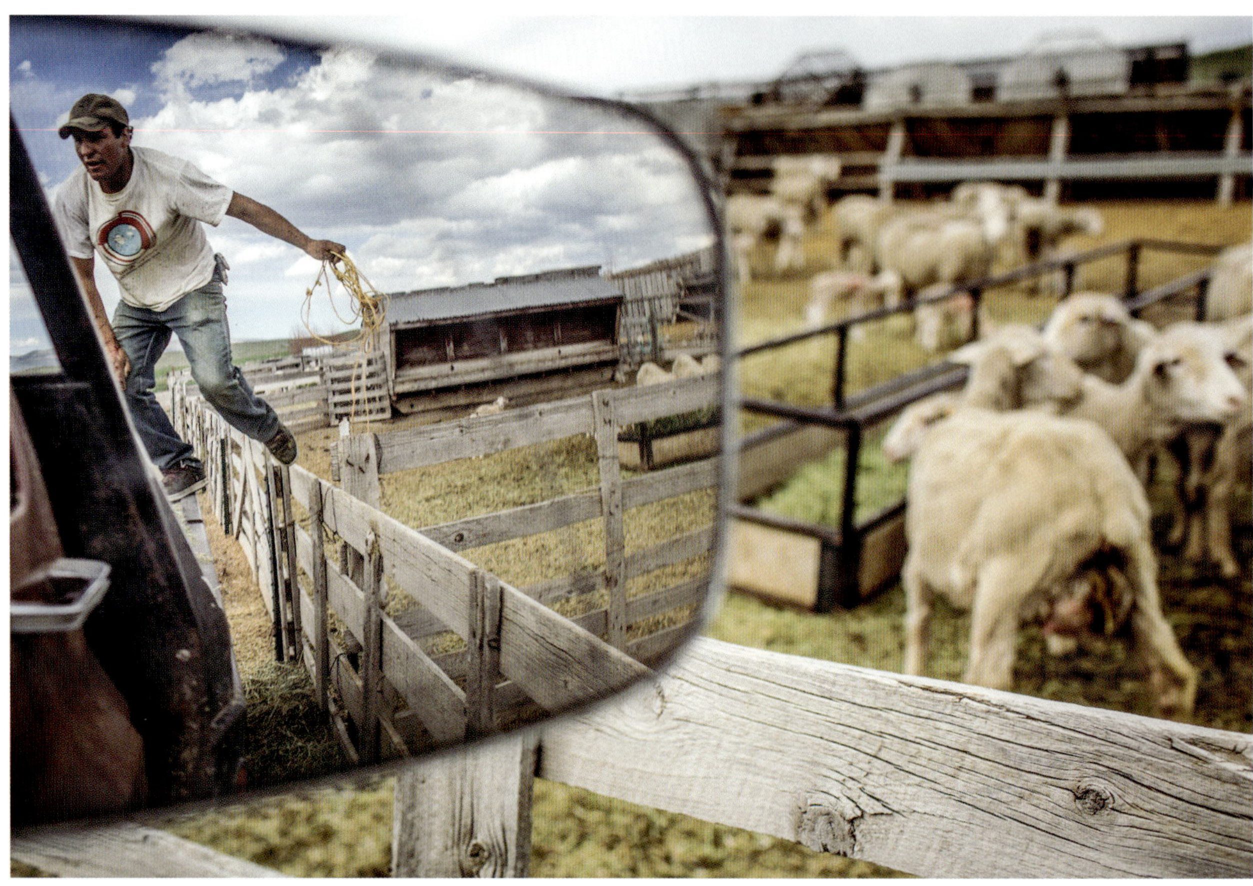

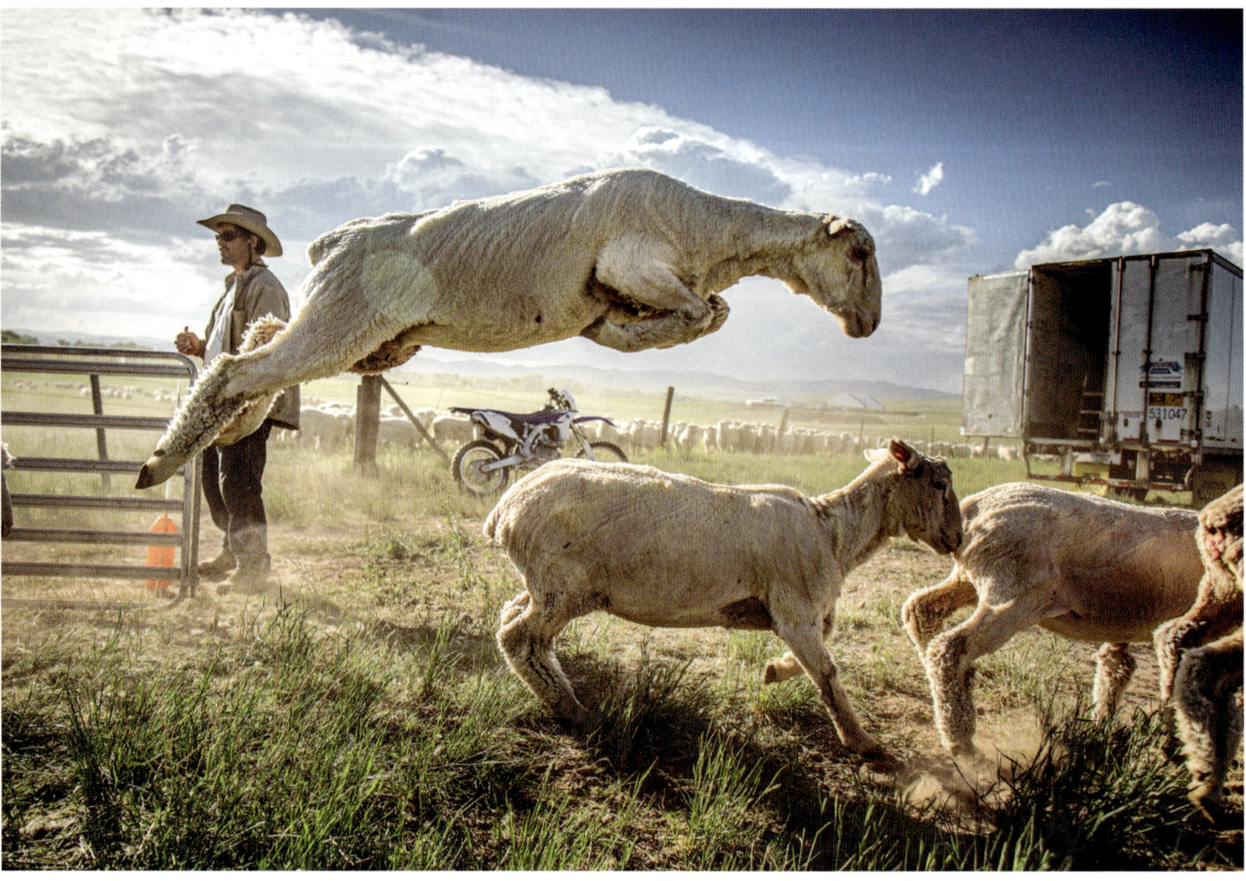

ABOVE: A ranch hand hops pens on the Helle Rambouillet sheep ranch near Dillon, Montana.
BELOW: John Helle releases freshly sheared sheep from their enclosure.

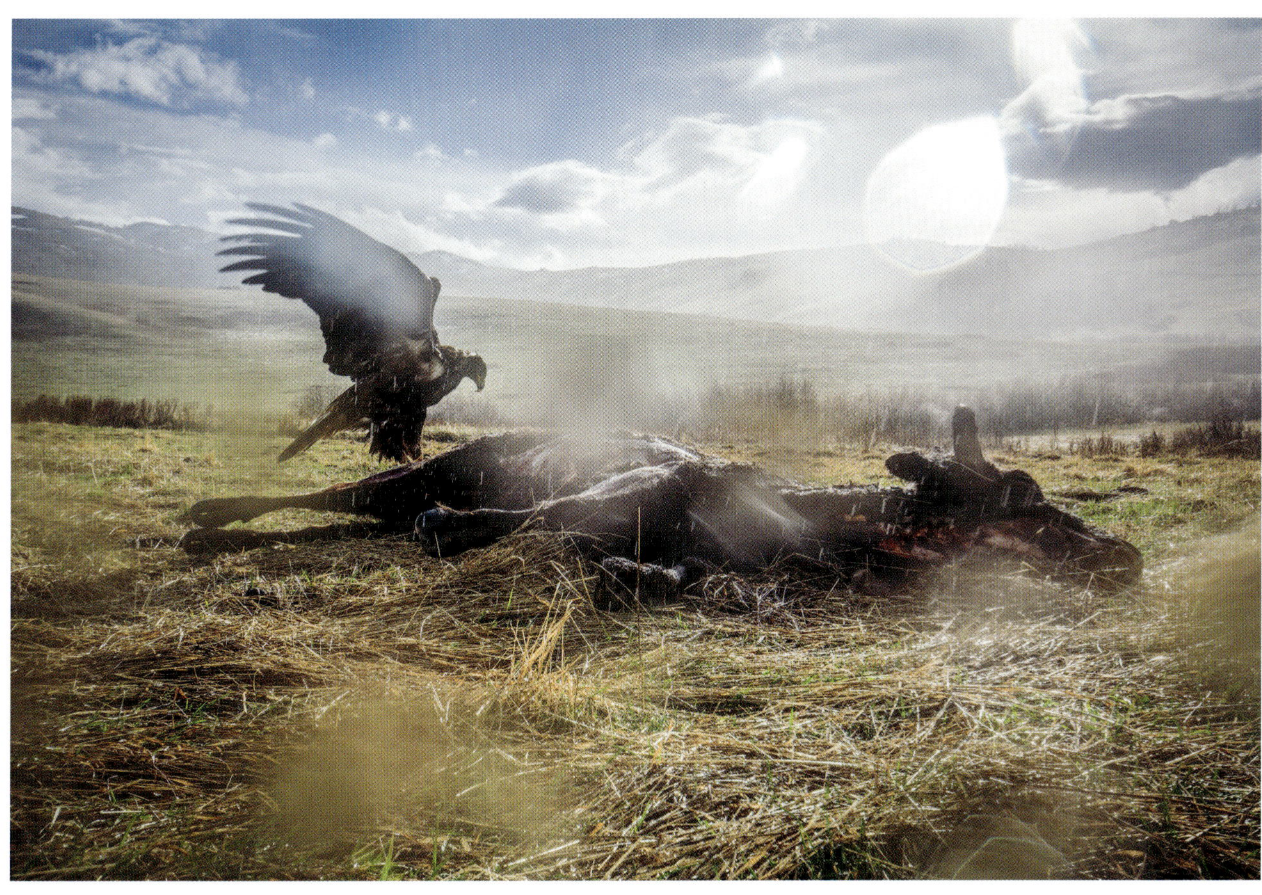

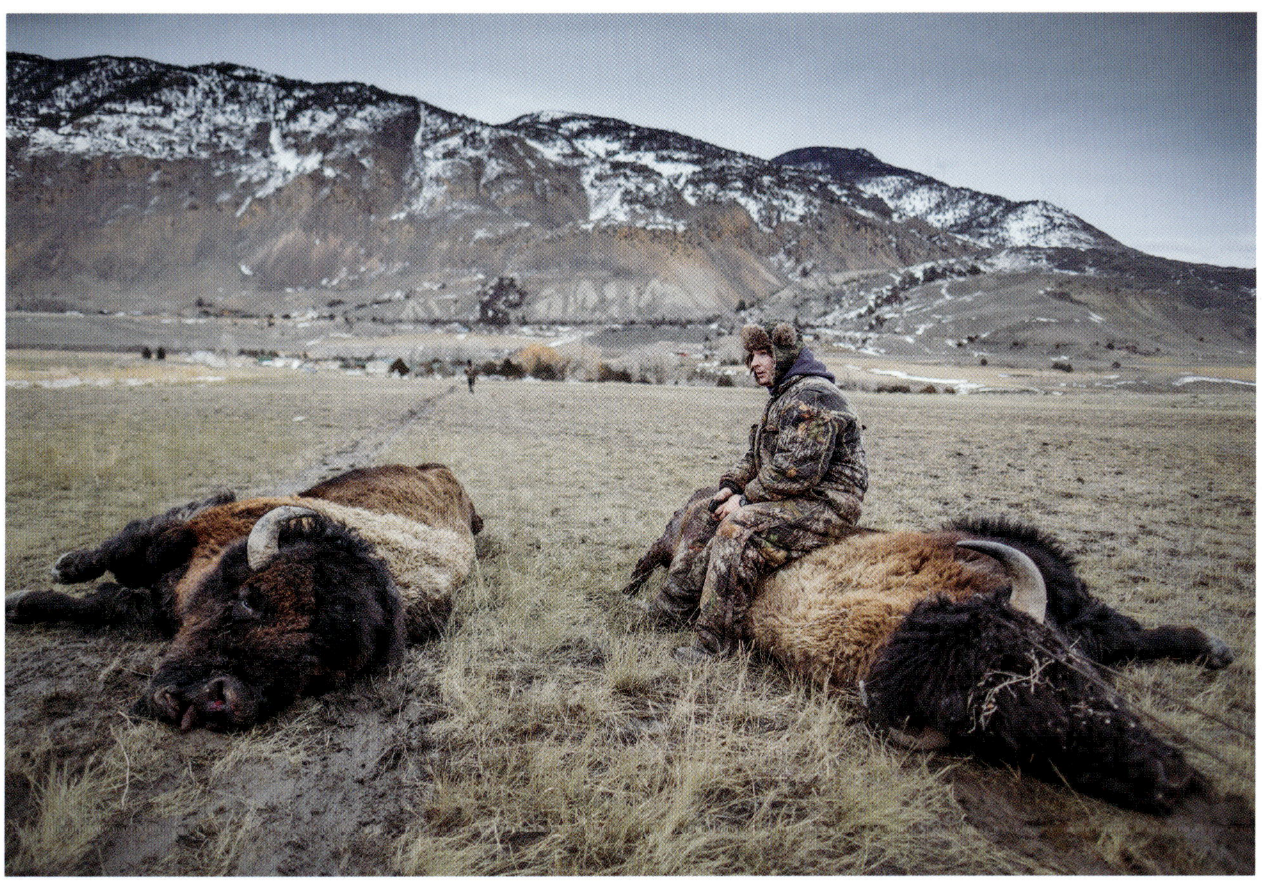

ABOVE: A golden eagle scavenges the carcass of a young bull on the Flying D Ranch.
BELOW: Bison harvested during the annual tribal hunt that takes place every autumn outside of Yellowstone National Park.

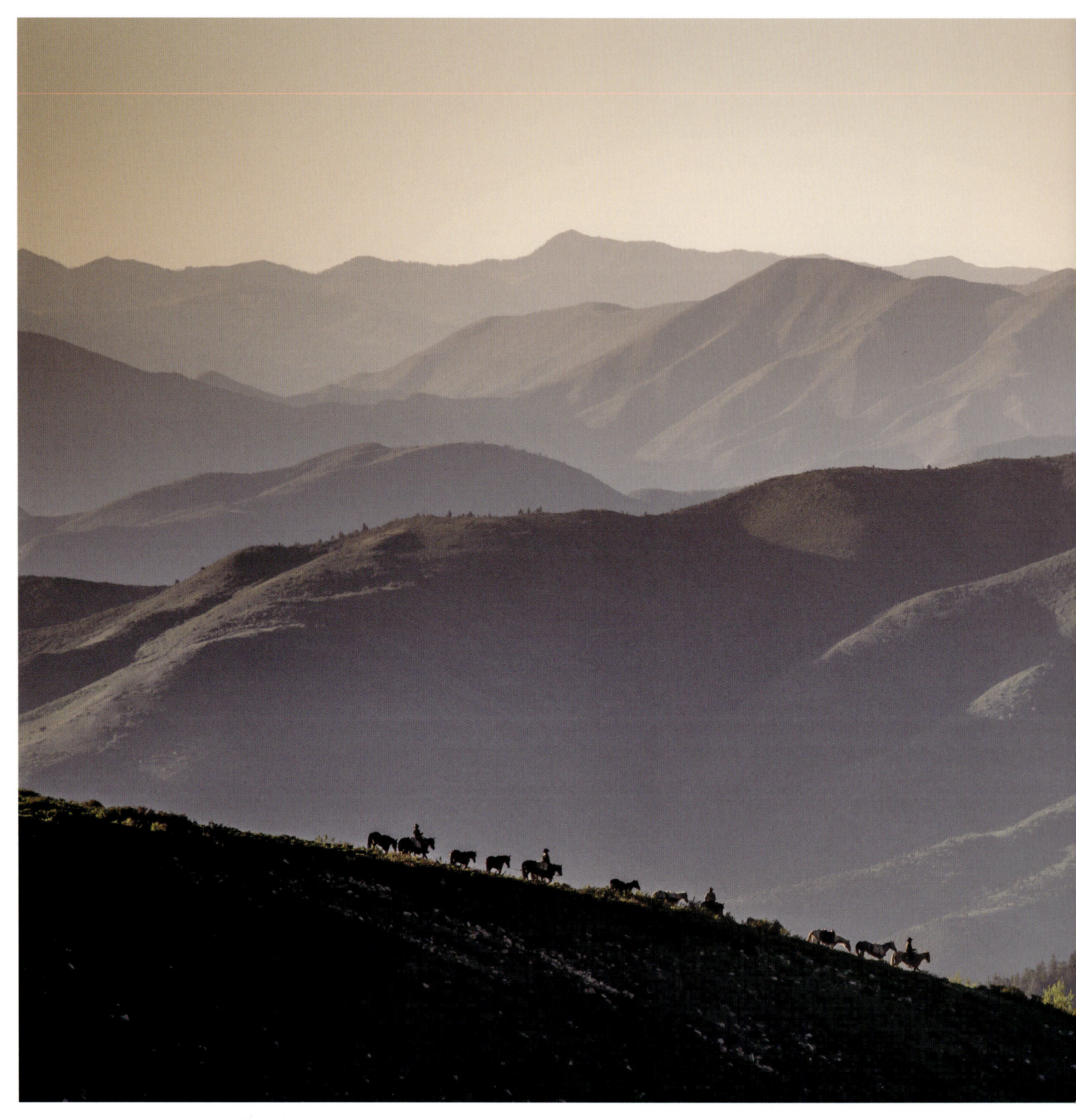

A horse train of wild mustangs is led through the Unita wilderness of Utah. **OPPOSITE, ABOVE AND CENTER:** The Stephens boys at home on their ranch, Colorado.
OPPOSITE, BELOW: Ben Masters leads a team of riders and wild mustangs through the Unita Wilderness of Utah.

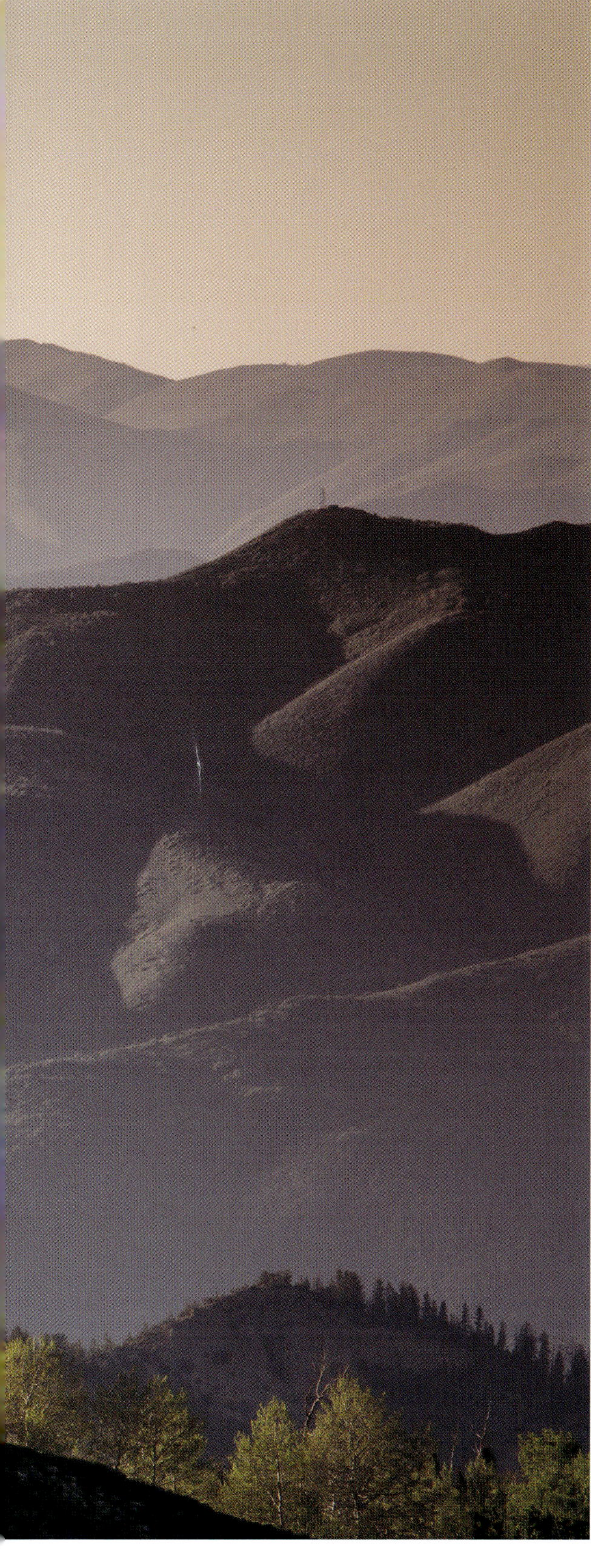

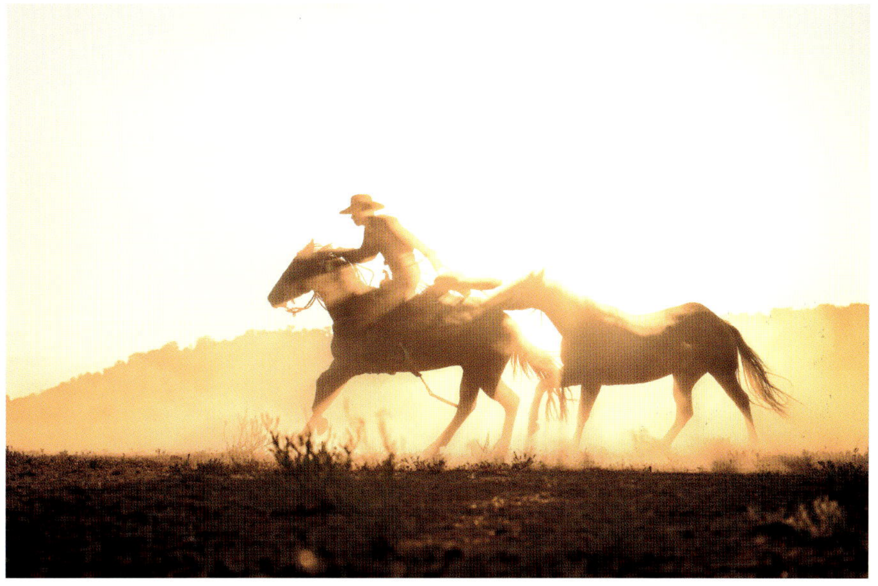

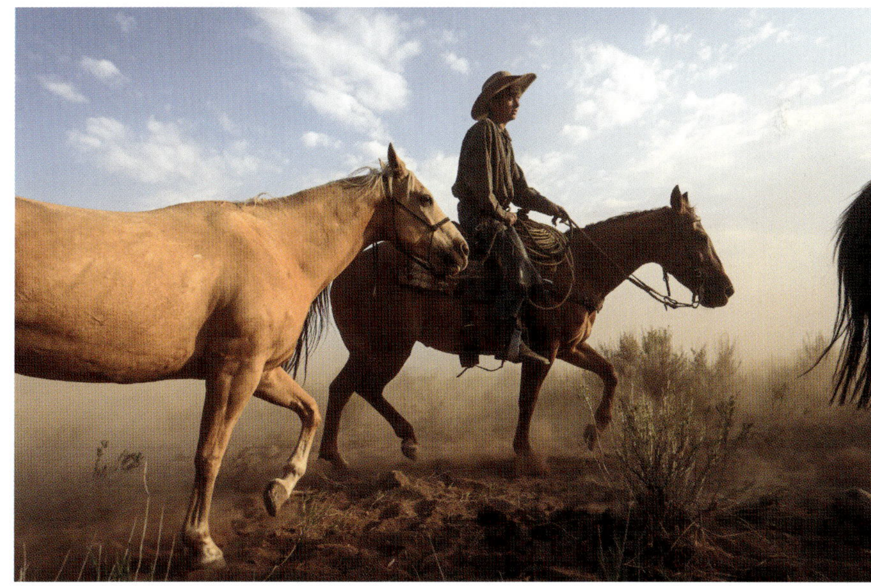

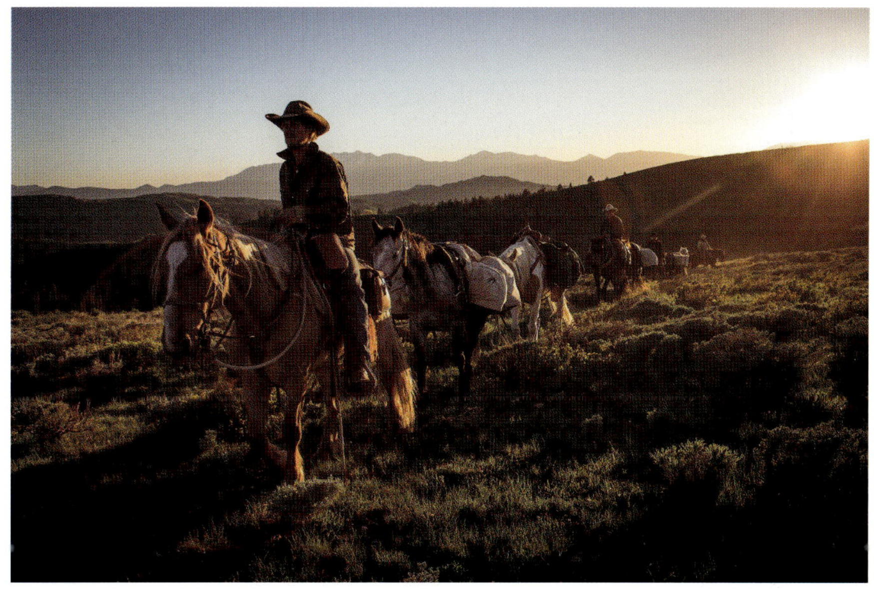

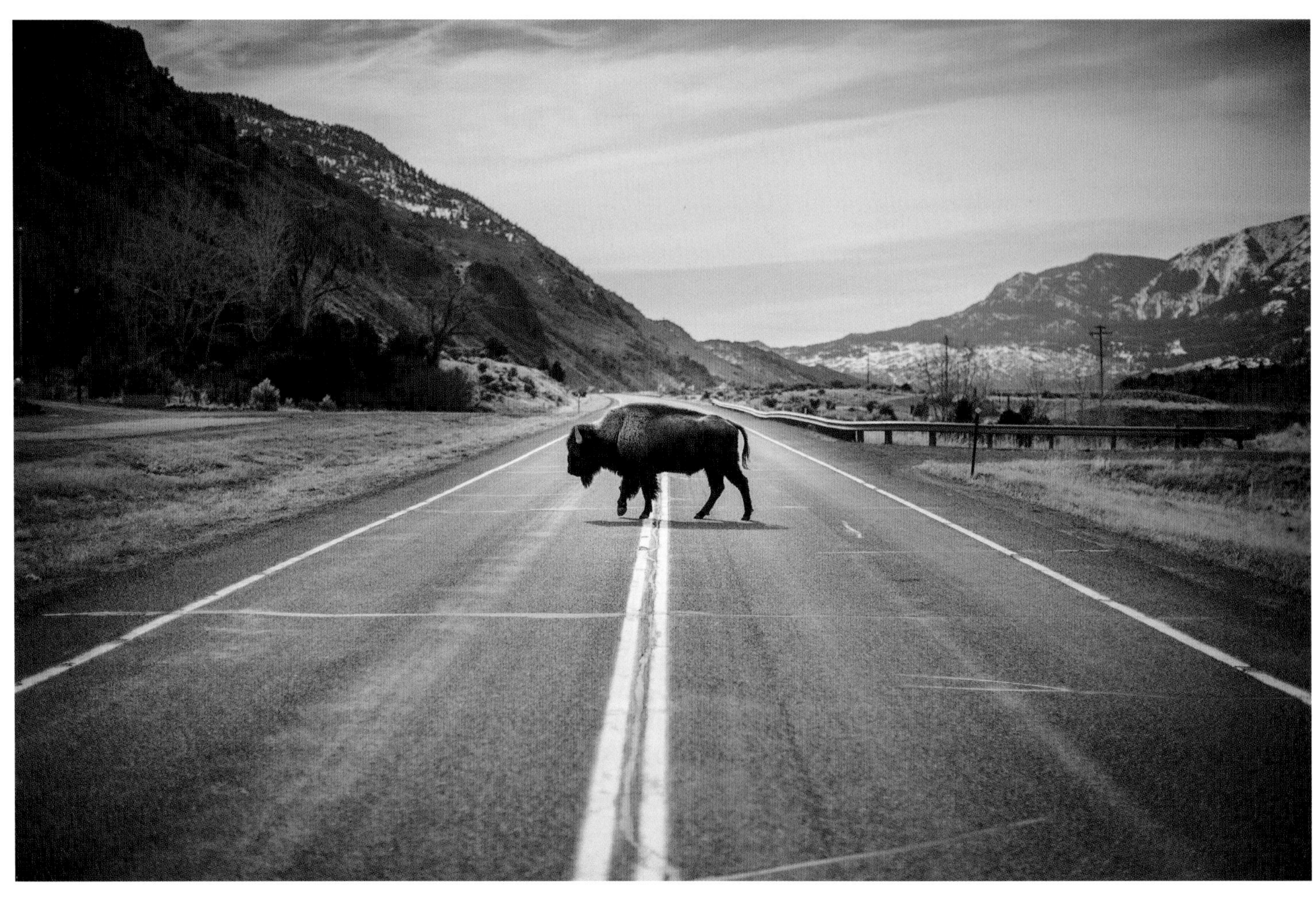

The intersection of wildlife and humans in Montana.

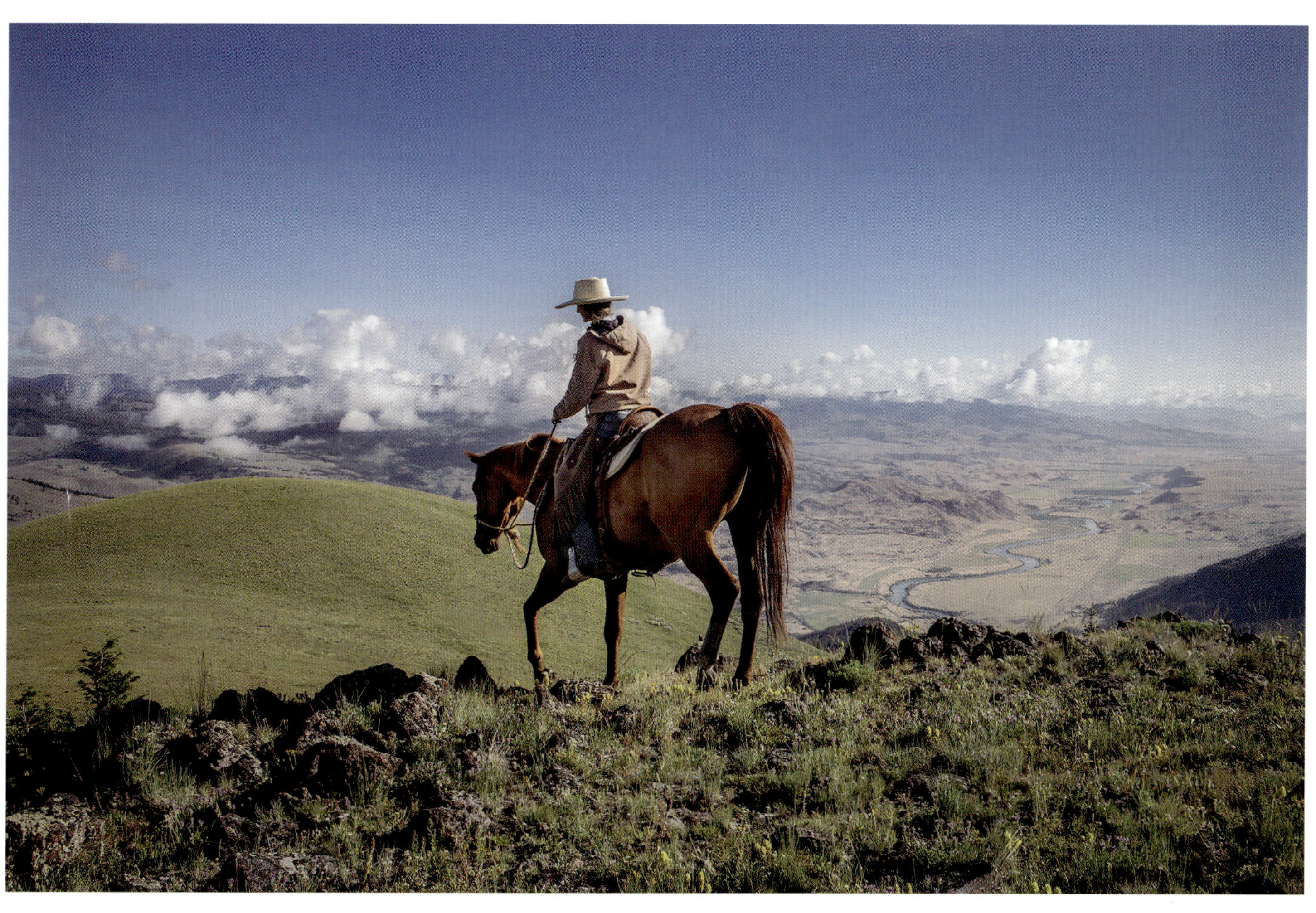

Hilary Zaranek rides above Paradise Valley on the border of Yellowstone National Park. **FOLLOWING:** Desert juniper in Colorado.

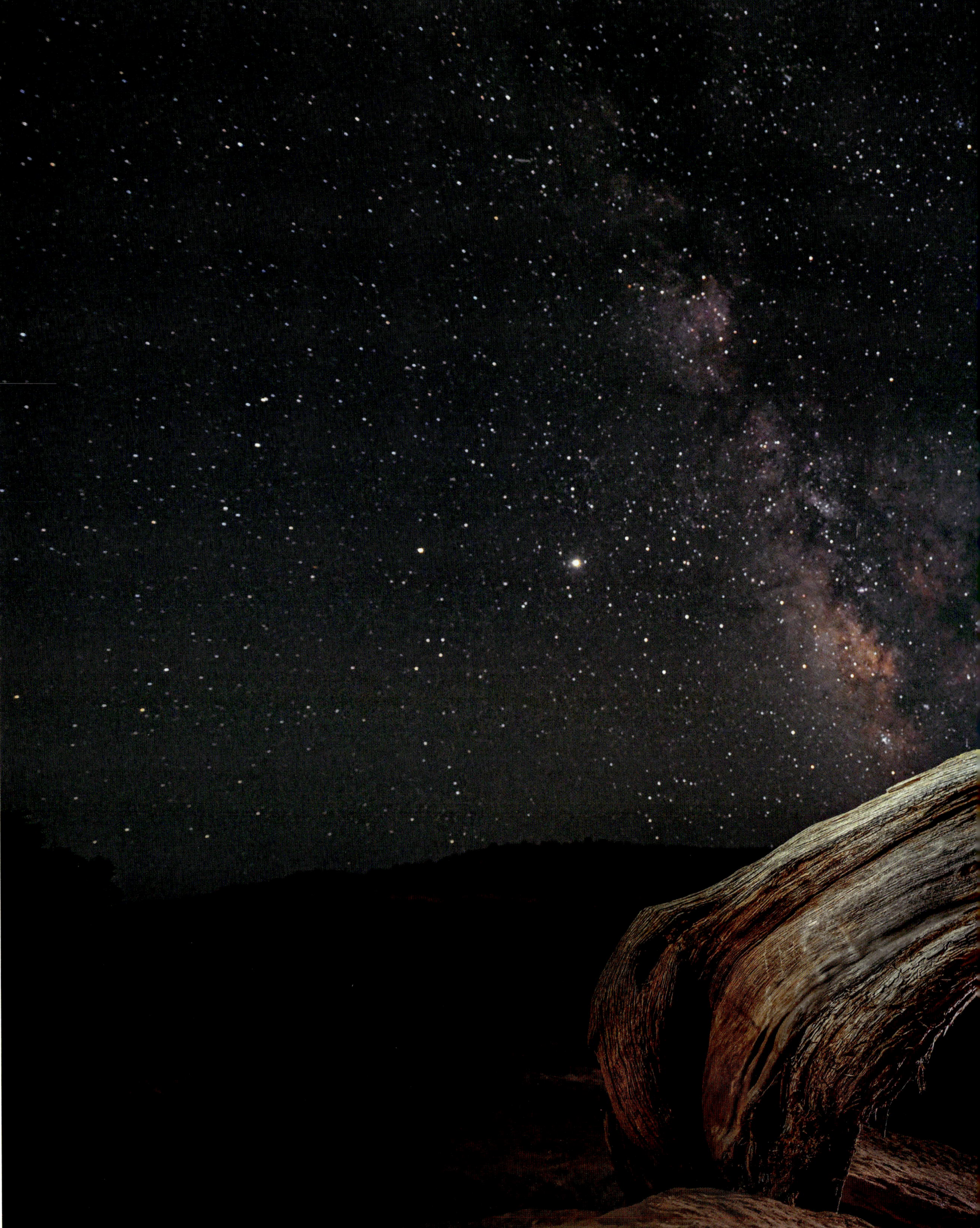

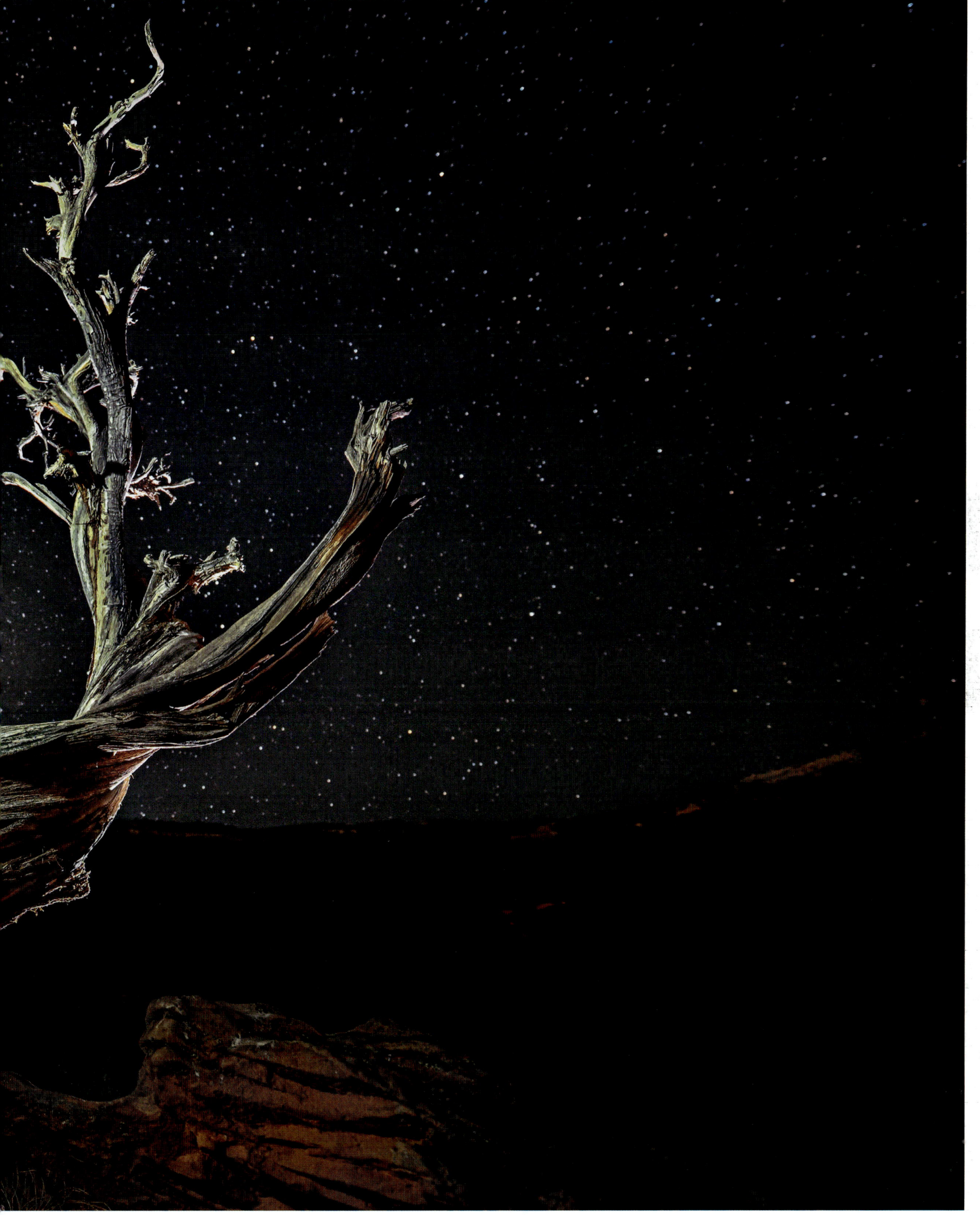

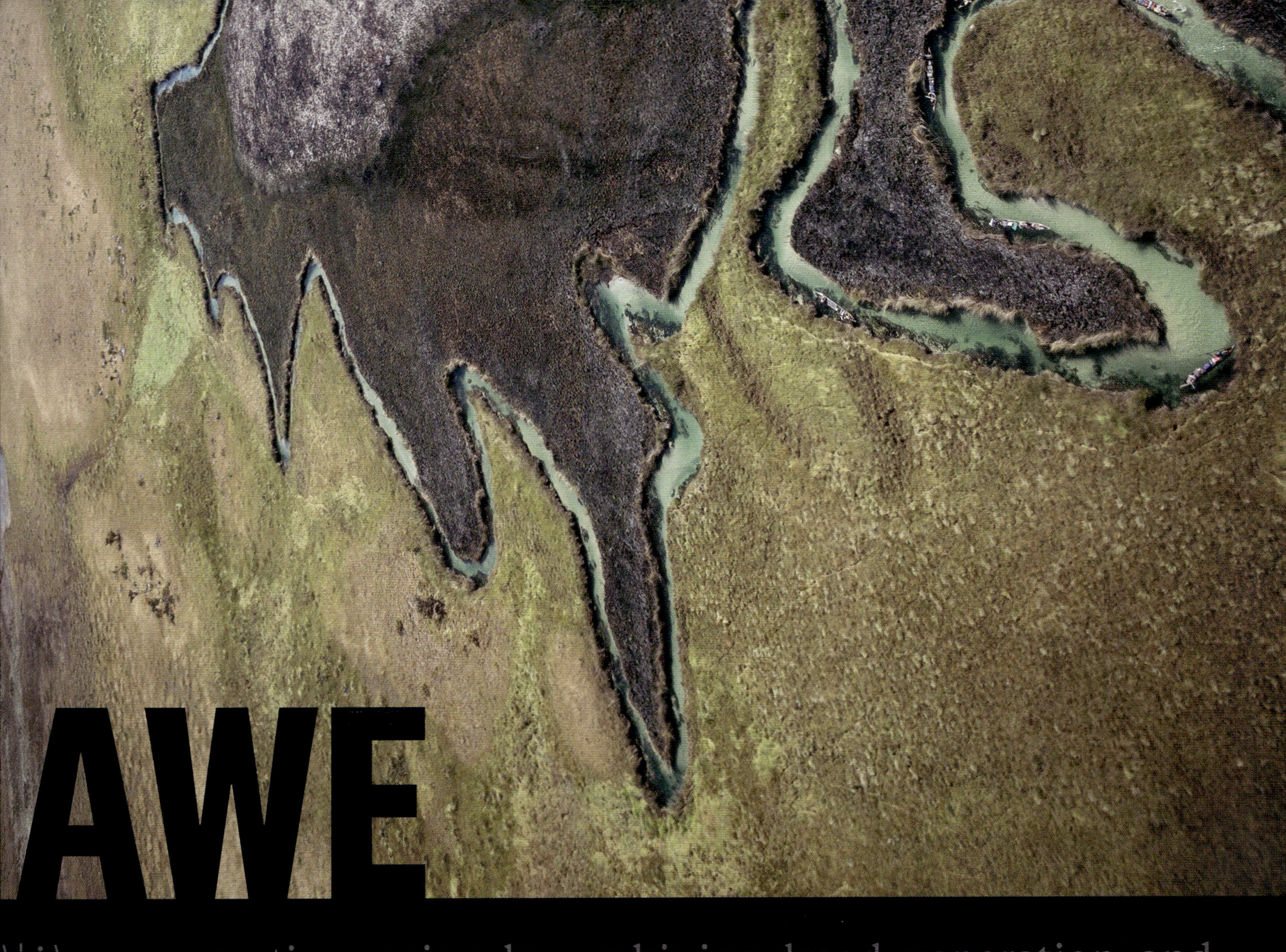

AWE
\'ȯ\ n: an emotion variously combining dread, veneration, and wonder that is inspired by authority or by the sacred or sublime;

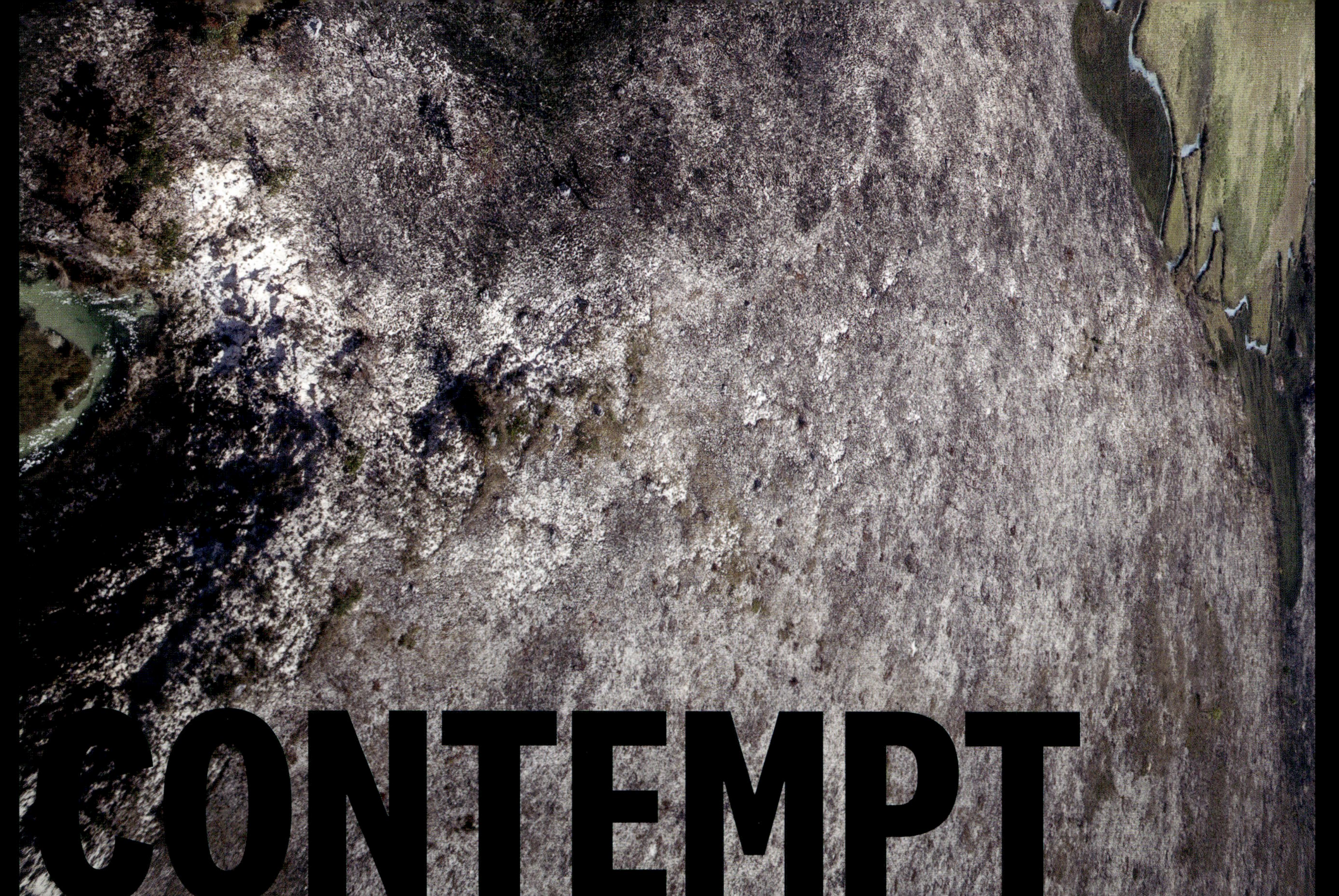

CONTEMPT

\kən-ˈtem(p)t\ *n*: lack of respect or reverence for something; the act of despising

A RIVER IN AFRICA

Angola, Namibia, Botswana, and the Okavango Delta

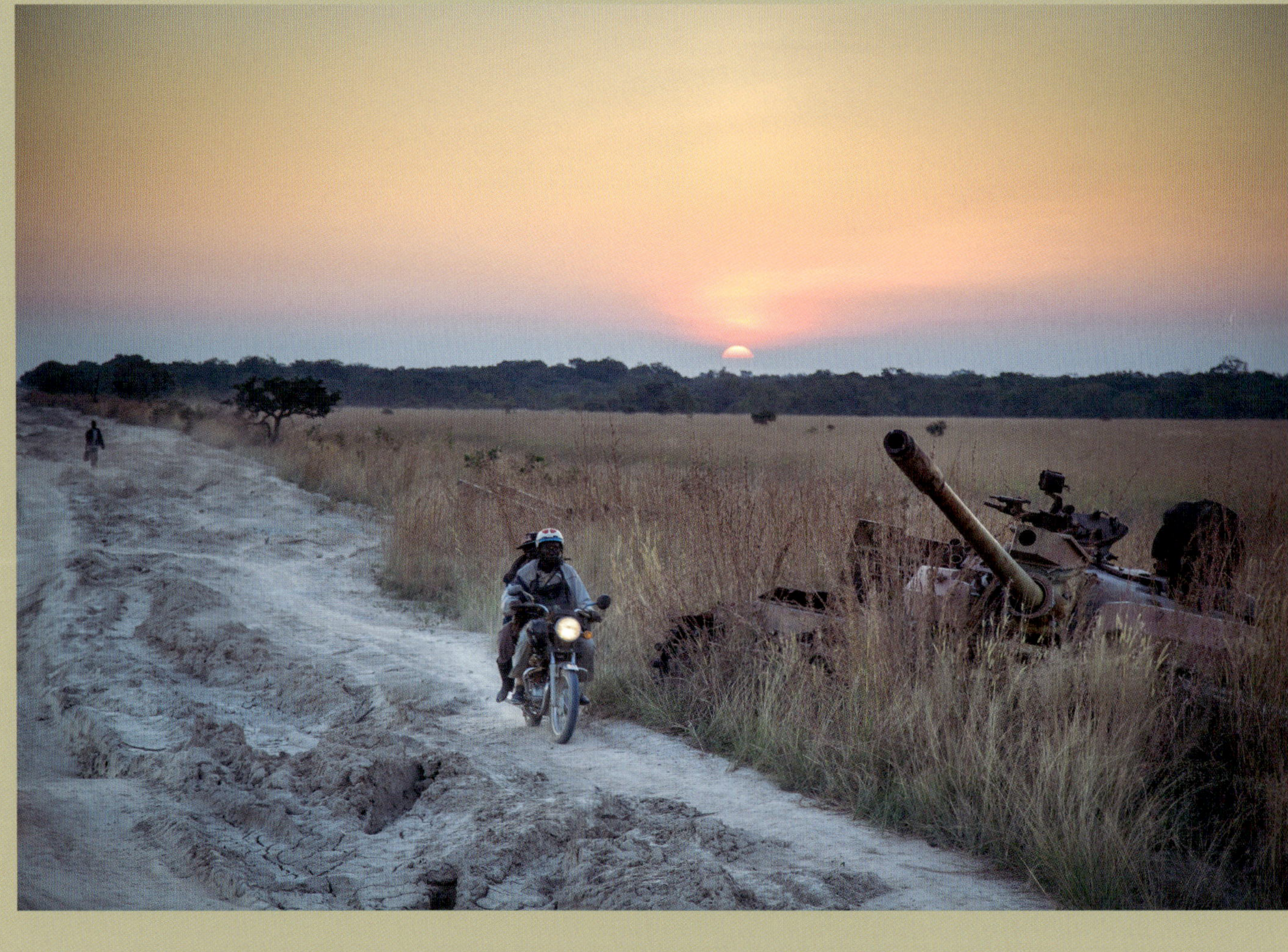

The radio crackles again and I watch as everyone around me shoves in earplugs and does one last visual survey to make sure no one is in the blast radius. The last man in the field is mostly silhouetted by the low sun as he walks back toward the vehicles with a military stride.

A hand raises. A hush settles. The hand drops.

I feel the detonation before I hear it. Eight anti-tank landmines ignite in a daisy chain, thrusting a gray cloud hundreds of feet into the sky. The shock wave blasts us with sand, and I feel a small tick inside my head as if my brain has gently bounced against the back of my skull. Orange specks of molten metal whisper as they cut through the air, followed by the gentle pitter-patter of falling debris that sounds like rain. And just as quickly, it's silent again. Eight landmines destroyed. Hundreds of thousands still hidden, waiting to disrupt the fragile peace.

I've been in Angola for nearly two months on assignment for *National Geographic*. Our team has been conducting a 2,000-mile scientific survey of the Cuito River from its source in the Angolan Highlands as part of Dr. Steve Boyes's *Into the Okavango* project. What we assumed would be a gentle float through a wilderness forgotten by the outside world has turned into a tireless march through razor grass and sweltering heat. We've been charged by hippos and capsized dugout canoes full of food and electronics. At first consideration, this seems like a needless exercise in suffering. Because of all the great rivers in Africa, the Cuito is an obscure one to follow, until you consider that it's the source of 70 percent of the Okavango Delta's water.

The delta itself lies downstream in Botswana. During its annual flood, eleven cubic kilometers of water spill across the plains and marshlands, creating one of the planet's most pristine and diverse ecosystems. Parched savannah dampens into deep green as braided channels of clear water twist though an enormous patchwork of islands. Massive herds of buffalo and zebra march across the expanses while elephants rumble and African wild dogs yip. Baboons taunt leopards, cheetahs slink, and termites build tall mounds while kudu and lechwe watch for lions. Hyenas cackle, and rhinos snort. At the end of the flood, the green fades back to brown and the earth cracks until the water comes again. The Okavango Delta is the beating heart of southern Africa and without the Cuito River, it wouldn't exist at all.

Ironically, it was Angola's civil war that has helped to protect the precious waterways. Near the end of the conflict, the United Nations estimated that there were nine to fifteen million landmines in the country. Much of the dense forests of the highlands were simply too dangerous to navigate until the unexploded ordinance was cleared. As much as the war decimated the biodiversity of the region upstream, it in some ways kept the Okavango Delta protected downstream.

It's 2015 and the war is over now. Thankfully, every day more landmines are removed. But as the humanitarian crisis slowly abates, a new threat arises. As soon as an area is cleared, people move in. Old-growth forests are cleared, burned for charcoal, and replaced with seasonal agriculture. Dams are needed for electricity and new fields require water. Domestic demands, foreign money, and internal pressure can too easily sway environmental policy, impacting the future of the rivers, wildlife, and people downstream. The race to clear the mines and protect the citizens creates a new race to legislate and protect the vast, interconnected ecosystem.

A low haze of smoke and dust has settled into the valley, and everything smells like burnt grass and gunpowder. It's hard to reconcile that something as contemptible as war could somehow play a role in protecting anything. To my eyes, the Okavango Delta is one of the planet's last, best places and a beacon of hope for what the world can be. I turn on the camera screen and scroll through the pictures of the explosion. The frame isn't perfect. But very few things in a war zone ever are.

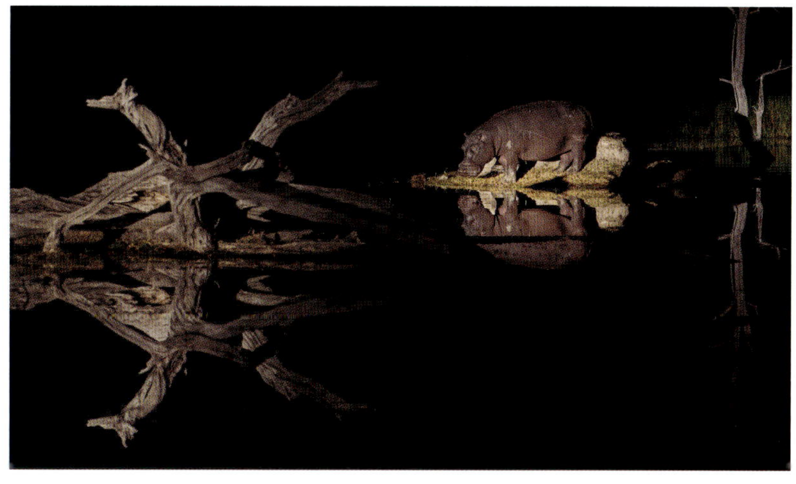

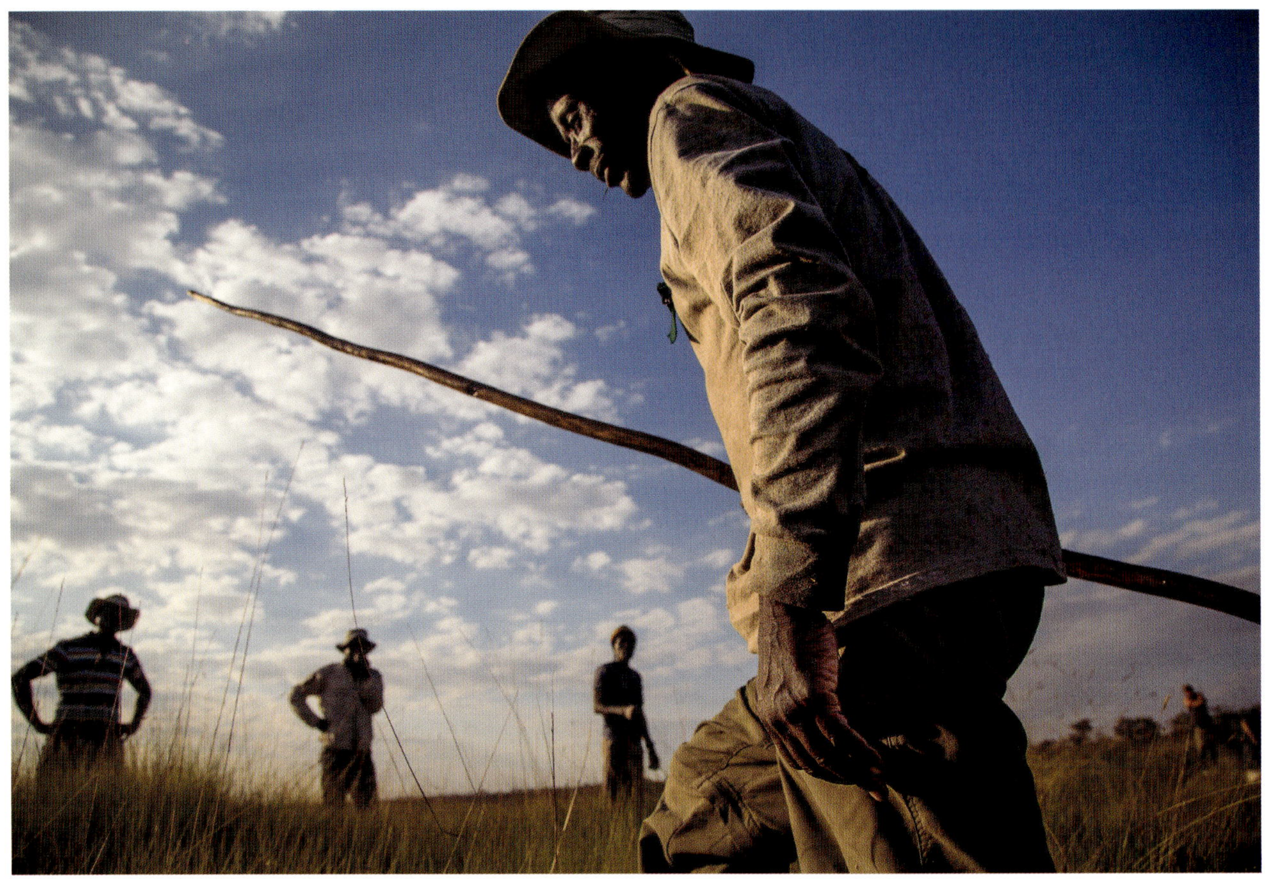

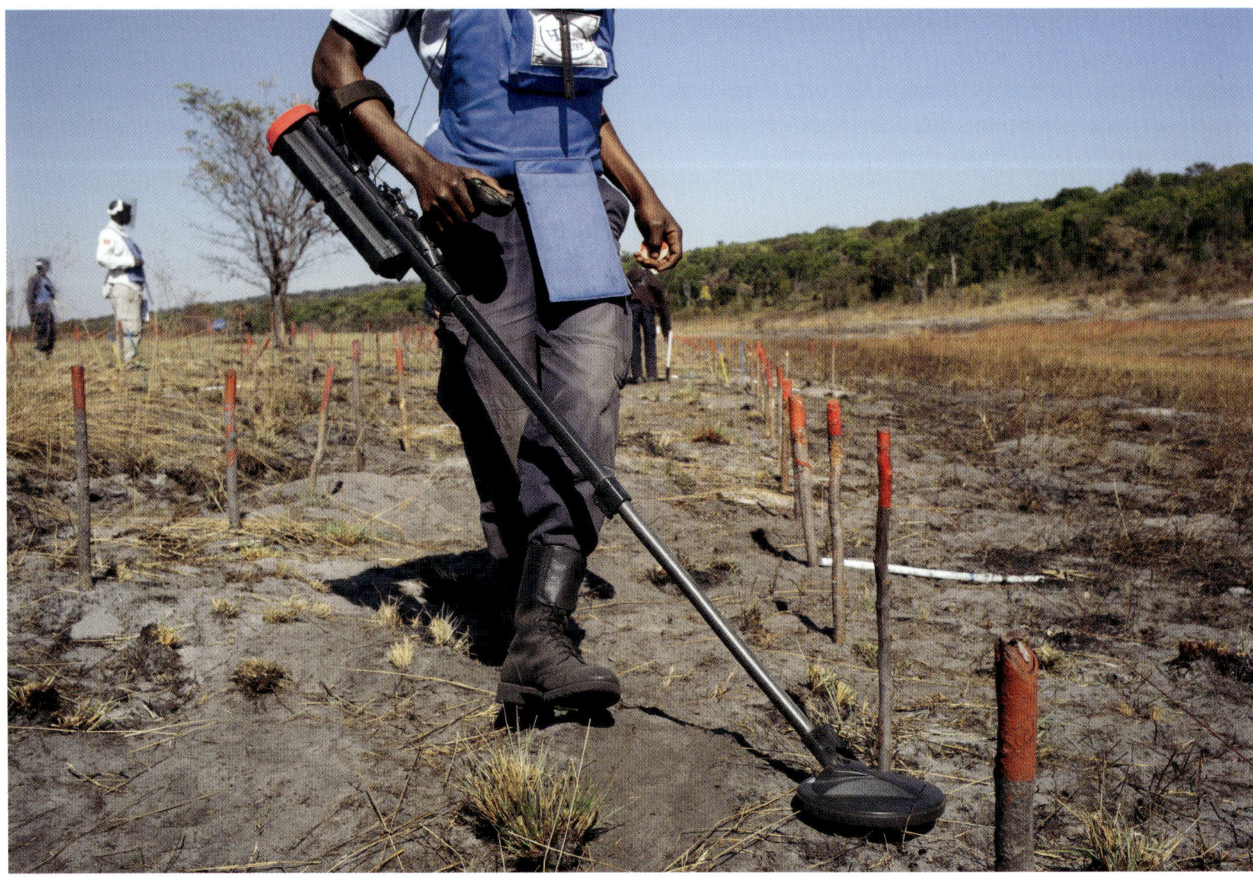

ABOVE: Water Setlabosha, a Bayei poler (an indigenous gondolier) and expedition guide, climbs from the river at the end of the day. **BELOW:** A HALO Trust employee uses a metal detector to locate unexploded landmines. The HALO (Hazardous Area Life-Support Organization) Trust is a nongovernmental organization that primarily works to clear land mines and unexploded ordinance in war-torn areas.

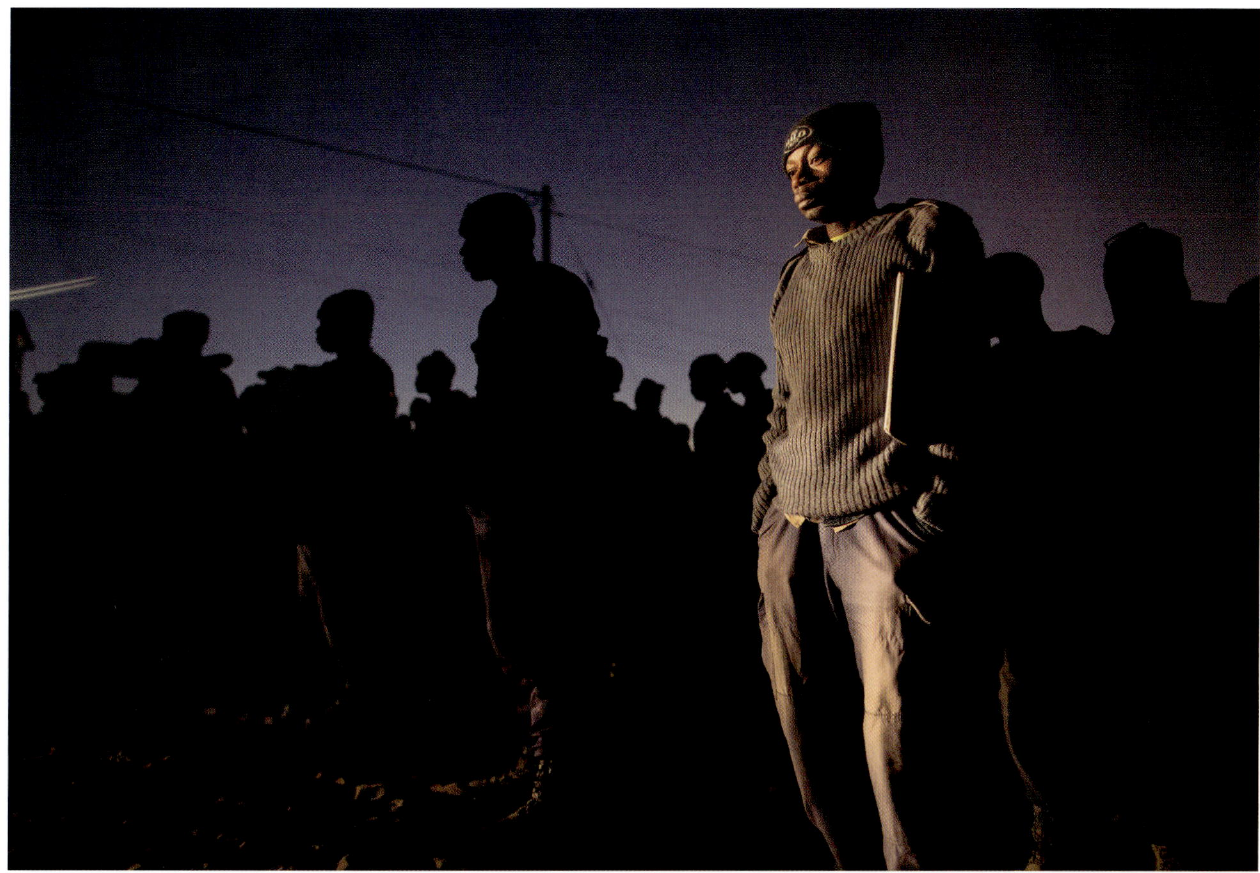

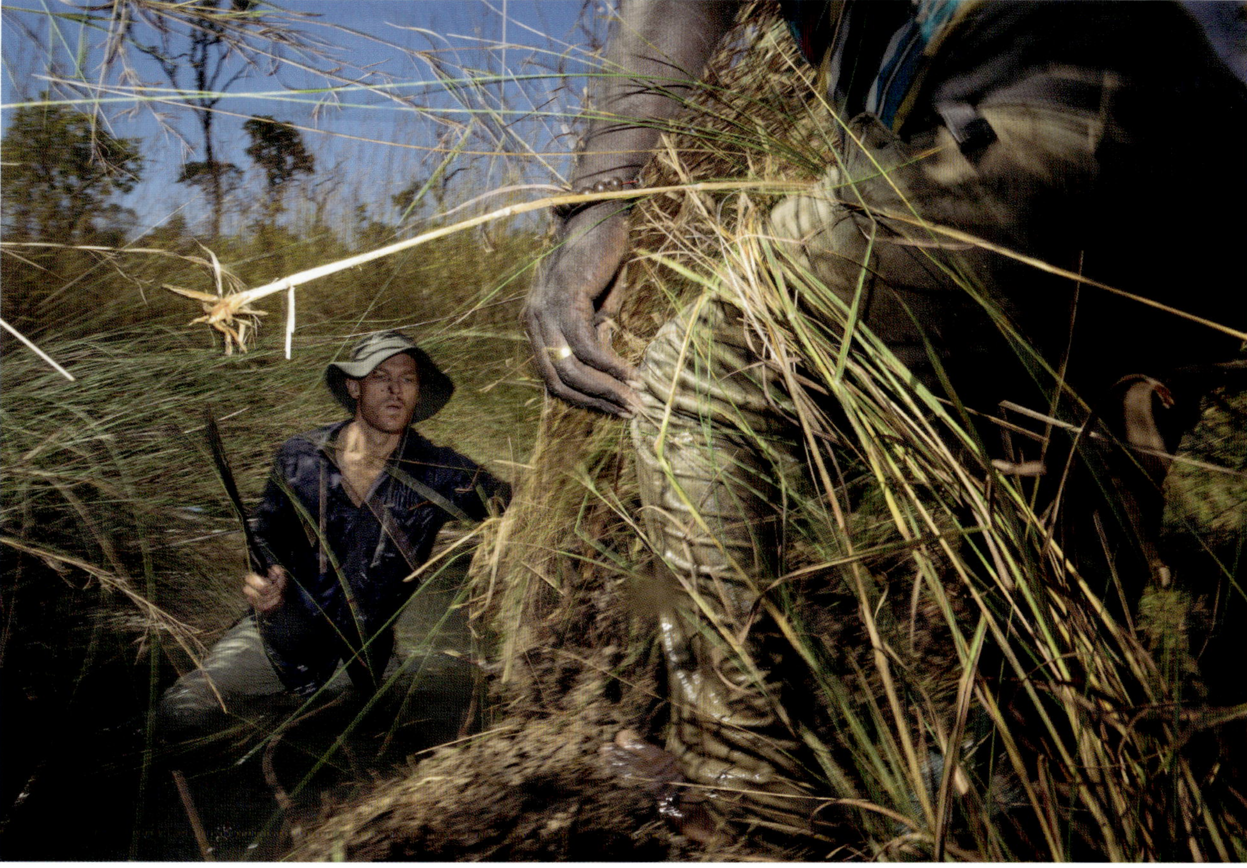

ABOVE: Angolan employees of the HALO Trust line up for predawn roll call before heading out to the minefields to continue the dangerous work of removing unexploded landmines left over from the civil war; Cuito Cuanavale, Angola. **BELOW:** South African photographer James Kydd cuts through the narrow banks of the upper Cuito River to allow passage of the mokoros, the traditional dugout canoes used to navigate the waterways of the region.

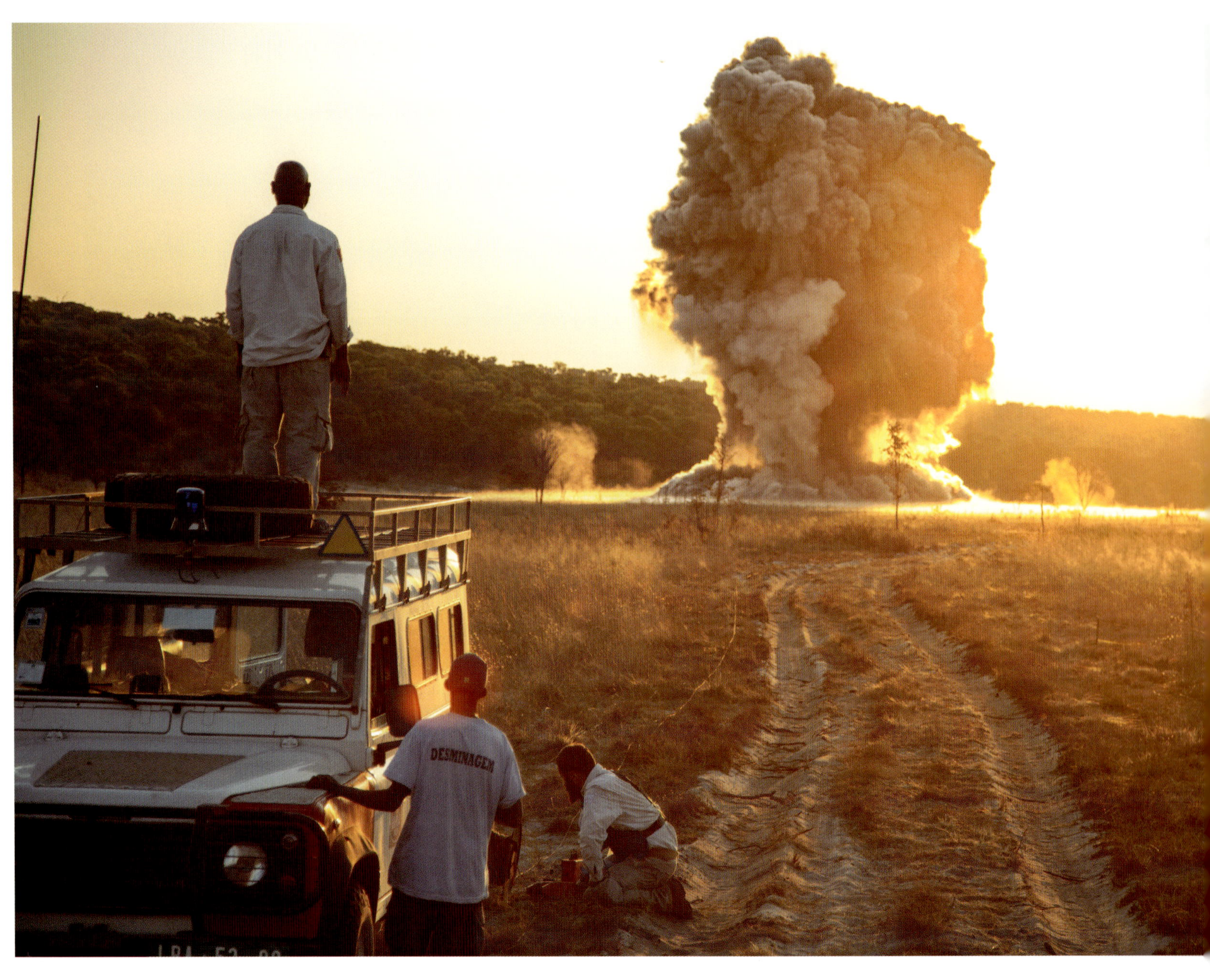

HALO Trust employees detonate unexploded anti-tank mines near Cuito Cuanavale, the site of the largest tank battle on the continent of Africa since World War II.
OPPOSITE: Civilian landmine victim; Cuito Cuanavale, Angola.

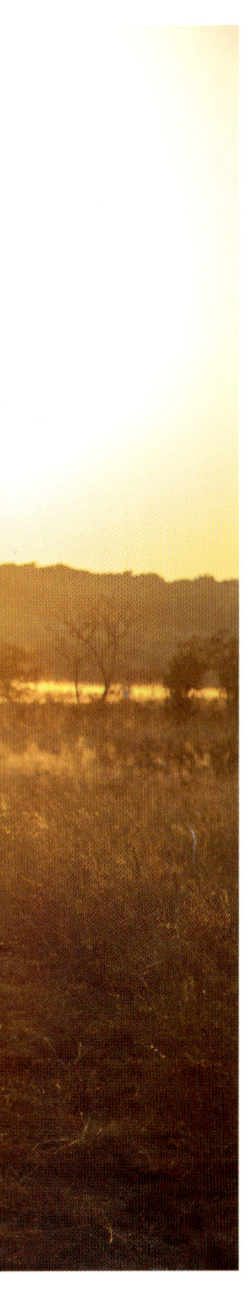

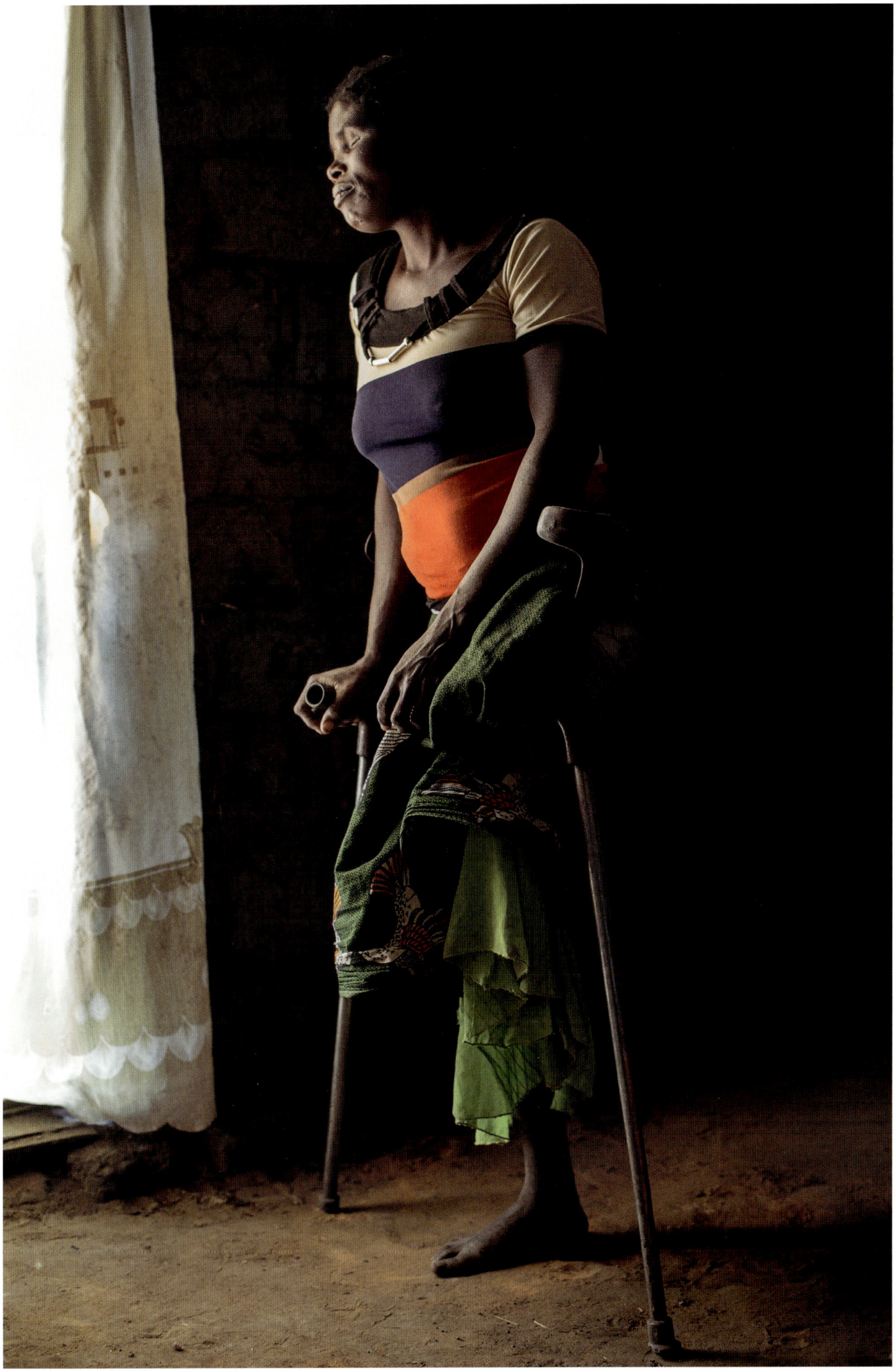

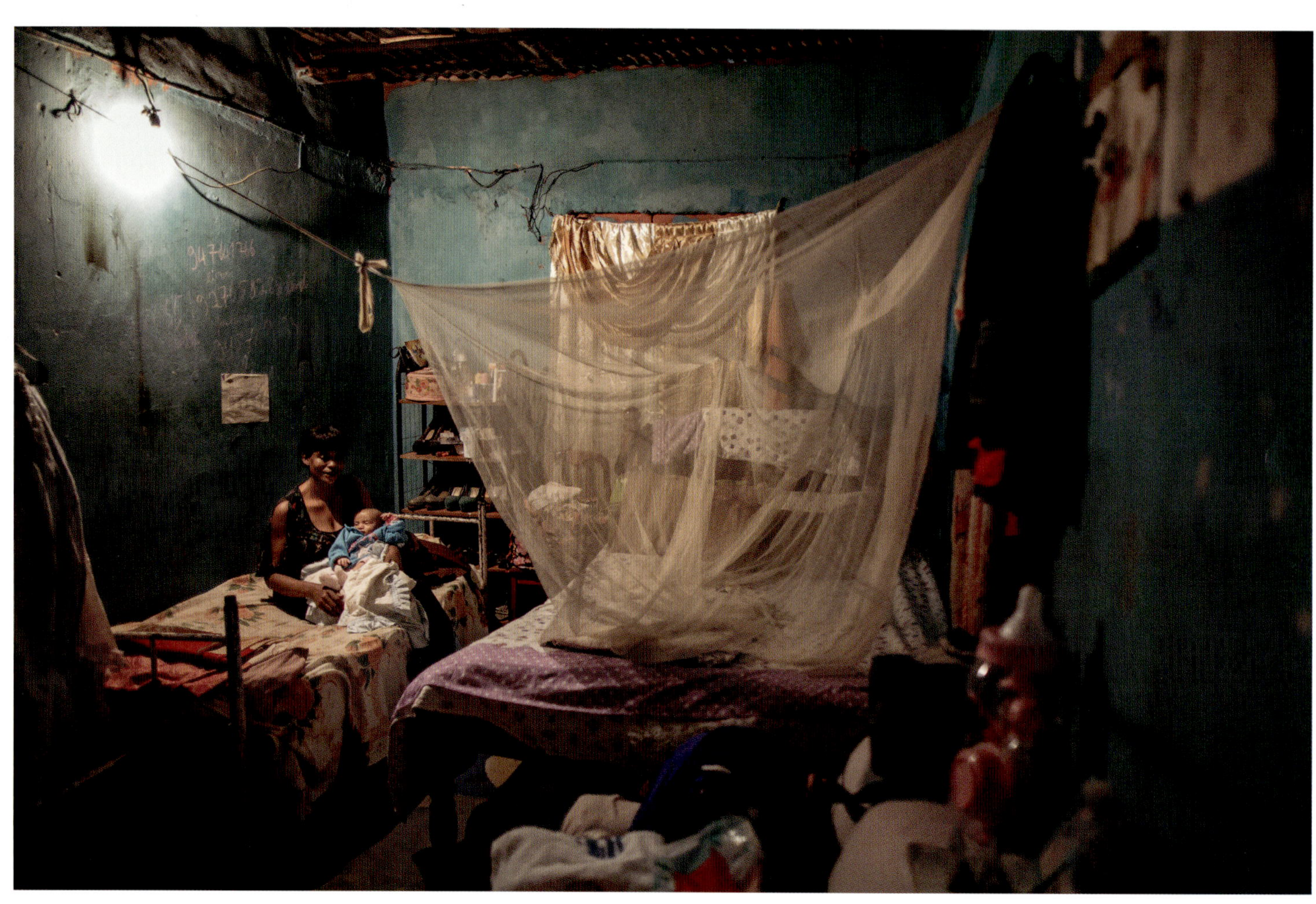

Lola, a resident of Luanda and caretaker of a city park, nursing her child; Angola. **OPPOSITE, ABOVE:** A Luchazi grandmother and grandchild stand in the door to their home in the Angolan Highlands. **OPPOSITE, BELOW:** Trading with a Luchazi community for chickens and an axe; Angolan Highlands.

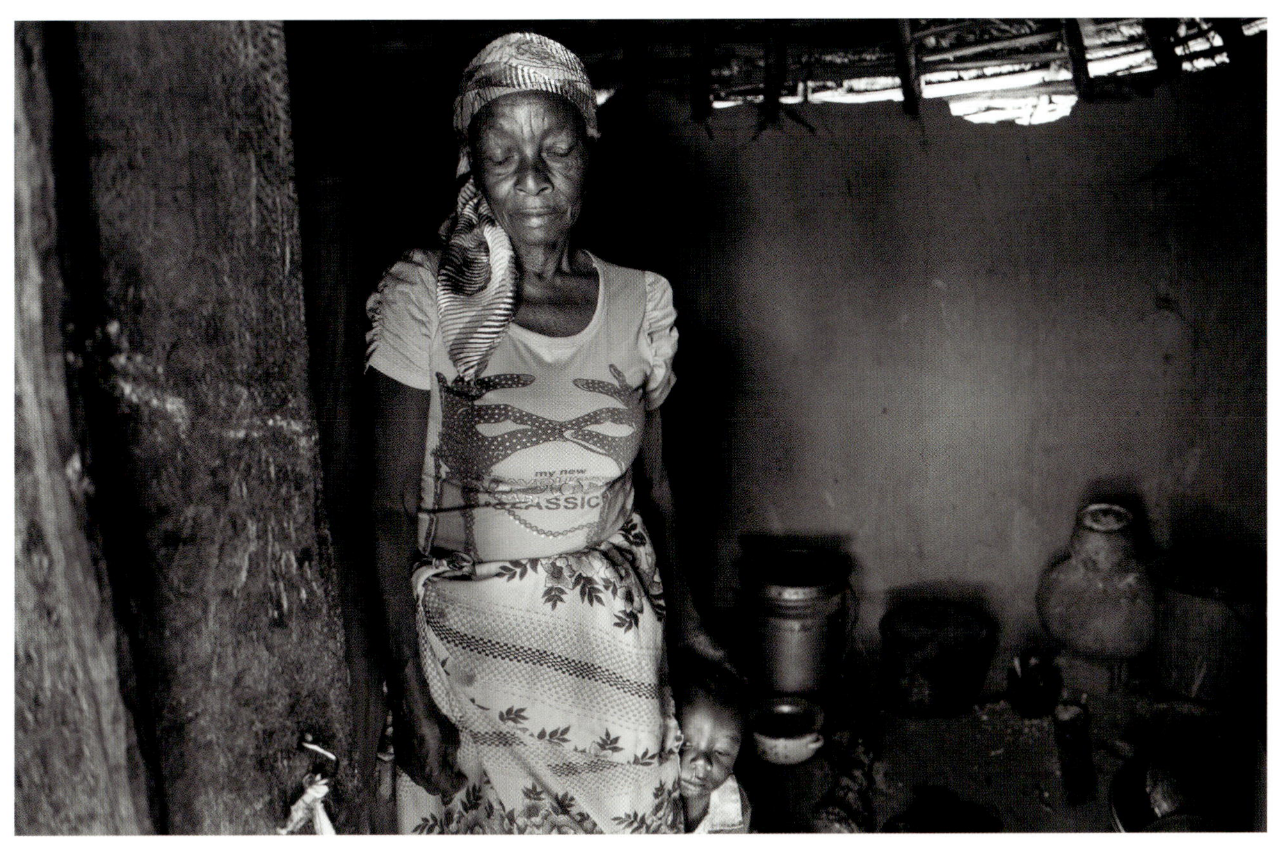

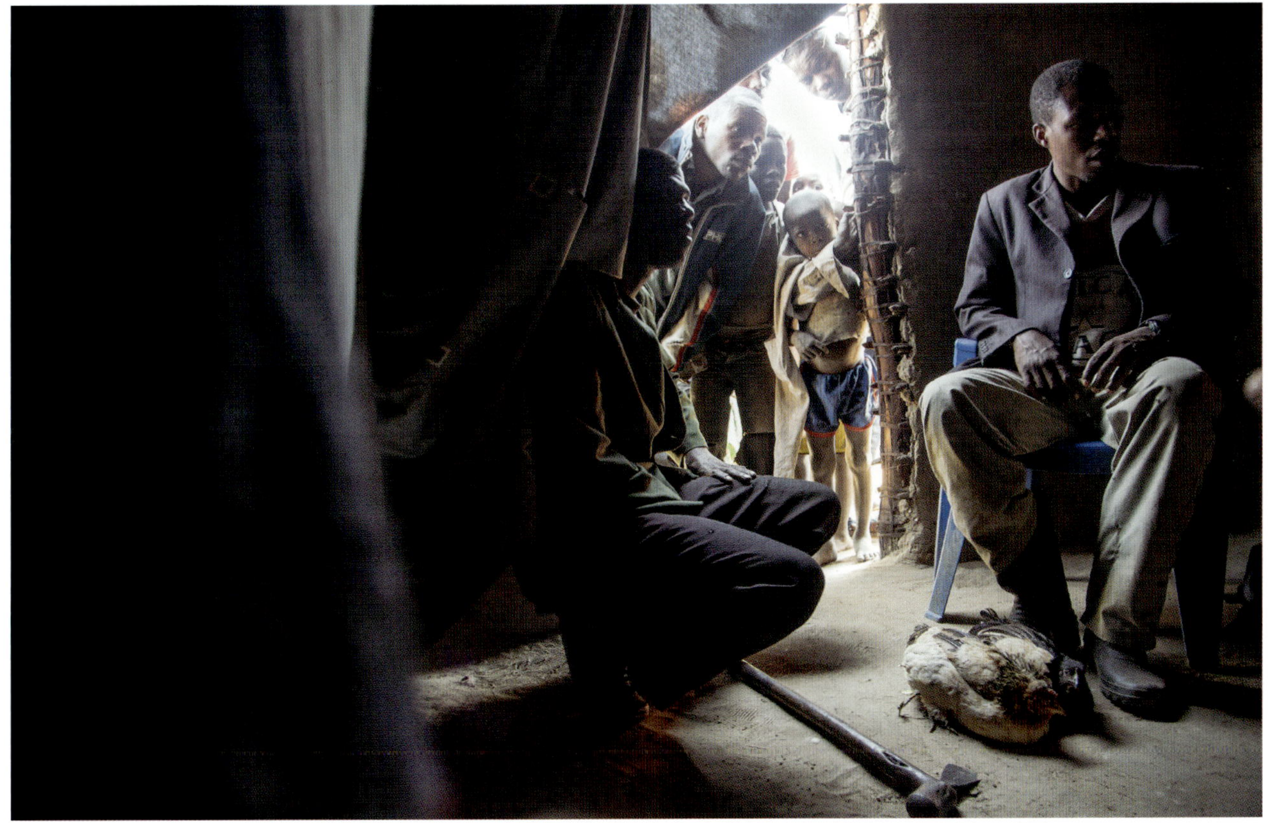

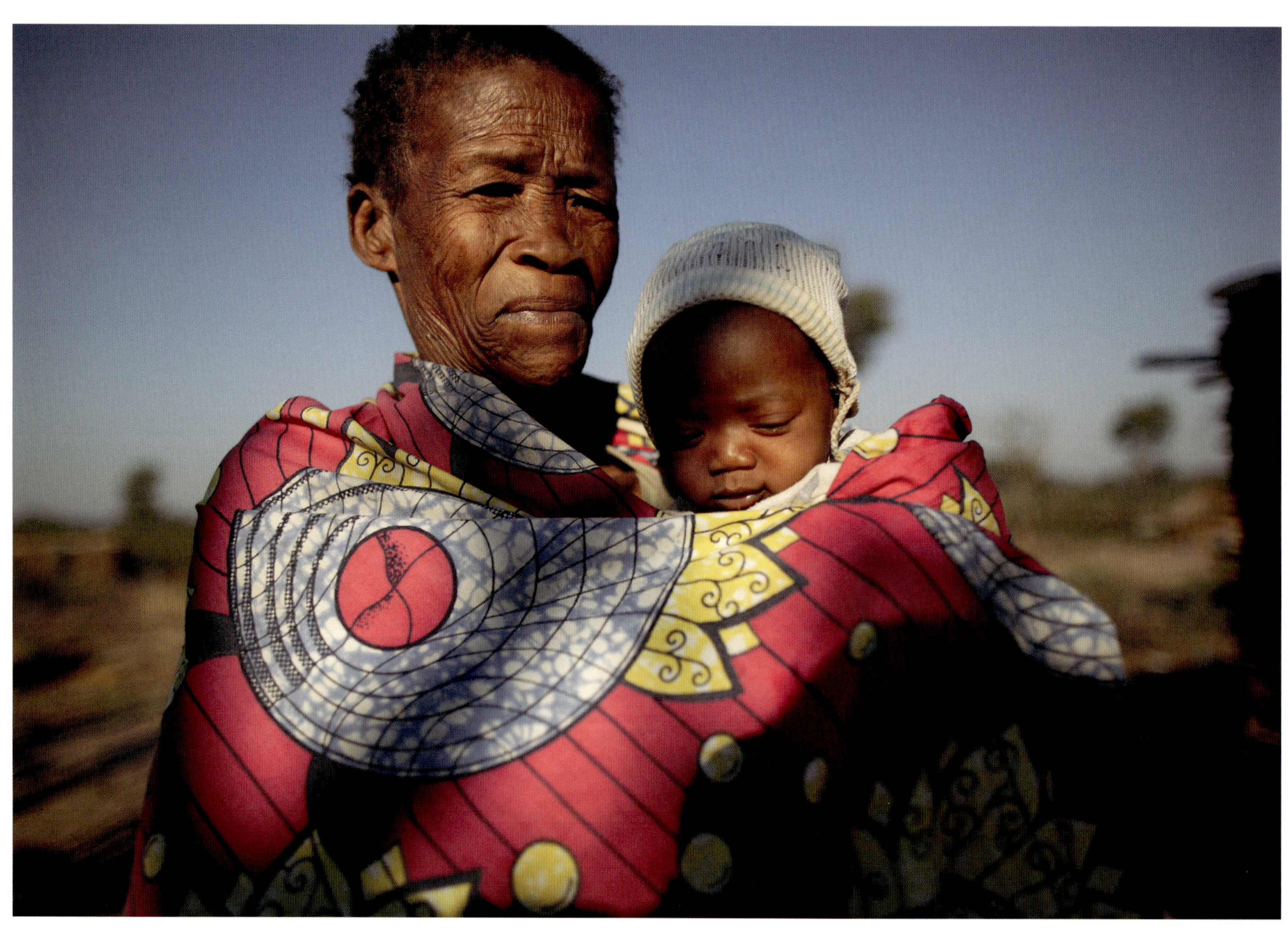

Khoisan great-grandmother and child.

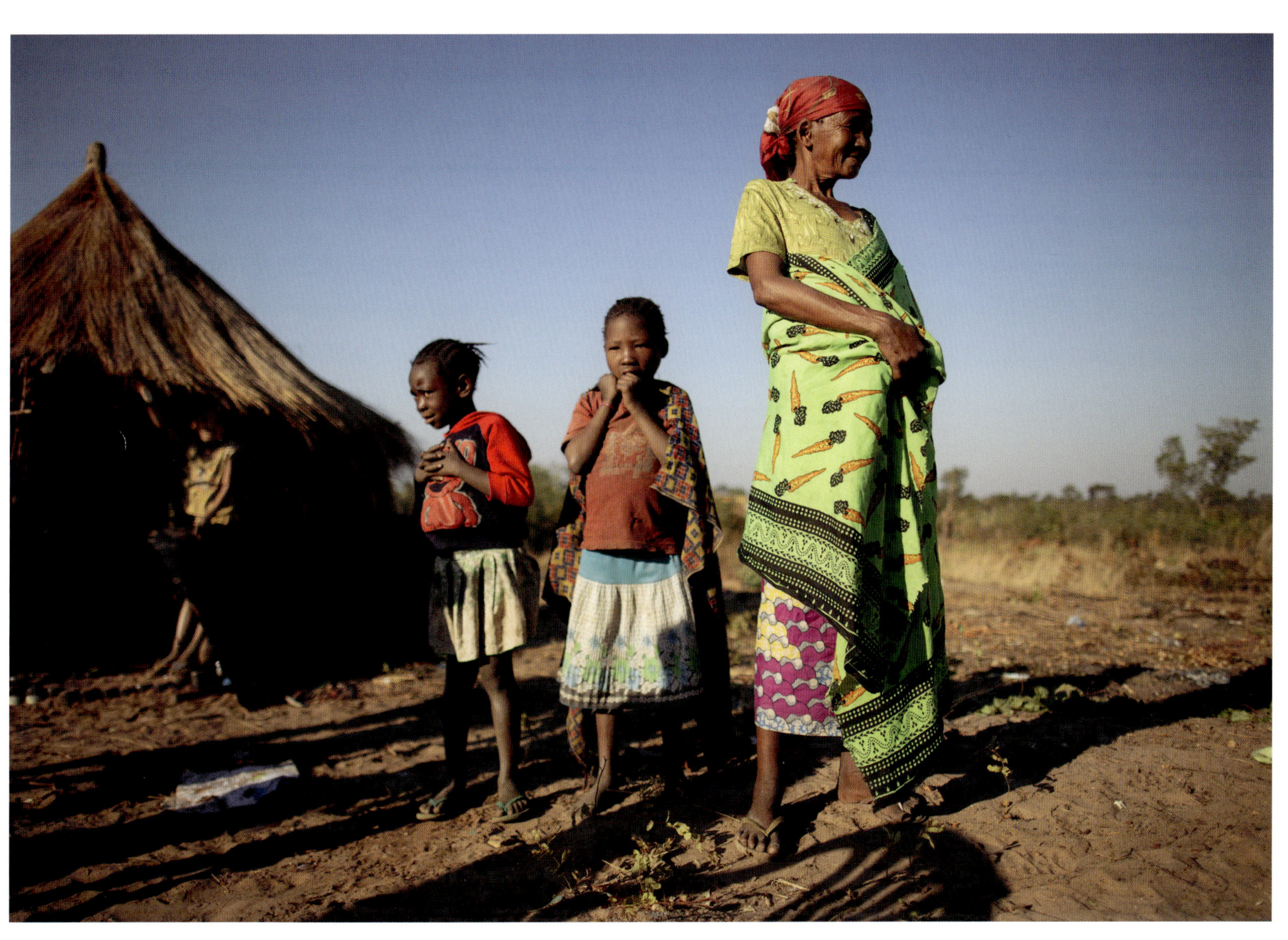

Members of a Khoisan family near their home on the outskirts of Cuito Cuanvale, Angola.

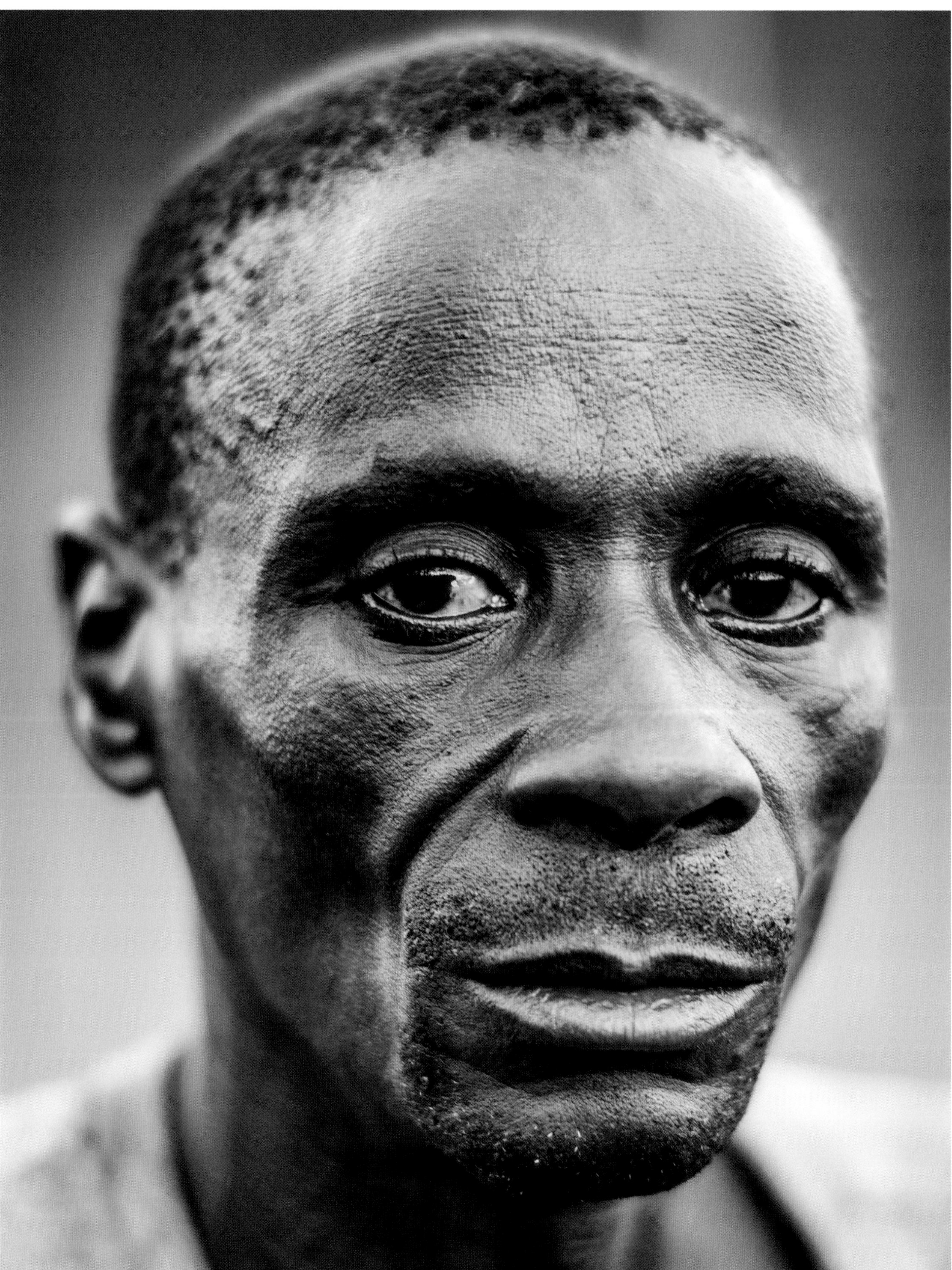

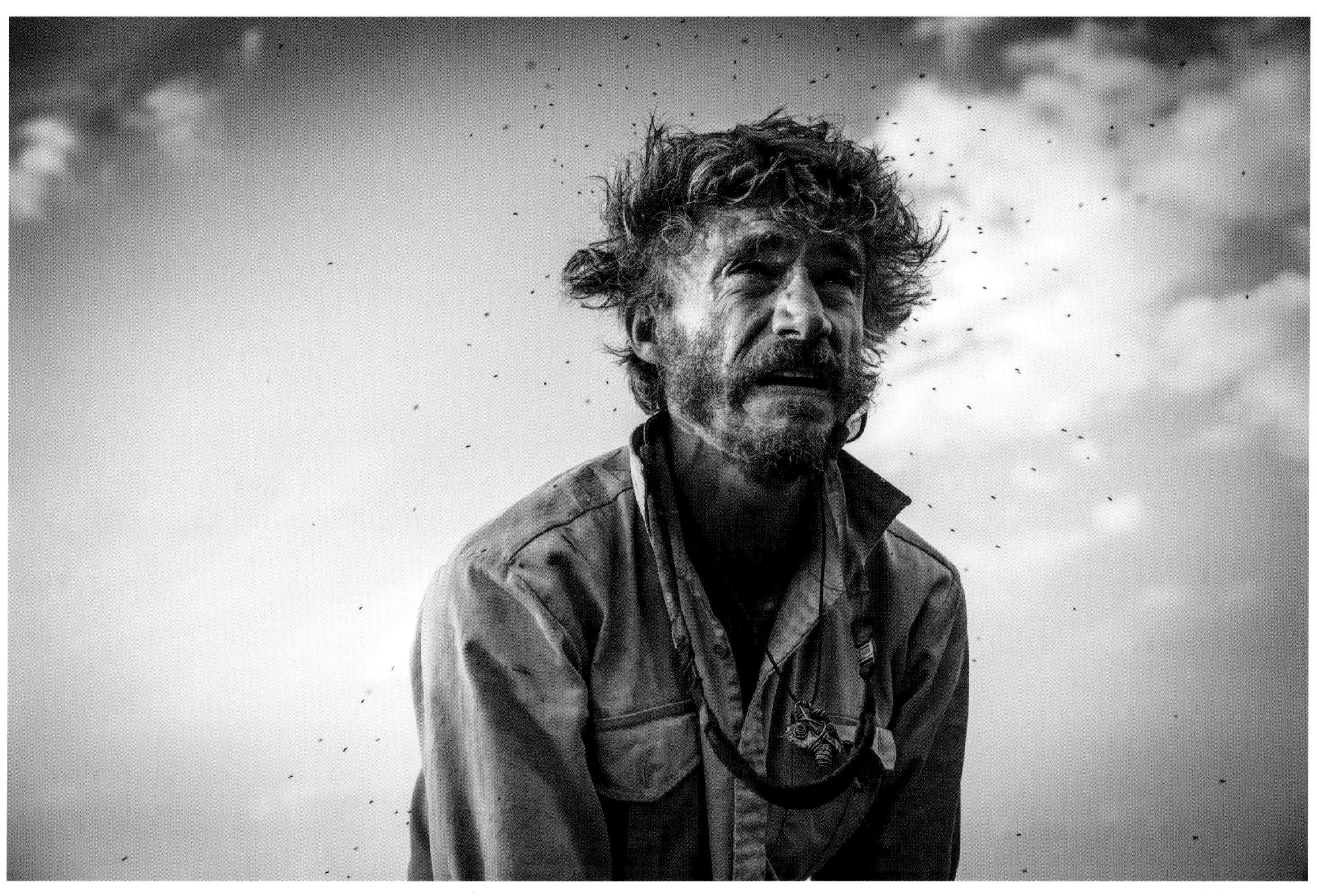

South African biologist and expedition leader Dr. Steve Boyes swarmed by sweat bees on the banks of the Cuito River. **OPPOSITE:** Water Setlabosha, Bayei poler and river guide.
FOLLOWING: Angolan children playing on Karl Marx Beach near Luanda.

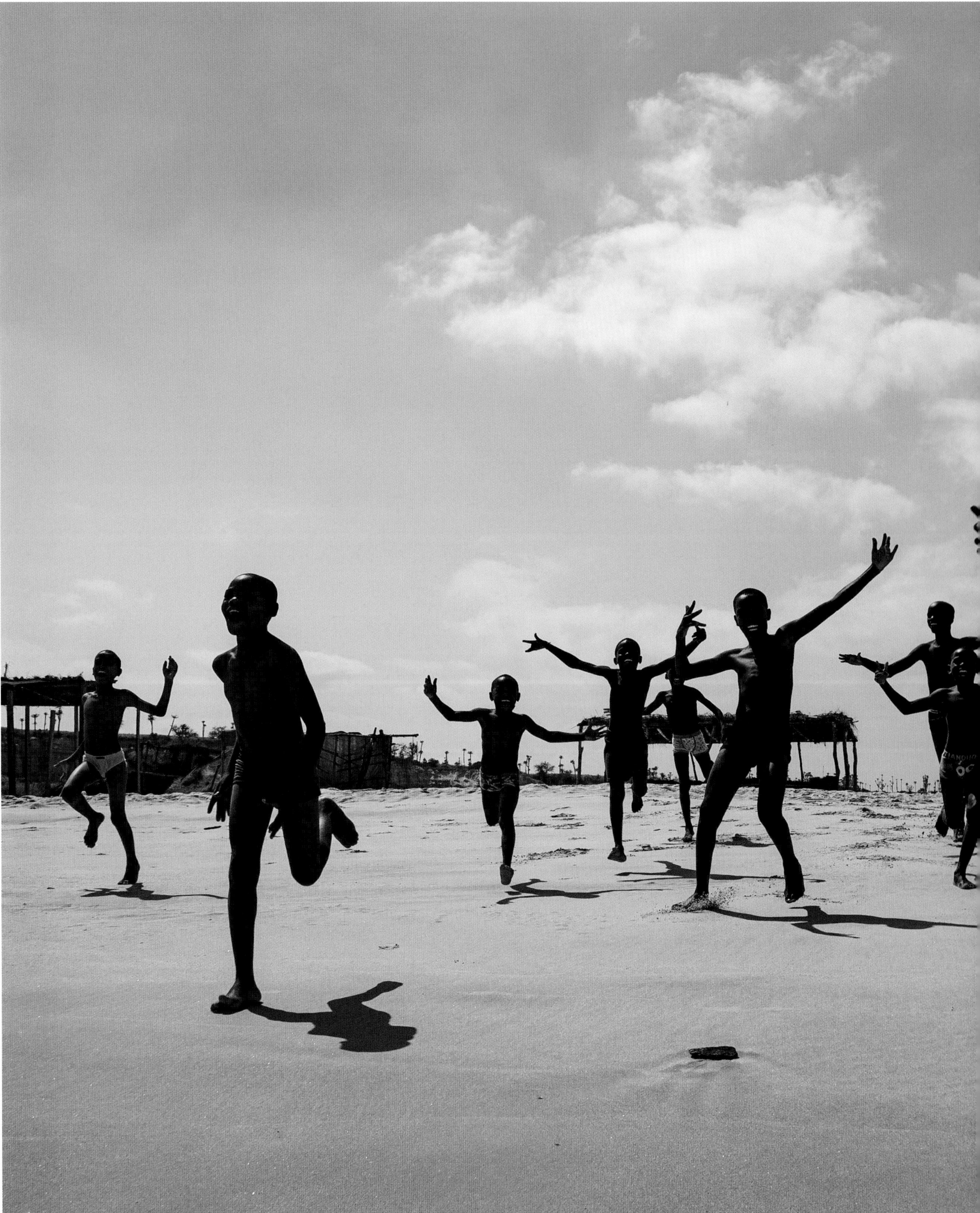

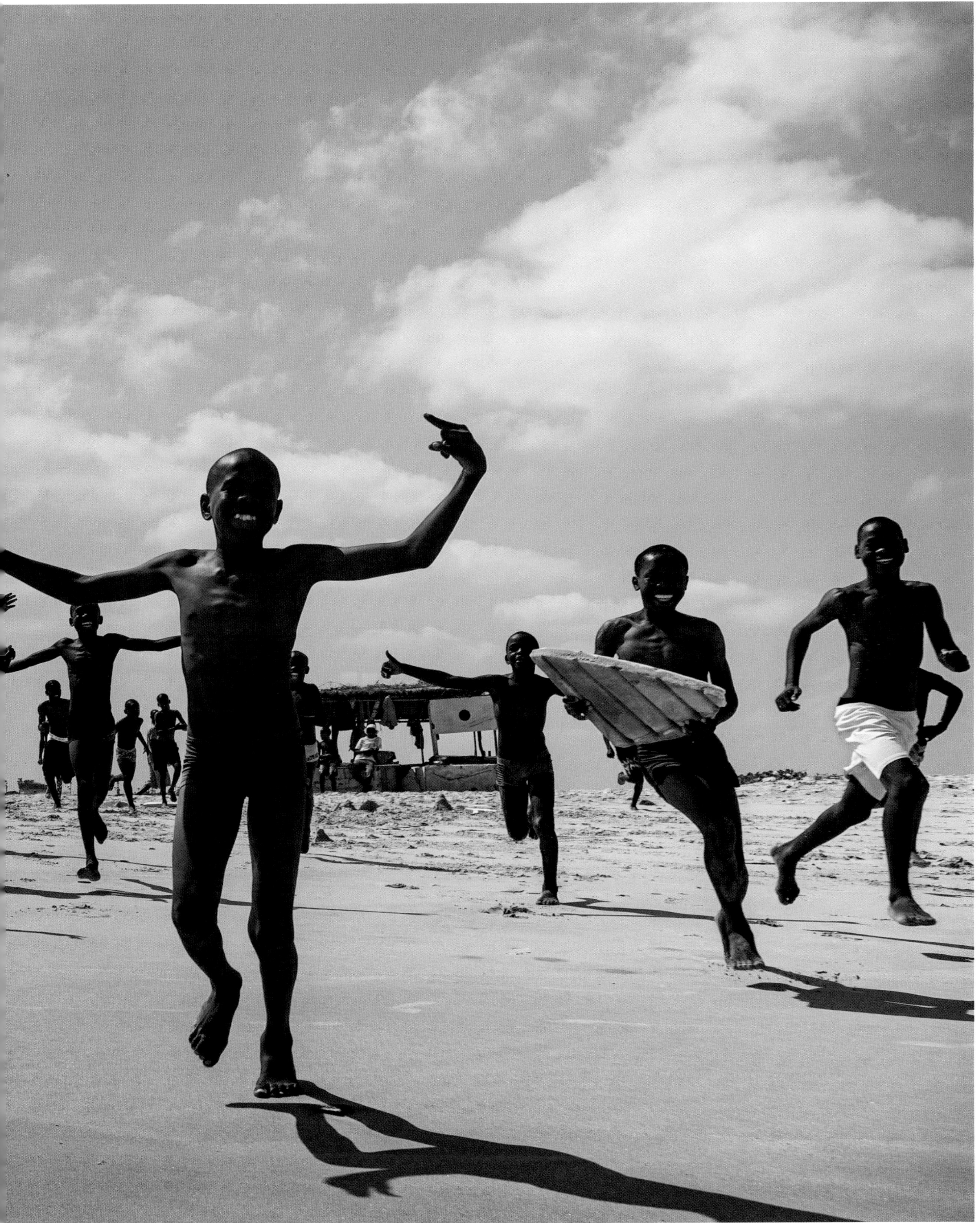

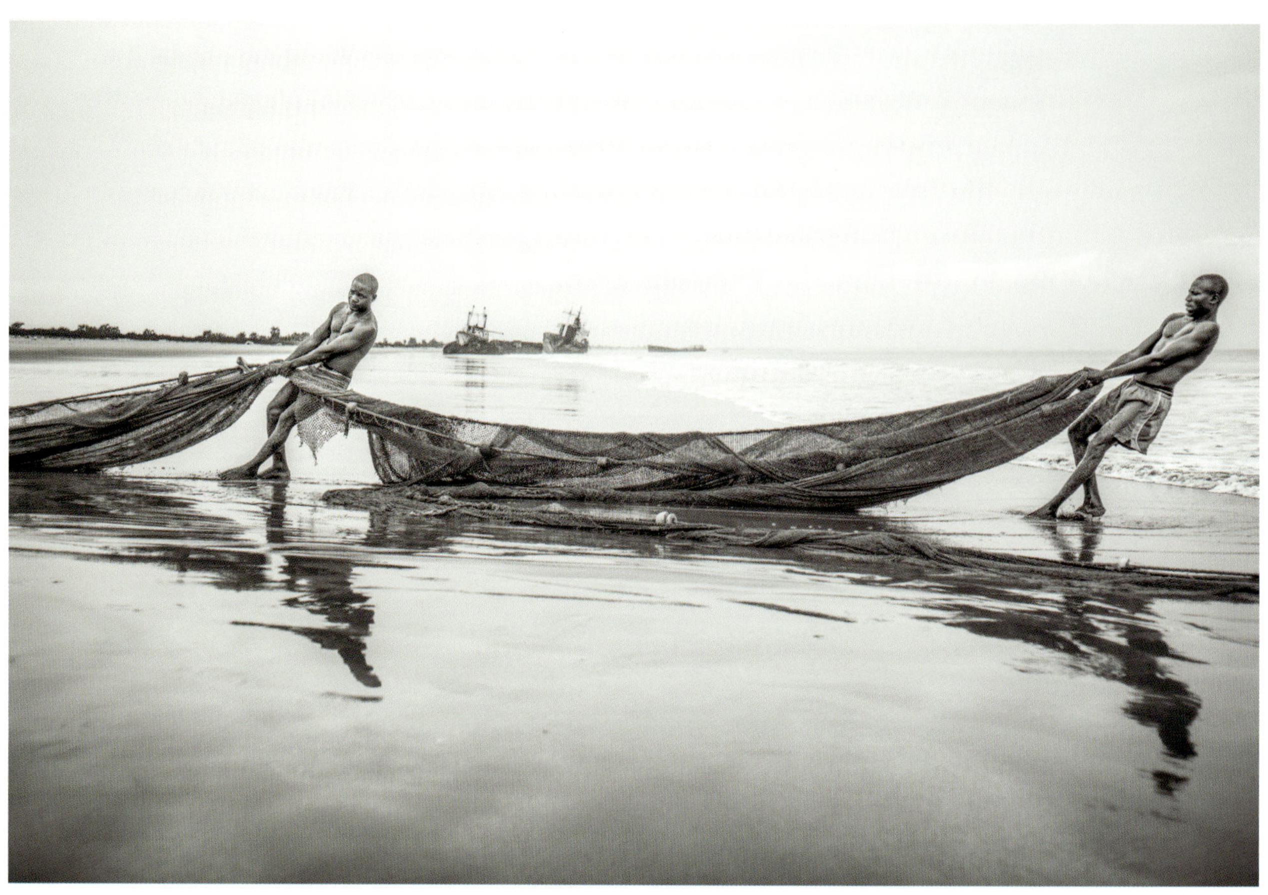

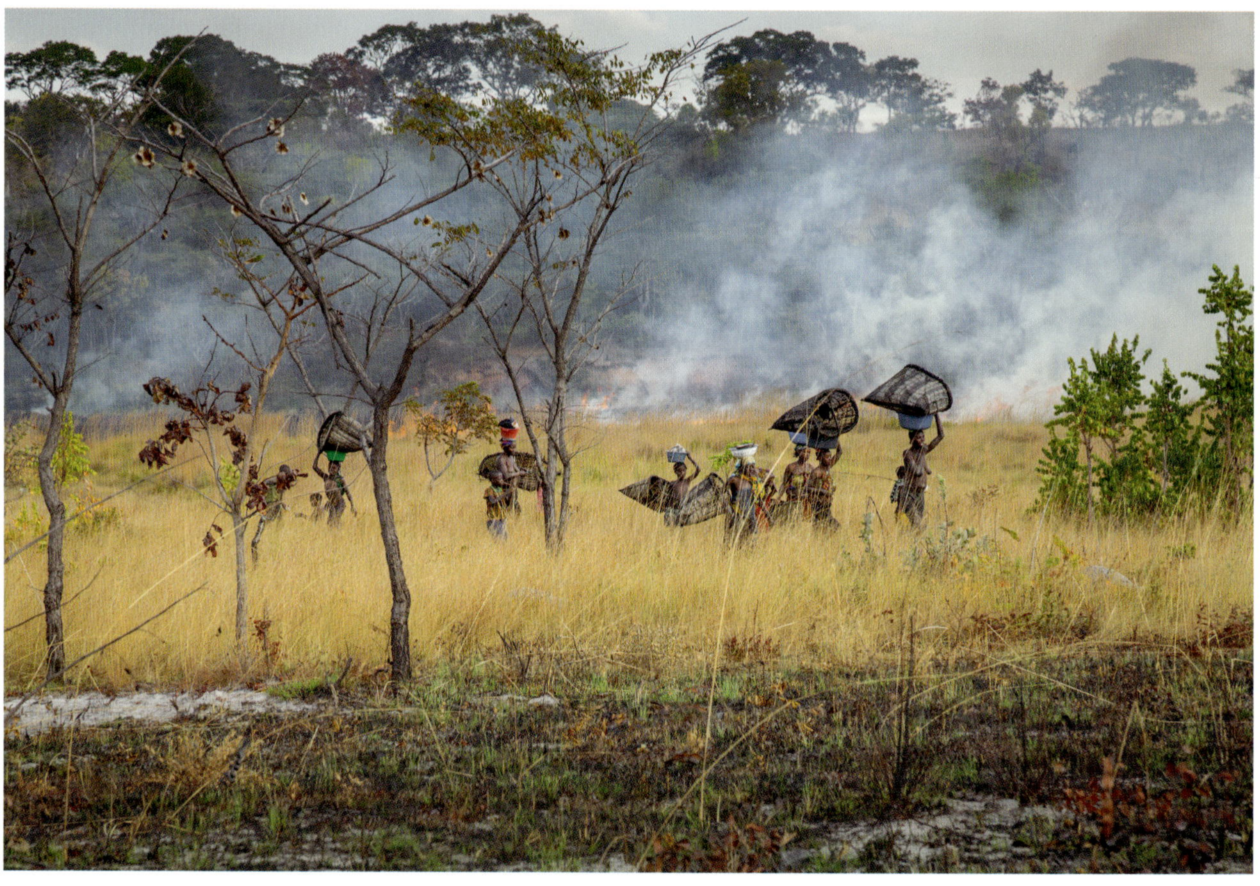

ABOVE: Fishermen pull their nets into the water; the derelict ships of Karl Marx Beach are in the distance. **BELOW:** Luchazi women and children traverse grasslands on their way back to their village as a brushfire burns behind them.

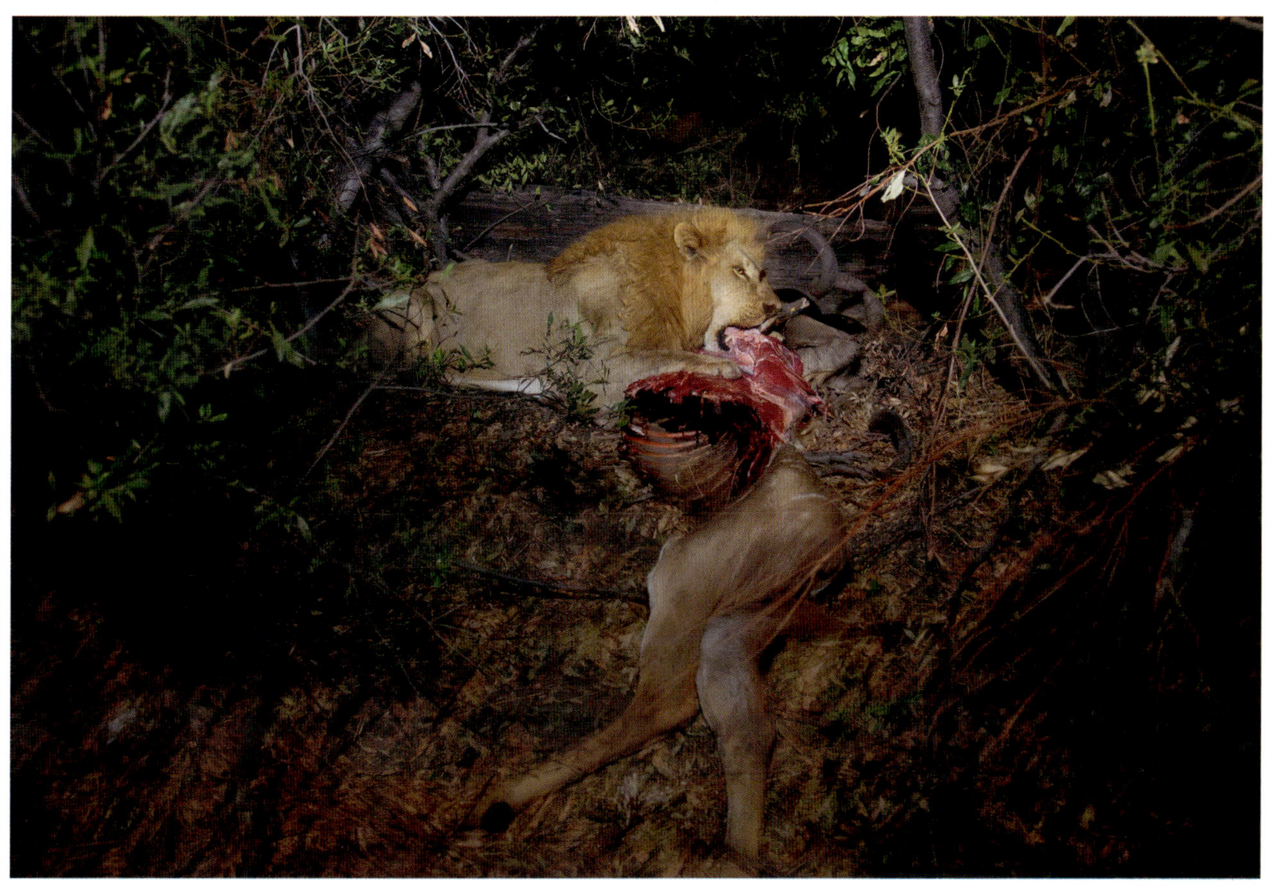

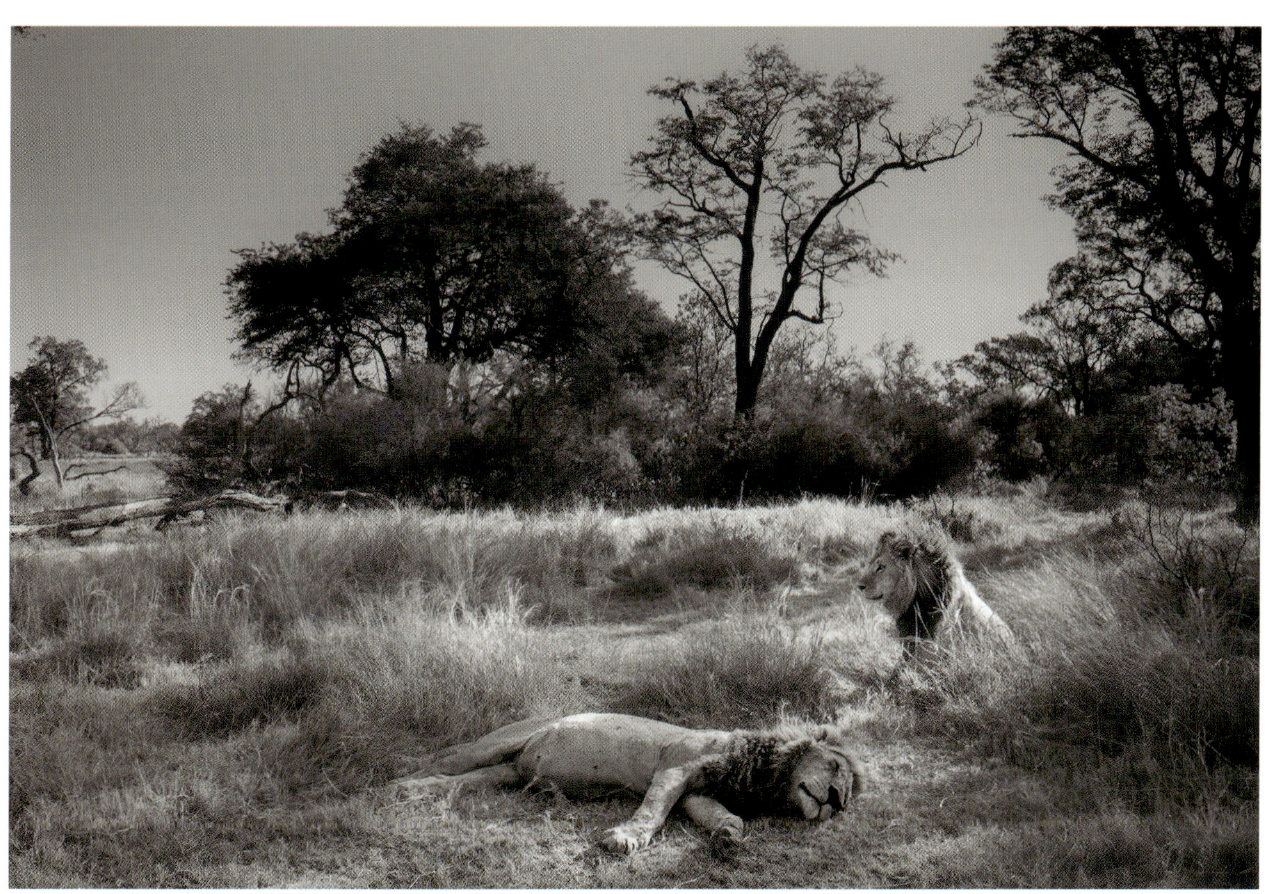

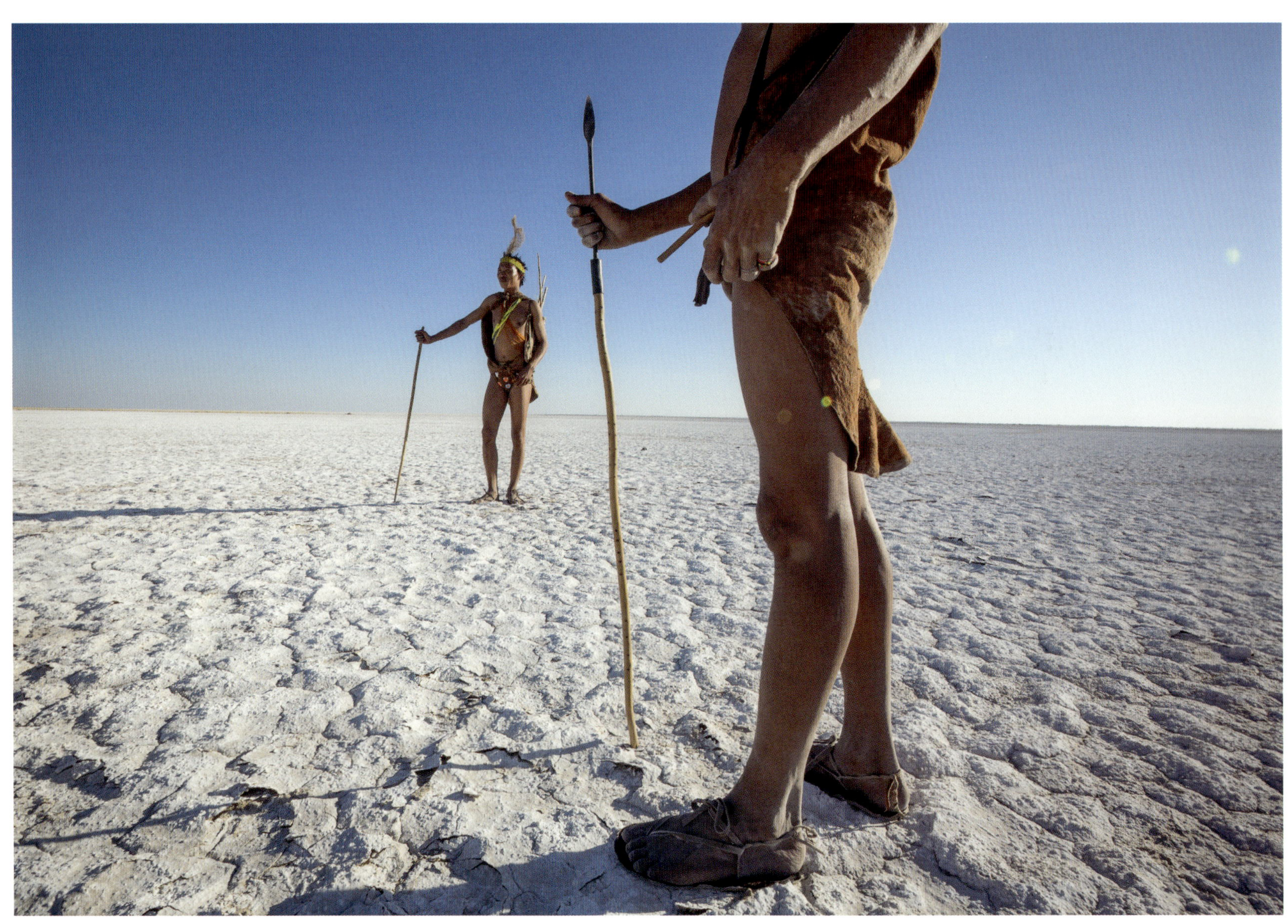

Xoma Xkgao (background) and Xoma Xwii (foreground), Khoisan "Bushman" in the Makgadigadi Pans. The Khoisan are perhaps the most genetically ancient humans and have populated southern Africa for 140,000 years. Marginalized through language, racism, and politics, most of them live in deep poverty. Xoma Xkgao and Xoma Xwii now lead "Bushman experiences" for tourists, sharing, and, in some ways, sustaining their ancient lifestyle while simultaneously forcing questions about cultural tourism and the plight of marginalized communities displaced by modernization.

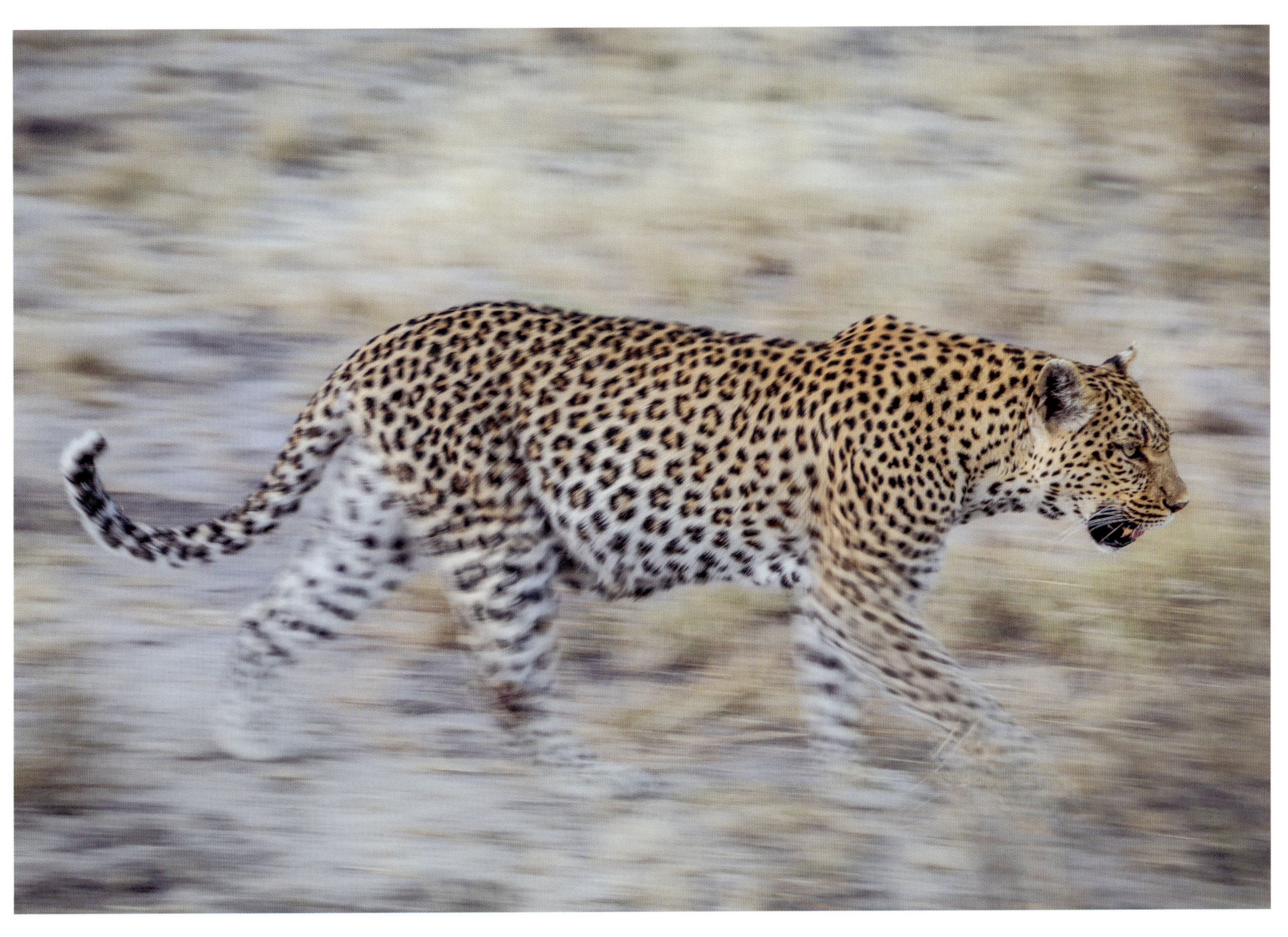

Leopard, Okavango Delta, Botswana. **FOLLOWING:** Elephants traversing the wetlands of the Okavango Delta.

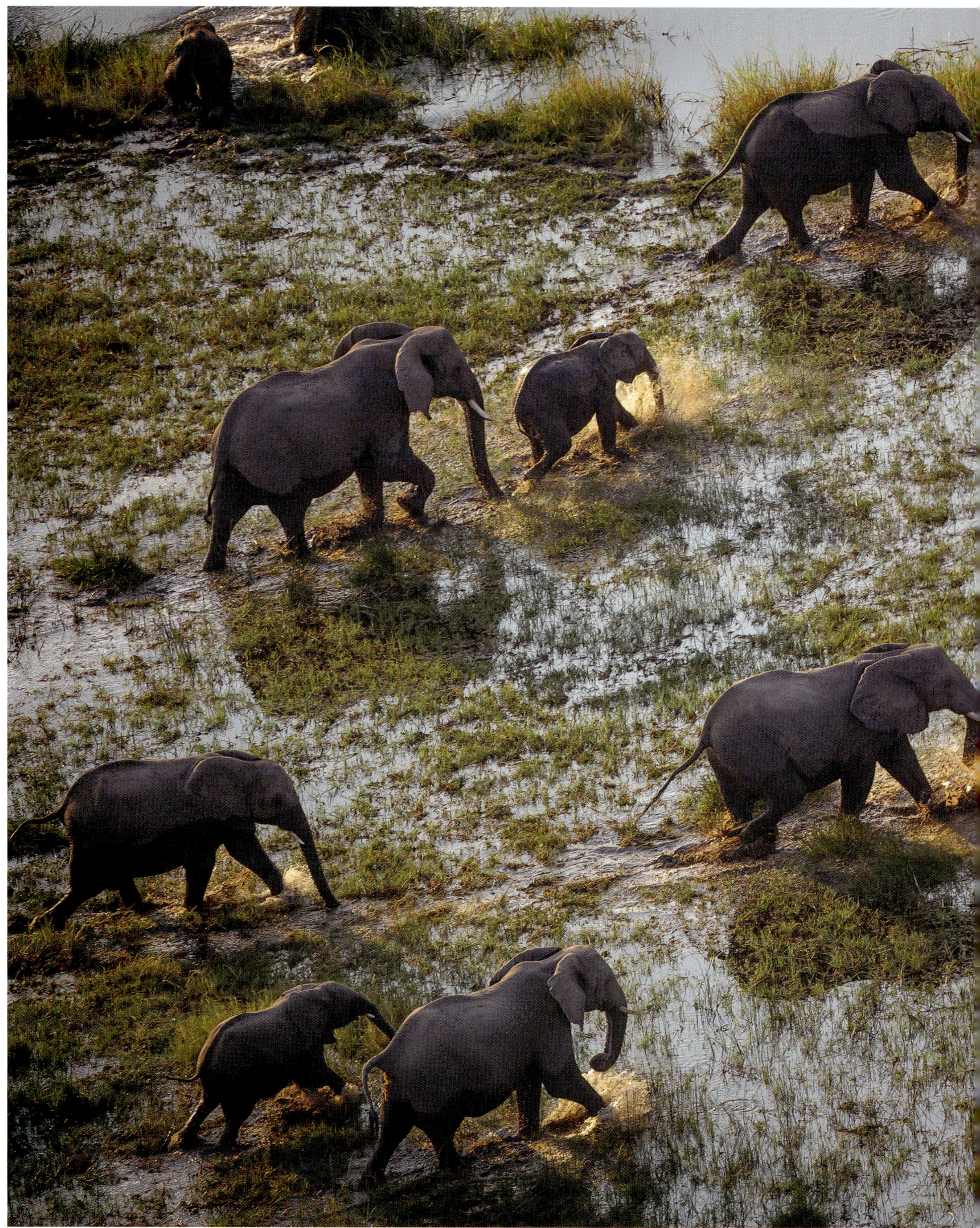

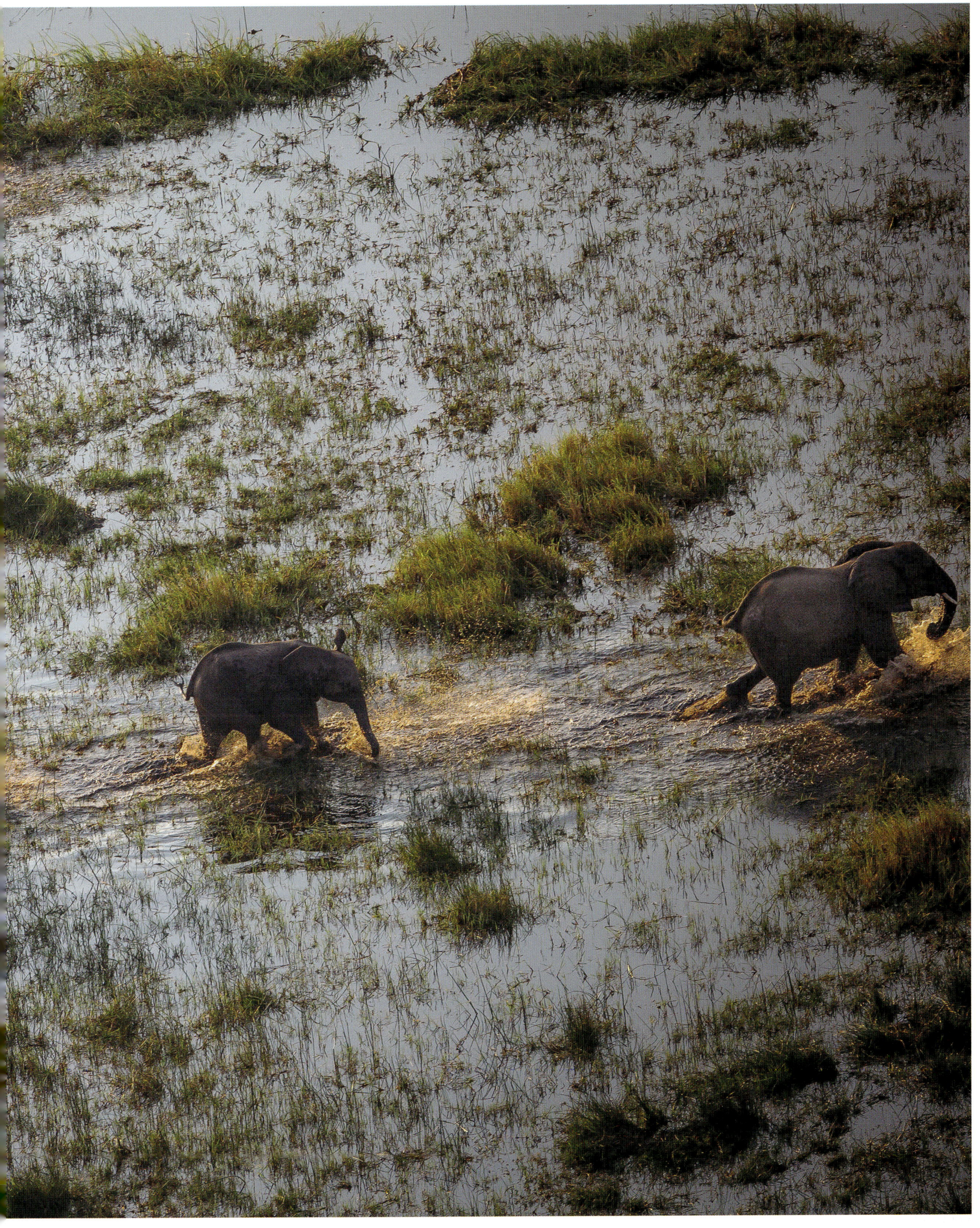

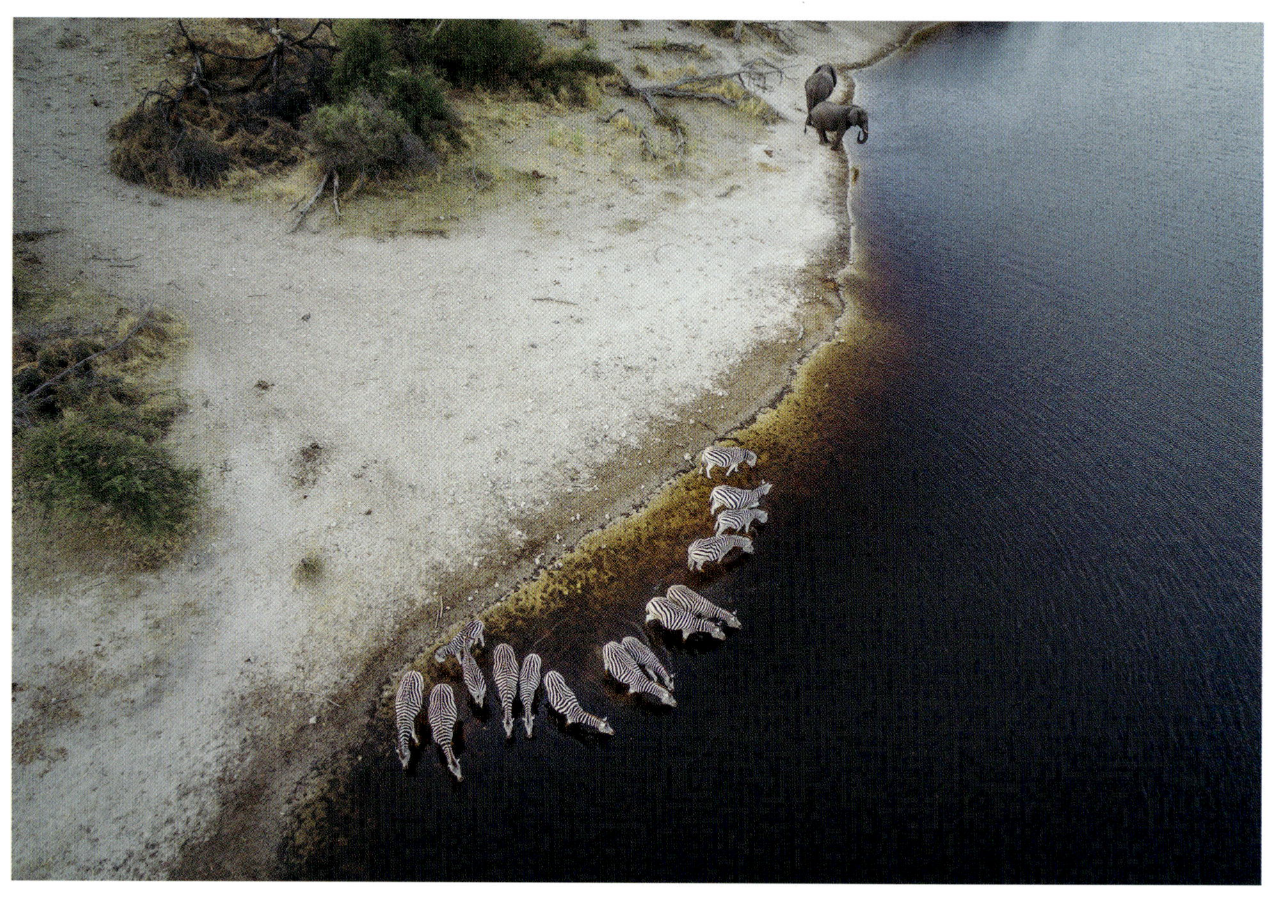

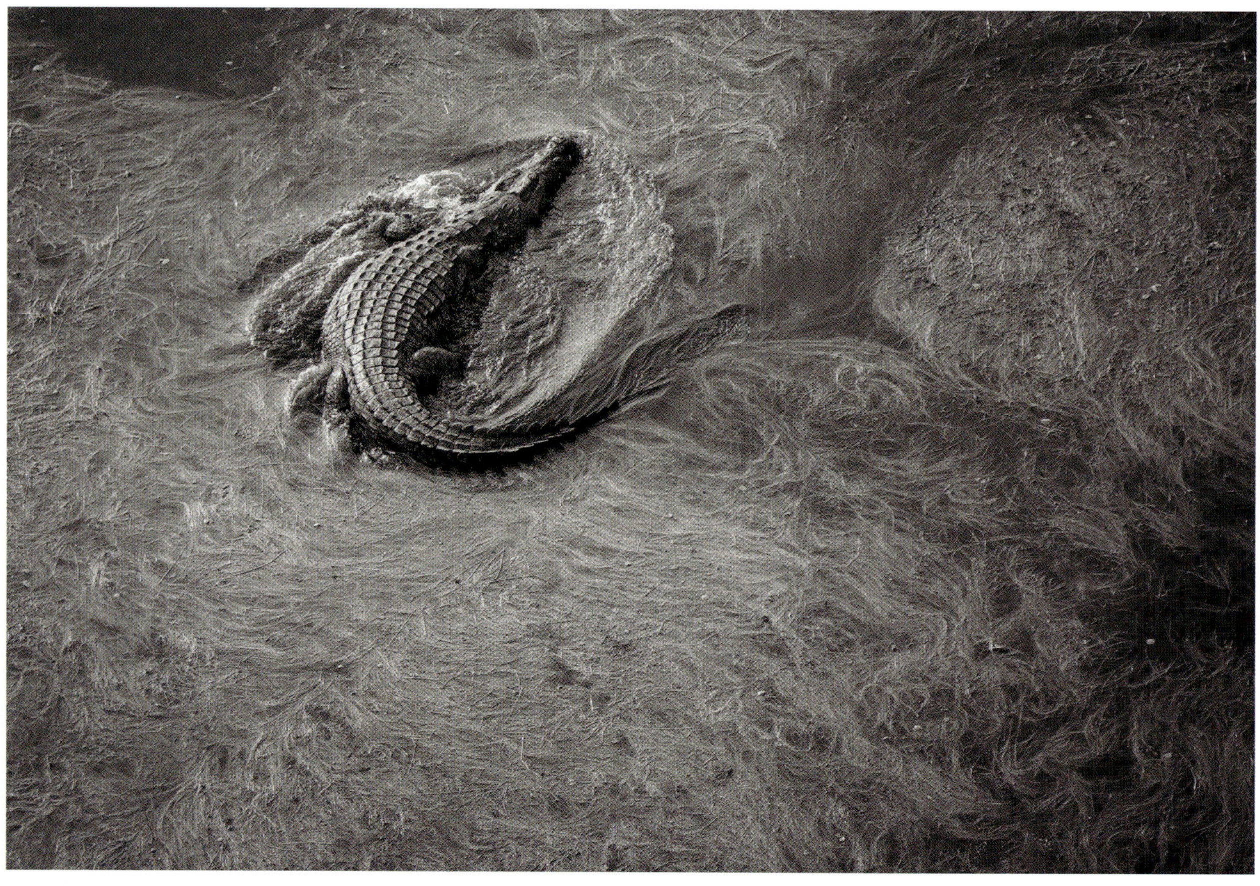

ABOVE: Zebra and elephants water near Meno A Kwena tented camp, Botswana. BELOW: Crocodile, Okavango Delta.

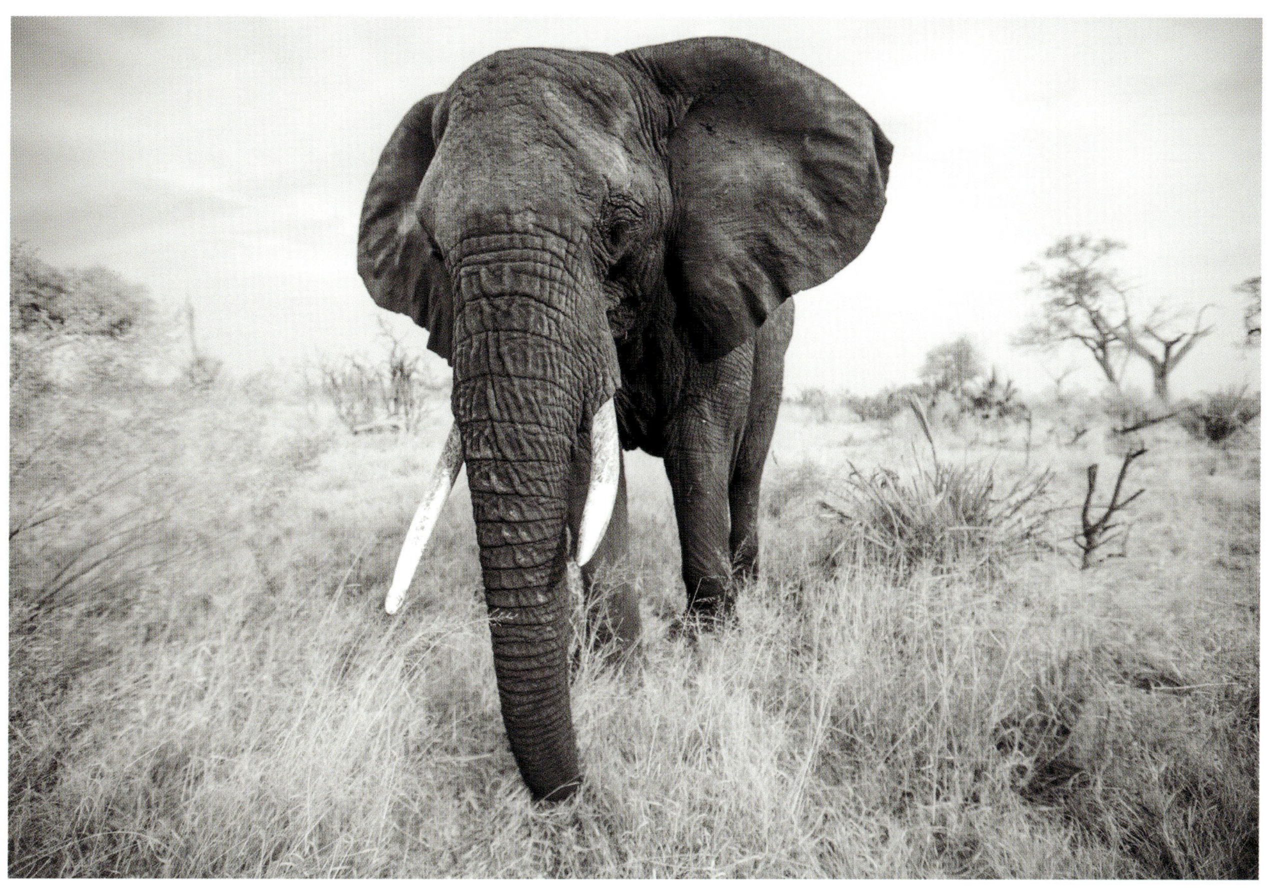

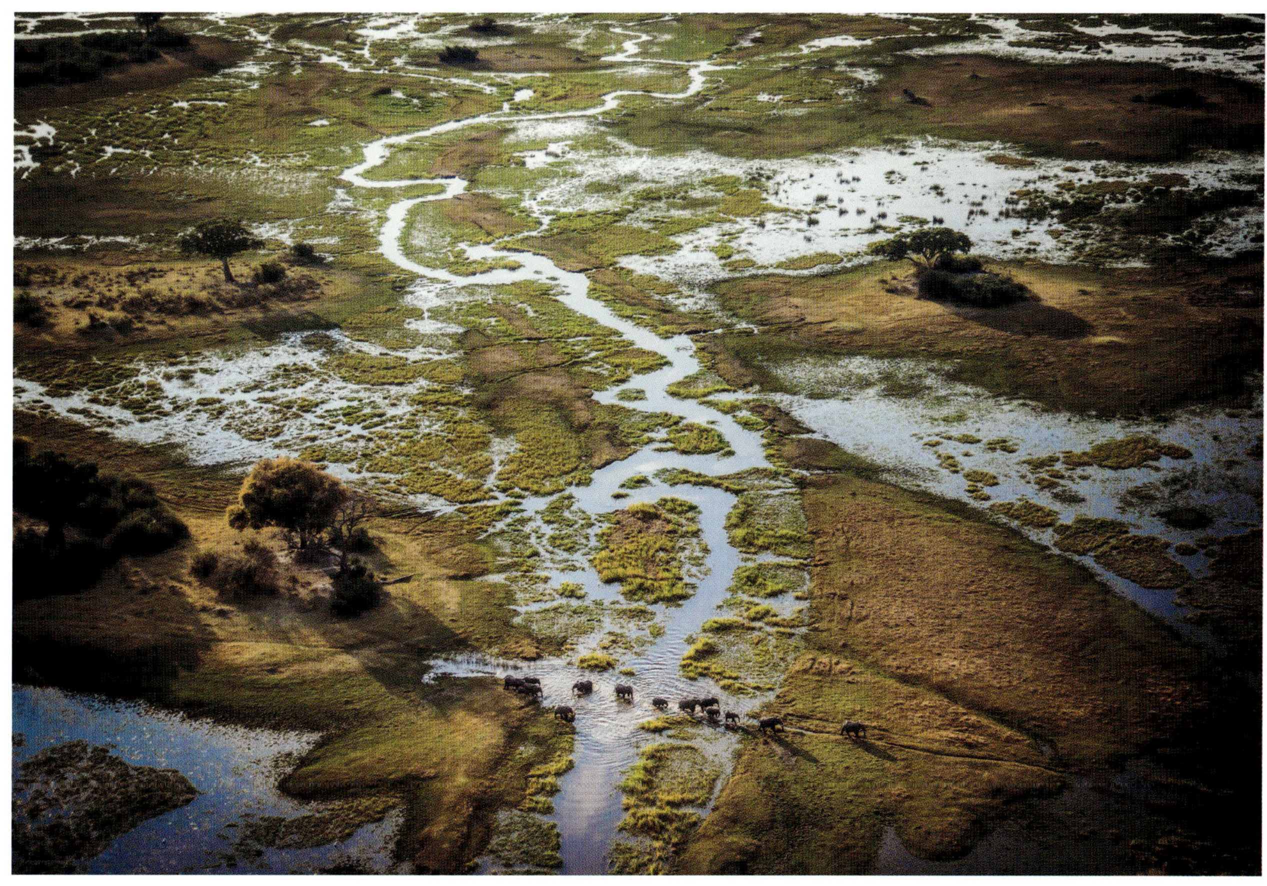

ABOVE: Bull elephant, Okavango Delta. **BELOW:** Elephants crossing the channels of the Okavango Delta.
FOLLOWING: The Cuito River spills over a waterfall in the Angolan Highlands.

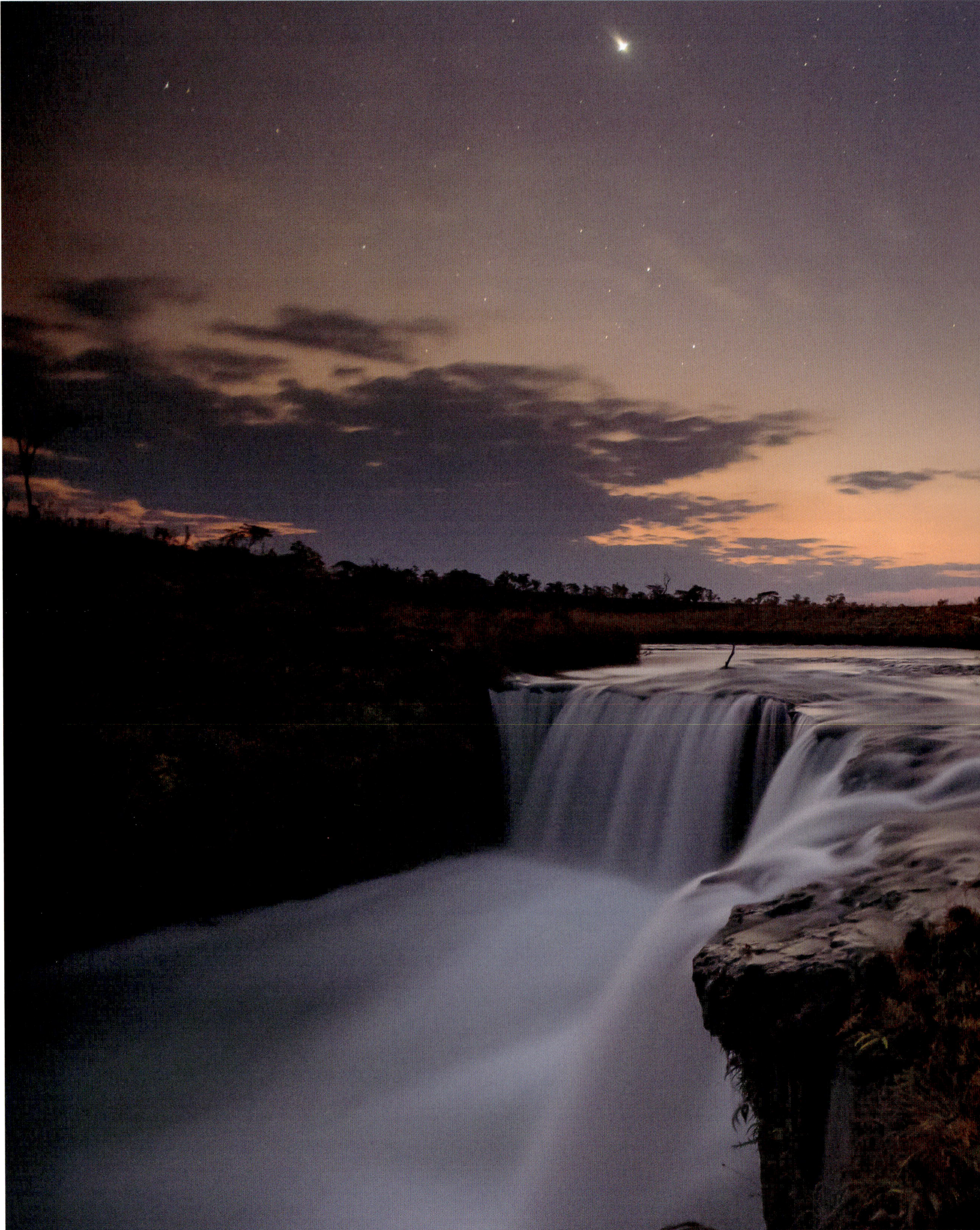

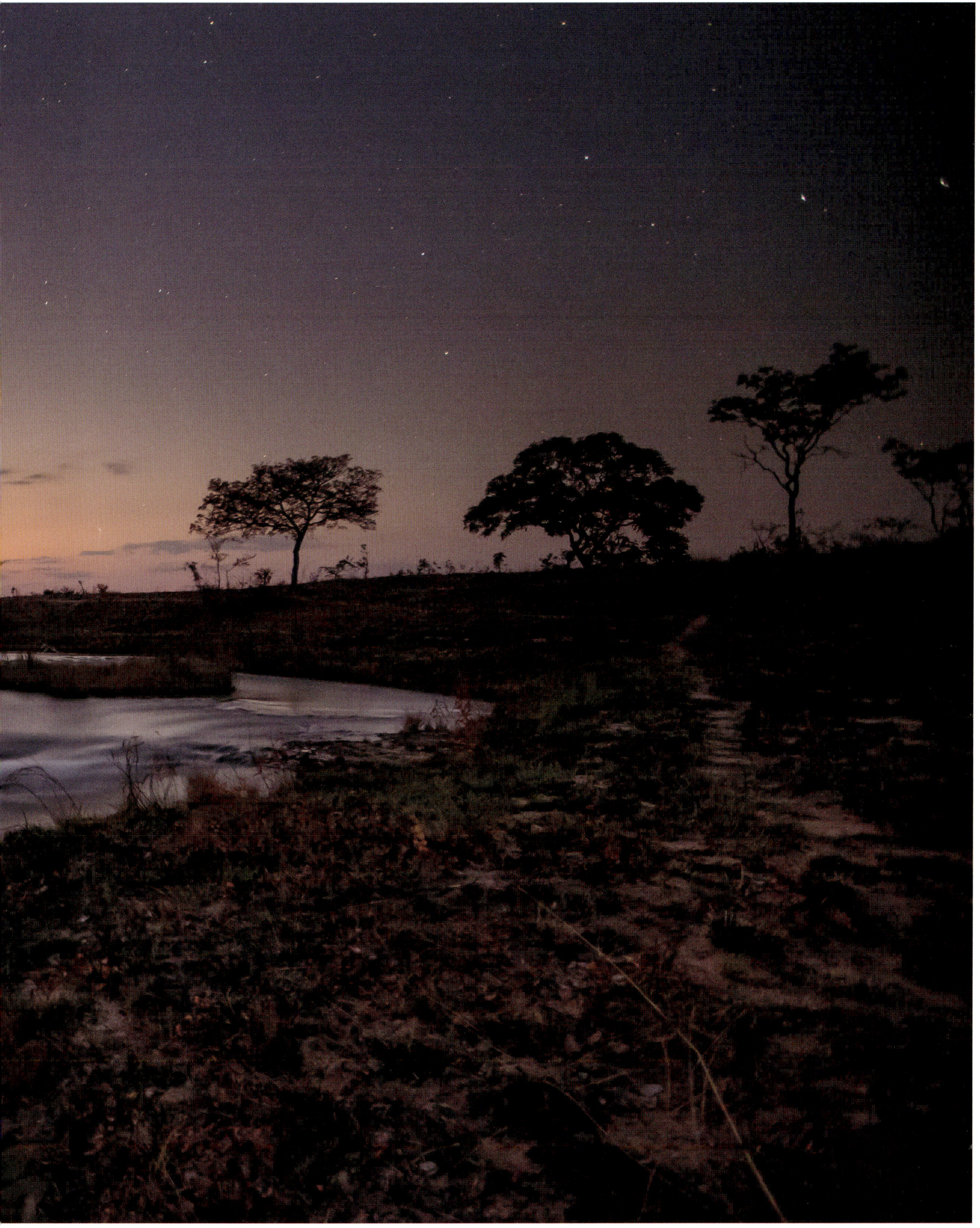

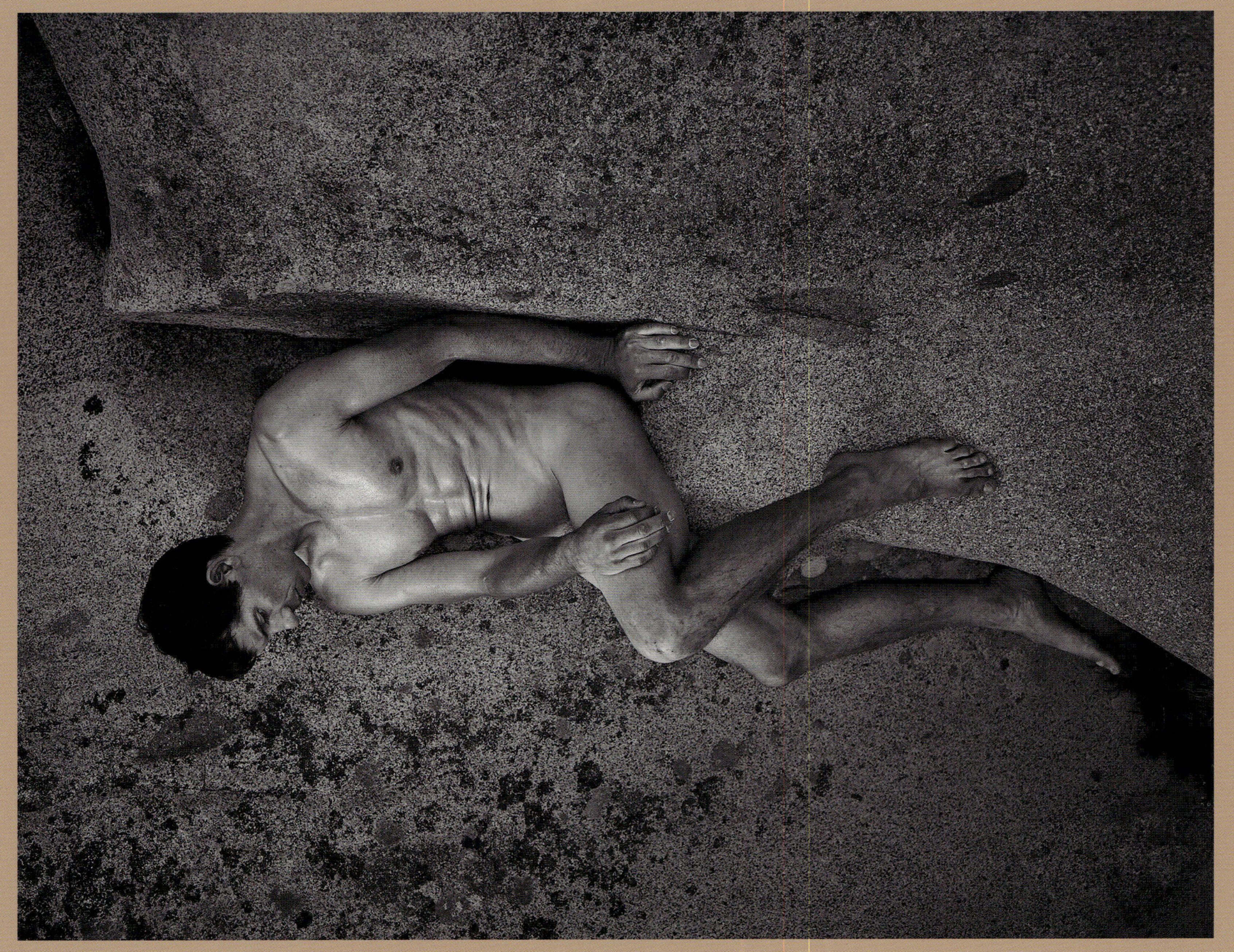

SUPERHUMAN SUPER HUMAN
Lake Tahoe, California, and Red Lodge, Montana

I'm sitting in a tent under the north face of Everest at 21,000 feet. It's June 3, 2017. Tired of reading, sick of playing cards, and fingers too cold to write, I scroll mindlessly on my phone. It buzzes and I ignore it. I'd rather keep watching a puppy slam into a glass door on Instagram. It buzzes again. And again. I open a text before jumping immediately to the news.

My friend Alex Honnold has just completed the first-ever ropeless ascent of El Capitan in Yosemite Valley, a nearly 3,000-foot wall of granite polished so smooth that it reflects a low sun like glass. At this moment, Alex is inarguably the greatest athlete in the world. For 3 hours and 56 minutes, it seems as if he stepped outside of Earth's gravity.

Two years later the film of the ascent, *Free Solo,* wins the Academy Award. Shortly after, ESPN asks me to photograph Alex for *The Body Issue,* a magazine that celebrates the many varied bodies of the world's best athletes by photographing them nude. In black and white, Alex's body appears to be made of stone.

A few months later, I'm bouncing up a rough gorge in Nepal in an old Land Cruiser covered in dust. I try to peel a hardboiled egg, but the shell is annoyingly stuck to the skin inside and I'm leaving dirty fingerprints all over the whites. My phone buzzes. Whatever it is, it can wait . . . I'm hungry. The truck's shocks moan as the tires dip in and out of deep potholes that have slowed the drive to a crawl. My mouth is dry, and I can taste the dust that's collected in tiny black *Vs* in the corners of my lips. My phone buzzes again. I'll get it later . . . I have an egg to peel and swallow before the sulfur smell of bad farts fills up the whole car. Again, the phone. I want to throw it out the window but think better of it and throw the mutilated egg instead. I smear big greasy fingerprints across the screen and the phone glows. Apparently Dad has liver cancer.

Back home, my dad rolls from his bed and I take pictures of his nearly naked frame. His legs are skinny, atrophied, and marked from immunotherapy. He smiles and groans and uses a cane to stand and walk to the bathroom, taking care not to trip over the dog, who doesn't understand why he can't bend over to pet her. He opens the medicine cabinet and scratches his back before counting out the morning dose: 1, 2, 3, 4 . . . 7. His skin is stretched smooth across a hunched back being pulled back to the earth. Gravity always wins.

Alex Honnold is one of the best athletes ever, mythologized by his incomprehensible athletic ability. Dad is dying and the whole process seems cruel. One body reminds me of infinite potential. The other displays the inescapable finitude of humanity. Both bodies are representations of the stimulus applied over the course of a life. Alex's body reflects countless hours moving over stone. Dad's body reflects eight decades of life and the cancer that will eventually claim it. Alex appears superhuman. Cancer seems inhumane. I didn't know it at the time, but I look at the pictures now and see that all I really wanted to do was to make them both fully human again.

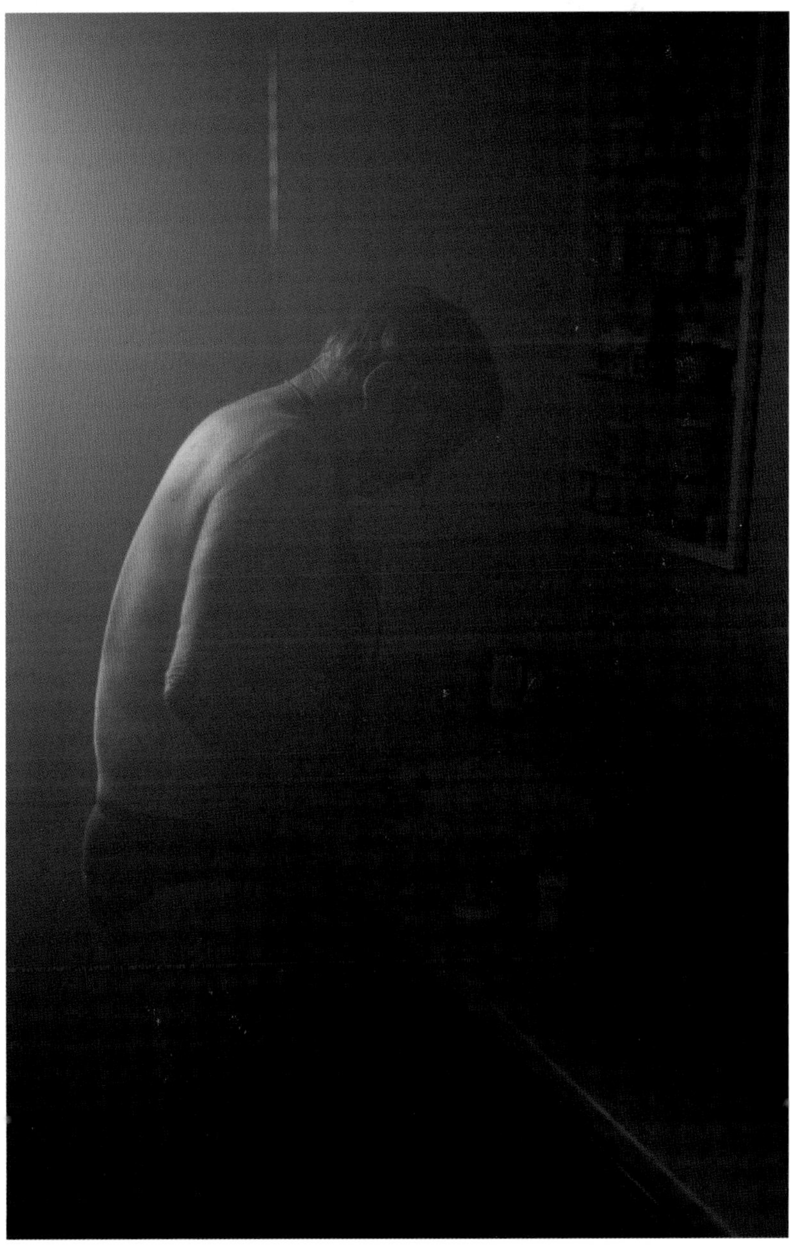

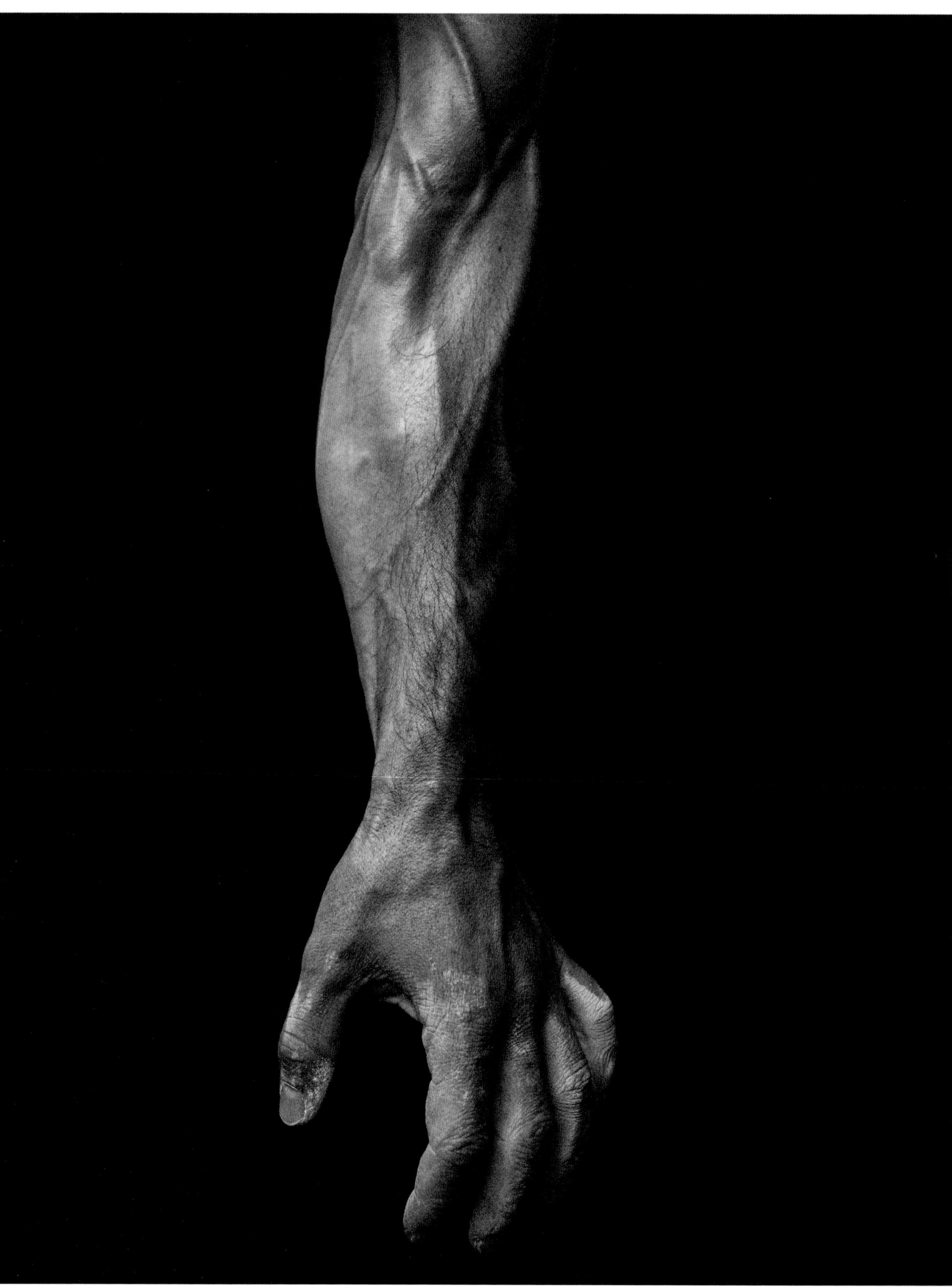

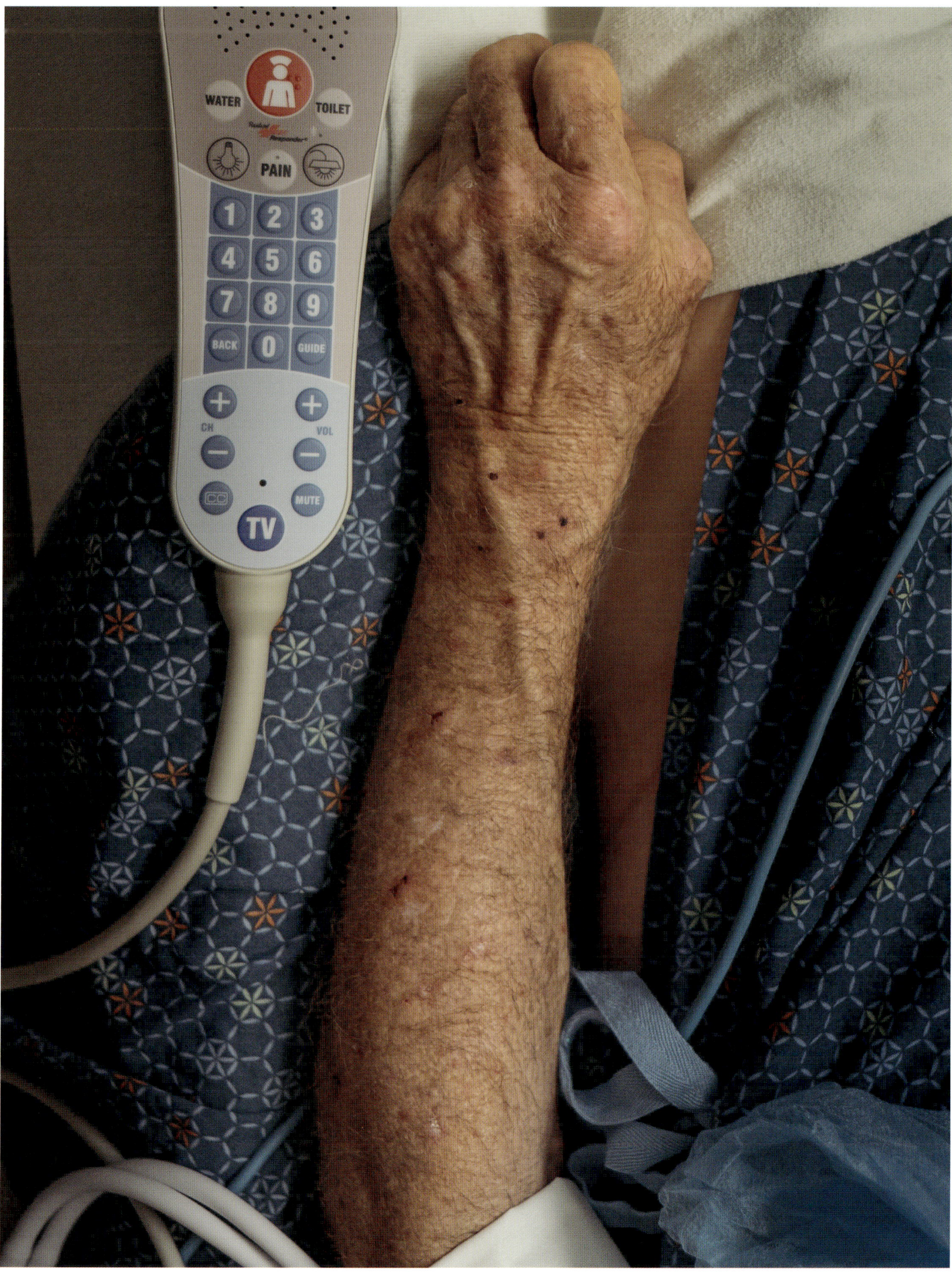

WATER
TOILET
PAIN
1 2 3
4 5 6
7 8 9
BACK 0 GUIDE
CH
VOL
CC
MUTE
TV

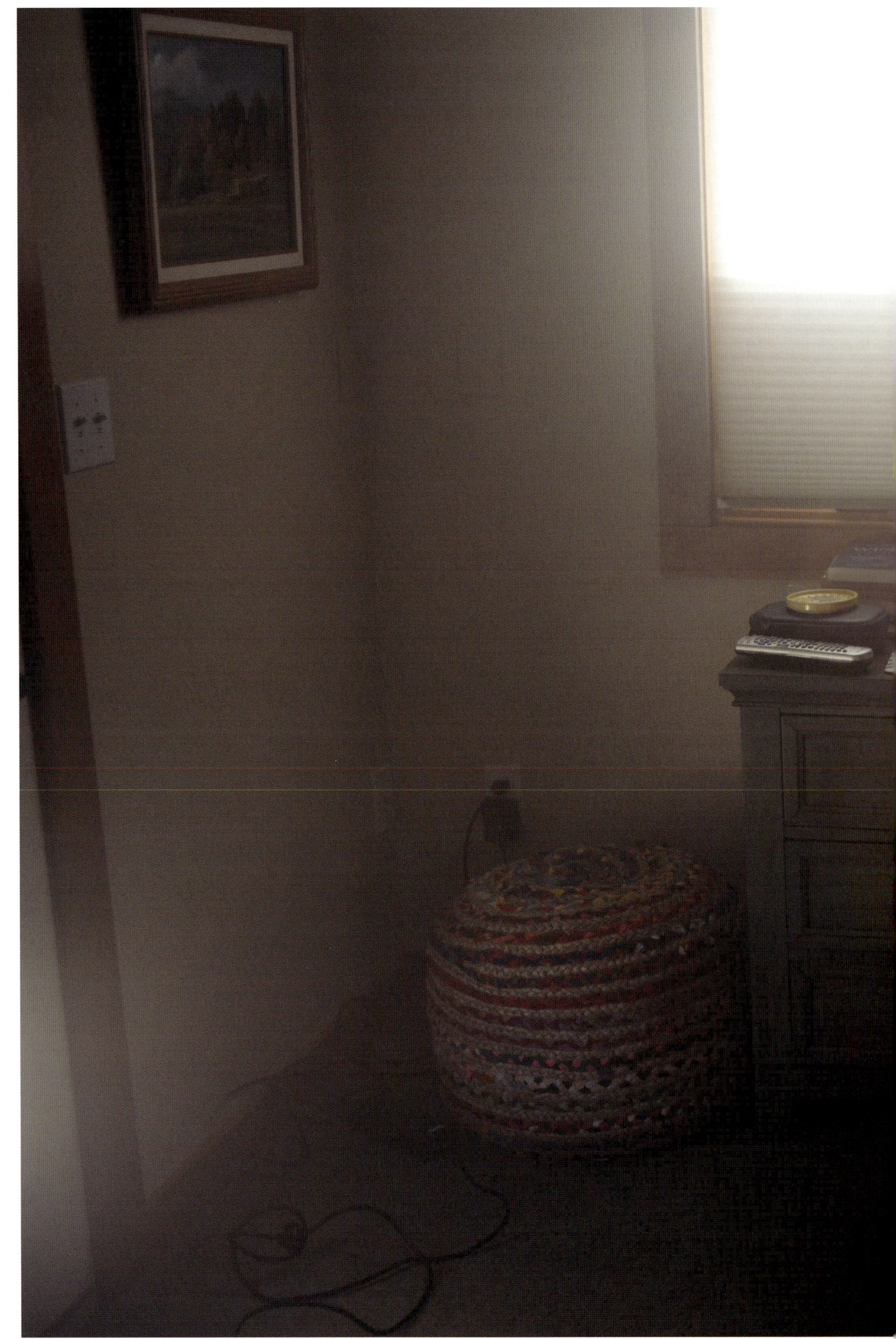

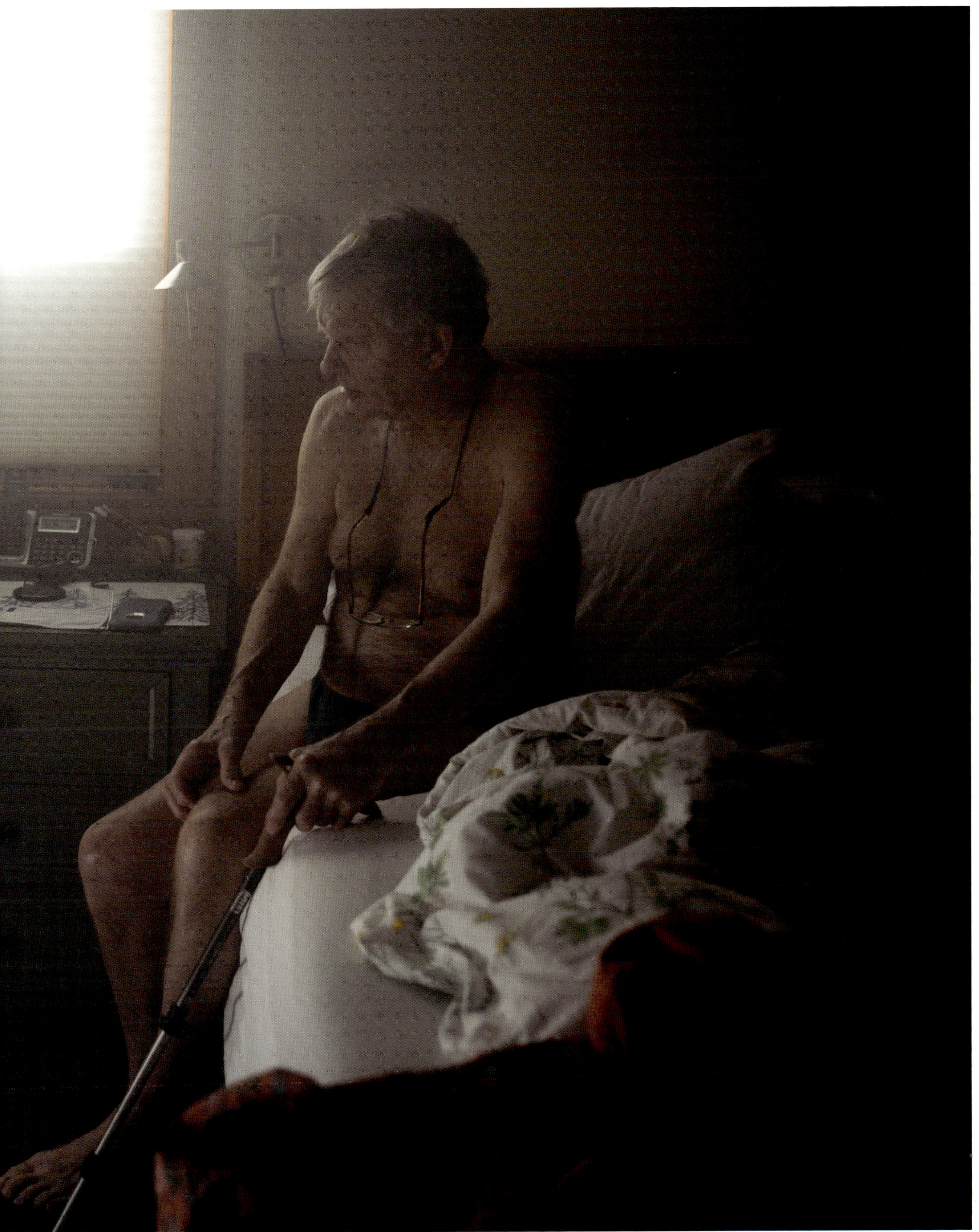

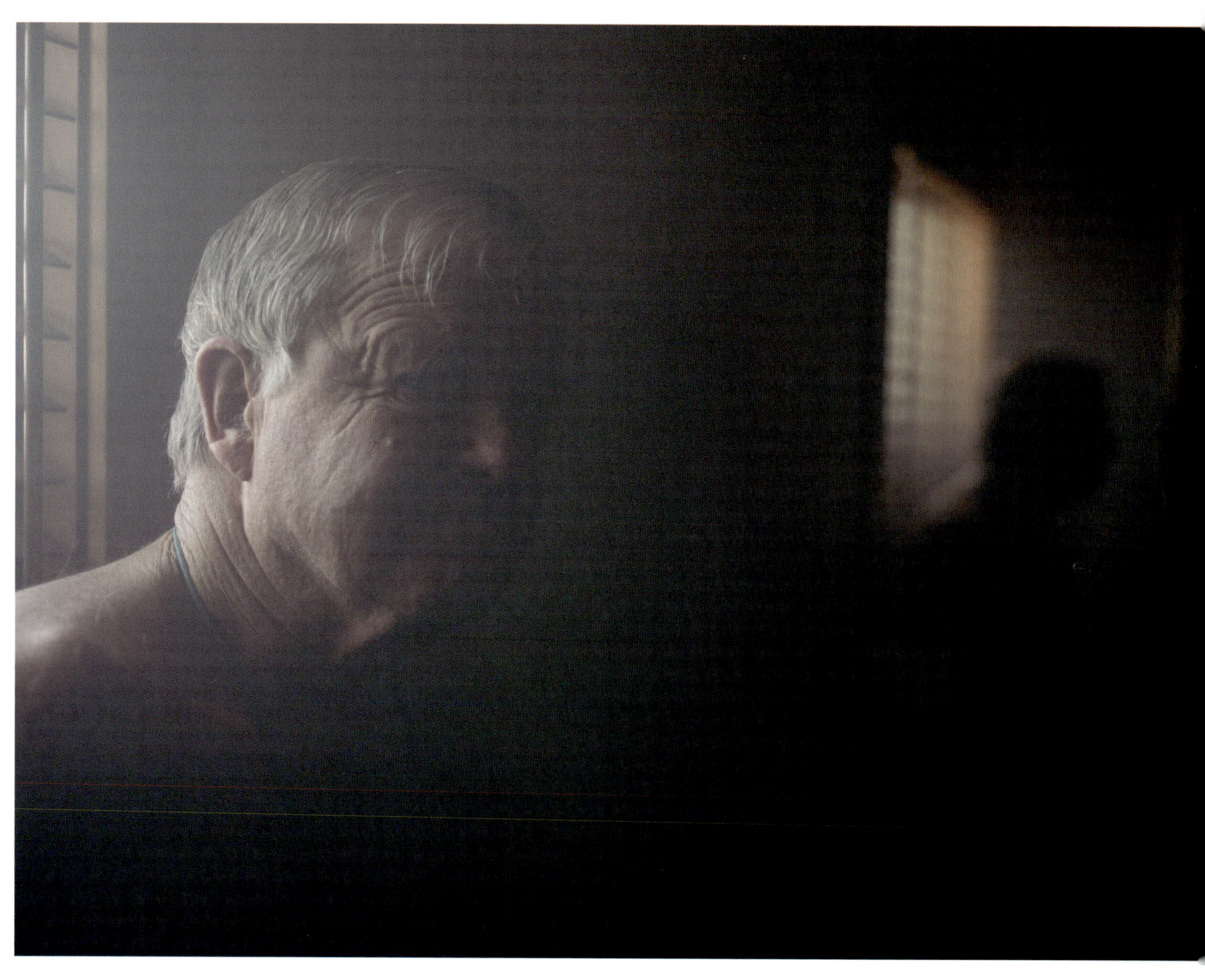

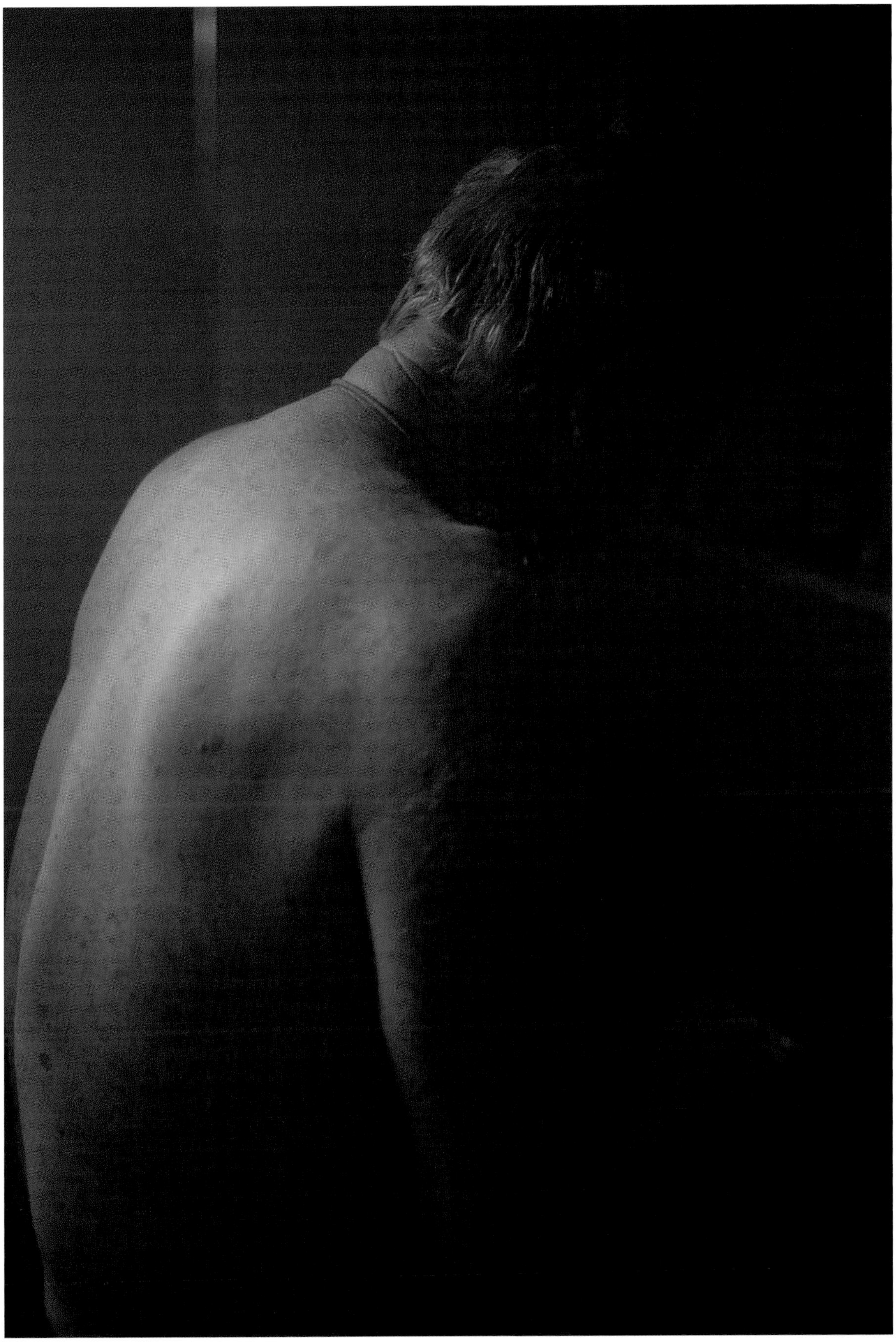

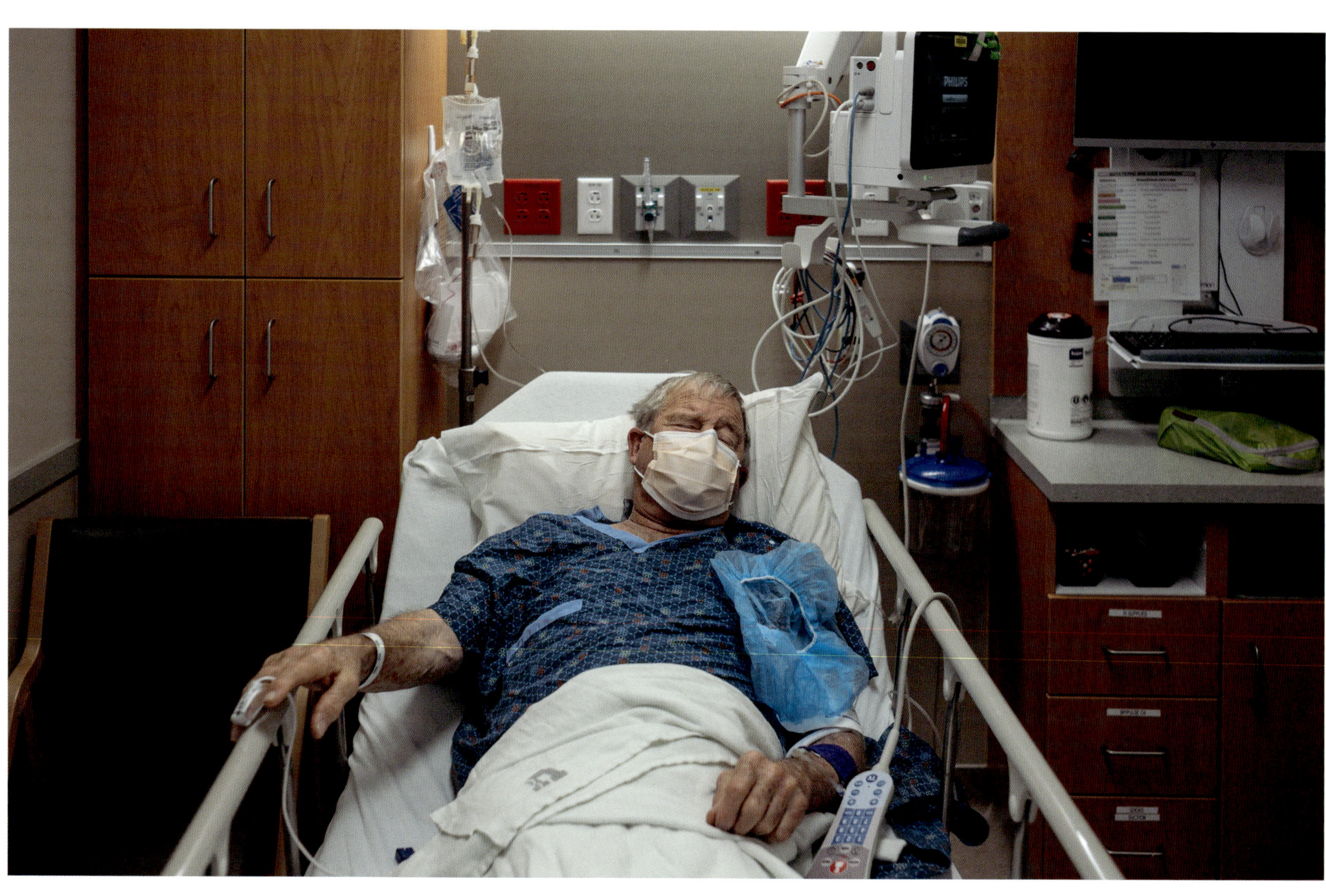

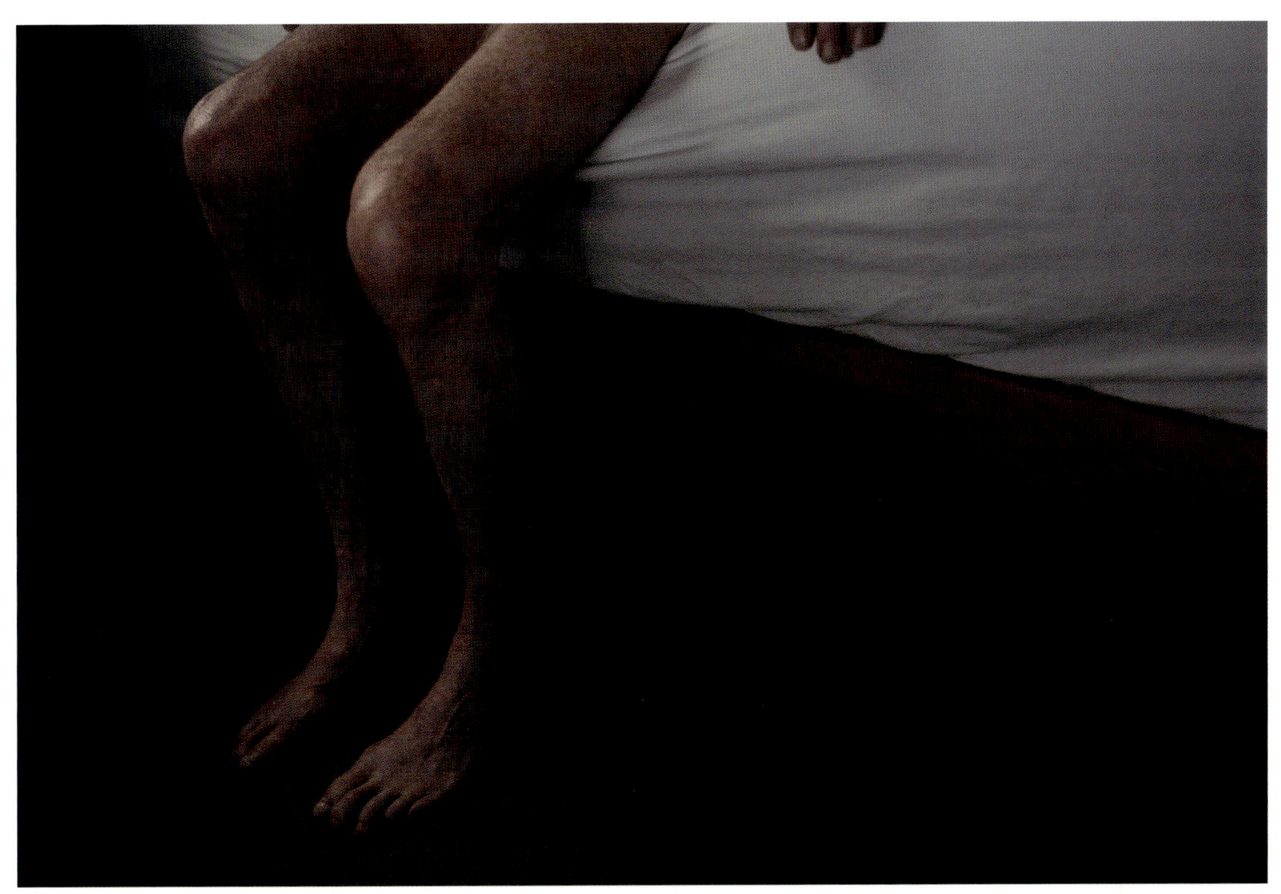

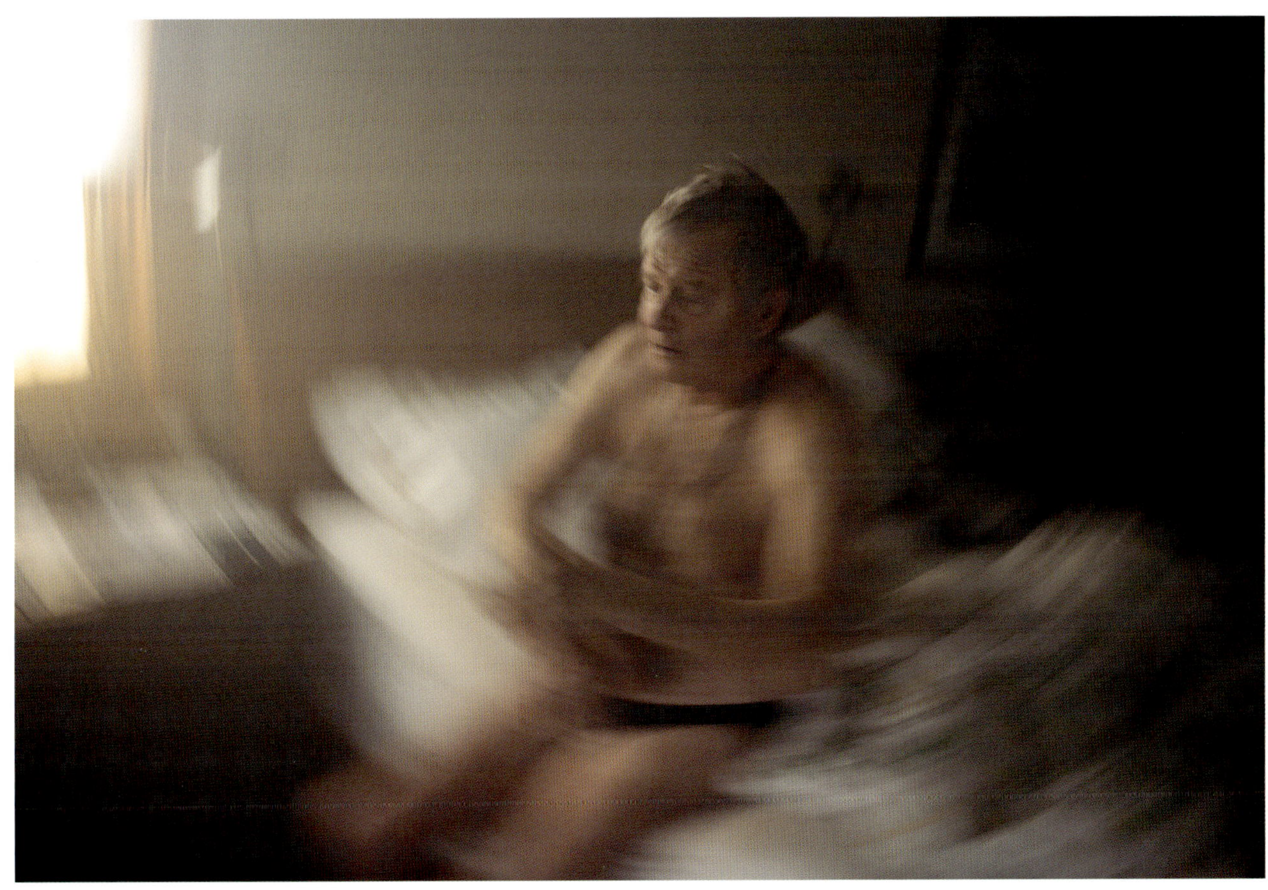

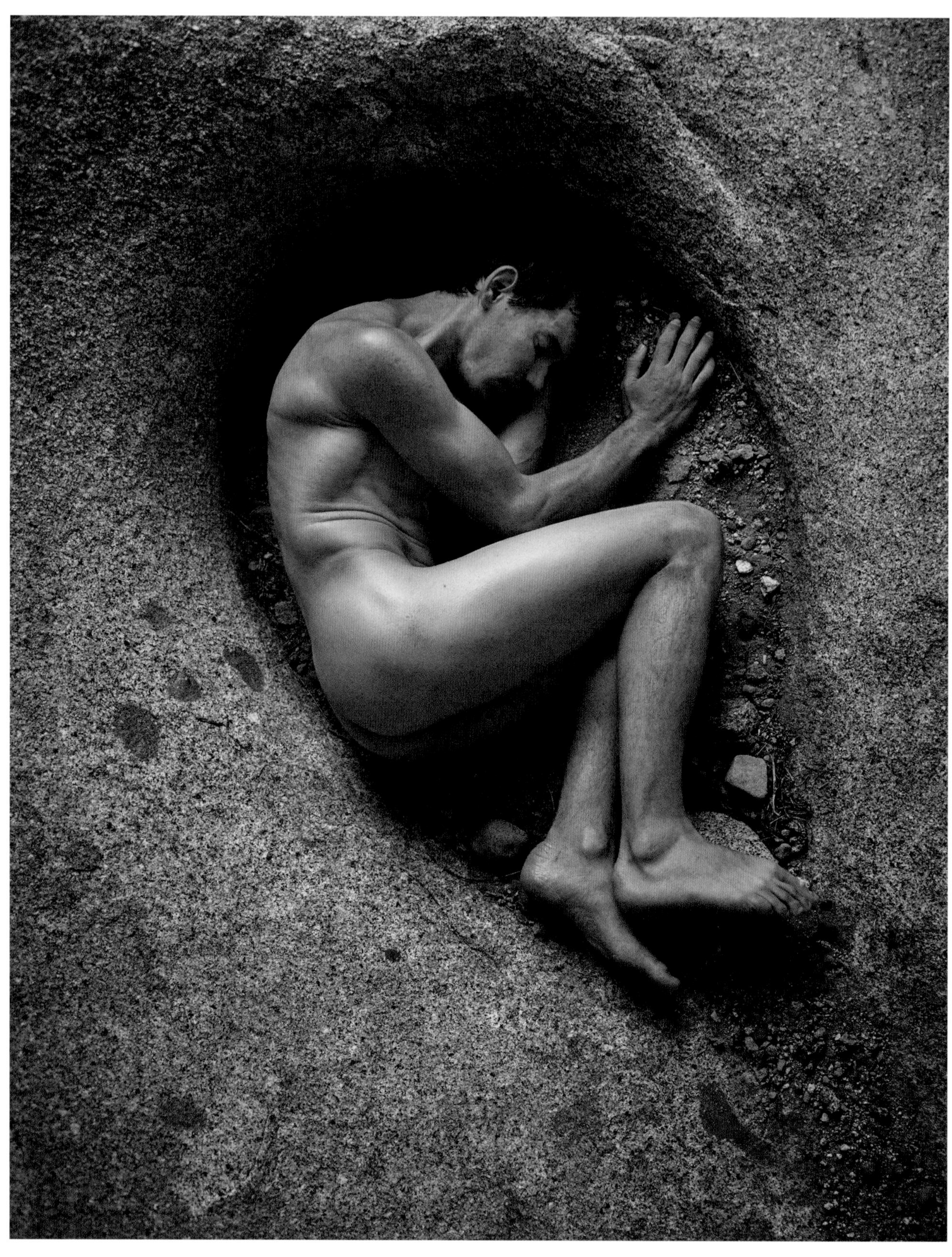

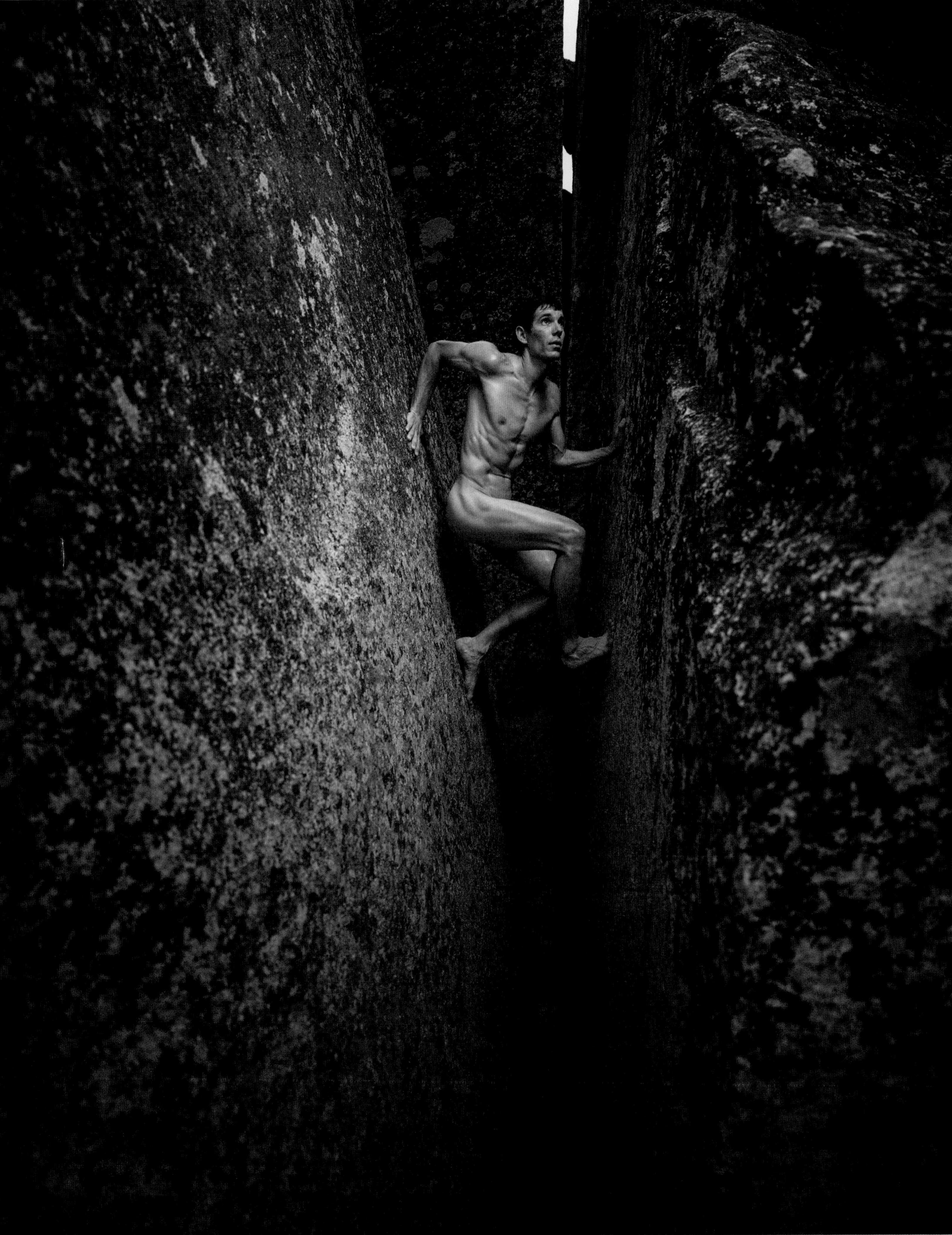

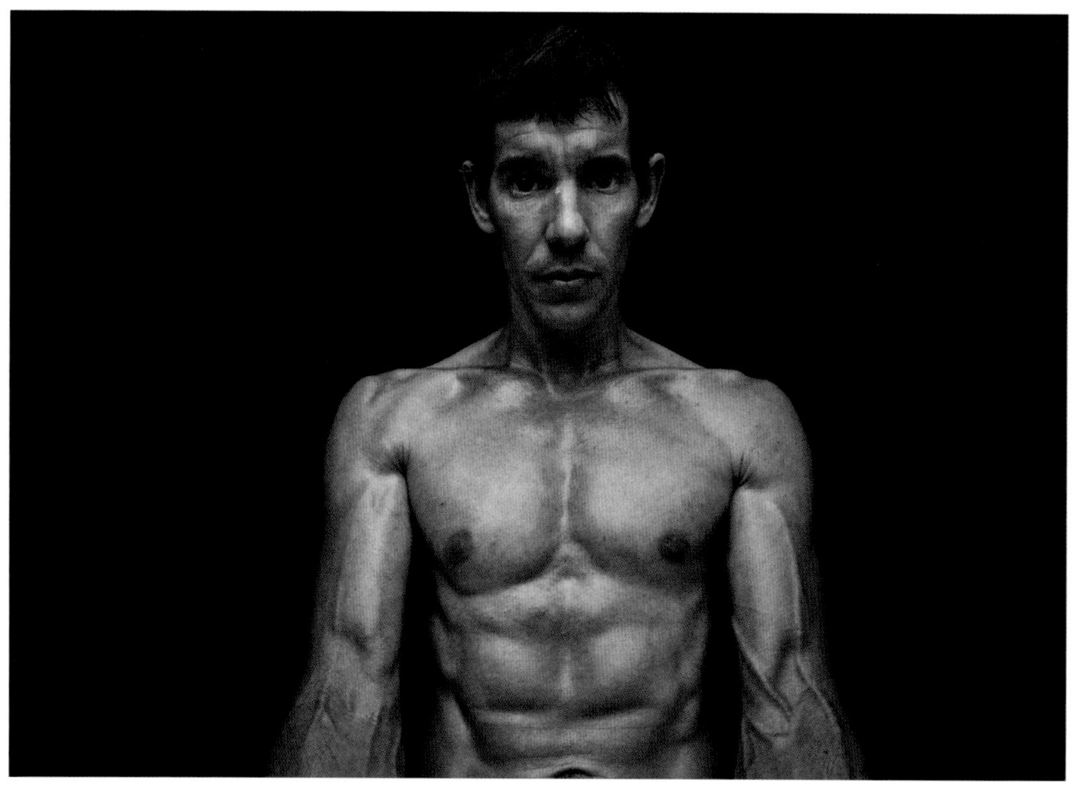

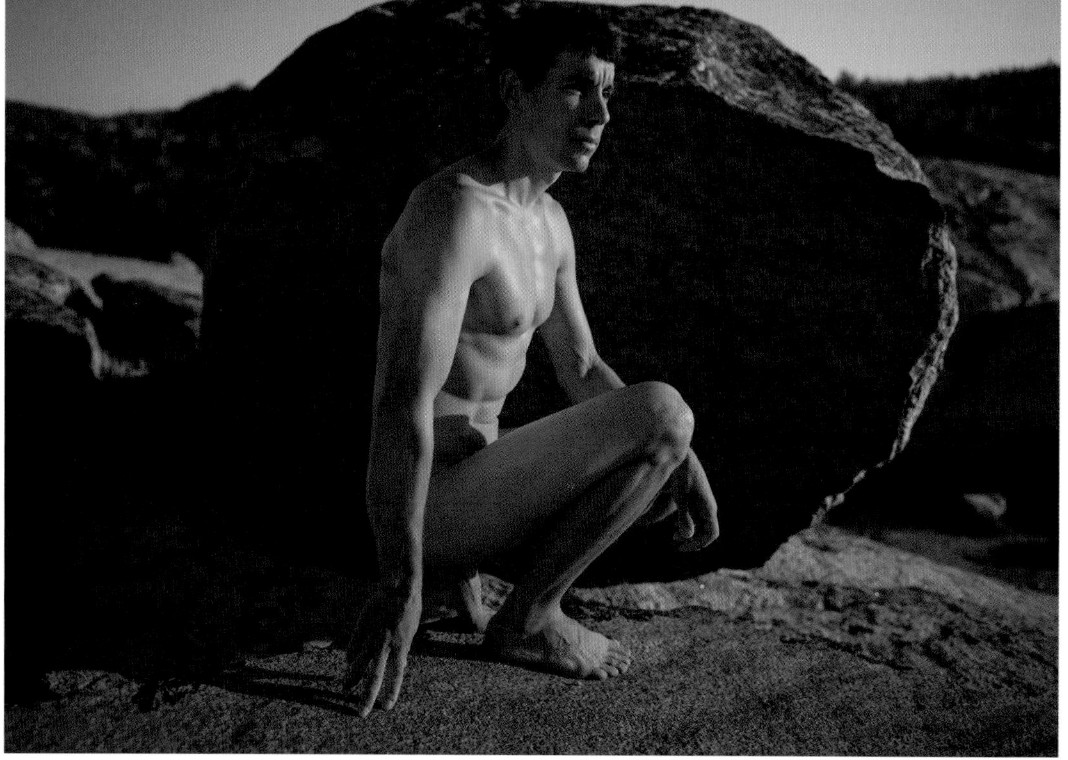

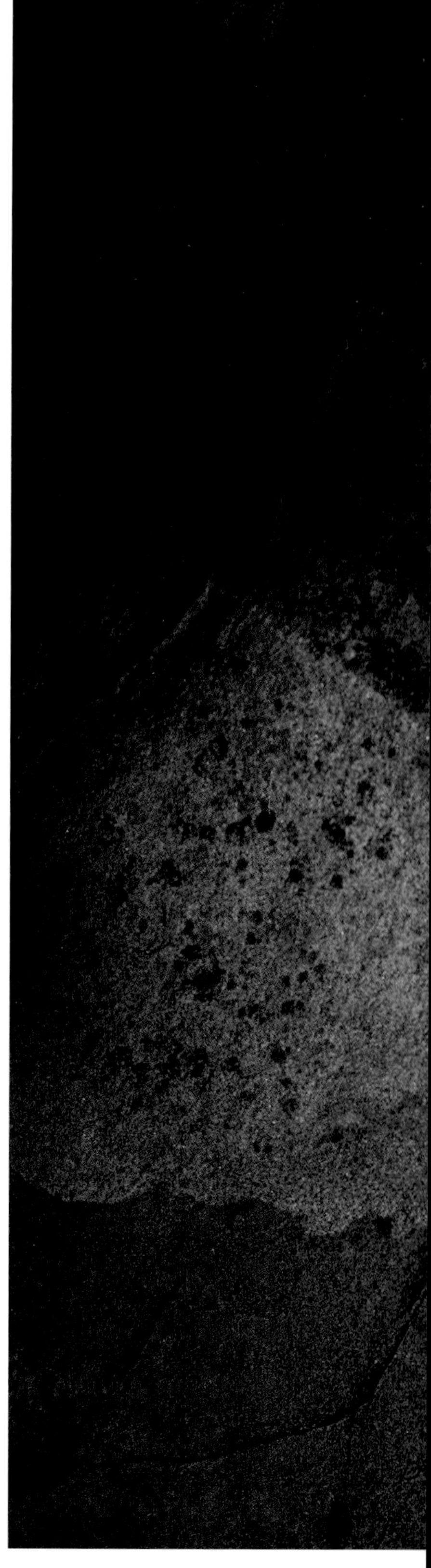

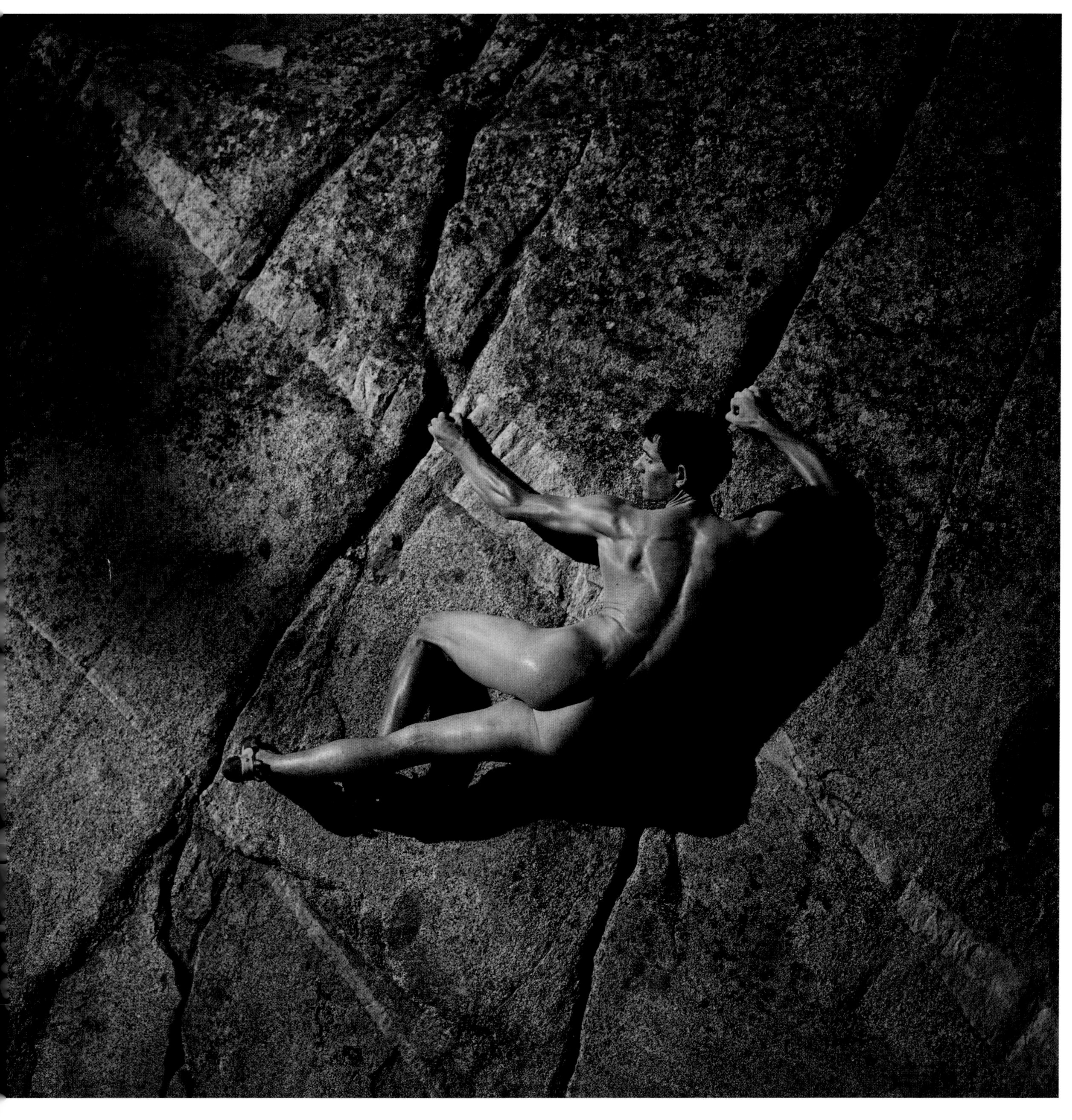

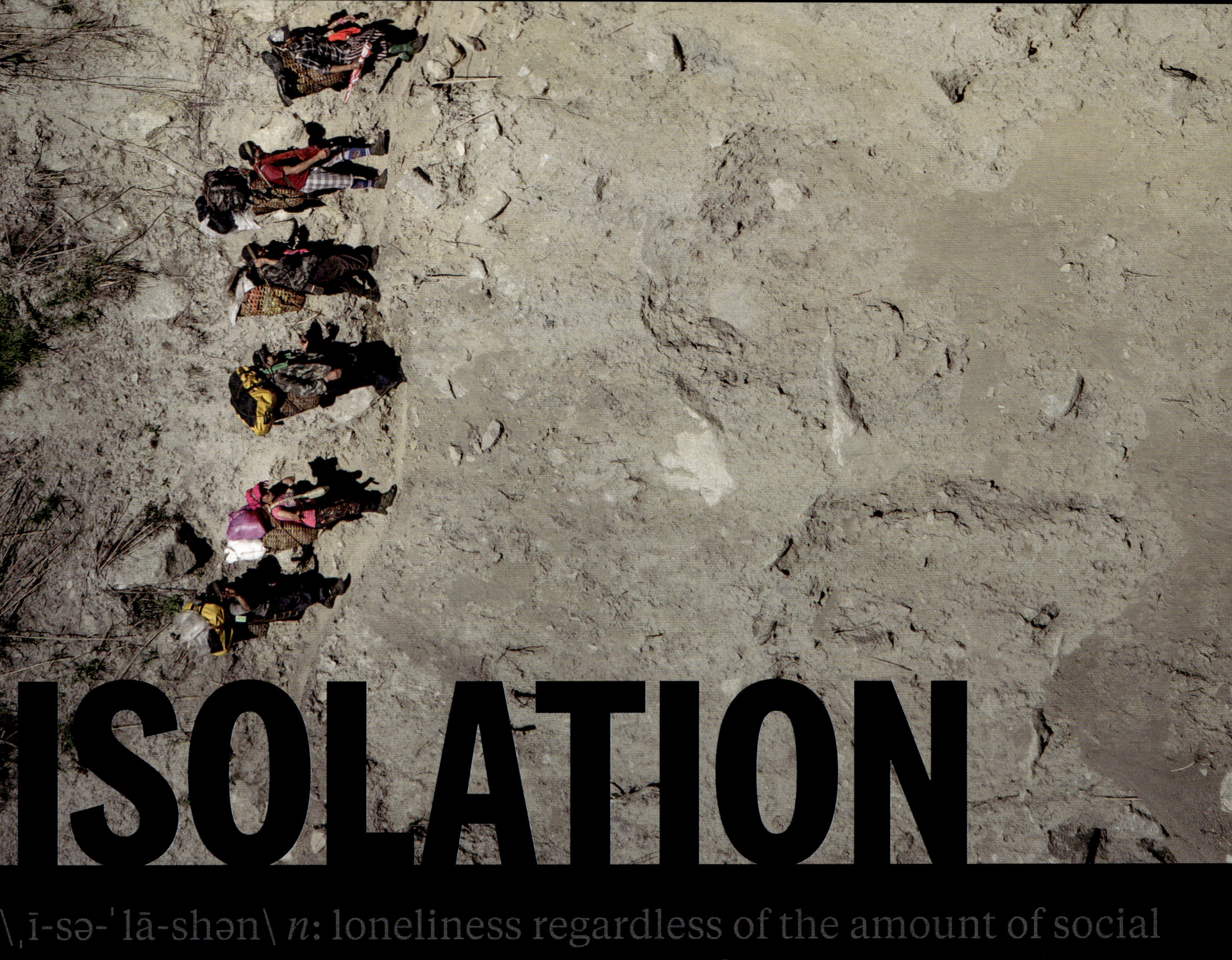

ISOLATION
\ˌī-sə-ˈlā-shən\ n: loneliness regardless of the amount of social contact; also, alone, separate, or apart from

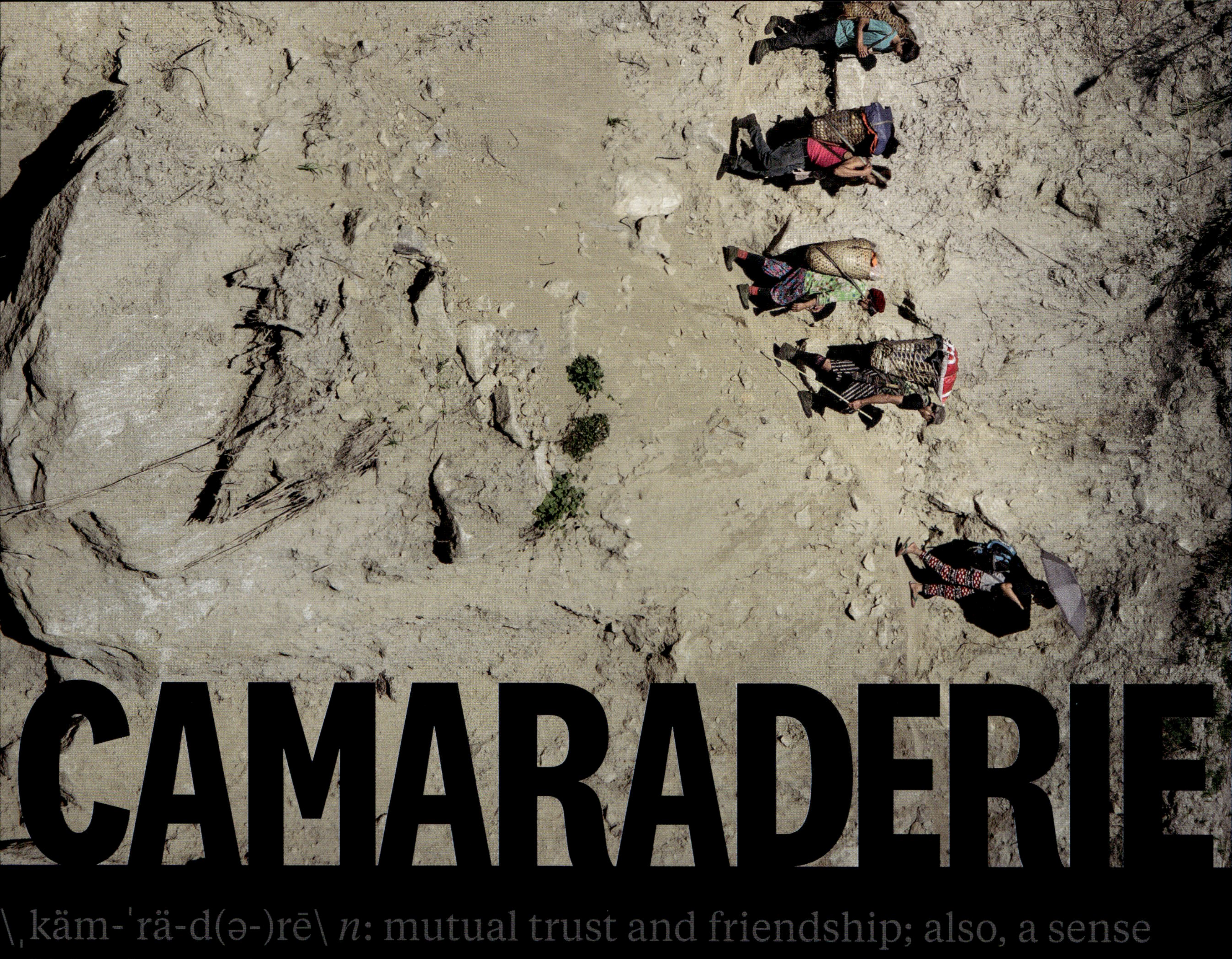

CAMARADERIE
\ˌkäm-ˈrä-d(ə-)rē\ n: mutual trust and friendship; also, a sense of kinship or belonging based on shared experience or deep

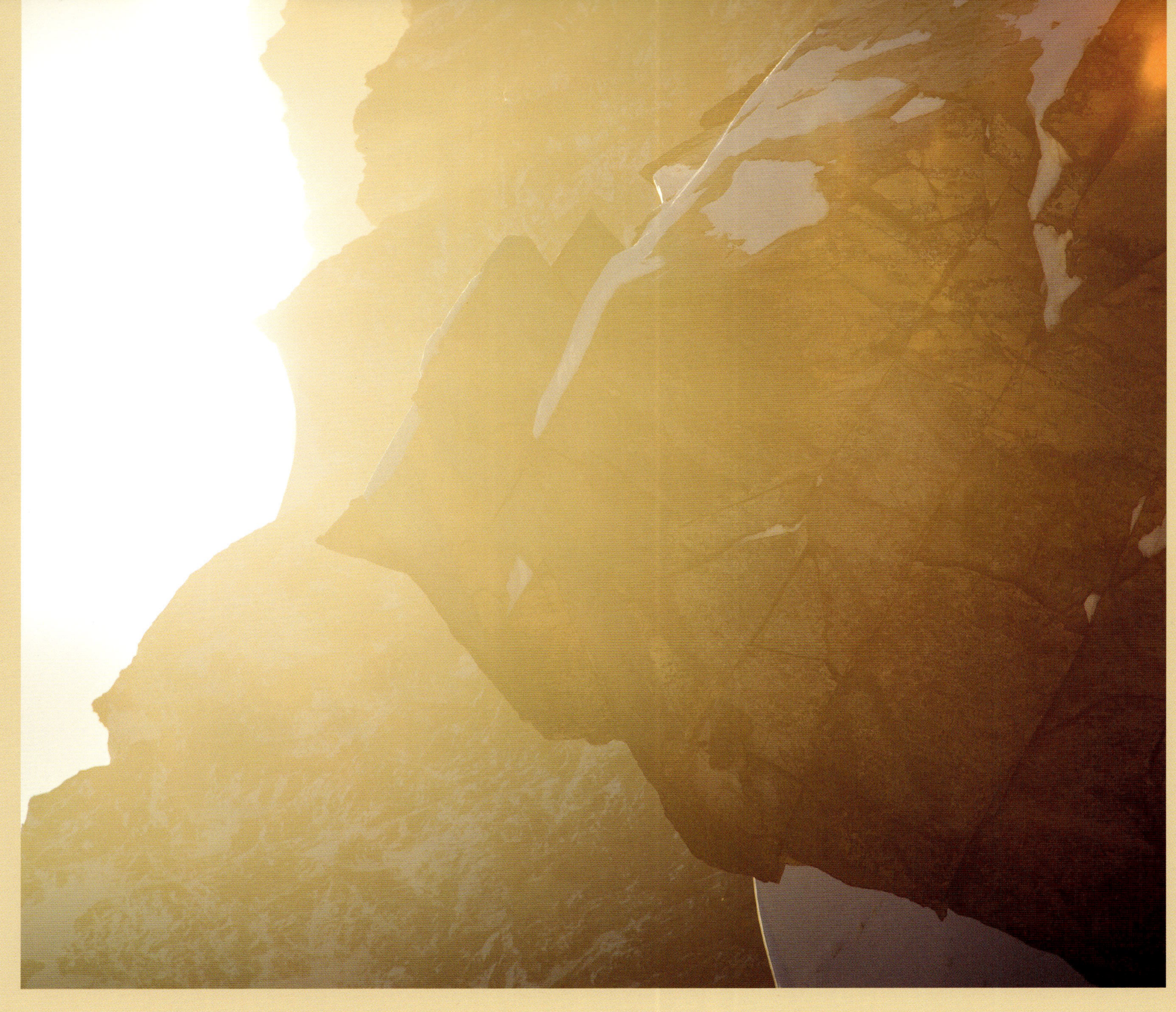

BULLET HOLES IN A MAP Myanmar

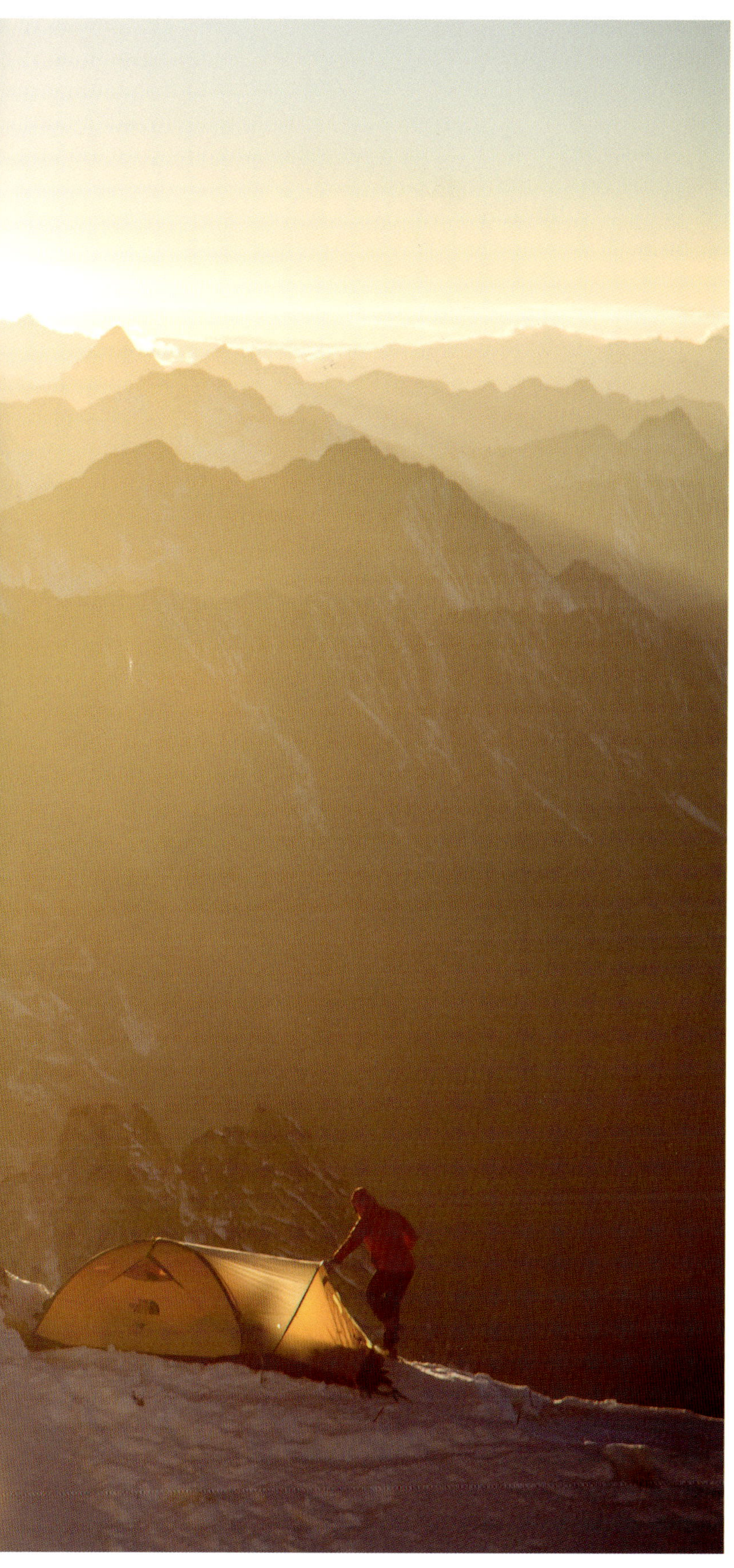

Forty-one days ago, five of us landed in Myanmar and wandered into the humid chaos of Yangon. Tuk Tuks and scooters buzzed past us in braided lines that seemed to have no order. We took the "Death Railway" north, a boat up the Irrawaddy River, and an overnight bus to Bagan. When we reached the Kachin region, still misty in the fog of a decades-long, bloody civil war, we were put on house arrest before being allowed to mount 125cc motorbikes and drive sixty-eight miles through the jungle. Finally, when the roads disappeared, we shouldered heavy packs and walked 125 miles to the foot of the Himalaya. It took us thirty days to reach the base of Hkakabo Razi, the highest mountain on the eastern tip of the range. The war locked the mountain away from the outside world, creating a geographic mystery. Our job is to measure its height.

But now, I'm descending back to our camp just below 20,000 feet. After a week of climbing, we realized that we were too strung out, too run down, and too isolated to complete the climb safely. We overestimated ourselves and underestimated the objective. We failed. It's a blow that will either cement us together or splinter us as a team. Both will end up being true. Either way we're bonded, welded together by a journey that has taken us farther than we knew we could go. Bonds this deep are cellular—even if we lose track of the people we share them with. Bonds this deep can transcend death.

Hilaree kicks her boot against the ice, sending a small explosion of backlit ice crystals into the air. Six years from now, the mountains stretching behind her will claim her body and life when she slips and falls near the summit of Manaslu, the eighth highest mountain in the world. These places have a way of taking more than we mean to give. I take another picture of her before she tucks back into the tent that has no business being where it is. After she dies, I'll look back on this picture again and again when I need to be reminded of how precious life is and how every relationship makes us somehow more complete.

LEFT: The late Hilaree Nelson, professional climber and expedition co-leader, camped just below 20,000 feet on Mount Hkakabo Razi, southeast Asia's highest mountain.

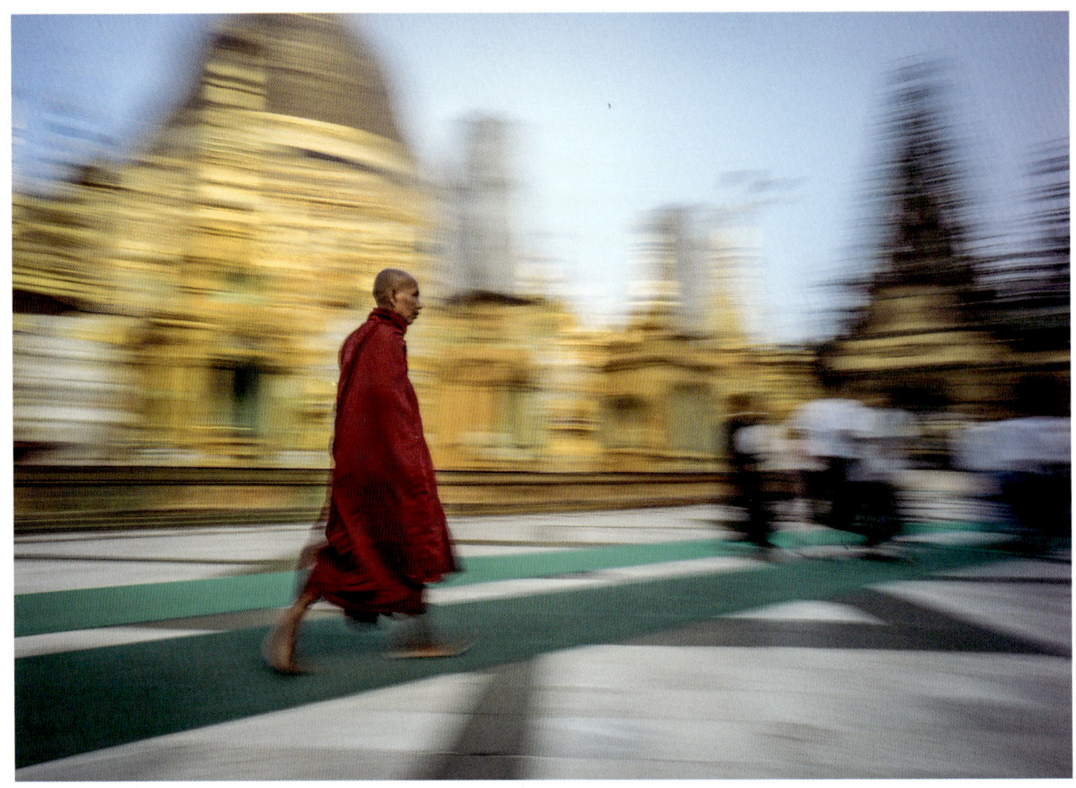

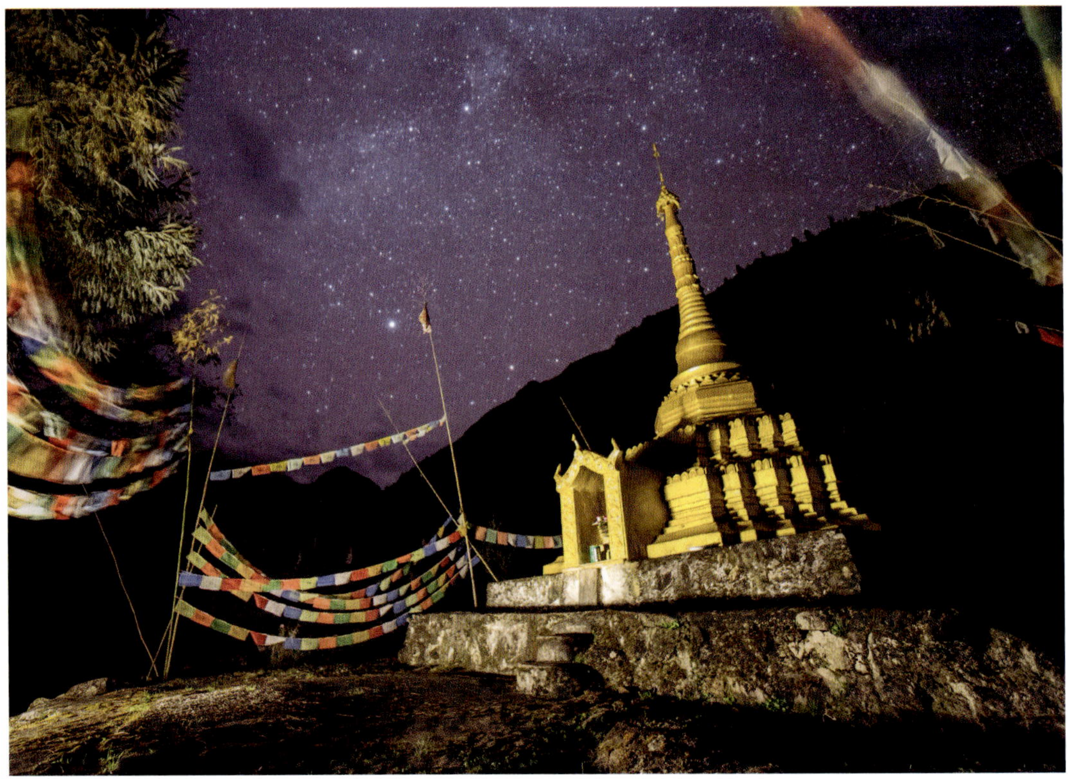

ABOVE: Monk, Shwedagon Pagoda, Yangon. BELOW: A Buddhist shrine in Dahongdam, the last village on the trail to Mount Hkakabo Razi. OPPOSITE: Monks underneath Mingun Pagoda near Mandalay (inspirational credit to Steve McCurry). FOLLOWING: Gawdawpalin Temple, Bagan (formerly Pagan). The city was founded in the second century and, from the ninth to thirteenth centuries, was capitol of the Pagan Kingdom, the first kingdom to bring together the territories that would eventually become Myanmar.

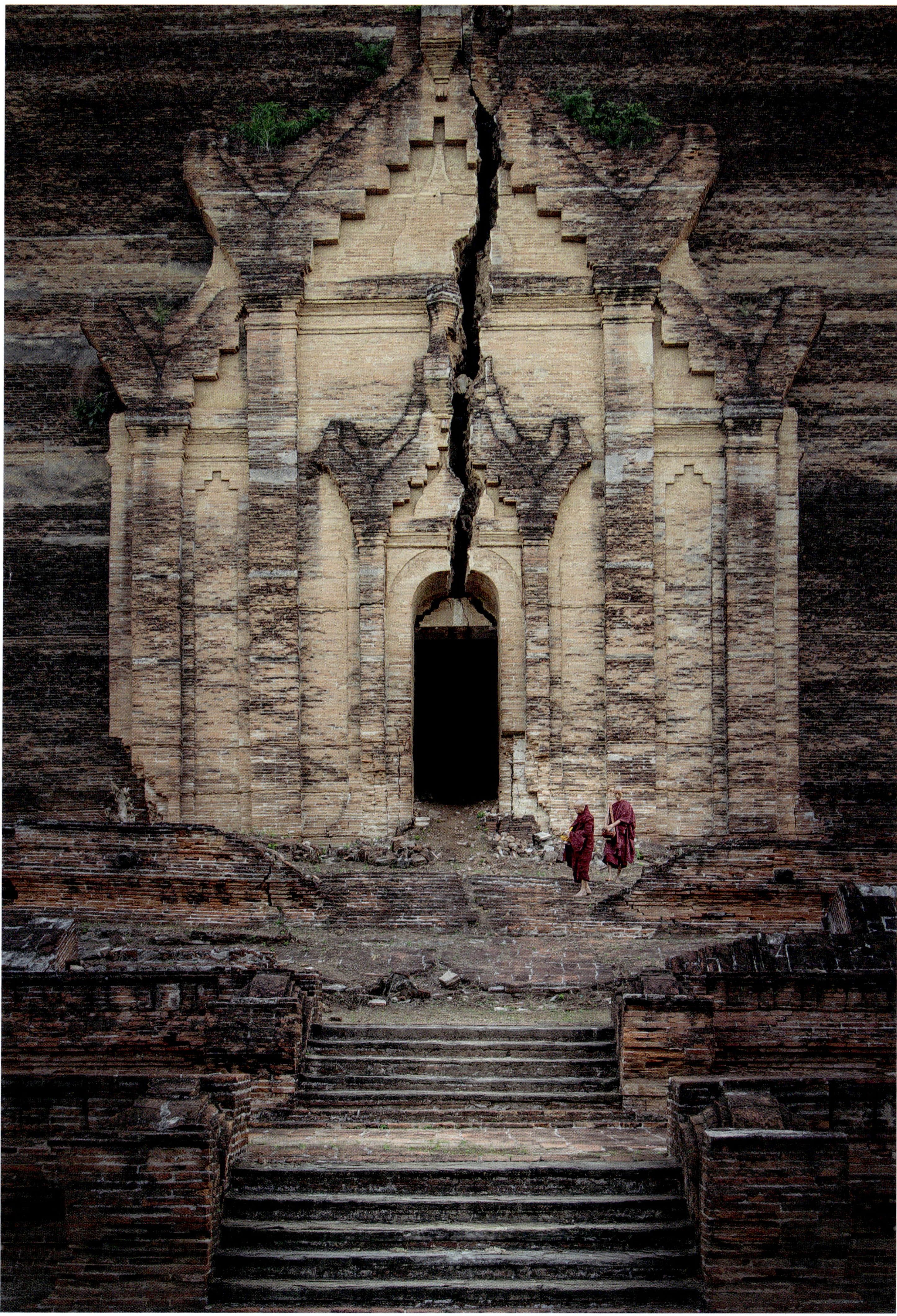

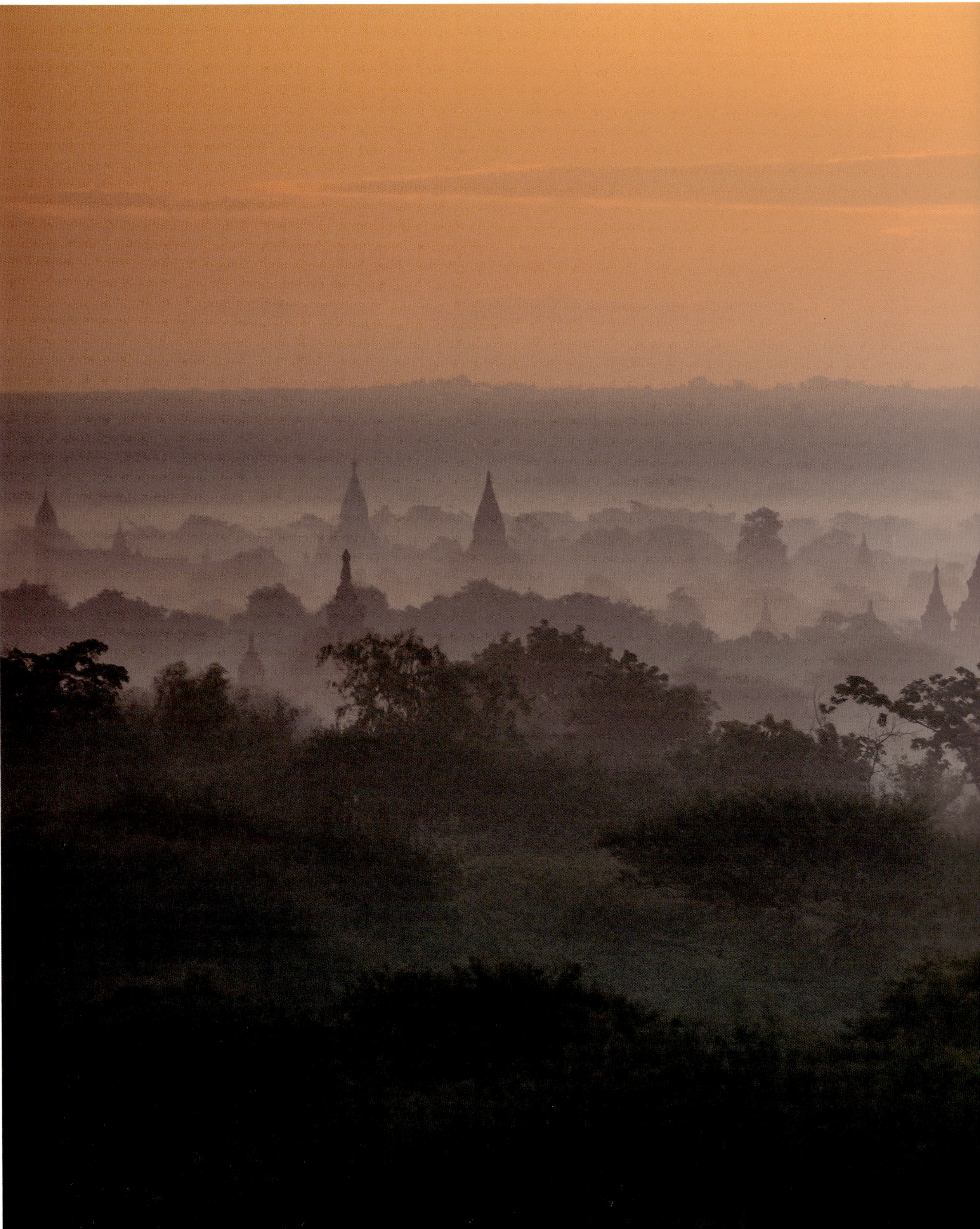

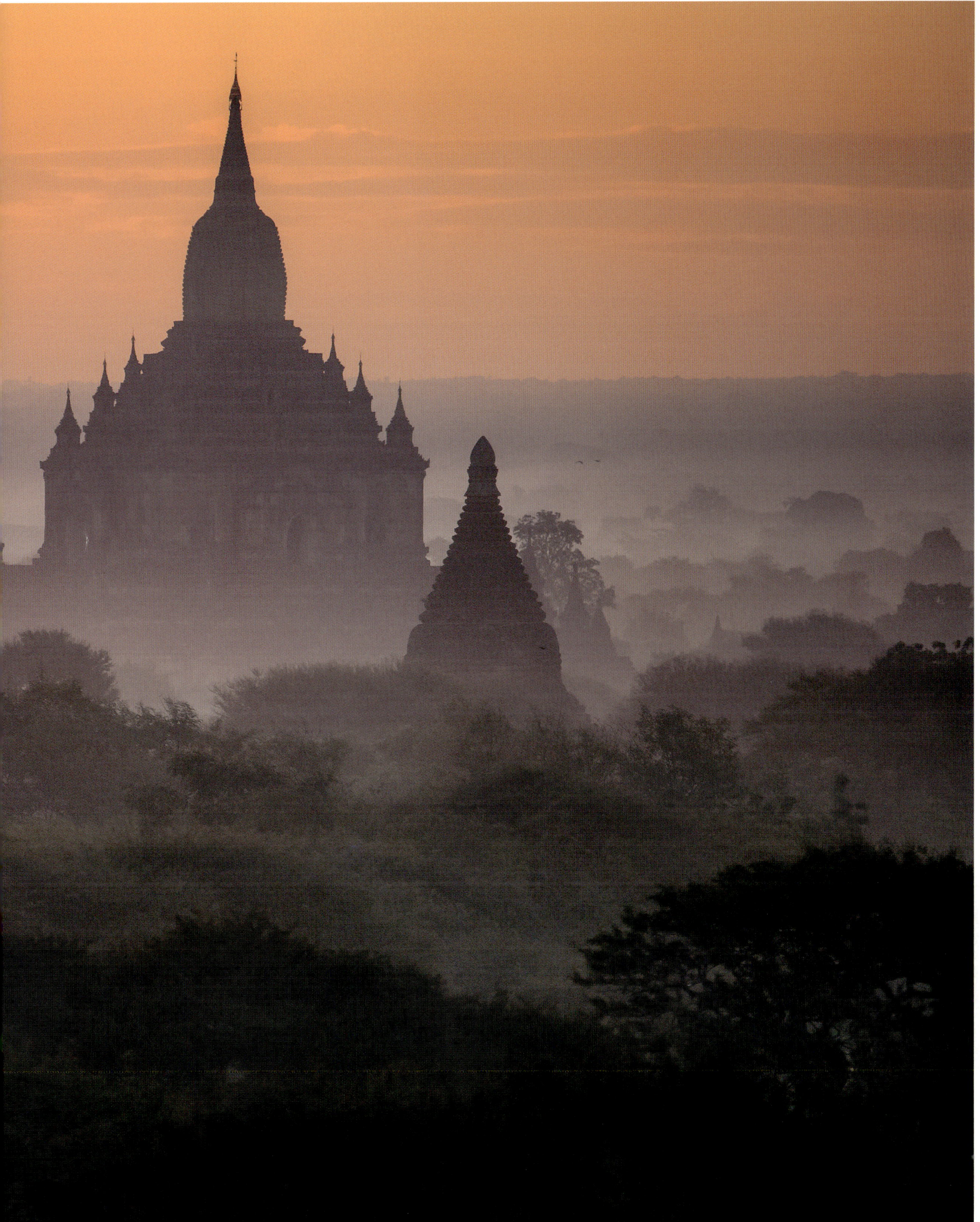

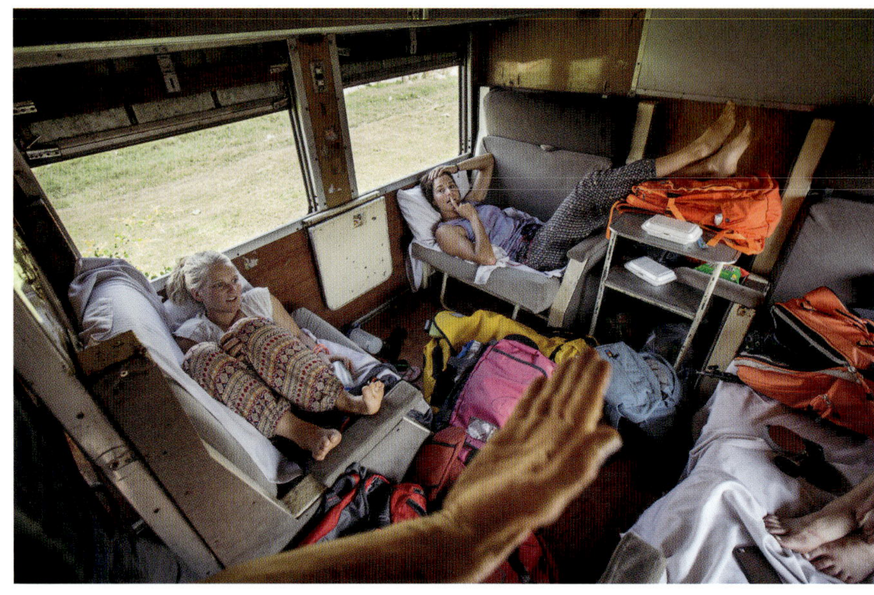

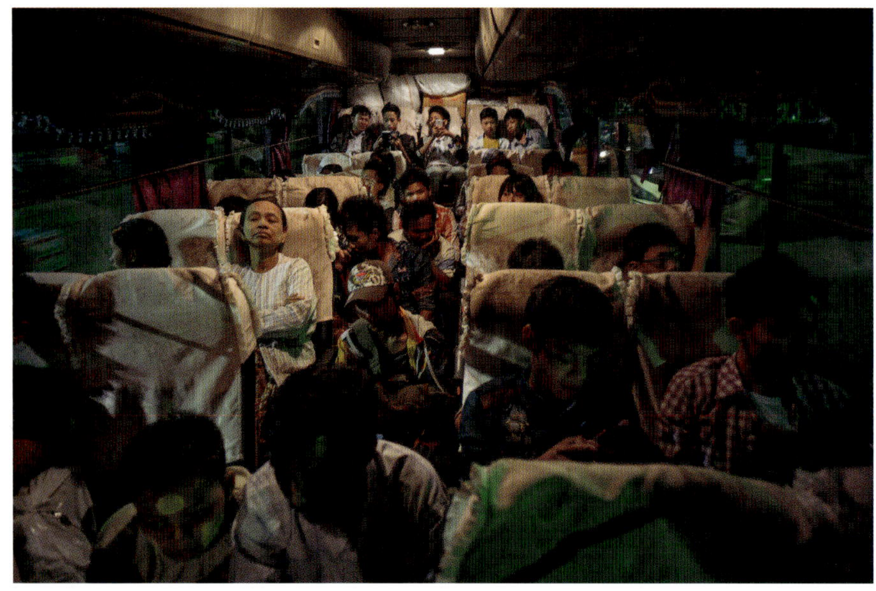

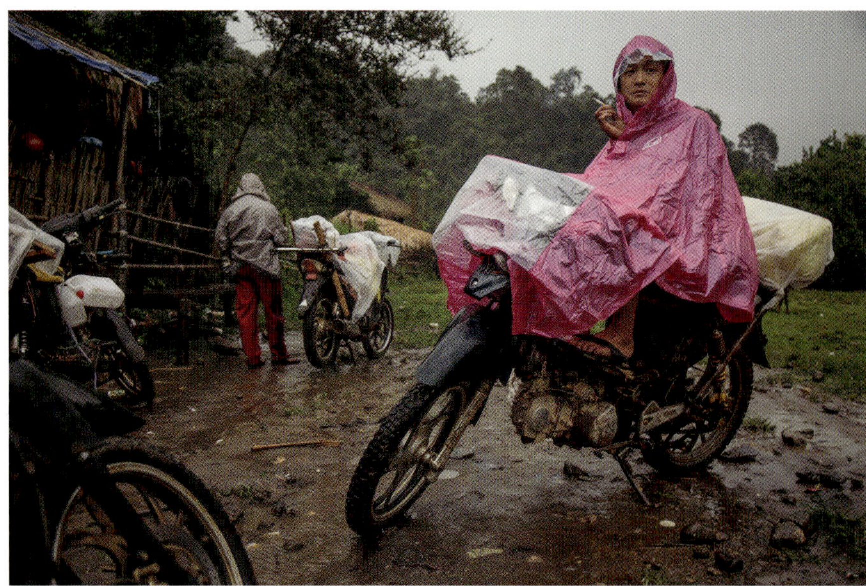

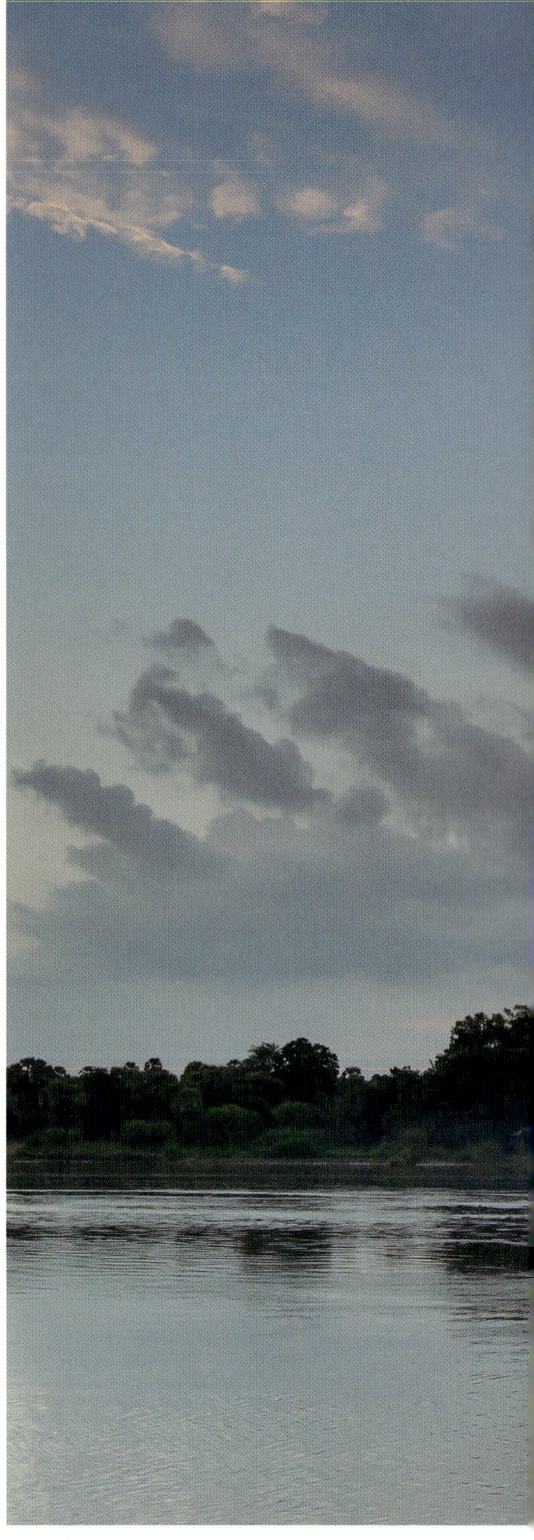

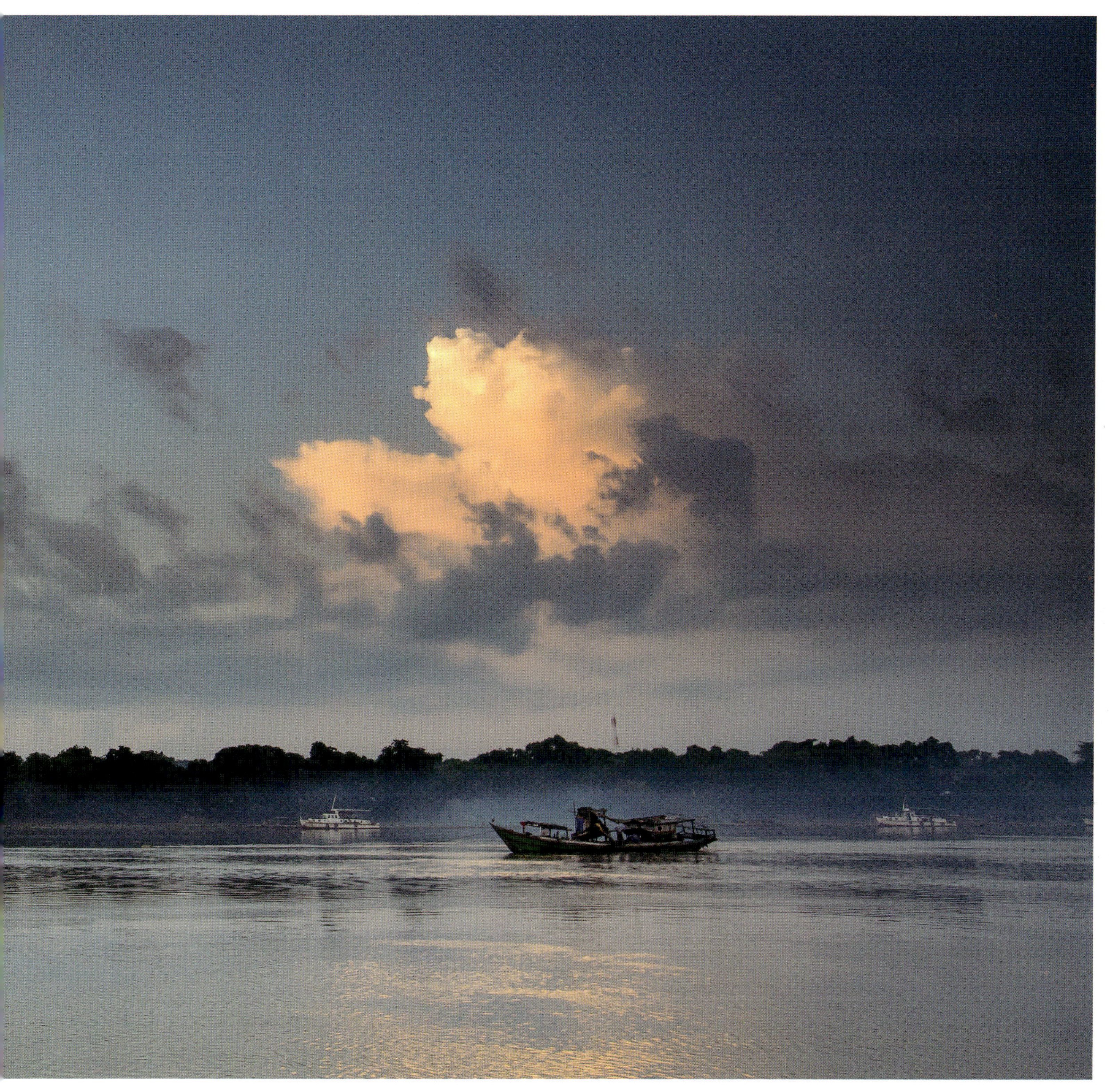

Dawn on the Irrawaddy River, the largest and most important commercial waterway in Myanmar. It was first used for trade and transport in the sixth century. **OPPOSITE, ABOVE:** American climber Emily Harrington (left) and Hilaree Nelson (right) ride the Siam-Burma Railway, also known as the Death Train. **OPPOSITE, CENTER:** A packed overnight bus the team took to Bagan. **OPPOSITE, BELOW:** One of the motorcyclists the team hired to transport us from Putao to the end of the road, roughly sixty-eight miles into the jungle.

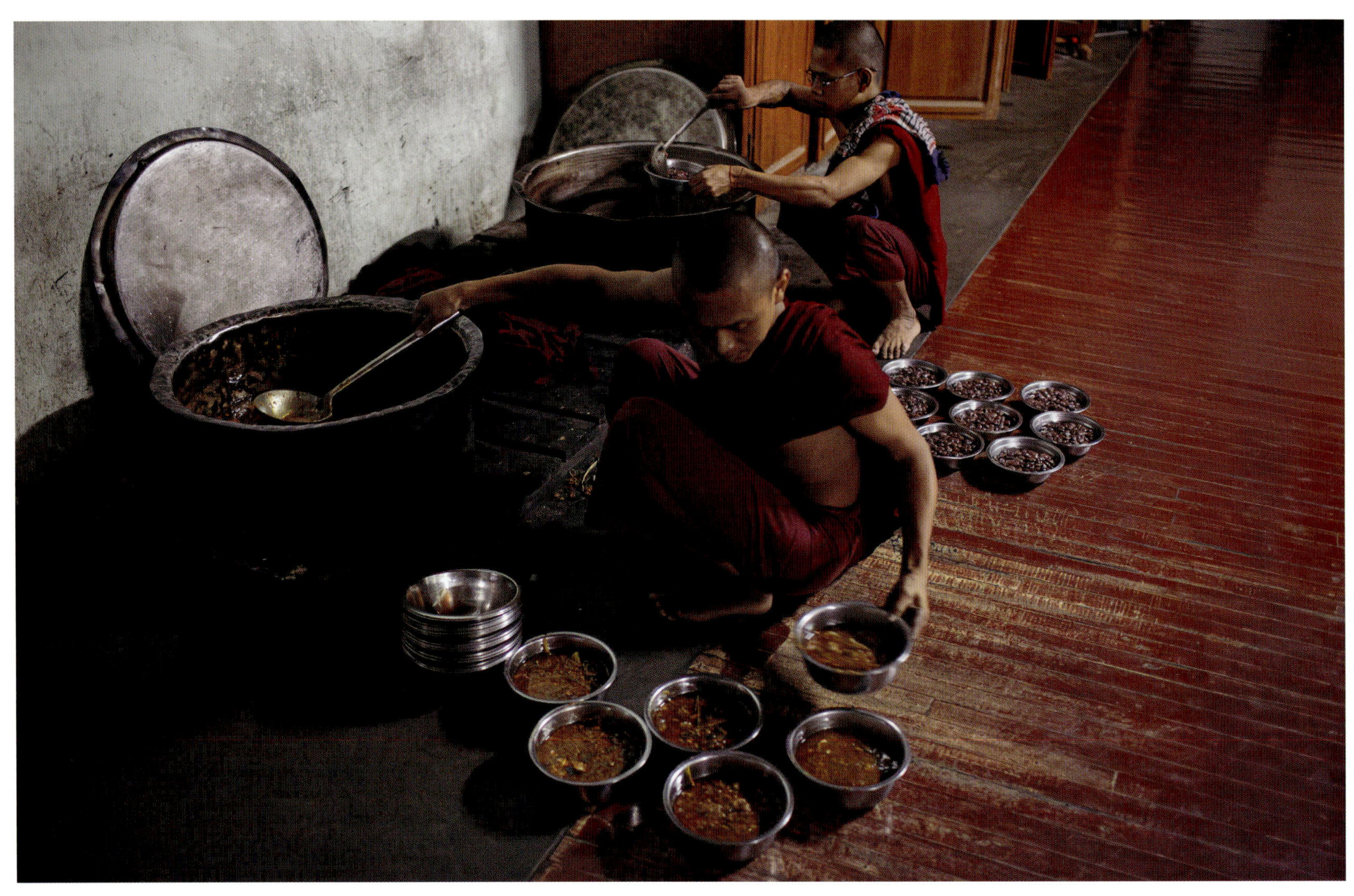

Monks prepare morning meals in Mandalay.

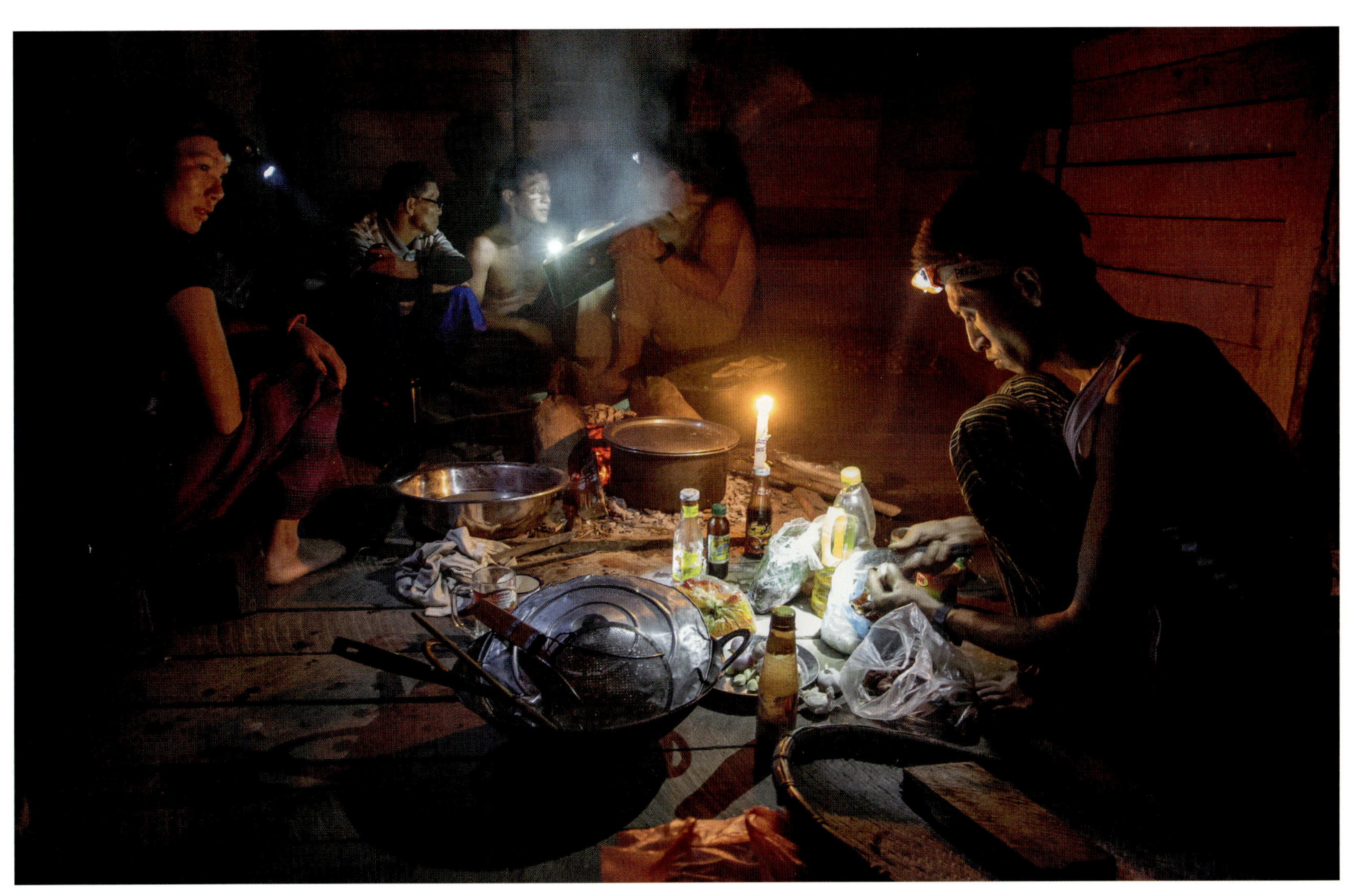

The team takes shelter in a small hut at the end of the road and the beginning of the walk into the jungle.

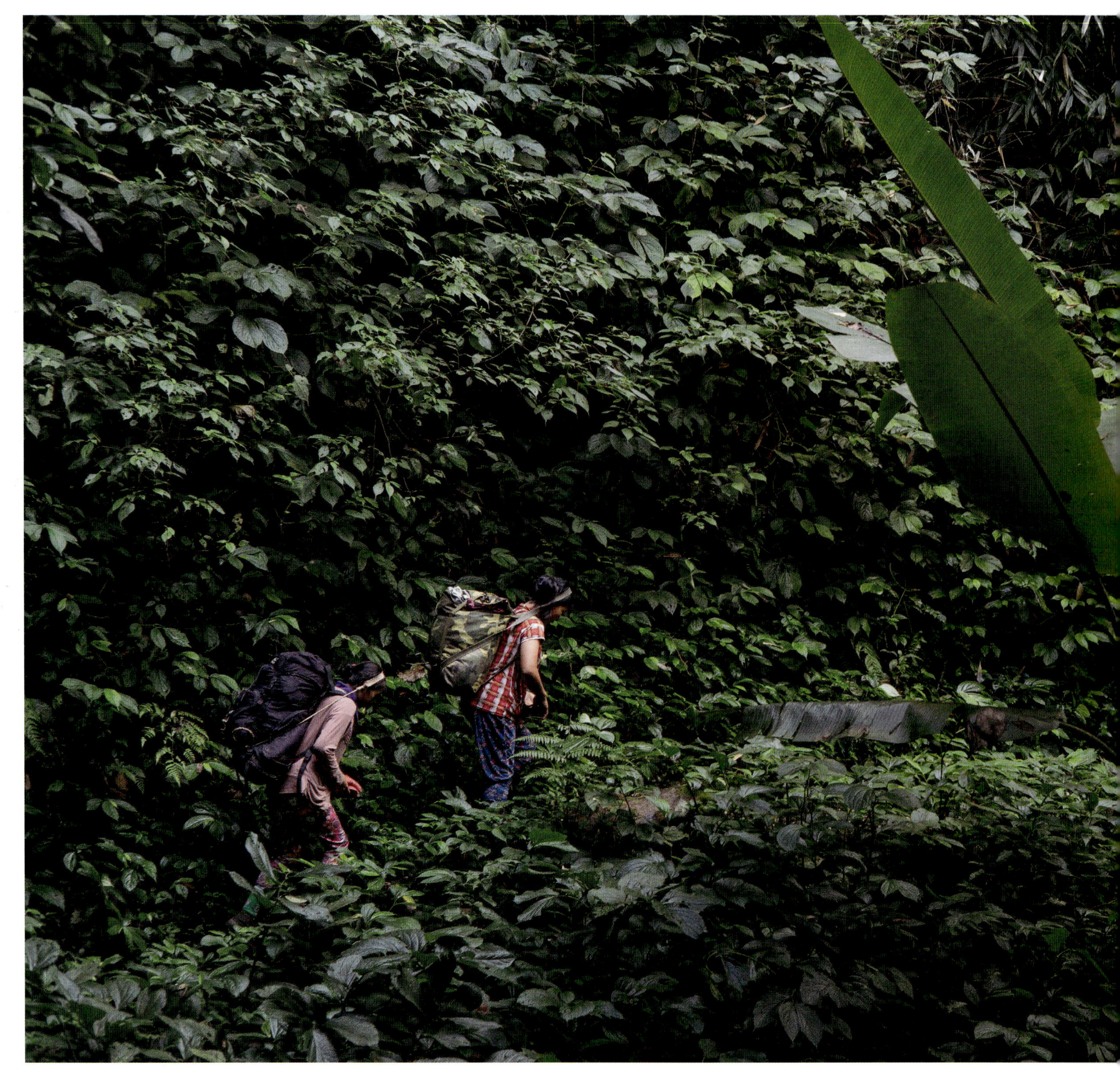

Two Rawang porters carry loads through the dense jungle of the Kachin Region. After roughly 100 miles of walking, the trail was little more than a faint depression through the foliage and often required bushwhacking to pass. In total, the team walked 125 miles to the base of the mountain, made possible only through local support and the tireless work of the porters and support staff. **OPPOSITE, ABOVE:** A team member crosses a long, modern suspension bridge over the Tamai River. As the crew made its way deeper into the jungle, the style and safety of the bridges deteriorated. **OPPOSITE, CENTER:** A porter crosses a bamboo suspension bridge. **OPPOSITE, BELOW:** Porters cross a downed tree used as a makeshift bridge close to the foot of the mountain.

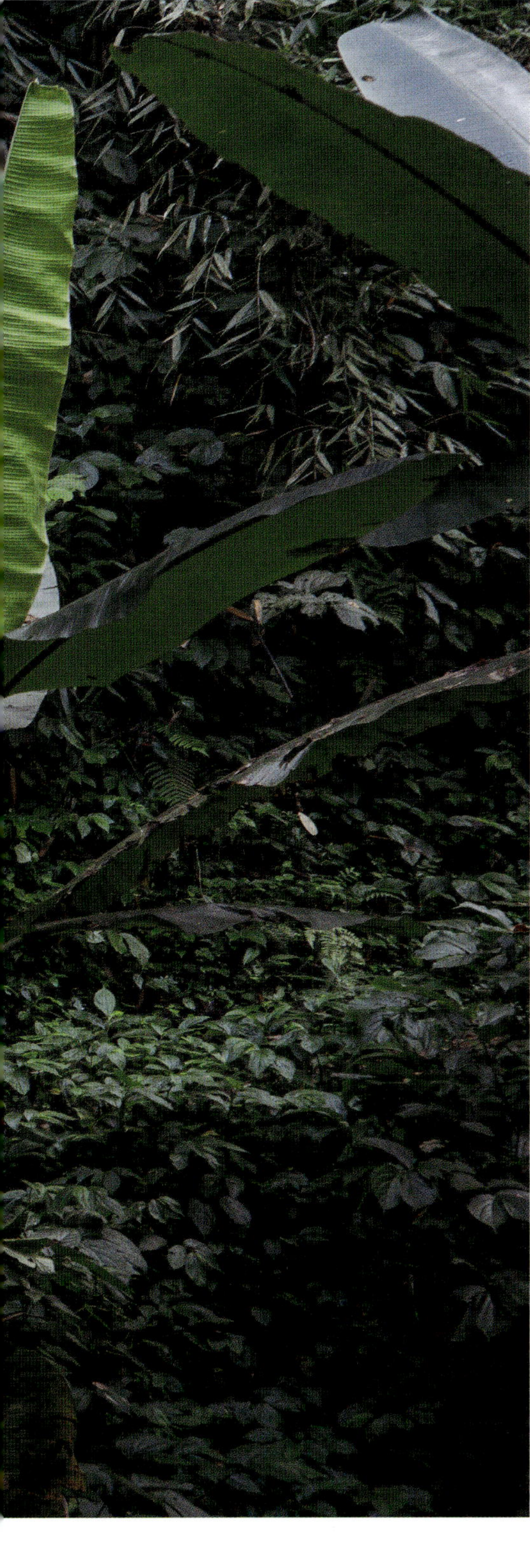

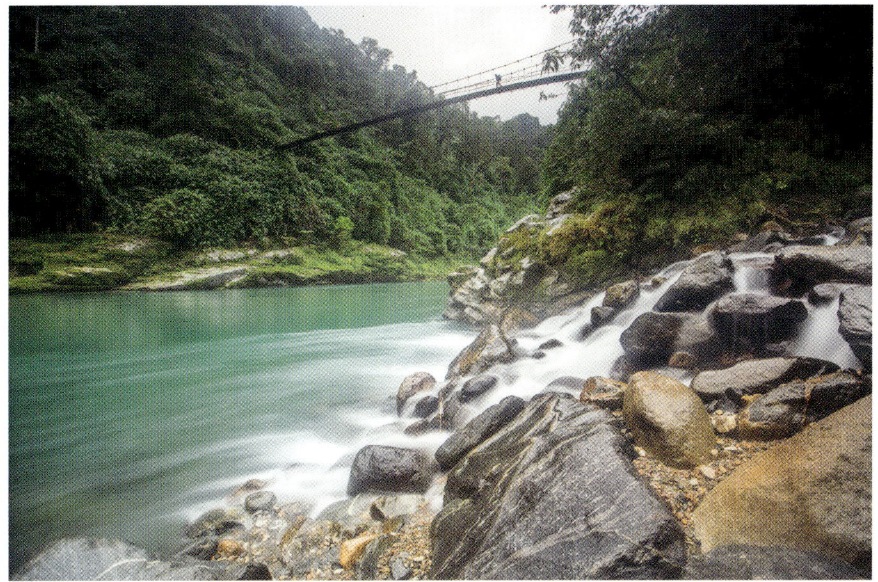

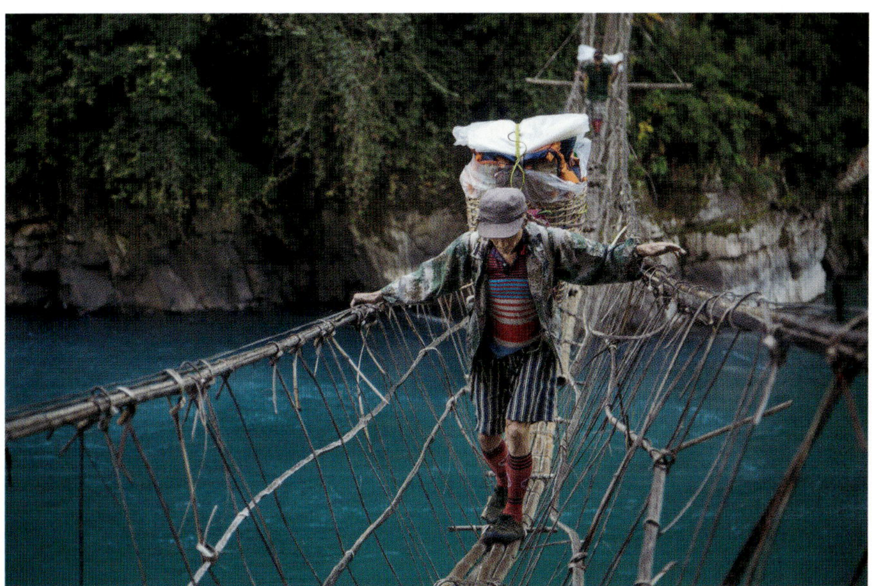

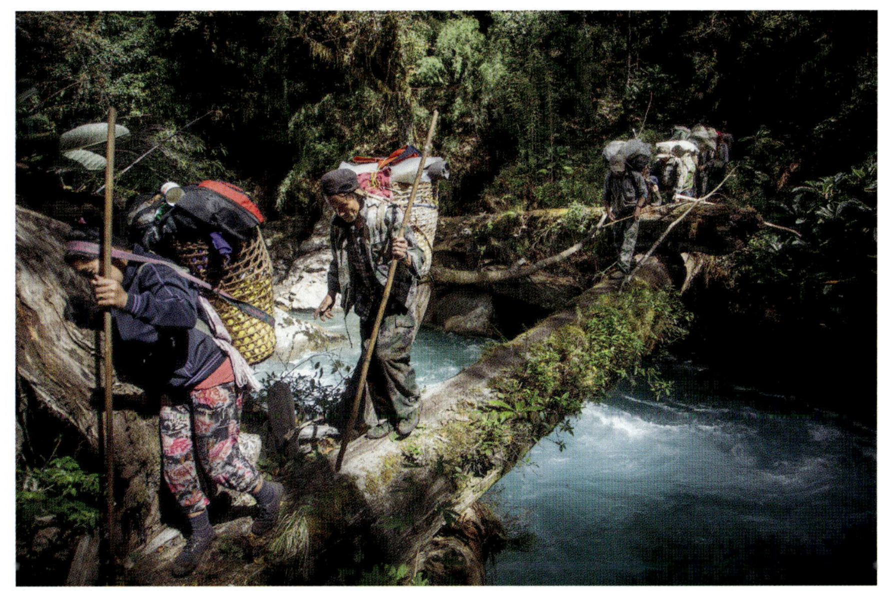

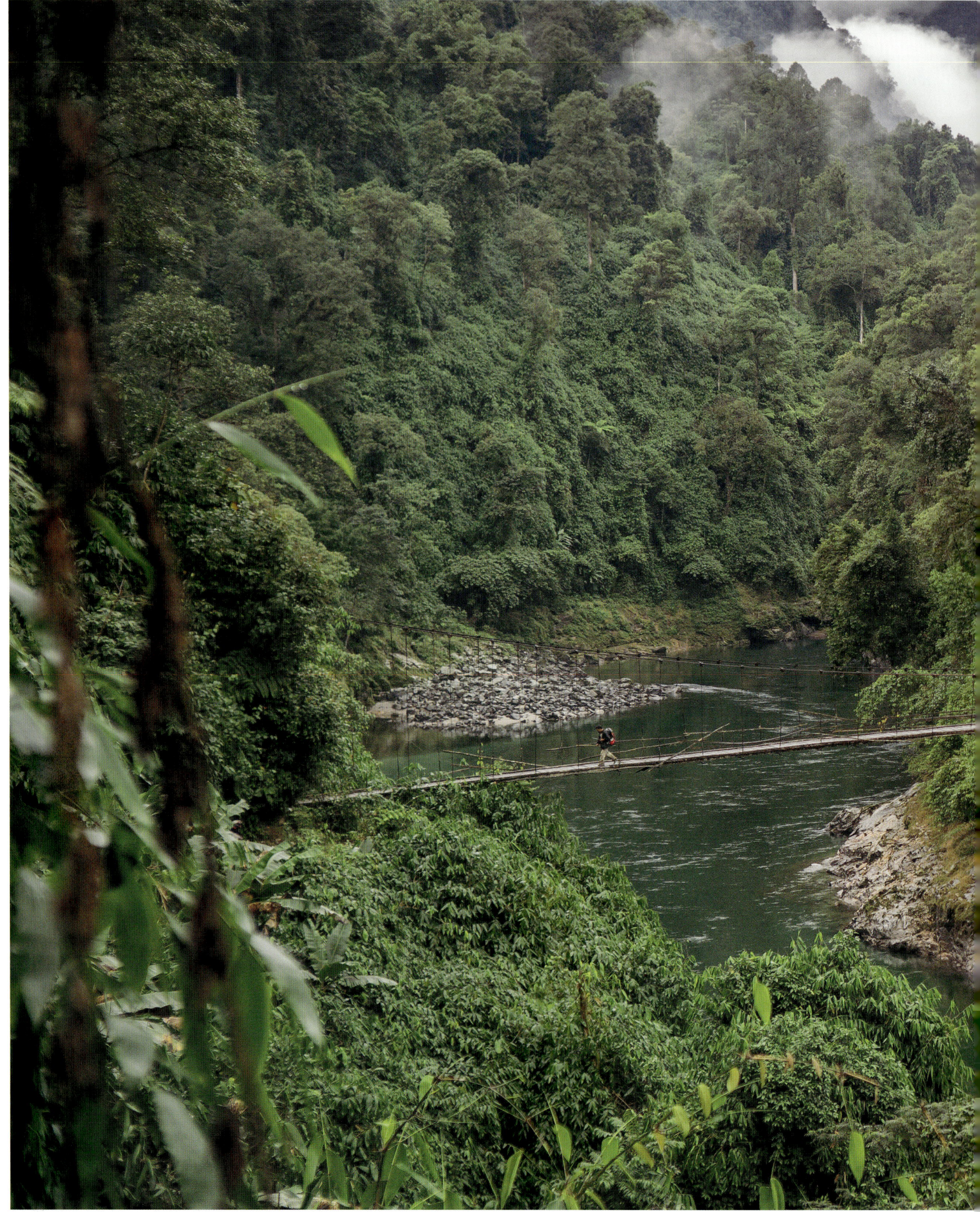

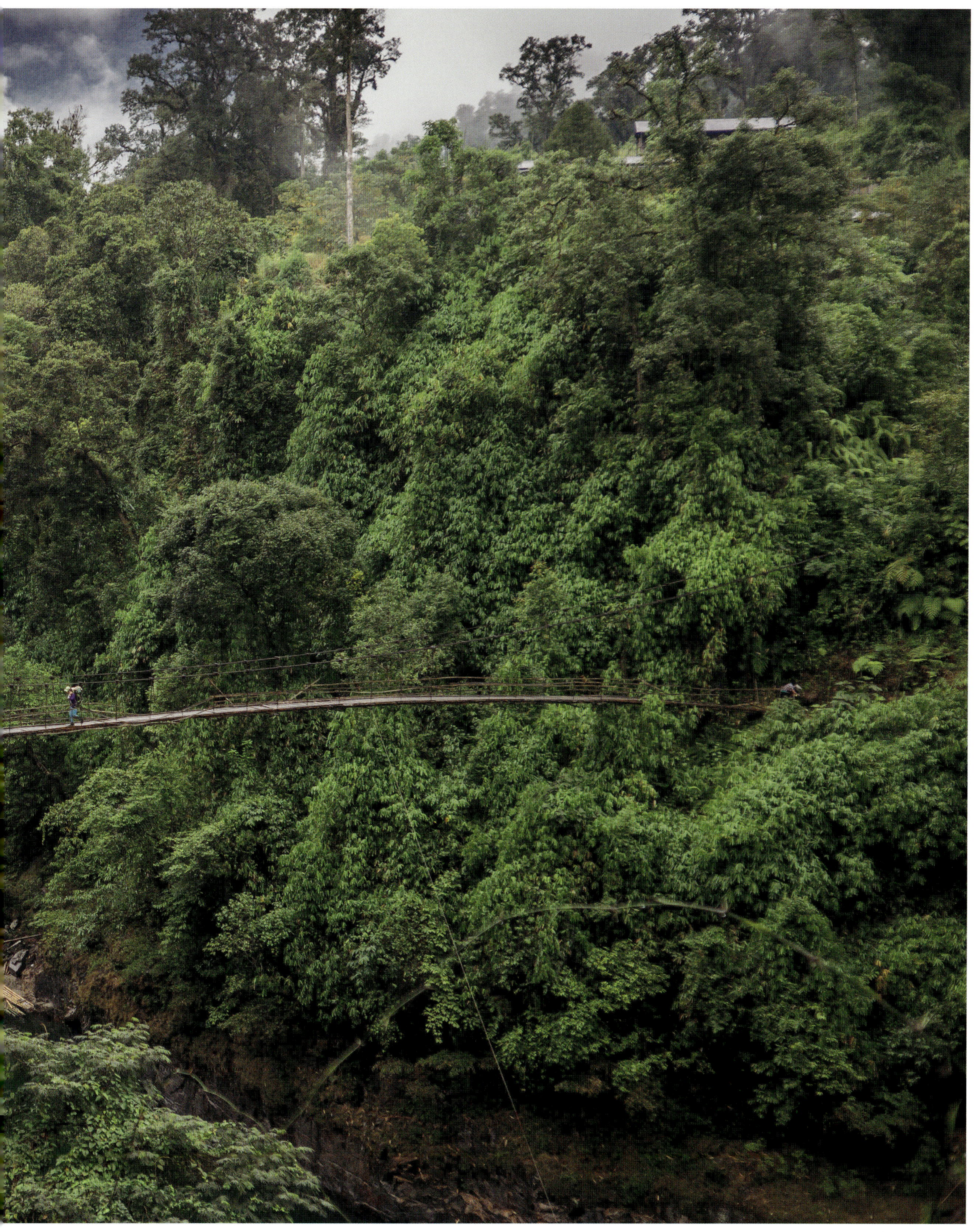

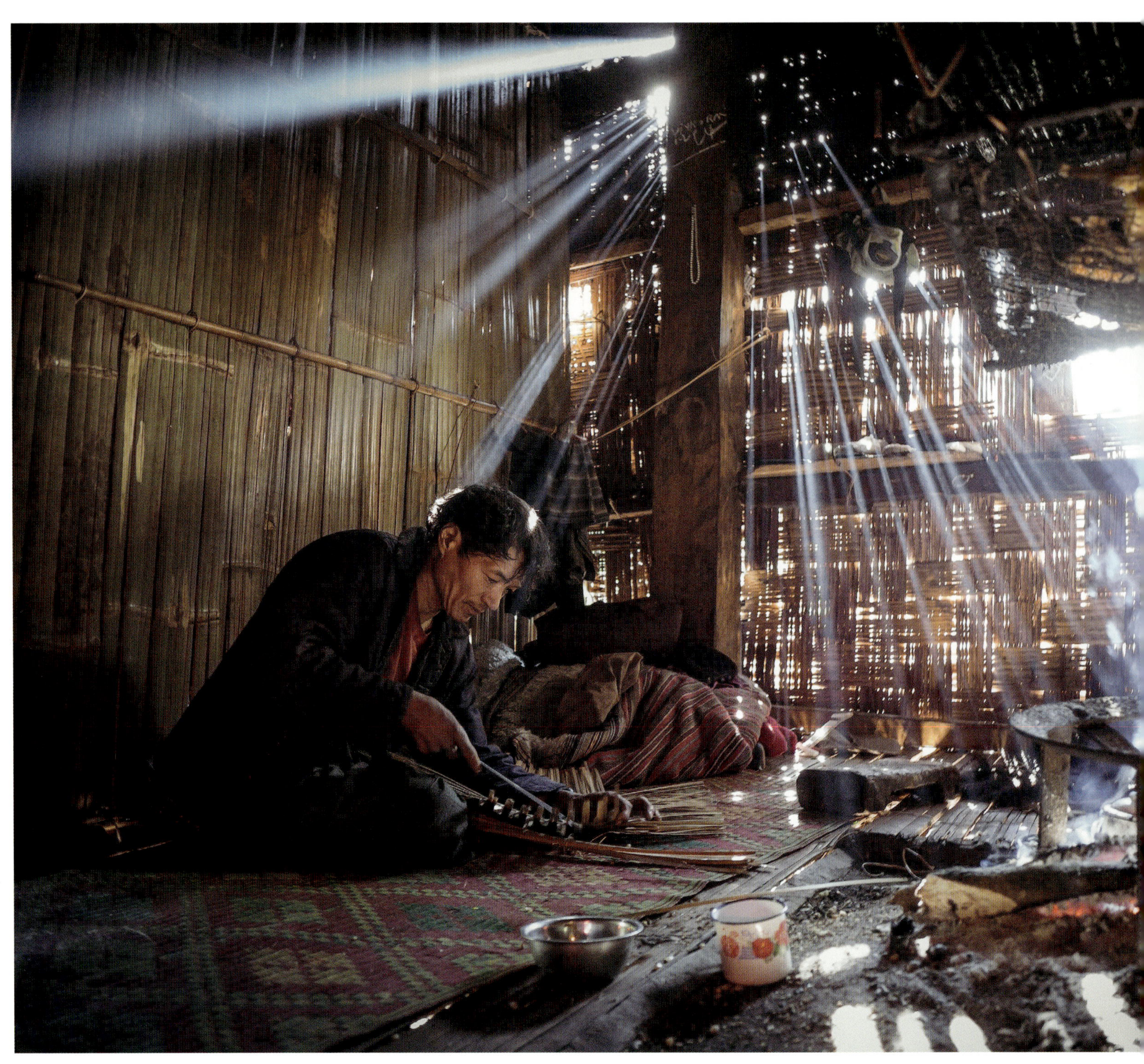

Inside the home of one of the many Rawang families that opened their homes to us along the trail. **OPPOSITE, ABOVE:** A group of porters rests on the trail. The team hired whole families to help ferry gear. We had hoped for about sixty porters, but were only able to find thirty-five or so, eventually forcing us to leave gear behind. Expeditions of this nature require thousands of pounds of climbing, camping, and photo and film gear, as well as food and fuel to support the entire team for weeks if not months. **OPPOSITE, BELOW:** American writer and expedition co-leader Mark Jenkins takes a break in Pangmandim on the road home.

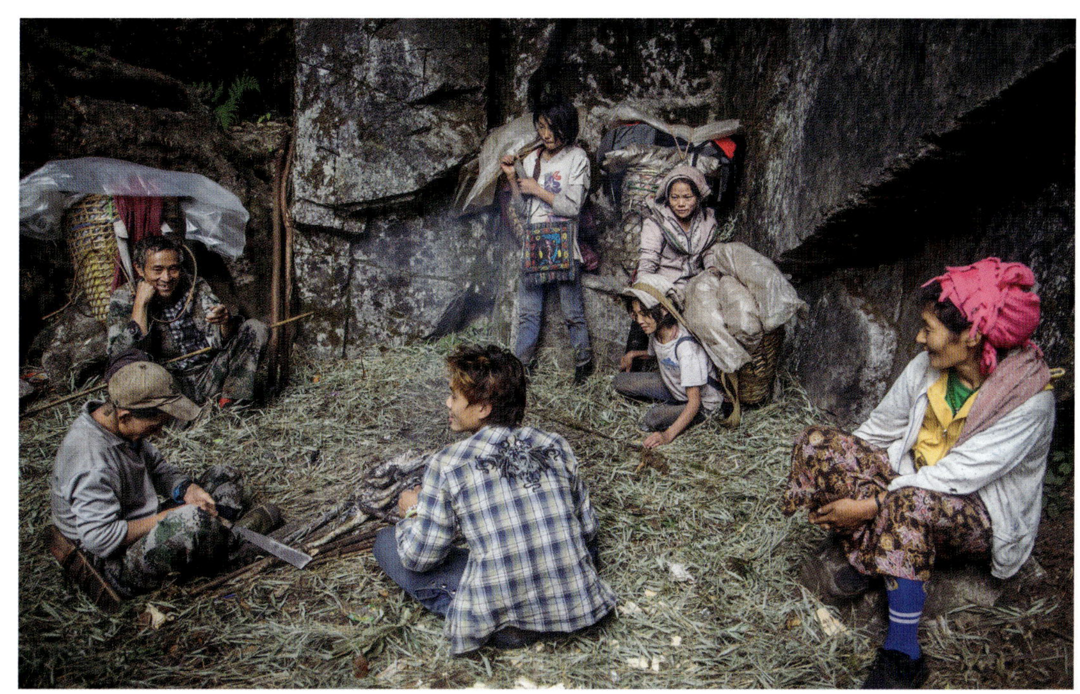

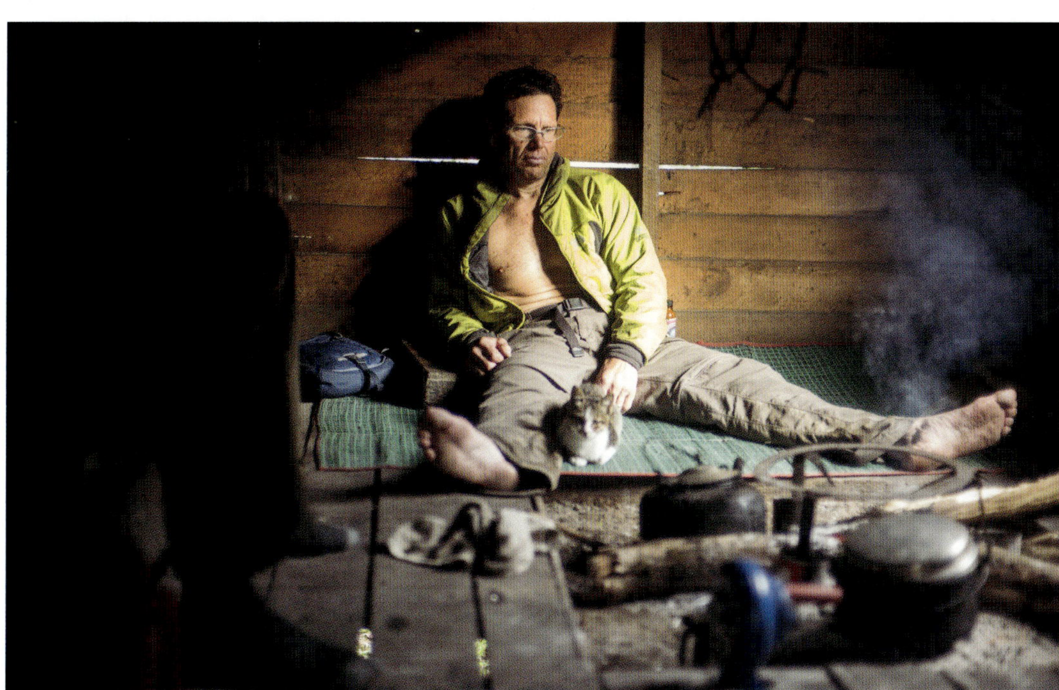

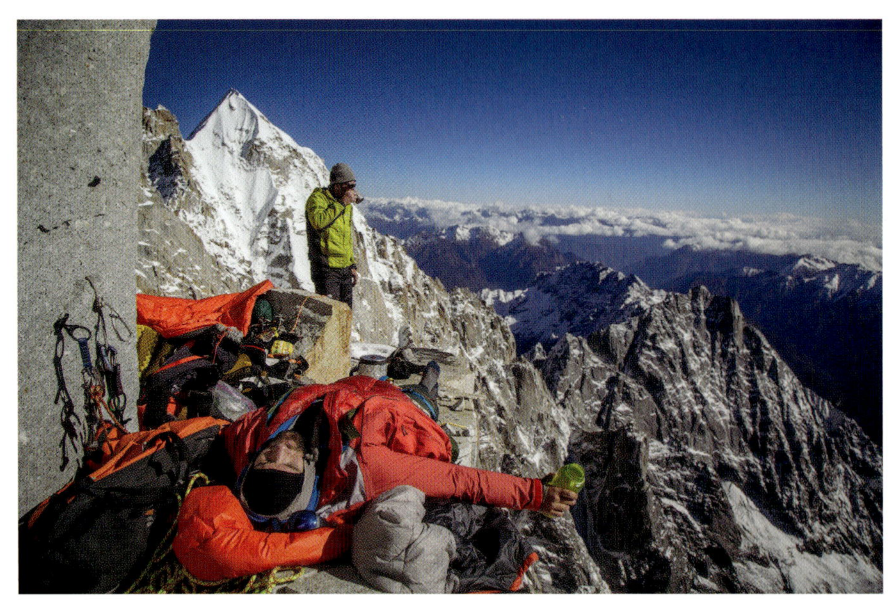

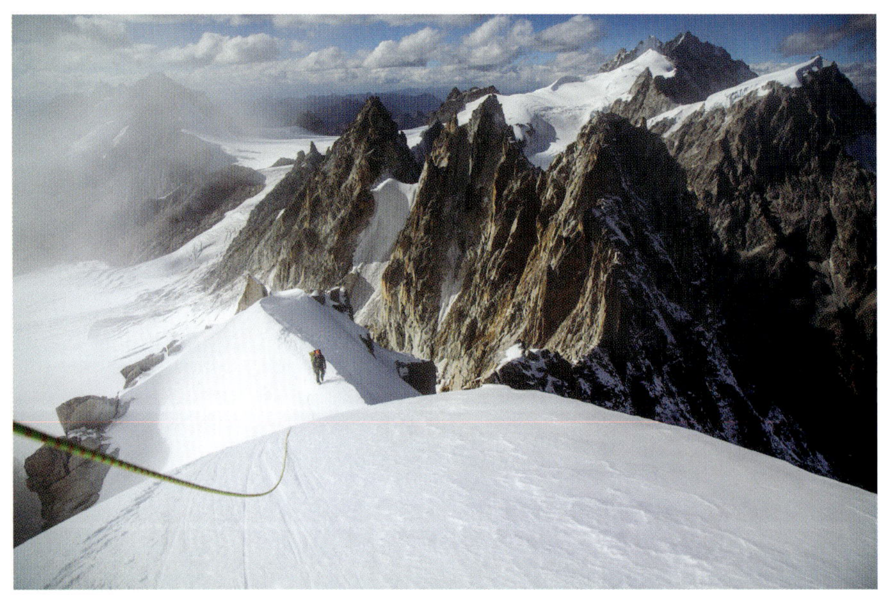

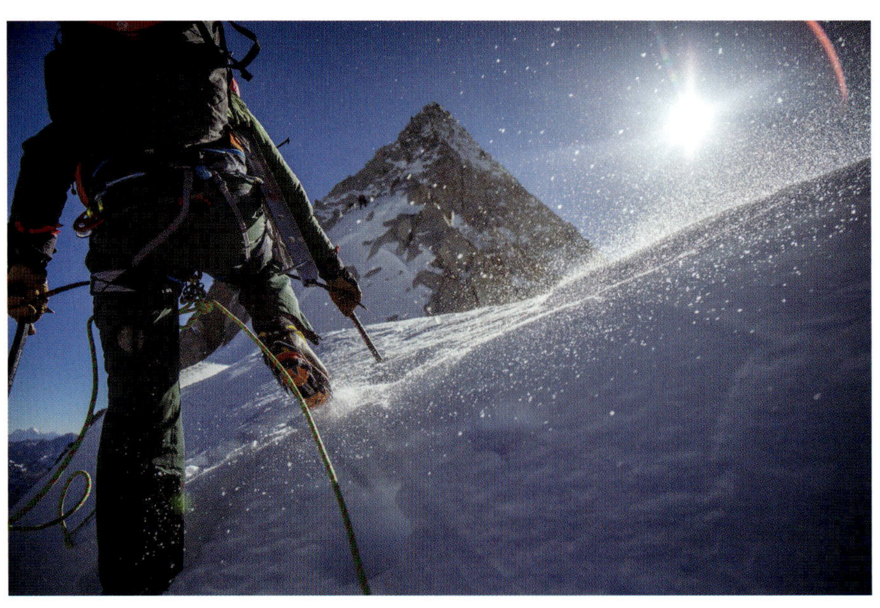

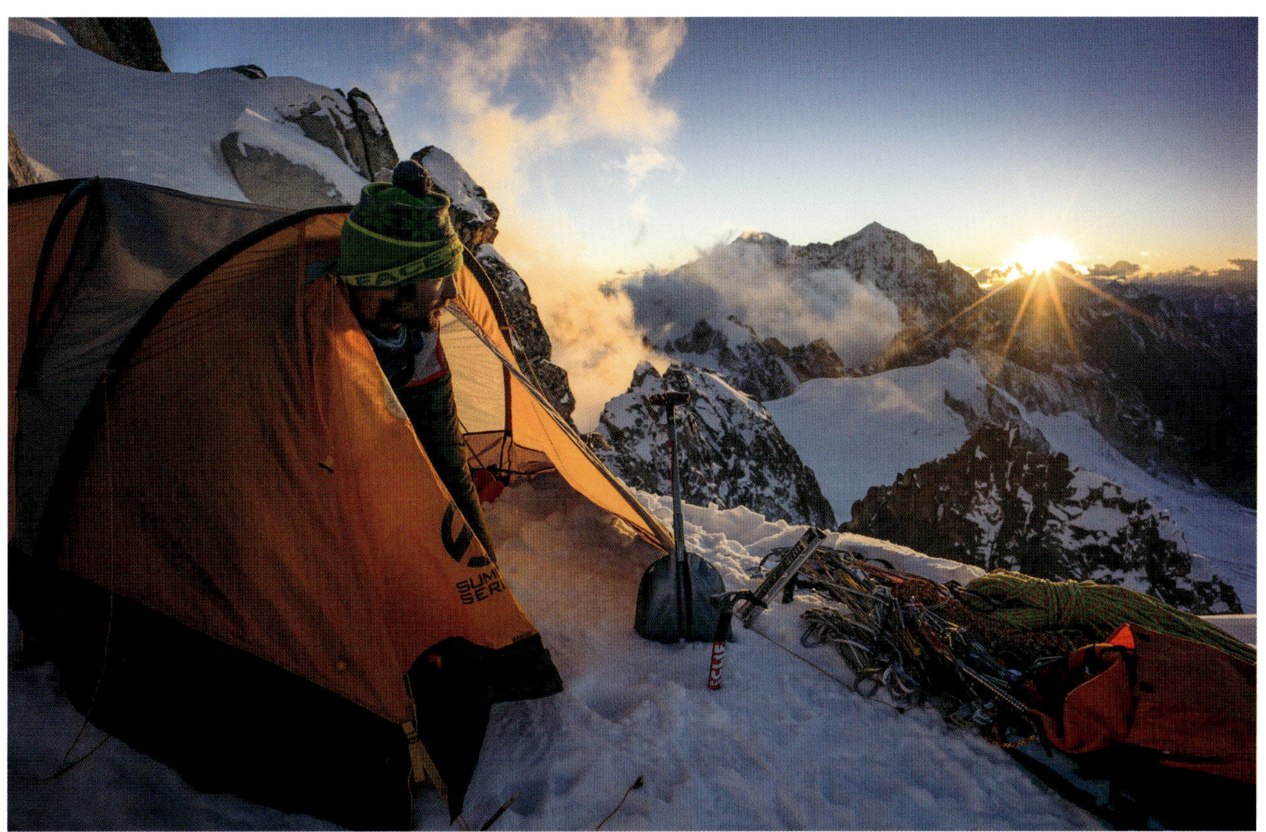

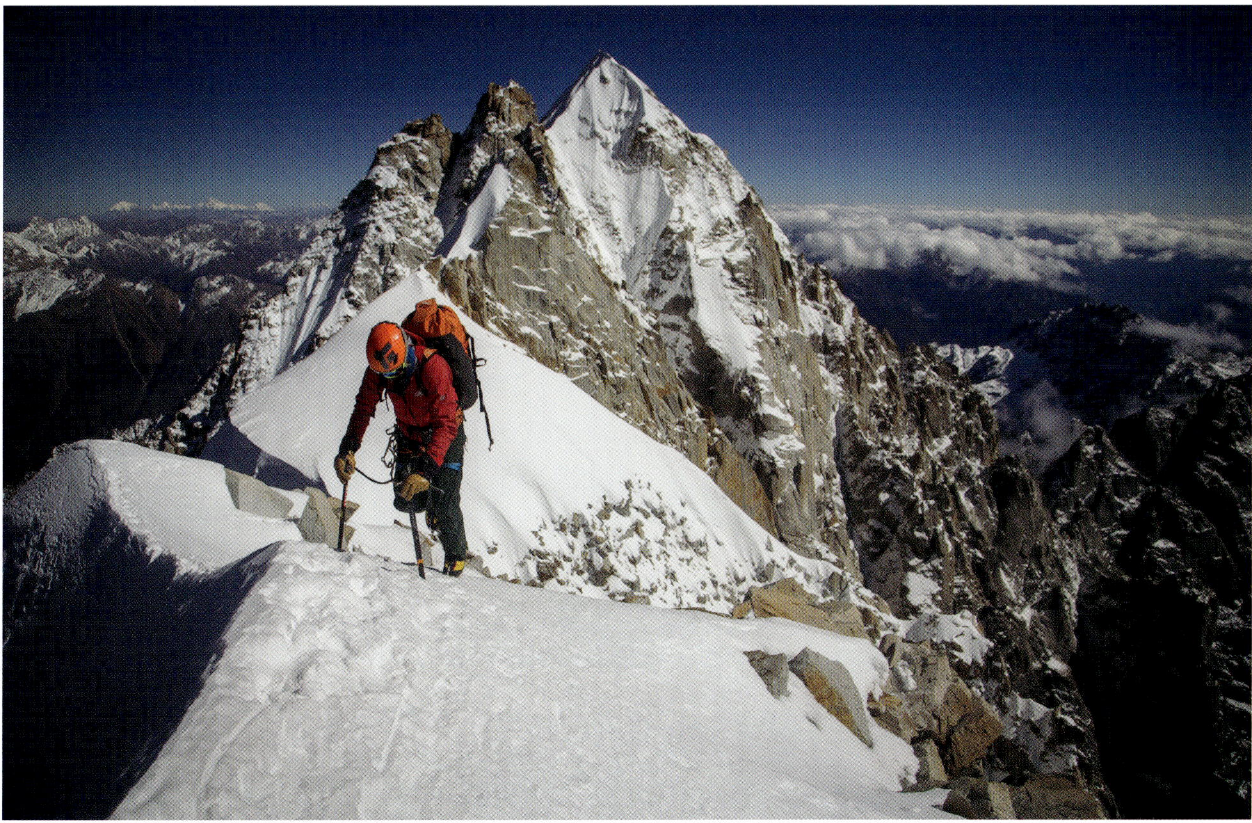

ABOVE: American climber Renan Ozturk surveys the weather before leaving for the summit. **BELOW:** Renan Ozturk reverses the route on the descent. The team turned around short of the summit after forty-one days. **OPPOSITE, ABOVE:** Renan Ozturk (foreground) and Mark Jenkins (background) rest on a ledge above 20,000 feet, still on the ascent. **OPPOSITE, CENTER:** Renan Ozturk climbs an exposed ridge to camp 2. **OPPOSITE, BELOW:** Renan Ozturk leaves camp 2 for the summit attempt on day thirty-nine of the journey.

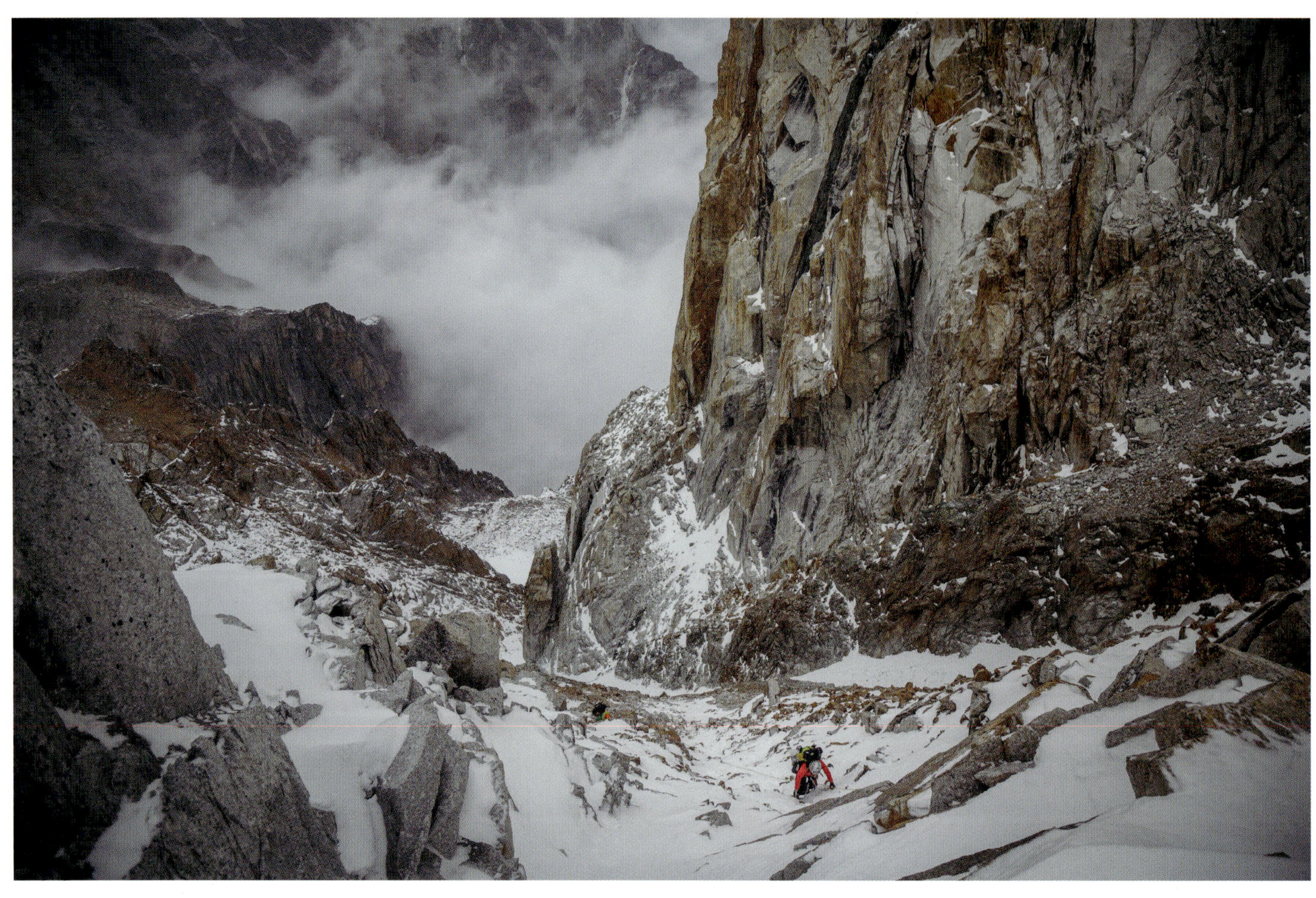

Emily Harrington navigates a mixed couloir below camp 1.

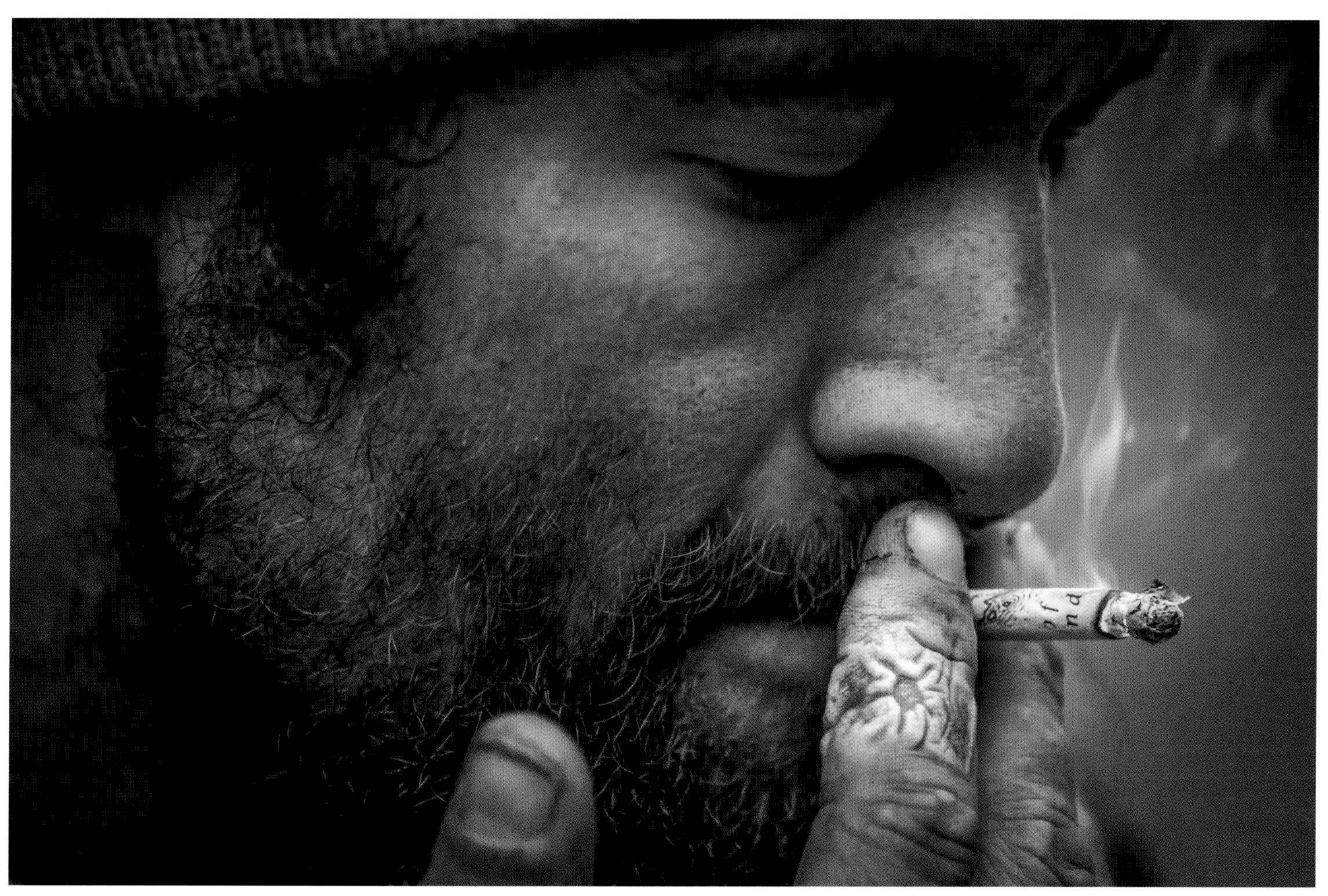

Renan Ozturk smokes a cigarette, exhausted. After the team ran out of rolling papers, we used pages from a shared copy of Emma Larkin's *Finding George Orwell in Burma*. **FOLLOWING:** Mark Jenkins navigates the still mysterious upper reaches of Mount Hkakabo Razi.

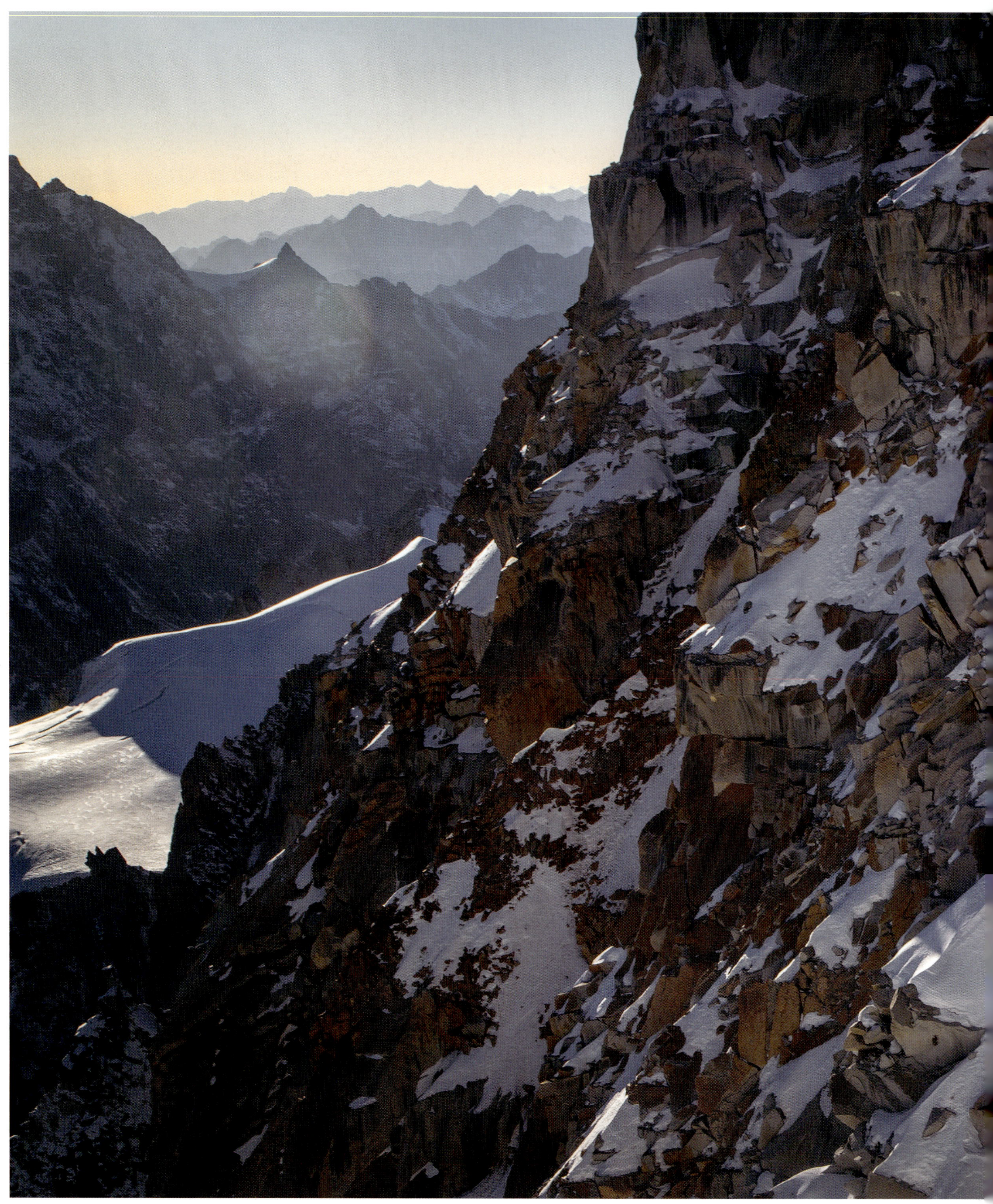

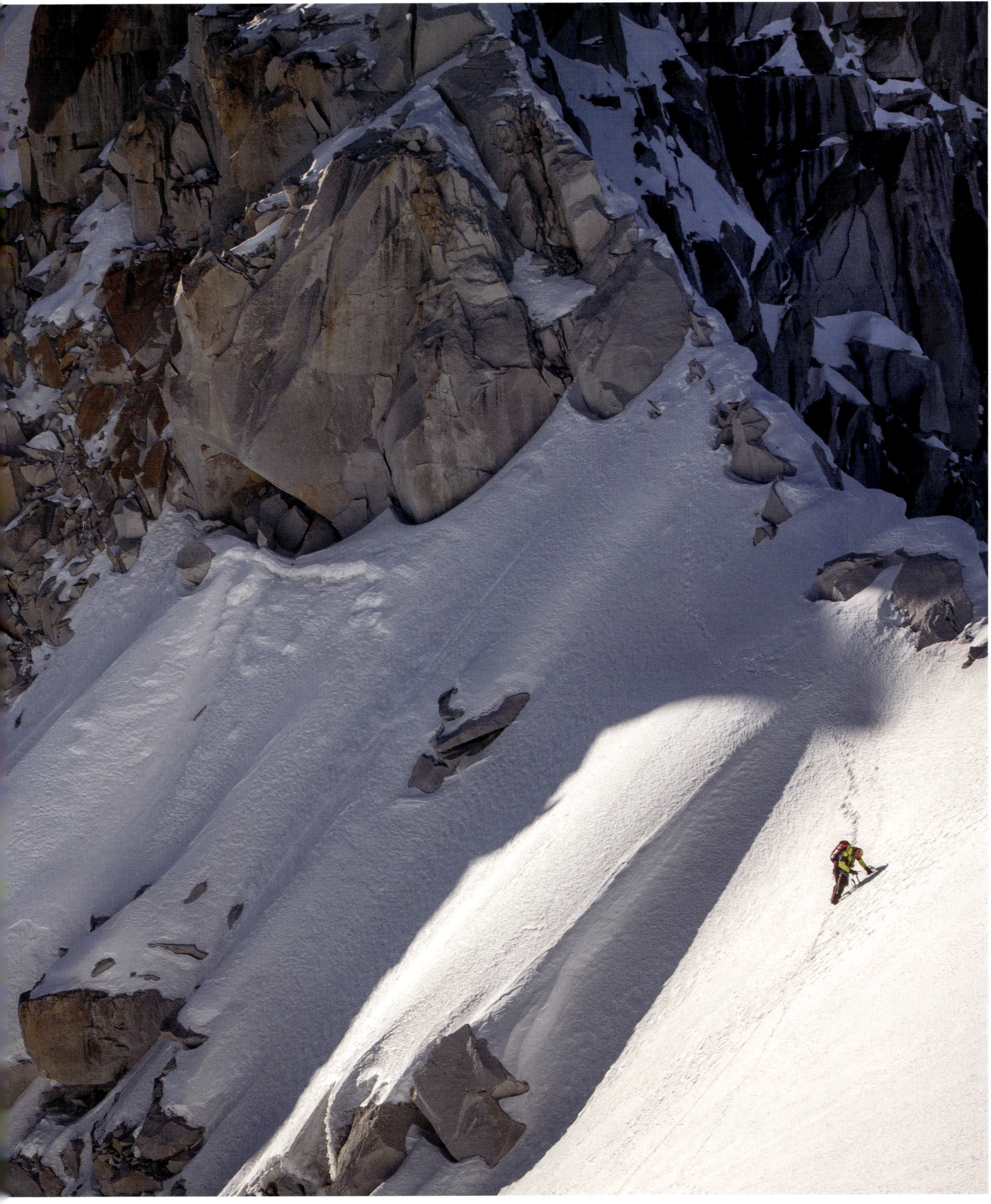

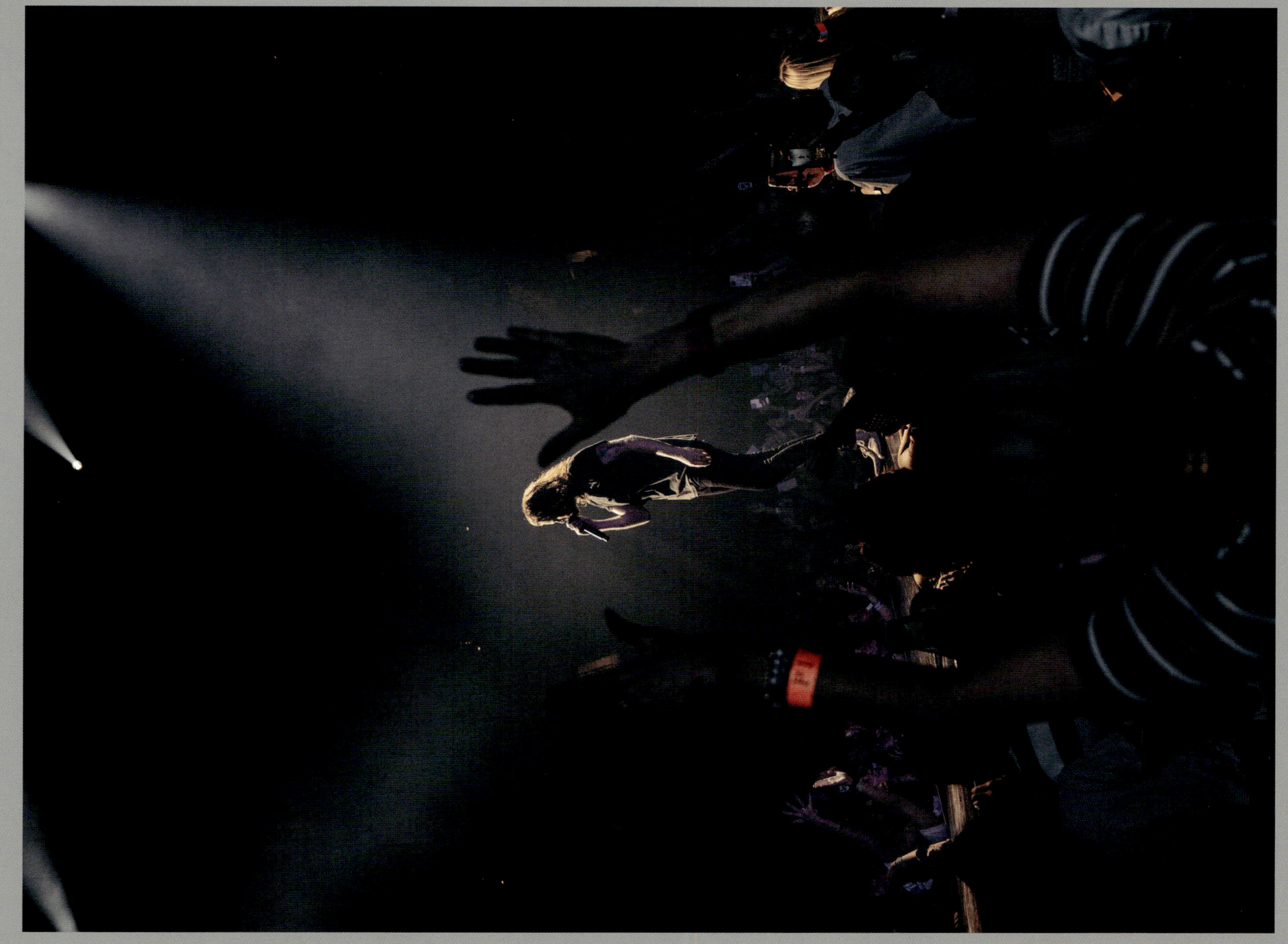

ON SCREAMS AND SILENCE On Tour with the Lumineers

There are three levels of sound that come from an audience at a live show. First, there is the murmur and hum of laughter and voices as people mill around, get drinks, and catch up with friends. When the lights go down, the level goes up and a palpable tension washes over the crowd. They wait.

Finally, the band takes the stage and what seems like a fever pitch of screams heightens into something so forceful and joyous that it overwhelms the space, pushing against eardrums and walls until the first chord hits. This is the connective and collective power of music.

My relationship with the Lumineers started with a deep friendship with the cofounder of the band, Jeremiah Fraites. We "met" via Instagram and became fast friends. He and his wife, Francesca, helped usher me through a painful divorce as I watched them grow their family and release two albums. It took years before I even brought my camera around, being careful not to mix my work with our friendship. Seven years into our relationship, Jer invited me to come on tour with the band for a week. Of course, I said yes.

I'm backstage with Wesley Schultz, the other cofounder of the Lumineers, in a nearly silent room as he goes over a set list and hums. It's the quiet that no one sees. It's the calm before the storm. A humidifier is sending a small stream of vapor into the air as he blows into a straw in ascending notes, warming up vocal cords that have been vibrating for months on end, thrusting out poetry over a sea of screaming fans hungry for the energy and emotion unique to music. He picks up a guitar and walks into the bathroom. I sit on the toilet and film as he strums across the strings and begins to sing. As much as the sounds are beautiful, it's a lonely scene and I feel like an intruder separated by a camera and the silence between songs.

Three stops into my time with them, I'm beginning to understand how much touring extracts from a band. Night after night, they step onto a stage and sweat their lives and art into an ocean of anonymous faces. When the lights come on and the buzz of the shows settles over the discarded cups and sticky arena floor, they pack up their family and crawl into cramped tour buses, driving into a late night and waking up in a new city to do it all again.

The road is a polar place, oscillating between masses of feverish fans and the quiet that follows. And as much as the stage connects the band to the audience, it also isolates them in a way that only musicians know. Balance seems scant, if not a myth itself.

Wesley lets his voice settle against the tiles of the bathroom and crawls out of the guitar strap. I can hear the low rumble of the audience through the walls as Gregory Alan Isakov finishes the opening set. Soon, the lights will go down, the darkness filled with the thunder of an audience screaming to connect.

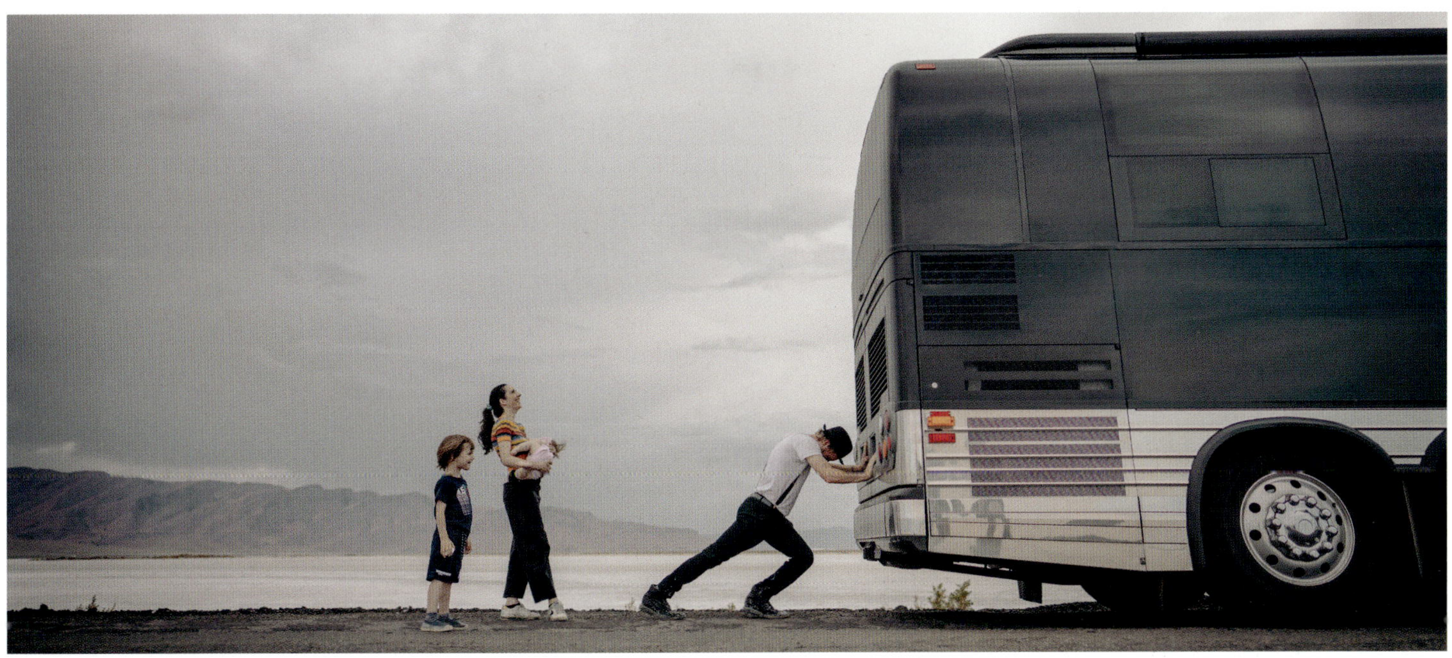

OPPOSITE: Wesley Schultz sings to a sea of fans. **ABOVE:** Jeremiah Fraites, with his family, pretends to push a tour bus through the salt flats outside of Salt Lake City, Utah. **FOLLOWING:** Nic Close and Shawn Lobb tune and wait to hand off guitars during rehearsal in Denver, Colorado.

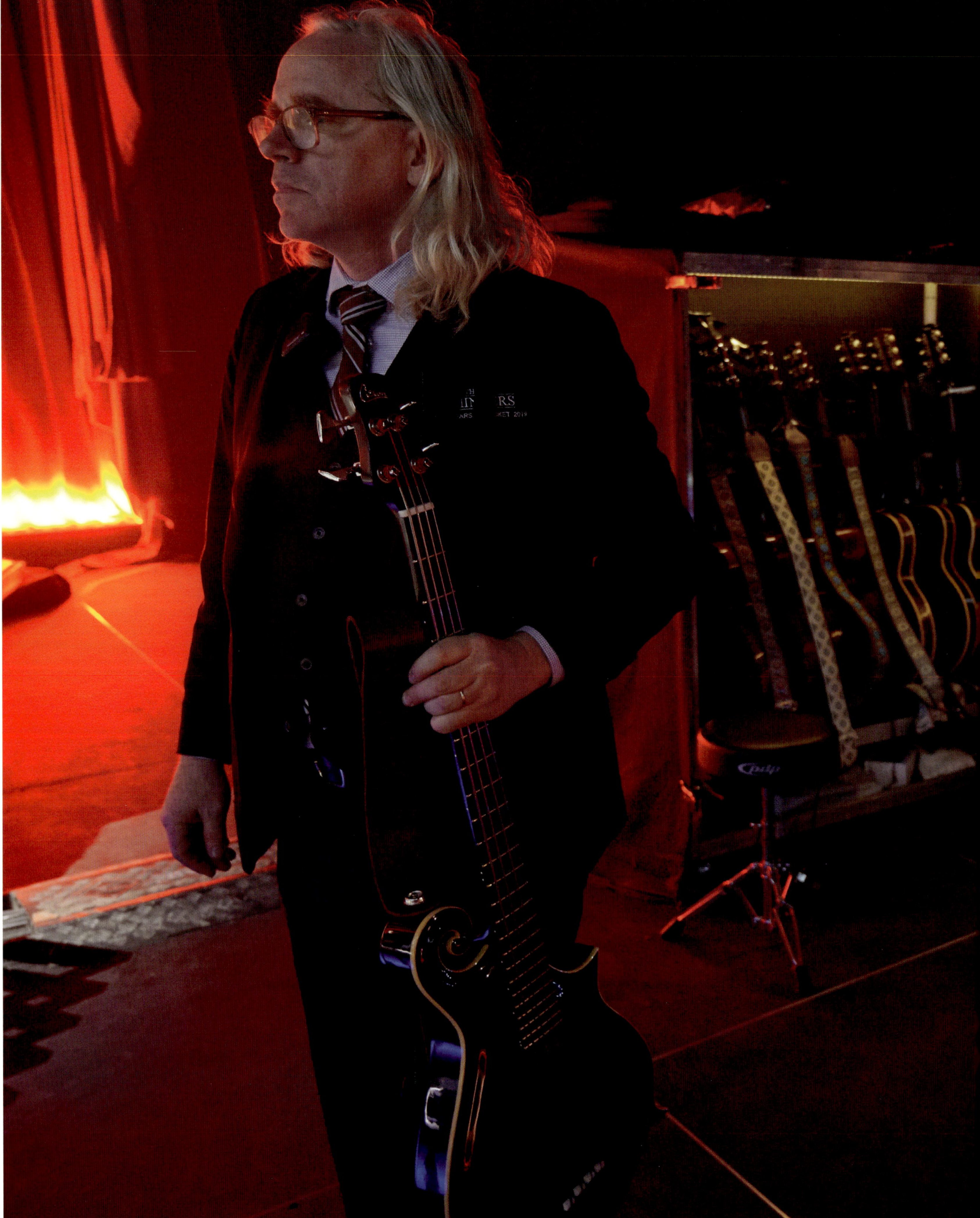

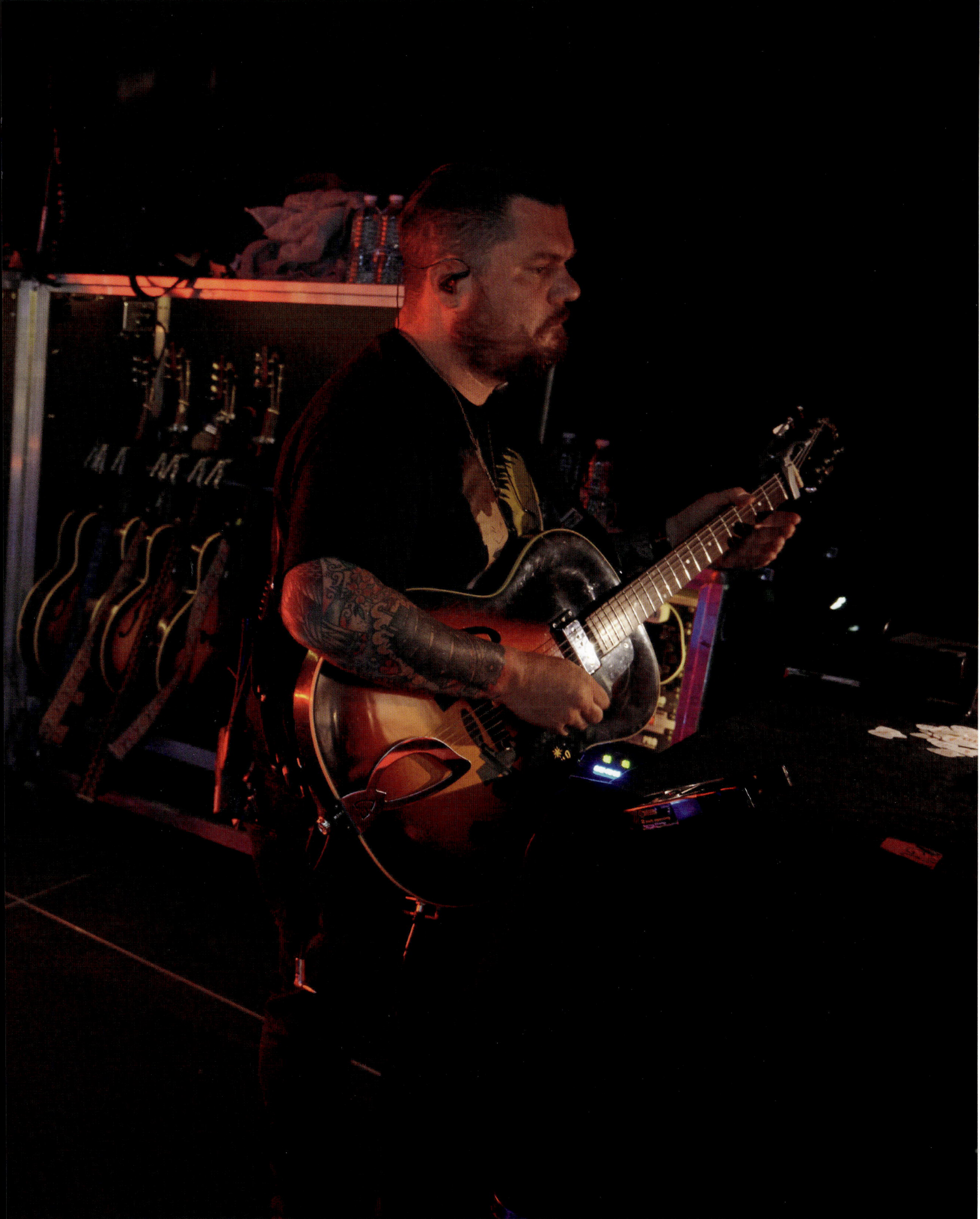

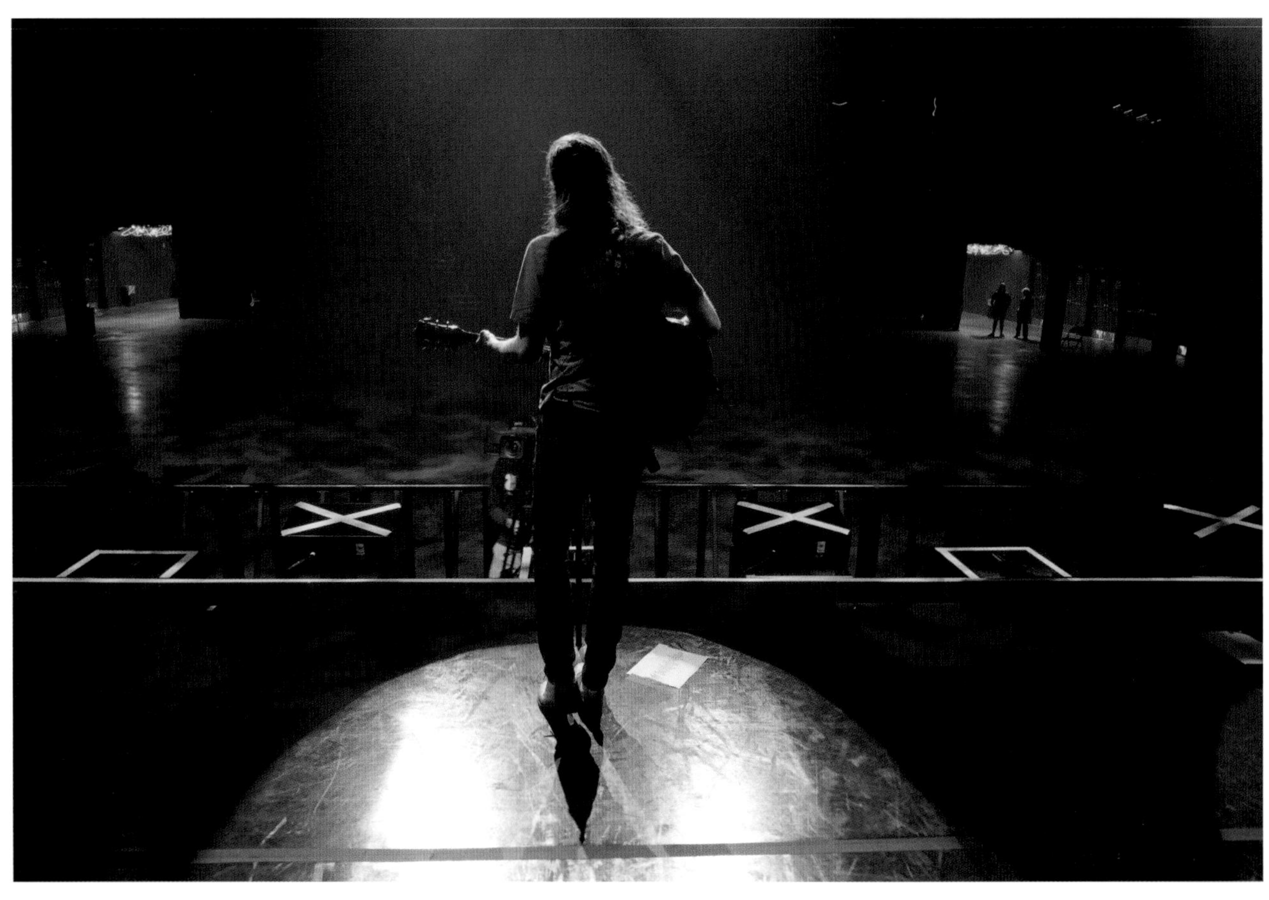

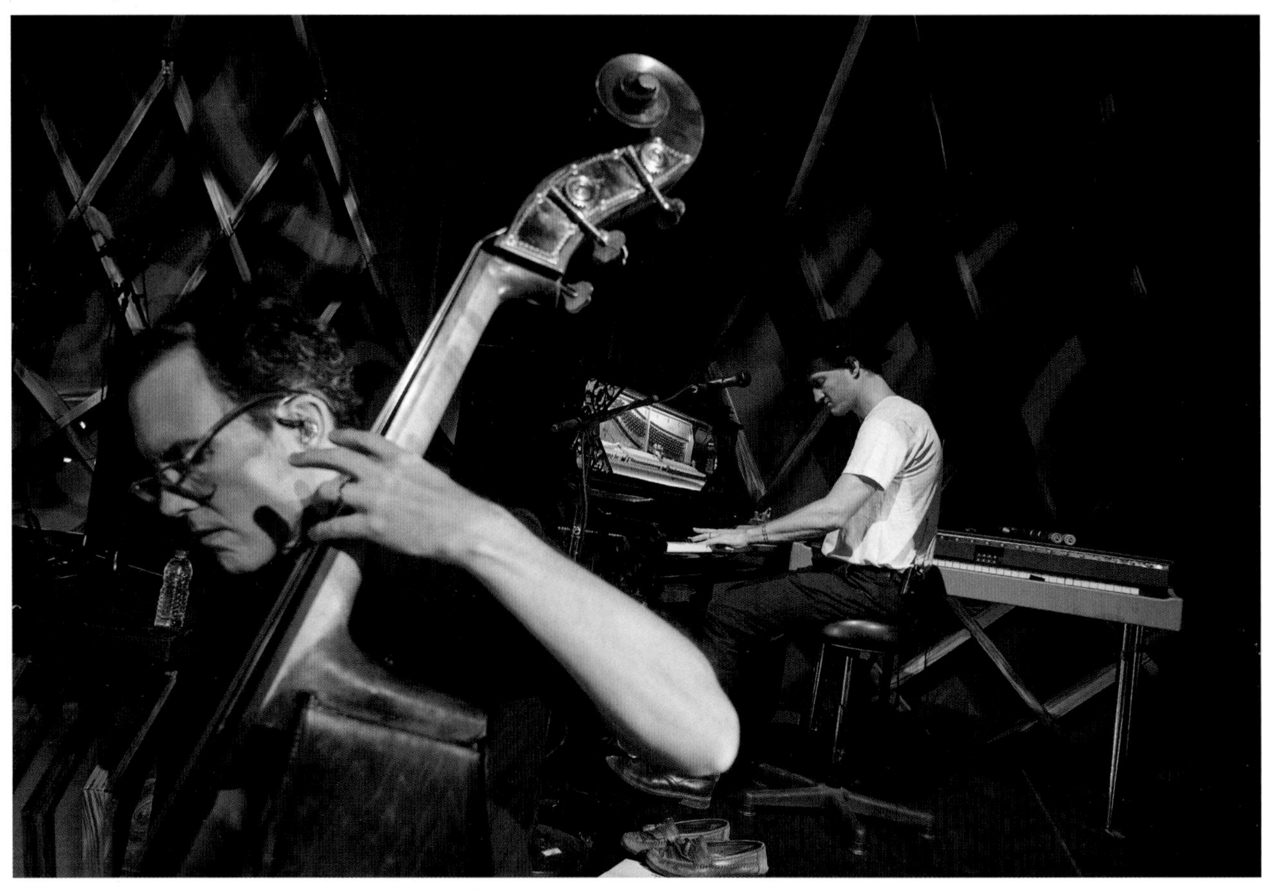

ABOVE: Wesley Schultz rehearses before an empty venue. **BELOW:** Byron Isaacs (foreground) and Jeremiah Fraites (background) rehearse.

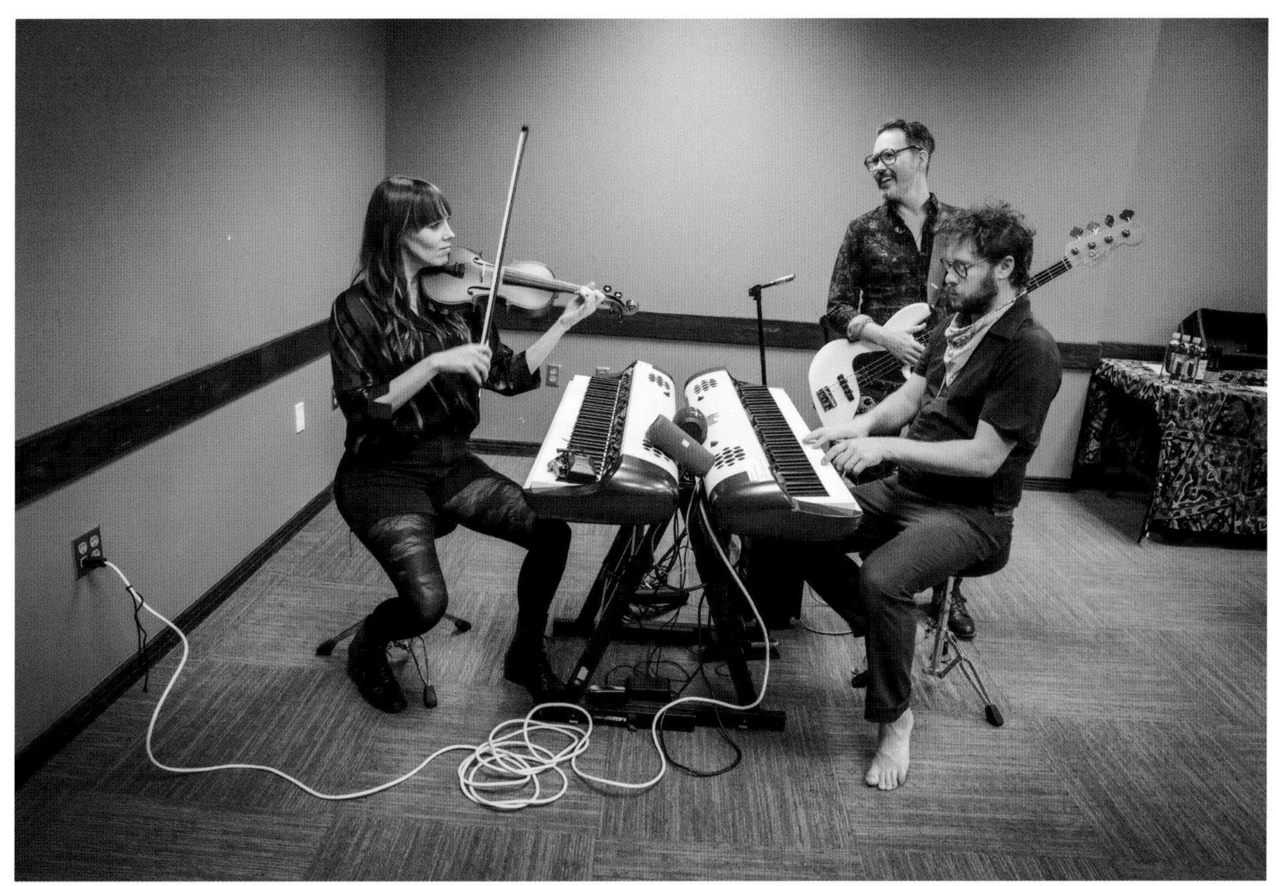

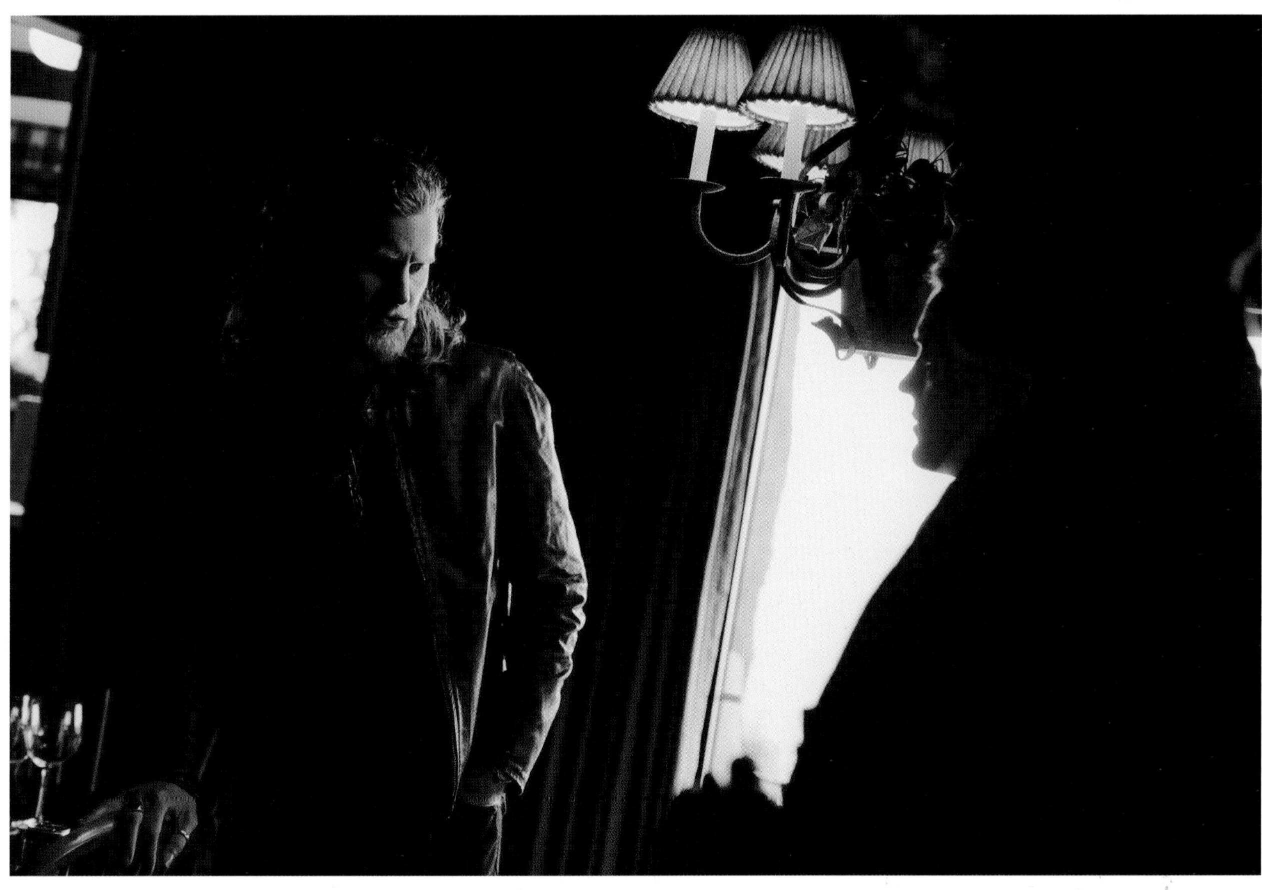

ABOVE (LEFT TO RIGHT): Lauren Jacobson, Byron Isaacs, and Stelth Ulvang rehearse backstage.
BELOW: Wesley Schultz in a makeshift greenroom before a private show on Victoria Island, Canada. **FOLLOWING:** Nic Close before the fans.

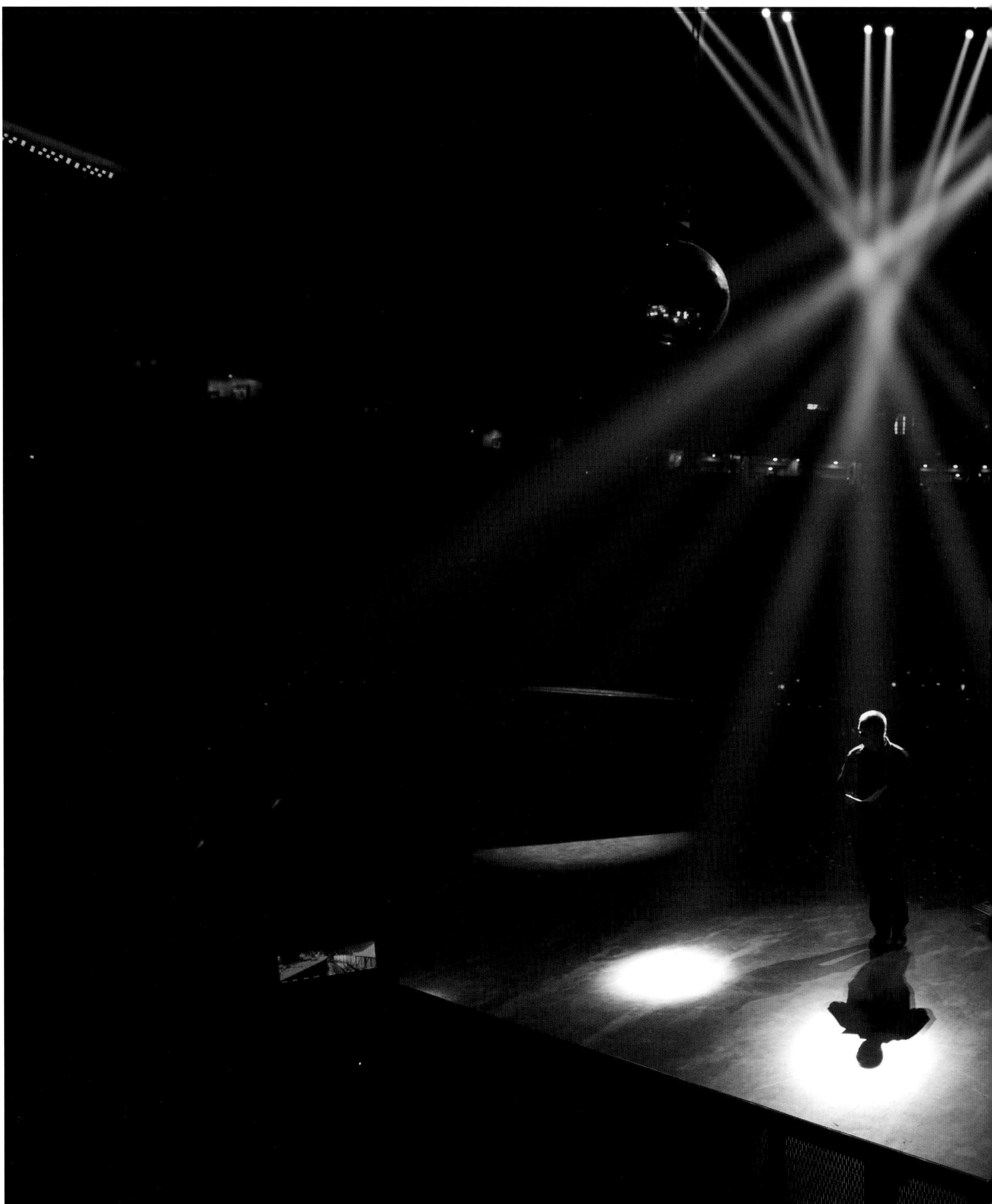

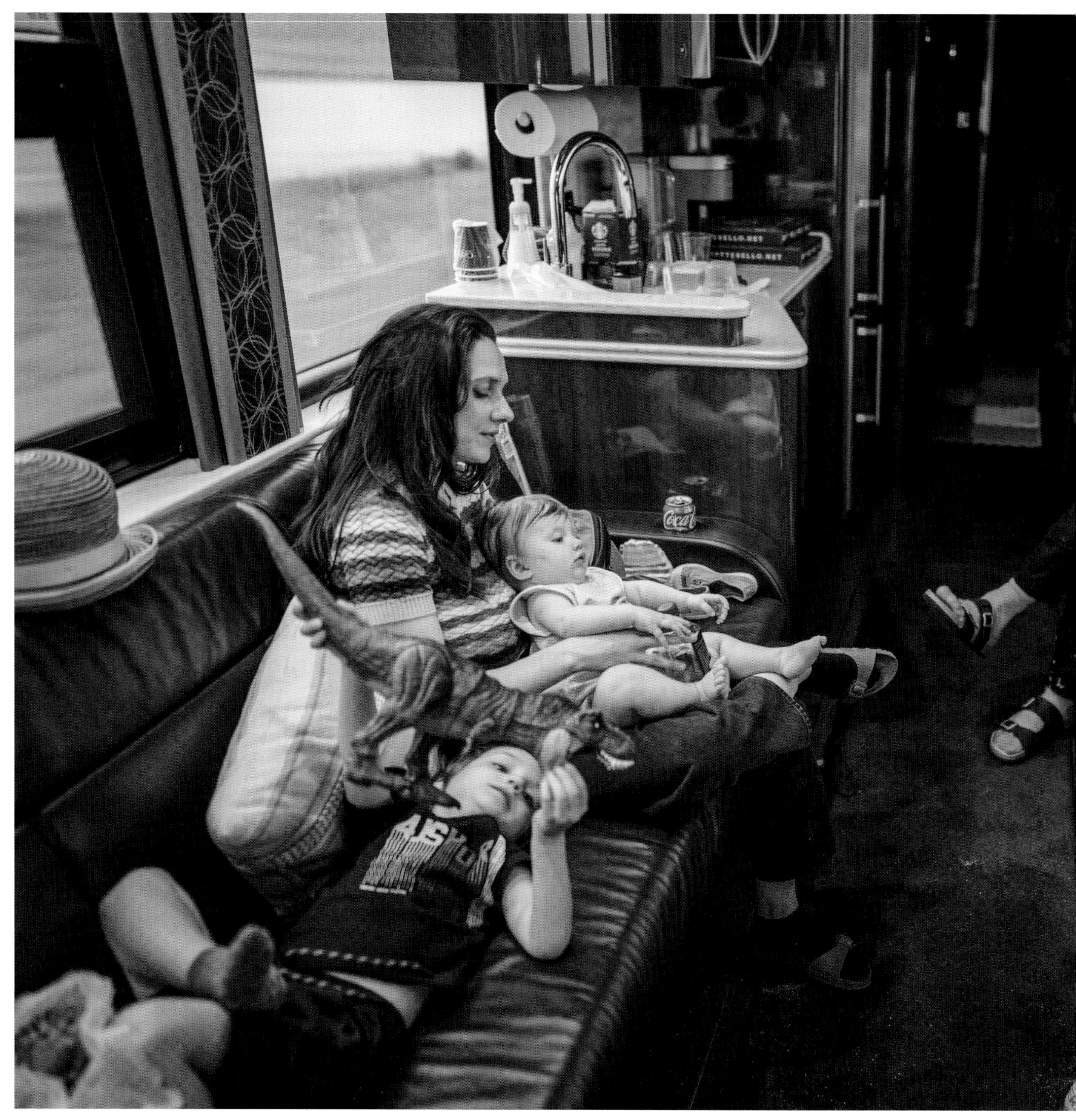

Family life on the Fraites tour bus, traveling between Salt Lake City and Denver. **OPPOSITE, ABOVE:** Wesley Schultz warms up his voice in a bathroom backstage. **OPPOSITE, CENTER:** Lauren Jacobson curls up backstage before the show in Vancouver, Canada. **OPPOSITE, BELOW (LEFT TO RIGHT):** Nick Bell, Ryan Dobrowski, and Lauren Jacobson on the road to somewhere. **FOLLOWING:** Brandon Miller enjoys the quiet while warming up his fingers.

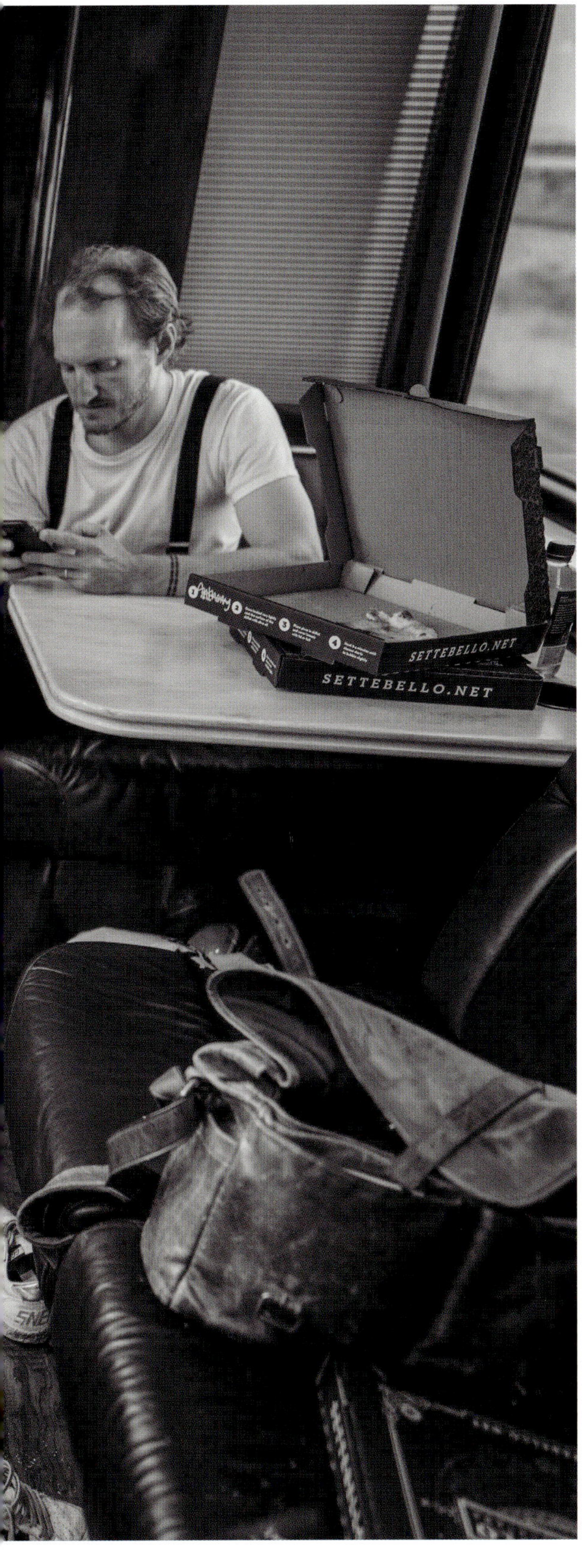
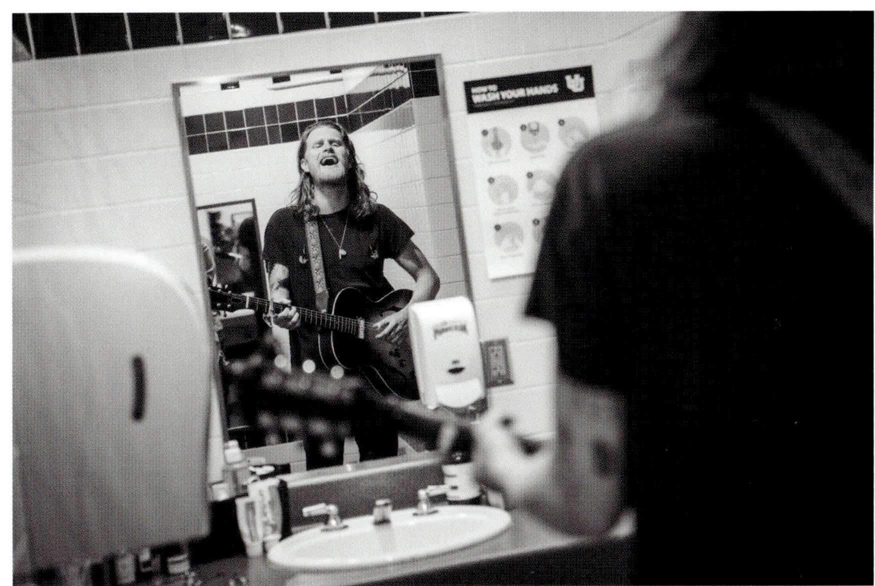
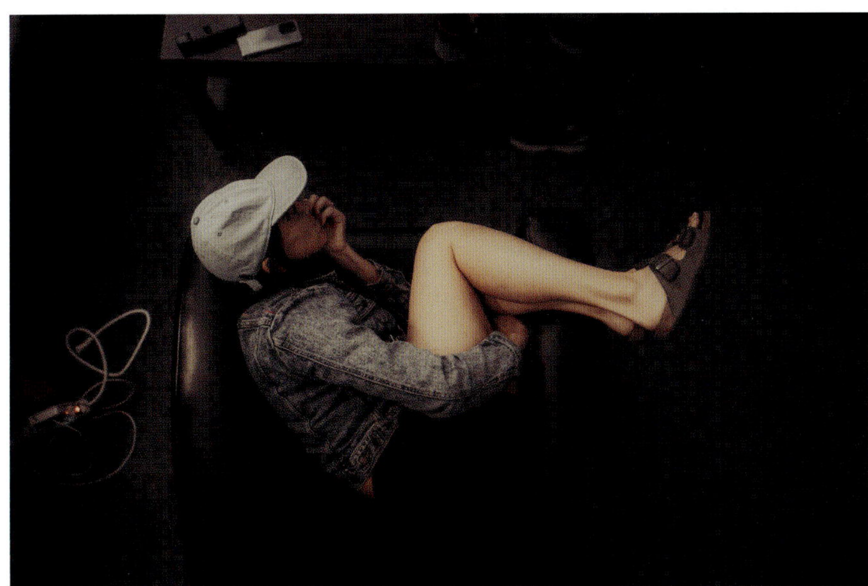
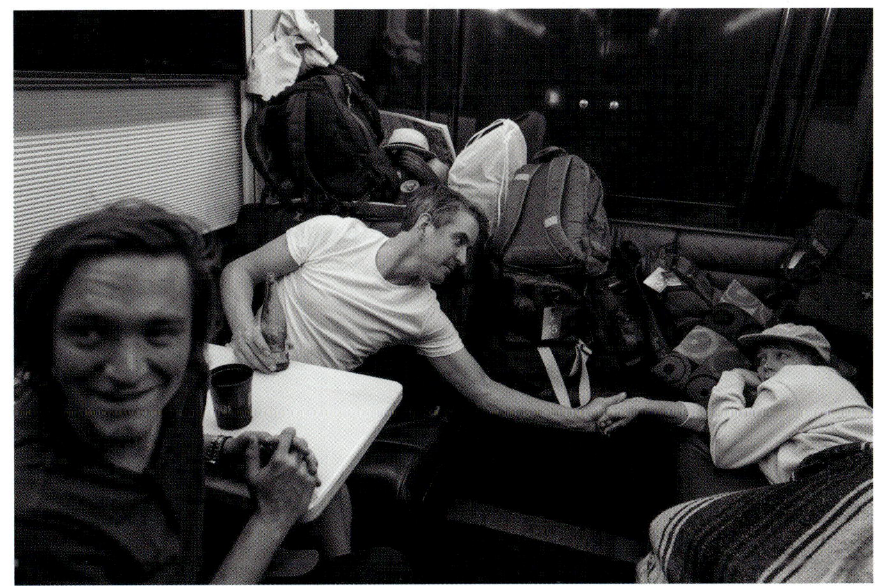

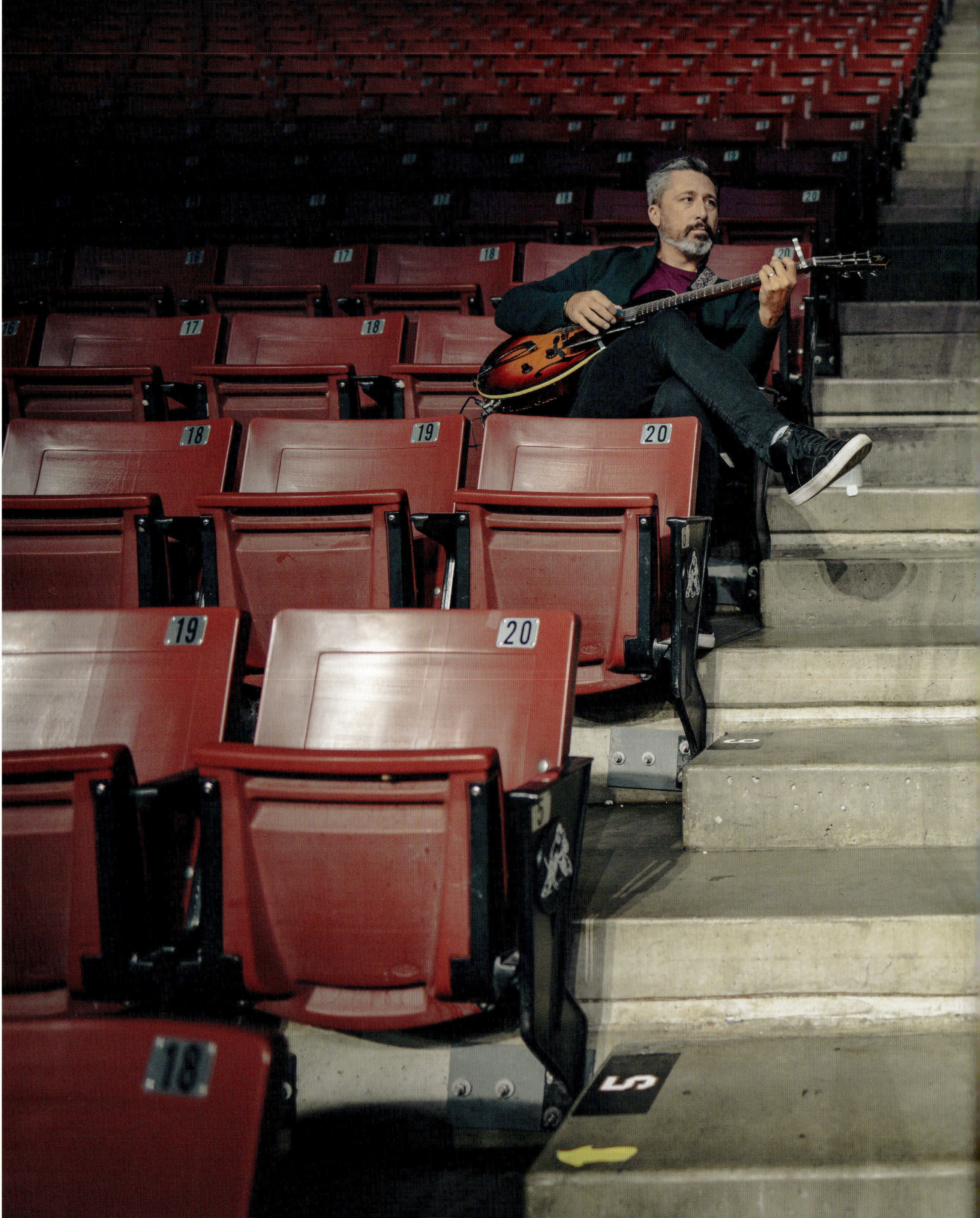

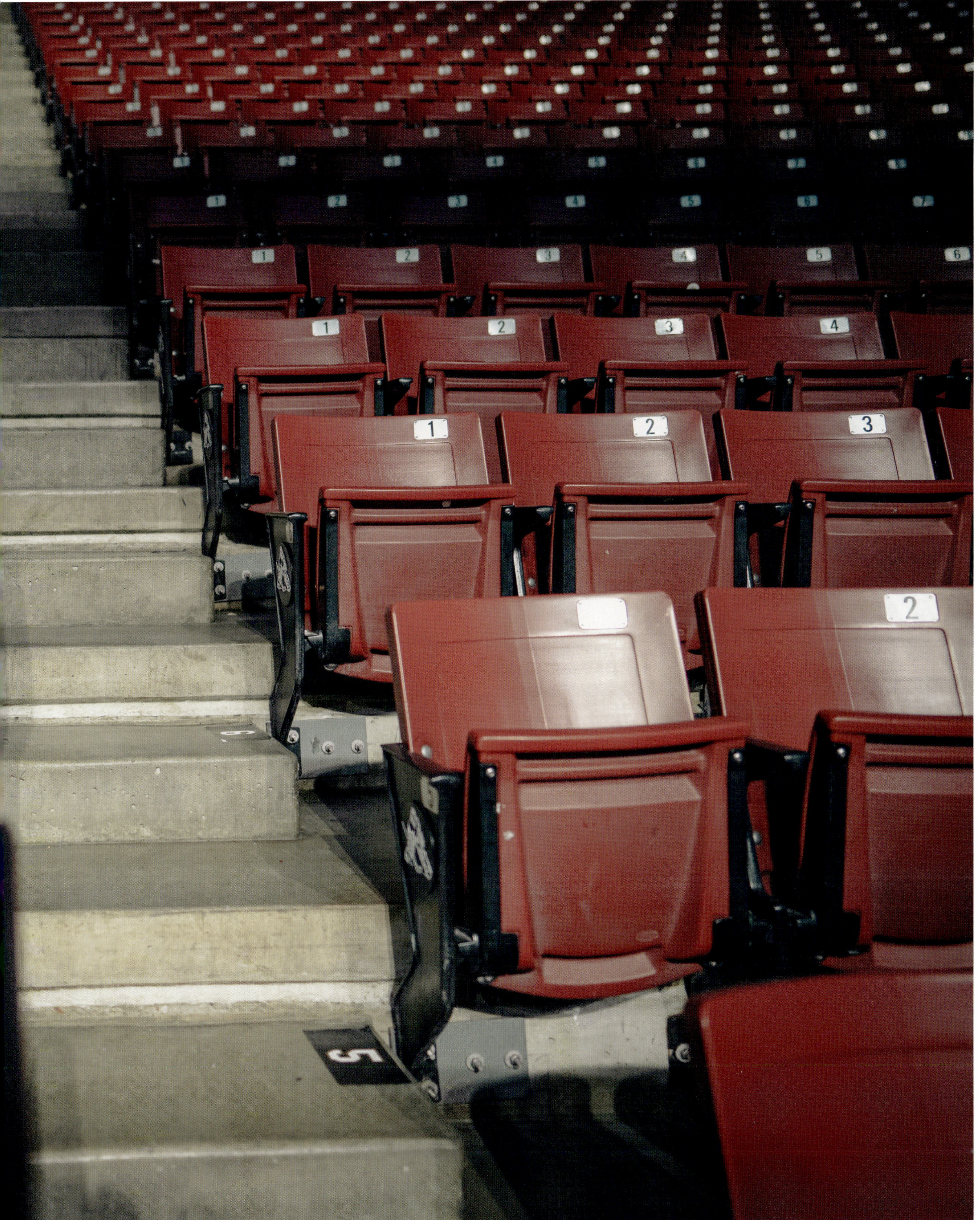

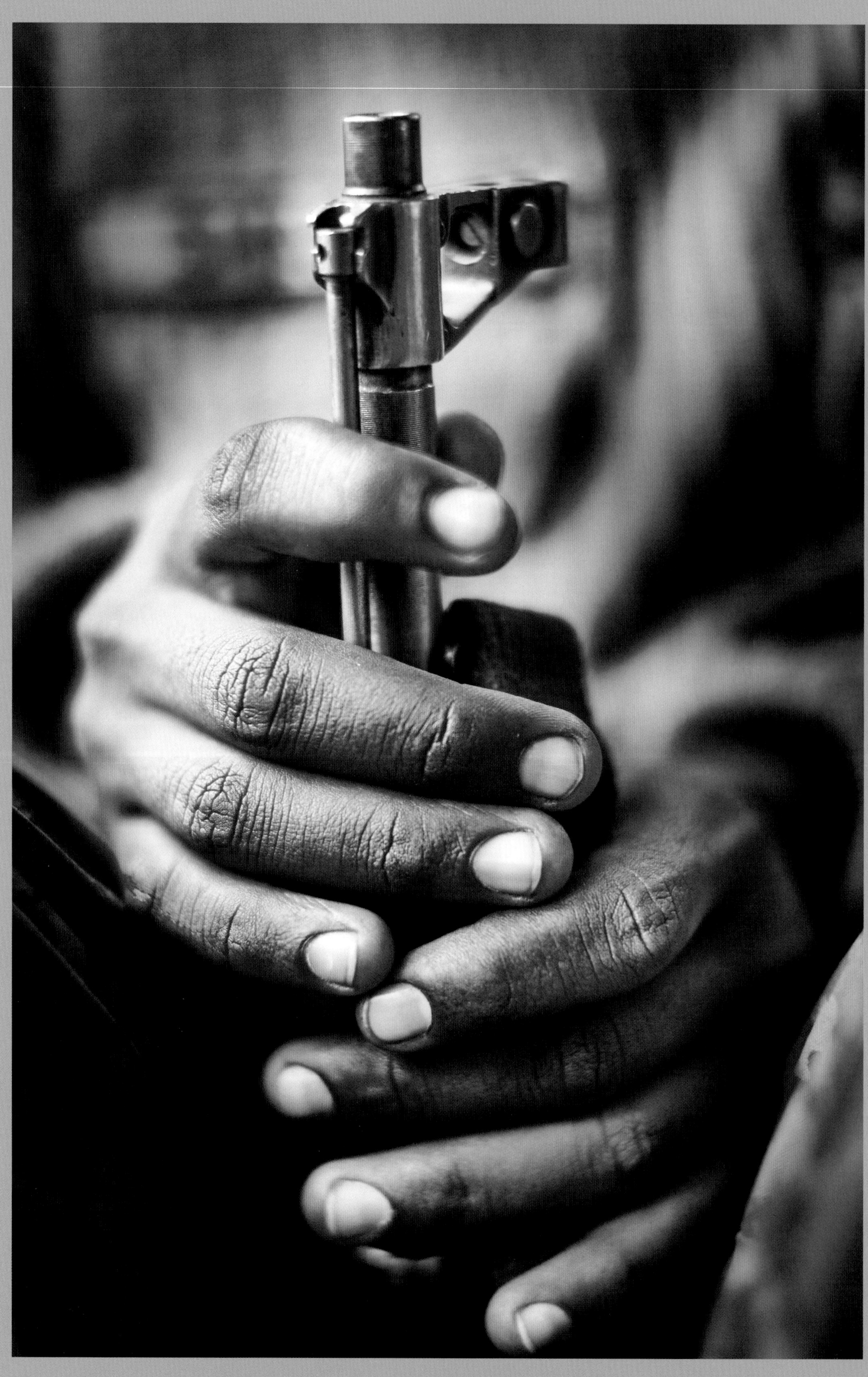

ICE MARTYRS

The Siachen Glacier
Conflict, Pakistan

In 1947, Mikhail Timofeyevich Kalashnikov invented what is now the most widely used shoulder weapon in the world, the AK-47. Known for being nearly indestructible, the rifles have become synonymous with war.

Throughout the world, they are often the weapon of choice, perfect for rugged terrain like the Karakoram Himalaya of Pakistan stretching out behind the five soldiers perched on a boulder in front of me.

The sharp granite teeth of the Trango Towers rise over their shoulders as they hold their weapons nonchalantly. This is the harshest battlefield in the world and the scene of the highest ground conflict in human history. Freddie Wilkinson and I are here for *National Geographic,* embedded with the Pakistani Army covering the Siachen Glacier conflict with India, which, as it turns out, is largely the fault of the US State Department.

After the partition of Pakistan and India in August 1947, the same year the AK-47 was created, new boundaries needed to be drawn. But when the mountains proved too treacherous to survey, the team responsible demarcated point NJ9842 and declared that the border continued "thence north to the glaciers," which left a lot of room for interpretation. In 1975, India noticed that American maps indicated that the Siachen Glacier was Pakistani territory, but declared that the land was theirs. Nine years later, in 1984, a mountaineering expedition that accessed the disputed territory through India finally thrust the region into open conflict.

I watch a soldier check the safety on his AK and say something to the other men in Urdu. They laugh. I adjust my flash and stare through the viewfinder, waiting for their faces to settle.

Despite a ceasefire declared in 2003, both India and Pakistan maintain a heavy military presence here. Soldiers live year-round at altitudes pushing 20,000 feet, their camps often dug precariously into sharp ridges. It's hard to understand why such an inhospitable and uninhabitable piece of land is worth dying for. But then again, war often doesn't make sense, even to those who are fighting.

Even if the soldiers keep each other safe, the terrain can and does claim lives. The danger here is no longer bullets and shelling, but rather avalanches, altitude, and exposure. In 2012, 140 soldiers and military contractors were killed at Gayari in a single avalanche that buried them under heaps of ice, boulders, and rubble.

The soldiers in front of me are quiet now, waiting for me to make a picture. I raise my hand to signal quiet. A rock falls somewhere to my right, and I can faintly hear water rushing from the tongue of the enormous Baltoro Glacier. Aside from that, the only sound is the shutter of my camera, the pop of the flash, and the tiny metal clicks of the men adjusting their rifles.

OPPOSITE: A Pakistani Army soldier holds the muzzle of his AK-47. **BELOW:** Soldiers stand for a portrait near their encampment on the Baltoro Glacier as it climbs toward Conway Saddle, the highest ground Pakistan holds in the Siachen border conflict with India. (At the request of the Pakistani military forces, names and ranks of soldiers are withheld.)

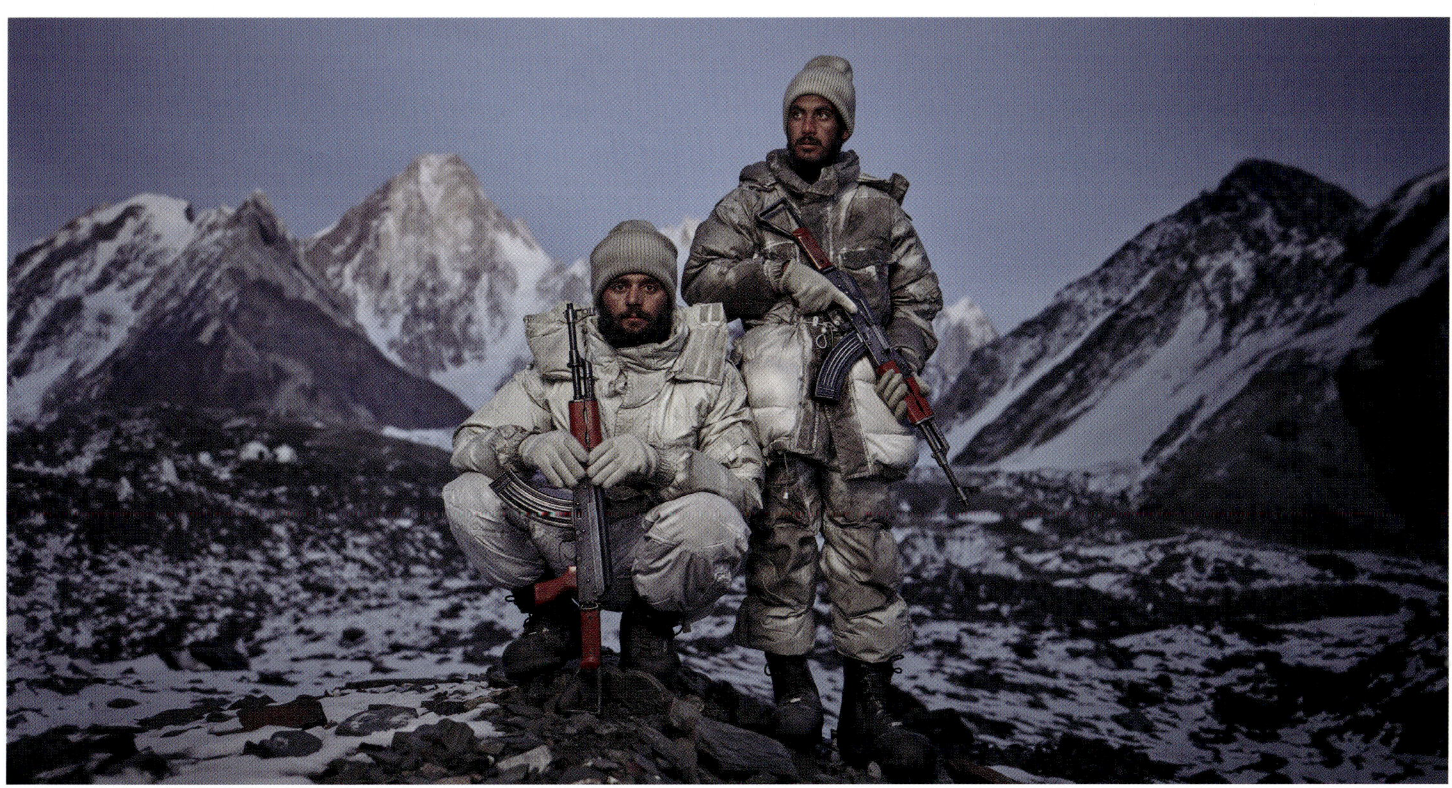

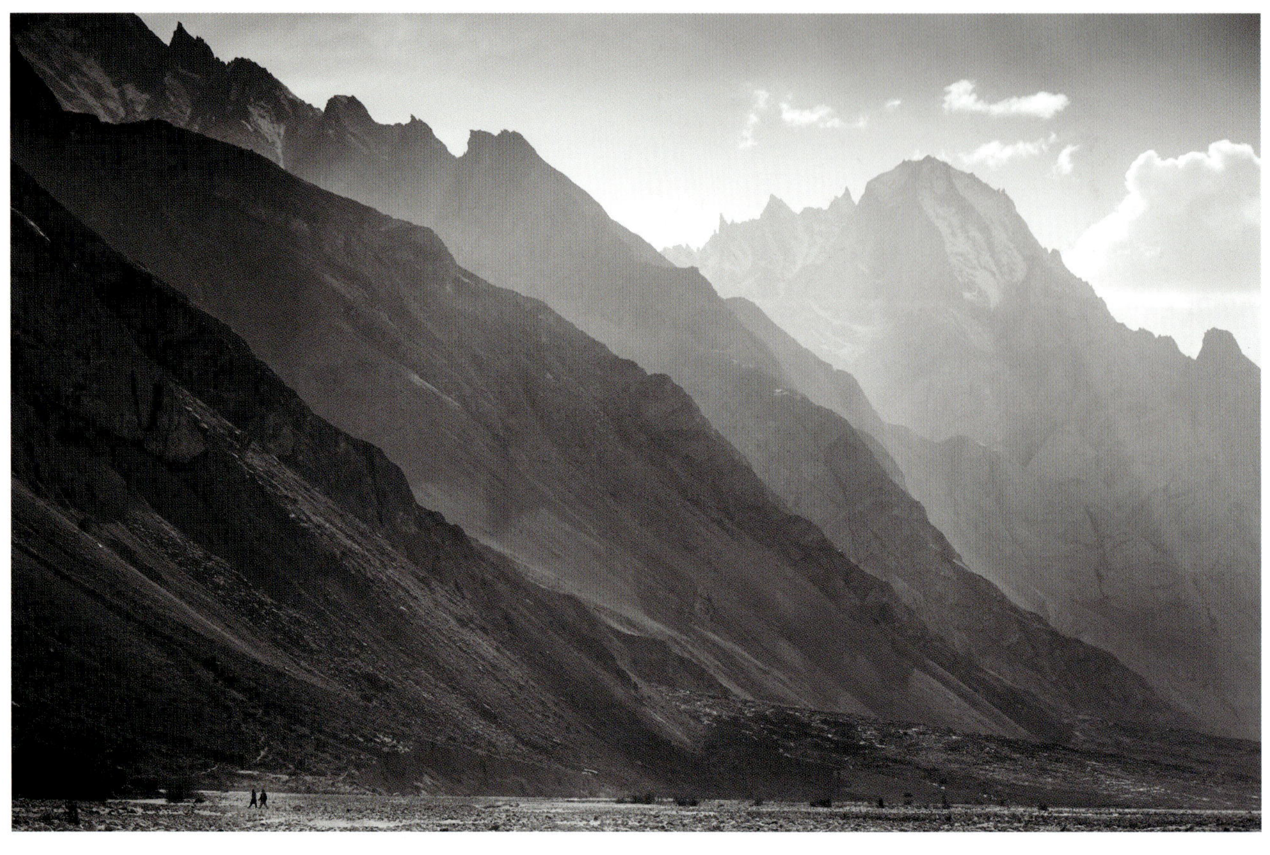

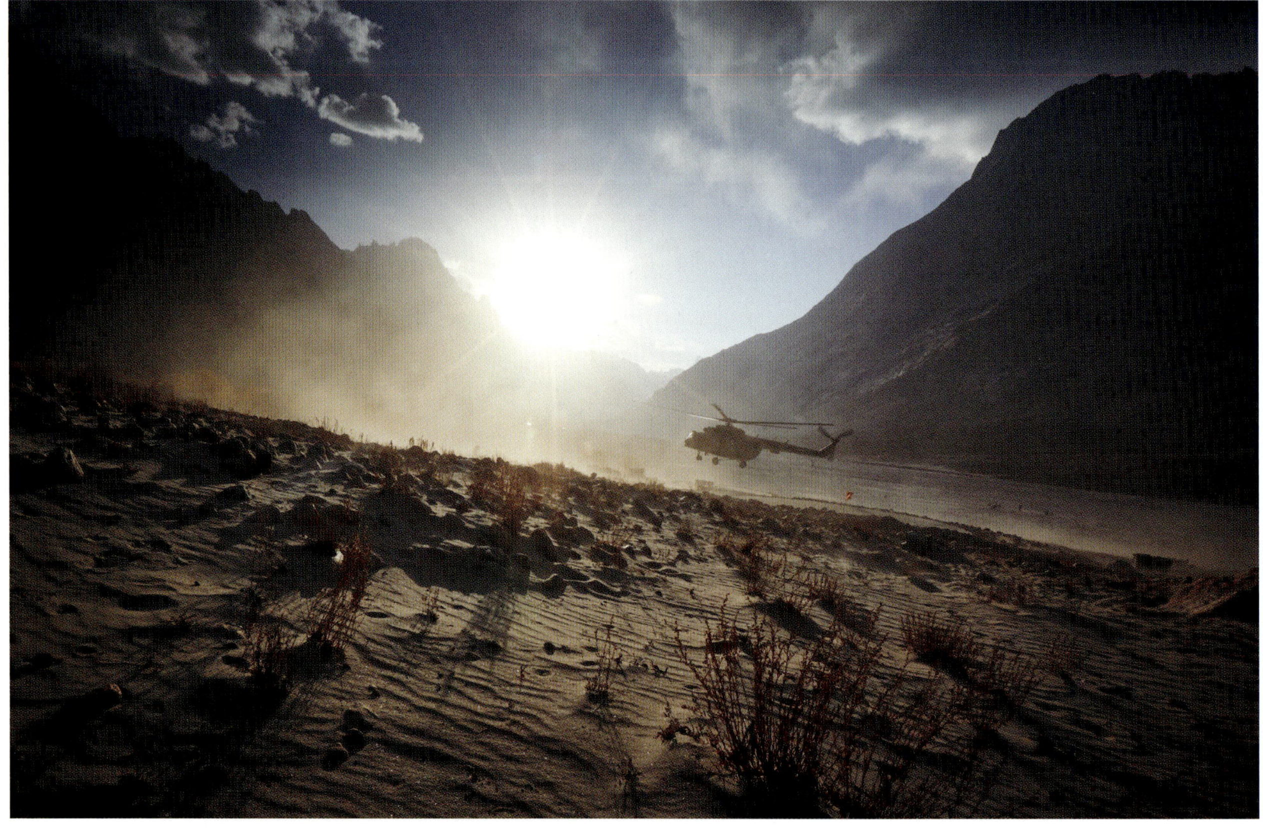

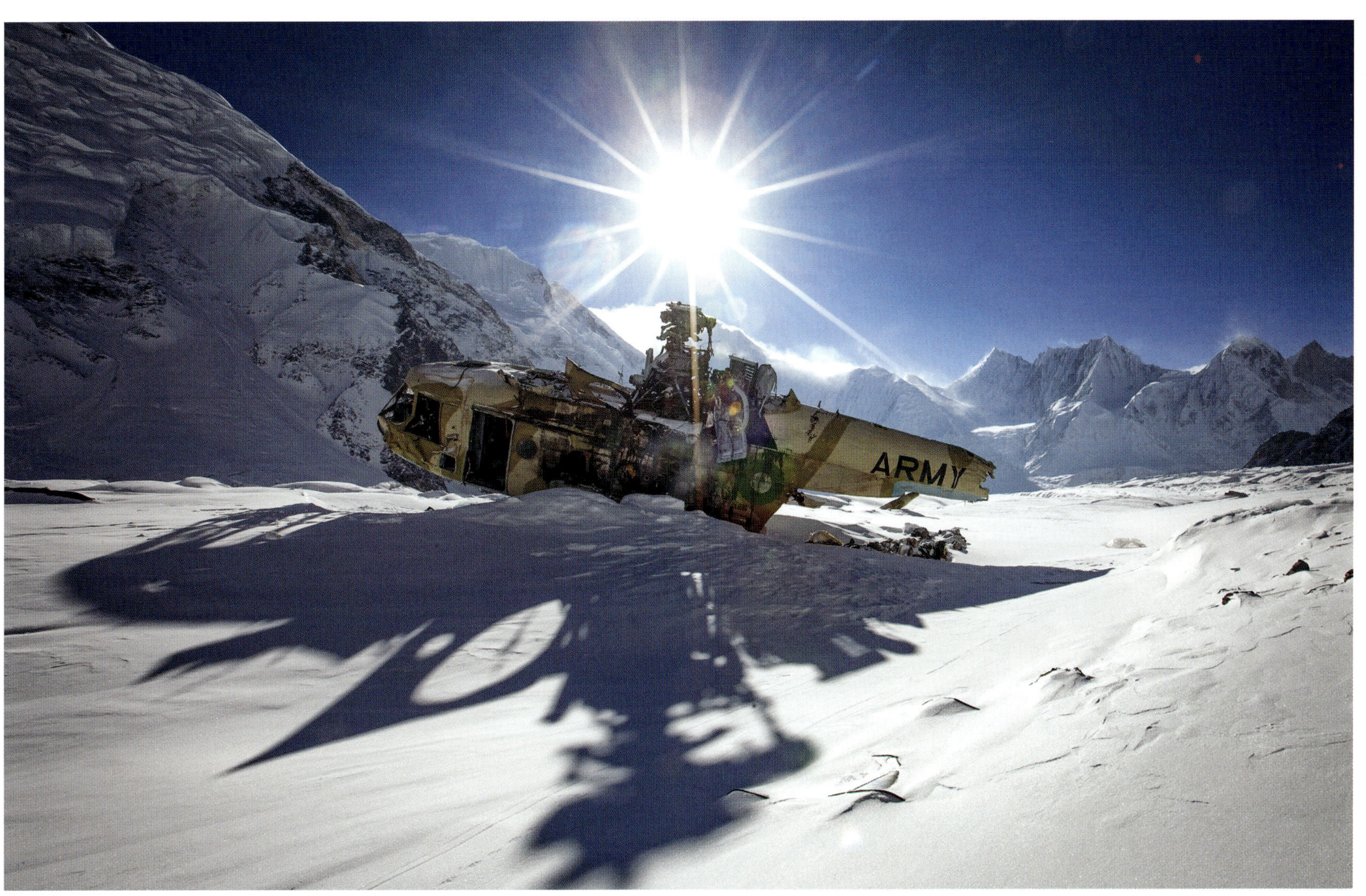

The carcass of an MI-17 helicopter, frozen in the ice at a forward-operating post near the head of the Godwin Austen Glacier. **OPPOSITE, ABOVE:** Soldiers walk below the rugged terrain surrounding the Line of Control, the line held through the mountains that divides the former princely states of Jammu and Kashmir. **OPPOSITE, BELOW:** An MI-17 helicopter lands at the Paiju administrative post. **FOLLOWING:** Soldiers of the 62nd Brigade beneath the Trango Towers at the terminus of the Baltoro Glacier.

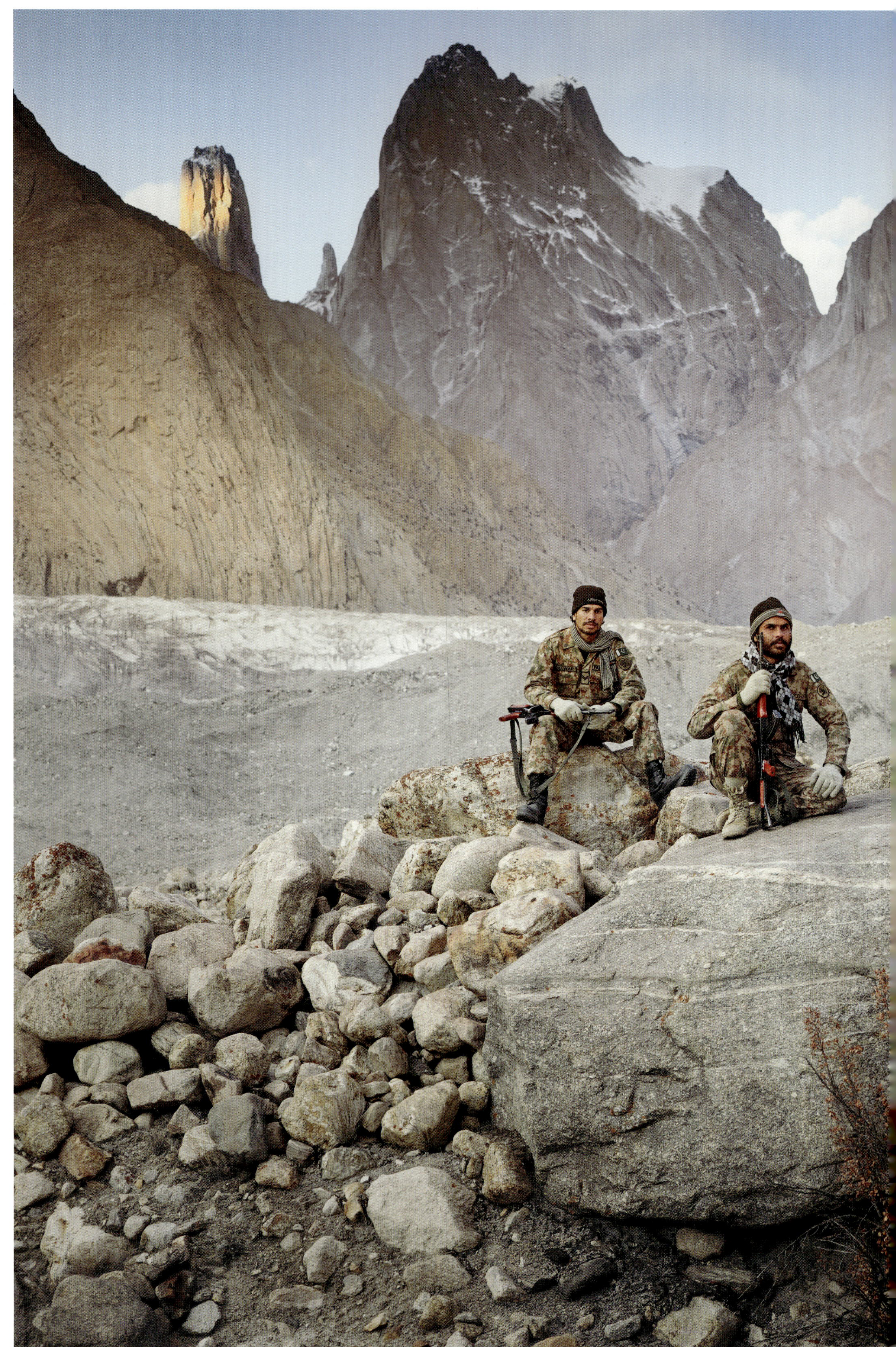

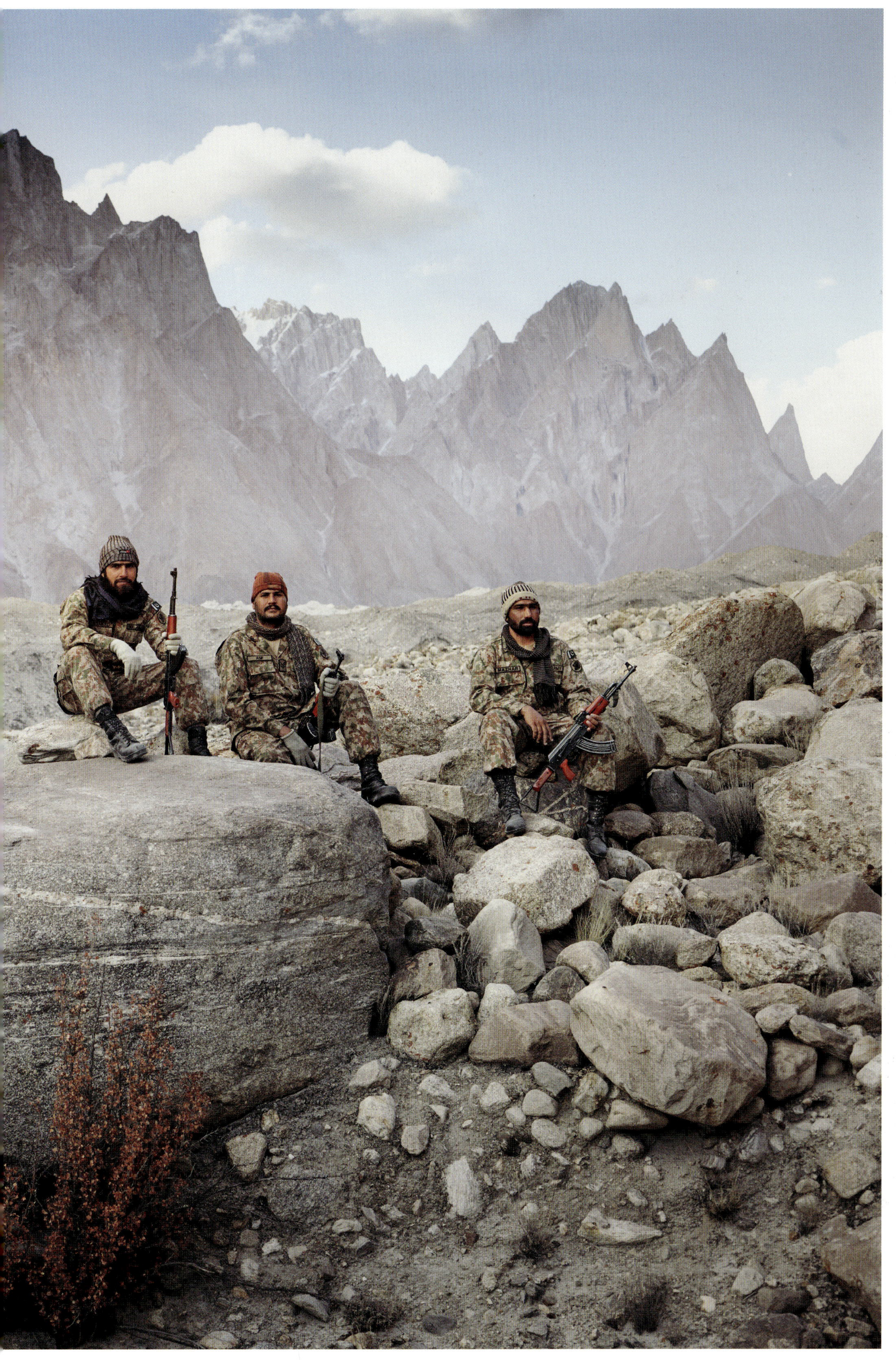

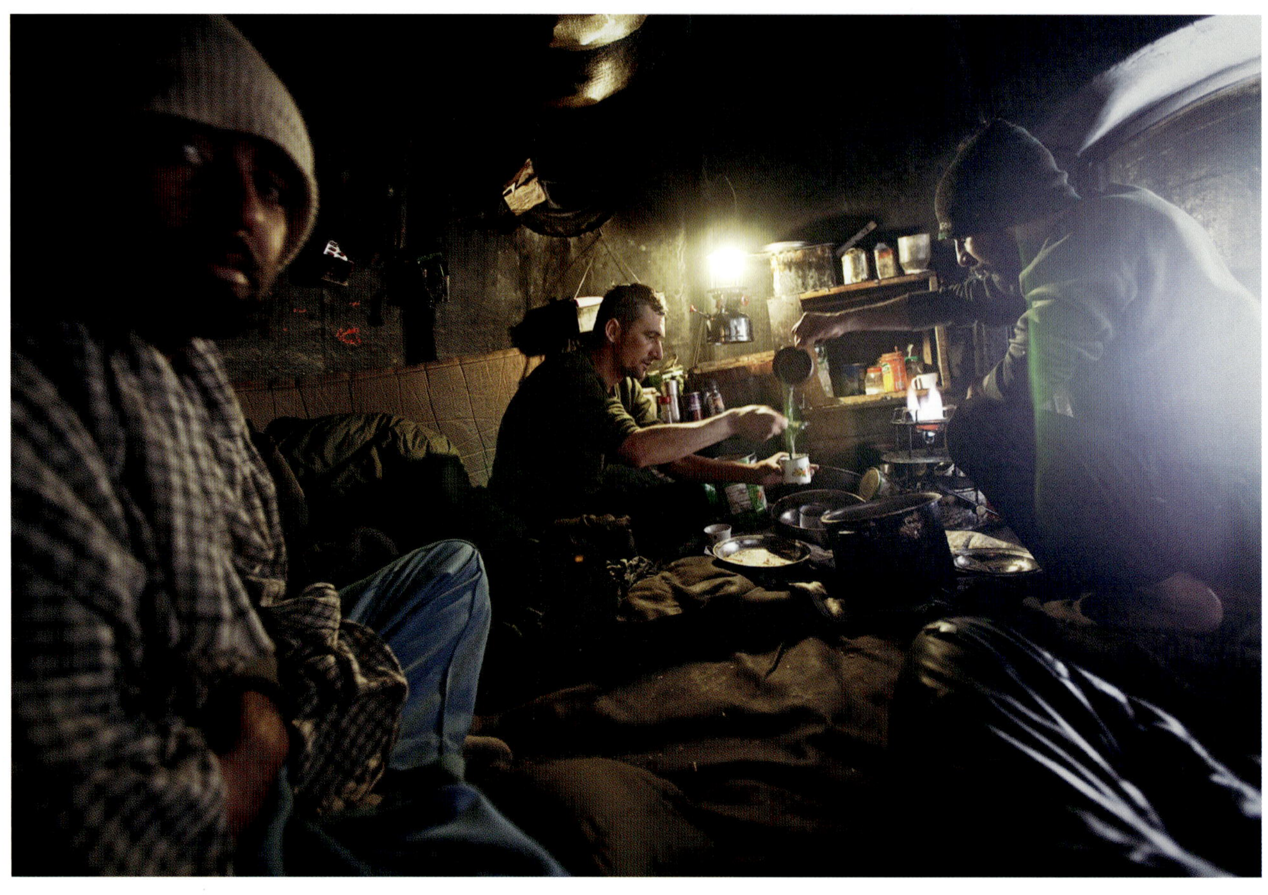

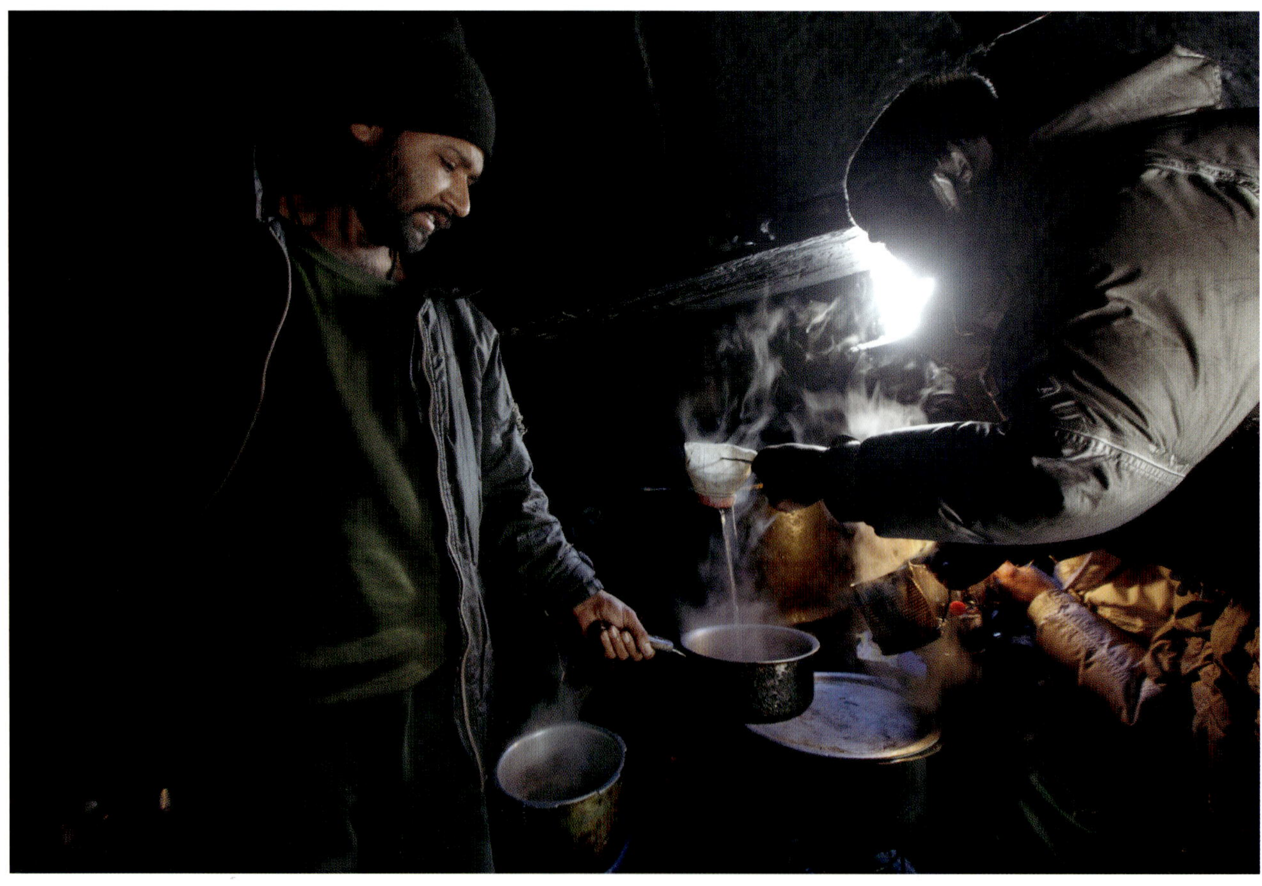

Inside soldiers' quarters. Men at the higher posts live four or five to a single fiberglass igloo.

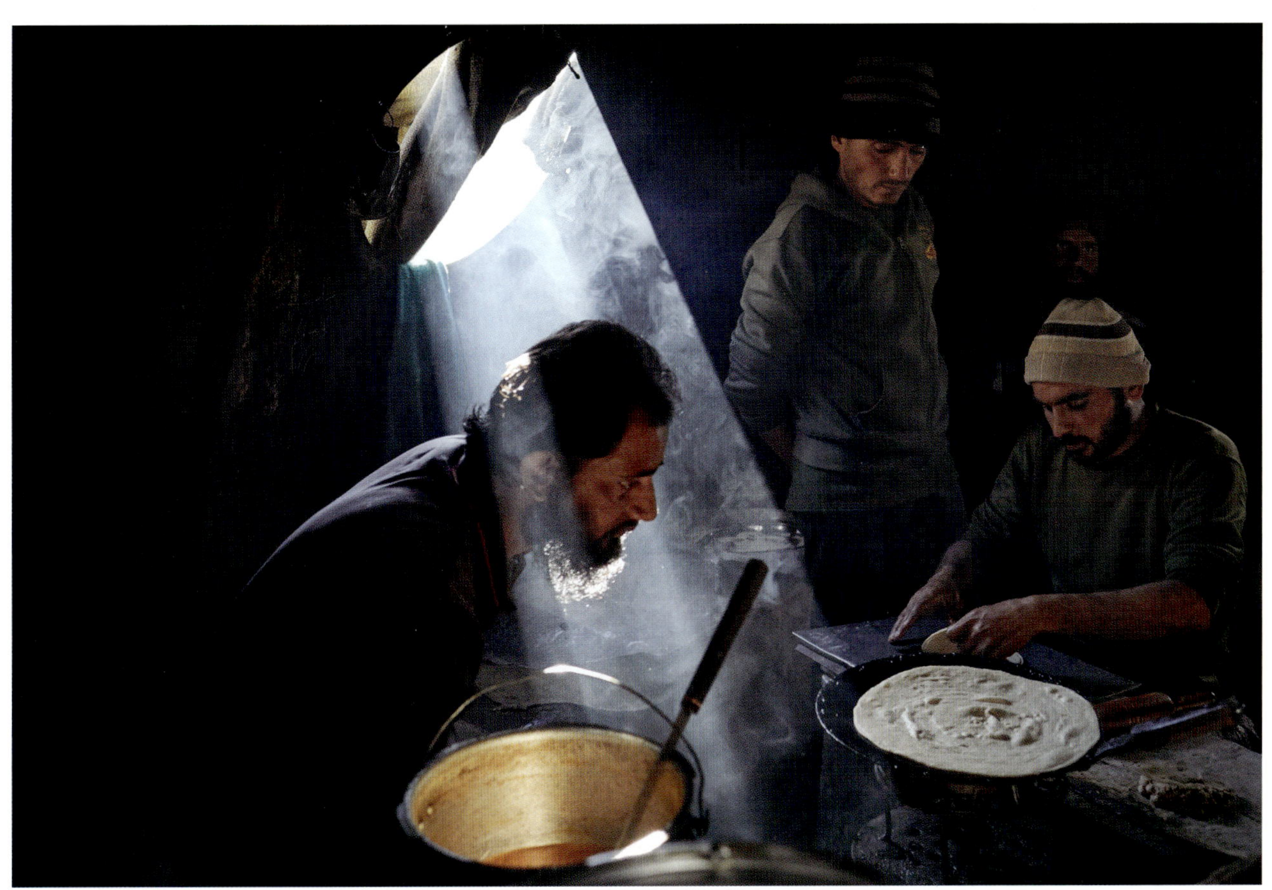

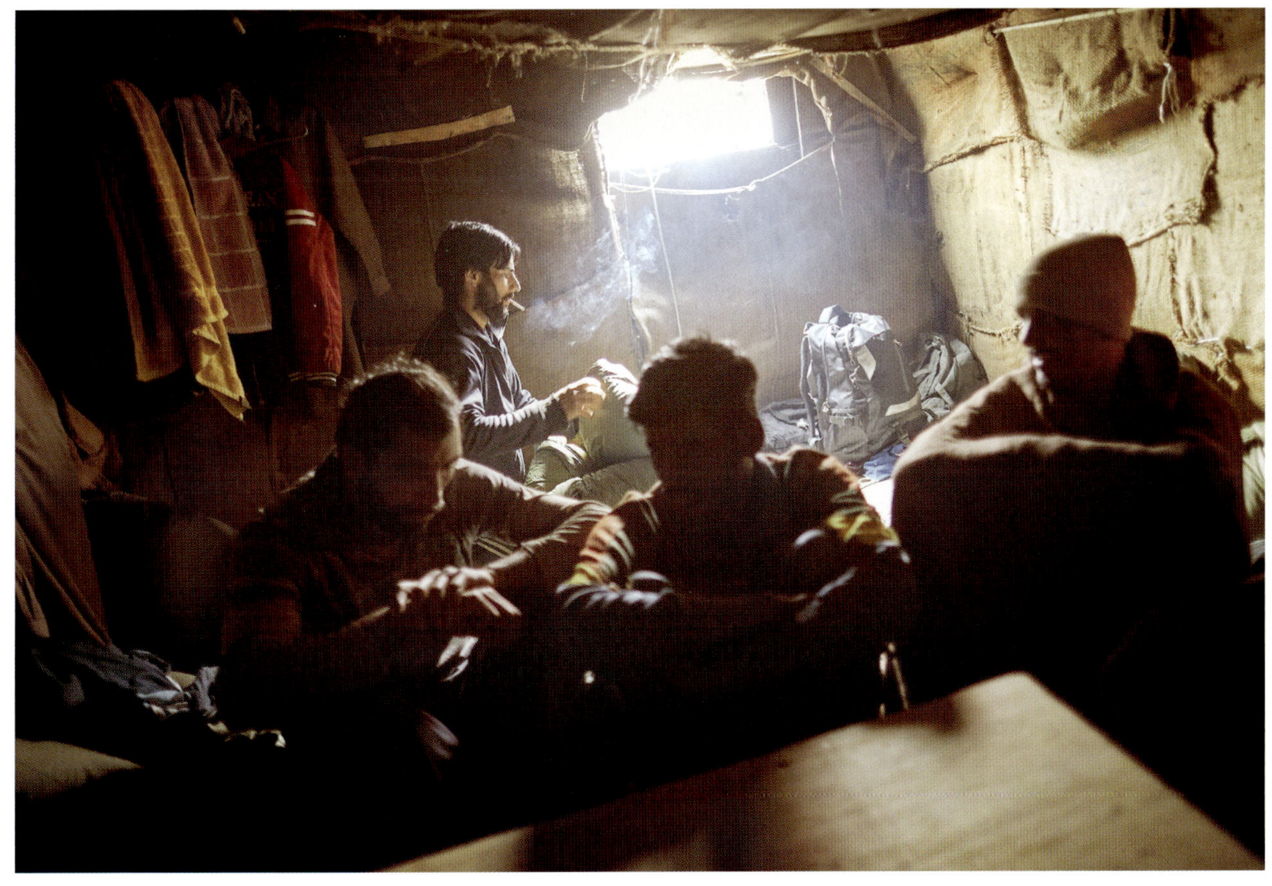

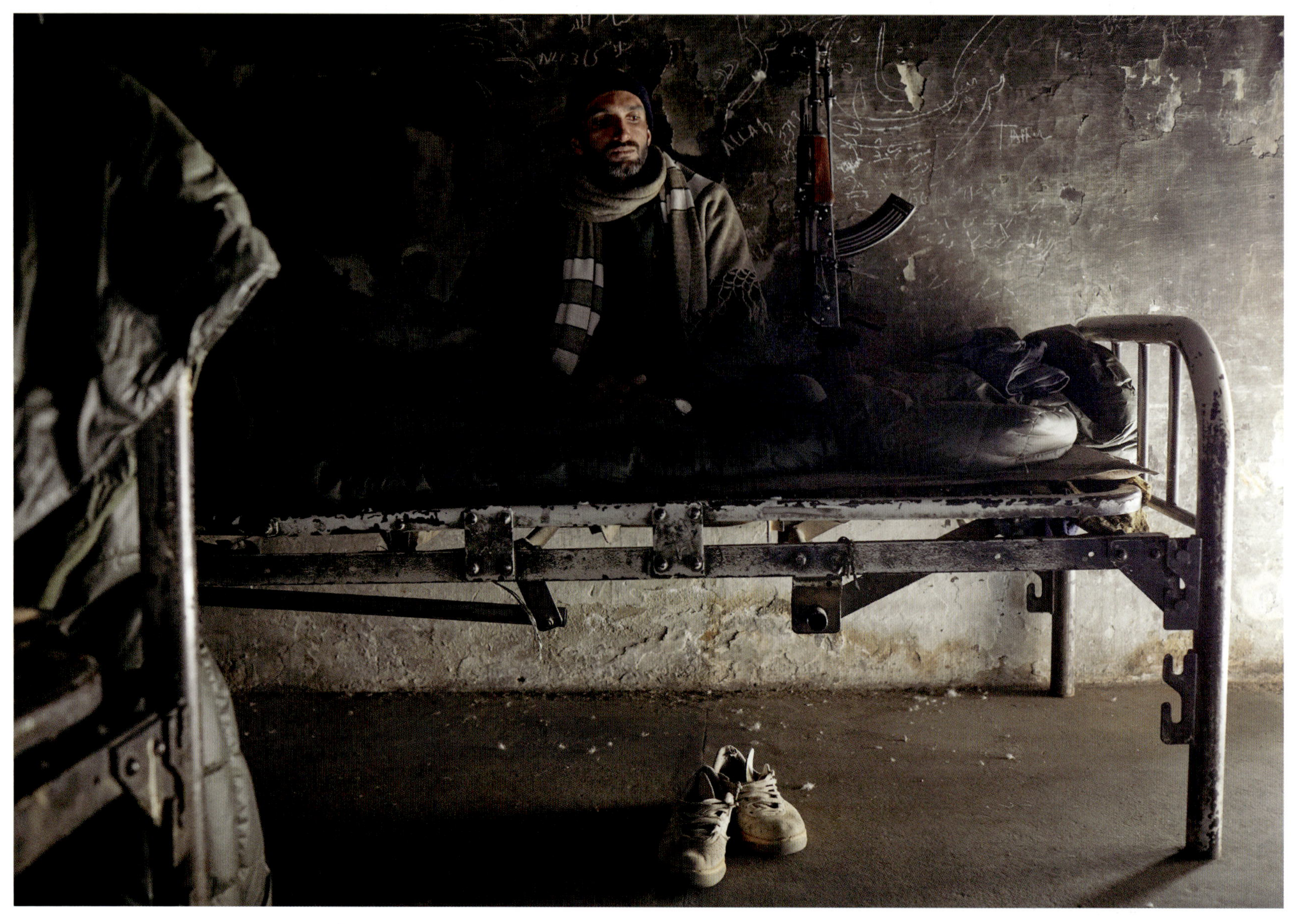

A soldier at the Gora I camp finds a moment of quiet. For many soldiers, the isolation of the terrain is as challenging as the altitude and cold.

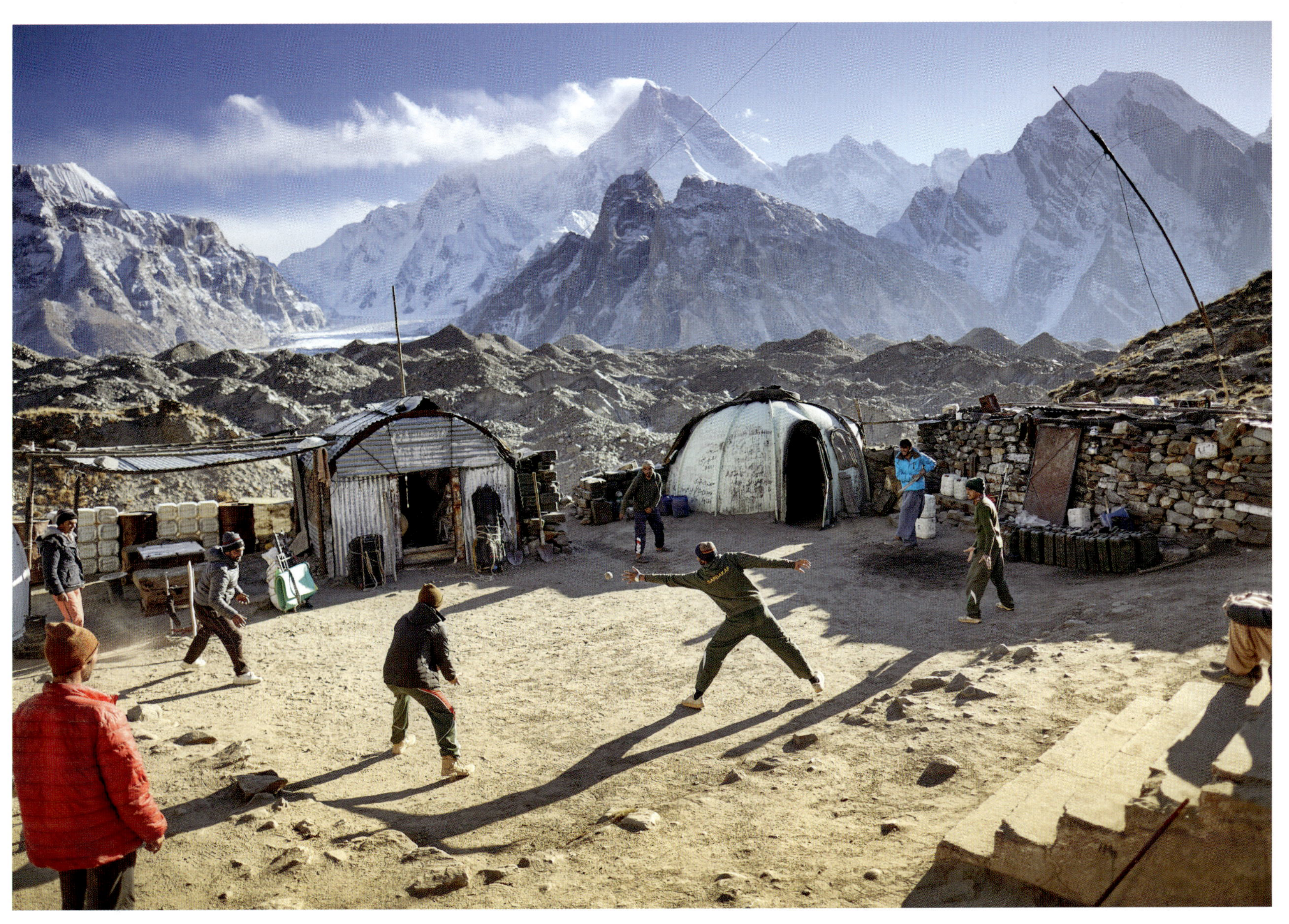

Soldiers play a breathless game of cricket at 13,700 feet with Masherbrum rising to 25,659 feet just behind them.

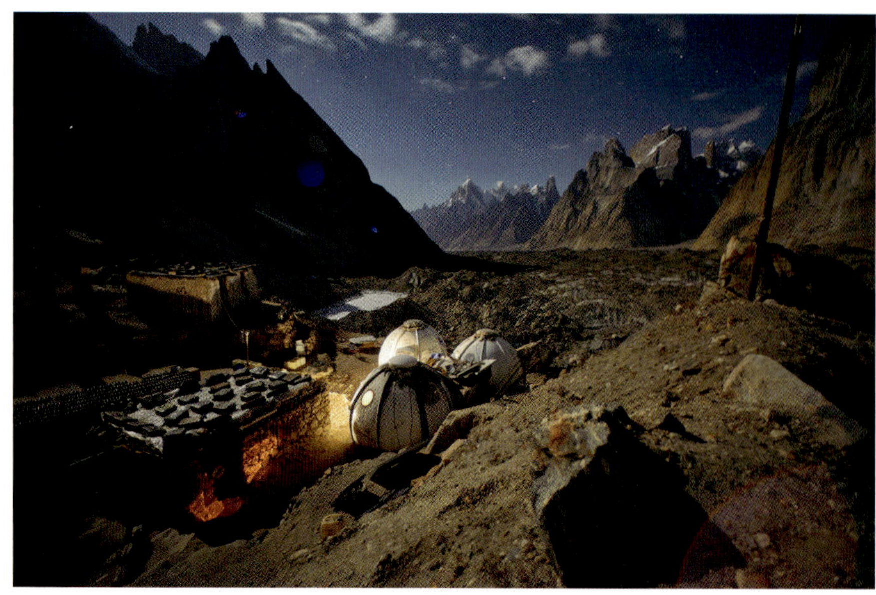

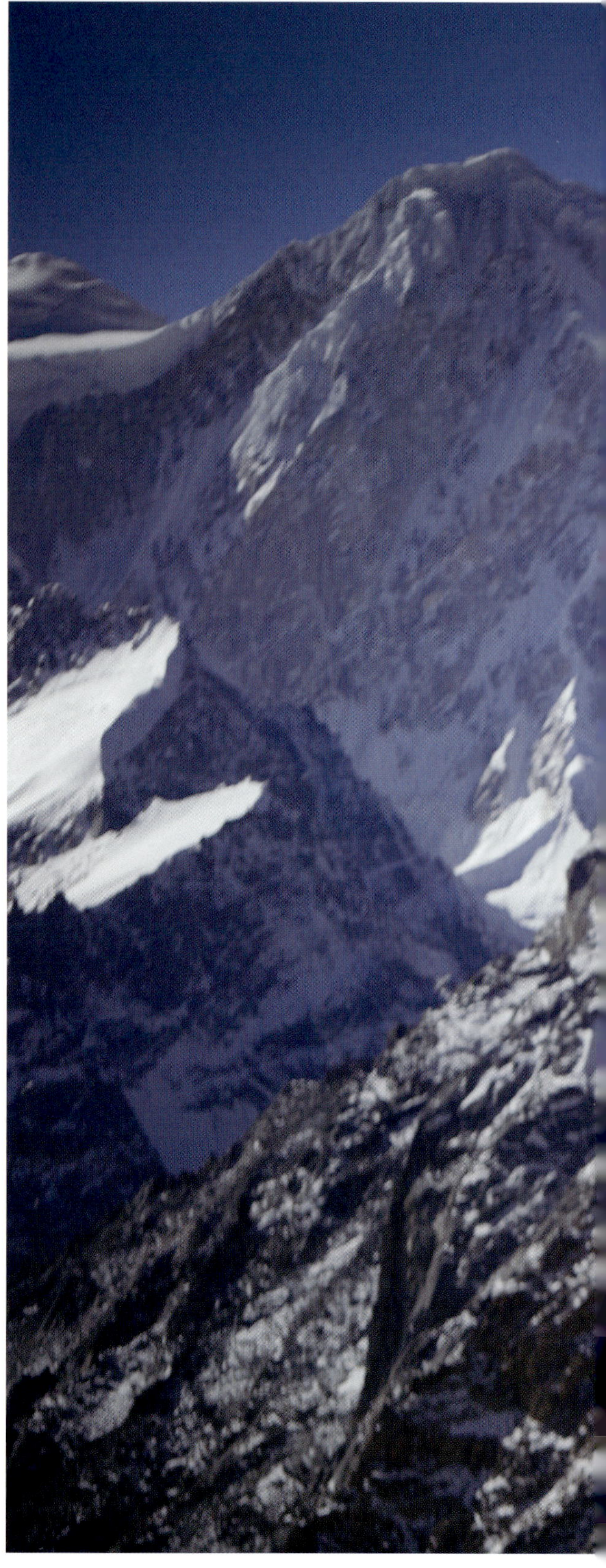

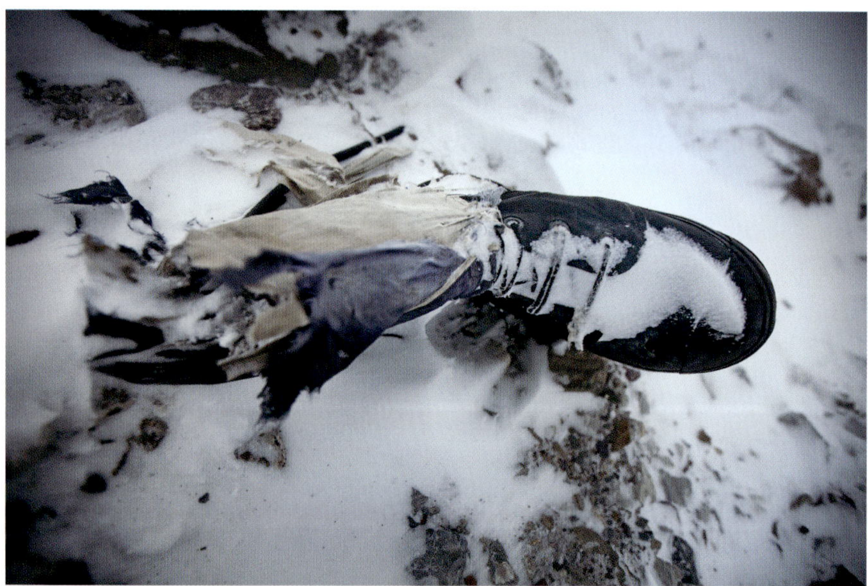

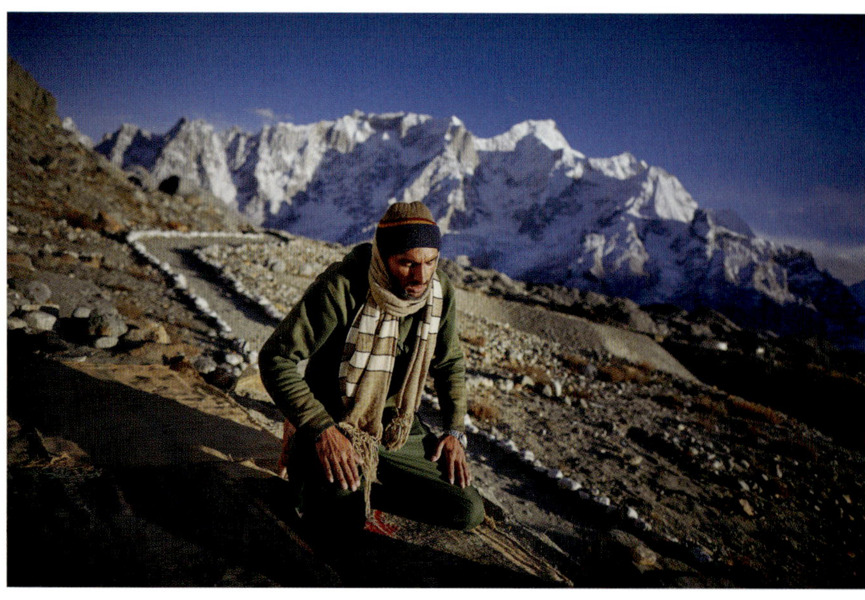

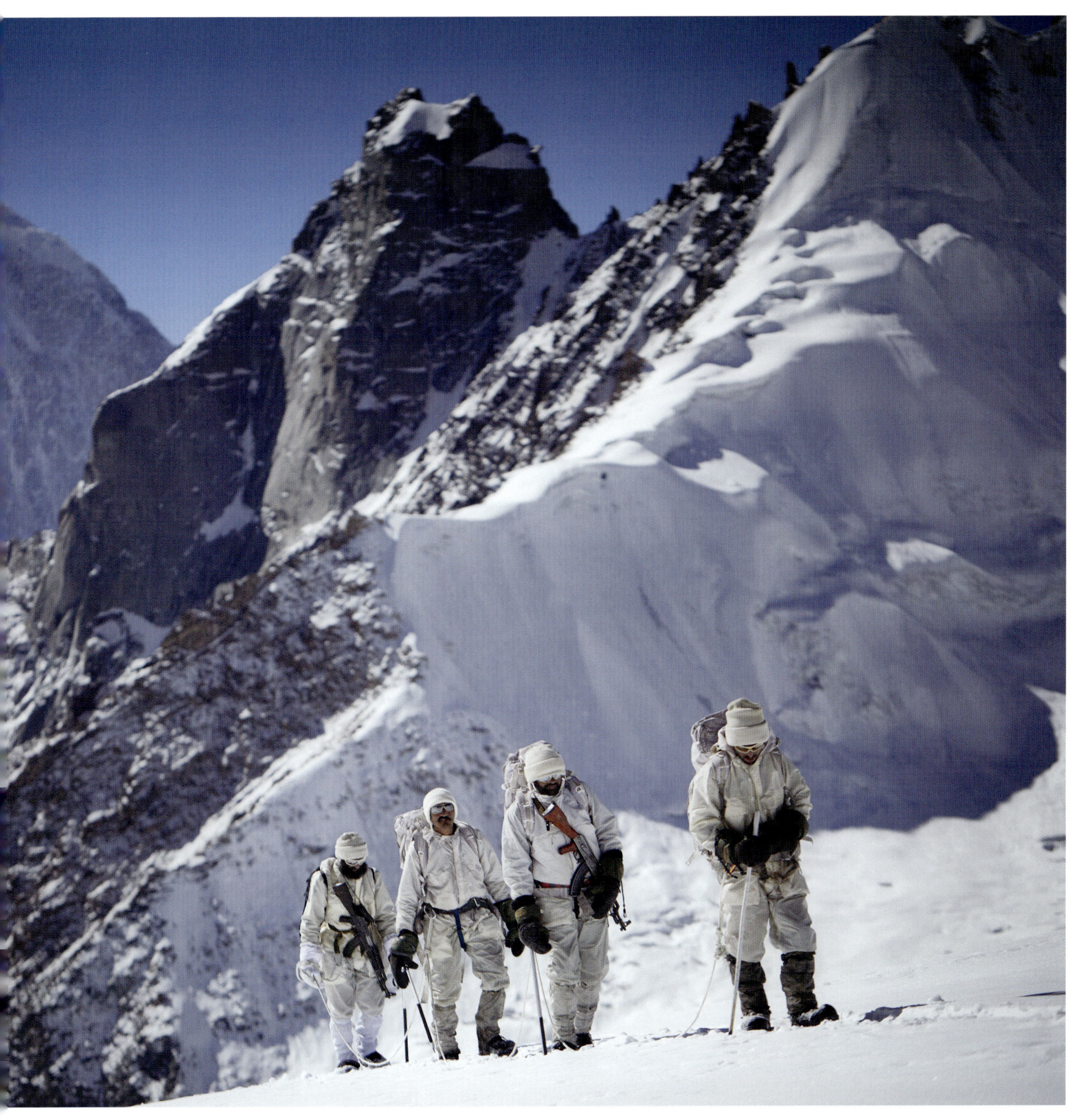

Soldiers cross the Gyong Glacier at 17,500 feet, taking care not to fall into the large crevasses hidden by fresh snow. **OPPOSITE, ABOVE:** Nightfall over the small post at Urdukas. **OPPOSITE, CENTER:** The foot and boot of a deceased soldier frozen in the ice. **OPPOSITE, BELOW:** A soldier prays near Gora I post. **FOLLOWING:** A soldier and his weapon.

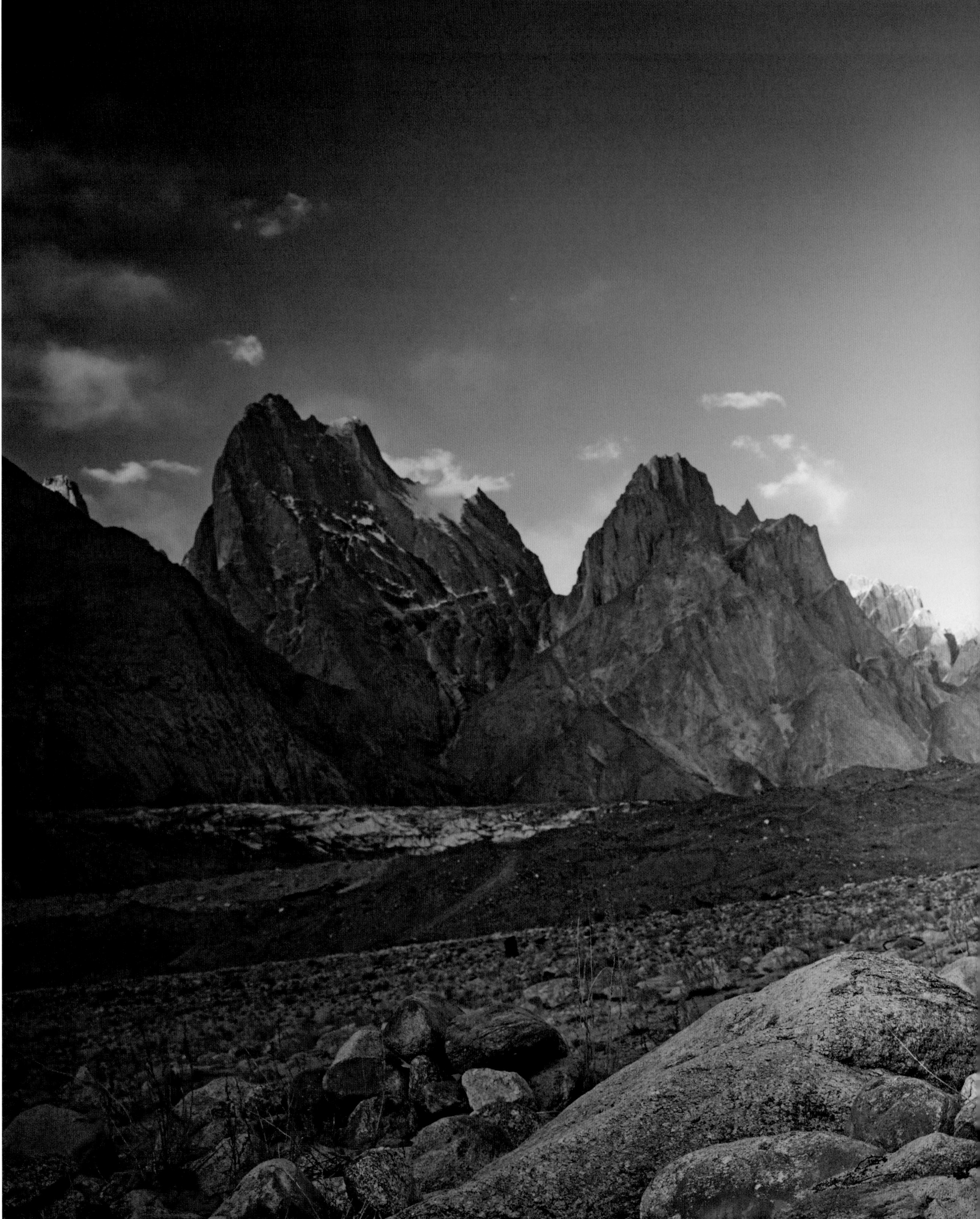

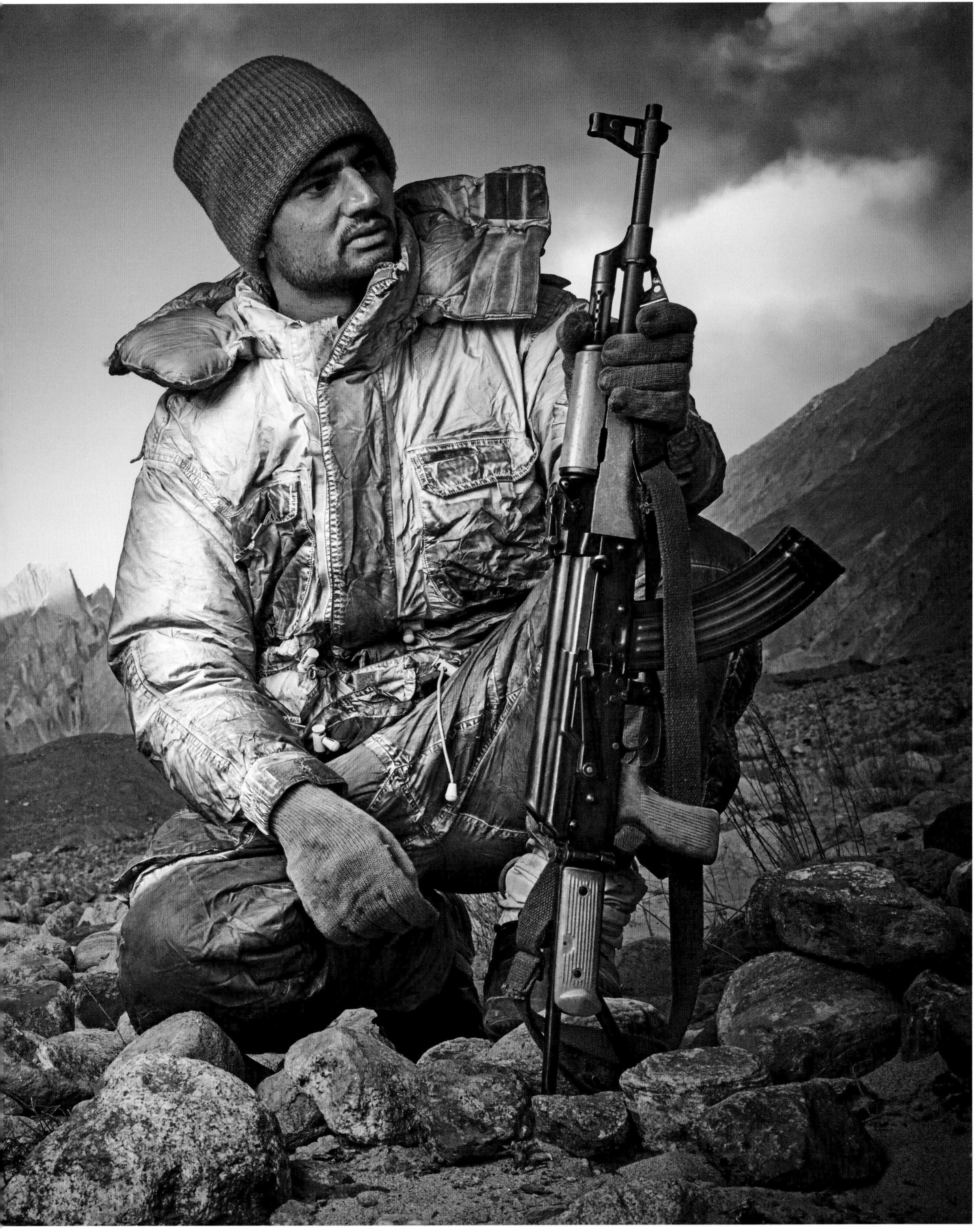

A LESSON ON BELONGING

Queen Maud Land, Antarctica

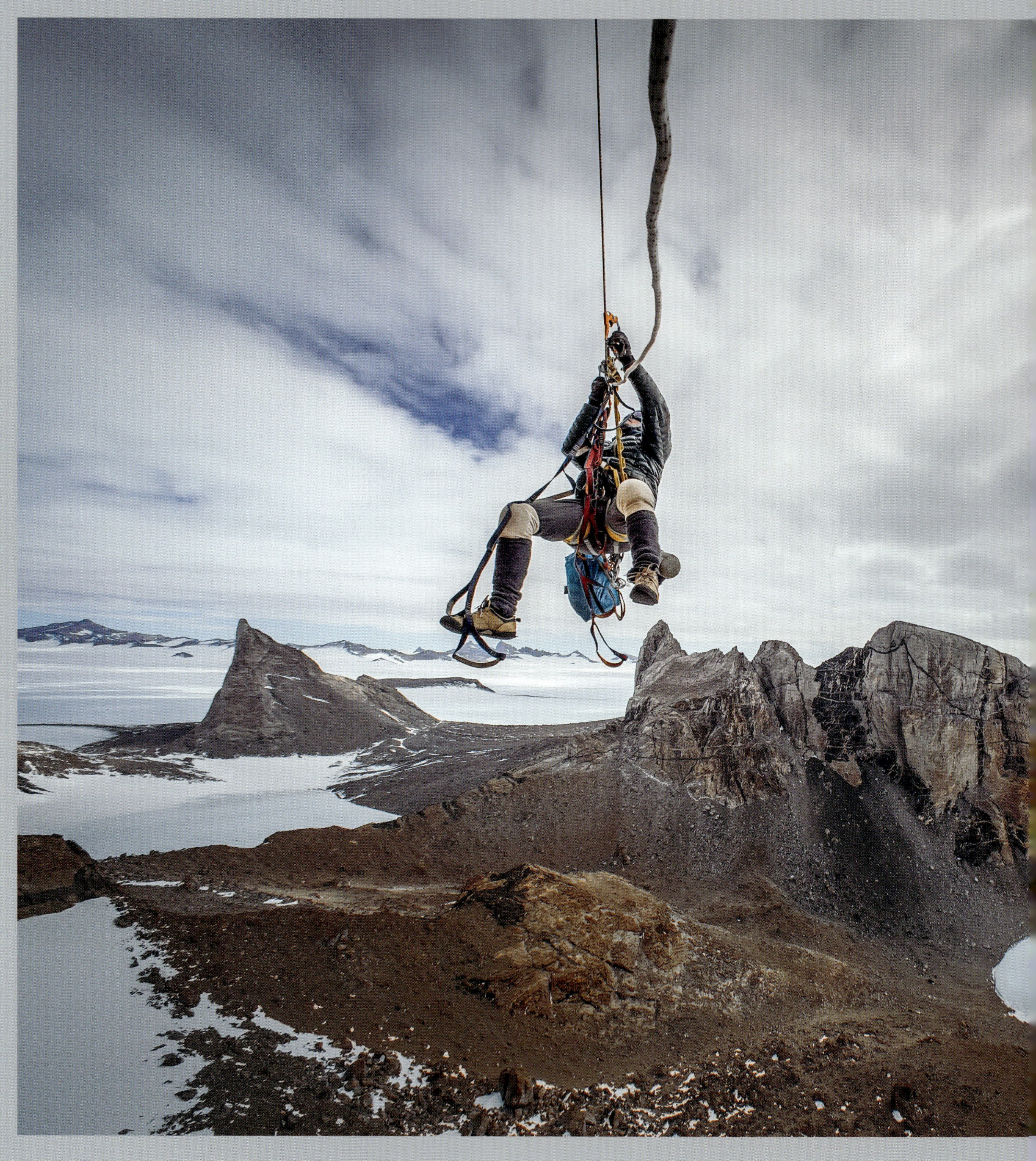

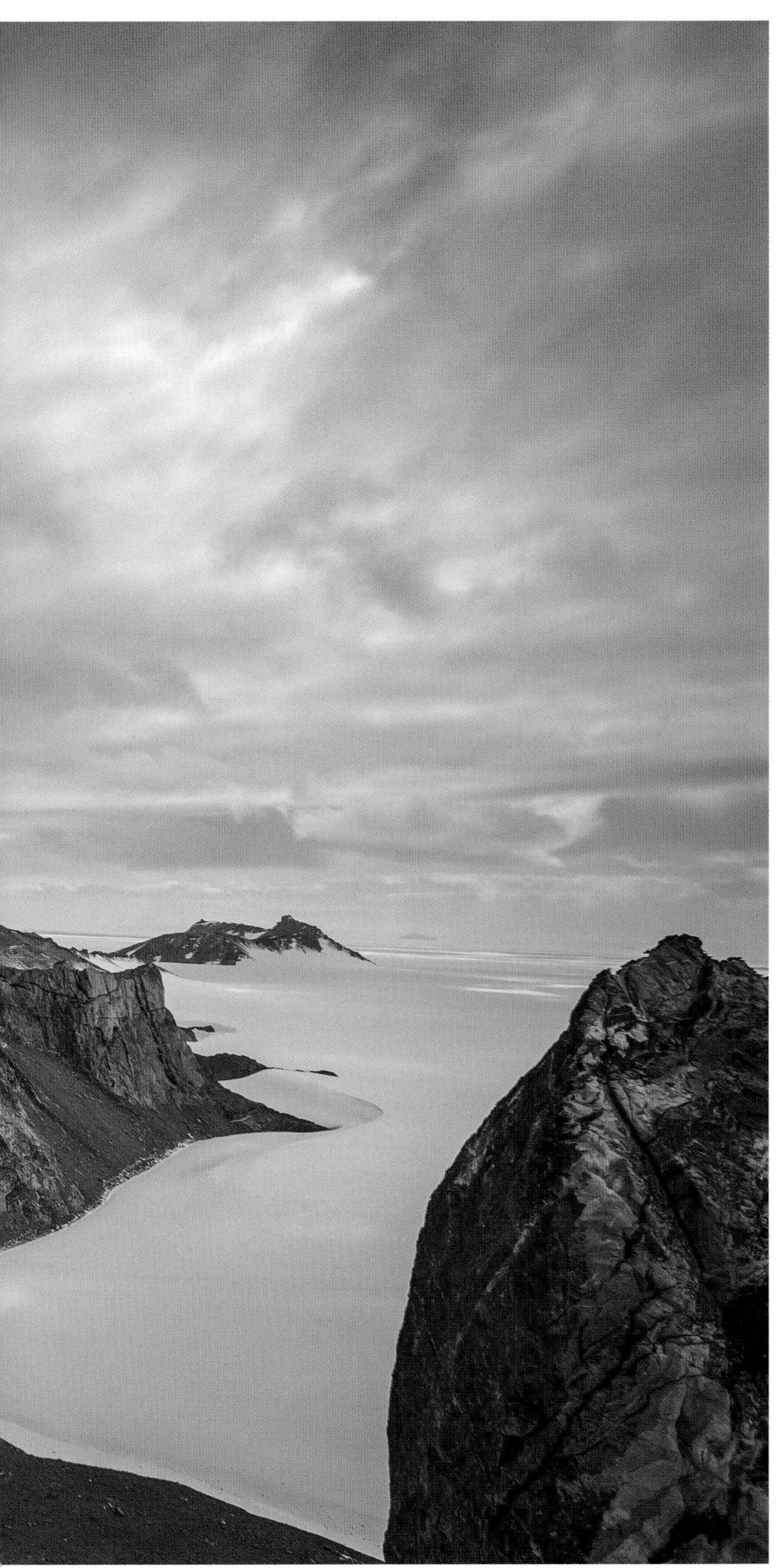

American explorer Mike Libecki ascends a rope on the first ascent of Bertha's Tower in the Wohlthat Range. **FOLLOWING:** An Illyushin Il-76 delivers people, equipment, and supplies to Novolazarevskaya Station. All inland travel and research for this region of the continent is staged here.

Mike Libecki is swinging above the expanse of Antarctica and it occurs to me that a climbing rope always looks too thin.

After thirty days alone in the Wohlthat Range of Queen Maud Land, I can't help but wonder about the sanity of what we're doing. If anything goes wrong, there is no escape hatch. Wind at speeds of 100 miles per hour regularly tears at our tents, lifting us off the ground and threatening to send us tumbling through the rocks. No planes fly overhead. No lights disrupt the night that never comes as the sunset and sunrise coalesce into a single orange event. We are hopelessly alone, tied to each other by a nylon thread that looks impossible.

We're on assignment for *National Geographic,* surveying the range and trying to climb a sharp granite tooth. But the underlying theme of this experiment is simpler: Survive. When the old DC-3 plane dropped off Mike, Freddie Wilkinson, Keith Ladzinski, and me a month ago, it all seemed so safe. But as soon as the buzz from the propellers faded, a heavy silence settled, and I haven't been able to shake it since. Even when the katabatic winds are tearing at our basecamp, there's a palpable quietness beneath, reminding us how isolated we are. The only safety is in each other, and that has created an unshakeable bond.

I've spent a thousand days just like this one. Inhospitable places indifferent to life have a way of bonding you to anything that breathes. On days when we aren't climbing, Keith and I chase birds with cameras, marveling at how something so delicate can be so robust. Everything here seems in danger of being swallowed by the landscape—and we are no different.

The holidays are coming. I think of rooms filled with people and tables set with food. I think of the warmth of a busy kitchen and a cacophony of voices humming over dirty plates. I think of how much I take connection for granted until I'm thrust into an environment that amplifies my finitude. I also think of how lonely it can be even when I am surrounded by people. Somehow here, despite the isolation or because of it, I feel more connected than ever.

After forty-six days, I hear the whine of the propellers coming to pick us up. We've climbed and skied and photographed. We've lost tents and gear, blown away or buried. We've lost weight and sweat and pretense. We are raw, boiled down to our most basic selves. When we ask the pilot why he returns year after year to this place, flying in dangerous conditions, his answer makes us laugh. It's also strangely familiar: "Well, first you do it for the experience. Then you do it for the money. And finally, you do it because you don't fit in anywhere else."

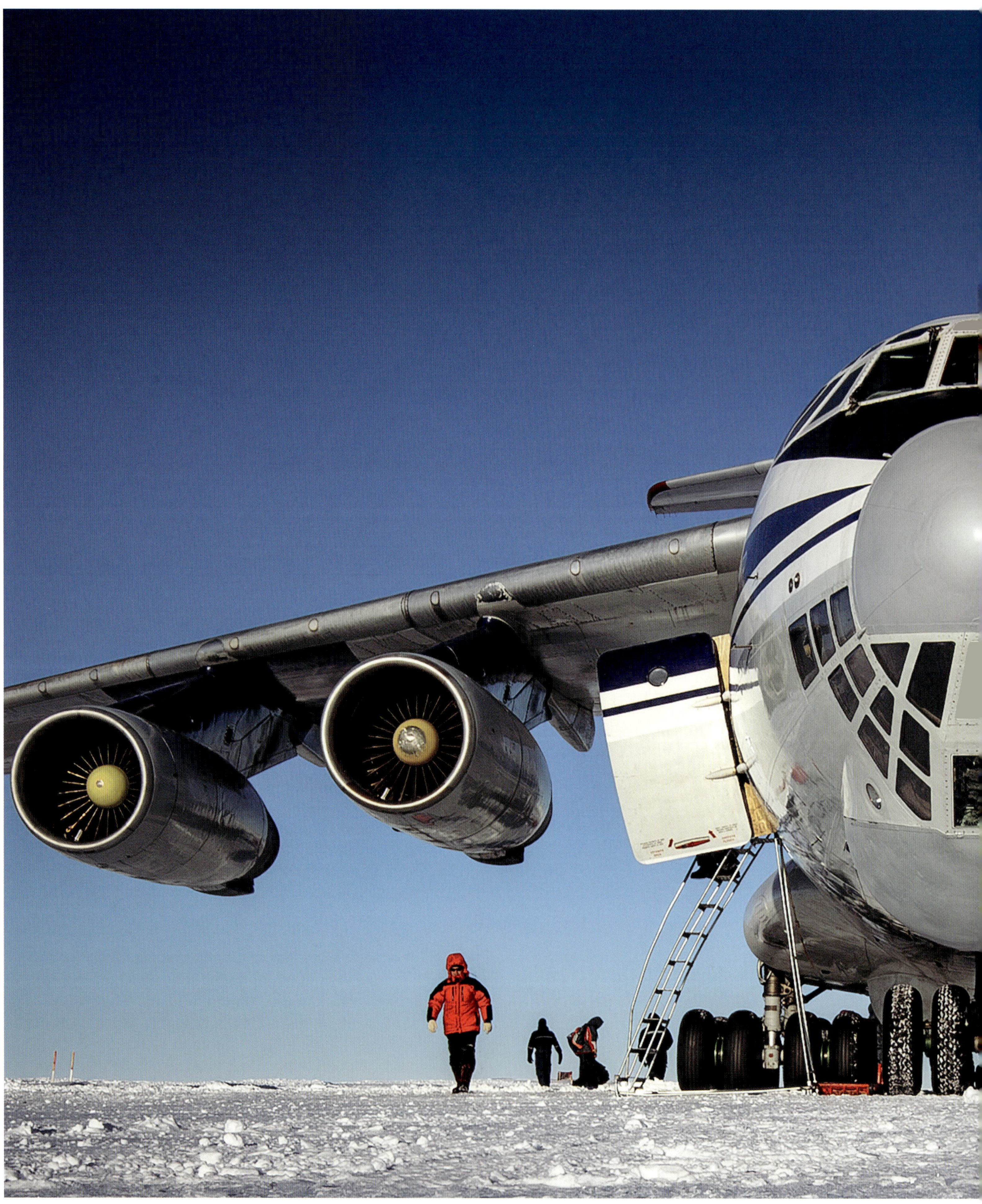

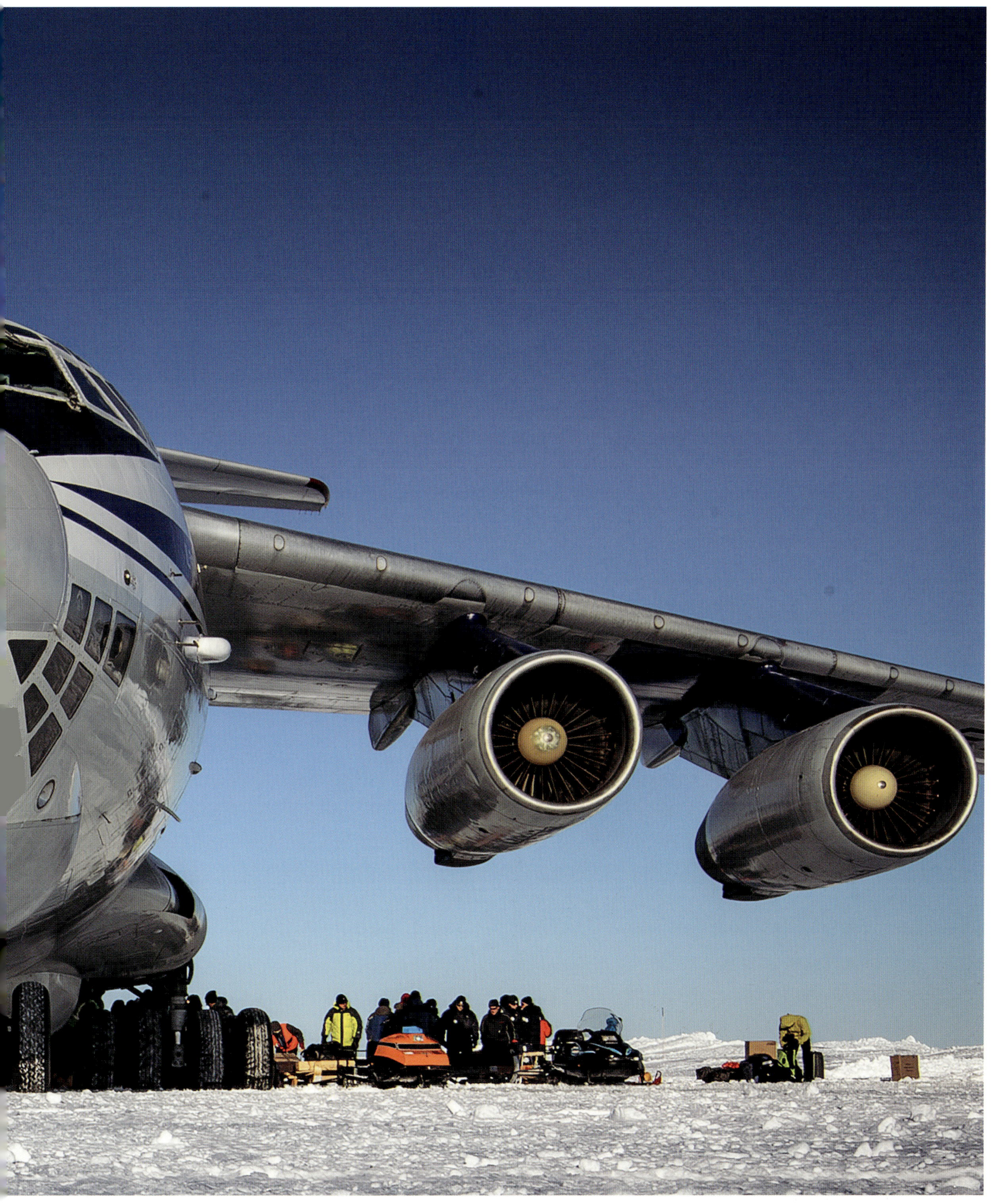

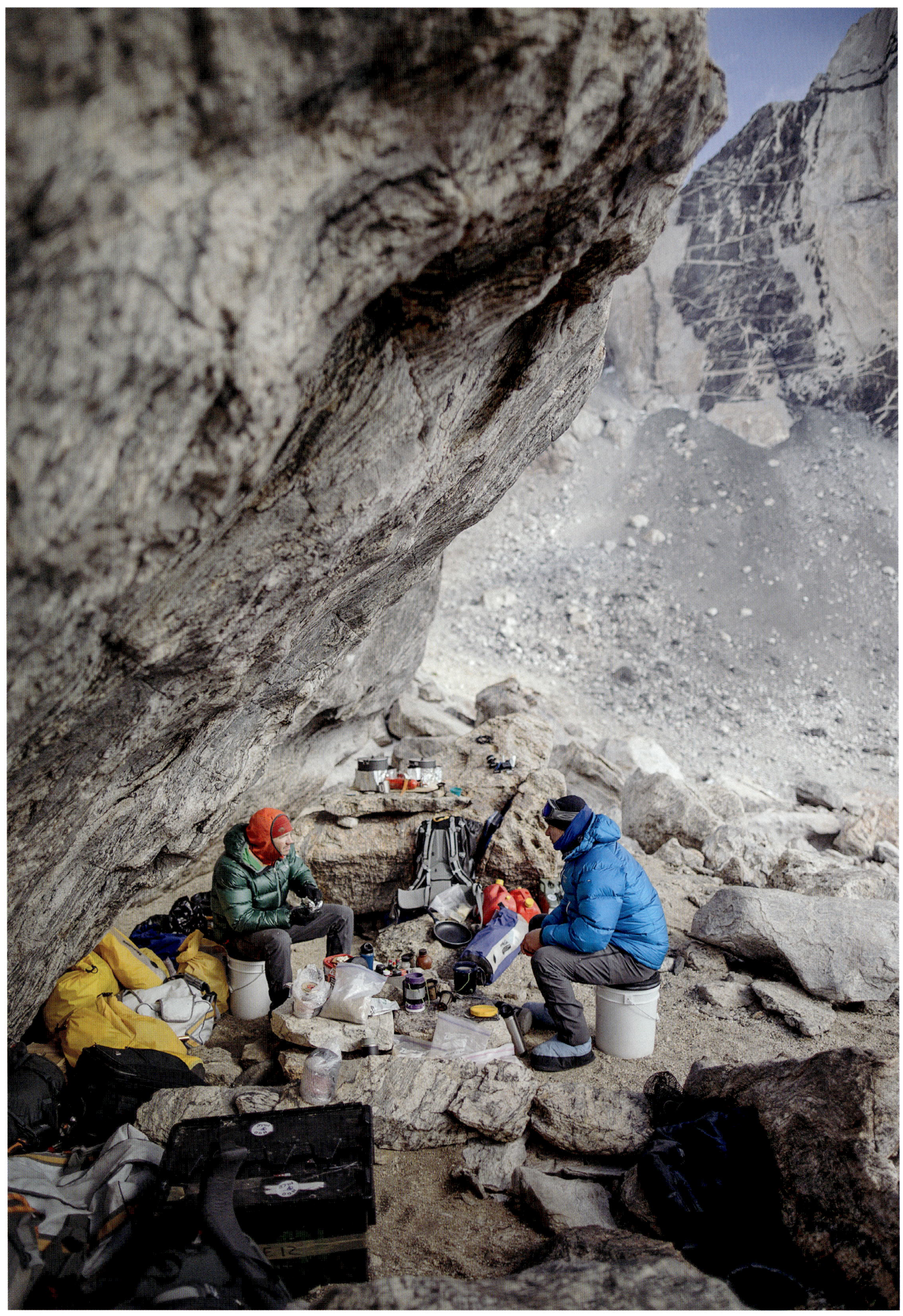

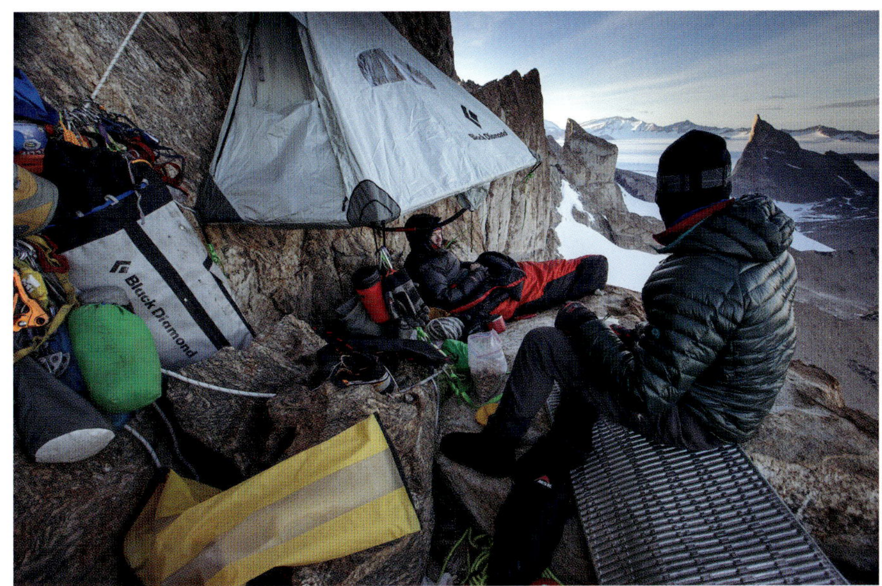

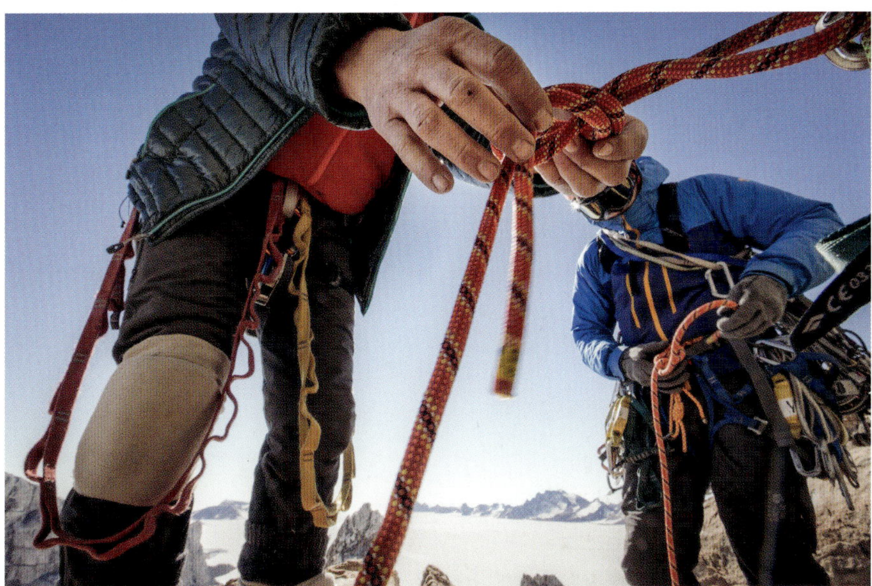

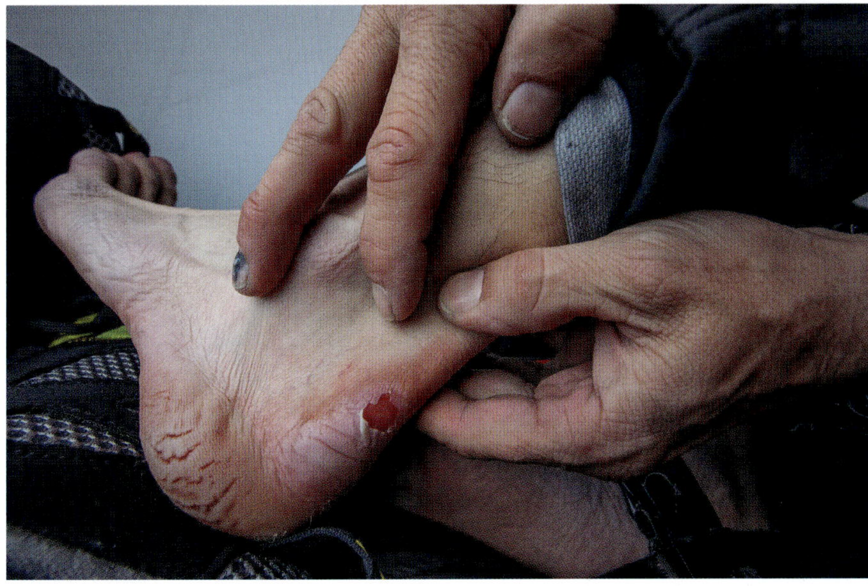

ABOVE: American climber and writer Freddie Wilkinson (left) and Mike Libecki (right) at a bivouac 1,500 feet up Bertha's Tower. **CENTER:** Mike Libecki deals with ropes while Freddie Wilkinson readies himself for climbing. **BELOW:** Blisters and blood on American photographer Keith Ladzinski's heel after a long day of surveying the range by ski and foot. **OPPOSITE:** Freddie Wilkinson (left) and Mike Libecki (right) at camp in the Wohlthat Range.

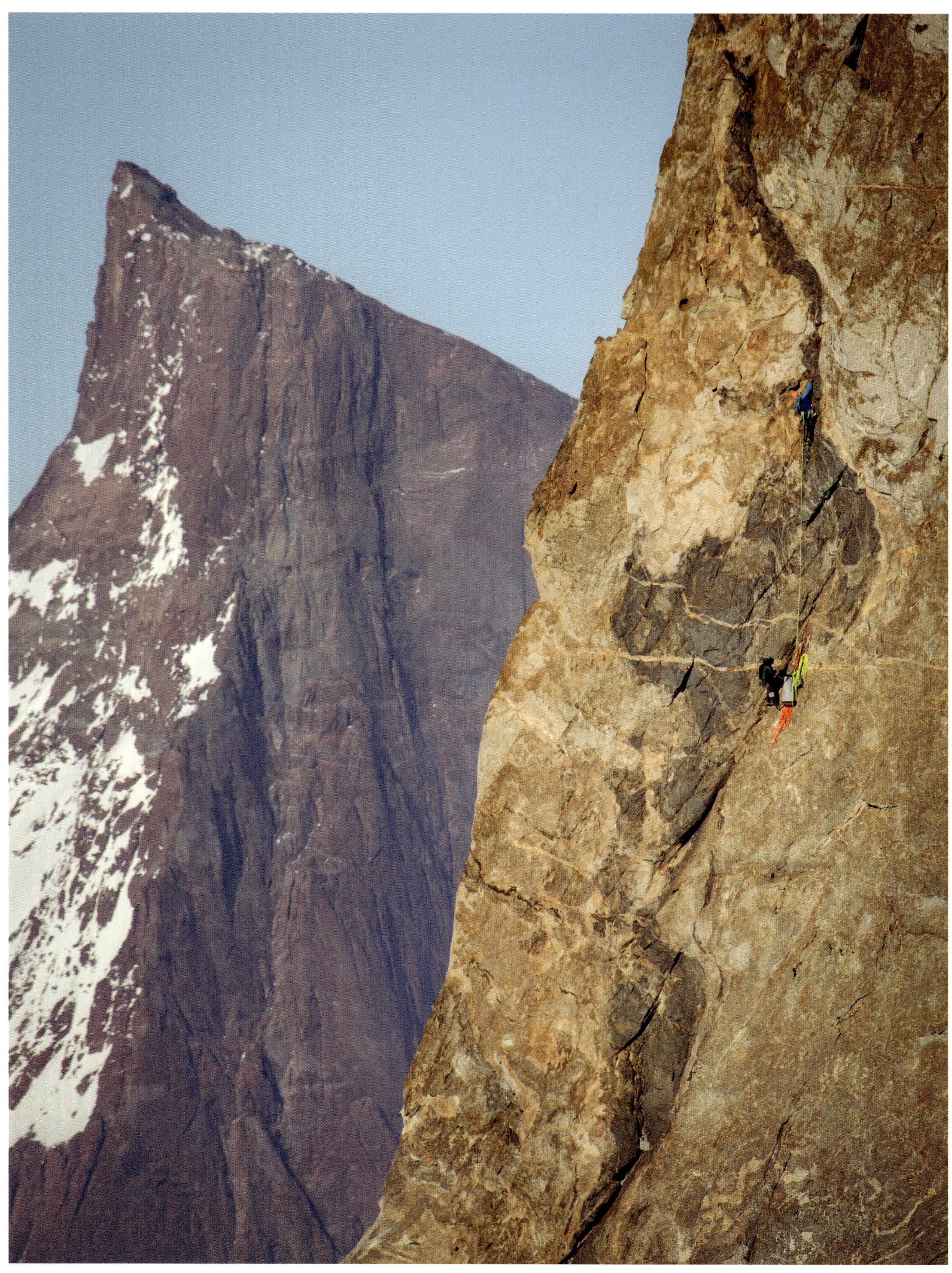

Freddie Wilkinson (top) and Mike Libecki (bottom) make slow, steady progress on the first ascent of Bertha's Tower.

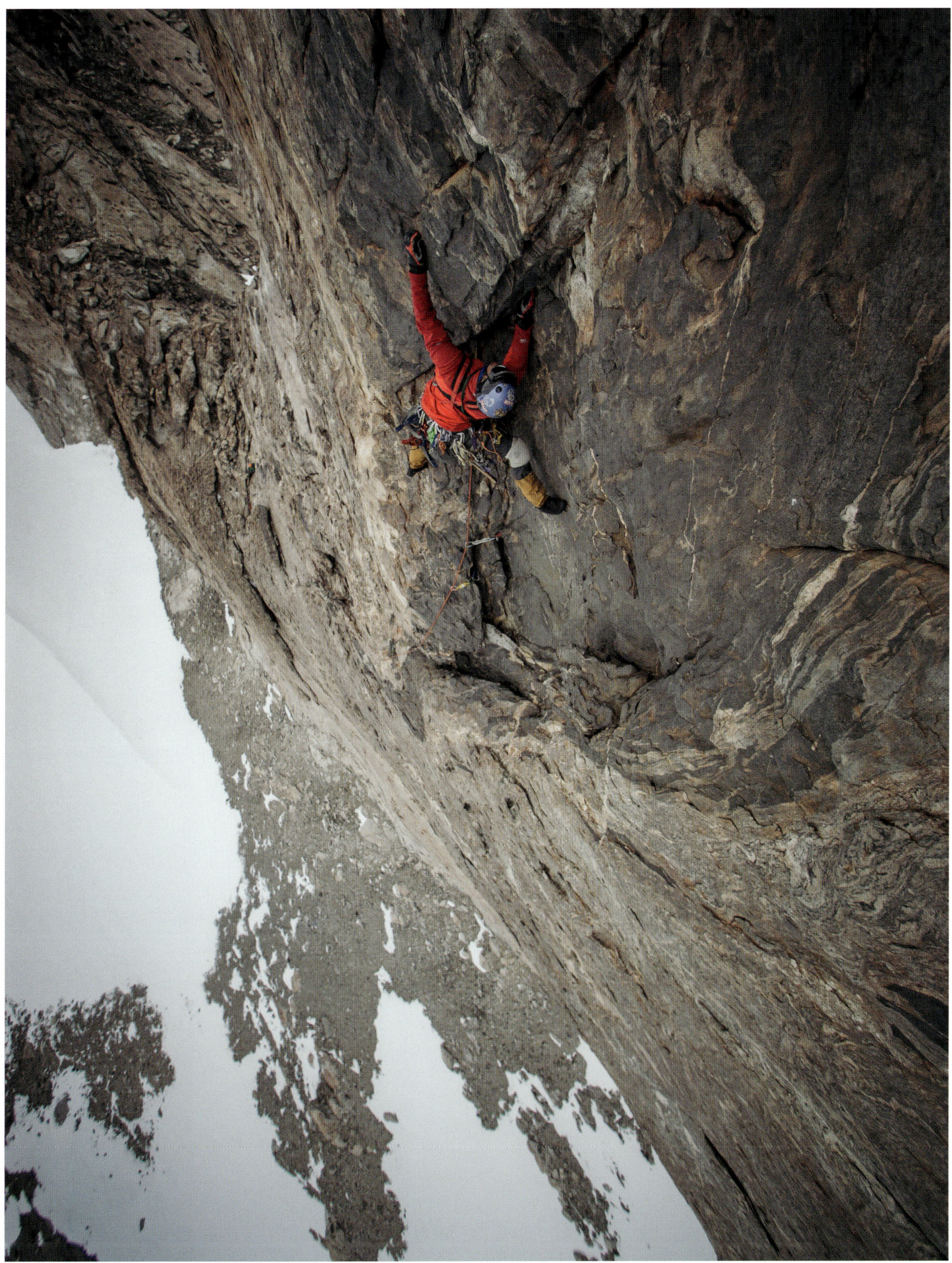

Mike Libecki leads through sharp, shattered, and unstable granite.

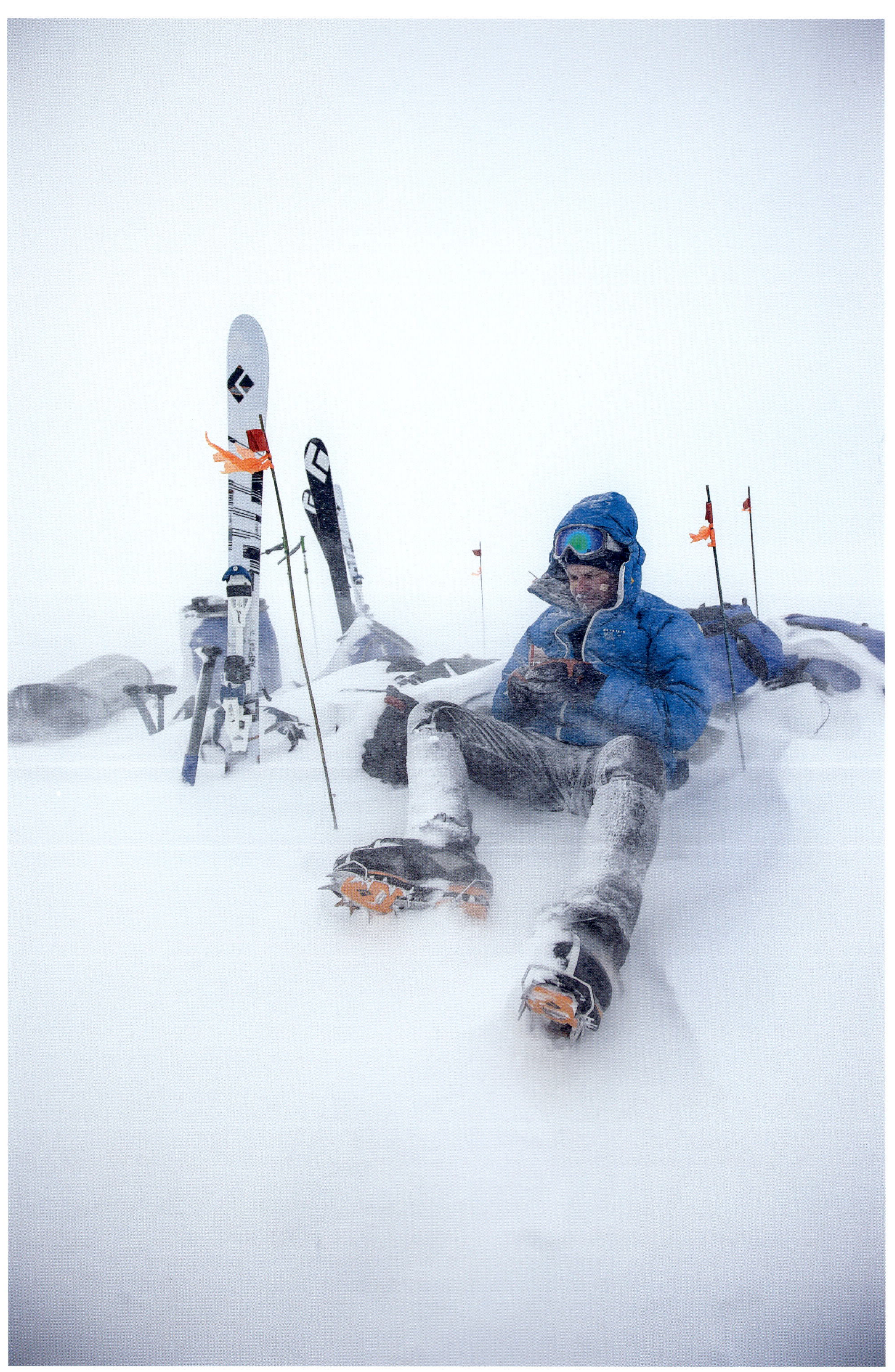

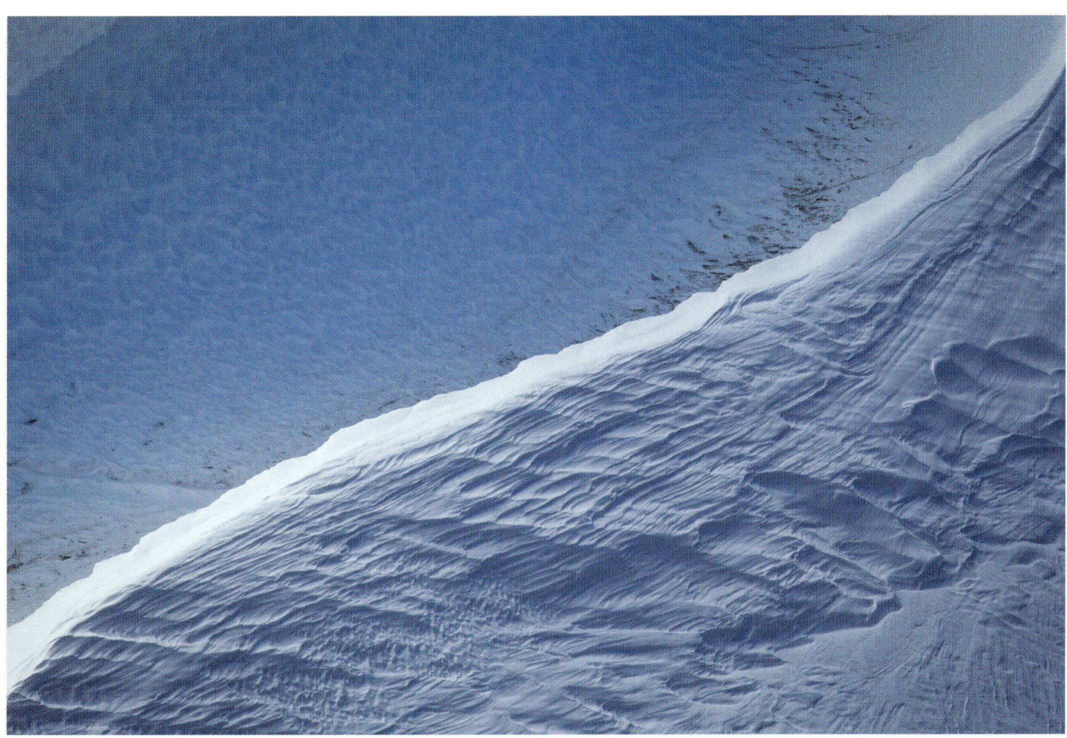

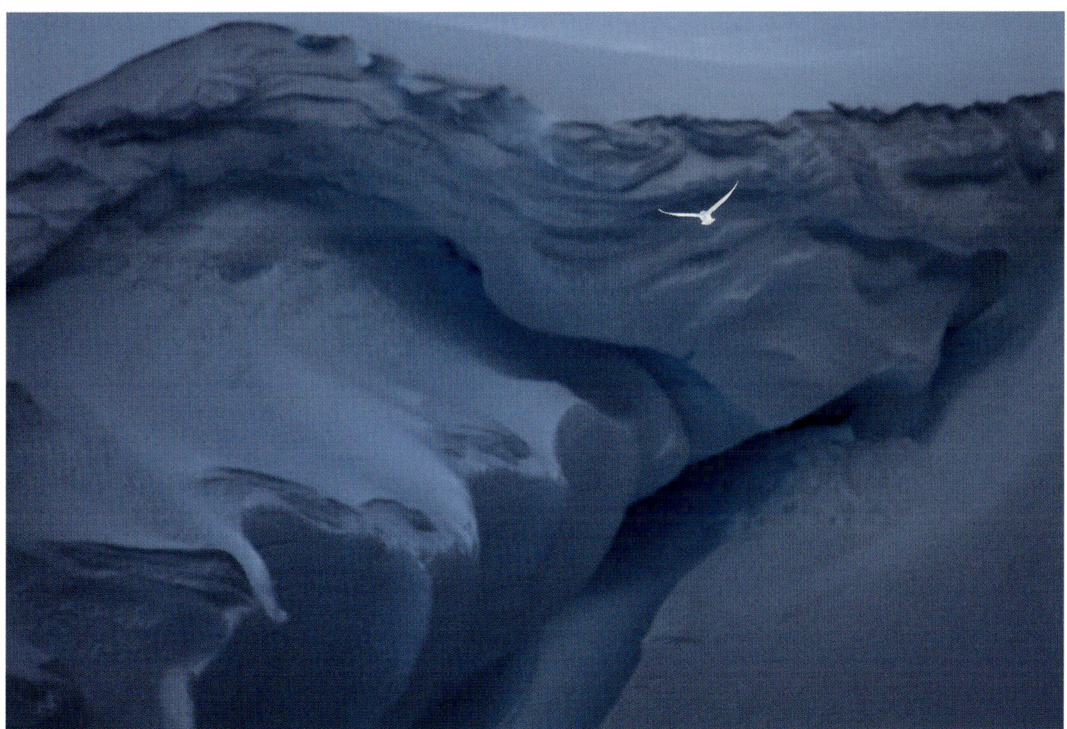

ABOVE: Ice and snow formations sculpted by the katabatic winds. **BELOW:** A snow petrel rides air currents beneath enormous cornices. **OPPOSITE:** Mike Libecki sits amid buried gear, buffeted by katabatic winds, while attempting to move camp back onto the ice.

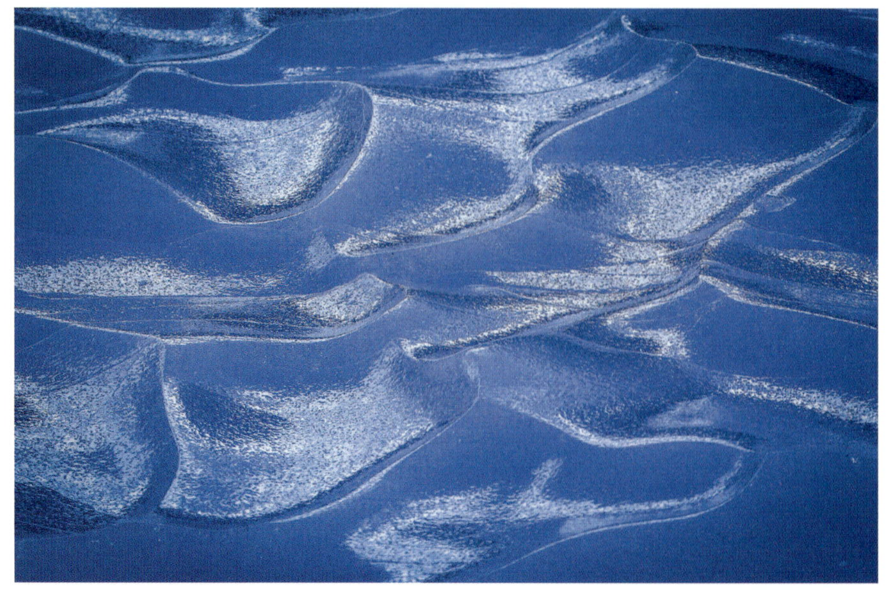

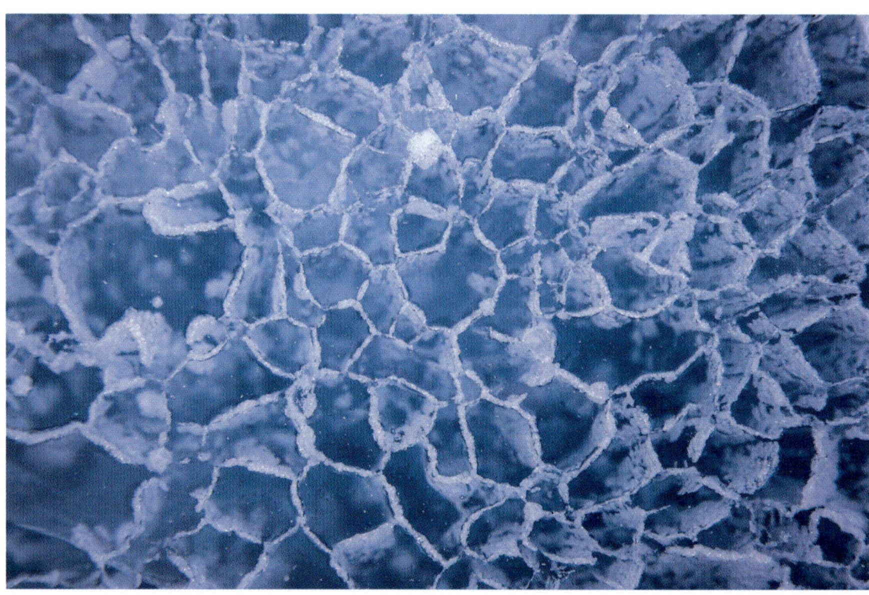

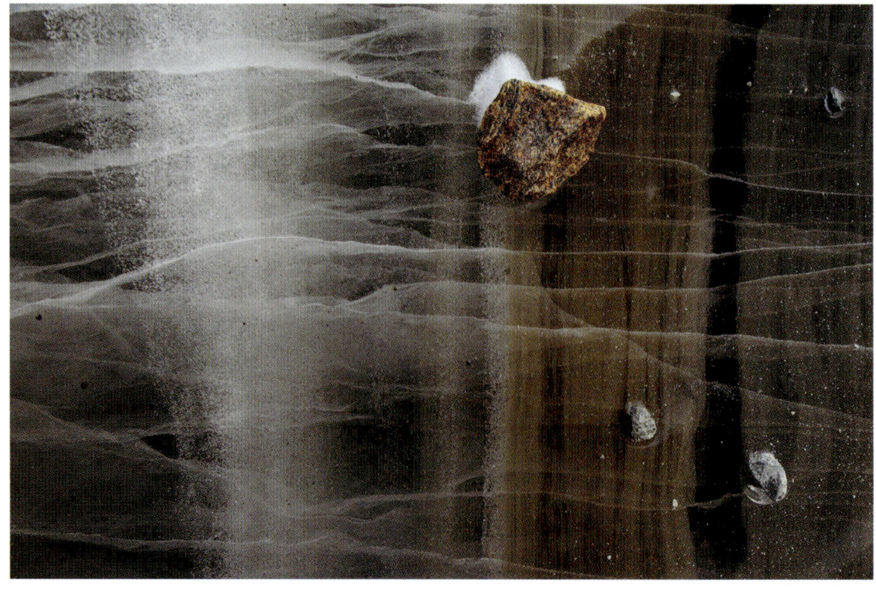

Ice in its many forms. **OPPOSITE:** Mike Libecki (left) and Freddie Wilkinson (right) circumnavigate the Wohlthat Range amid a sea of ice. **FOLLOWING:** Keith Ladzinski fights through a ground blizzard with the granite teeth of Queen Maud Land behind.

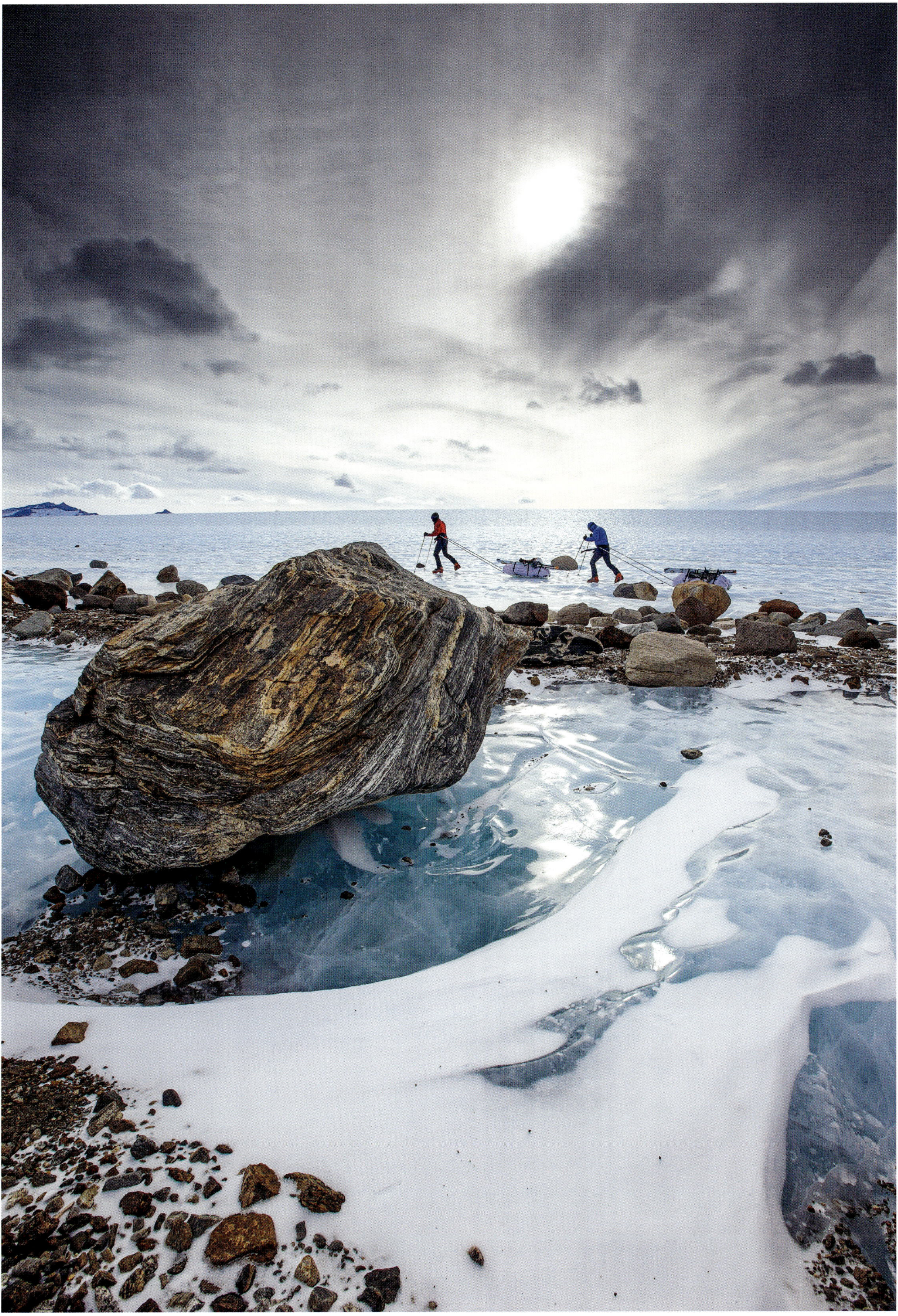

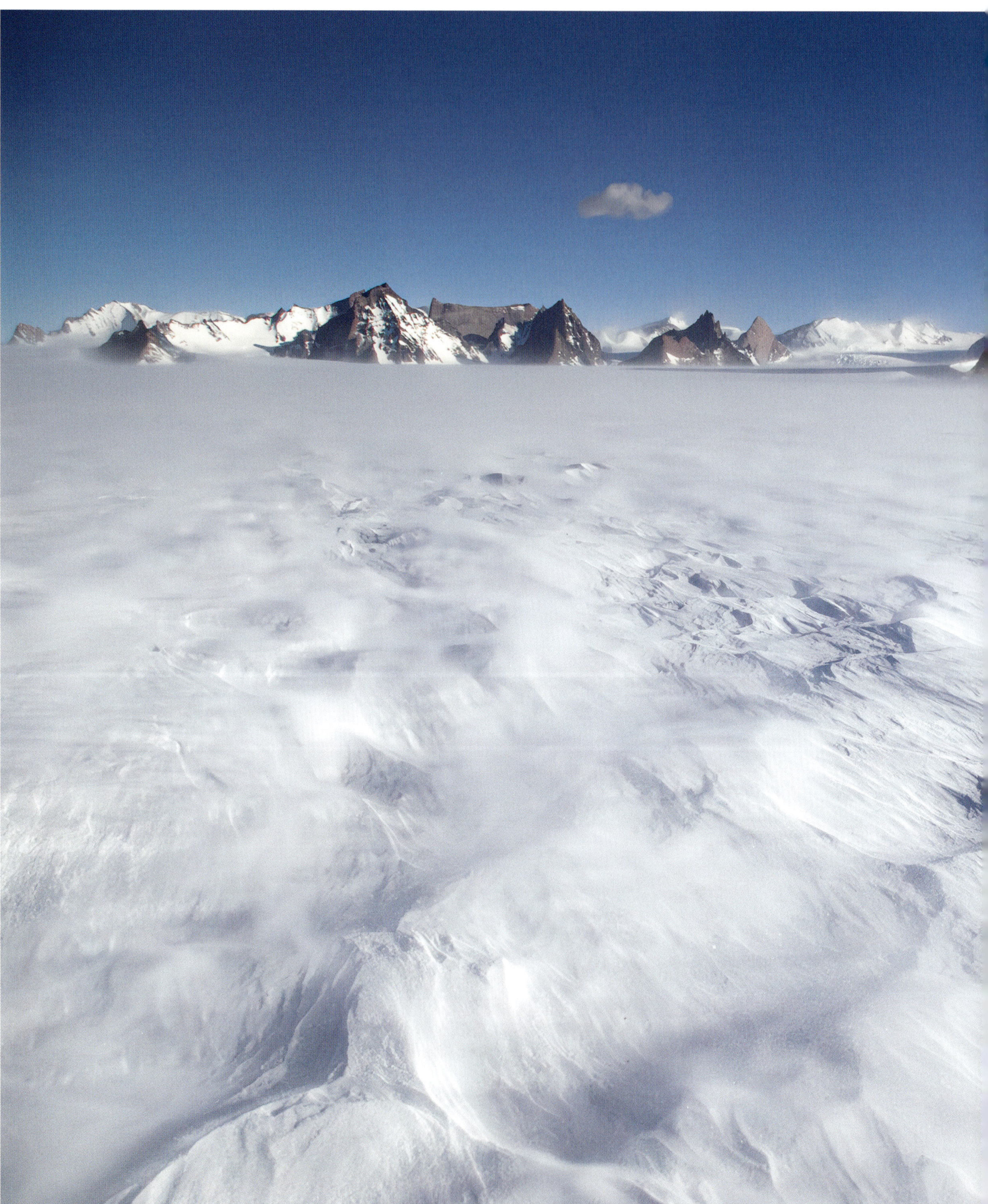

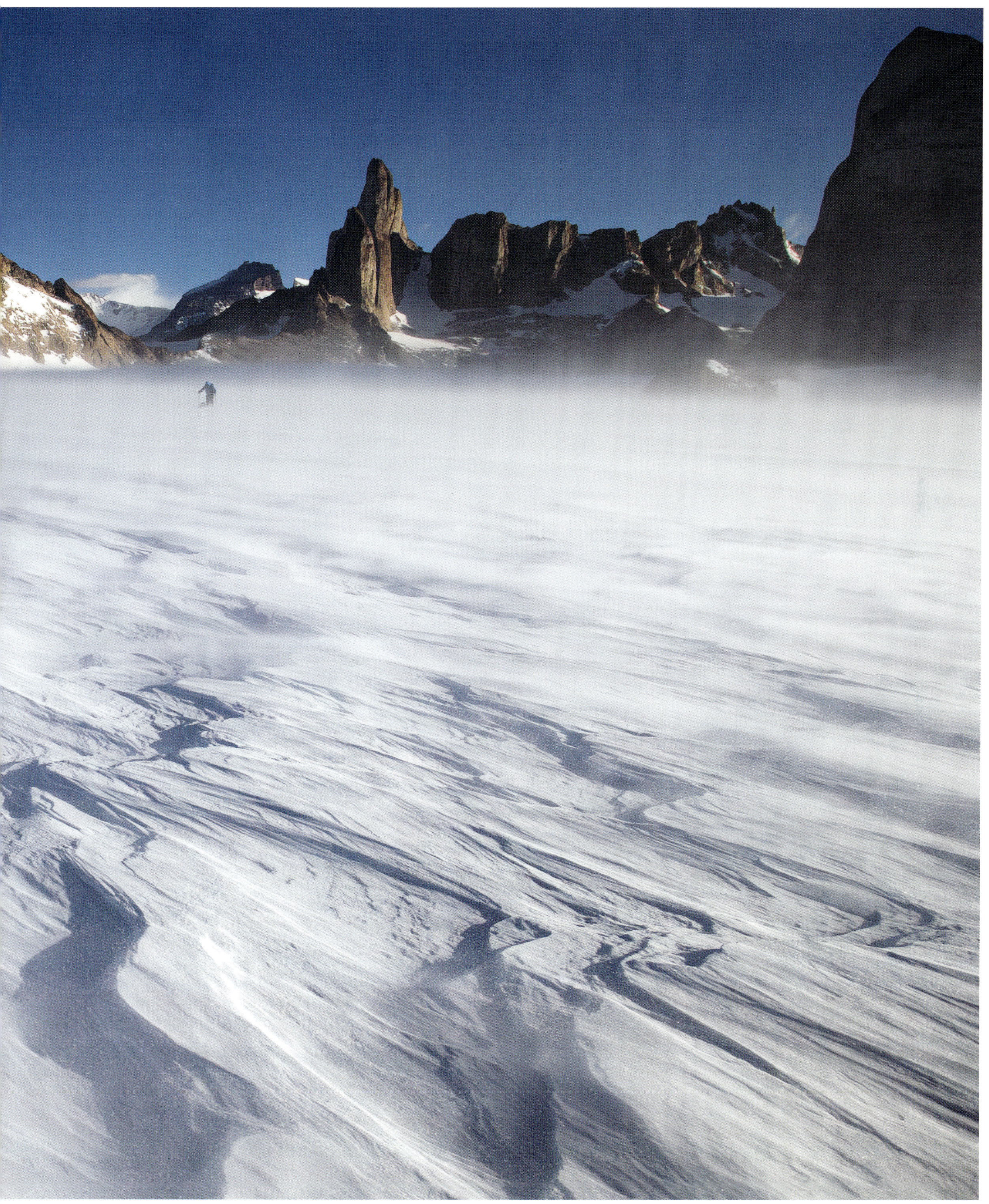

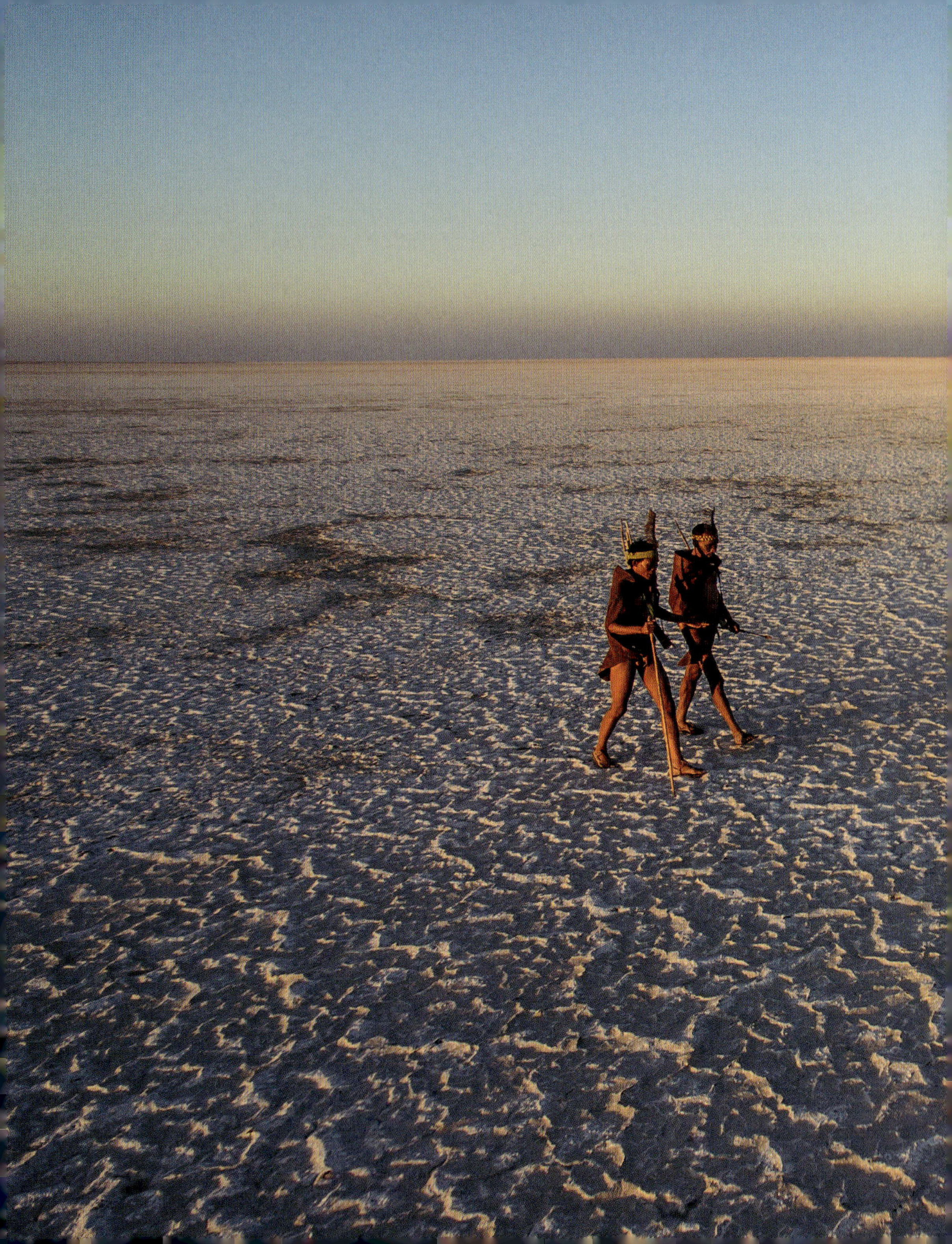

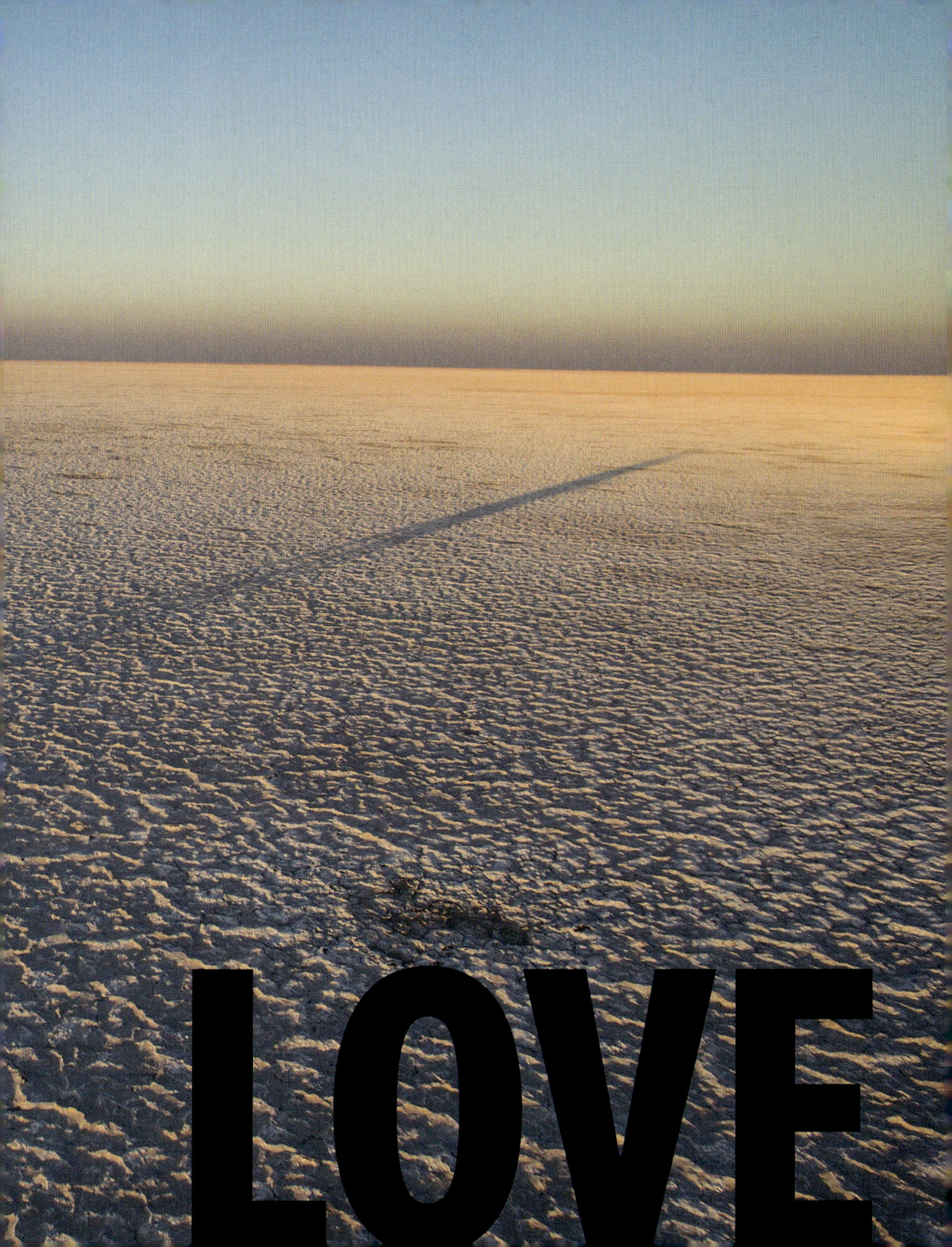

LOVE

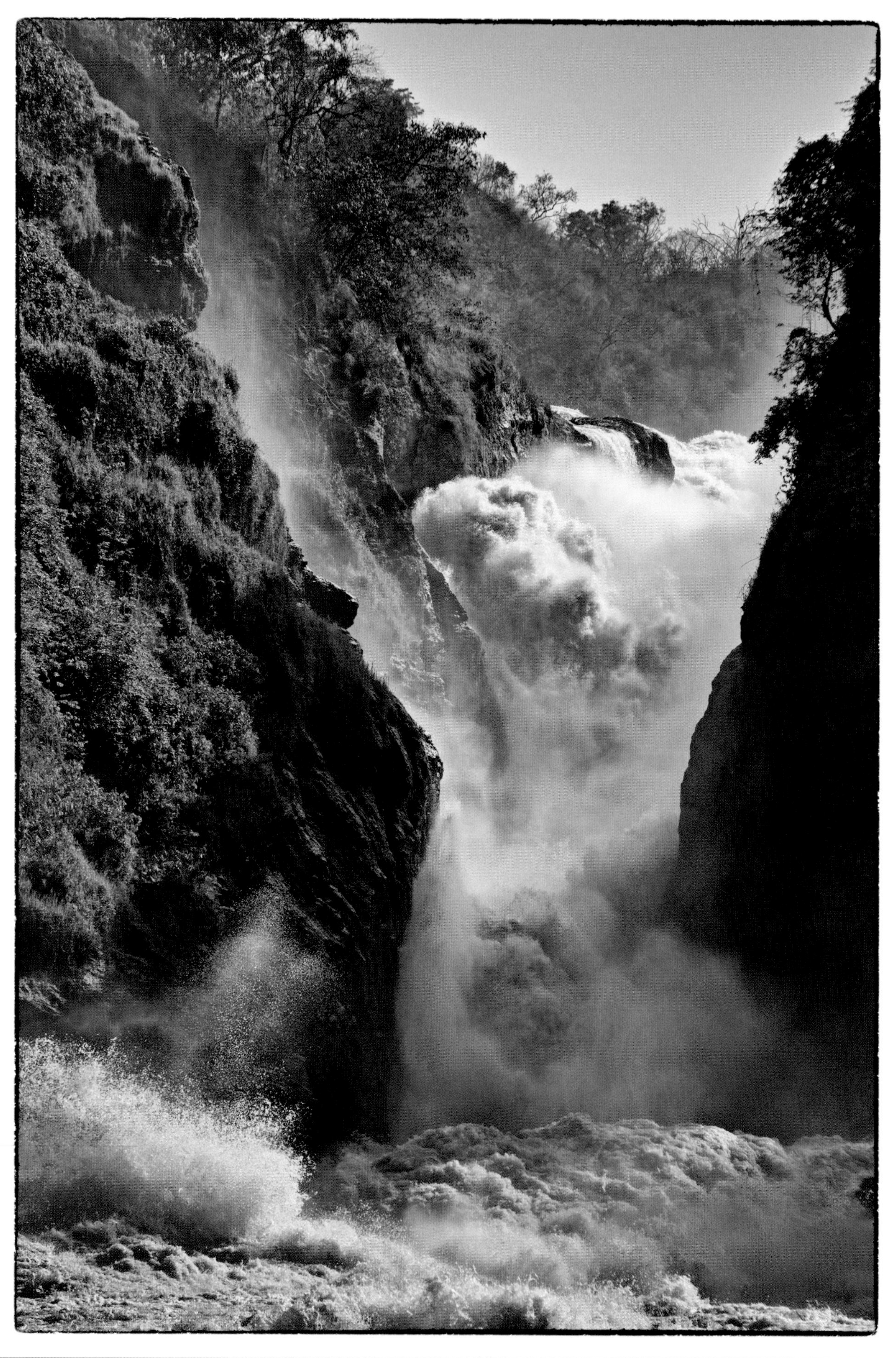

In Jewish mysticism, the word _gadol_ is interchangeable with _love_ and _big_.
Abraham used it to describe God.

In English, *love* is generally used to describe something finite, leaving us with incomplete and nebulous definitions. Science has a hard time defining *love* at all because it intersects, overlaps, and expands far beyond what we can measure. And yet despite how big love is, it's accessible to everyone at every moment.

The kind of love I'm struggling to describe makes room for everything: it is an umbrella raised above humanity in all its ugliness and splendor. Humans are messy. The world isn't perfect. There is pain and loss and war and extinction. There is inequity and racism and hate. But those realities are also woven together with astonishing beauty, wonder, compassion, and kindness. In many ways, they rely on each other. Somehow, love is a singular duality.

That I've been so fortunate to witness the world from both ends of its geographic poles is a gift I don't take for granted. That my experience mirrors the label that was applied to my brain at a young age is a happy accident. Because of my mind's polarity, at times I've been exposed to such immeasurable darkness that it's been hard to see love at all. On the other hand, I've been struck by love's capacity to permeate and break apart the horrors that life throws at us. I used to believe that art was born of struggle and pain. Now I understand true art to be love making itself seen, even amid the most tragic circumstances. Where it seems to be an expression of darkness, art is the *heart's* hopeful response and the method we use to make sense of it all.

Love is not something that I claim to understand in its entirety, but photographs help. Pictures provide a pathway to feel the heartbreak and joy of the world and our place in it. They give us the opportunity to define what makes us hurt and what makes us whole. And yet as helpful as they are, photographs are just an invitation; reminders of what we're already a part of. It's another of life's strange paradoxes that sometimes we have to stop looking in order to see. What is illuminated in that quietude is astonishing and marvelous. Love holds all of it. Love is all of it.

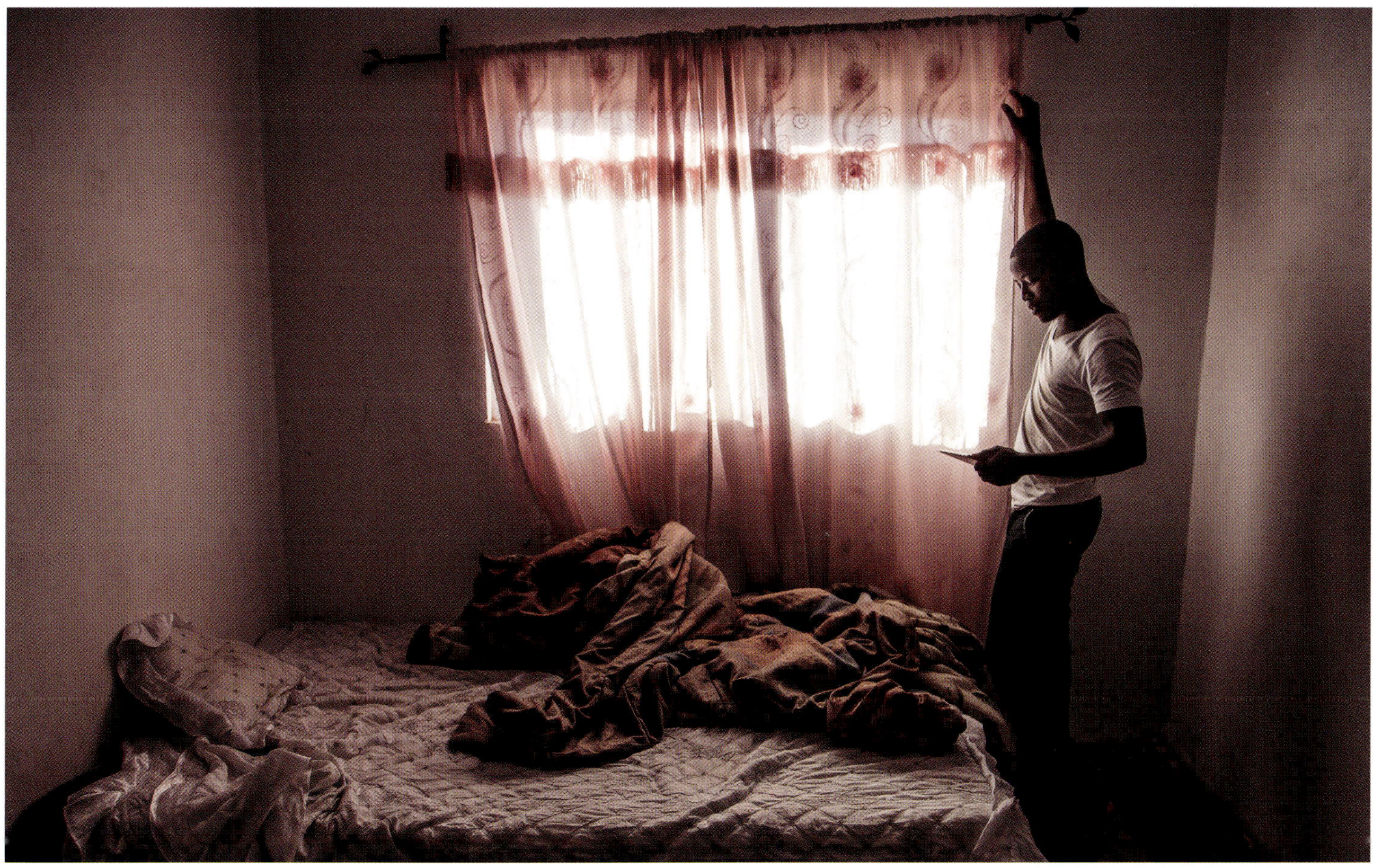

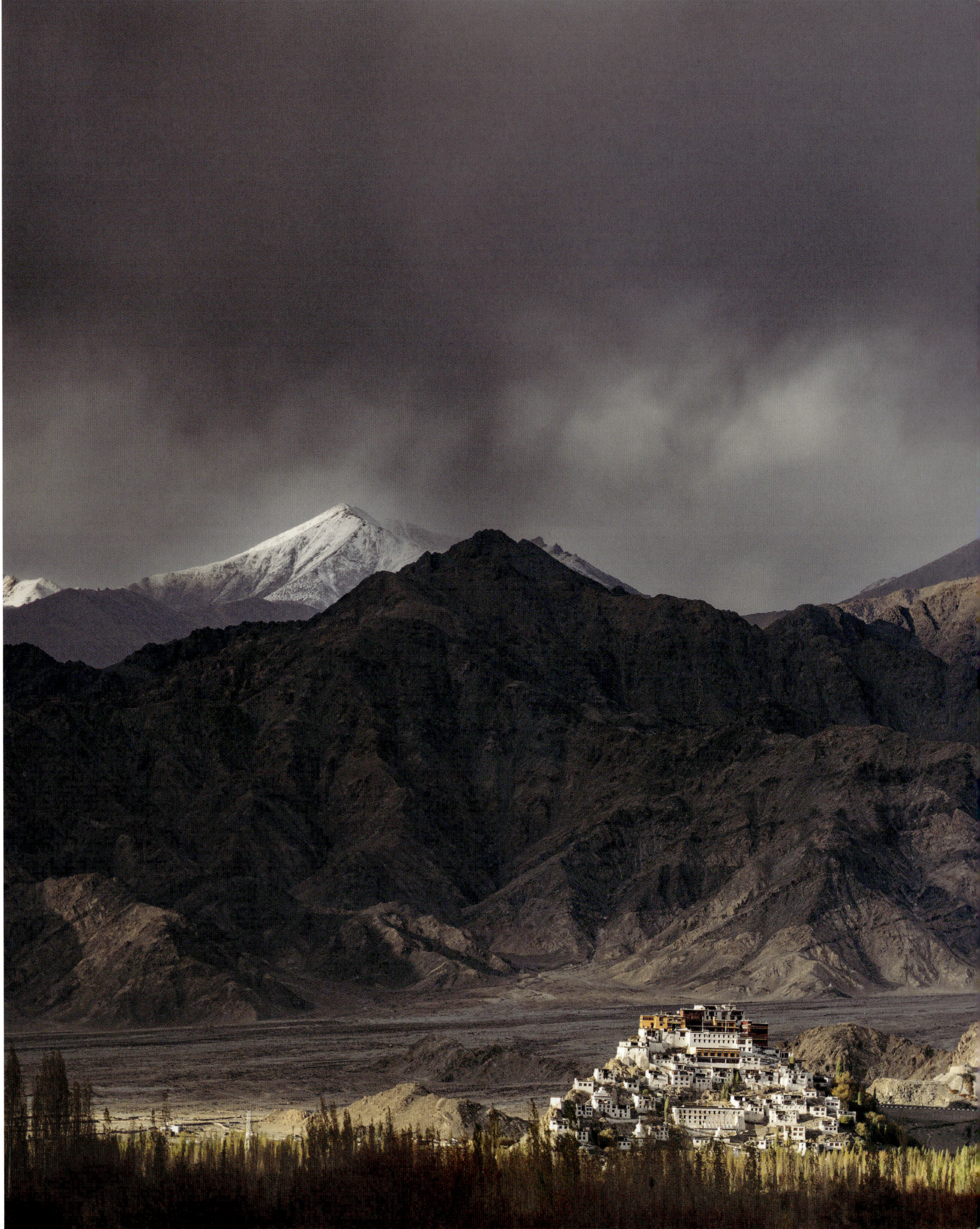

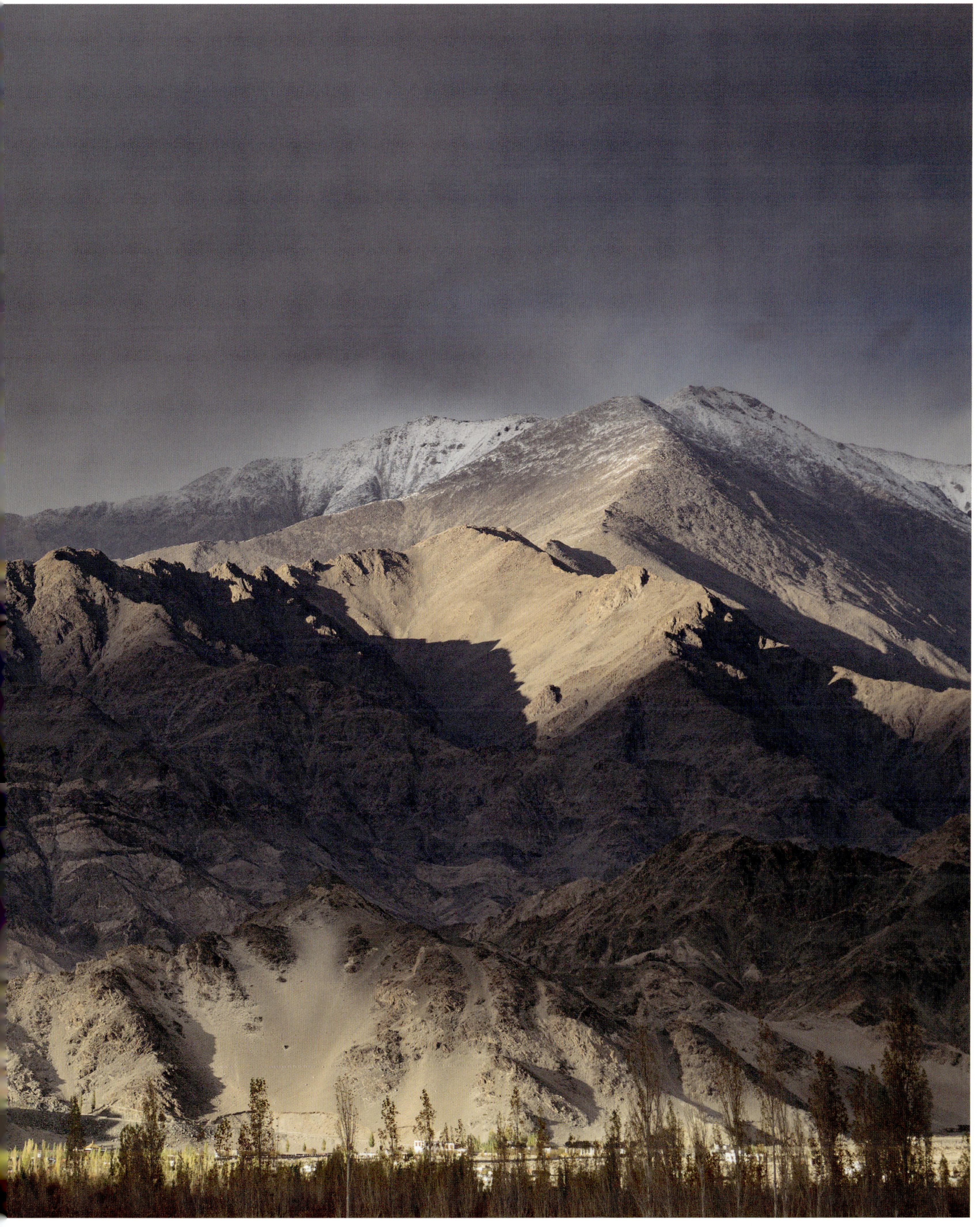

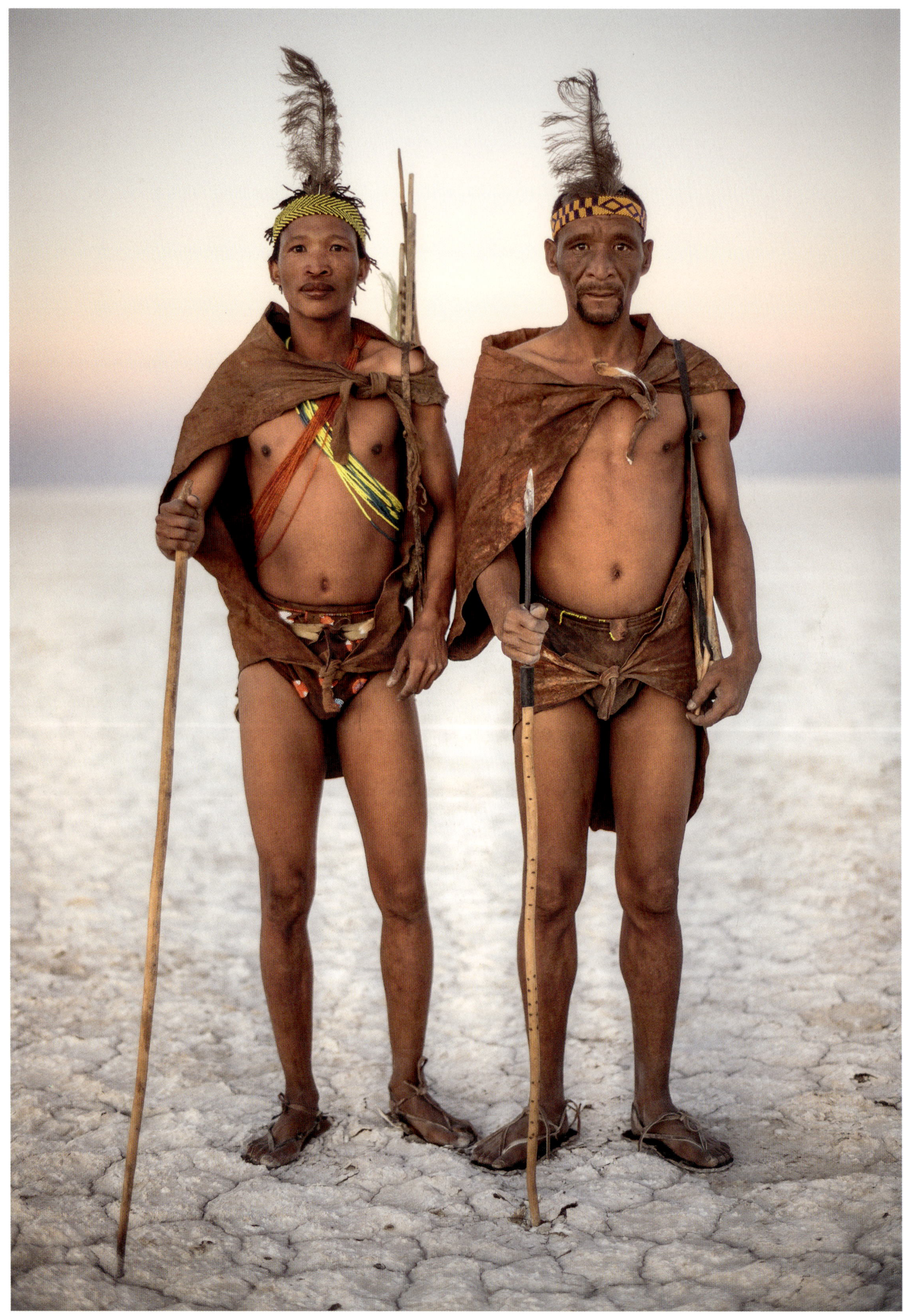

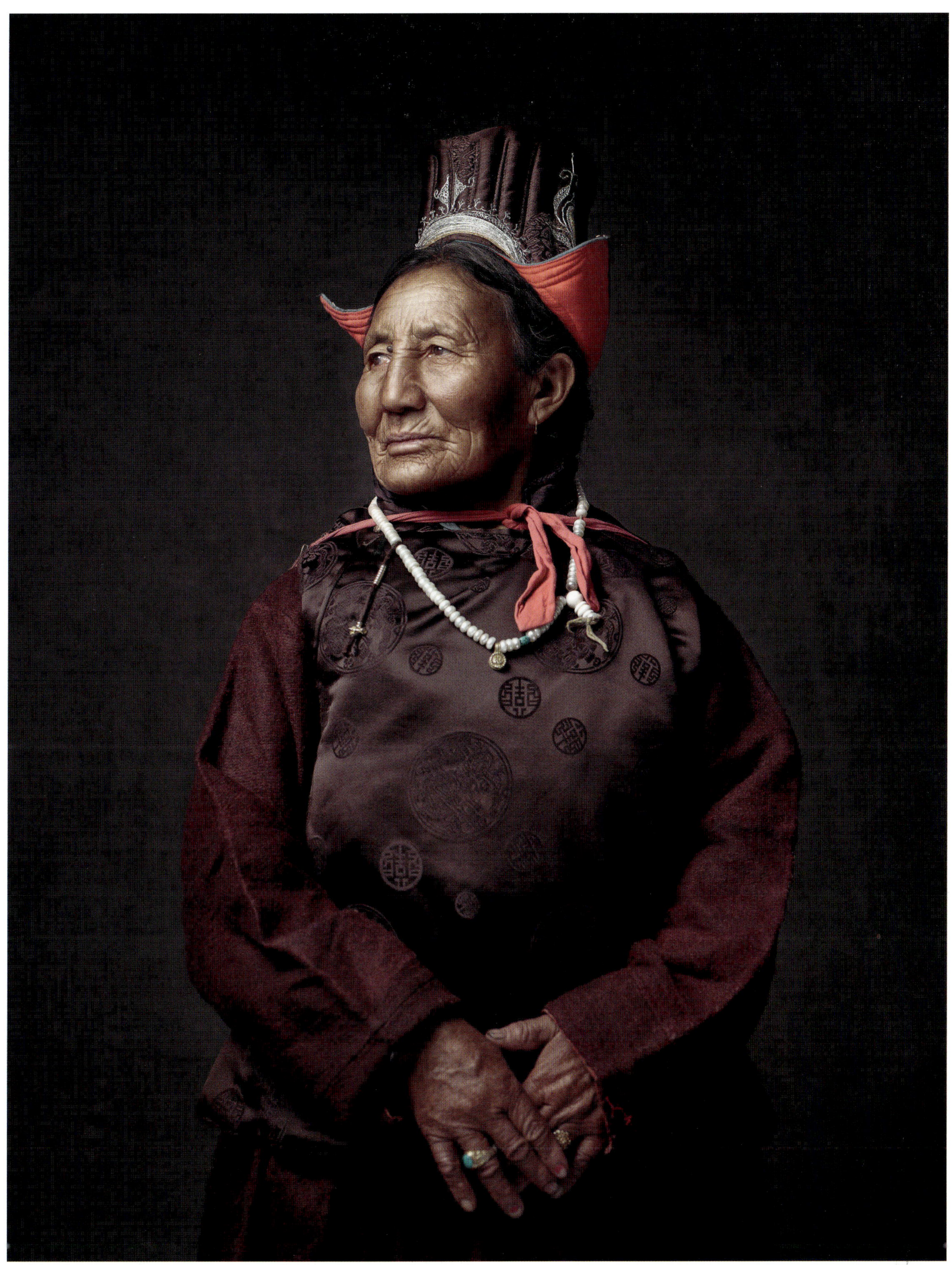

Ladakhi elder, India. **OPPOSITE:** Xoma Xkgao (left) and Xoma Xwii (right), Botswana.
FOLLOWING: Honey hunting, the practice of harvesting Himalayan beehives for their honey on the steep, overhung cliffs of the lowland jungles, Nepal.

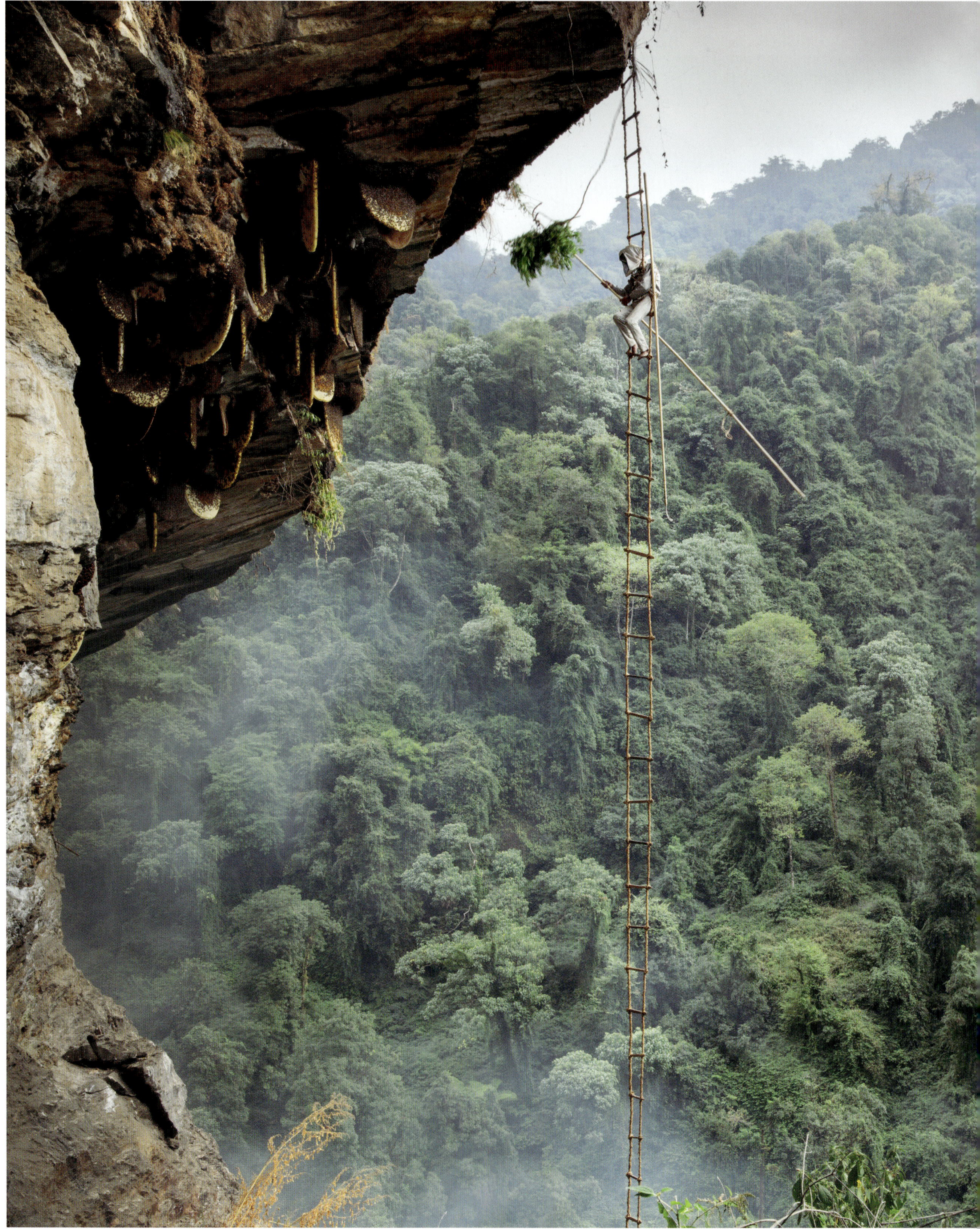

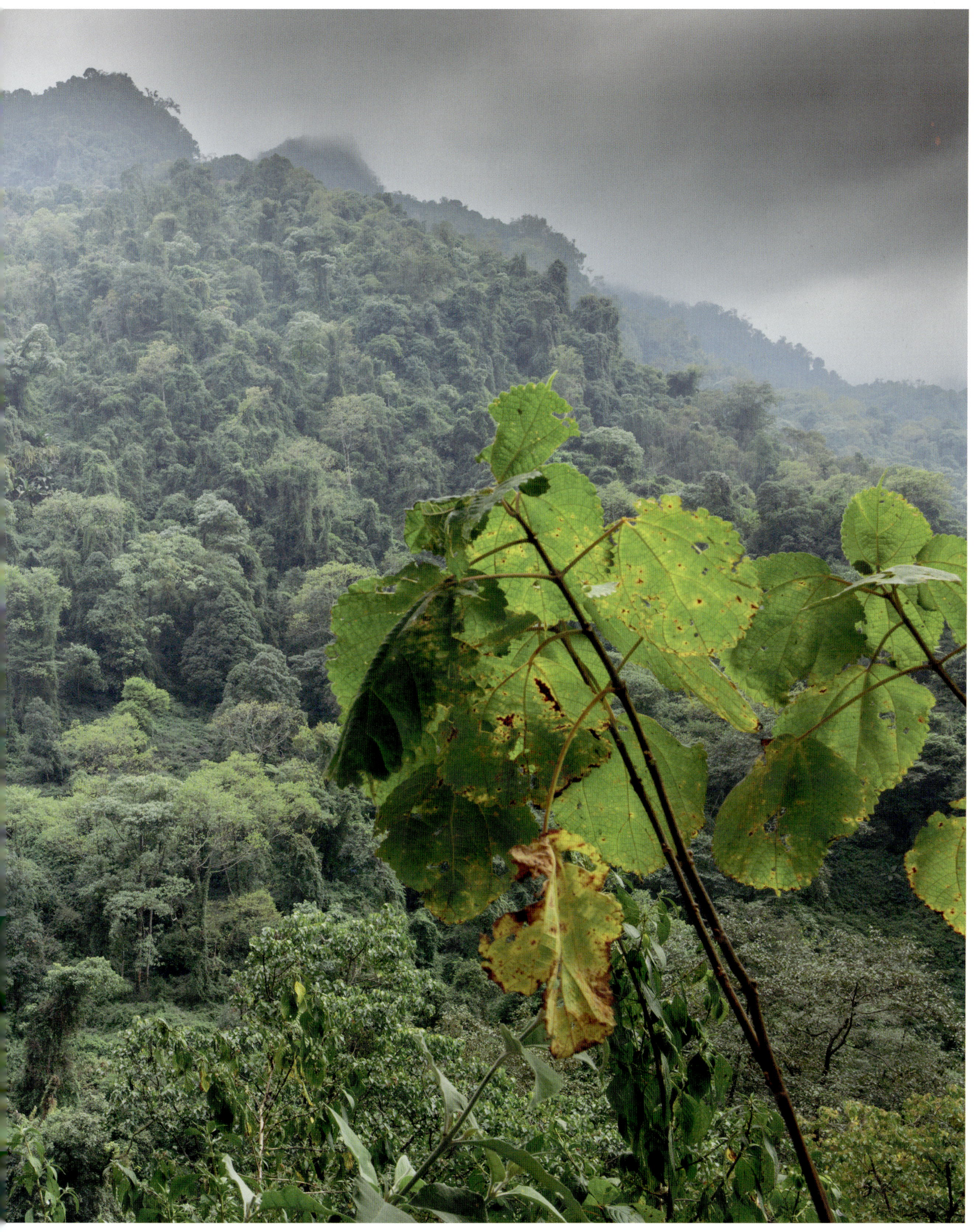

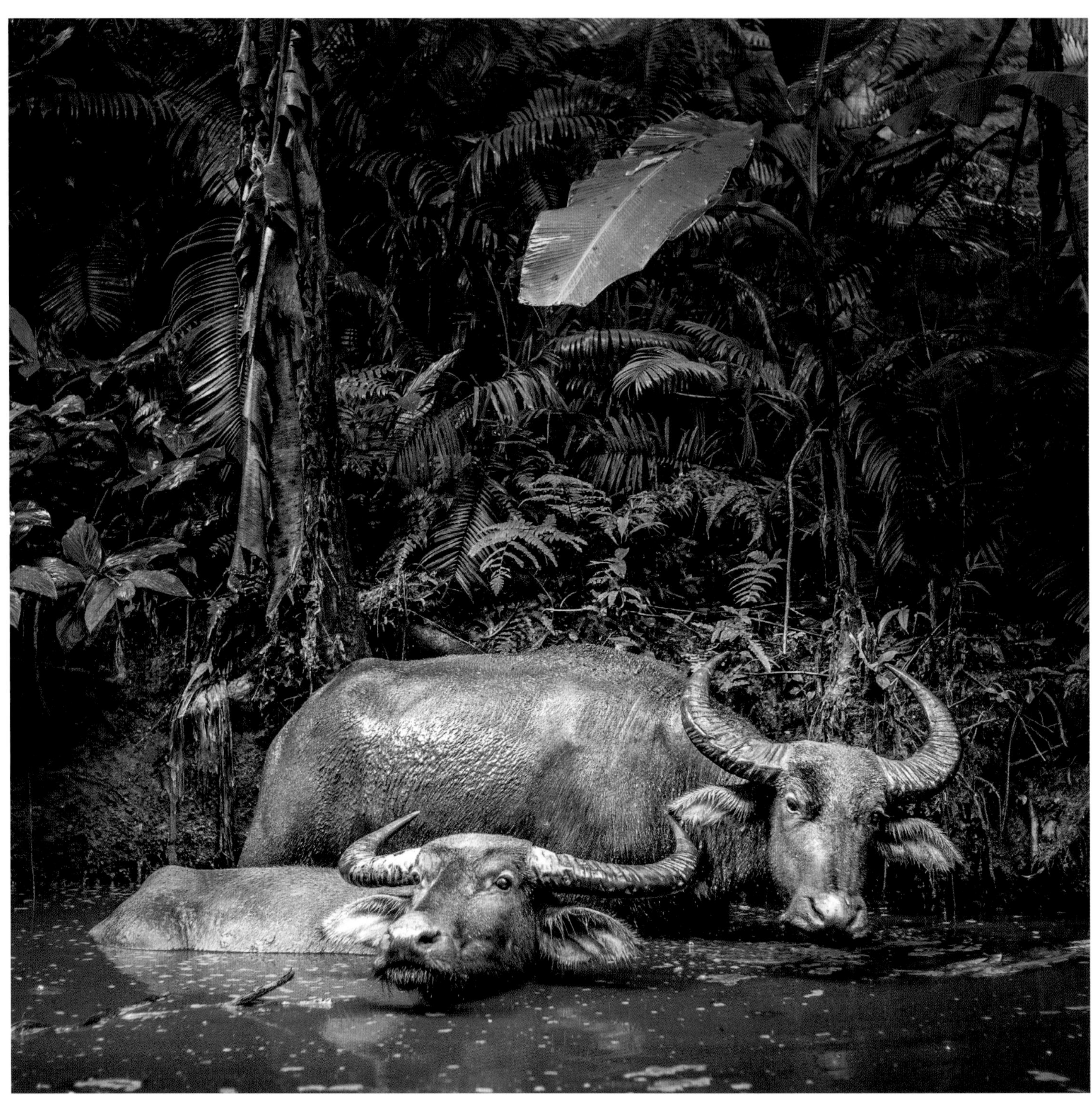

Water buffalo, Myanmar.

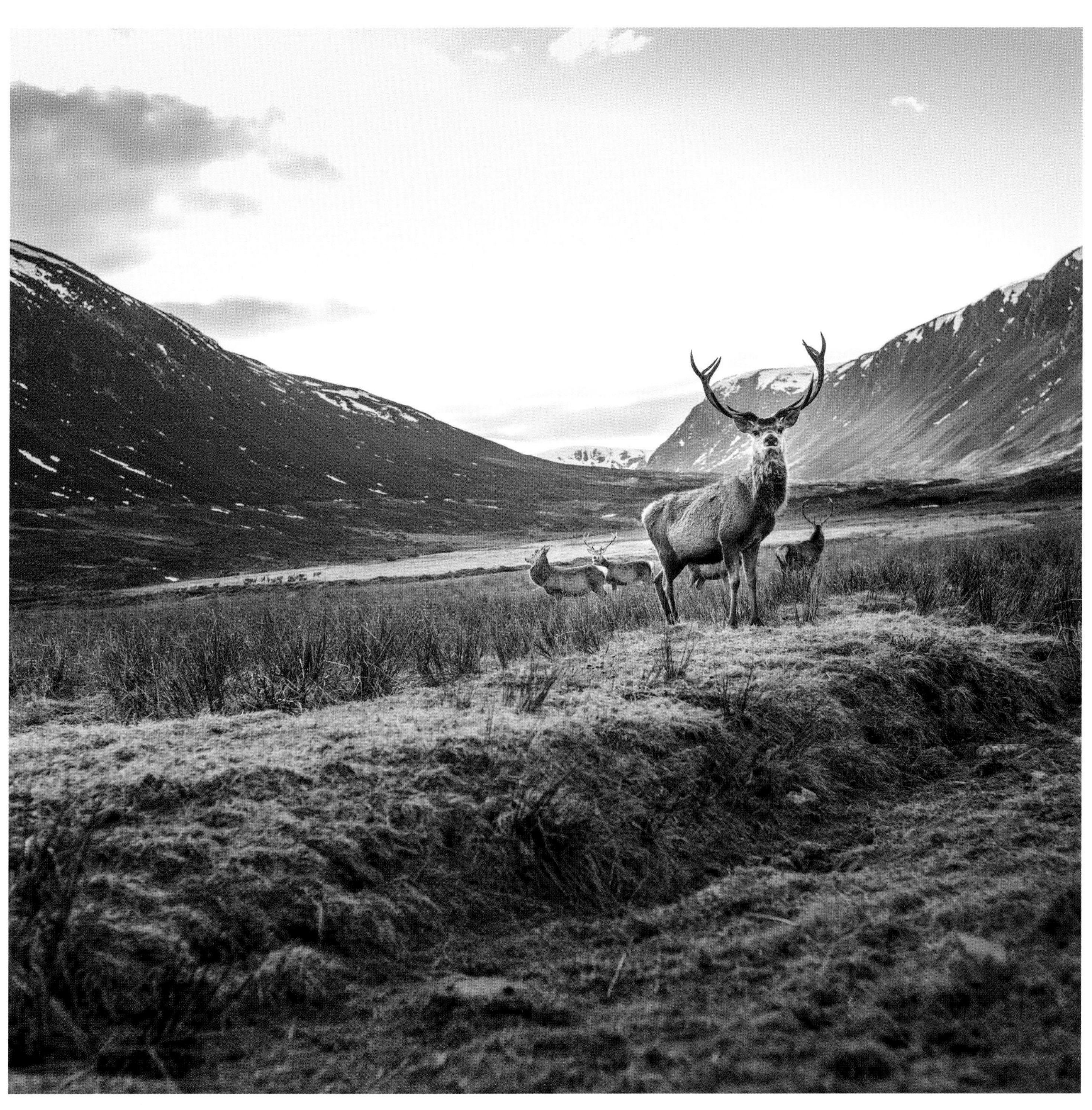

Scottish red deer, Scottish Highlands. **FOLLOWING:** Krenkel Station, Heiss Island, Franz Josef Land, Russia.

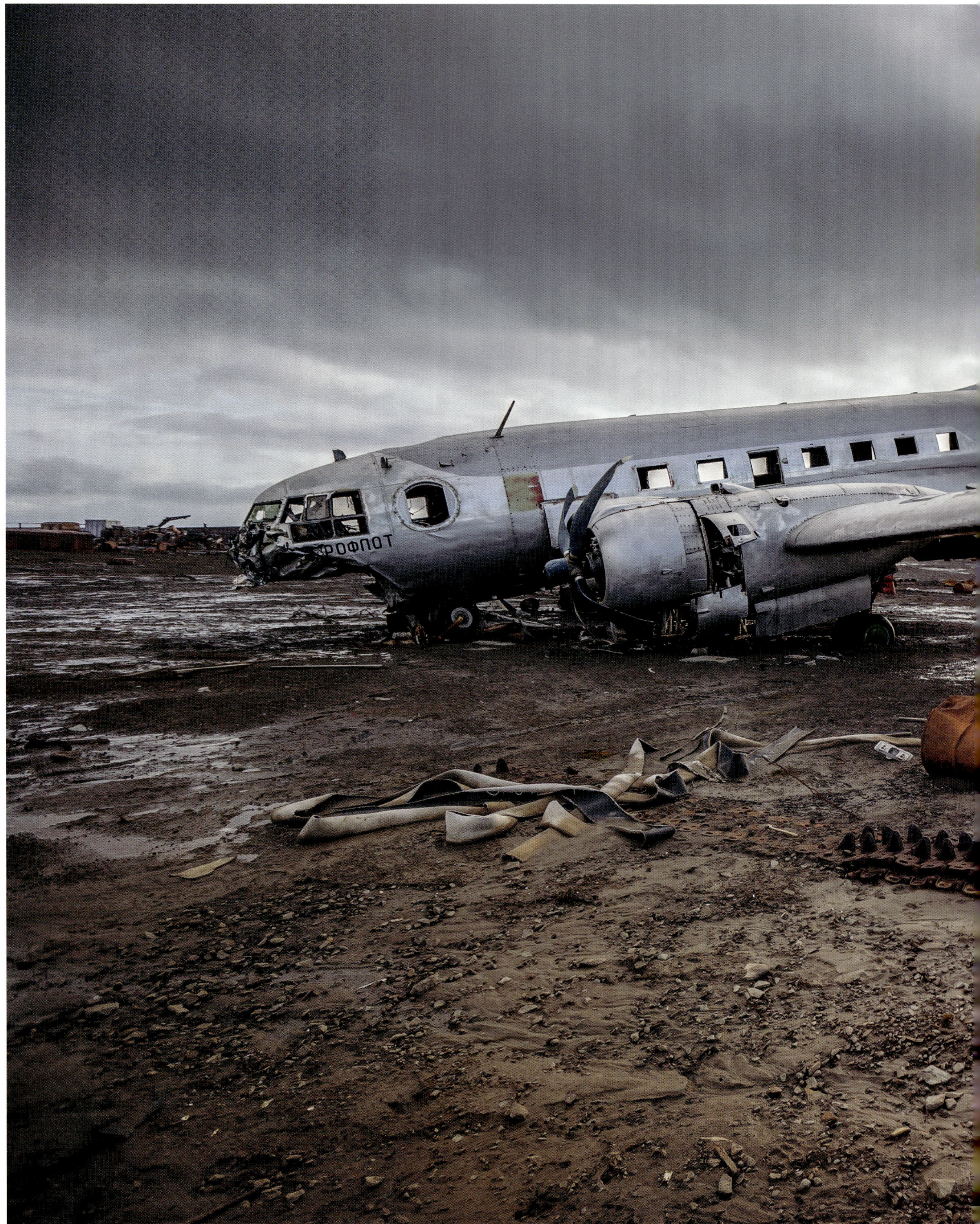
РОФЛОТ

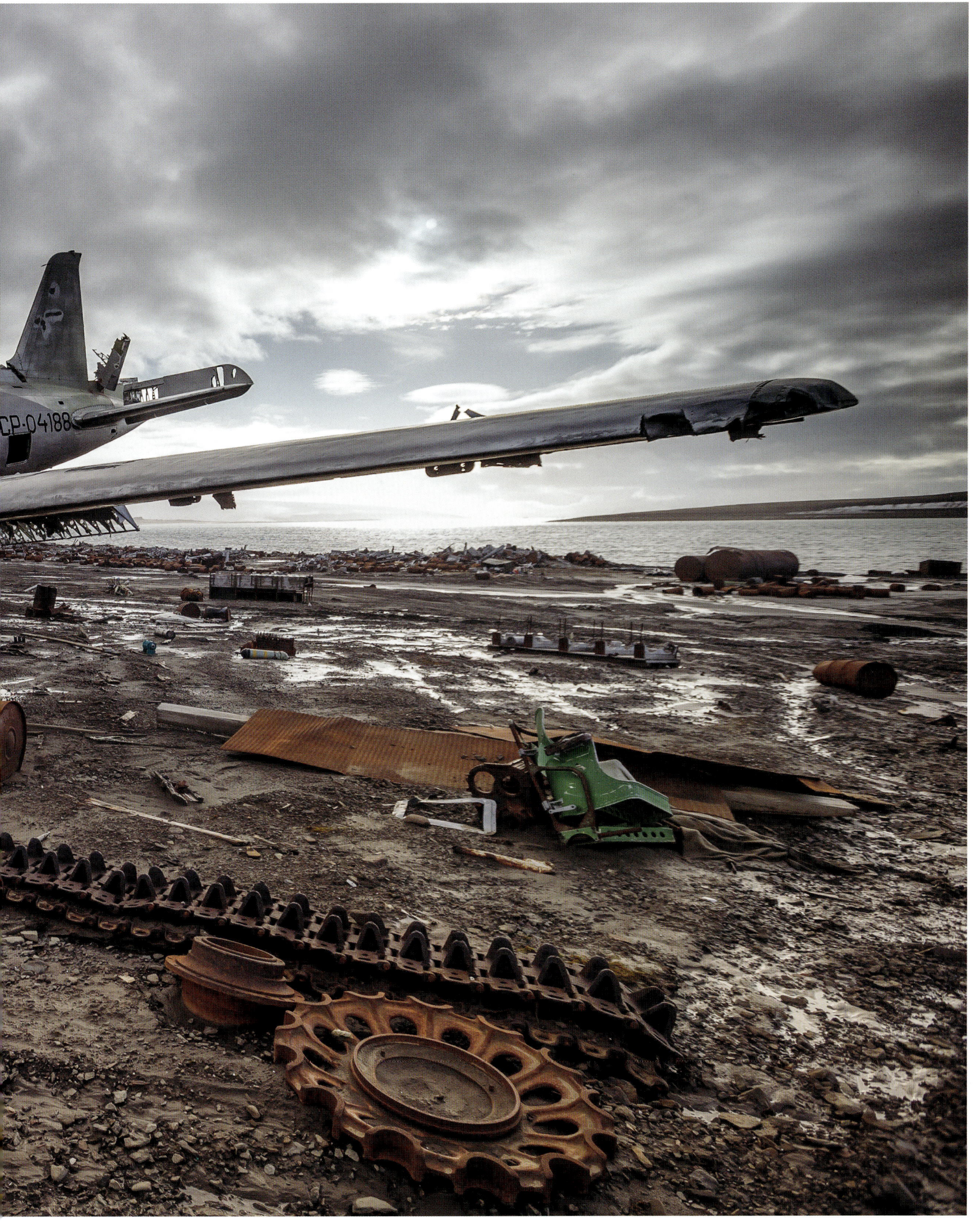

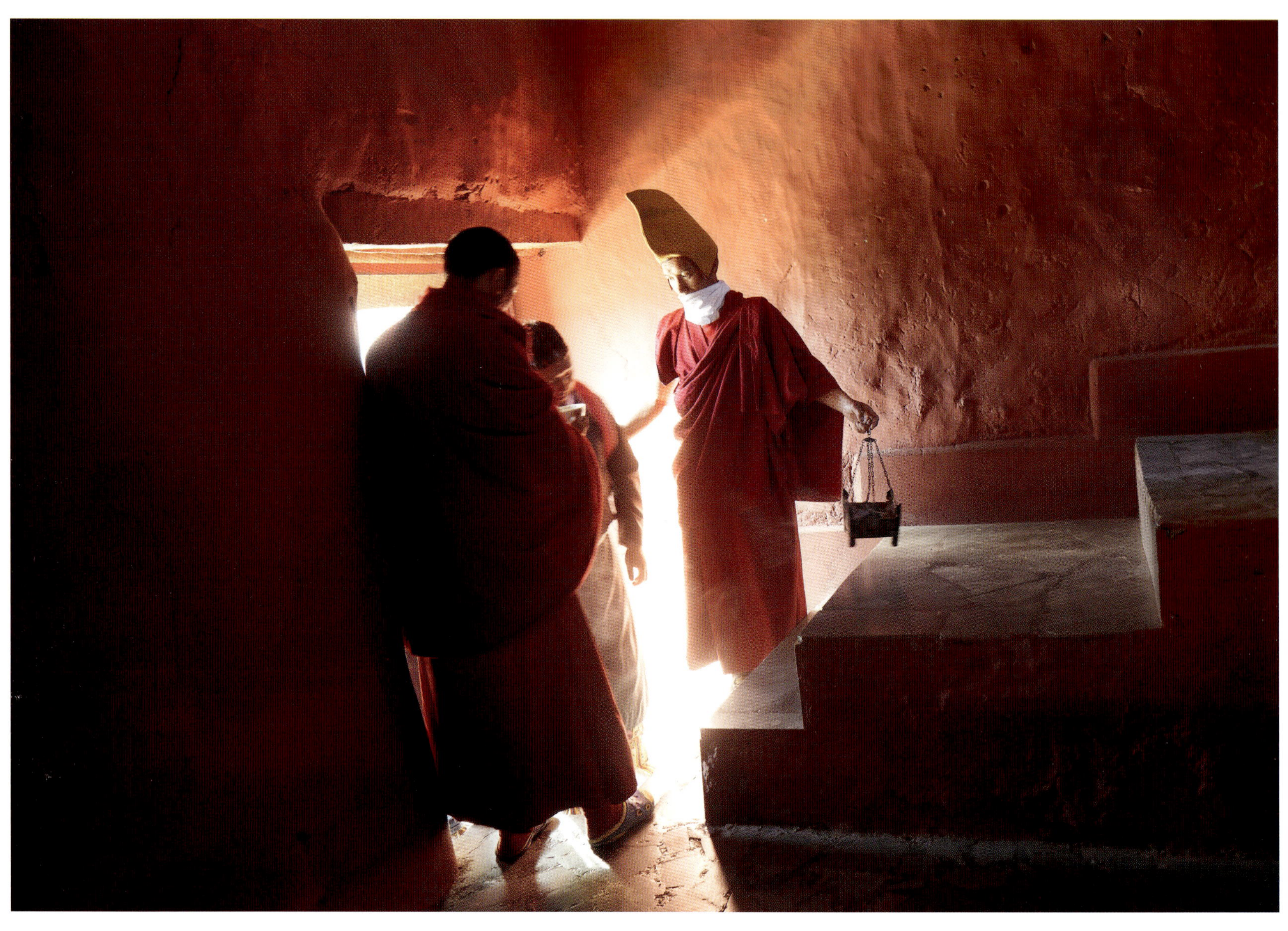

Monks welcome an oracle, Ladakh, India.

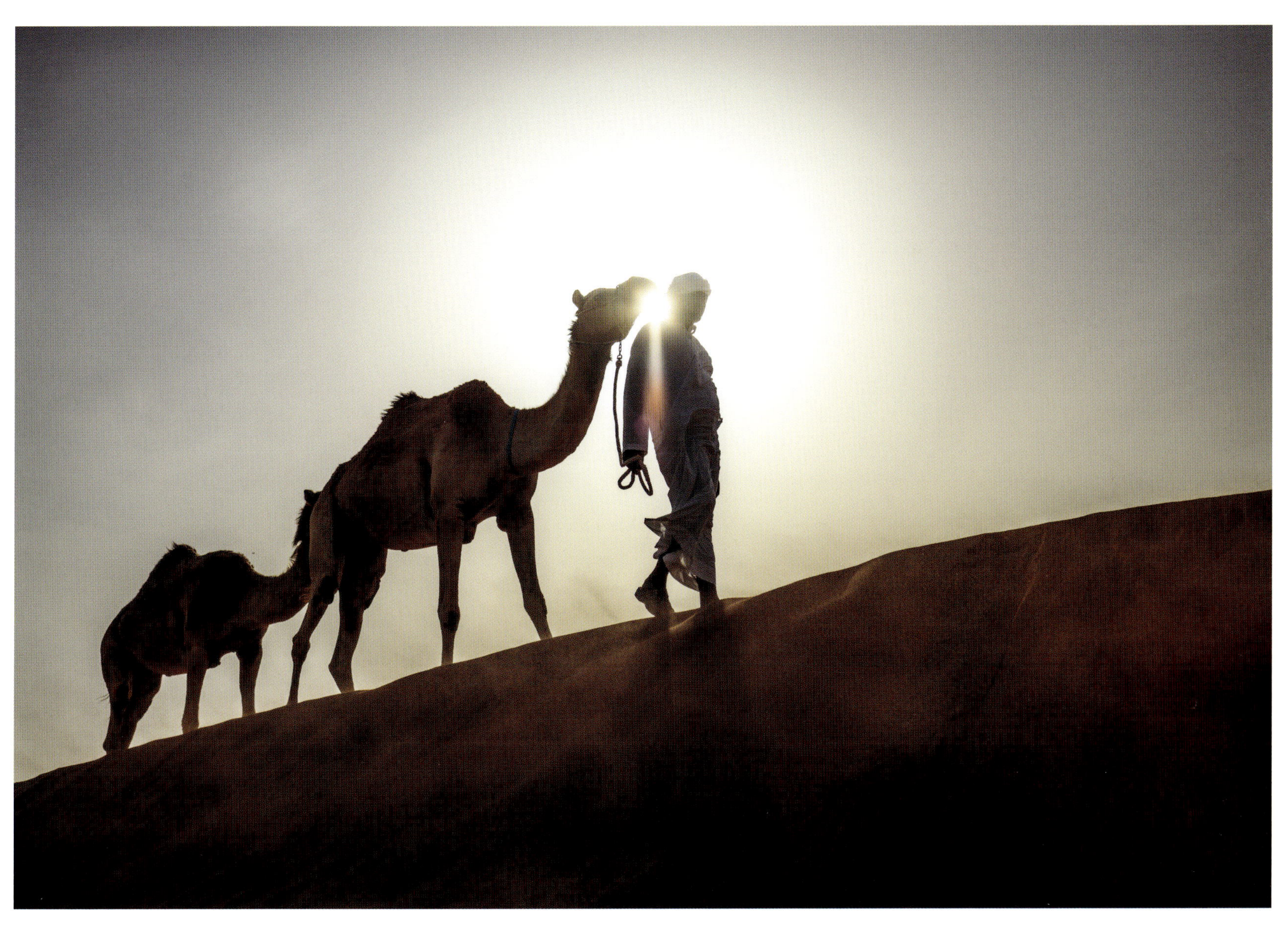

Camels and driver, United Arab Emirates. **FOLLOWING:** Elephant, Uganda.

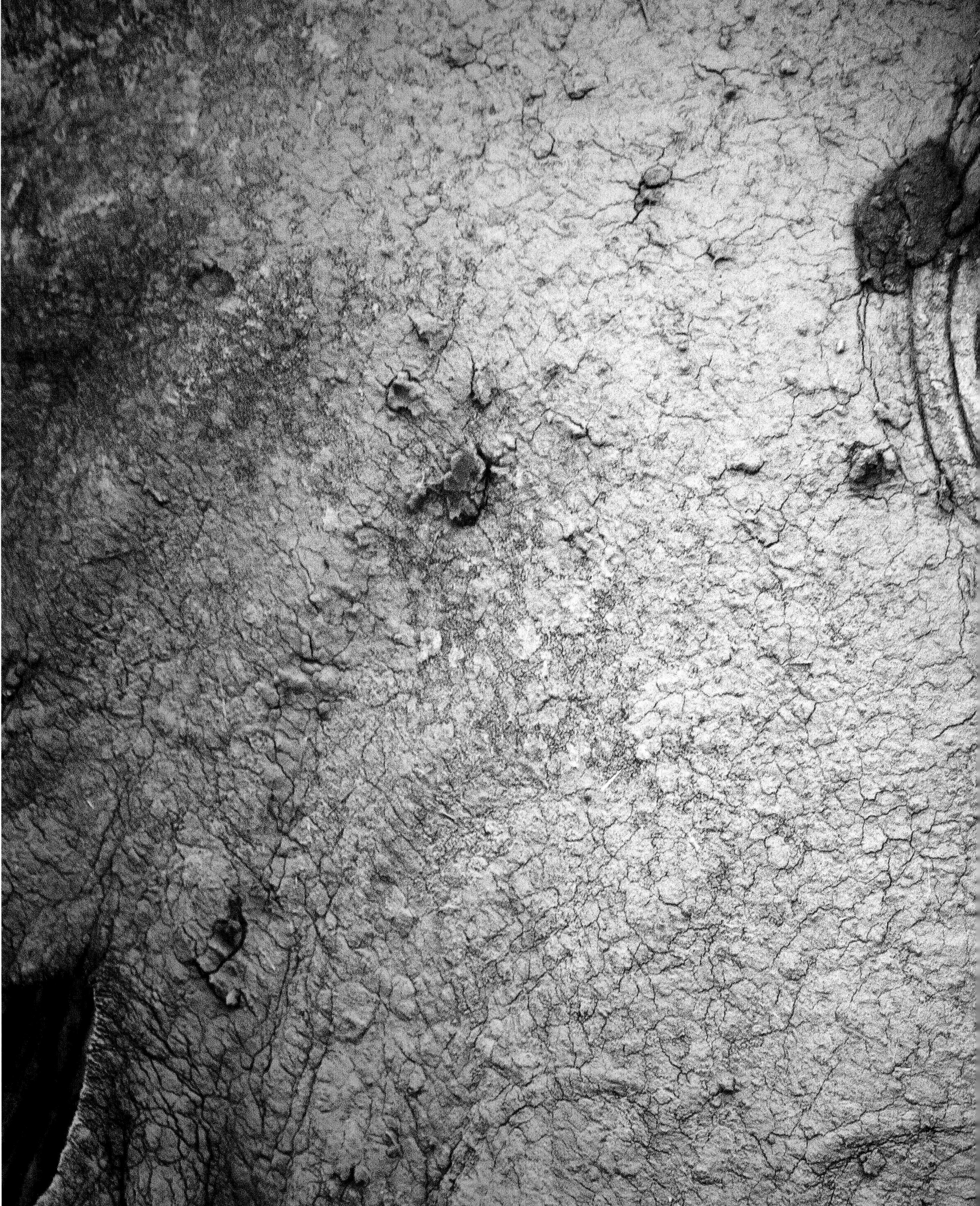

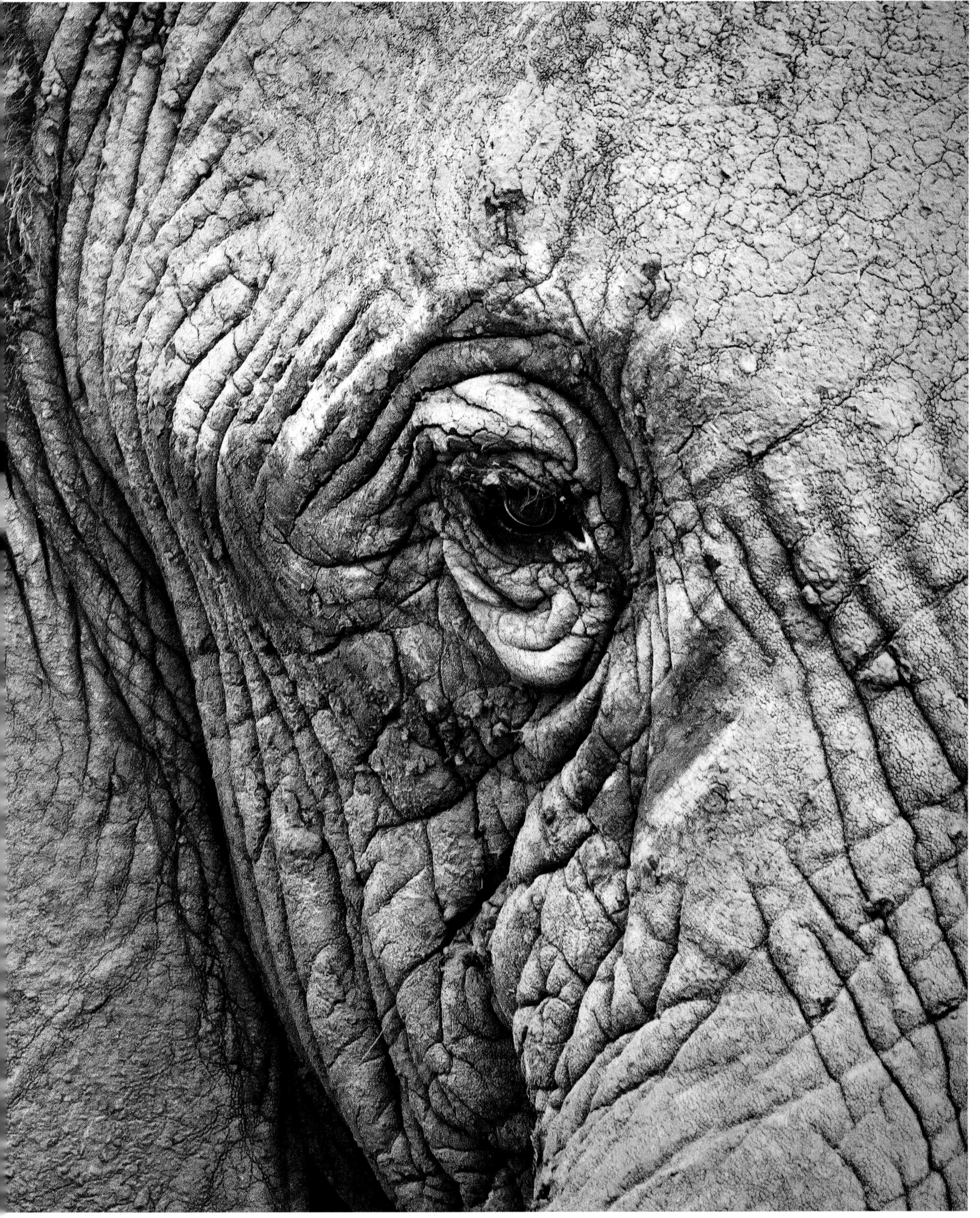

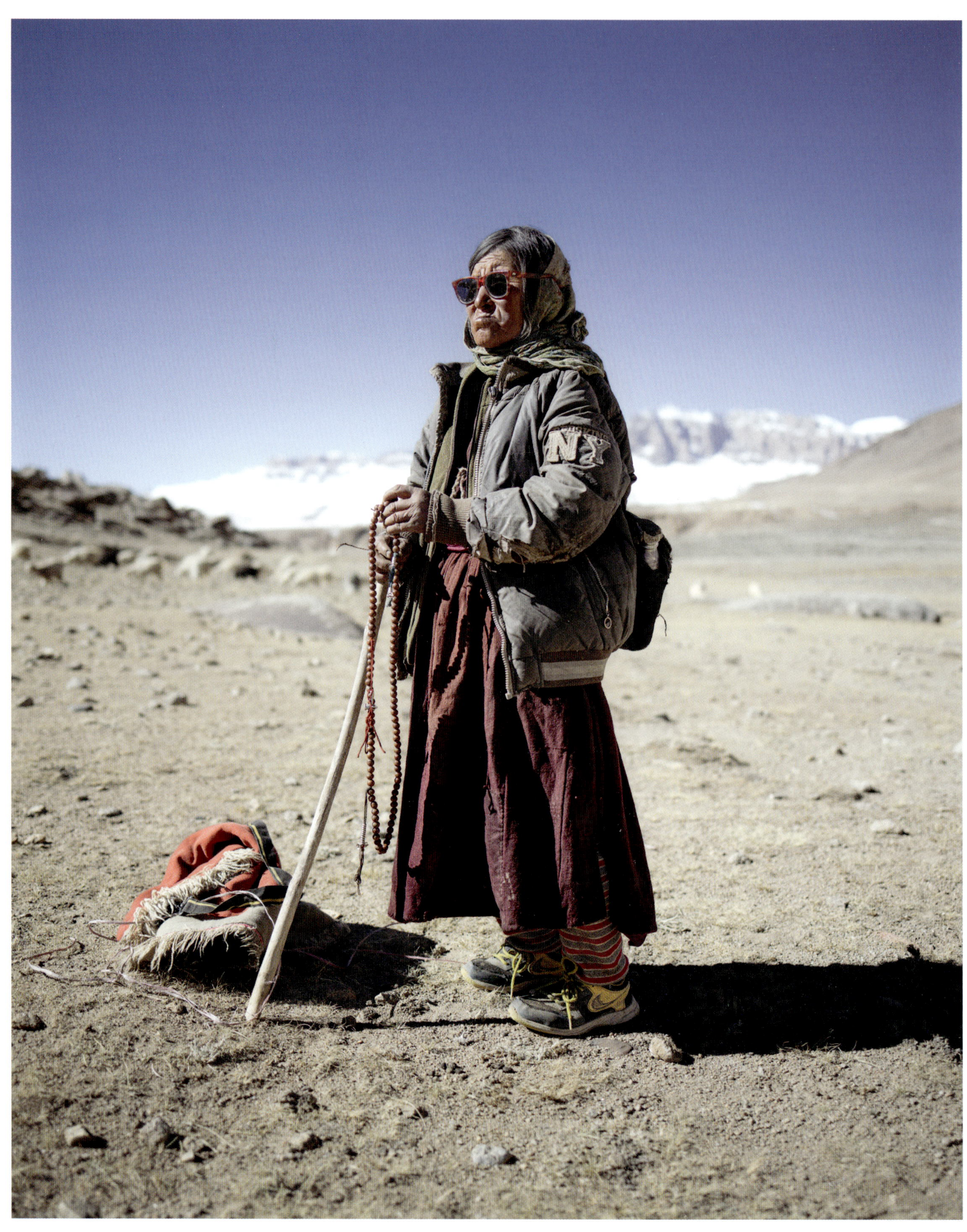

Goat herder, Ladakh, India. **OPPOSITE:** Skin and ink, USA. **FOLLOWING:** Raphael Slawinski, Icefields Parkway, Canadian Rockies.

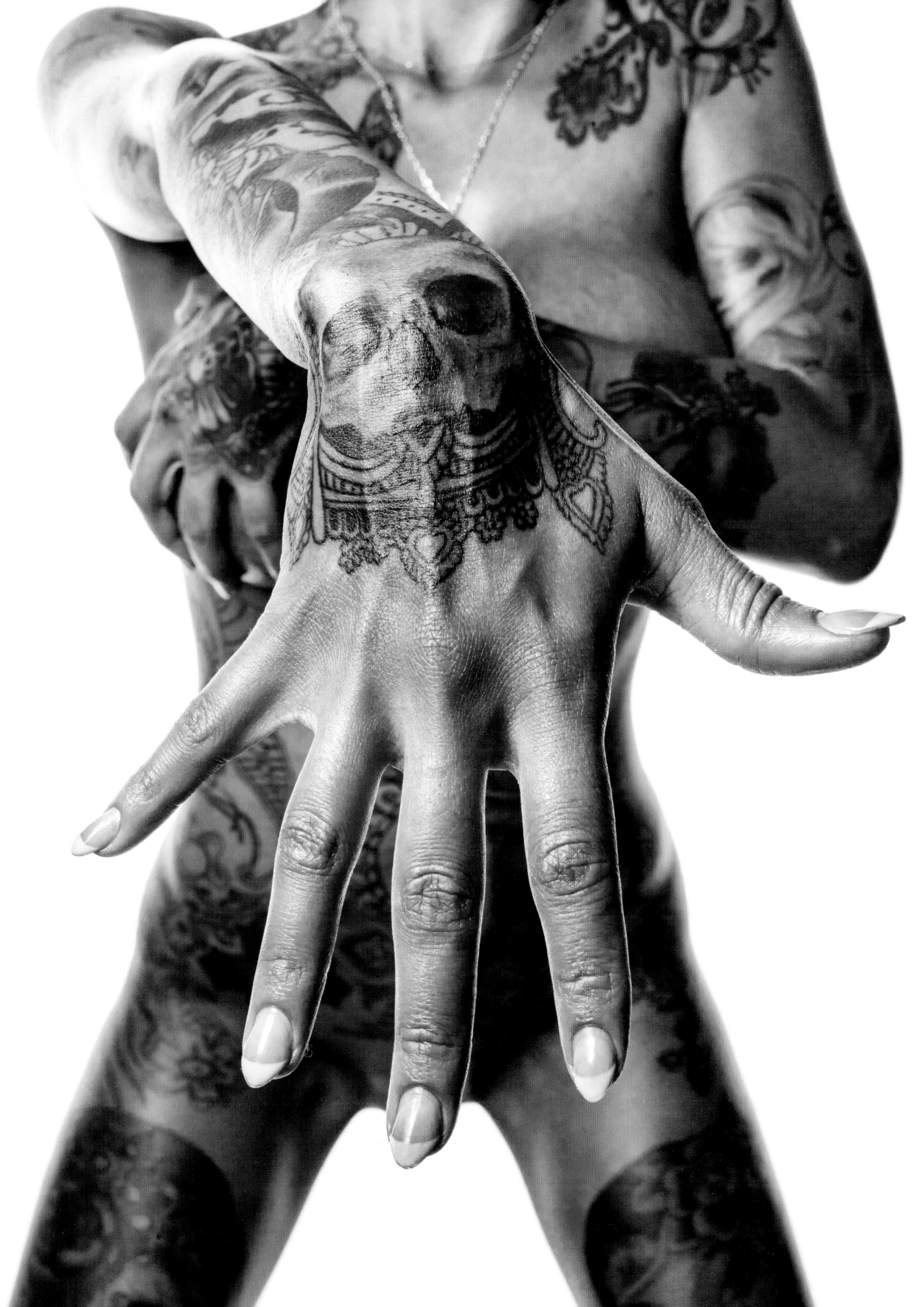

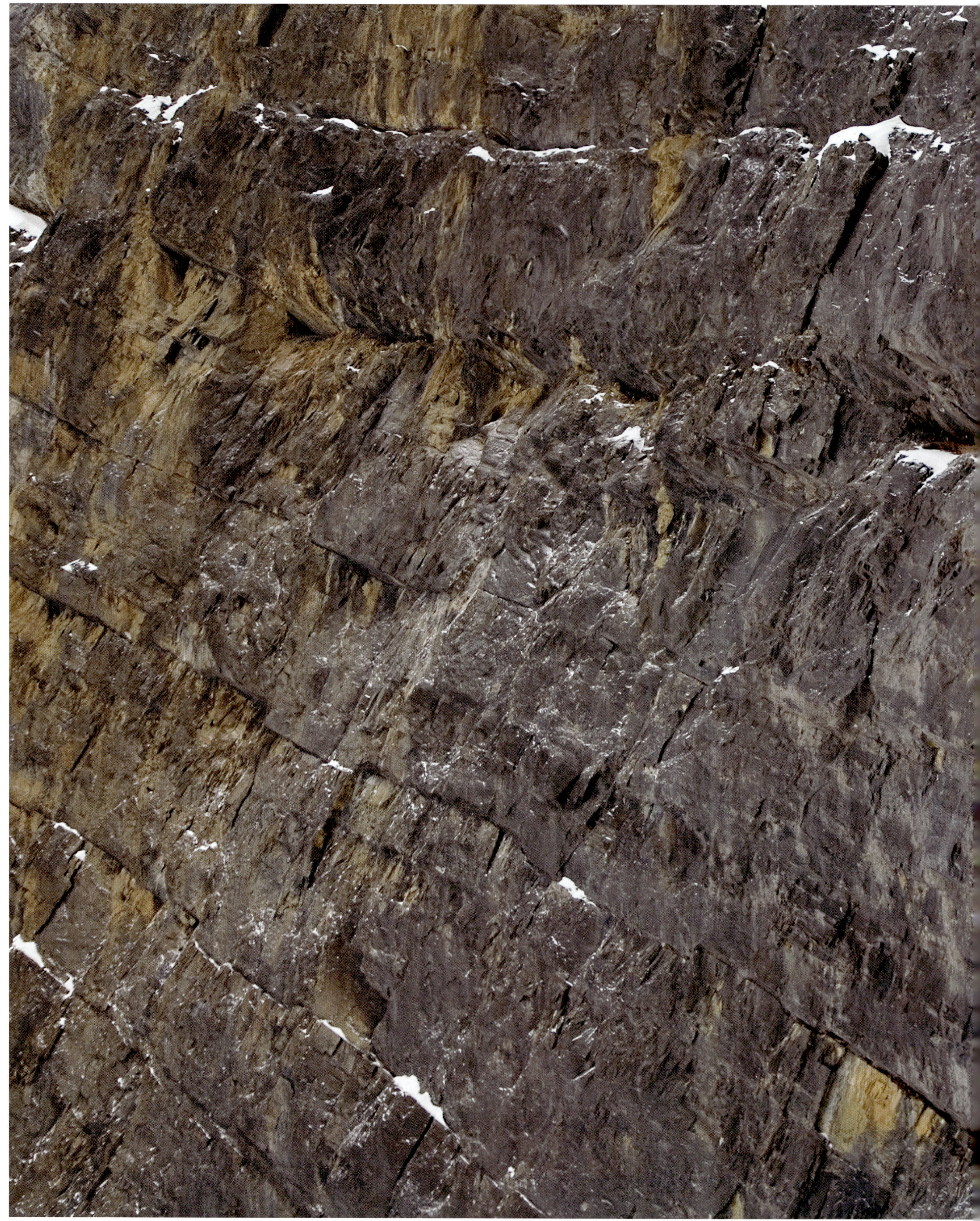

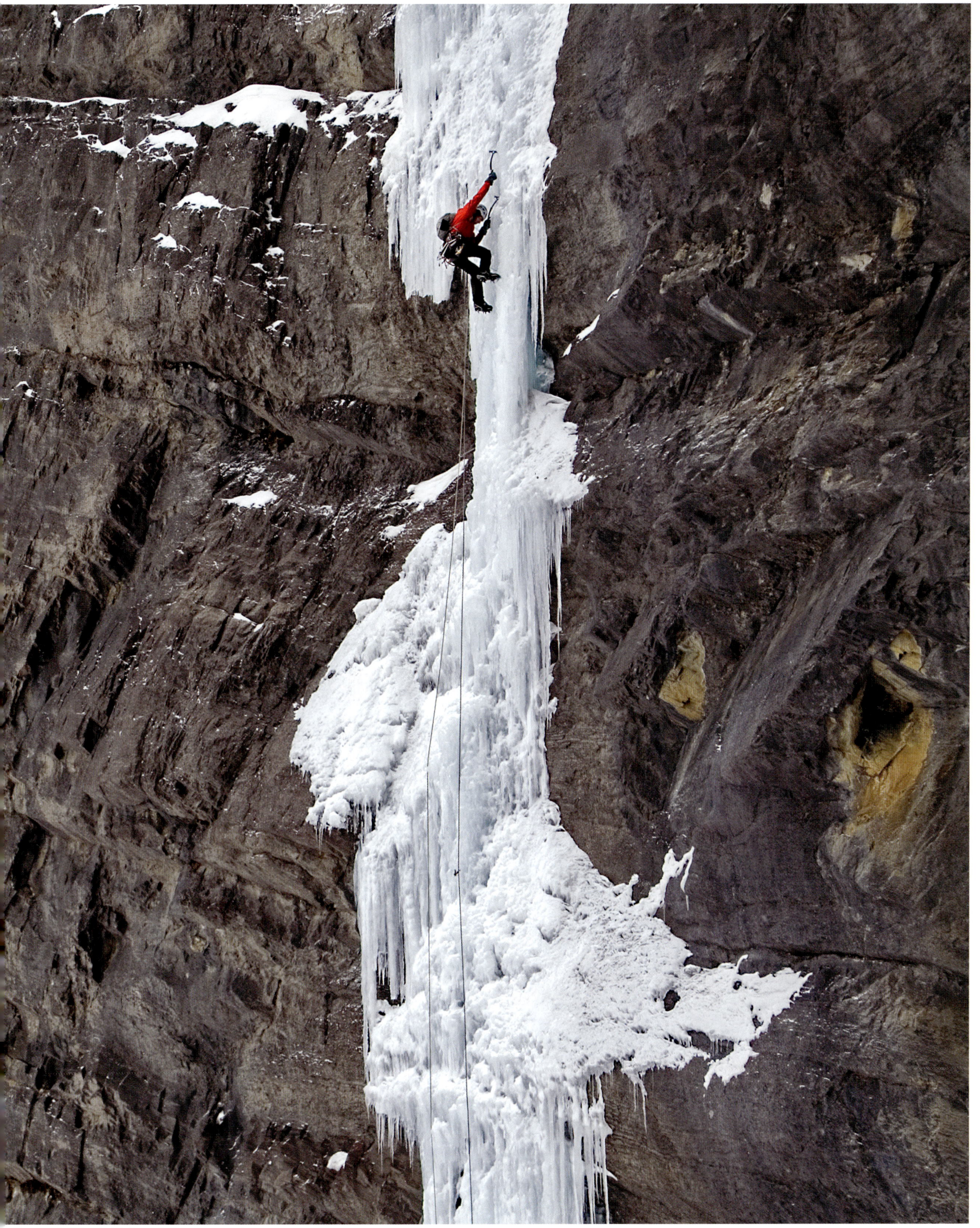

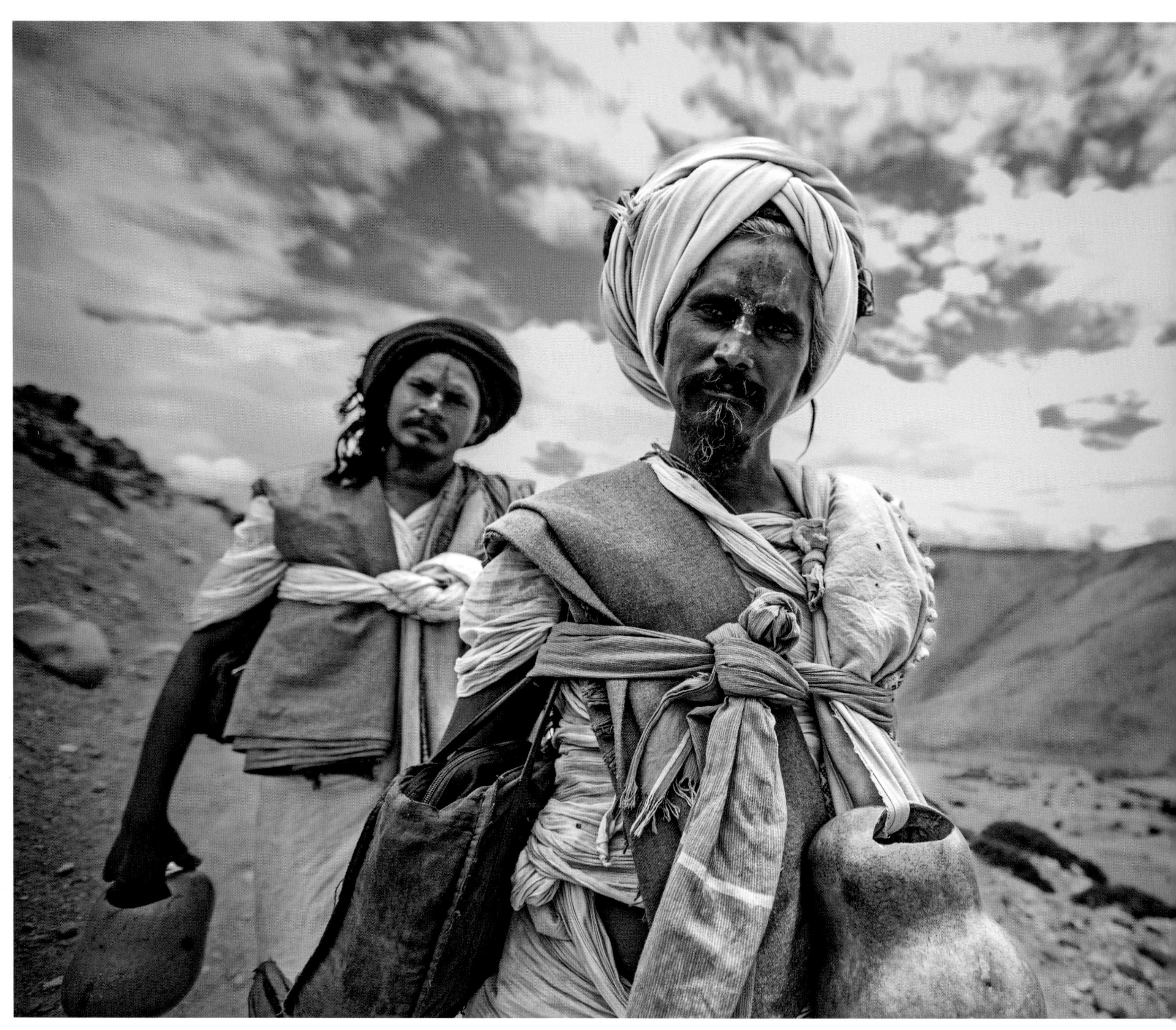

Pilgrims, Mustang, Nepal. **OPPOSITE:** Day laborer's hand, Sri Lanka. **FOLLOWING:** Prayer and food, Mustang, Nepal.

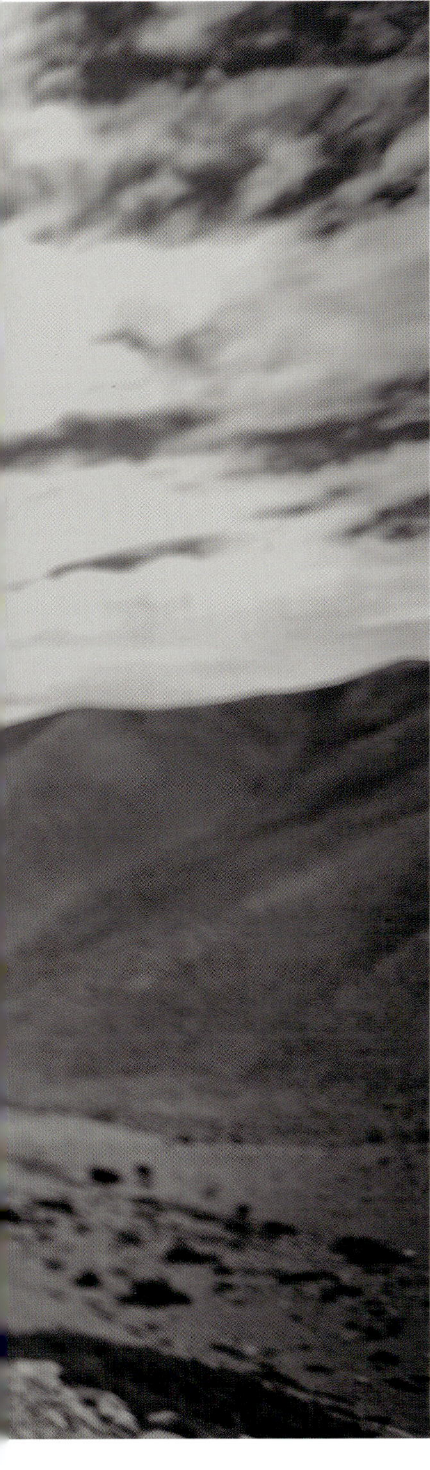

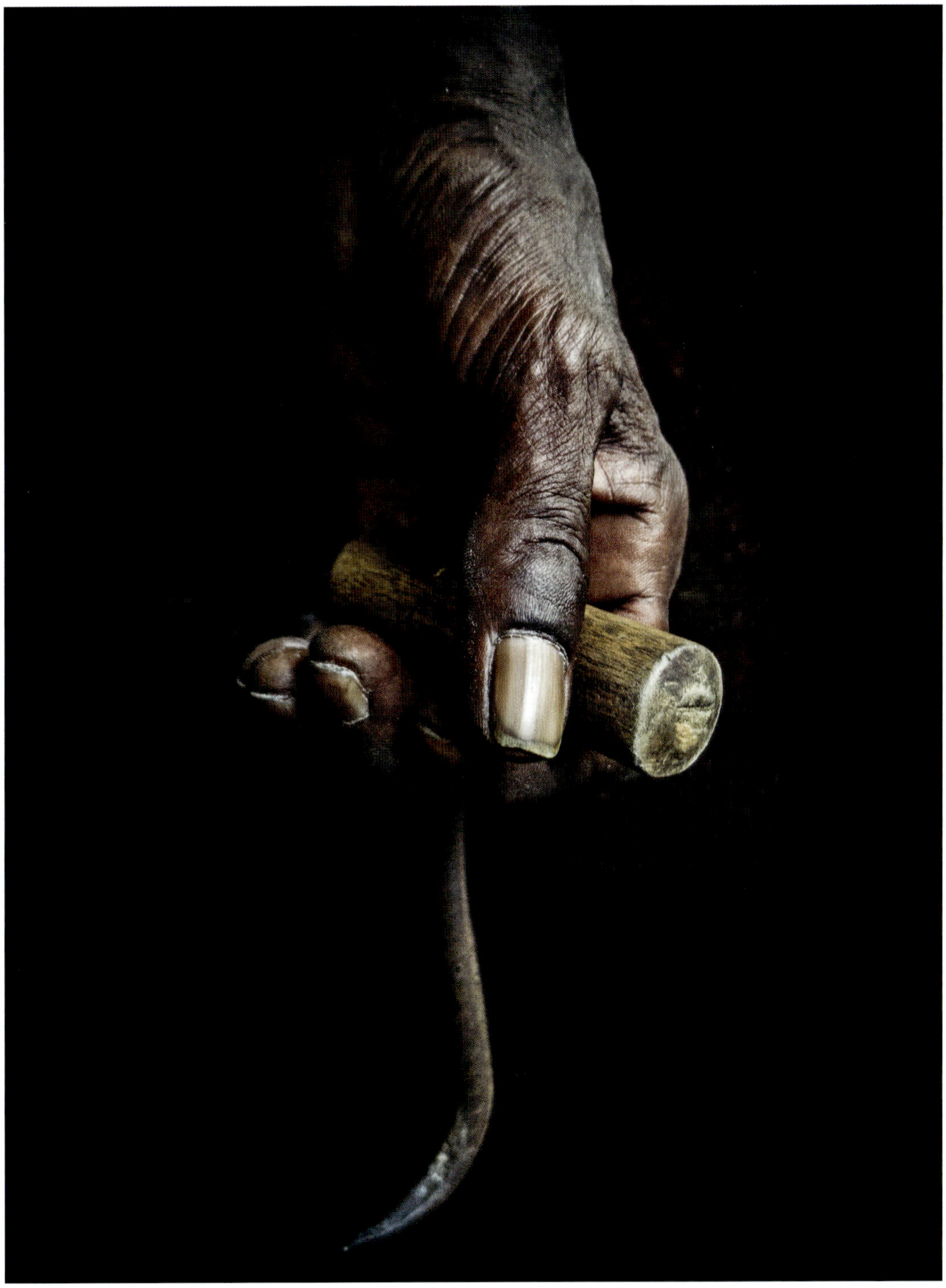

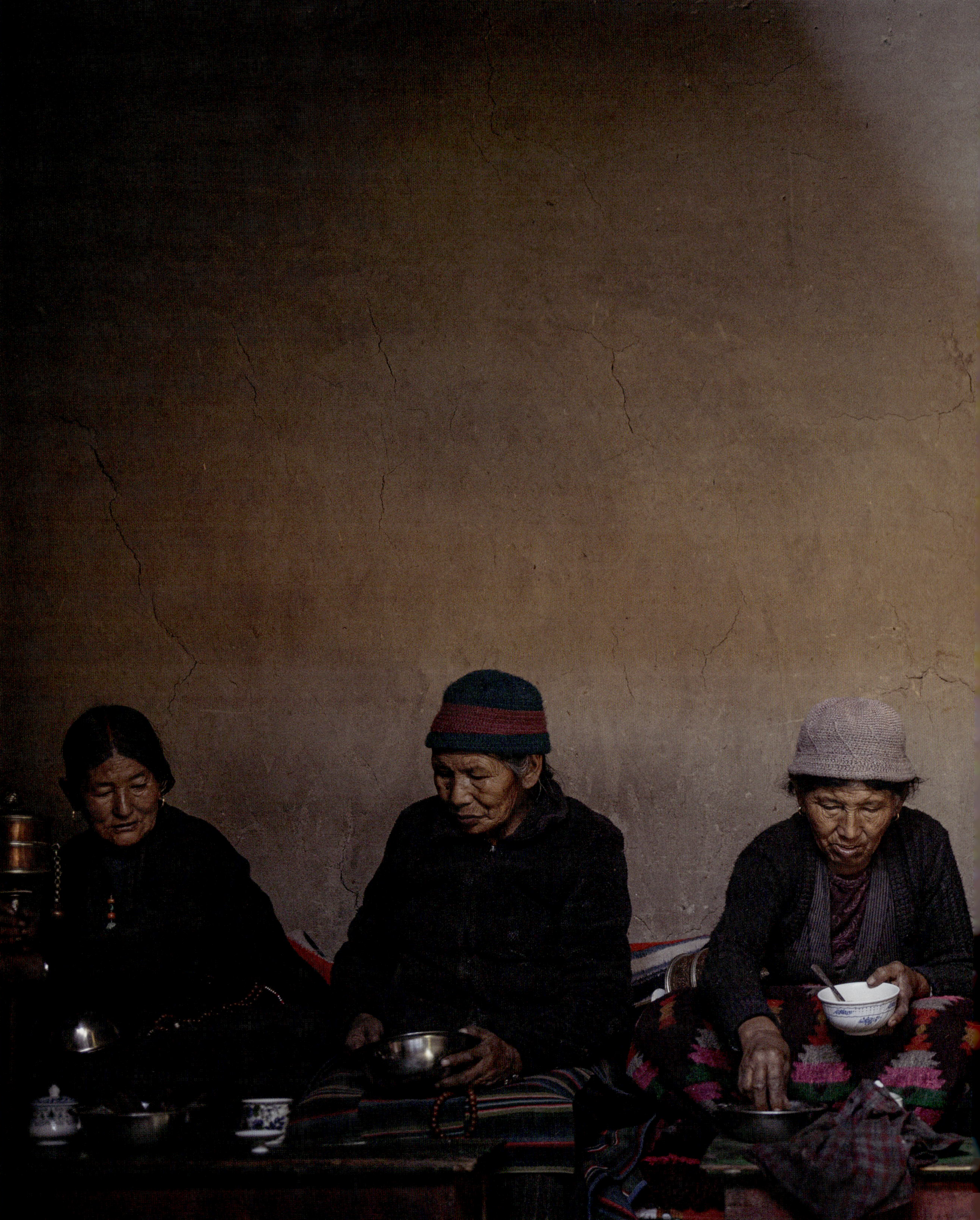

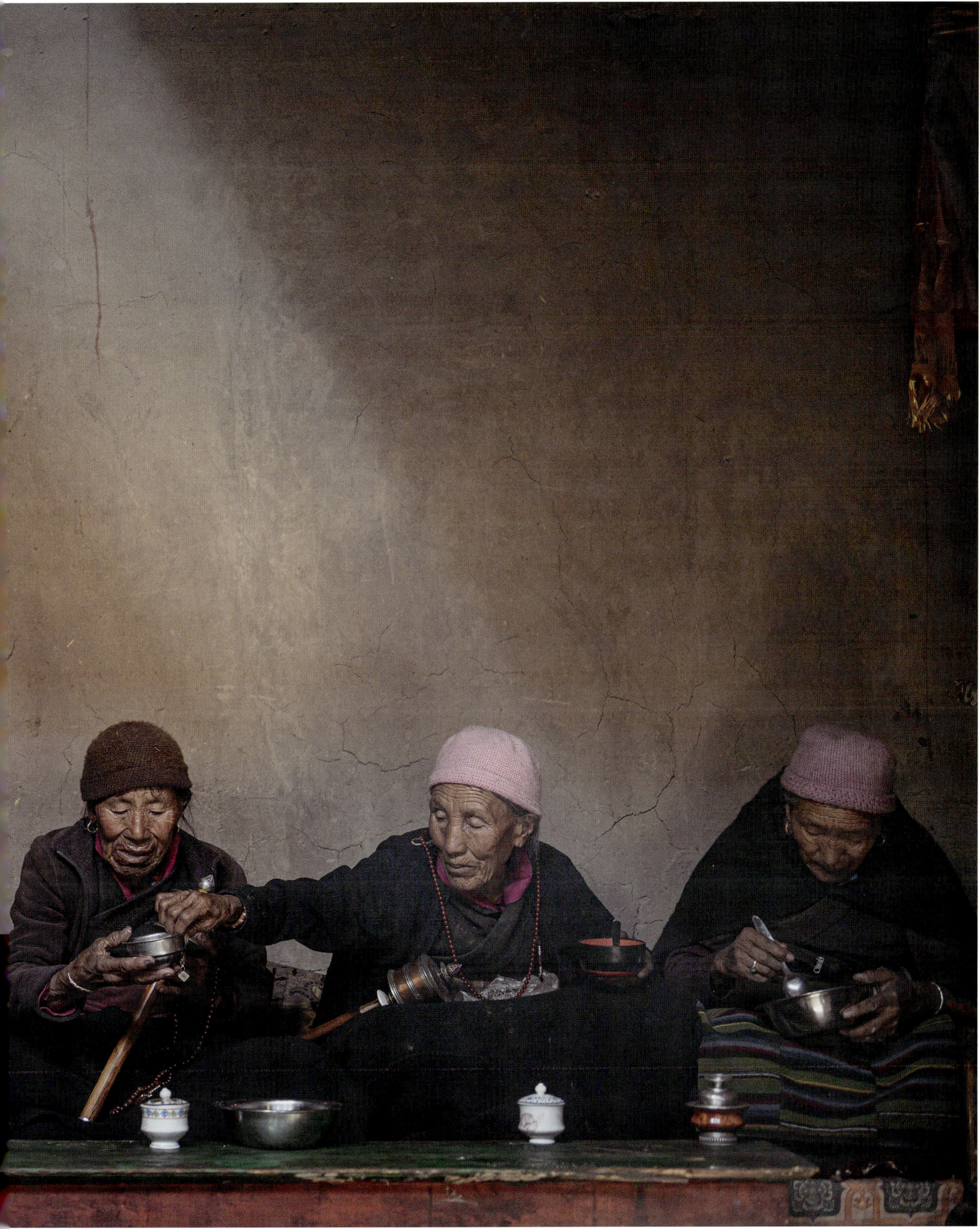

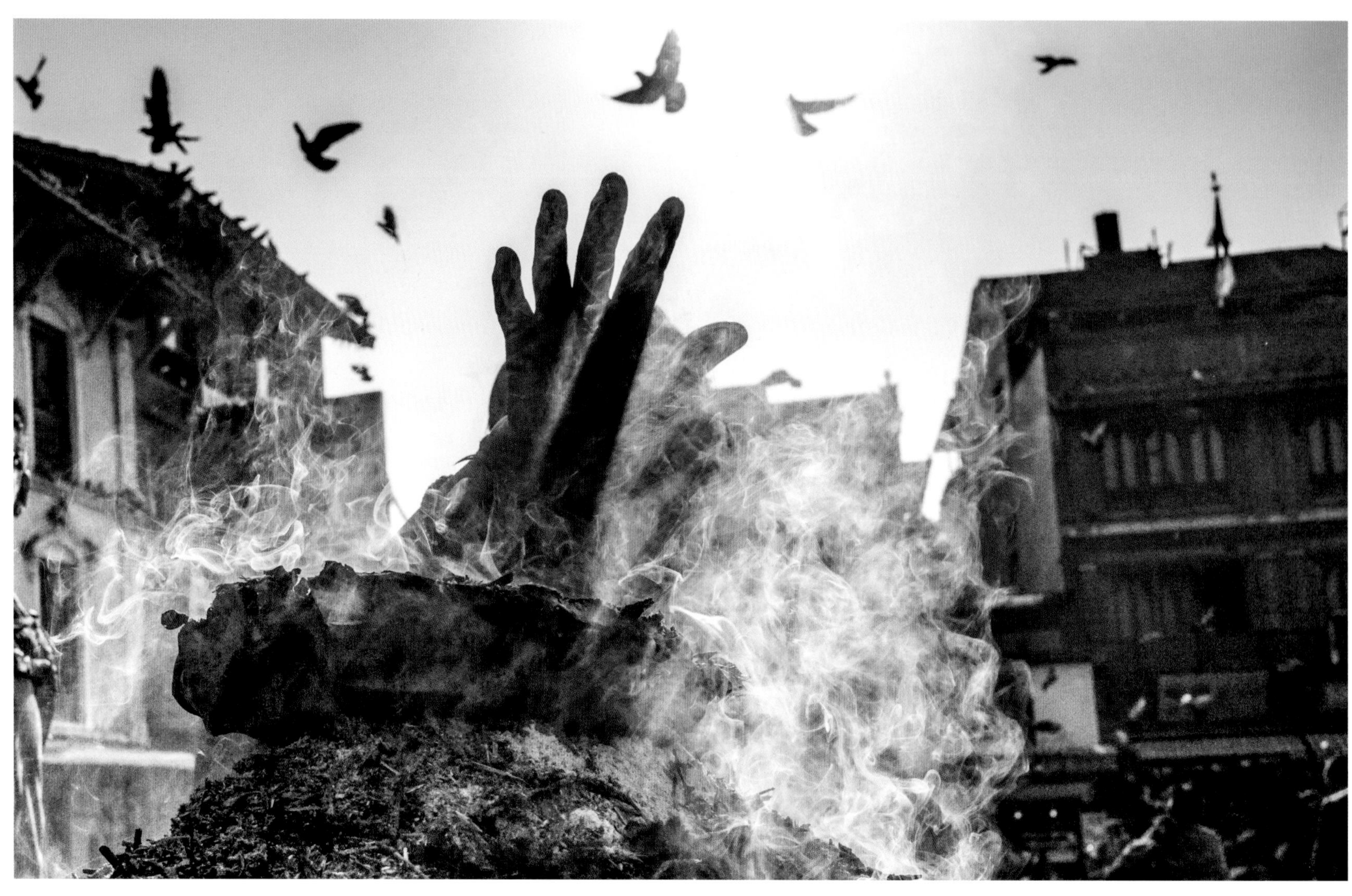

Juniper smoke and faith, Boudhanath, Nepal.

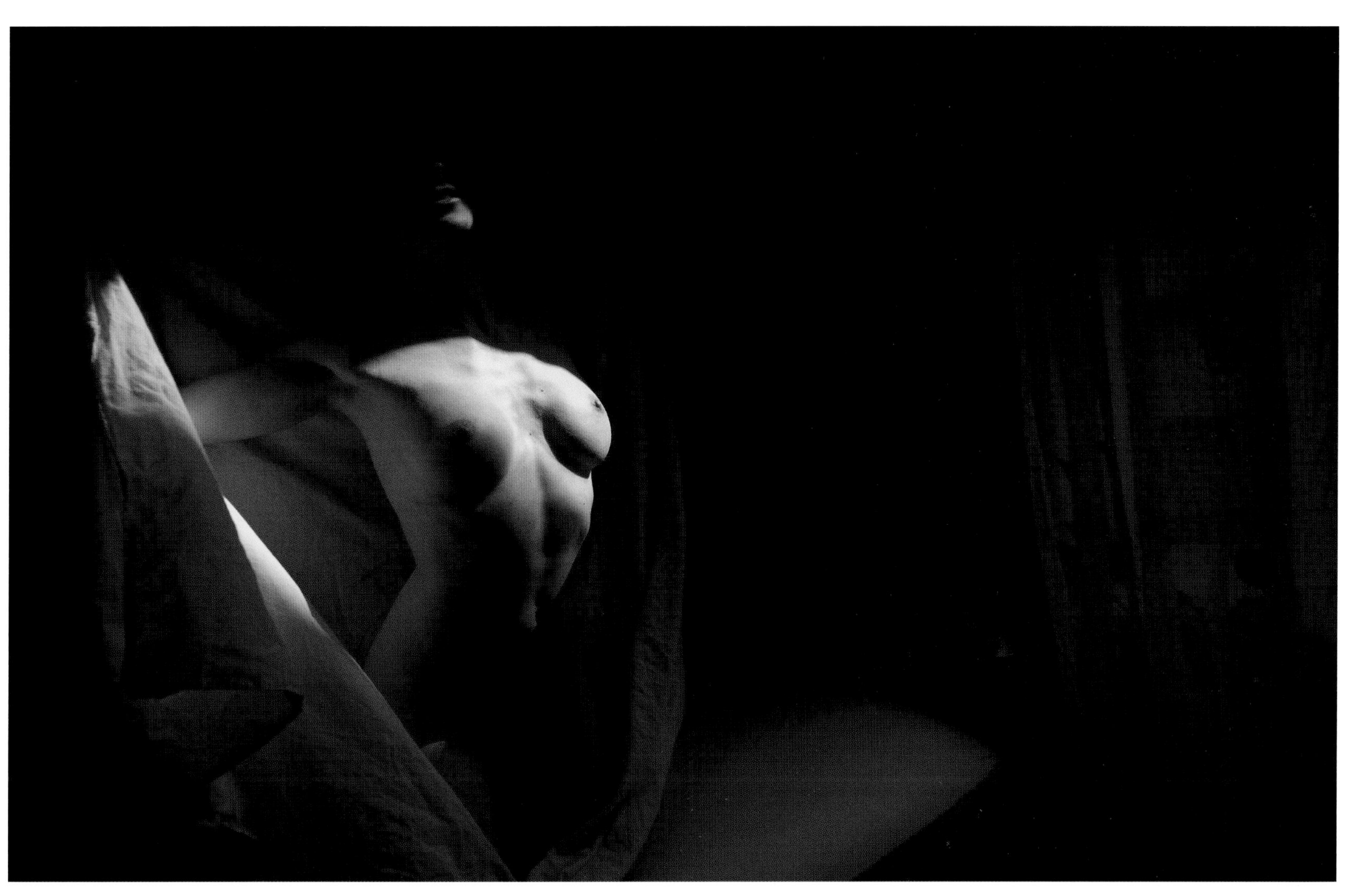

Light and form, Manhattan, New York. **FOLLOWING:** Amony, a former child soldier, on the border of Uganda and South Sudan. **PAGES 312–313:** Stilt fisherman, Sri Lanka. **PAGES 314–315:** Polar bear, Russian Arctic. **PAGES 316–317:** Nepali children, Mustang.

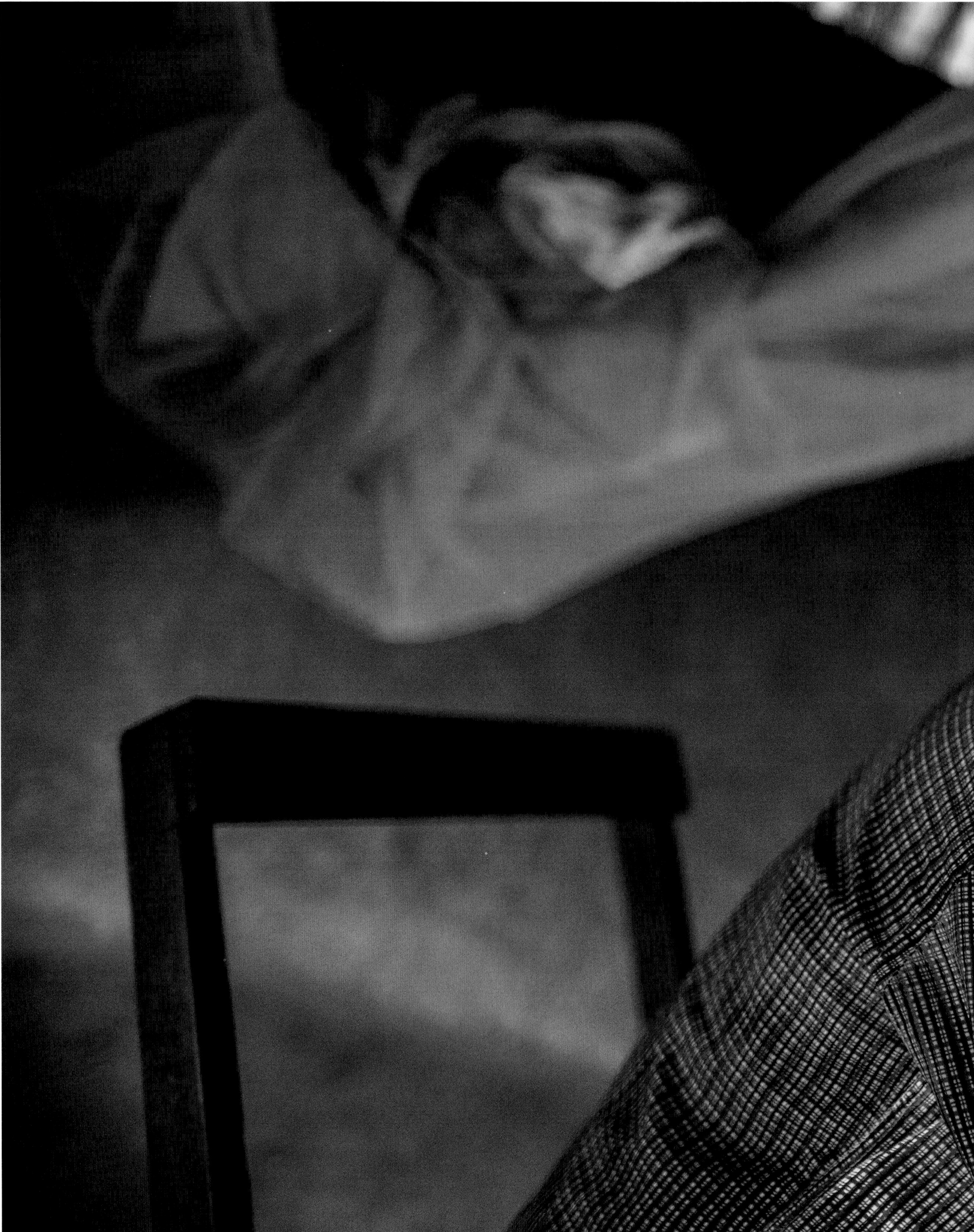

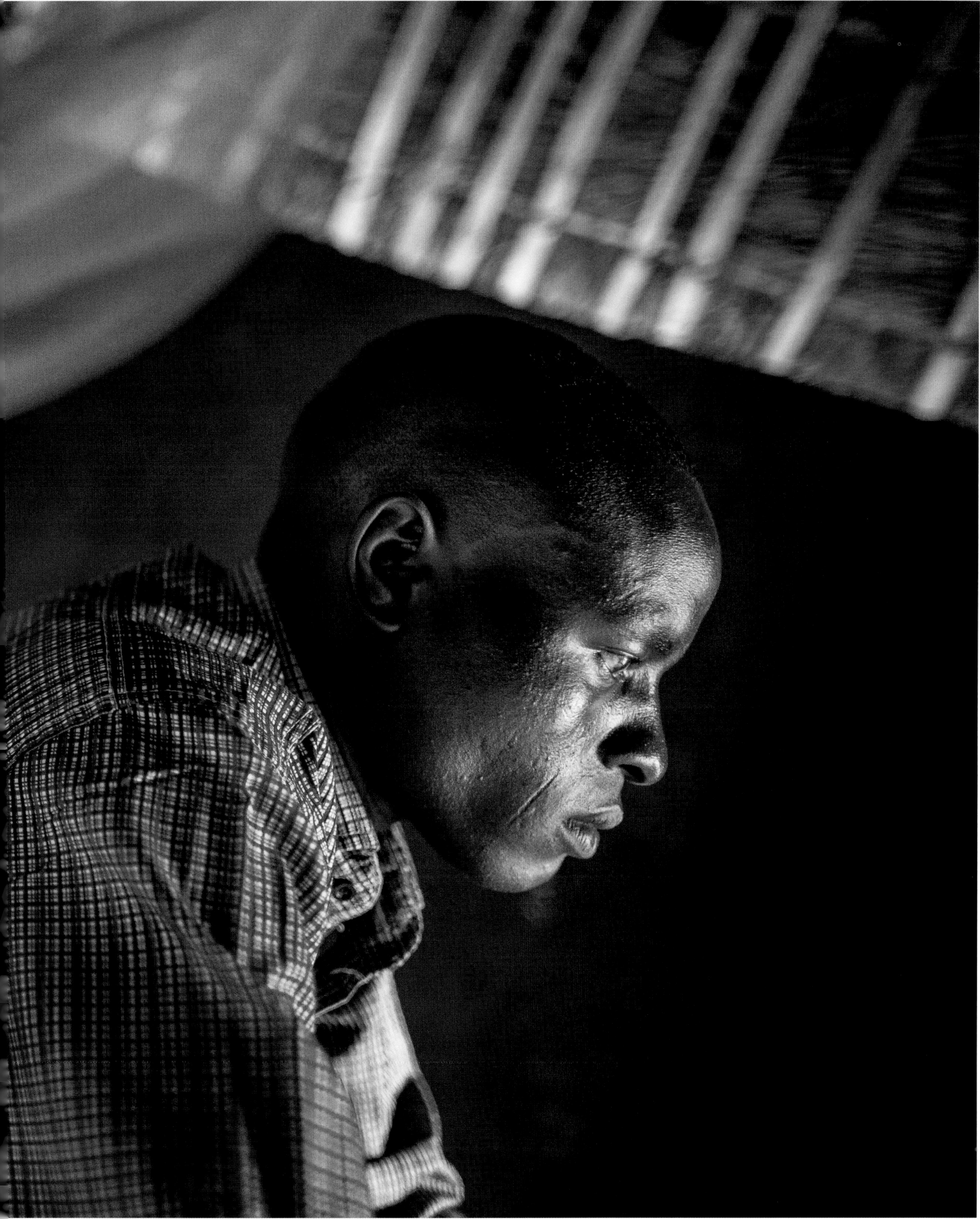

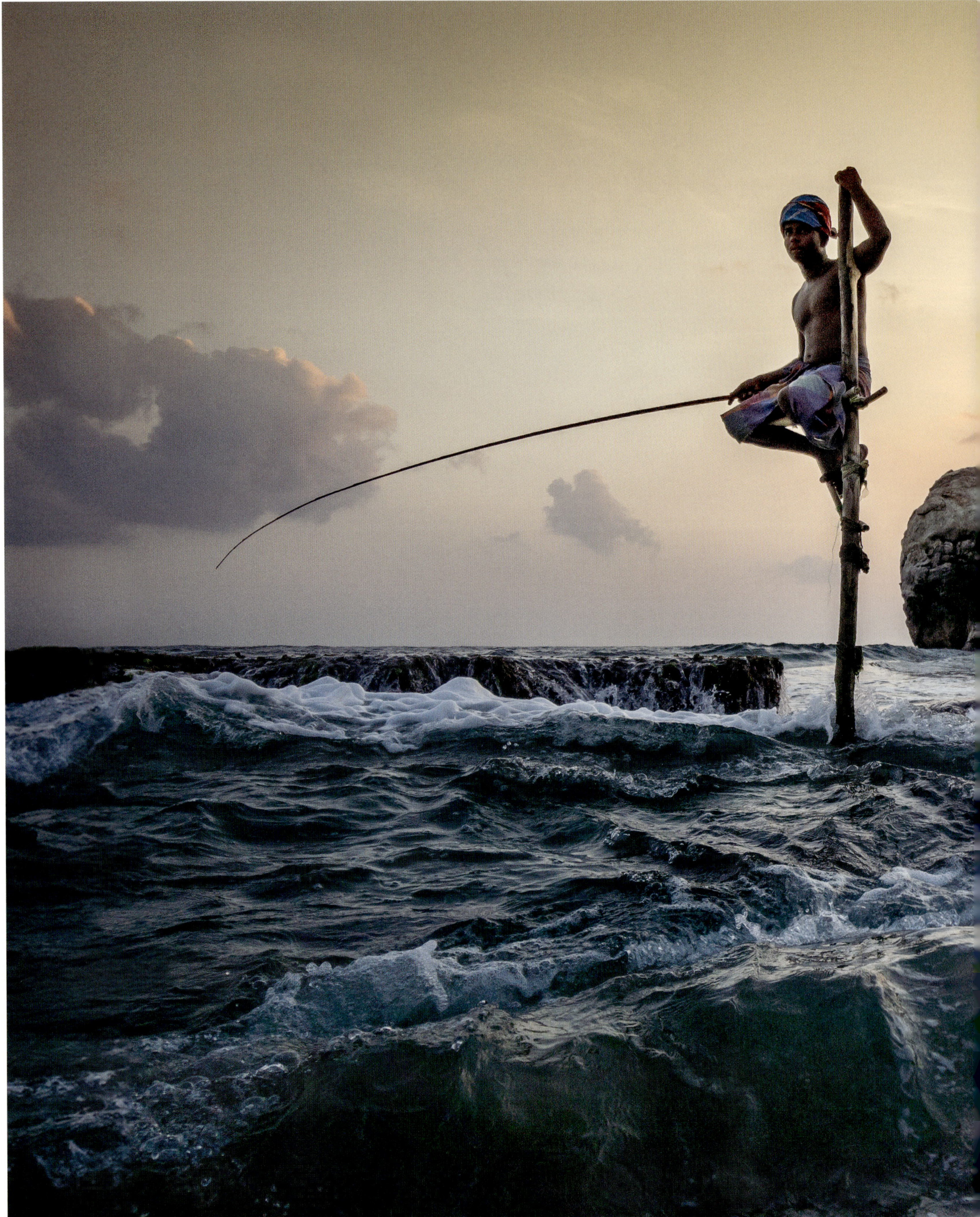

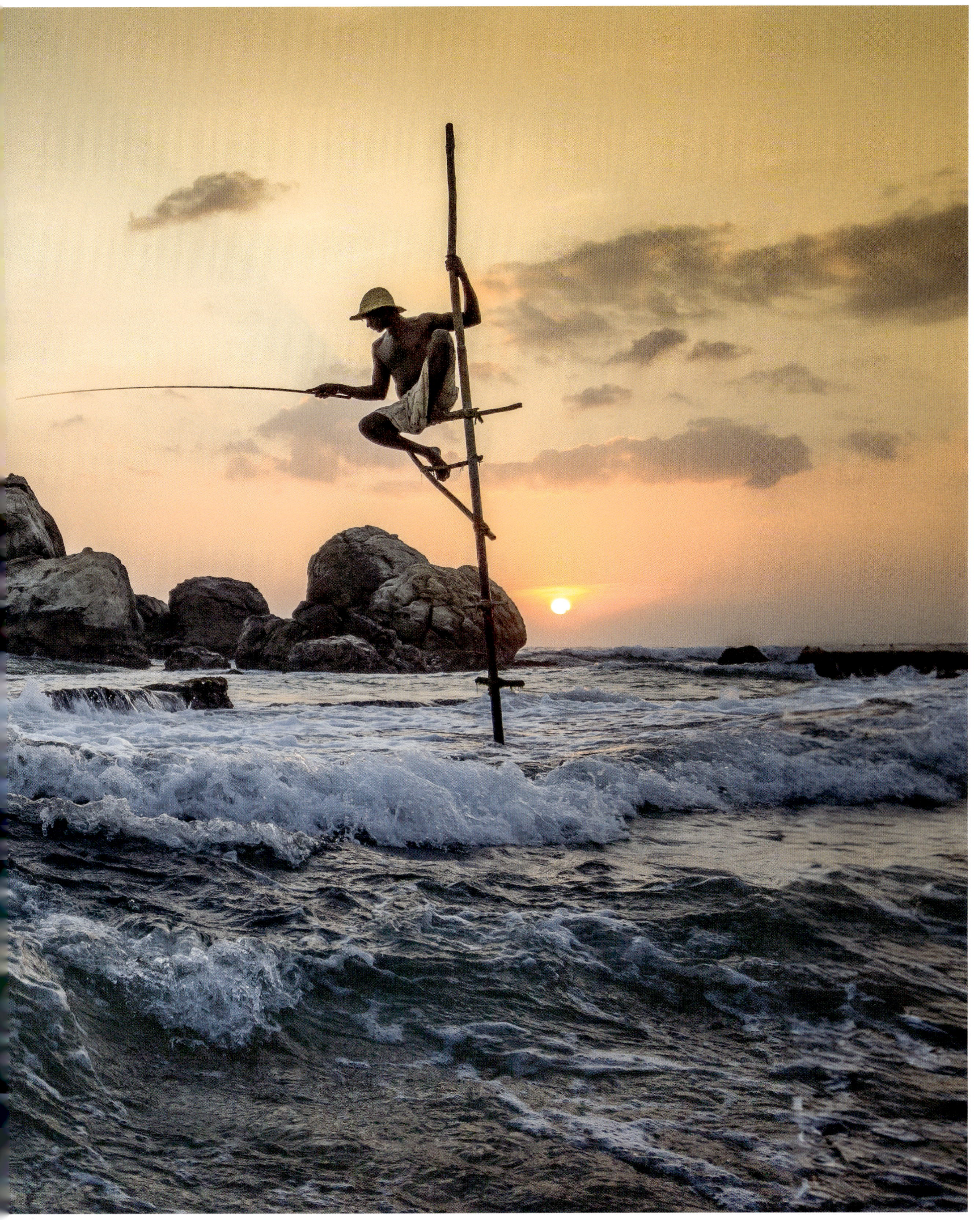

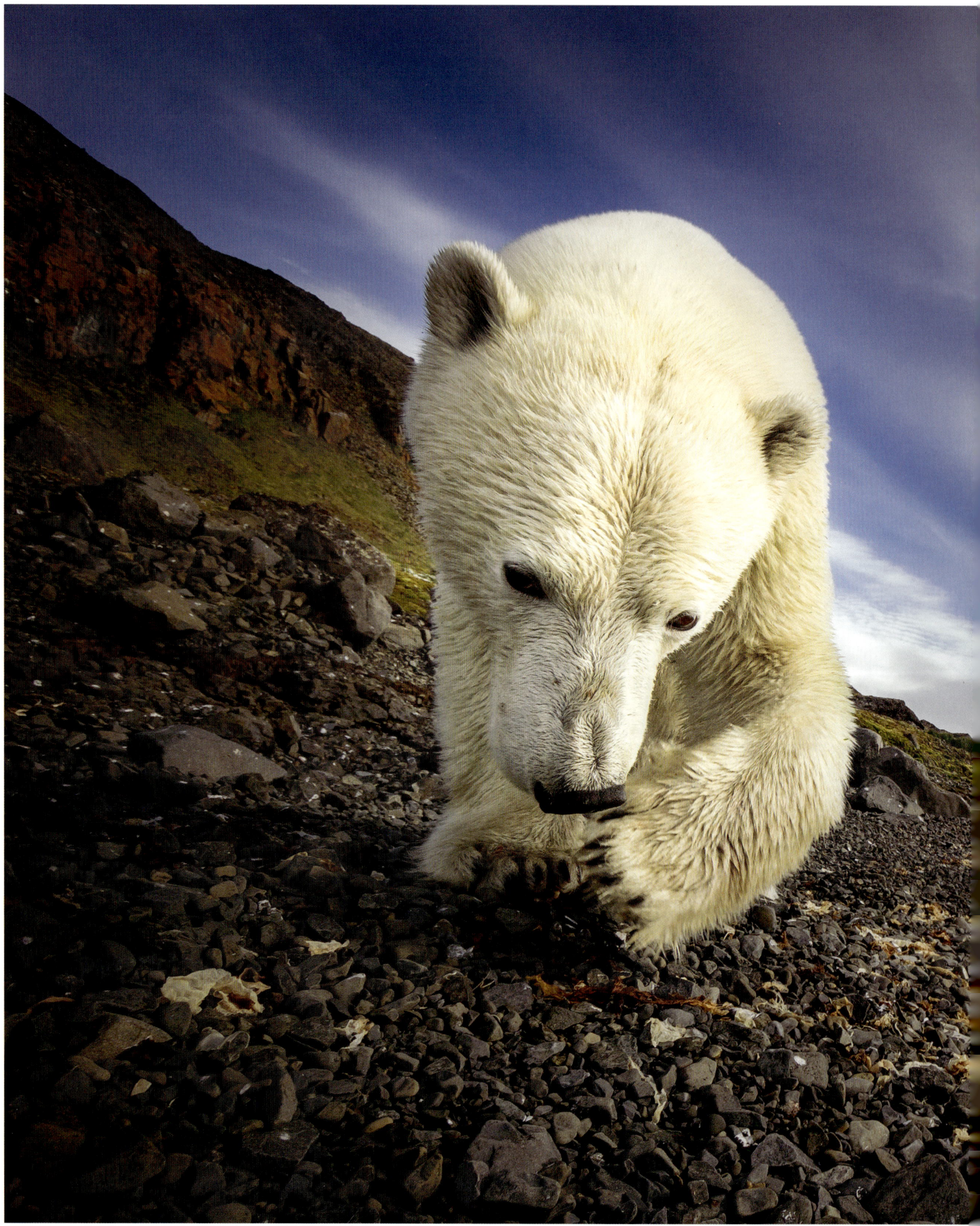

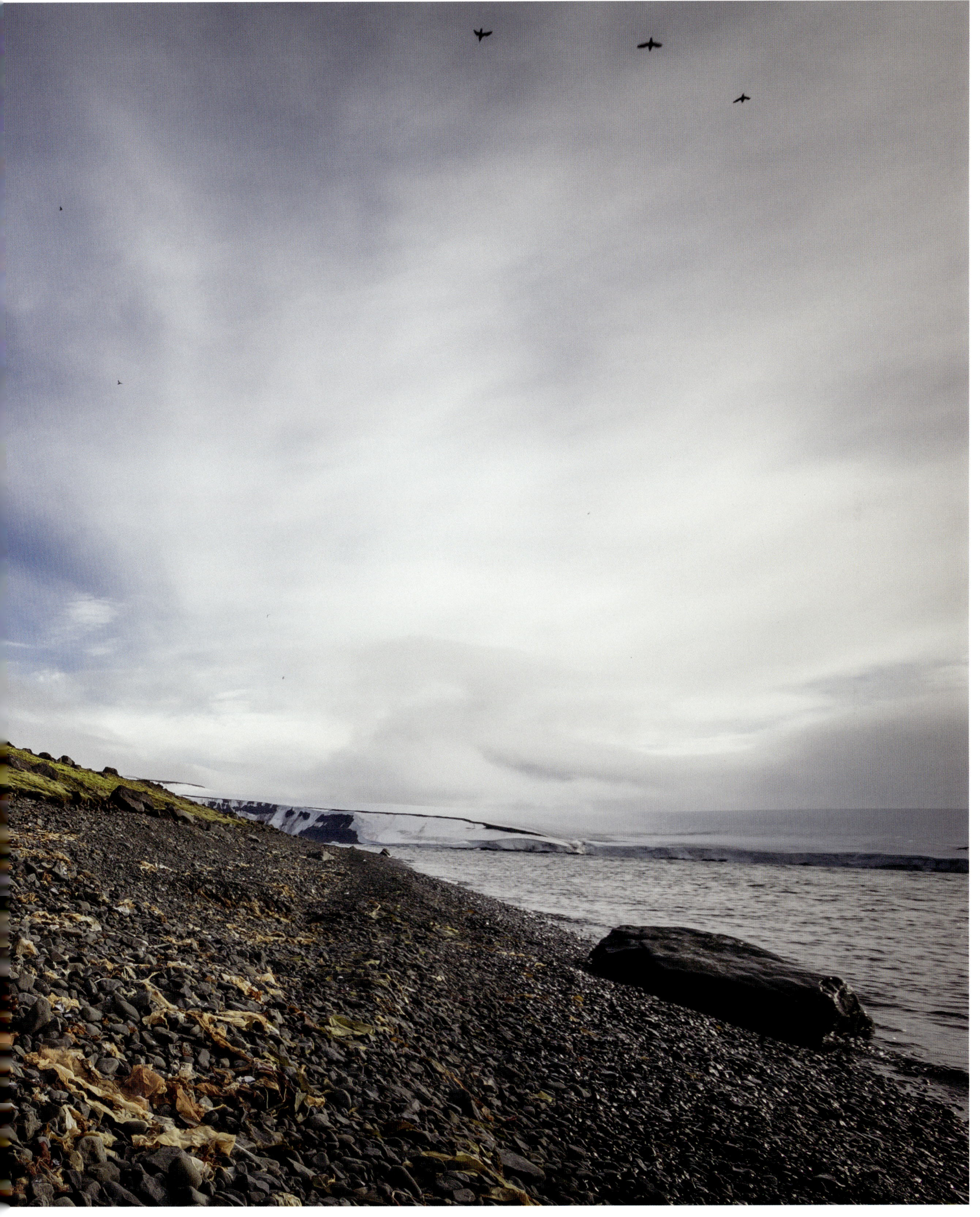

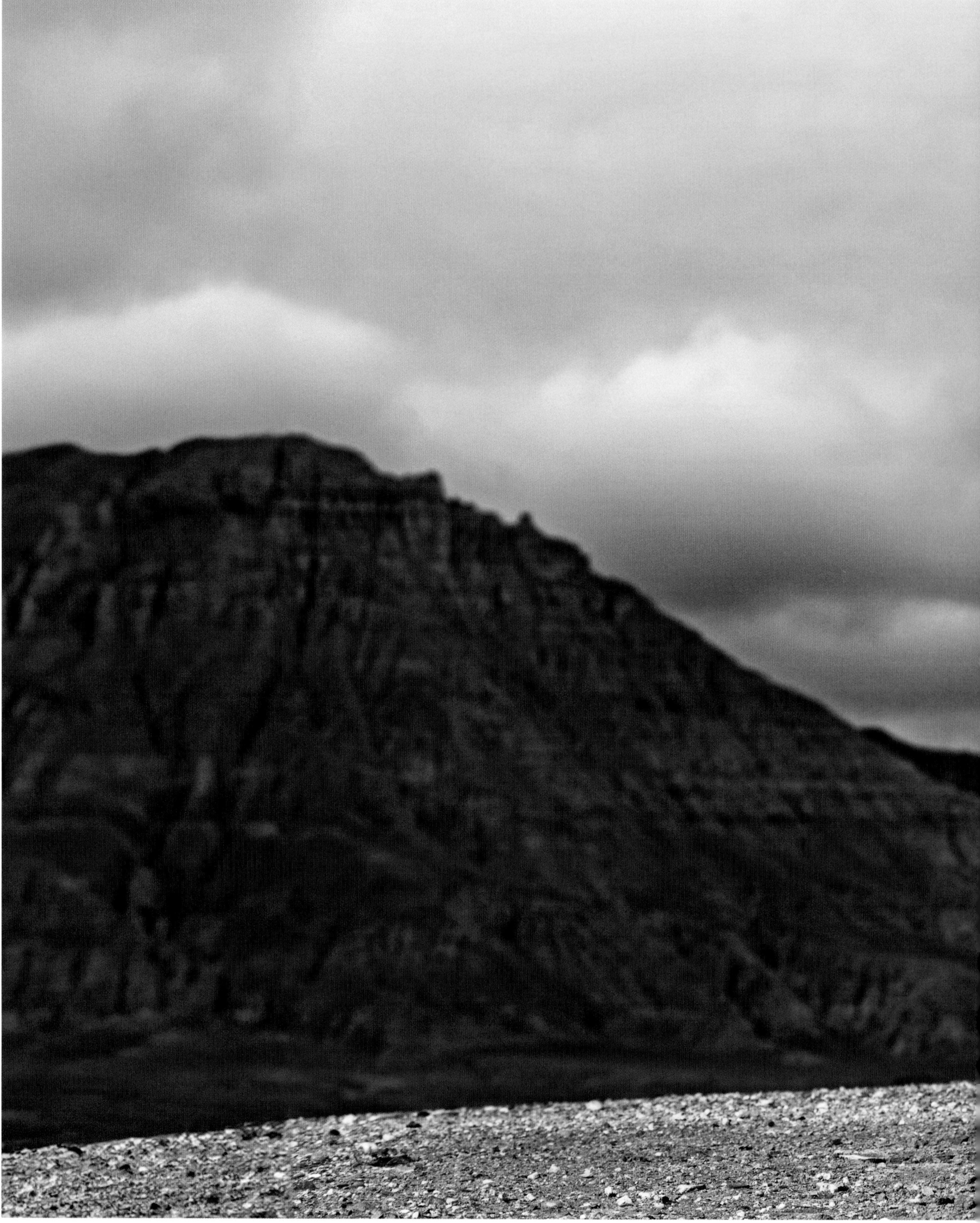

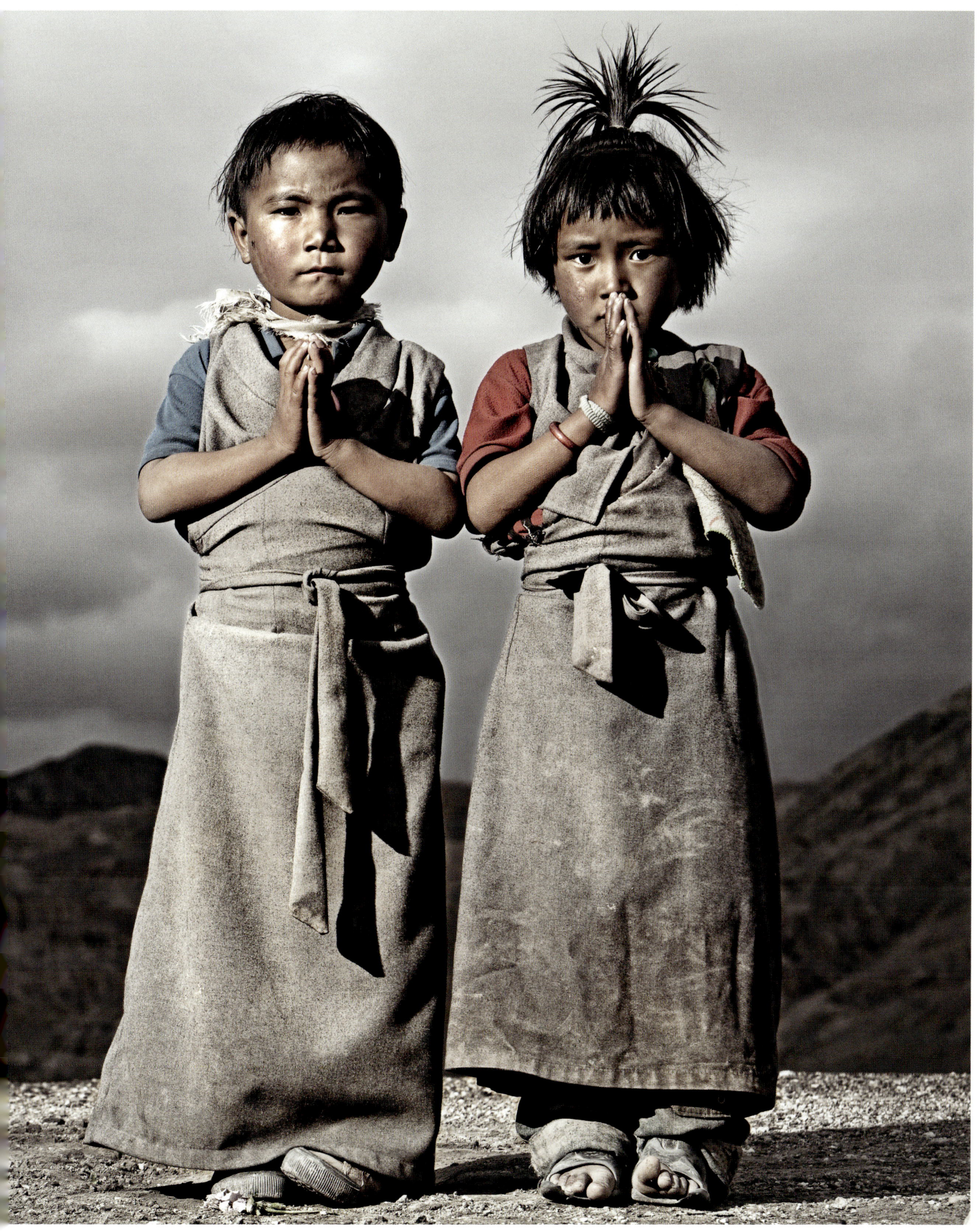

ACKNOWLEDGMENTS

Everything in this book, including the images, are collaborations and I can in no way take sole responsibility for them. I've been fortunate to have so many allies, creative and adventure partners, mentors, editors, and guides along the way. Andrew Phelps, to whom the book is dedicated, was my first photography mentor. Without his urging, my life would never have taken the shape it has. Adam Clark and Lee Cohen, ski photographers in Utah, were my first real-life examples of photographers actually making a living pursuing this craft full-time; they introduced me to my first real clients, Patagonia and Black Diamond. Barb Penoyar and Bill Cannon gave me my first jobs as a photo assistant, and I worked for Bill for seven years, using the money I made to go on small climbing trips and expeditions. Chris Johns gave me my first assignment for *National Geographic*. I owe huge thanks to my creative collaborators, including Haliy San Miguel, Kurt Muchler, Susan Welschman, Sara Leen, Todd James, Kathy Moran, Whitney Johnson, David Quammen, Peter Gwin, Mark Synott, Freddie Wilkinson, Mark Jenkins, Enric Sala, Paul Nicklen, Dr. Steve Boyes, Jimmy Chin, Keith Ladzinski, Marco Grob, David Guttenfelder, Bill Allard, George Steinmetz, Randy Olson, Lynn Johnson, Jodi Cobb, Andy Mann, Steve McCurry, Charlie Hamilton James, Aaron Huey, Andy Bardon, Gary Knell, and Susan Goldberg as well.

To *all* the photographers, editors, writers, and designers I've had the privilege of working with, thank you. Thank you for the team behind the scenes that supported me along the way, including Stacy Gold, Rachel DeRuyter, Gina Martin, Sara Snider Papademetriou, Alice Keating, Melissa Schneider, Malou Anderson-Ramierez, and Dre Ramirez.

For all of my climbing and adventure partners, athletes, and mentors, of which there are just too many to name, I am forever indebted.

Thank you, Mom, for the 1984 Ricoh point and shoot. Thanks, Dad, for holding the calm as I made my way.

For the incredible guidance and design collaboration for the heart illustration in the table of contents, I owe a huge thanks to Gaspar Costa. Thank you to my incredible editor, Julie Bennett, who, alongside designer Kelly Booth, brought this book to life. A massive thanks to my agent, Susan Canavan, as well, who found me a home with Ten Speed Press. Thank you to Vacheron Constantin, who has supported my artistic development over the past six years. I am so grateful.

Thank you to the incredible men of my "Treehouse," including Kenny Kane, Giovanni Messner, Erik Foster, Andrew Kline, Nick McCutchen, Sina Monjazeb, Jeff Fleeher, Matt Nichols, Arturo Muyschondt, Marcus Kowal, Ron Mathews, Martin Morse, Tobey Maguire, Jack Osborn, and Reinaldo Marcus Green.

Thanks to Lauren Taus for helping me refine and distill the concept of this book and thanks to Tim Ferriss for the "dash." It was insight that made it better.

The bulk of this work was made alongside two of the most important people in my life: Sadie Quarrier and Mark Stone. Without you, most of this work never would have happened, let alone been as meaningful as it was. Thank you for holding the wheel when I threatened to spin out. Thank you for your patience, kindness, and creative contributions. Thank you for the ceaseless love and support in the pursuit of these pictures. Your names are attached to almost every image in this book, and I am truly eternally grateful.

Lastly, thank you to Jessica Camacho for your love, tireless support, insight, curiosity, pursuit of growth, and energy to get it all across the finish line. I love you.

Photography would mean nothing if it weren't for those who consume it. My deepest gratitude to all of you for loving art and the world we live in. Thank you.

CORY RICHARDS is an internationally renowned photographer, filmmaker, and author of the memoir *The Color of Everything*. He is the first and only American to climb one of the world's 8,000-meter peaks in winter. His documentation of the climb and aftermath of the experience was made into the award-winning documentary *COLD* and appeared on the cover of the 125th anniversary issue of *National Geographic*. Richards is a *National Geographic* Adventurer of the Year, Photographer Fellow, and a two-time recipient of an Explorers Grant. He has photographed twelve feature assignments for the magazine and has an active speaking career, in which he leads discussions about conservation, mental health, leadership, and vulnerability. Richards lives in Los Angeles.

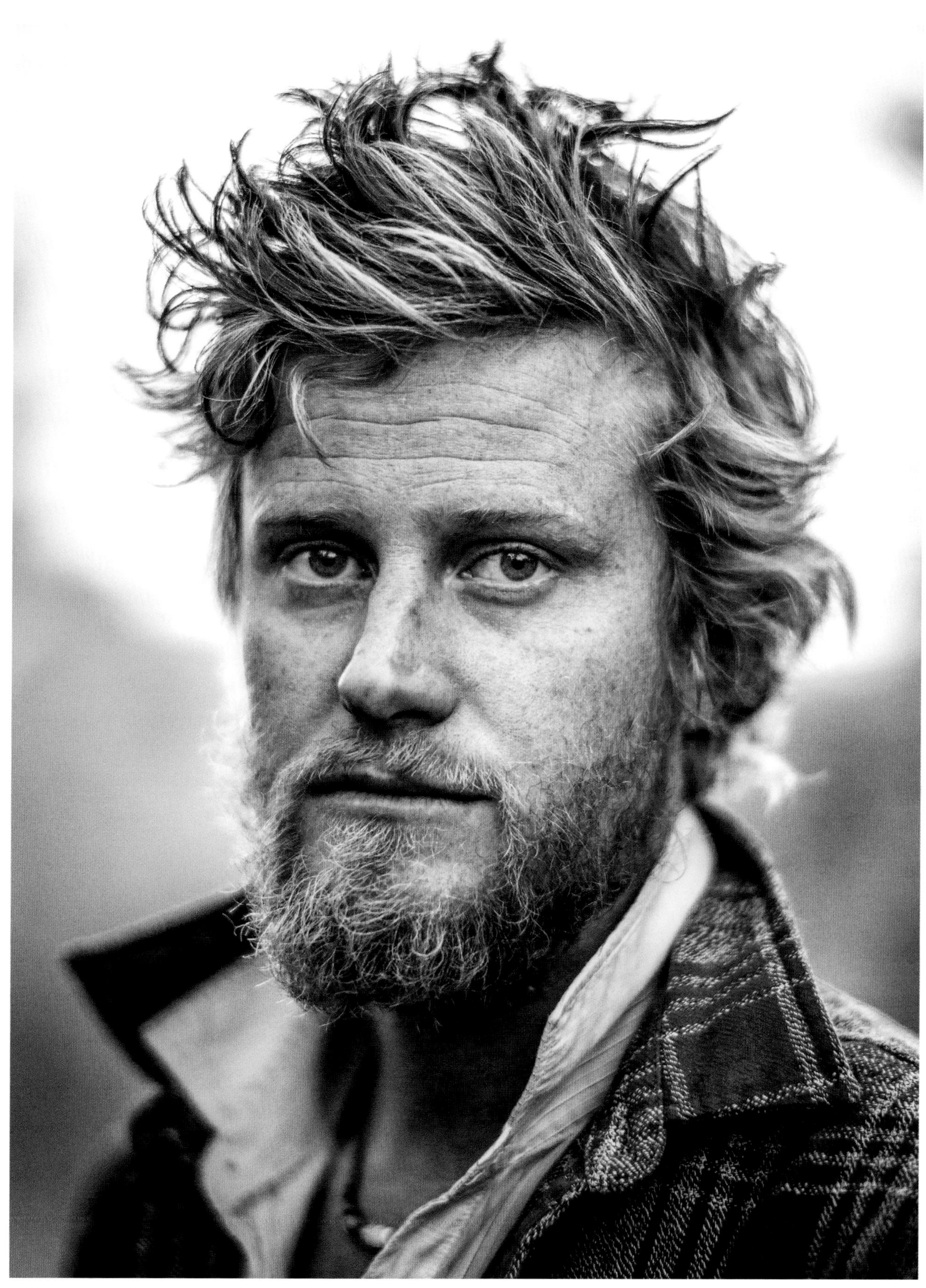

Author's Note: When names are withheld from photo captions, it is at the request of the subjects due to sensitive content, or because the information was not able to be recorded.

Typefaces: Klim Type Foundry's National 2 Condensed and Tiempos Text.

Library of Congress Cataloging-in-Publication Data
Names: Richards, Cory, author, photographer. Title: Bi-polar : photographs from an unquiet mind / Cory Richards. Identifiers: LCCN 2023058442 (print) | LCCN 2023058443 (ebook) | ISBN 9781984862419 (hardcover) | ISBN 9781984862426 (eBook) Subjects: LCSH: Photography, Artistic. | Richards, Cory. | Bipolar disorder—Patients—Biography. | Mountaineers—United States—Biography. Classification: LCC TR647 .R4245 2024 (print) | LCC TR647 (ebook) | DDC 779.092—dc23/eng/20240304

LC record available at https://lccn.loc.gov/2023058442
LC ebook record available at https://lccn.loc.gov/2023058443

Hardcover ISBN: 978-1-9848-6241-9
Ebook ISBN: 978-1-9848-6242-6

Printed in Malaysia

Editor: Julie Bennett | Production editors: Terry Deal and Ashley Pierce
Designer: Kelly Booth | Production designer: Mari Gill
Illustration and hand lettering: Cory Richards
Production manager: Serena Sigona
Prepress color manager: Jane Chinn
Copyeditor: Michael Richards | Proofreader: Monika Dziamka
Publicist: Felix Cruz | Marketer: Joey Lozada

10 9 8 7 6 5 4 3 2 1

First Edition

COVER: Ama Dablam, Khumbu Valley, Nepal.
PAGE 1: Bridegroom, Ladakh, India.
PAGE 2: Rudolph Island, Franz Josef Land, Russia.
PAGE 4: Renan Ozturk, Hkakabo Razi, Kachin, Myanmar.
PAGE 318: Author photo by Mark Stone.

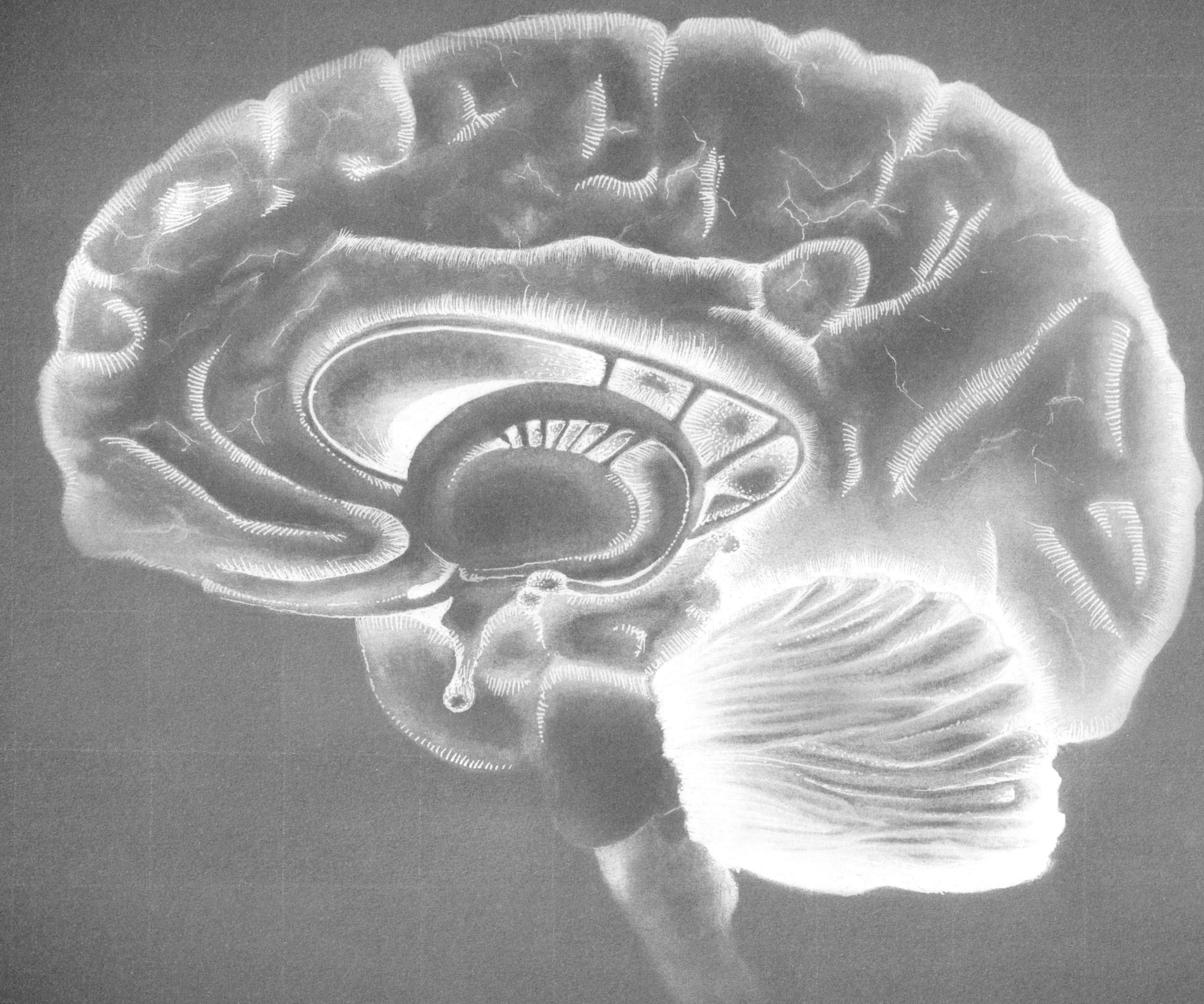
N
S

I think I chased pictures to quiet the noise in my mind, to
slow down the world, to stop it. I kept trying for twenty
years, striving for the stillness of those little moments.
One hundredth of a second. One thousandth. But I learned
that photography doesn't really work that way. And what I
thought was presence was just framing, light, serendipity,
and time. Looking, looking, looking. I noticed a lot, but often
in exchange for witnessing the moment itself. And after a
while, I forgot what I was looking at at all. A second would
blend into a collection of fragments and the fragments
would come together as something I never saw. It was fast.
It was fun. But it was never soft, even in periods of slow

Maybe photography is a trade-off — of of the photographer's
presence so others can have a moment of their own. Maybe
photography is just that — and maybe that's what we need
now, more than ever, in a world that seems to move faster
than we can keep up with. Pictures remind us to notice what
we're part of. Or maybe that's high and self-important
praise for an art that relies more on the world then on the
artist. Maybe. That's okay. Maybe none of this makes sense. Maybe
it's all bullshit. That's okay too.